COST-EFFECTIVENESS OF PSYCHOTHERAPY

COST-EFFECTIVENESS OF PSYCHOTHERAPY

A Guide for Practitioners, Researchers, and Policymakers

Edited by
Nancy E. Miller
Kathryn M. Magruder

New York • Oxford Oxford University Press 1999

Oxford University Press

Oxford New York
Athens Auckland Bangkok Bogotá Bombay Buenos Aires Calcutta
Cape Town Chennai Dar es Salaam Delhi Florence Hong Kong Istanbul
Karachi Kuala Lumpur Madrid Melbourne Mexico City Mumbai
Nairobi Paris São Paulo Singapore Taipei Tokyo Toronto Warsaw

and associated companies in
Berlin Ibadan

Published by Oxford University Press, Inc.
198 Madison Avenue, New York, New York 10016

Oxford is a registered trademark of Oxford University Press

Library of Congress Cataloging-in-Publication Data
The cost-effectiveness of psychotherapy : a guide for practitioners, researchers, and policymakers / edited by Nancy E. Miller, Kathryn M. Magruder.
p. cm.
Includes bibliographical references and index.
ISBN 0-19-511458-2
1. Psychotherapy—Cost effectiveness. 2. Psychotherapy—Cost effectiveness—Research. 3. Mental health services—Utilization.
I. Miller, Nancy E. II. Magruder, Kathryn M.
RC480.5.C62 1998
338.4′361689′14—dc21 97-43075

1 3 5 7 9 8 6 4 2

Printed in the United States of America
on acid-free paper

In Memory of Carl A. Taube

Prescient trailblazer, developer of the nation's first NIMH program in Mental Health Economics, Carl dedicated his career to determining how the principles of supply, demand, and organization of mental health services might contribute to making the health care system more equitable and cost-effective. He was responsible for creation of the first community of scholars committed to using methods of economic analysis as a means for forging policy solutions to address the nation's most pressing problems in the delivery of mental health services.

and

In Honor of Agnes Rupp

Director, NIMH Program in Mental Health Economics, for her impressive leadership, unique expertise, and personal generosity in further expanding the focus of economic studies and moving the field forward to meet the growing demands for systematic cost-effectiveness information on mental health interventions in the coming century.

For Family and Friends

For our colleagues at the National Institute of Mental Health, and with special thanks to the lights of our lives, Walter, Jacob, Jennifer, and Katie and Adam for their love, encouragement, and support.

Nancy E. Miller
Kathryn M. Magruder

Acknowledgments

This volume has benefitted from the assistance, encouragement, and contributions of many individuals. We are grateful to Grayson Norquist, Darrel Regier, and Tom Lalley of NIMH, who helped provide the initial impetus for exploring these services research issues in depth, and to Jane Steinberg and David Shore, of the Division of Clinical and Treatment Research, who provided vital support for this work. Agnes Rupp gave unstintingly of her time, and was instrumental in helping to shape many of the key economic papers included here.

In addition, we wish to express our appreciation to William Hargreaves, who contributed prescient, clear, and thoughtful reviews of our economics chapters, and to thank John P. Docherty, Richard G. Frank, Kenneth I. Howard, A. John Rush, and Kenneth B. Wells, whose respective views of the "big picture" pertaining to the economics of psychotherapy contributed so fruitfully to the organization of this volume.

Not to be forgotten is the generous assistance of Lynn G. Gordon of the Fetzer Institute, who provided us the opportunity to add a series of international perspectives pertaining to psychotherapy service utilization patterns in nations with single-payer systems, and the helpful support of Walter Reich, of the Project on Health, Science, and Public Policy, of the Woodrow Wilson International Center for Scholars.

A special thank you goes to Janice Huque and Janet Sorrells for their efficient administrative support, and without whom we could not have handled the volume of work required.

Finally, we express warm appreciation to Joan Bossert of Oxford University Press, who skillfully guided us through the publication process with her prodigious editorial know-how, contagious enthusiasm, and superb judgment.

To all the above, we express our profound thanks.

Note

Earlier versions of some papers were presented at the sponsored international conference entitled "The Cost-Effectiveness of Psychotherapy: Developing Clinical and Services Research Models in an Era of Health Care Reform," National Institute of Mental Health. That meeting was collaboratively sponsored by the Project on Health, Science, and Public Policy of the Woodrow Wilson International Center for Scholars and by the Fetzer Foundation. The preparation of this volume took shape following the conference, with manuscripts included here, solicited de novo. The volume comprehensively reflects the speed of change characterizing the delivery and financing of the nation's mental health care, and chronicles the resulting repercussions on the nature and focus of psychosocial treatment research.

Disclaimer

The opinions expressed herein are those of the individual authors only and do not necessarily reflect the official position of the NIMH or the NIH.

Contents

Contributors

Stewart Agras, M.D.
Department of Psychiatry and Behavioral Sciences
Stanford University
Stanford, CA

Bengt-Åke Armelius, Ph.D.
Department of Applied Psychology
University of Umea
Umea, Sweden

David H. Barlow, Ph.D.
Department of Psychology
Boston University
Boston, MA

Gary R. Bond, Ph.D.
Department of Psychology
Indiana University and Purdue University
Indianapolis, IN

James A. Clardy, M.D.
Department of Psychiatry
University of Arkansas for Medical Sciences
Little Rock, AR

Elizabeth M. Corbitt, Ph.D.
Epidemiology Research Director
Rehabilitation Research and Training Center
on Drugs and Disability
School of Medicine
Wright State University
Dayton, OH

John P. Docherty, M.D.
Department of Psychiatry
Cornell University Medical College
White Plains, NY

Ellen P. Fischer, Ph.D.
Department of Psychiatry
University of Arkansas for Medical Sciences
Little Rock, AR

Edna B. Foa, Ph.D.
Department of Psychiatry
Medical College of Pennsylvania
Philadelphia, PA

Richard G. Frank, Ph.D.
Department of Health Care Policy
Harvard University Medical School
Boston, MA

Michael J. Goldstein, Ph.D.
(deceased)
Department of Psychiatry
University of California, Los Angeles
School of Medicine
Los Angeles, CA

Jodi Halpern, M.D., Ph.D.
Department of Psychiatry
University of California, Berkeley
Berkeley, CA

William A. Hargreaves, Ph.D.
Department of Psychiatry
University of California, San Francisco
San Francisco, CA

Andrew Healy
Center for the Economics of Mental Health
Institute of Psychiatry
London, England

Heidi L. Heard, B.A.
Institute of Medical and Social Care Research
University of Wales
Bangor, Wales, UK

Stefan G. Hofmann, Ph.D.
Phobia & Anxiety Disorders Clinic
Albany, NY

Jan A. Hollenberg, M.S.
Department of Psychiatry
University of Arkansas for Medical Sciences
Little Rock, AR

Steven D. Hollon, Ph.D.
Department of Psychology
Vanderbilt University
Nashville, TN

Kenneth I. Howard, Ph.D.
Department of Psychiatry and Behavioral Sciences
Northwestern University Medical School
Chicago, IL

Lisa H. Jaycox, Ph.D.
The RAND Corporation
Santa Monica, CA

Horst Kächele, M.D.
Department of Psychotherapy
University of Ulm
Ulm, Germany

Mark S. Kamlet, Ph.D
The H. John Heinz III School of Public Policy and Management
Carnegie Mellon University
Pittsburgh, PA

Robert M. Kaplan, Ph.D.
Department of Family and Preventive Medicine
University of California, San Diego
La Jolla, CA

T. Michael Kashner, Ph.D.
Dallas VA Medical Center
Dallas, TX

Leah Kleinman, Dr.P.H.
MEDCAP International
Bethesda, MD

Richard P. Kluft, M.D.
Department of Psychiatry
Temple University School of Medicine
Philadelphia, PA

Martin Knapp, Ph.D.
Centre for the Economics of Mental Health
Institute of Psychiatry
University of London
London, England

Janice L. Krupnick, Ph.D.
Department of Psychiatry
Georgetown University
Washington, DC

Judith R. Lave, Ph.D.
Graduate School of Public Health
University of Pittsburgh
Pittsburgh, PA

Anthony F. Lehman, M.D., M.S.P.H.
Department of Psychiatry
University of Maryland School of Medicine
Baltimore, MD

Robert J. Lueger, Ph.D.
Department of Psychology
Marquette University
Milwaukee, WI

Marsha M. Linehan, Ph.D.
Department of Psychology
University of Washington
Seattle, WA

Wolfgang Lutz, Ph.D.
Department of Psychology
Northwestern University
Evanston, IL

Kathryn M. Magruder, M.P.H., Ph.D.
Department of Psychiatry and Behavioral Sciences
Medical University of South Carolina
Charleston, SC

John C. Markowitz, M.D.
New York Hospital–Cornell Medical Center
Cornell University Medical College
New York, NY

Zoran Martinovich, Ph.D.
Department of Psychiatry and Behavioral Science
Northwestern University Medical School
Chicago, IL

Thomas G. McGuire, Ph.D.
Department of Economics
Boston University
Boston, MA

Lisa S. Meredith, Ph.D.
The RAND Corporation
Santa Monica, CA

Adolf-Ernst Meyer
(deceased)
Department of Psychotherapy and Psychosomatic Medicine
University of Hamburg
Hamburg, Germany

Nancy E. Miller, Ph.D.
Office of the Director
National Institutes of Health
Bethesda, MD

James Mintz, Ph.D.
Department of Psychiatry
University of California, Los Angeles School of Medicine
Camarillo, CA

Lois Imber Mintz, Ph.D.
Department of Psychiatry
University of California, Los Angeles
Los Angeles, CA

James E. Mitchell, M.D.
Department of Psychiatry
University of North Dakota
Fargo, ND

Cindy L. Mosley, B.B.A
Department of Psychiatry
University of Arkansas for Medical Sciences
Little Rock, AR

Brian D. Neighbors, Ph.D.
Department of Psychology
Oklahoma State University
Oklahoma City, OK

Pierre R. Nunez
Department of Psychiatry and Behavioral Sciences
Northwestern University Medical School
Chicago, IL

Mark Olfson, M.D.
Department of Clinical Psychiatry
Columbia University
New York State Psychiatric Institute
New York, NY

Glenys Parry, Ph.D.
Director of Research
Community Health Sheffield NHS Trust
Sheffield, England

J. Christopher Perry, M.D.
Psychiatry Research
Jewish General Hospital
Montreal, QC
Canada

Carol B. Peterson, Ph.D.
Eating Disorders Research Program
University of Minnesota
Minneapolis, MN

Paul A. Pilkonis, Ph.D.
Western Psychiatric Institute and Clinic
Department of Psychiatry
University of Pittsburgh Medical Center
Pittsburgh, PA

Harold Alan Pincus, M.D.
Office of Research
American Psychiatric Association
Washington, DC

Rainer Richter, Ph.D.
Department of Child and Adolescent Psychiatry
University of Hamburg
Hamburg, Germany

A. John Rush, M.D.
Department of Psychiatry
University of Texas Southwestern Medical Center
Dallas, TX

Joel Sadavoy, M.D.
Mount Sinai Hospital
Toronto, ON
Canada

Stephen M. Saunders, Ph.D.
Department of Psychology
Marquette University
Milwaukee, WI

Herbert C. Schulberg, Ph.D.
Department of Psychiatry
University of Pittsburgh School of Medicine
Pittsburgh, PA

Martha Shumway, Ph.D.
Department of Psychiatry
University of California, San Francisco
San Francisco, CA

G. Richard Smith, Jr., M.D.
Department of Psychiatry
University of Arkansas for Medical Sciences
Little Rock, AR

Roland Sturm, Ph.D.
Economist
The RAND Corporation
Santa Monica, CA

Teh-Wei Hu, Ph.D.
Department of Economics
School of Public Health
University of California, Berkeley
Berkeley, CA

Helmut Thomä, M.D.
Department of Psychotherapy
University of Ulm
Ulm, Germany

John T. Vessey, Ph.D.
Department of Psychiatry and Behavioral Sciences
Northwestern University Medical School
Chicago, IL

Kenneth B. Wells, M.D., M.P.H.
UCLA Neuropsychiatric Institute and Hospital
University of California, Los Angeles
School of Medicine
Los Angeles, CA

Introduction

Services and Cost-Effectiveness Research for Psychotherapy

Overview

Psychotherapy is one of the predominant modes of mental health treatment today, yet relatively little is known about how psychotherapy is used, its cost, or its outcome, in "real world" settings. The absence of such information, since the advent of health care reform efforts, has public health officials, practitioners, researchers, and policymakers facing serious questions regarding accountability—how well do these therapies achieve their intended goals, and at what cost.

As market pressures for change mount in response to escalating health care costs, as the conflicting needs to improve quality and control costs confront state and federal policymakers, and as the focus of health care delivery moves from a perspective of understanding and curing illness to one extolling better care for more people at less cost, coverage for, and access to, psychotherapy services has become increasingly constrained.

In response to the public health need for scientifically based information, this book has been designed to serve as a guide to this rapidly developing area of inquiry: It consolidates and reviews what is known about the efficacy, effectiveness, and cost-effectiveness of psychosocial interventions tailored for specific disorders; it charts new paths as to where the field must move next, and most importantly, provides a state-of-the-art introduction to understanding and implementing the approaches economists commonly use to evaluate the cost-effectiveness of treatments. The book documents what we know empirically, what we need to find out, and how to do the studies which need to be done, while also providing a comprehensive overview of the methods, tools, and measures needed.

This volume describes the metamorphosis of psychotherapy from a decentralized, fee-for-service cottage industry, to a massive market-driven, largely for-profit, health care system. It also charts the development of psychotherapy as a scientific field of research, tracing the development of the various methods and shifts in research emphasis over the course of several decades.

The findings of many of the world's most distinguished mental health investigators are included here, with each underscoring urgent research concerns pertaining to mental health economics. In response to the burgeoning call for "evidence-based medicine," this handbook is designed to serve as a guide, bringing together two disparate fields of research which have not previously intersected: psychotherapy and economics.

The volume includes clear descriptions of key research instruments, critical assessments of the pros and cons of alternative research designs, the next steps in developing means of assessment of cost and outcome in psychotherapy, and tips for avoiding methodologic and ethical pitfalls when using measures of economic evaluation. Large-scale surveys and meta-analyses document what is known about who uses psychotherapy in the United States, who provides it, what it costs, and where it is delivered. Finally, reports on cost and status of psychotherapy in western nations utilizing single-payer health care systems provide useful models against which to compare our own national psychotherapy delivery system.

At the heart of the book, national and international experts in health economics clarify key methodological issues in assessing cost-benefits, cost-utilities, and cost-effectiveness specific to psychotherapy. These experts discuss ways in which the cost-effectiveness of specific treatments can serve as useful decisionmaking tools for designing and financing mental health benefit plans. Also included is an overview of the efficacy and effectiveness literature in psychotherapy, taking into account those disorders which, while commonly encountered in clinical practice and perceived to incur high health care costs, are rarely studied systematically. Finally, data pertaining to the differential cost-effectiveness of combination treatments and to the relative efficacy of pharmacotherapeutic versus psychotherapeutic interventions, are systematically discussed. As such, this volume stands apart from many reviews of psychotherapy research, by virtue of moving away from an exclusive emphasis on what is available in the psychotherapy research literature on short-term, symptomatic outcomes, and moving toward construction of an evidentiary base geared toward assessing the effect of interventions—as practiced in the community—on costs, work, quality of life, and functional capacities over the long term.

Now that it is no longer sufficient to demonstrate empirically the most efficacious behavioral intervention for treatment of a targeted psychiatric disorder, without also determining broader questions of cost and quality of outcome, this volume provides tools essential to begin tackling what is certain to emerge as one of the pivotal mental health care issues of the 21st century.

Walking Through the Book

Organized into six primary parts, this book sets forth a number of the key challenges facing research on behavioral treatment interventions from the point of view of multiple stakeholders. In order to provide the reader with a more detailed introduction to some of the book's central themes, highlights from each part will be described here.

Part I: Defining Psychotherapy

In broadly detailing some of the major concerns facing the field of psychotherapy research today, John Docherty opens the volume with a historic overview of the growth of psychotherapy as both intervention and science, tracking the growing disparities between scientific advances in therapeutics, and the development of psychotherapy practice as a cottage industry. Until recently, psychotherapy, like much of medicine, remained relatively unconstrained by limits of time, data on outcomes, financial expenditures, or by growing evidence of significant regional variation in practice patterns unrelated to outcome.

Increased scrutiny of costs, however, has brought into sharp focus several important issues which impinge on psychotherapy research. The advent of a market-driven health care economy has stimulated and radically changed the types of research questions now being posed by both private and public sectors. In the context of a fee-for-service system where public health accountability was seldom discussed, efficacy studies did not encompass population-based variables, nor yield information regarding the utility of psychotherapy for the vast majority of clinical conditions encountered in practice. Accordingly, treatment as usual—which typically includes heterogeneous patients with multiple disorders treated by generalists, without access to training in psychotherapy treatment manuals or ongoing supervision—has rarely been studied.

Since the advent of the 1993 Health Security Act, the absence of data pertaining to the cost-effectiveness of psychotherapeutic interventions has continued to be a serious impediment to more wide-spread consideration—by federal actuaries and economists—of psychotherapy as a benefit. In coming years, it can be anticipated that evidence pertaining to these public health needs will increasingly come to dominate the public research agenda.

Given that psychotherapy and pharmacotherapy represent the two primary modes of treatment for mental disorders, Steven Hollon next undertakes an exhaustive examination of the efficacy, effectiveness, and cost-effectiveness of psychotherapy and pharmacotherapy, both alone and in combination, across a variety of disorders. In the course of his review, Hollon focuses on the truthfulness of some commonly accepted assumptions about efficacy and effectiveness research.

For example, he looks at evidence from efficacy research to determine the validity of the following assumptions:

- while psychotherapy may be sufficient in the treatment of the less severe disorders, medication is essential to treatment and prophylaxis of more severe disorders
- psychosocial interventions are as effective as medication in the treatment of the less severe disorders
- psychotherapy may have broader, more enduring effects over time than pharmacologic agents
- the combination of drugs and psychotherapy work better than either modality alone

Hollon's findings in some instances are surprising and suggest significant research questions which have yet to be addressed.

In discussing common beliefs pertaining to effectiveness research, Hollon also examines evidence for the hypotheses:

- most treatments perform better in controlled clinical trials than they do in naturalistic settings
- drugs are less labor-intensive, depend less on the level of skill of the practitioner, and therefore are significantly less expensive to use than psychosocial interventions
- drugs are more cost-effective than psychotherapy over the short-term

Hollon concludes his comprehensive review by emphasizing that cost-effectiveness research on psychotherapy is still very much in its infancy, and adds that the quality and quantity of economic appraisals will have to increase and improve if psychotherapy research is to make any contribution to arguments for sustaining its use.

The next chapter attempts to make sense of the rapid changes in the field of psychotherapy research. In "Linking Efficacy and Effectiveness Research in the Evaluation of Psychotherapies," A. John Rush underscores the urgent need to expand effectiveness studies aimed at evaluating what is actually delivered in practice, how, and to whom, and the effects such treatment has on representative populations and on systems of care. Because services systems research typically uses the system as the unit of analysis, Rush notes, its results can more adequately serve as a guide to administrators, purchasers, and payers in setting priorities for resource allocation.

In his overview, Rush calls for considerable streamlining of the research process, advocating a more flexible approach wherein both efficacy and effectiveness can be established simultaneously. In many ways, he suggests, the issues facing psychotherapy researchers are similar to those confronting practitioners using disease-management protocols, treatment algorithms, and/or clinical guidelines. In these decision-tree models, beneficial effects cannot be definitively attributed to any one particular element or step in the process, since there may well be more than one active ingredient in any treatment. Each treatment intervention involves multiple steps, usually administered in a specified sequence recommended by the protocol, but ultimately defined, in part, by a patient's response to prior steps in the treatment process.

Because management decisions to restrict the number of psychotherapy sessions contradicts available scientific data, Rush suggests that those responsible for authorizing care should also be responsibile for sponsoring scientifically objective evaluations of the outcomes of their decisions. The for-profit health care sector has yet to produce peer-reviewed results, published in the public domain, that evaluate the appropriateness of company policy decisions. There is every reason to believe, Rush contends, that a single-minded focus on the bottom line will affect not only cost, but quality of services, and hence treatment outcome. Rush recommends that managed care organizations which limit access to treatment, should face the legal, economic, and ethical consequences of failing to provide such documentation. Systems of care that define preferred treatments and the methods to implement them, he concludes, have an obligation to support the conduct of effectiveness research in psychotherapy.

In keeping with Rush's concern about moral responsibility in the era of managed care, ethicist Jody Halpern ponders how important it is for the field to develop an explicit approach to the trade-offs in value inherent in today's delivery of psychosocial treatment services. Her chapter grapples with two fundamental questions for an industry run on free market principles. First, what are the goals of health care, and second, how is health care to be allocated fairly? Both are salient, and neither has been significantly addressed by the public or by the psychotherapy research community. She notes that we have not yet, as a society, begun to evaluate the relative worth of competing goals of treatment.

Halpern emphasizes that it is imperative that investigators educate the public on an ongoing basis, not only regarding the benefits of, but also the limitations of, economic analyses for assessing the relative worth of treatments. While cost-effectiveness studies can deliver a common currency for assessing the individual and societal benefits to be derived from psychotherapy, they also pose the potential danger that investigators will adopt a solely economic construct of values (or utilities) as the basis for decisions on the worth of psychotherapy. More explicit attention is needed to better clarify the context, values, and underlying assumptions so often overlooked in economic research. Clearly, the cost-effectiveness of treating patients varies markedly, depending upon which stakeholder's vision is used in defining the outcomes.

Halperin cautions that psychotherapy services researchers cannot avoid addressing this gap in values at the heart of effectiveness research simply by ranking treatments in terms of their cost-effectiveness. Because there is no one definitive approach to making such recommendations, the way that certain parameters are selected for study is certain to reflect implicit values. Research can be more fairly representative of societal ideals if it is guided by societal consensus regarding which benefits of psychotherapy are most important, and how best to distribute such benefits fairly.

Part II: Psychotherapy Service Utilization Patterns in the United States

This section provides an overview of systematic evidence on patterns of psychotherapy use and access. The chapters in this part represent the few large-scale surveys that have been done in this area. They document what is known about who uses psychotherapy, who provides it, what it costs, and where, in the United States, it is provided. These findings focus on the relationship of patterns of service utilization to course and outcome and can usefully be contrasted with those reported in the book's final section, which features assessment of similar variables, but in the context of single-payer health care systems in North America and Europe.

Mark Olfson and Harold A. Pincus base their discussion on data from the National Medical Expenditure Survey, a household survey that provides detailed information on medical events and associated interventions. Data have been statistically adjusted to be generalizable to the United States population. Of relevance to this volume are the nearly 80 million outpatient psychotherapy visits made in 1987, 91% of which were to a mental health specialist. The average psychotherapy user made about 11 visits in a year, and 45% of all users reported that they paid for their own treatment (26% paid with private insurance, 17% through Medicaid). While patterns of use and profiles of users are almost certain to be very different a decade later, this data set provides a rich and useful baseline from which to measure some of the changes that coincide with the onset of managed care.

Lisa Meredith, Roland Sturm, and Ken Wells of the RAND Corporation have been involved for many years in analyzing the Medical Outcomes Study, a large study of health care delivery and outcomes for several medical conditions, including depression. They use data from this rich study to describe patterns of psychosocial counseling for depressed patients in typical medical practice. Though counseling is quite different from formal psychotherapy, there are studies that support the notion that even brief counseling interventions for depression in typical general medical practice can be effective. The longitudinal data presented in this chapter represent usual general medical practice as opposed to practice under research conditions or in the specialty mental health sector. The descriptive findings suggest that patients of mental health specialists tend to be about twice as likely to receive counseling as those of other providers, and that fee-for-service patients are more likely to receive counseling than those under prepaid plans. Counseling was significantly associated with improved outcomes for the sickest depressed patients. An update of this study, with better measures of "psychotherapy" and of "counseling," under the current medical practice and payment structures would be most welcome.

Robert Lueger and colleagues investigate the realities of patients who are actively seeking mental health services, entering psychotherapy, and continuing in psychotherapy. As in the previous chapter, because the data are based on secondary analyses of large epidemiologic data sets, certain assumptions had to be made about what constitutes psychotherapy. Based on a previous finding that a minimum of eight mental health sessions typically produces a 50% improvement, psychotherapy was defined as minimally constituting that number of visits. Of those who made at least one mental health visit, college graduates, whites, those with higher incomes, and those in their twenties were more likely to enter psychotherapy. Using the "readiness to change" model proposed by Prochaska and associates, the authors argue that the most difficult process in seeking help is first realizing that an actual problem exists. Type of insurance coverage (fee-for-service, HMO, or self-pay) was not related to help-seeking, but once in treatment, HMO patients experienced shorter durations of treatment than self-pay or fee-for-service patients. The approach taken by these investigators emphasizes the patient's point of view, including reference to some of the issues and barriers that people face in coming to understand the nature of their problem, and whether or not to seek and continue in mental health care. The full exploration of these issues has important implications for access to mental health care.

Part III: Assessing Costs and Benefits of Psychotherapy: The Economic Evaluation of Psychotherapy Services

The impetus for developing this volume has come from the interest expressed by policymakers, employer-purchasers, and the public and private health care sectors, in more accurately assessing and tracking the cost and value of the health care provided to the mentally ill. This section, which describes state-of-the-art economic strategies for measuring and comparing costs, benefits, and risks of psychotherapeutic services, is what makes the contents of this volume different from any other. All chapters in this part are written from the perspective of health economics, covering principles of economic analysis in detail. Daunting but necessary to consider are the complexities of health studies, particularly mental health and psychotherapy studies. It is clear from reading the chapters in this section that there are a number of different analytic tools and approaches that health economists use, all of which could be applied to the economic study of psychotherapy. What is not stated explicitly, but only comes through after reading the section as a whole, is that as important as the economic tools are, the economic questions about psychotherapy must be thought through carefully. For example, we must be careful to decide if the cost-effectiveness question is asked from the patient, provider, family, or societal point of view. Nearly all of the authors in this section argue that much larger sample sizes are needed for economic analyses than for the usual clinical studies.

Judith Lave and Charlie Schulberg provide a cogent argument for integrating cost-effectiveness analyses within randomized controlled clinical trials. This chapter is based on their own experience of "piggy-backing" a cost-effectiveness study onto an existing three-arm randomized controlled trial on treatment of depression. They review the pros and cons of other common data sources. Claims data sets, for example, typically have large numbers of patients and are relatively inexpensive, but are limited for mental health research given the few outcome variables of interest, the self-selection of patients into different treatment groups, and because of questionable diagnostic precision. Data sets based on cohort studies have the advantage of being able to build in costs and outcome measures prospectively, and tend to have high generalizability since patients are able to self-select into various treatment conditions; however, there may be factors influencing the outcome that are not measured and differentially affect the comparison groups. Clinical trials with random assignment of patients have the advantage of random assignment, but the disadvantages of usually being relatively small for cost-effectiveness studies, and sometimes having high refusal rates prior to study entry. Furthermore, patient respondent burden is increased, and there can be difficulties in establishing working relationships among such disparate trained professionals as economists, mental health clinical researchers, and mental health clinicians. Despite these difficulties, information gained from cost-effectiveness analyses within clinical trials can provide precise comparative results, and the richness and completeness of the clinical data gathered can offer unexpected opportunities to analyze outcomes. Increasing sample sizes and agreement on a standardized set of outcome measures (so as to facilitate meta-analyses) could help maximize the utility of this approach. Although not mentioned by Lave and Schulberg, random assignment studies with multiple sites could also increase the sample size and generalizability of this study design, thus dramatically adding to the value of cost-effectiveness analyses.

In the context of providing an overview of the types of cost-effectiveness research, Bill Hargreaves, Martha Shumway, and Teh-Wei Hu contrast the amount of information available on the cost-effectiveness of psychotherapy versus the information available pertaining to the cost-effectiveness of pharmaceutical treatments, drawing attention to the serious paucity of data regarding psychosocial treatment interventions, and the unbalanced economic literature on mental health interventions.Since there is little profit motive to study the cost-effectiveness of psychotherapy, this trend is apt to continue, unless other funding sources are identified.

Hargreaves and his coauthors point out the main components involved in measuring psychotherapy costs and effectiveness. For example, psychotherapy quality and client suitability are two issues to consider immediately, in addition to the unit of resource (e.g., session of therapy, etc), and the direct and indirect costs (such as mental health care, physical health care, other services, family and informal care, lost productivity, research costs). Even when these aspects can be measured precisely, it may be difficult to attribute cost to emotional versus physical problems. A key point made in this chapter is the importance of analyzing costs and outcomes from the different payer perspectives, and typically there are a number of "payers" (e.g., the client, the client's family, the employer, the insurance company, public health services payers). There is a need for good effectiveness measures (different stakeholders may be concerned with different effectiveness measures) that are standardized, in order to study increments in effectiveness per dollar spent.

Mark Kamlet and Leah Kleinman introduce the concept of cost-utility analysis (CUA) as a sub-category of cost-effectiveness of psychotherapy, which measures and then values the impact of an intervention on a patient's health-related quality of life. The authors point out that while randomized clinical trials are the gold standard for examining health interventions, the short duration of the trial may limit their usefulness for cost-utility analysis; however, with some planning, these data can be incorporated into CUA. The first thing necessary for CUA is actual costs (resources consumed), as opposed to what is charged. In addition, there should be attention to the difference between marginal versus average costs. For example, the last unit of service conceivably may be different in cost from the first. Another point is that transfer payments (e.g., unemployment compensation) are not included in CUA, but resource use is. The authors caution that, ideally, data on the subjective experience of participants should be captured, even after the study is finished. This is especially true for conditions which are long lasting, as many mental health problems are. Last, the authors assert the need to capture total resource use, as opposed to health system use. Even though health system use may include out-of-pocket costs, transportation, and family burden, there are many other non-health system costs, such as criminal justice or social welfare systems costs, that may be involved. Also discussed in this chapter is the need for data on Quality-Adjusted-Life-Years (or QALYs) for the denominator of the CUA. As in previous chapters, Kamlet and Kleinman emphasize the need to establish which utility will be used in the CUA—the patient's? the provider's? the insurance company's? the family's? Finally, the authors review studies in which utility measures have been developed for a range of severe mental illness and CUA is conducted for several maintenance interventions, including psychotherapy.

In setting the stage for their discussion of medical offsets in psychotherapy, Michael Kashner and A. John Rush cogently detail the history of health care cost-containment in the United States. Beginning with the Flexner Report in 1910, touching upon the Hill-Burton Act of the 1940s, and documenting the government's move to implement utilization review and medical fee schedules in the 1970s and 1980s, the authors discuss how federal efforts to promote market solutions to cost-containment eventually yielded the HMOs, PPOs, and other forms of managed care familiar today. Because the potential for realizing medical offsets is appealing to those concerned with cost-containment, the chapter outlines key assumptions of the economic theory pertaining to demand for health care. The authors follow this with a review of the empirical literature on cost-offsets. On the one hand, these studies suggest that investments in mental health care in general, and in psychotherapy specifically, might serve to reduce medical costs, as a result of averting additional health care costs which would otherwise have been consumed had the patient not received the targeted treatment. The chapter also explores the empirical literature on general medical offsets of mental health care using Donabedian's framework for explaining how utilization of psychotherapy might conceivably lead to lower medical costs. On the other hand, Kashner and Rush balance this hypothesis, with a potentially different rationale, suggesting that psychotherapy utilization could paradoxically escalate medical care costs: other illnesses might be discovered, patients may learn to value their health more, and there may be increased contact with a health system that does little to discourage inapporpriate use of medical care. For these reasons, cost-offset studies should be evaluated in the context of the particular managed care environment involved and with respect to changes in patient health outcomes. The authors' review of the mental health cost-offset literature shows that there are serious methodologic and measurement flaws that limit the generalizability of these findings. In response, the authors suggest a variety of methodologic improvements, ranging from the recommendation that cost-offset research be directly linked with changes in health outcomes, to the stipulation that, rather than focusing on traditional cost-offset research techniques that assess rates of utilization, a more reliable, consumer-based, and valid approach might be to estimate cost-offsets as a response to changes in *access* to psychotherapy.

Andrew Healey and Martin Knapp point out that while more conventional forms of economic evaluation such as cost-effectiveness, cost-benefit, and cost-utility analyses have the capacity to compare psychotherapy to different treatments, these approaches depend on analysis of aggregate, or group, databases. The authors suggest that a valuable supplementary source of data resides in information obtained from individual-level data sets. Because studies of interpatient variation in cost and outcome have attracted little research attention, the authors describe how to go about carrying out such studies, while emphasizing the benefits from using this approach to supplement more traditional economic measures. Knapp and Healey also discuss their conceptual framework for the "production of welfare" approach which, while relatively well known in Great Britain and parts of Europe, is unfamiliar to American investigators. This approach enables investigators to encompass linkages among needs, resources, and outc)mes. Based on consideration of how costs, patient characteristics, therapy type, and outcomes all interact, the approach can optimally assist policymakers and administrators to direct the efficient and equitable allocation of resources in the provision of psychotherapy.

In concluding this section, Richard Frank and Tom McGuire present some of the issues involved in determining an appropriate pricing structure for psychotherapy. Their discussion is based on the experience of these two economists in the recent health care reform initiative of 1992–1993, and cogently outlines the very real problems they were confronted with, when arguing policy issues around psychotherapy coverage in the context of a finite budget and competing health concerns. After describing the proposed coverage for mental health care, the authors illustrate a number of the issues that arise in cost estimation. Chief among these are concerns raised by the actuarial community, which are also voiced by many lay people. Given these concerns, methods of cost-estimation tended to err on the side of caution. In particular, it was estimated that if benefits were extended to the uninsured, such coverage could result in costs 245% higher than costs for the typical person who is currently insured. Alternate approaches, such as using data from demand research, yield considerably lower estimates of utilization growth. Estimates of reduced medical care use following psychosocial treatment (see chapter by Kashner and Rush) may also contribute to lower total health costs, but variability of such estimates is considered too great to factor in reliably. It is clear that more careful attention needs to be paid to the concerns raised in this chapter when formulating psychotherapy pricing benefits. This chapter is an important accounting of the different ways that policy questions can be analyzed, depending on the economic assumptions that are made.

Part IV: Measures for Studying Psychotherapy Costs and Outcomes

This section addresses one of the main problems in studying the cost-effectiveness of mental health treatments, that is, defining what the outcomes should be and how to measure them. In clinical treatment trials, the usual approach is to examine disease specific outcomes—typically, change in number and severity of symptoms. In mental health services research there is an interest beyond mere symptom reduction to various functional domains. Fortunately, a number of top researchers have given attention to developing appropriate measures for the study of these outcomes. This section reflects the state of knowledge with regard to quantifying functional outcome assessments. Included are in-depth reviews of the types of outcome measures most salient to policymakers, to health care maintenance organizations, to purchasers, and to consumers, but heretofore rarely used by clinical investigators. These chapters chart the course of the shift in clinical research away from a focus on short-term, symptomatic outcomes, toward longer-term functional and economic measures of general health, work, consumer preference, and subjective quality-of-life indicators.

One of the key issues in studying the effectiveness of any treatment is how to evaluate response to that treatment. Such monitoring of interim responsiveness is essential in the real world so that clinicians know when to take correctional action such as modifying the dose, augmenting with adjunct treatment, changing the treatment entirely, or reassessing the diagnosis. In their chapter, Ken Howard and colleagues tackle these important issues by presenting two useful models in psychotherapy: the "dose-response model" and the "phase model." Developed from Howard's earlier work, the dose-response model shows that improvement in psychotherapy follows a log-linear model, with most improvement occurring in the early sessions, with slowing rates of improvement as the number of sessions increase. According to this model, 50% of all patients will show improvement by eight sessions of psychotherapy, 75% will be improved by 26 sessions, and 85% by 65 sessions. This model can be a useful way of comparing therapies, particularly when associated cost data are available. It can also be useful in establishing guidelines for the number of therapy sessions for various diagnostic conditions. The "phase model" consists of three categories of outcomes (remoralization, remediation, and rehabilitation) through which psychotherapy patients progress sequentially. Instruments to measure attainment levels in these phases have been developed. Both the "dose-response" and the "phase" models provide a conceptual framework that can help to guide detailed cost-effectiveness studies.

Clardy and colleagues argue that the assessment of outcomes in clinical practice is integrally linked to patient characteristics, treatment process, and treatment value. Researchers need to measure these aspects carefully. Patient characteristics (or case-mix) can often play a role in what type of treatment the patient seeks as well as the prognosis for treatment. For example, in treatment of depression, more educated patients may prefer psychotherapy to pharmacotherapy, and education (independent of treatment) may be related to more favorable outcomes. Similarly, treatment process (including the type of treatment, its dosing, frequency, and setting) are also important determinants of outcomes. Although "dosing" is typically thought of in relationship to pharmacotherapy, the concept is equally valid for psychotherapy. Researchers need to decide which outcomes are important to measure in their study (for example, work productivity, quality of life, overall health status) and which instruments to use. Last, they need to collect information on cost of treatment for even a rudimentary determination of the value of health improvement relative to the cost of care provided. The approach advocated in this chapter is relatively straightforward, and if more clinical psychotherapy researchers followed it, the field would be in a significantly stronger position to comment on the effectiveness and cost-effectiveness of psychotherapy for various disorders.

Robert Kaplan details the theory behind health-related quality-of-life measures and their relevance to mental health services research. While quality-of-life measures grew out of the study of general health conditions, the construct is also applicable and important to mental health conditions. Such measures allow for comparison between mental health and general medical outcomes. Components for quality-of-life study include mortality, morbidity, utility (or relative importance of certain states), and prognosis. Using these concepts, two important measures have been developed: Quality Adjusted Life Years (QALYs) and Disability Adjusted Life Years (DALYs). Both measures can help to determine the impact of psychotherapy relative to other treatments (including combined treatments), as well as overall success of mental health treatments relative to treatments for medical conditions. As hard decisions are being made concerning how resources should be allocated, it is critical that the relationship of mental health treatments to quality of life be demonstrated.

Given the importance of this subject, Tony Lehman provides a careful review of the components of quality of life and its importance to the mental health field. Arguing that quality of life reflects the significance to the patient of clinical changes (and is therefore a critical part of mental health outcomes assessments), Lehman lays out the dimensions of quality of life and their domains. Broadly, quality of life is composed of functional status (what an individual is capable of doing), access to resources, opportunities to use one's abilities to pursue interests, and a sense of well-being. Within these dimensions are life domains, such as health, family, social relations, work, financial status, and living situation. Various quality-of-life measures have been developed, including measures for general quality of life, health-related quality of life, and disease-specific quality of life. As an introduction to the reader, Lehman briefly describes 15 quality-of-life measures, including 11 for severe and persistent mental illness, one for schizophrenia, and three for anxiety and affective disorders. While not an exhaustive review, this chapter makes it easier for the reader to investigate some of these measures for his/her own use.

Jan Krupnick discusses the importance of taking into account both symptom and functional measures in both research and clinical settings. Knowledge of the functional improvements associated with various mental health treatments is as important to clinicians in choosing a treatment and assessing its effectiveness in a given patient, as is knowledge of symptom improvements. Because functional improvement follows a different trajectory than symptom improvement, it is critical not to stop treatment early based on symptomatic outcomes alone. Underscoring the importance of functional improvement to both patients and providers, the chapter reviews a number of outcome measures that are currently in use in managed care settings, as well as some psychotherapy-specific measures. Despite advances in developing these measures, there is a need for more diagnosis-specific measures that could be used to measure the disability typically associated with particular disorders. Advances in functional measurement methodology should translate to improved patient care, better science, and better policy decisions.

Despite the centrality to life satisfaction that is universally placed on the ability to carry out meaningful work, there is a paucity of research findings about work function in the mental health treatment literature. In their chapter on assessing work function, Jim Mintz, Gary Bond, and Lois Imber Mintz articulate the gap that exists between the psychiatric treatment literature and the rehabilitation literature in measuring work function. The most commonly used instruments to measure work function are part of social function measures—and there has been only one new social function measure since 1980. Clearly, with the changes in work (and changes in the work force), there is a need for updated work assessment instruments. This chapter discusses concepts that are central to the notion of work function, but not necessarily easily measured, such as employment, primary and multiple roles, money and productivity. More provocative is the variable relationship between mental symptoms and work capacity. In some disorders, such as depression, the correlation between symptoms and work capacity is strong, but in others, such as in chronic and severe conditions, correlations are weak. The study of work function is vital to assessing mental health outcomes, and may be even more vital to psychotherapy outcomes specifically, because psychotherapy can target particular functions. Enhancing the measurement of productivity, a component of indirect costs, is clearly an area ripe for additional research.

Part V: Examining Efficacy and Cost-Effectiveness of Psychotherapy

This section critically reviews the psychotherapy efficacy literature on disorder-specific controlled clinical trials, demonstrating that the lion's share of rigorous empirical studies to date have focused largely on treatment of schizophrenia and of major affective disorder. Nevertheless, this section also takes into account those disorders commonly encountered in clinical practice—but rarely studied in academic settings, despite the fact that they are perceived to incur high medical costs.

Diagnoses ranging from post-traumatic stress disorder and dissociative disorder, to bulimia and borderline personality disorder are discussed in terms of available estimates on cost, outcome, and cost-effectiveness. Clinical questions pertaining to the relative efficacy of pharmacotherapy versus psychotherapy for treatment of specific disorders are also discussed, as are recommendations for development of cutting-edge hybrid research designs, better able to yield practical answers to cost and outcome comparisons.

In his review of psychotherapy for major mood disorders, Rush highlights the primary obstacles to translating findings from studies of affective disorder into routine practice. Conversely, he also emphasizes key questions to be posed in evaluating routine clinical practice, in light of efficacy findings. He observes that while a continuum is believed to exist between efficacy and effectiveness outcomes, such that symptom improvement is automatically assumed to lead to enhanced psychosocial functioning, improved quality of life, and reduced service utilization, the empirical basis for such a presumption remains far from established.

Rush's meta-analytic review of the mood disorder efficacy literature concludes that different psychotherapies appear to be equivalent in efficacy, just as all antidepressant medications appear to be about equally efficacious. He ponders whether these efficacy findings actually generalize to clinical practice sites with "real world" patients treated under routine treatment conditions. There is growing consensus that the transfer of positive findings from efficacy trials to front-line care is not necessarily predictable. Variables such as patient recruitment bias, diagnostic accuracy, flexibility of treatment, and service system contingencies, all can impact the efficacy of psychotherapy.

Michael Goldstein reviews evidence for the efficacy of psychotherapy, behavioral interventions, social skills training, and family therapy for patients diagnosed with schizophrenia. He notes that psychosocial treatment development research in schizophrenia has moved from a predominant focus on efficacy, to one on effectiveness, emphasizing attention to the cost-effectiveness of treatment delivery. He draws attention to the value of psychoeducational family intervention, which has proceeded through pilot development and controlled clinical trials, but as yet, is unavailable on the front lines, because the intervention awaits development of an applied, cost-effective means to implement it, and disseminate information about it. Psychoeducational family programs reduce patient relapse following hospital discharge, even when contrasted with controls receiving pharmacotherapy alone. While medication comprises the most common type of outpatient therapy in the United States for schizophrenia, from a cost-effectiveness perspective, it would be useful to show how each relapse averted—by virtue of ancillary psychoeducational interventions—might produce cost savings. Despite the ability of these methods to enhance quality of life, work, and social function, without ancillary data from cost-effectiveness studies, it is unlikely that these or any other behavioral advances will be successfully incorporated into routine care.

Stefan Hofmann and David Barlow discuss how anxiety disorders incur significant personal costs, imposing direct and indirect costs in terms of inappropriate medical services delivered and reduced work productivity. Despite the wide prevalence of these disorders, there has been little work assessing the financial burden of anxiety disorders on society. As with schizophrenia, psychopharmacologic treatment remains a common and efficacious form of intervention for the spectrum of anxiety disorders, however, when the drugs are stopped relapse rates rebound. The authors' review of the anxiety treatment literature suggests that many psychosocial interventions are at least as good as existing pharmacologic approaches, and in addition, appear to have more enduring effects. Nevertheless, despite the availability of studies demonstrating the efficacy of behavioral interventions, pharmacologic approaches typically receive top preference in clinical practice, often to the exclusion of psychosocial approaches entirely. In part, this is because patients are unaware these treatments exist and therefore fail to request them. In addition, effective psychosocial interventions are not often available to the majority of individuals who might benefit from them. Problems pertaining to information dissemination about useful treatments, treatment accessibility, practitioner education, and public relations must clearly be addressed.

In considering dysthymic disorder, a syndrome previously dismissed as a subcategory of major depression, John Markowitz draws attention to the fact that such disorders may incur higher costs and cause more chronic dysfunction than major depression. Affecting nearly 3% of American adults, dysthymia is commonly associated with other comorbid psychiatric disorders, including anxiety, substance abuse, and dependent, avoidant, borderline, and/or self-defeating disorders. Results from the RAND Medical Outcomes Study comparing patients with major affective disorder, dysthymic disorder, and subsyndromal depressive symptoms showed that at two-year follow-up, dysthymic patients manifested the worst functional outcomes of all groups. Given its early onset and long duration, dysthymia may impair productivity throughout the course of a working career, while remaining both underdiagnosed and untreated. Prior to the advent of DSM-III, dysthymic disorder was considered neurotic in nature, and psychotherapy was the treatment of choice. Over the past decade, pharmacotherapy has eclipsed psychotherapy as a first line treatment for chronic depression. The absence of systematic information pertaining to the effectiveness of psychosocial treatments is disturbing, given the high treatment failure rates reported with medication alone. Only about half of dysthymic individuals receiving pharmacologic agents tend to respond—some cannot tolerate the side effects, others have medical contraindications, and/or refuse to take medications. Until recently, there were no federally funded outcome studies of the psychotherapy of dysthymic disorder, and no systematic effectiveness, or cost-effectiveness, studies undertaken. Research is needed to test the cost-effectiveness of acute and maintenance time-limited therapies, with attention to serial and combined applications of psychotherapy and pharmacotherapy. Follow-up assessments can help determine whether treatments have more than a transient effect on chronic, entrenched symptoms and dysfunctional patterns of functioning. As economic pressures on mental health services continue to tighten and as numbers of psychotherapy visits covered by third-party payers continue to shrink, the need to to define effective and cost-effective psychotherapy for dysthymic patients represents an important research priority.

Jaycox and Foa review cost-effectiveness in the treatment of post-traumatic stress disorder (PTSD). An anxiety disorder with an estimated lifetime prevalence of 9% in the general population, the disorder occurs in response to extreme stress, and is accompanied by feelings of terror and/or helplessness during the experience. The authors report rates of PTSD resulting from combat experience, terrorism, accidents and natural disasters, and assaults (including sexual assaults, child molestation, domestic violence), and draw attention to those professions that are at risk for developing PTSD (e.g., law enforcement officers, emergency room technicians, fire fighters, and disaster workers). Traumatic experience puts these individuals at risk for depression and suicide. While individuals with PTSD may "self-medicate" anxiety symptoms by using drugs and alcohol, there are few programs available to treat PTSD and substance abuse disorders within an integrated approach, despite extensive rates of comorbidity. PTSD patients incur high health care system costs and show increased utilization of doctor visits, emergency room visits, psychiatric hospitalizations, and outpatient psychotherapy. While a variety of interventions have been developed to treat PTSD (e.g., supportive counseling individually or in groups, brief psychodynamic psychotherapy, hypnotherapy, pharmacotherapy, cognitive-behavioral therapy, eye-movement desensitization and reprocessing, critical incident debriefing), few controlled outcome studies have been staged. The authors discuss estimates for core PTSD treatment costs, but, generally, there is little evidence pertaining to cost-effectiveness.

There are good reasons, say James Mitchell, Carol Peterson, and Stewart Agras, for the paucity of economic data pertaining to the cost-effectiveness of treatments for eating disorders. Anorexia nervosa, the disorder studied for the longest duration, is difficult to track because prevalence rates are low, access to care is problematic, the disorder often requires hospitalization which makes randomization difficult, and because many anorexic patients are treatment-resistant and manifest high rates of morbidity and mortality. Because of these strategic and methodologic barriers, investigators have been slow to engage in studies of anorexia. More information is available on the cost-effectiveness of treating bulimia nervosa, given its higher prevalence, low rates of hospitalization, and lesser number of interventions, but nevertheless, the number of studies is modest. This chapter reviews the research literature on treatment comparisons, examines predictors of treatment response, and presents evidence on mediators of treatment. Estimated costs of bulimia treatment to health care systems, and to patients, are calculated, and an analysis of the comparative cost of using cognitive behavioral treatment, versus treatment with fluoxetine hydrochoride, is discussed. The authors call for development of psychotherapy research which uses more naturalistic designs, includes more heterogeneous patient groups, uses samples which are generalizable, tracks drop-outs and nonresponders over time, and establishes working ties with practitioners working on the front lines.

Paul Pilkonis, Bryan Neighbors, and Elizabeth Corbitt discuss the chronic, pervasive maladaptive behavior patterns that constitute personality disorders (PDs). They review the literature on efficacy of psychosocial and pharmacologic treatments, discuss problems pertaining to comorbidity—both among Axis II disorders, and between Axis I and II disorders—and attempt to identify costs associated with these disorders. Three main categories of PDs are described, including the odd or eccentric cluster A (including paranoid, schizoid, and schizotypal), the externalizing or dramatic Cluster B (including antisocial, borderline, histrionic, and narcissistic), and the internalizing or anxious Cluster C (including avoidant, dependent, and obsessive-compulsive disorders).

Cluster B is the most socially disruptive and most costly PD, and is often characterized by emotional instability, poor impulse control, chronic anger, suicidality and self-mutilation, as well as eating disorders and substance abuse. Such debilitating problems lead to repeated episodes of hospitalization, sporadic ability to work, and high suicide rates. These individuals are often inadequately diagnosed and treated. For example, a 22% prevalence rate of personality disorders identified in a community sample followed from age 14 to 47 revealed that despite continuing evidence of impairment and increased morbidity and mortality rates, few individuals ever received appropriate psychiatric attention or even accurate diagnoses.

The effect of comorbidity on course of illness has not been adequately addressed, with the exception of studies which have evaluated the impact of a comorbid PD on course and treatment of affective disorder, where prevalence estimates of PDs among depressed patients range from 30 to 81%. Comorbid PDs lead to worse prognoses, and are associated with earlier onset of depression, more suicidal ideation and suicide attempts, and worse treatment outcomes. Comorbid PDs may be even more common with anxiety, somatoform, and substance abuse disorders than with affective disorders.

There are few psychotherapy outcome studies which primarily focus on patients diagnosed with PDs. Among the completed studies, methodologic difficulties—whether small Ns, heterogeneous samples, diverse diagnostic procedures, inconsistent change measures—often limit the ability to draw conclusions about differential efficacy. With the exception of Linehan's work (discussed below), there are no data on cost-effectiveness linked to PDs, despite the obvious need to collect such information. The degree of functional impairment associated with severe PDs suggests that major costs accrue from chronic problems in work, family and interpersonal functioning, substance abuse, and inappropriate utilization of health care services.

Linehan and Heard describe the economic parameters of borderline personality disorder (BPD), noting that despite the high costs incurred by BPD, it is one of the least studied of the chronic psychiatric disorders. Affected individuals are characterized by chaotic relationships, confused identities, and typically have a pattern of multiple, discontinuous psychotherapies and pharmacotherapies, along with various legal system involvements, ranging from filing for bankruptcy to imprisonment for criminal offenses. Employment histories are problematic, and a significant percentage receive some combination of unemployment, public assistance, housing subsidies, and the like. The greatest health care costs of BPD typically result from repeated hospitalizations for suicidal or self-injurious behavior. Many costs associated with the disorder are difficult to estimate, such as the degree to which the patient constitutes a financial burden to family and friends. Considering the severity of BPD, Linehan and Heard note that the absence of therapies with proven efficacy is disturbing. Pharmacotherapy trials suggest that while medication effects may be significant, medicated patients suffer high rates of treatment attrition, and the clinical benefit derived appears modest at best. Vis à vis psychotherapy, clinical trial data from Linehan's Dialectical Behavior Therapy (DBT) suggest that compared to routine mental health care, DBT has a better benefit-cost value (monetary value of benefits minus costs) than does standard treatment, and is more cost-effective (ratio of nonmonetary benefits to monetary costs). Additional studies are needed in order to address BPD outcomes in conjunction with assessment of direct and indirect costs of providing the treatment.

In his discussion of dissociative identity disorder (DID), which until recently was called multiple personality disorder (MPD), Richard Kluft documents this complex chronic dissociative form of psychopathology, characterized by lesions of identity and memory. He underscores the confusing clinical presentation with which these polysymptomatic patients often present, and notes that prevalence of DID in national and international studies is unexpectedly high, particularly in psychiatric inpatients, in subgroups with chemical dependency, and in those with childhood histories of sexual abuse. Cases with symptoms referable to DID spend an average of seven to eight years in the mental health care delivery system prior to accurate diagnosis, and estimates suggest that in the years spent in treatment prior to correct diagnosis, close to $185,000 dollars could be expended on nonspecific psychiatric treatment. Because individuals are not typically diagnosed until the fourth decade of life, they commonly sustain adverse economic outcomes in terms of greater likelihood of underachievement, disability, and absenteeism. Kluft reviews screening measures, structured interviews, specialized mental status examinations, and psychological test batteries for diagnosis of DID, and describes a number of targeted interventions and treatments. There is considerable need for systematic data pertaining to the utility and cost-effectiveness of these heretofore untested treatment interventions.

Despite impressive progress characterizing the field of psychotherapy research over the course of the past several decades, taken together, the papers in this section reflect immense gaps in systematic knowledge pertaining to some of the most costly and chronic of mental disorders. The section is rich with ideas for advancing a new research agenda in psychosocial treatment research, which can help provide research-based guidance to enhance mental health practice and policy.

Part VI: Psychotherapy Service Utilization Patterns: An International Perspective

In this section, experts from other nations discuss the role of psychotherapy in the context of their respective national health care systems, touching upon how, and whether, psychotherapy is rationed, describing who is eligible to administer psychosocial treatment, how costs are determined, and estimating the proportionate share of the national health care budget accounted for by mental health expenditures. In the face of the federally supported movement to embrace managed care in the United States, these papers lend an international perspective to this book, outlining the different ways in which single-payer systems work, and underscoring the varying degrees of support available for psychosocial interventions in different countries.

Sadavoy and Perry describe the system of psychotherapy services delivered in Canada. The authors relate how the Canadian government initiated universal national health care in 1984, establishing a decentralized system which remained the predominant responsibility of each of the ten provincial governments. As a result of cuts in funding, neither federal nor provincial-based data pertaining to outlays relevant to psychotherapy are collected. Although Sweden and Germany define required credentials for psychotherapists, Canada—and until recently, England—have not done so. Initiating and terminating treatment remain decisions made at the practitioner's discretion, and no outcome criteria or effectiveness measures are in place in any Canadian jusisdiction. As in the U.K., waiting lists for long-term psychotherapy are lengthy, and primary-care physicians find ascertainment of needed psychiatric services for their patients difficult to obtain. Psychotherapy funded by the Provincial Health Services covers only physicians, with the result that the private fee-for-service psychotherapy domain remains entirely nonmedical, conducted by psychologists and social workers. Eighty percent of all psychotherapy conducted in Canada, however, is carried out by psychiatrists on an individual outpatient basis, with the annual cost per patient (latest figures available) of $782 Canadian, and with an average treatment episode duration of 7.8 sessions.

Horst Kächele, Rainer Richter, Helmut Thoma, and Adolph-Ernst Meyer review the history and current status of psychotherapy services in the federal republic of Germany. The authors trace how psychotherapy and psychosomatic medicine developed on a trajectory independent from psychiatry in Germany, but today comprise an essential part of the mandatory curriculum for all medical students. There is strong societal consensus in Germany regarding the effectiveness of psychoanalytic psychotherapy. Findings of significant reduction in rehospitalization rates in those receiving psychotherapy, as opposed to treatment as usual, were instrumental to the government's decision to include psychodynamic and psychoanalytic psychotherapies as benefits to be provided by the national health insurance companies. Insurance companies were also impressed by a series of cost-benefit studies which estimated the impact of psychotherapy on chronic somatic and psychosomatic disorders. These positive results, particularly in the realm of work function benefits, which were sustained over time, helped shape German mental health care policy.

The health insurance system in Germany ensures that necessary medical treatment is available to all, regardless of ability to pay. Patients, in fact, are not permitted to make direct payments for care, yet are free to select their own physicians. The cost of insurance premiums, however, is steep, comprising approximately 14% of an individual's income. It is typically the therapist's task to justify his recommended therapy to the insurance company in terms of medical necessity, cost, and effectiveness. In addition to access to short-term therapies, three years of psychoanalysis for treatment of a diagnosable illness is also fully covered by public health insurance. Moreover, nearly 40% of all patients receive psychotherapy as inpatients. In Germany, an 8000-bed inpatient psychotherapy service provides up to six weeks of intensive multimodal psychotherapy. The chronically ill can be provided with intensive psychoanalytic inpatient treatment with duration of stay up to nine months. 50% of the psychotherapy workforce are MD's and 50% are clinical psychologists. Government estimates, however, based on epidemiologic prevalence data, suggest that six-to-seven times more outpatient therapists are needed. Compared to the availability of therapists in other countries, this represents a large number of practitioners, yet the budget for outpatient psychotherapy amounts to only 0.39% of the total budget of German health insurance companies.

The situation in England, as Glenys Parry suggests, is one rapidly undergoing change, with the advent of a more market-based approach to delivery of Britain's health care. While not able to be as generous in the psychosocial treatment arena as the German insurance companies, the British National Health Service (NHS) has taken the lead in sponsoring efforts to develop evidence-based practice and effectiveness information. The NHS provides health services to the people of Britain free of charge, purchased via approximately 100 local health authorities, each of which targets the needs of individual localities. Services are delivered through provider organizations (NHS Trusts), which exercise relative autonomy in benefit design and service provision. Primary-care physicians serve as gatekeepers to specialists, and purchase psychotherapy services on behalf of their beneficiaries. In Britain, formal psychotherapy services have long waiting lists, with many who potentially could benefit from treatment, failing to receive it. Less than 50% of health authorities have yet attempted to systematically assess their locality's need for psychotherapy. Nevertheless, the NHS aims to enhance psychosocial service delivery via development of evidence-based practice, promotion of cost-effective methods, utilization of clinical guidelines, clinical audits, and enhanced professional training.

Parry reports that in 1993–1994, the latest year for which data are available, expenditures on mental health comprised approximately 12% of total NHS expenditure. Systematic review revealed delivery of a broad range of psychosocial therapies, by a diverse range of professionals, many of whom were unlicensed and unregulated. As part of its mandate to oversee adequacy and quality of mental health treatment, the NHS Executive commissioned and published advice to researchers on how to integrate economic analyses when staging controlled clinical trials. Stimulated by this, The Mental Health Foundation, a British charity, has begun funding research on the economic evaluation of psychotherapy services. In 1994, the NHS commissioned a systematic review of the empirical psychotherapy literature on efficacy and effectiveness. Findings revealed a dearth of good studies of psychodynamic schools of treatment—the most frequently practiced modality in all four countries reviewed—but did locate evidence for efficacy of Interpersonal Psychotherapy (IPT) and of Cognitive Behavioral Therapy for depression.

Front line practitioners in the U.K., however, found these studies of marginal relevance, in the absence of research on more widely practiced treatment modalities. The studies were also criticized for their poor generalizability, their minimal attention to comorbid conditions and to individual differences, and for their intensive focus on symptom remission to the exclusion of criteria related to function and quality of life. The absence of efficacy data, the report emphasized, does not constitute evidence of ineffectiveness. At the same time, there appears to be growing sentiment in Britain, suggesting that standard practice should be better informed regarding the use of clinical guidelines and benchmarks for "best-practices," based on reviews of service evaluation data, clinical consensus, and research findings. On the local level, health authorities express a preference for seeing treatment effectiveness—not efficacy—tested via field trials and service evaluation methods, in hopes of revealing gaps in knowledge and gaps in practitioner skill. There is growing interest in matching patient complexity and severity of illness with therapist skill level.

A different type of universal health care system is in place in Sweden. In his chapter, Bengt Åke Armelius shares information regarding the nature, costs, and variegated training supporting the delivery of psychosocial treatment services in his nation. Armelius indicates that the total cost for psychiatric care provided by the state is about $123 per person per year, while the average daily cost for inpatient care is approximately $230. The maximum out-of-pocket capital cost for any form of health care in Sweden is $200 annually and the cost for health care per visit is about $20. Sweden has an even higher proportion of mental health specialists than Germany, with its approximately ten psychiatrists, nine psychologists, and nine social workers per each 100,000 in population. The preponderance of psychiatric care delivered in Sweden takes place within the official welfare system.

The nation is divided into 114 psychiatric sectors which are responsible for all types of care. The two types of psychosocial interventions delivered in outpatient settings include the formal psychotherapies, which are largely provided by psychologists, and the "supportive talks" which are provided by psychiatrists and social workers with limited training in psychotherapy. Formal psychotherapies are predominantly delivered to those diagnosed with personality disorders, anxiety, depression, and to a lesser extent, to those in acute psychologic crisis—but are rarely delivered to those diagnosed with substance abuse or psychosis.

As a result of escalating health care costs, the trend in Sweden lately has been away from the formal psychotherapies, and toward increased emphasis on "supportive talks." Presently, there are approximately 3300 patients on waiting lists for psychotherapeutic services in Sweden, because funds are insufficient to support all in need. About half of all reimbursement for psychotherapy in private practice is paid out-of-pocket by the patient him/herself—given that general health insurance can only be used to reimburse physicians, and not psychologists. Nevertheless, psychologist-psychotherapists in Sweden are required to be formally trained, authorized, and licenced, with duration of training in psychodynamic approaches extending to a decade beyond completion of basic education. Psychiatrists and social workers rarely have access to this intensive form of training. Sweden recently reorganized its service delivery organization, placing greater emphasis on early psychotherapeutic intervention in the family unit in an effort to prevent the onset of chronicity in first-break schizophrenics and in disturbed individuals with borderline personality disorder. While all four of the single-payer systems described above are laudable, signs of financial stress are evident in each one, as national health services attempt to grapple with mounting demand and rapidly increasing costs.

A Blueprint for the Psychotherapy Research Agenda

This volume has enumerated many reasons for investment in building a services research field for psychosocial treatment that integrates economic variables, employs more naturalistic designs, includes more heterogeneous patient groups, uses samples which are generalizable, tracks drop-outs and non-responders, and establishes close working ties with practitioners working on the front lines.

The volume includes many important recommendations pertaining to the distribution, utilization, and costs and benefits of psychotherapy. It may be useful for the reader to consider several of the following potential points, in thinking about moving the field of psychotherapy research forward into the 21st century. These include:

1. Collecting epidemiologic data pertaining to psychotherapy utilization, cost, and outcome: This focus might determine why such a high proportion of psychotherapy users manifest no diagnosis (but nevertheless feel the need for treatment); illuminate characteristics of the 10% of high-end users who account for 90% of psychotherapy services expenditures; and assess whether those patients with multiyear chronic and relapsing disorders are the ones receiving prolonged treatment in "real world" clinical settings.

2. Studying the impact of benefit design on psychotherapy utilization and outcome: This topic might include determining the effects of price-sensitivity on demand for services; or assessing what motivates choices about purchase of psychotherapy services under various constraints.

3. Developing a psychometrically sound Core Battery to assess cost and outcome of psychotherapy services, designed for use across clinical and services research domains.

4. Evaluating cost, treatment, and posttreatment outcomes of patients receiving sequential, maintenance, and/or continuation psychotherapies. This emphasis might consider the impact of psychotherapy followed by a prescribed next step, such as medication, or another type of psychotherapy, for treatment nonresponders.

5. Assessing dose-response relationships and thoroughness of treatment response in naturalistic settings. This focus might entail studies designed to evaluate the impact of adequacy, length, and frequency of psychotherapy on sustained remission; determining whether posttreatment effects of time-limited therapies are most profound in the less severely ill, for example, or assessing whether clinically remitted, or just somewhat improved, but still symptomatic, treatment response, affects course of illness, and therefore, cost.

6. Determining whether the acute psychotherapy interventions used in randomized, controlled clinical trials actually improve clinical course, outcome, and cost over the long term in naturalistic practice settings.

7. Developing innovative cost-effective research design and statistical methods for use across psychosocial clinical and services domains.

8. Developing studies of utilization, cost, and outcome of psychotherapy in primary-care settings.

9. Developing research partnerships with the private sector.

10. Designing mechanisms to expedite the transfer of effective psychotherapy technologies, for example providing for systematic conduits among professional organizations, states, and municipalities, to support the use of empirical data in shaping clinical practice, linking efficacy and services researchers with the postgraduate educational system, in order to incorporate training in effective treatments on a continuing basis.

In closing this rich tour of the state of the art, it may be useful to draw readers' attention to two recent publications which nicely complement the aims of this volume, and which may further assist in advancing an economics/psychotherapy research agenda for the nation.

The first, entitled *Cost-Effectiveness in Health and Medicine* (Gold, M. R., Siegel, J. E., Russell, L. B. and Weinstein, M. C., Eds., Oxford University Press, 1996) details findings and recommendations from a multidisciplinary Panel on Cost-Effectiveness in Health and Medicine convened by the U.S. Public Health Service. The panel of economists, ethicists, psychometricians, and clinicians produced a thoughtful report pertaining to the use, conduct, and limitations of cost-effectiveness analysis as a decision-making tool in the delivery of medical care. While focused on medical costs and conditions in general, and not on mental health per se, nevertheless the volume's clarity of approach in measuring costs and effectiveness, evaluating outcomes, discounting, and dealing with uncertainty, serves as an excellent introduction to these concepts.

The second book, *Cost-Outcome Methods for Mental Health*, by William Hargreaves, Martha Shumway, Teh-Wei Hu, and Brian Cuffel (Academic Press, 1998), focuses specifically on cost-effectiveness studies as they apply to psychopharmacologic and psychosocial treatment interventions. The authors serve as lucid guides to readers unfamiliar with economics, helping them to consider new perspectives in services research design, in key economic concepts and tools, while also describing how to make optimal use of cost-effectiveness findings to guide mental health practice and policy.

The mental health service delivery system has changed dramatically over the past twenty years, and even more so over the last five. As the system of care in the United States has been transformed from a hospital based, public monopoly into a diversified market primarily controlled by managed-care organizations, economic considerations are certain to loom ever larger in shaping policy decisions regarding the quality and cost-effectiveness of psychotherapy outcomes. Efforts by the federal government to enhance the quality of health care strongly emphasize the importance of evidence-based practice and innovation for treating conditions which are prevalent, costly, and understudied. As such, the blueprint for psychotherapy research outlined above should serve as a useful springboard for addressing and repairing the considerable gaps in research evidence available for support of psychosocial treatment practice. As pressures for quality, effectiveness, and cost containment continue to mount at the dawn of a new century, the integration of economic variables into psychotherapy outcome studies will become increasingly necessary and desirable.

1

DEFINING PSYCHOTHERAPY

1

Market-Based Health Care Reform and the Cost-Effectiveness of Psychotherapy

John P. Docherty

We have entered a new era of health care reform, an era which represents a very fundamental shift in the paradigm of health care delivery in this nation. The structure and agenda of this new outlook in health care have been generated by three key problems: cost, quality, and access. Our entire health care system is being reorganized to address these three issues. This book is about the participation of psychotherapy and psychotherapy research in this new era of health care reform. The chapters in this book, under the heading of "cost-effectiveness," reflect the field's initial efforts to actively grapple with, and effectively participate in, forwarding these national goals.

This chapter places psychotherapy cost-effectiveness research within a sociopolitical and historical perspective. It reviews the nature of cost, quality, and access issues in mental health care, the specific impact of these issues on highlighting current problems in psychotherapy research and practice, and new directions emerging for resolving these problems.

Cost, Quality, Access, and Mental Health Care

Cost

Several historical facts reflect the critical nature of the cost factor in mental health care. First, in recent decades, there has been a vast expansion of available services and their concomitant costs. For example:

- The number of private psychiatric hospitals grew nearly 200% between 1970 and 1988, from 150 to 444 (Redick, Witken, Atay, & Manderscheid, 1992).
- Between 1965 and 1990, the number of inpatient episodes in mental health organizations in the United States increased steadily from 1,565,525 to 2,262,474; whereas the number of psychiatric outpatient episodes nearly quintupled from 1,071,000 to 5,810,405, and the number of partial care admissions increased almost 10-fold from 55,486 to 544,201 (Redick et al., 1994a).

Second, the dollars spent on mental health care services and research increased substantially:

- The National Institute of Mental Health (NIMH) budget increased from $1,119,000 in 1945 to $178,067,000 in 1979, to over an estimated $661,290,000 in 1996, and this current estimate does not include Substance Abuse and Mental Health Services Administration (SAMHSA), which represents about $2 billion in federal funding (National Institutes of Health, 1996).
- Total expenditures by mental health organizations in the United States, as measured in current dollars, increased more than eightfold between 1969 and 1990, from $3.3 to $28.4 billion (Redick et al., 1994b).
- While policymakers viewed the problem of escalating costs in general medicine as daunting when they manifested a 300% increase over the consumer price index (CPI), the situation was signifi-

cantly more grave in the behavioral health field. For example, in 1990, the increase in total mental health care costs was almost three times that of general health care costs.

Beyond the absolute cost issues, as Frank and McGuire point out (see chapter 13), the well-substantiated finding of greater demand for ambulatory mental health care than general medical office care has led policymakers and their advisers to be particularly wary of extending benefits for mental health coverage.

Quality

In addition to problems with escalating costs, numerous studies have demonstrated problems with quality, including failures in diagnosis and failure to provide appropriate or adequate treatment. The mental health field also reflects problems, endemic in general medical care, of wide regional variation in practice patterns, which are seemingly unrelated to clinical variables. Illustrative examples of quality problems include the following:

- Primary-care clinicians have been regularly found to substantially underdiagnose the depressed patient in the primary-care setting (Docherty, 1997). One study found that primary-care clinicians accurately diagnosed only 44% of patients with *DSM-III* depressive disorder. On the mental health specialty side, however, this statistic was "balanced" by considerable overdiagnosis, with a rate of 164% (Schulberg et al., 1985).
- Strupp's series of landmark studies demonstrated the prevalence of negative attitudes by the therapist toward the patient as a frequent cause of treatment failure (Sachs, 1987; Strupp & Binder, 1984).
- Hofmann and Barlow point out (see chapter 21) that although specific, demonstrably effective psychosocial treatments are available for the treatment of phobia, three recent surveys in different cities have shown that only 15–38% of phobic patients *in treatment* are receiving psychosocial interventions that have been demonstrated to be efficacious in randomized clinical trials.
- Linehan and Heard (see chapter 27) note that the only psychosocial treatment that has been demonstrated to be efficacious by randomized clinical trials for the treatment of borderline personality disorder is not only the least costly but also the least frequently utilized.

Similar quality problems exist in the use of psychopharmacology and with treatment resource allocation. For example:

- It has been repeatedly shown that insufficient dose or duration of antidepressant treatment accounts for most treatment nonresponse and relapse in depressed patients. However, virtually all studies of the treatment of depressed patients in the community have found problems. Findings from the Program on the Psychobiology of Depression are illustrative. Out of 88 outpatients, 29% received no antidepressant somatotherapy, another 24% received very low or unsustained levels, and only 19% received at least 200 mg of imipramine (or its equivalent) for four consecutive weeks (Keller, Lavorie, & Klerman, 1986).
- A 12-year longitudinal study by Segal, Cohen, and Marder (1992) demonstrated that in chronically mentally ill sheltered-care residents, despite recommendations to the contrary, the mean daily dosage of neuroleptics has nearly doubled since 1973.
- A study with 83 patients treated with carbamazepine at a VA medical center in Iowa City found that only one patient was monitered according to recommended criteria during the first three months of treatment (Sabotka, Alexander, & Cook, 1990).
- Psychiatrists in Omaha and Lincoln, Nebraska, were found to demonstrate significantly different practice patterns. According to Blue Cross/Blue Shield small area analysis data, psychiatrists in Omaha submit a significantly larger number of claims per patient than do psychiatrists in Lincoln. The observed/expected claims were 86% higher than expected for Omaha, and only 89% of the standard for Lincoln (Hrdy, Hoppe, & Bouda, 1993).
- A 1989 study in Illinois demonstrated wide variation in length of stay for psychiatric inpatients with similar disorders admitted to one of five units within a psychiatric facility. Physician practice patterns were found to account for a significant proportion of this variation, and this finding persisted even after case mix variation was controlled (Lyons, O'Mahoney, & Larson, 1991).

In summary, although we have been benefiting greatly from the development of new knowledge, we suffer from the lack of systematic application of this knowledge to patient care.

Access

For all of health care, the access problem—the ability of all of the citizens of the United States to receive adequate and appropriate care—is an acute and serious one. It is represented most clearly by the recent increase in the number of uninsured Americans—at last count, over 40 million. However, the problem in mental health care is even more acute.

Several major studies have found extremely low rates of utilization of mental health services by the mentally ill, suggesting the presence of substantial barriers to access to mental health care. For example, data from the Epidemiological Catchment Area study found that less than 30% of individuals with a mental illness receive any professional help. Less than half of individuals with an affective disorder receive treatment, only one of every three individuals with anxiety receive any kind of treatment, and only approximately one in five chemically dependent individuals are treated (Narrow, Regier, Rae, Manderscheid, & Locke, 1993; Regier, 1993).

Findings from the National Comorbidity Study, currently the definitive national survey of the prevalence of mental illness and its treatment in the United States, revealed exceptionally low rates of treatment utilization for both lifetime and annual periods:

Lifetime Utilization

- Only 42% of individuals with a lifetime history of a psychiatric or substance abuse disorder have ever received *any* professional treatment for their disorder (Kessler et al., 1994).
- Only 26.2% of individuals with a lifetime history of at least one disorder have received care from a mental health professional (Kessler et al., 1994).

Annual (12-Month) Utilization

- Only 20.9% of individuals with a 12-month history of any psychiatric or substance abuse disorder have received any professional treatment for their disorder in the past year (Kessler et al., 1994).
- Only 11.5% of individuals with a 12-month history of at least one disorder have received care from a mental health professional in the past year (Kessler et al., 1994).

A New Paradigm for Mental Health Practice and Research

Increasing societal awareness and concern with the problems of cost, quality, and access in health care has created a new mandate in medicine. The new mandate is to simultaneously reduce costs, increase quality, and enhance access to care. This mandate has, in turn, generated a shift in paradigm for both mental health practice and research. The new paradigm, in the area of practice, is represented by "managed care," and the new paradigm in research is "effectiveness studies." The rapid emergence of these two new paradigms, managed care and effectiveness studies, underscores problems that have long characterized both psychotherapy research and practice, offer the development of new methodologies that promise to resolve those problems, and finally, also boldly define a new set of problems for the field to resolve.

Implications of the New Paradigm for Psychotherapy Practice

Over the last 40 years, the practice of psychotherapy has undergone extraordinary growth. Beginning in the 1940s, with the introduction of psychoanalytic psychotherapy based on the work of Freud and his early followers, psychotherapy rapidly took hold in this country, coming to be considered an essential component of general health care. Mahoney (1995) estimated that by 1993, there were over 400 distinctly described forms of psychotherapy. Furthermore, not only did the number of psychotherapies multiply, but the number of practitioners and disciplines involved in providing psychotherapy also multiplied, growing to include not only psychiatry, clinical psychology, and social work, but also a host of other generic and categorical counseling disciplines. The emphasis of this era of psychotherapy development was on growth, expansion, differentiation, and invention. However, the unfolding of health care reform has brought into sharp, and in some cases uncomfortable, focus critical problems in both the structure and the functioning of this field. Key problems include the following.

The Procrustean Couch Psychotherapy as a social enterprise has long had a "cottage industry" structure, consisting primarily of individual practitioners working out of individual offices, treating individual patients, the treatment often being uncoordinated with other aspects of the patient's health care. The cumulative impact of these forces has led over time to a problem similar to that described in Homer's Odyssey, wherein Procrustes would seize travelers and tie them to a bed, either stretching them or cutting off their legs to ensure their bodies fit the bed frame. Thus, patients who seek help from individual clinicians who are limited in their range of knowledge and training, and who are in situations where they and their patients lack adequate access to other subspecialties, and where there is no formal method of systematic evaluation, face a dilemma similar to that encountered by the Odyssean travelers. Patients risk receiving whatever treatments, interventions, and theories of pathology a particular provider has been trained to deliver, rather than the services they actually need. In the absence of any effective system of coordination and integration, it is virtually impossible to ensure that patients will receive the most appropriate and effective form of treatment provided by the most skilled practitioner available. There has been little means of ensuring that those most in need of psychotherapeutic services, or those capable of benefiting most from psychotherapeutic services, will actually receive them. Furthermore, the capacity to carry out more cost-efficient psychotherapeutic services, such as group treatments, is inherently limited because of theoretical considerations, which emphasize the intrapsychic dynamics of the individual; because of socioeconomic forces resulting from lack of systematic patient flow to individual practitioners; and, research data to the contrary, because group treatment modalities are seen as "second-class" treatments, much like a private versus semiprivate room.

Unfocused Goals The increase in health care costs appears to be the product of the increased demand for health care, the development of new technologies and methods of health care, and a continuing expansion of the definition of health care. The field of psychotherapy has not been exempt from this tendency toward expansiveness. Definitions of the purpose of psychotherapy, by many major historical figures in the field, reflect this optimistic expansionism, an expansion that many would regard as well beyond the bounds of what should be appropriately thought of as health care. For instance, Carl Rogers (1951) defined the aim of psychotherapy as an effort to "increase peace of mind; to give the individual a more satisfying adjustment within himself, as well as more satisfying relationships to others, and to his environment." In the 1960s, Alan Watts (1990) wrote "Psychotherapy is concerned with bringing about changes of consciousness, changes in our ways of feeling our own existence, and our relation to human society and the natural world." Around the same time, Jerome Frank (1991) reflected a similar perspective when he wrote, "As institutions of American society, all psychotherapies, despite their diversity, share a value system that accords primacy to individual self-fulfillment or self-actualization. This includes maximum self-awareness, unlimited access to one's own feelings, increased autonomy and creativity."

The psychotherapy field has, unfortunately, never dealt explicitly and definitively with the question of what range of problems pertaining to self-realization should be integrated within the boundaries of health care.

At the individual patient level, this state of affairs is reflected in the problem Herbert Schlesinger (p. 00) has characterized as "shifting goals," that is, the tendency of psychotherapy to slide from topic to topic, without a clear rationale for the transition, and without clear termination points. In more recent years, with the advent of targeted, time-limited interventions, often empirically based and manual-guided, treatment aims have become much more clearly defined, although the limitations of manual-guided treatments have become increasingly clear.

Professional Competence Psychotherapy practice has been largely characterized by an absence of oversight or regulation. There are few legal impediments to opening a practice as a psychotherapist, regardless of level of training. Moreover, the requirement of testing for competency in psychotherapy, even within established disciplines, either at an initial or especially on an ongoing basis, typically is absent. As a result of the need to protect confidentiality and establish an atmosphere that will promote trust and self-disclosure, psychosocial treatment is usually conducted in privacy. Increasing recognition in recent years of the frequency of inappropriate sexual fraternization between patient and therapist has focused public attention on the potential for negative therapeutic outcomes, on enhanced professional training focused on these issues, and on more attention to development and enforcement of professional codes of ethics.

Lack of Dependency of Psychotherapy Practice on Research Over a decade ago, Morris Parloff (1982) referred to the relationship between psychotherapy research and psychotherapy practice as an "anaclitic depression," reflecting the view that psychotherapy as a field of practice had not shown the same reliance upon scientific research as had other areas of medical health care. Glenys Parry, in her chapter "Psychotherapy Services in the English National Health Service" (this volume), describes good reasons for the reluctance of practicing psychotherapists to base practice decisions on research findings. These good reasons have to do with problems of generalizing from clinical trials designed to maximize internal validity (thereby minimizing generalizability), applying nomothetic findings to individual cases, and the virtual absence of research on widely practiced therapies, on common psychiatric disorders, and on comorbid conditions. Nonetheless, these "good reasons" have come to sound increasingly self-serving, and the absence of studies of psychoanalysis, for example, is perceived to be the failure of the practitioners of that treatment to fulfill an essential responsibility. There was, and remains, a tendency for clinicians to describe their work more as artistic and hermeneutic, rather than as based on empirically based outcome studies. Within the context of health care reform and managed care in the United States, such traditions have become increasingly less acceptable, as quantification of treatment outcomes is increasingly monitored, and studies of effectiveness, in contrast to "efficacy," yield information more relevant to practitioners on the front lines.

Implications of the New Paradigm for Psychotherapy Research

The Focus on Efficacy at the Expense of Effectiveness Research As the move toward managed care has brought to light critical issues in psychotherapy practice, it has also highlighted the critical limitations inherent in current psychotherapy research methodologies, and their fundamental emphasis on "efficacy," at the expense of "effectiveness" studies.

The goals of effectiveness research are substantially different from the efficacy studies that have received the lion's share of psychotherapy research attention as it has evolved over the last four decades. (See also chapters 2 and 3 pertaining to this issue, this volume.) Effectiveness research is concerned with understanding what relative value is obtained by providing a health care intervention to a population of individuals, and by further understanding the variables which can enhance that value. The efficacy of the therapies involved (i.e., the improvement in outcome specifically attributable to the therapy under highly controlled conditions) is only one component of the variance in effectiveness.

Efficacy Paradigm Contributions Nevertheless, within the context of efficacy research, a number of substantial achievements have been made. Over the last 40 years, psychotherapy research has adapted a credible methodology from psychopharmacology, with which to conduct randomized controlled clinical trials. The field has developed consensual methodologies for standardizing therapies, for selecting and training therapists, and for defining and selecting homogeneous patient samples (Docherty & Streeter, 1996; Imber, 1992). Useful methods have been developed to reliably measure therapists' adherence to manualized treatments. These methods may eventually provide the underpinnings for designing tools to monitoring practitioner competence in the field (Luborsky & Barber, 1993; Rounsaville, O'Malley, Foley, & Weissman, 1988; Shaw & Dobson, 1988; Svartberg, 1989). These activities have led to a body of progressive research that has, over the last 10 years, yielded a number of demonstrably efficacious treatments for alleviating major disorders, including depression (Docherty & Streeter, 1993), agoraphobia (Craske & Rodriguez, 1994), panic (Barlow, 1992), obsessive-compulsive disorder (Foa, Kozak, Steketee, & McCarthy, 1992), and schizophrenia (Docherty, Herz, & Gunderson, 1993; see part V, this volume).

In the course of this work, major advances have been achieved in defining and demonstrating the strong, even singular, contribution to outcome of the therapeutic alliance (Hartley, 1993; Safran & Wallner, 1991) and of identifying key common curative factors in psychotherapy (Luborsky, 1993).

Limitations of Efficacy Randomized Clinical Trials: Generalizability and Cost Despite these achievements, however, psychotherapy research has, as yet, made only marginal impact on psychotherapy practice. Empirically validated treatments, such as interpersonal psychotherapy and cognitive behavior therapy for depression, and exposure-based treatments for phobia and obsessive-compulsive disorder, have begun to make some inroads. Yet the influence of these targeted treatments has been remarkably small, in contrast to the vast amount of psychotherapy practiced in this country. The extent to which this lack of import is due not only to long-standing social and economic factors, but also to inherent limitations of the randomized controlled clinical trial and of the efficacy research paradigm as a basis for defining practice, has necessarily become more fully acknowledged with the advent of managed care.

Emphasis on Homogeneity. The limitations of efficacy research derive from two inherent aspects of the randomized controlled trial. The first is its requirement for homogeneity, which limits generalizability, and the second is the amount of time and expense necessary to conduct a properly designed efficacy study. Though efficacy studies provide a credible core body of research regarding the impact of well-defined therapies on well-defined patient groups with carefully trained and closely monitored therapists, this model yields limited information pertaining to individual differences and regarding the usefulness of psychotherapy for the vast majority of clinical conditions as they are encountered, and treated, in daily practice.

The Problem of Comorbidity. Efficacy studies fail to assess patients with psychiatric comorbidity, that is, the simultaneous presence of several diagnosable disorders such as addiction, major affective disorder, and borderline personality disorder, especially in patients with the most severe conditions, patients with concomitant acute and/or physical disease, patients from minority groups, and patients over 60 years of age. Robert Michaels once summarized the findings of the 500 studies reported in the Smith, Glass, and Miller landmark meta-analysis of psychotherapy efficacy studies (Smith, Glass, & Miller, 1980) by saying that this work definitively demonstrated "that psychotherapy conducted by psychiatric residents was an effective treatment for female undergraduates in large urban universities who were suffering from snake phobias."

Practitioner Variance. In addition, as regards practitioners, although a body of systematic data suggests the presence of substantial differences in patient outcomes among therapists trained to deliver particular forms of therapy, minimal attention has been paid to the variance in outcome contributed by therapist competence and skill. Few data are available regarding the characteristics of therapists necessary to successfully conduct particular types of therapeutic interventions. For example, type and extent of training, personal characteristics of practitioners, and level of oversight necessary to insure that therapy is adequately delivered in the ordinary clinical setting remain unknown (Howard et al., 1996).

Limited Breadth. With regard to specific families of therapies themselves, knowledge is also limited. For example, despite their longevity in the history of psychotherapy, no randomized controlled clinical trial on the efficacy of long-term psychotherapy has been published to date. It is estimated that of the 400 psychotherapies, reasonably adequate efficacy data are available on only 7 or 8 (Norcross, 1995).

Narrowly Defined Outcomes. Finally, data on outcomes collected in efficacy studies tend to be unduly limited, most studies being largely focused on measuring change in the presence and severity of symptomatology. In one of the most studied syndromes, major depression, only 10 of the hundreds of studies that have been conducted have measured the effect of treatment on work function (Mintz, 1992; see chapter 19, this volume).

Paradigm Limits. Beutler (1991) has emphasized the ultimate futility of attempting to generate all the empirical information necessary to direct clinical practice, given the current model of efficacy research paradigm, noting, "There are nearly one and one-half million potential combinations of therapy, therapists, phases, and patient types that must be studied in order to rule out relevant differences among treatment types" (p. 228).

Generalizability, Cost, and Time Factors. In addition to the considerable problem of clinical representativeness, two major difficulties posed by the efficacy paradigm limit the development of health care policy and the guidance of management decisions regarding psychotherapy practice. First, the amount of time, effort, and cost entailed in undertaking such complex studies has substantially hampered the development of new and useful knowledge. It takes years, under the current model, to determine whether even minor modifications in treatment technique might introduce clinically or even fiscally relevant improvements in outcome. Second, the requirement of homogeneity in efficacy research seriously impedes the generalizability of findings, thereby minimizing the probability of wide-scale technology transfer to the front lines. These deficits in the knowledge base, impediments to the transfer of knowledge, and impracticality in a process aiming to integrate continuous treatment refinements remain critical problems underlying the national research effort to enhance the quality, decrease costs, and extend access to care.

Attention to Economics. Last, but certainly not least, in the current managed-care environment, with a few notable exceptions (Kamlet et al., 1995; Krupnick & Pincus, 1992; Rogers, Wells, Meredith, Sturm, & Burnam, 1993; Sturm et al., 1994; Sturm & Wells, 1995), there has been minimal attention in the empirical literature to determining the cost-effectiveness, cost-benefit, or cost utility of psychotherapeutic interventions. From a public policy and a national health plan standpoint, the absence of such data represents a serious deficiency for the field.

The Future Is Now!

In light of current sociopolitical trends and the current status of research in psychotherapy, the need to address certain specific issues is clear. Critical consideration should be focused on the following areas.

Paradigm Shift

Emphasizing Psychotherapy Services Research The first is a fundamental reconceptualization of the research paradigm for developing and implementing psychotherapeutic interventions in health care. Randomized controlled clinical trials and efficacy testing will be sharply de-emphasized in the era of managed care, and "horse races" between "schools" of therapy will no longer be considered as important as therapist competence, quality of the alliance, patient satisfaction, and long-term cost-effectiveness. There will be an accelerating move away from studies largely focused on internal validity and a significantly heightened services research emphasis on effectiveness and cost-effectiveness studies, staged in naturalistic settings.

Developing Population-Based Methods Second, in the context of a rapidly changing health care environment, there is a pressing need for the development of new models of population-based psychotherapy intervention assessment. Compelling examples of such work include Howard's "Phase and Dose Effect Model" (1986, 1994), Seligman's (1995) recent consumer satisfaction survey research, and Sturm and Wells's (1995) analysis of reduction of functional impairment through use of psychotherapy undertaken in the context of the RAND Medical Outcomes Study, in addition to many other excellent examples contained in this volume (e.g., see chapters 6, 14, 15, 16, and 19).

Including and Enhancing Economic Measures Third, there needs to be a new emphasis on inclusion, and development, of agreed-upon criteria for the conduct of cost analyses, which will be considered key components of psychotherapy investigations. The application of cost analysis to psychotherapy studies has been rudimentary at best; to date, the methodology used remains highly variable. This state of affairs hinders the capacity to develop cumulative archives of empirically verified information across studies and, in efforts to secure research support, leads to widely disparate reviews of identical grant applications. Methods development and research consensus meetings pertaining to cost evaluations of psychosocial treatment interventions must be urgently pursued.

The Assessment of Outcome

Expanding Scope of Outcomes Four decades of psychotherapy research have yielded a sophisticated, scientifically based methodology for assessing outcome in behavioral health care, largely based on the Food and Drug Administration (FDA) model of controlled clinical trials for demonstrating the short-term safety and efficacy of pharmaceutical agents. As in that model, the presence or absence of symptomatology has constituted the primary aim of outcome studies. Despite lip service to the contrary, assessment of functioning, client satisfaction, and quality of life have been rarely included in treatment study designs (Mintz, Mintz, Arruda, & Hwang, 1992). Because the focus of past research has been largely on symptomatology, generalizations from symptomatology to overall health status have often been misleading. Empirical data now suggest, that the impact of an intervention on the timing and ultimate level of recovery of work functioning, for example, is significantly slower than impact on depressive symptomatology (chapter 19, this volume).

Considering Stakeholder Perspectives It is imperative that such distinctions be clearly delineated both in the conduct of research investigations and in the uses to which research data are put. We are dealing here not with an arcane issue but with a very real matter. The outcome measures selected in a treatment study have very real implications for the shaping of health care policy, in both the public and private sectors. With the advent of this new era, as health plans grow increasingly reliant on quantification and cognizant of the need for the rational use of finite resources, the nature of the outcome measures selected will have real and significant implications for the patients served (see chapter 18, this volume). For example, despite the intense interest of employer health plan purchasers in impact of treatment on work function and quality of life, measure of work and client indices are still not included. Similarly, in considering the plight of the severely mentally ill, how might one appropriately determine the value of an intervention for a permanently disabled schizophrenic patient? Clearly, methodologies must be developed for gathering a wide range of outcome data efficiently and for the benefit of quite different stakeholders.

Moving From Measures of Adherence to Provider Competency

Policymakers, employers, and patients are increasingly vocal in their demands for accountability on the part of the providers of health care. For-profit health plans increasingly track the impact of provider performance on patient outcomes. The development of scientifically based methods to accredit and monitor the competence of therapists will be an increasing focus of research attention in coming years. Current experiments in "provider profiling" have been limited, more often involving data on utilization rather than on any assessment of quality of care delivered. While efficacy research has yielded methods to reliably assess a therapist's adherence to a manualized treatment intervention (whose validity has never been demonstrated), more crucial efforts to systematically and validly define and measure therapist competence have been minimal at best. A critical new task for the field is the development of valid methods for more effectively selecting good candidates for psychotherapy and for tracking continuing performance of therapist practitioners. Such methods must be effective, sensitive, and nonintrusive. The rapid determination, through research, of methodologies that actually work is critical. In the absence of such data, current business trends will introduce, and already are introducing, untested methods of provider profiling calculated to yield de facto clinician assessments.

Scope of Psychotherapy

Prioritizing Access A looming question for health care policy involves delineating the type of populations and the scope of psychotherapeutic services to be included under the rubric of health care. This question, these days, is ultimately dependent upon which party pays for these services. For example, many plans and purchasers are currently experiencing tension between whether coverage should be provided for the severely disabled mentally ill, or for the worried well, or for both. Two issues are involved. The first entails the prioritization of populations for access to psychotherapeutic treatments.

Delineating "Medical Necessity" The second entails ethical judgments of value, regarding which aspects of human life should be included within a communally supported health care system (see Halpern, this volume). These issues are often fought out around the development and application of certain "criteria" for eligibility for certain "benefits." For example, with regard to the severely disabled, the debate revolves around questions of "medical necessity" versus "social necessity," as constituting the primary criterion for the provision of services. For the worried well, it centers on debates over "medical necessity" versus "medical appropriateness" criteria, that is, delineating those interventions essential to treat an illness versus delineating interventions that are useful, but not necessary, for treatment. These are highly complex issues. From a strictly medical point of view, for example, it may be determined that treatment of marital distress, while a useful and a valuable personal social good, should not be included within a health care system. On the other hand, an employer, recognizing the disruption in work productivity that can attend such a state of affairs, might be, and often is, eager to include such "treatment" within the health care benefit.

The Role of Choice: Restricted Versus Unrestricted Provider Panels

A key issue facing the field is the tension between the quality of the individual doctor-patient *relationship* and the efficiencies to be gained by managing a well-run *system*. For instance, minimal data are available on which to base empirical determinations regarding the advantages and disadvantages pertaining to the relative balance between "restricted practitioner panels" and those comprised of "any willing provider." While it is clear that there are competent and incompetent therapists, and that the capacity of a system to select therapists who are stable, competent, and of high integrity will enhance care, the variance accounted for by "system-centered" issues versus that accounted for by "person-centered" issues remains to be determined. Such data will be increasingly called for in the development of elegant models of care that accommodate patient preference, strengthen the odds of developing a strong therapeutic alliance, and enhance the overall integrity of the system of care.

Confidentiality, Privacy, and Research Risk

In order to gather the data necessary to conduct effectiveness studies, support accountability, and develop an information system for continuous improvement in quality, the confidentiality of the therapeutic relationship may be placed at increasing risk. The impact of such risk on treatment outcomes has yet to be determined. Because confidentiality in the doctor-patient relationship may constitute a critical underpinning of the therapeutic alliance, the impact of current changes raises practical and ethical concerns in need of sustained empirical and ethical inquiry.

Financing Research

Prior Narrow Base of Support Funding for psychotherapy research has—from the inception of such activity in the late 1940s to the present—been almost entirely government-supported, and that government support has been derived almost entirely from the National Institutes of Health, too narrow a base to support such a highly utilized service. The field itself has been deficient in supplying funds to support its own research activities, due in large part to the "cottage industry" structure of the field. Individuals in private offices are unlikely to generate a pool of dollars sufficient to support useful efforts in research and development. Moreover, professional societies, such as the American Psychiatric Association and the American Psychological Association, have also failed to step up to the plate and develop independent sources of funding for this central activity of their respective professions. Most important, there has been no industrial base in psychotherapy, analogous to that in pharmaceuticals, to support R & D.

Prospects for Funding From Managed Care and Pharmaceutical Industries This lack of an organized industry for the provision of psychotherapy may be changing, since some of the larger managed-care organizations now have the capacity to provide support for research on cost-effective patient outcomes, customer satisfaction, and provider performance. The profitability of these enterprises may be consistent with the setting aside of funds for activities meant to further their corporate mandate. As demands to demonstrate quality improvement as well as cost control increase, research on the utility of psychosocial interventions will be of inherent value for the economic well-being of health care plans. There are excellent examples of such emerging centers of research activity, for example, Group Health Cooperative of Puget Sound.

There is also recognition growing in the pharmaceutical industry that the effectiveness of various medications can be enhanced by psychosocial programs, especially those which facilitate compliance. There is a linked recognition that increased compliance is associated with increased use of medications and thus may support the economic interest of these companies. This concordance of a social good and economic interest augurs well for the growth of support from pharmaceutical companies for psychosocial interventions that will effectively remedy those issues that have impeded patient compliance.

Cost Offsets in the Context of Multiyear Health Plans The absence of definitive data regarding the "cost offset effect" (i.e., the extent to which general medical and surgical care costs are reduced by psychotherapeutic interventions) should also be pursued with a greater interest (see Kashner and Rush, this volume). For HMOs, in particular, it will be both useful and prudent to more clearly determine what psychosocial interventions, with what kind of practioners and what categories of patients, prevent the inappropriate use of expensive medical services.

The exploration of the effectiveness of long-term approaches would also be enhanced by policy changes that would require a capitated medical plan to assume a multiyear responsibility for an individual subscriber. Recent legislation allowing for the portability of insurance plans may encourage such activity.

Finally, it is clear that in order for psychotherapy research to fulfill its promise, a significant enhancement of the psychotherapy services research funding base is needed. As health care reform proceeds and innovative systems of care and new forms of organization develop, steps must be taken to ensure that such broadened support for psychotherapy research will be forthcoming.

References

Barlow, D. H. (1992). Cognitive-behavioral approaches to panic disorder and social phobia. *Bulletin of the Menninger Clinic*, 52(2 Suppl. A), A14–28.

Beutler, L. E. (1991). Have all won and must all have prizes? Revisiting Luborsky et al.'s verdict. *Journal of Consulting and Clinical Psychology*, 59(2), 226–232.

Craske, M. G., & Rodriquez, B. I. (1994). Behavioral treatment of panic disorders and agoraphobia. *Progress in Behavioral Modification*, 29, 1–26.

Docherty, J. P. (1996). Barriers to the diagnosis of depression in primary care. *Journal of Clinical Psychiatry*, 57(suppl 14), 5–10.

Docherty, J. P., & Dewan, N. A. (1995). *Outcomes assessment monograph*. Washington, DC: National Association of Psychiatric Healthcare Systems (NAPHS).

Docherty, J. P., Herz, M. I., & Gunderson, J. (1993). *Psychosocial treatment in psychiatry: A task force report of the American Psychiatric Association*. Washington, DC: American Psychiatric Association.

Docherty, J. P., & Streeter, M. J. (1993). Progress and limitations in psychotherapy research: A focus on depression. *Journal of Psychotherapy Practice and Research*, 2(2), 100–118.

Docherty, J. P., & Streeter, M. J. (1996). Measuring outcomes. In L. Sederer & B. Dickey (Eds.), *Outcomes assessment in clinical practice* (pp. 8–18). Baltimore: Williams & Wilkins.

Foa, E. B., Kozak, M. J., Steketee, G. S., & McCarthy, P. R. (1992). Treatment of depressive and obsessive-compulsive symptoms in OCD by imipramine and behavior therapy. *British Journal of Clinical Psychology*, 31(Pt. 3), 279–292.

Frank, J. D., & Frank, J. B. (1991). *Persuasion and healing: A comparative study of psychotherapy* (3rd ed.). Baltimore: Johns Hopkins University Press.

Hartley, D. E. (1993). Research on the therapeutic alliance in psychotherapy. In *American Psychiatric Association Annual Review* (Vol. 4, pp. 532–549). New York: Basic Books.

Howard, K. I., Cornille, T. A., Lyons, J. S., Vessey, J. T., Lueger, R. J., & Saunders, S. M. (1996). Patterns of mental health service utilization. *Archives of General Psychiatry*, 53(8), 696–703.

Howard, K. I., Kopta, M. S., Krause, M. S., & Orlinsky, D. E. (1986). The dose-effect relationship in psychotherapy. *American Psychologist*, 41(2), 159–164.

Howard, K. I., Orlinsky, D. E., & Lueger, R. J. (1994). Clinically relevant outcome research in individual psychotherapy: New models guide the researcher and clinician. *British Journal of Psychiatry*, 165, 4–8.

Hrdy, S. A., Hoppe, M., & Bouda, D. W. (1993). Psychiatrists practice patterns: A comparison of Omaha and Lincoln. *Nebraska Medical Journal*, 78(9), 299–305.

Imber, S. D. (1992). Then and now: Forty years in psychotherapy research. *Clinical Psychology Review*, 12, 199–204.

Kamlet, M. S., Paul, N., Greenhouse, J., Kupfer, D., Frank, E., & Wade, M. (1995). Cost utility analysis of maintenance treatment for recurrent depression. *Control Clinical Trials*, 16(1), 17–40.

Keller, M. D., Lavorie, P. W., & Klerman, G. L. (1986). Low levels and lack of predictors of somatotherapy and psychotherapy received by depressed patients. *Archives of General Psychiatry*, 43(5), 458–466.

Kessler, R. C., McGonagle, K. A., Zhao, S., Nelson, C. B., Hughes, M., Eshleman, S., Wittchen, H-U., Kendler, K. S. (1994). Lifetime and 12-month prevalence of DSM-III-R psychiatric disorders in the United States: Results from the National Comorbidity Survey. *Archives of General Psychiatry*, 51, 8–19.

Krupnick, J. L., & Pincus, H. A. (1992). The cost-effectiveness of psychotherapy: A plan for research. *American Journal of Psychiatry*, 149, 1295–1305.

Luborsky, L. L. (1993). How to maximize the curative factors in dynamic psychotherapy. In N. E. Miller, L. L. Luborsky, J. P. Barber, & J. P. Docherty (Eds.), *Psychodynamic treatment research: A handbook for clinical practice* (pp. 519–535). New York: Basic Books.

Luborsky, L. L., & Barber, J. P. (1993). Benefits of adherence to psychotherapy manuals, and where to get them. In N. E. Miller, L. L. Luborsky, J. P. Barber, & J.P. Docherty (Eds.), *Psychodynamic treatment research: A handbook for clinical practice* (pp. 211–226). New York: Basic Books.

Lyons, J. S., O'Mahoney, M. T., & Larson, D. B. (1991). The attending psychiatrist as a predictor of length of stay. *Hospital and Community Psychiatry*, 42(10), 1064–1066.

Mahoney, M. J. (1995). *Cognitive and constructive psychotherapies: Theory, reserach, and practice*. New York: Springer.

Mintz, J., Mintz, L. I., Arruda, M. J., & Hwang, S. S. (1992). Treatments of depression and the functional capacity to work. *Archives of General Psychiatry*, 49(10), 761–768.

Narrow, W. E., Regier, D. A., Rae, D. S., Manderscheid, R. W., & Locke, B. Z. (1993). Use of services by persons with mental and addictive disorders. Findings from the National Institute of Mental Health Epidemiologic Catchment Area Program. *Archives of General Psychiatry*, 50(2), 95–107.

National Institutes of Health (U.S.), Division of Public Information. (1996). *NIH Almanac 1995 1996* (96–95). Bethesda, MD: U.S. Department of Health Education and Welfare, Public Health Service, NIH.

Norcross, J. C. (1995). Dispelling the dodo bird verdict and the exclusivity myth in psychotherapy. *Psychotherapy*, 32(3), 500–504.

Parloff, M. B. (1982). Psychotherapy research evidence and reimbursement decisions: Bambi meets Godzilla. *American Journal of Psychiatry*, 139(6), 718–727.

Redick, R. W., Witkin, M. J., Atay, J. E., & Manderscheid, R. W. (1992). Specialty mental health system characteristics. In R. W. Manderscheid & M. A. Sonnenschein (Eds.), *Mental health, United States 1992* (pp. 1–20). DHHS Publication No. (SMA)94-3000. Washington, DC: U.S. Government Printing Office.

Redick, R. W., Witkin, M. J., Atay, J. E., & Manderscheid, R. W. (1994a). The evolution and expansion of mental health care in the United States between 1955 and 1990. *Mental Health Statistical Note, 210*, 1–700.

Redick, R. W., Witkin, M. J., Atay, J. E., & Manderscheid, R. W. (1994b). Highlighs of organized mental health services in 1990 and major national and state trends. In R. W. Manderscheid & M. A. Sonnenschein (Eds.), *Mental health, United States 1994* (pp. 77–99). DHHS Publication No. (SMA)94-3000. Washington, DC: U.S. Government Printing Office.

Regier, D. A. (1993). The linkage of health care reform and health services research. *American Journal of Psychiatry, 150*(11), 1613–1615.

Rogers, C. (1951). *Client-centered therapy: Its current practice, implications, and theory*. Boston: Houghton Mifflin.

Rogers, W. H., Wells, K. B., Meredith, L. S., Sturm, R., & Burnam, M. A. (1993). Outcomes for adults outpatients with depression under prepaid or fee-for-service financing. *Archives of General Psychiatry, 50*(7), 517–525.

Rounsaville, B. J., O'Malley, S., Foley S., & Weissman, M. M. (1988). The role of manual guided training in the conduct and efficiency of interpersonal psychotherapy for depression. *Journal of Clinical and Consulting Psychology, 56*, 681–688.

Sabotka, J. L., Alexander, B., & Cook, G. L. (1990). A retrospective study of compliance with recommended hematologic monitoring of carbamazepine. *DCIP, 24*(120), 1166–1168.

Sachs, J. S. (1987). Negative factors in brief psychotherapy: An empirical assessment. *Journal of Consulting and Clinical Psychology, 51*, 557–564.

Safran, J. D., & Wallner, L. K. (1991). The relative predictive validity of two therapeutic alliance measures in cognitive therapy. *Psychological Assessment, 3*(2), 188–195.

Schulberg, H. C., Saul, M., McClelland, M., Ganguli, M., Christy, W., & Frank, R. (1985). Assessing depression in primary medical and psychiatric practices. *Archives of General Psychiatry, 42*(12), 1164–1170.

Segal, S. P., Cohen, D., & Marder, S. R. (1992). Neuroleptic medication and prescription practices with sheltered-care residents: A 12-year perspective. *American Journal of Public Health, 82*(6), 846–852.

Seligman, M. E. (1995). The effectiveness of psychotherapy: The Consumer Reports study. *American Psychologist, 30*(12), 965–974.

Shaw, B. F., & Dobson, K. S. (1988). Competency judgements in the training and evaluation of psychotherapists. *Journal of Clinical and Consulting Psychology, 56*, 666–672.

Smith, M. L., Glass, G. V., & Miller, T. I. (1980). *The benefits of psychotherapy*. Baltimore: Johns Hopkins University Press.

Strupp, H. H., & Binder, J. L. (1984). *Psychotherapy in a new key*. New York: Basic Books.

Sturm, R., McGlynn, E. A., Meredith, L. S., Wells, K. B., Manning, W. G., & Rogers, W. H. (1994). Switches between prepaid and fee-for services health systems among depressed outpatients: Results from the Medical Outcomes Study. *Medical Care, 32*(9), 917–929.

Sturm, R., & Wells, K. B. (1995). How can care for depression become more cost-effective? *Journal of the American Medical Association, 273*(1), 51–58.

Svartberg, O. M. (1989). Monitoring the competence of dynamic psychotherapists: A practical demonstration. *Acta Psychiatrica Scandinavica, 80*(3), 292–296.

Watts, A., Naranjo, C., Taylor, E., & Crook, J. H. (1990). *From sentience to symbols: Reading on consciousness*. Toronto: University of Toronto Press.

2

Psychotherapy and Pharmacotherapy

Efficacy, Generalizability, and Cost-Effectiveness

Steven D. Hollon

Psychotherapy and pharmacotherapy represent the two primary modes of treatment for mental disorders and associated problems in living. There are few disorders for which each has not been tried, and both are widely used in the larger treatment community. Each has been shown to be effective in the treatment of a variety of overlapping disorders, and often, both are combined in the treatment of any given patient.

Nonetheless, it is still not clear how well the psychosocial interventions work under ideal conditions. This is the issue of efficacy, typically studied by outcome researchers using randomized clinical trials (RCTs) methodology. Moreover, it is increasingly clear that neither psychotherapy nor pharmacotherapy works as well in applied clinical settings as they do in controlled research studies. This is the issue of generalizability (or external validity), something that has now come to be referred to as *effectiveness* in the services research literature. Finally, surprisingly little is known about the actual costs associated with the two approaches relative to the benefits that each provides. This is the issue of cost-effectiveness, largely the domain of the health care economist. Addressing this issue is more complex than it first seems, but it is important nonetheless, particularly with respect to combined treatment.

This chapter examines the efficacy, generalizability (effectiveness), and cost-effectiveness of psychotherapy and pharmacotherapy, both alone and in combination, across a variety of disorders. There are gaps in the current state of knowledge, particularly with respect to generalizability and cost-effectiveness. In many instances, issues can only be raised for future consideration, since the necessary data currently do not exist to permit their resolution. Nonetheless, the issues themselves are important and likely to become even more so as managed care and third-party payers play an ever larger role in the delivery of mental health services.

This chapter is organized around several assumptions that most people hold about the relative value of drugs and psychotherapy. With respect to efficacy, these are (a) that although psychotherapy is often sufficient in the treatment of the less severe disorders, medication is essential to the treatment and prophylaxis of the more severe disorders, (b) that although drugs often work more rapidly, psychotherapy has broader and more enduring effects that last beyond the end of treatment, and (c) that the combination of drugs and psychotherapy works better than either one alone. With respect to generalizability (effectiveness), these are (d) that most treatments perform better in controlled research studies than they do in more naturalistic settings, and (e) that pharmacotherapy is more robust than psychotherapy because it depends less on the skill of the practitioner. Finally, with respect to cost-effectiveness, it is (f) that drugs are more cost-effective than psychotherapy (alone or in combination) in the short term. Some of these assumptions appear to hold (at least for some disorders), whereas others may not be as true as they first seem.

Relative Efficacy of Drugs and Psychotherapy

There is good consensus that drugs or other somatic interventions are essential to the treatment of the more severe disorders, particularly those that involve psychotic symptoms (National Advisory Mental Health Council [NAMHC], 1993). Standard antipsychotic medications remain the most effective means of reducing the more florid symptoms of psychosis, and the recently developed atypical antipsychotics show promise in relieving the negative symptoms of schizophrenia. Lithium and the newer anticonvulsant medications provide the most effective means of prophylaxis in the bipolar disorders. The antidepressant medications and electroconvulsive therapy (ECT) remain the treatments of choice for the most severe depressions (particularly those that reach psychotic proportions), and clomipramine and the newer selective serotonin reuptake inhibitors (SSRIs) appear to be promising in the treatment of severe obsessive-compulsive disorder. Similarly, the antidepressants and high-potency benzodiazepines appear to be helpful in the treatment of panic states that often underlie severe agoraphobia. The efficacy of each of these agents has been demonstrated in numerous controlled clinical trials. Although none is a panacea, each plays a key role in the treatment of the more severe disorders, particularly those that reach psychotic proportions.

However, the psychosocial interventions often play an important adjunctive role in the treatment of even the most severe disorders. For example, rehabilitation programs and behavioral skills training appear to help redress impairments in psychosocial functioning in schizophrenic patients and may allow the use of the newer low-dose neuroleptic drug strategies without any decrement in coping capacity (Liberman, 1994). Similarly, psychoeducational family therapy aimed at lowering the level of distress in the family and reducing the burden of illness on relatives has been shown to reduce subsequent risk of relapse in medicated schizophrenic patients (chapter 22, this volume). Such programs appear to have a similar effect in medicated bipolar patients (Clarkin et al., 1990) and cognitive therapy directed at concerns about medication-taking can enhance compliance in that same population (Cochrane, 1984).

The relative superiority of drugs to psychotherapy alone is less pronounced among even the more severe nonpsychotic disorders and quite possibly nonexistent among the less severe disorders. The newly developed cognitive behavioral therapies (CBTs) and interpersonal psychotherapies (IPTs) appear to be at least as effective as medications in the reduction of acute distress in mildly to moderately depressed outpatients and may enhance the breadth and stability of response relative to pharmacotherapy alone among even more severely depressed patients (Hollon, Shelton, & Loosen, 1991a; Weissman & Markowitz, 1994). Exposure-based therapies have been shown to be quite helpful in reducing compulsive rituals in obsessive-compulsive disorder and behavioral avoidance in severe agoraphobia and are often combined with medications (Christensen, Hadzi-Pavlovic, Andrews, & Mattick, 1987; Marks & O'Sullivan, 1988). CBT appears to be at least as effective and possibly longer-lasting than pharmacotherapy in the treatment of panic disorder and social phobia (see chapter 21, this volume). The same can be said with respect to the relative efficacy of psychotherapy (particularly CBT and IPT) in the treatment of bulimia (see chapter 25, this volume). Exposure-based behavior therapy is clearly superior to pharmacotherapy (or any other form of psychotherapy) in the treatment of the specific phobias. There is little evidence, as yet, that drugs are particularly helpful in the treatment of the personality disorders, whereas dialectic behavior therapy appears to reduce the frequency of self-destructive behavior in patients with borderline personality disorder (see chapter 27, this volume).

Thus, the general rule appears to be that the more severe the disorder, the greater the relative efficacy of pharmacotherapy, although there are exceptions. The psychosocial interventions typically play a complementary role in even the most severe disorders and appear to be at least as effective as medications in the treatment of the less severe disorders. Moreover, there are indications that psychotherapy may produce broader and more enduring effects than medications. For example, IPT has been found to produce greater change in social functioning than medications in depressed outpatients, although this effect can take months to emerge (Weissman, Klerman, Paykel, Prusoff, & Hanson, 1974) and may not become evident until well after treatment is over (Weissman, Klerman, Prusoff, Sholomskas, & Padian, 1981). Bulimic patients treated with IPT also continued to improve following treatment termination (Fairburn, Jones, Peveler, Hope, & O'Connor, 1993; see chapter 25, this volume). These findings suggest that IPT may have a broader (if somewhat delayed) effect than medications alone (Weissman & Markowitz, 1994).

Similarly, CBT appears to have an enduring effect that reduces risk for symptom return well after treatment is over (see Hollon & Beck, 1994, for a review). For example, several studies have suggested that depressed patients treated to remission with CBT are at lower risk for relapse following treatment termination than patients treated to remission pharmacologically (Hollon et al., 1991a). Similar results have been found for patients with panic disorder (Clark et al., 1994; see also chapter 21, this volume), social phobia (Heimberg, personal communication, November 1995), and bulimia (Craighead & Agras, 1991). Although none of these findings can be considered conclusive, they are potentially quite exciting and suggest that psychotherapy may have broader and more enduring effects than are typically found with drugs alone.

Evidence for the superiority of combined treatment over either single modality is often indirect and based on qualitative integrations across multiple measures, since synergistic (or even additive) effects with respect to any given outcome are rare (Hollon, Shelton, & Loosen, 1991b). That is, combined treatment is rarely better than the more effective single modality on any given index of change, but it typically retains the specific benefits associated with each (Hollon & Fawcett, 1995). Thus, when drugs are faster, than psychotherapy, combined treatment is faster, too; when psychotherapy has broader or more enduring effects than pharmacotherapy, combined treatment does as well. Moreover, combining the two modalities increases the likelihood that any given patient will be exposed to something to which he or she will respond and that at least one component of treatment will be properly implemented. Whether these gains justify the greater costs associated with combining drugs and psychotherapy is a separate issue that will be addressed in a subsequent section, but it does appear that combined treatment provides some pragmatic advantages over either single modality alone.

Conspicuous by its absence in the previous discussion was any mention of the more traditional dynamic-eclectic or humanistic-experiential approaches to psychotherapy. Although these interventions are widely practiced in applied treatment settings, they have rarely been compared to pharmacotherapy in controlled clinical trials. This may reflect a sense on the part of their advocates that the therapy process is too complex to be adequately represented in the typical efficacy study (Stiles & Shapiro, 1989). Nonetheless, the fact remains that there are few direct comparisons between drugs and the more traditional approaches to psychotherapy.

Those studies that have compared these more traditional interventions to pharmacotherapy have not been particularly supportive, although many of the early studies involved psychotic populations for whom drugs may have been indicated (Hollon & Beck, 1978). Moreover, it is not clear that the traditional psychotherapies have been adequately implemented in even those comparisons involving nonpsychotic populations, since the majority of those trials have been conducted by researchers with investments in other approaches. In the nonpharmacological literature, most types of psychotherapy have been found to be superior to minimal treatment controls, and differences between the respective approaches in specific studies can often be attributed to allegiance effects on the part of the investigators (Luborsky, Singer, & Luborsky, 1975; Smith & Glass, 1977). Whether this will prove to be true with respect to comparisons to medication remains to be seen, but the fact remains that (with the exception of IPT) the more traditional dynamic-eclectic and humanistic-experiential therapies have rarely been tested in studies in which they have been adequately implemented.

The absence of evidence does not necessarily mean that these interventions are less effective than pharmacotherapy, but it does represent a gap in the current state of knowledge. A recent survey by a leading consumers' magazine found that most patients thought that psychotherapy (regardless of type) improved the quality of their lives and that adding medications did little to enhance their satisfaction ("Mental Health," 1995). Although most of the respondents had less severe disorders (limiting the generalizability of the findings) and assignment to treatment was not random (so that it is difficult to draw causal inferences), these findings suggest that it may be premature to dismiss the more traditional forms of psychotherapy (Seligman, 1995).

Moreover, there is the strong sense that the way treatment is conducted in efficacy studies bears little resemblance to the way it is conducted in the field (Seligman, 1995). In most efficacy studies, patients are randomly assigned to treatment of a predetermined length, and clinicians are constrained from varying the nature of what they do in response to their perceptions of their patients' needs (Persons, 1991). The implication is that randomized controlled trials have systematically underestimated the effects of the more traditional approaches to psychotherapy typically preferred in applied clinical settings. At the same time, there is little good evidence that clinicians are particularly adept at tailoring their interventions to their clients' needs in a manner that enhances treatment effects (Wilson, 1996).

With respect to efficacy, then, it appears that drugs may be essential to the treatment of the more severe disorders (with the newer psychosocial interventions playing a useful adjunctive role), but that the psychosocial interventions may be of at least equal efficacy for the less severe disorders. Moreover, there are indications that at least some psychosocial interventions may have broader and more enduring effects than pharmacotherapy, although the relevant studies are not yet conclusive. Finally, there are indications that combined treatment may be superior to either single modality alone, largely as a consequence of retaining whatever specific advantages are associated with either single modality. These conclusions need to be qualified by a recognition that the oldest and most widely practiced types of psychotherapy have rarely been tested relative to medications; the bulk of the existing trials have involved the newer cognitive behavioral, interpersonal, and psychoeducational family interventions. Thus, the existing empirical literature may say more about what could be done in clinical practice than it does about what already takes place. This is a point to which we now turn.

Relative Generalizability of Drugs and Psychotherapy

Demonstrating efficacy in controlled clinical trials is important, but it is not enough. A given treatment may perform well in a research context but may still not generalize to applied clinical settings. Why this should be the case is not always clear, but it is important to know whether treatments retain their effects when taken into applied clinical settings.

There are strong suspicions among clinical practitioners that they do not. Surveys find that practicing clinicians pay little heed to the controlled empirical literature and rely more on an informal network of case reports, workshops, and collegial interactions to inform their clinical practice (Cohen, Sargent, & Sechrest, 1986). One of the most widely voiced complaints of practicing clinicians over the years has been that psychotherapy research is of minimal relevance to them.

Not only are the types of therapies they prefer ignored in controlled trials, but the task faced by the practicing clinician is often quite different from that faced by scientists in research settings (Weisz, Weiss, & Donenberg, 1992). Research therapy typically involves homogeneous samples of patients treated by expert clinicians who can focus on a particular problem and who have been provided with special training and supervision in a specific, manual-based treatment. Clinical therapy, on the other hand, often involves heterogeneous samples with multiple problems treated by generalists who must chart a course through a range of problems without the luxury of recent training in any specific approach.

The implication is that treatment effects should not be as great in applied clinical settings as they are in controlled research trials. In fact, this appears to be the case in the child treatment literature, in which effect sizes for studies conducted in laboratory studies have been found to be far larger than those observed in applied clinical settings (Weisz et al., 1992). It is not clear that this is also the case in the adult treatment literature (Shadish and colleagues found little evidence of a comparable decrement in an as yet unpublished manuscript, but they may not have operationalized their constructs in a comparable fashion), but the general dissatisfaction of clinical practitioners with the relevance of the treatment outcome literature suggests that this might be the case.

If treatment effects are smaller in applied clinical settings, the question remains just why that is. As previously described, problems in generalizability can arise from any of several aspects of the treatment situation. For example, differences may exist in the nature of the patient samples selected or in the quality and nature of the treatment delivered. If the former, then the clear implication is that treatments developed in controlled research settings would not be as effective if applied to the same populations encountered in everyday clinical practice. If the latter, then there may be cause for trying to enhance the quality and nature of treatment as it is provided in those applied clinical settings. Current indications are that both may be true.

Recent studies suggest that rates of comorbidity are high in applied clinical settings (Kessler et al., 1994). This suggests that many of the patients seen in such contexts might fail to meet criteria for any controlled treatment trial, since most try to utilize specific inclusion and exclusion criteria designed to select relatively homogeneous samples. In general, one would expect that patients with multiple problems would be harder to treat than those with relatively discrete disorders. Thus, there appears to be considerable merit to the notion that the task faced by clinicians in applied clinical settings simply may be tougher than that faced by clinicians in controlled research trials, simply because the patients presenting for treatment are more likely to express multiple disorders that complicate the course of treatment.

On the other hand, it is not clear that the samples selected are necessarily as dissimilar as they first may seem. Although most controlled treatment trials do try to select samples that are relatively homogeneous with respect to the presence of the disorder of interest, they often vary with respect to the extent and nature of comorbidity allowed. Moreover, most studies adhere to a rough hierarchy of diagnostic severity when determining just which types of comorbid disorders to include and which to exclude. For example, treatment studies with depressed samples typically exclude patients with a history of schizophrenia or bipolar disorder but often include patients with comorbid anxiety or personality disorders. Finally, diagnostic ascertainment is far from perfect, and some disorders that would be considered grounds for exclusion are often missed (or misrepresented) in the screening process. For example, although it is known that there exists a high rate of comorbidity for substance abuse in depressed patients, researchers often fail to screen such patients out of their trials because the extent of current drinking goes undetected.

The implication is that samples selected for research trials may not be as dissimilar from those observed in applied clinical settings than is often presumed to be the case. Moreover, given the nature of the processes involved in patient recruitment and selection, it may be less true that the easiest patients gravitate to controlled research settings as seems to be believed. Many research studies are conducted in tertiary-care facilities that get the bulk of their referrals from the surrounding treatment community. Under such circumstances, it may be the case that at least some controlled treatment trials are overpopulated with patients who are passed along through the referral system precisely because they are difficult to treat.

The other major possibility is that treatments are not delivered with the same care or precision in applied clinical settings as they are in controlled research studies. To the extent that that is true, some portion of that lesser precision may be largely unavoidable; the demands of maintaining an active clinical caseload filled with large numbers of clients with diverse problems may simply tax the resources of any clinician, no matter how well trained. However, it may also be the case that part of the problem may lie in the nature of the training that clinicians receive or in the choices that they subsequently make. For example, a survey commissioned by Division 12 of the American Psychological Association found that most graduate programs provide insufficient training in precisely those interventions that have fared best in controlled clinical trials (Task Force on Promotion and Dissemination of Psychological Procedures [TFPDPP], 1995). Thus, treatments which have fared well in controlled trials tend to have difficulty penetrating applied clinical practice, and those treatments that are widely practiced have tended not to receive adequate tests in controlled clinical trials (Seligman, 1995).

There is nothing inherent in the nature of randomized controlled clinical trials that states that they must exclude difficult patients. One need look no further than the recent work by Linehan and colleagues with borderline patients to find an example of a program of research that focuses on a population that most clinicians find difficult to treat (see chapter 27, this volume). These were very difficult patients, all of whom engaged in repeated parasuicidal behaviors and most of whom were comorbid for other related problems such as anxiety or depression. As described by Linehan and Heard (chapter 27, this volume), those patients treated with dialectic behavior therapy, a newly developed intervention created specifically for this population, were less likely to engage in parasuicidal behaviors or require additional hospitalizations than were similar patients referred to "treatment-as-usual" (typically supportive expressive therapy) in the community. Nevertheless, few practitioners in the community currently have the ability to provide this type of treatment. Whether dialectic behavior therapy will prove to be as effective in applied clinical settings as it was in this controlled clinical trial remains to be seen, but if it does not, it is not likely to be because the patients studied were less difficult to treat than the typical borderline patient.

Other examples abound. It is likely that few clinicians in applied settings actually provide psychoeducational family therapy, despite clear indications it can reduce risk for relapse in medicated schizophrenic patients (see chapter 22, this volume). Barlow has written extensively about the difficulties in transferring technologies tested in controlled clinical trials to applied clinical settings (Barlow, 1980, 1981; Barlow, Hayes, & Nelson, 1984; chapter 21, this volume). Even the recent NIMH Treatment of Depression Collaborative Research Program has been criticized for failing to ensure that its two psychotherapies (CBT and IPT) were properly implemented at each of its three sites

(Jacobson & Hollon, 1996a, 1996b; Thase, 1994). In that study, although drug-placebo differences were robust across sites, the performance of each psychotherapy varied considerably in a manner that may well have been linked to prior experience with the approach (Elkin et al., 1989).

Clearly, questions remain as to just how well the effects of treatment generalize from controlled research trials, but the general consensus appears to be that treatment effects decay, for whatever reason, as the interventions are moved into applied clinical settings. A key question for our current purposes is whether that is more true for psychotherapy than it is for pharmacotherapy. Unfortunately, this is a question for which there is no clear answer. The general perception is that pharmacotherapy is more robust than psychotherapy, if for no other reason than that its effects are believed to depend less on the skill of the practitioner. However, surveys of clinical practice suggest that many patients receive pharmacotherapy that is far from adequate in terms of dosages (Keller et al., 1986) or are treated with drugs that are inappropriate to their clinical condition (Sturm & Wells, 1995; Wells, Katon, Rogers, & Camp, 1994). Moreover, this is particularly likely to be the case in general practice settings, which account for up to half of all prescriptions written for psychotropic medications.

The gap between those medication strategies that have been empirically validated in controlled research trials and what actually transpires in applied clinical settings, is reminiscent of what occurs with respect to psychotherapy. This disjunction has led to greater efforts at professional education (Regier et al., 1988) and the formulation of treatment guidelines targeted to physicians designed to rectify these limitations (American Psychiatric Association [APA], 1993a, 1993b; Depression Guideline Panel, 1993). These efforts, combined with the development of newer medications with less problematic side effect profiles, has led to greater congruence between the clinical trials literature and practice in applied clinical settings (see chapter 5, this volume).

Moreover, important differences probably do exist between psychotherapy and pharmacotherapy that make the process of maintaining treatment integrity more difficult in the case of the former. First, most practicing psychotherapists have an allegiance to a particular school of therapy or, at the least, differ in the level of expertise they possess with respect to the various interventions. It this regard, it is probably more difficult to switch between different types of psychosocial interventions than it is to switch between different medications. Second, it is simply more difficult to monitor what goes on during the psychotherapy process than it is during pharmacotherapy. There is less consensus as to what constitutes the necessary and sufficient conditions of change with respect to the former, and it is clearly easier to monitor dosage and plasma levels than it is to assess the actual moment-by-moment interactions between psychotherapist and patient (Chevron & Rounsaville, 1983; Waltz, Addis, Koerner, & Jacobson, 1993). Third, there exists a large and well-funded pharmaceutical industry that not only funds research and development (typically focused on short-term treatment) but is also more than willing to publicize new developments in patient care and to provide training to practitioners in their utilization. That this willingness to engage in educational activities is largely self-serving and driven by the profit motive is beside the point; nothing comparable exists with respect to the psychotherapies to fuel the dissemination of clinical innovations. For these and other reasons, we would expect that the effects of pharmacotherapy should be more robust in clinical settings than is the case for psychotherapy.

Overall, there appears to be reasonable consensus (but surprisingly few data) that the effects of treatment deteriorate as we move from controlled research trials to applied clinical settings. Precisely why this should be the case (or even whether this is the case) remains unclear, but it could derive from either differences in the nature of the patients treated (in which case, research trials could simply become more realistic in whom they select) or an inability or unwillingness to maintain the integrity of the treatments offered (in which case, efforts to improve the quality of clinicians' skills and to develop treatment guidelines appear indicated). Moreover, this apparent deterioration in effect appears to be a problem for pharmacotherapy as well, but one that is more readily resolved due to the greater simplicity of the task.

Relative Cost-Effectiveness of Drugs and Psychotherapy

Finally, there is a growing interest in assessing the differential benefits of drugs and psychotherapy relative to their costs (see chapter 8, this volume). In essence, if two treatments produce comparable outcomes, then the one which is less expensive (either in terms of its monetary costs or in terms of its freedom from undesirable complications) is likely to be preferred. Moreover, a less effective treatment might even be preferred over a more effective one, if it costs considerably less and its outcome is deemed sufficient. Decisions about what treatment to provide become more complex when the persons who benefit are not the same as the persons who bear the burden of the costs. Nonetheless, it is clear that information regarding the relative costs and benefits of drugs and psychotherapy will play an ever larger role in determining health care policy in the marketplace (Yates, 1994).

It is fairly well established that the provision of psychosocial interventions can reduce health care utilization and enhance the quality of life with respect to medical illness (Krupnick & Pincus, 1992). Nonetheless, the general perception with respect to the treatment of mental disorders and problems in living is that drugs are less labor-intensive and therefore less expensive than the psychosocial interventions. Formal analyses of the relative costs and benefits of drugs versus psychosocial interventions have been few, but those that have been conducted tend to be consistent with this belief.

Two recent studies illustrate the issues involved in conducting cost-effectiveness analyses with respect to the relative merits of drugs and psychotherapy. In the first study, maintenance pharmacotherapy was found to be more cost-effective than maintenance IPT (either alone or in combination with medications) in the prevention of recurrence in recovered depressed patients (Kamlet et al., 1995). This was not surprising, since maintenance pharmacotherapy was both more effective than maintenance IPT and comparable to combined treatment in the original efficacy study on which the economic analysis was based (Frank et al., 1990). In the second study, pharmacotherapy was found to be more cost-effective than CBT (either alone or in combination with medication) in the treatment of bulimia (Koran et al., 1995). This was somewhat more surprising, since combined treatment typically produced the best overall results in the original efficacy study on which the economic analysis was based (Agras et al., 1992, 1994). Given the relative novelty of these analyses, each will be discussed in greater detail.

In the study described by Kamlet and colleagues (also see chapter 10, this volume), patients with a history of recurrent depression were first treated to the point of recovery with a combination of imipramine pharmacotherapy and interpersonal psychotherapy (IPT), then randomized into one of five conditions and followed for the next three years (or until they exhibited a recurrence of depression). The five conditions were (a) maintenance imipramine pharmacotherapy plus maintenance IPT, (b) maintenance imipramine pharmacotherapy alone, (c) maintenance IPT plus pill-placebo, (d) maintenance IPT alone, and (e) maintenance pill-placebo. Results indicated that the maintenance medication strategy (with or without IPT) was more effective in preventing recurrence than maintenance IPT (with or without pill-placebo), which was, in turn, more effective than maintenance on a pill-placebo alone (Frank et al., 1990).

To conduct the cost-effectiveness analysis, Kamlet and colleagues first estimated the costs of the respective treatments, taking into account both the direct costs (e.g., the costs of medications and laboratory assays for drugs and the costs required to reimburse clinicians for their time in treatment) and indirect costs to the patient (e.g., transportation to and from the clinic). They next estimated the effect of each treatment on expected lifetime health as measured in quality-adjusted life years (QALYs). This index takes into account not only how long a person is likely to live (mortality), but also how much he or she is likely to value the time that he or she does have (morbidity). Estimates of the likely impact of various disorders on quality of life typically are made by asking respondents to indicate how many years of life they would be willing to "trade off" to be free of a particular disorder. Studies have found that most people would be willing to sacrifice up to half of their remaining years if it meant being free of depression (Sackett & Torrence, 1978). The costs associated with each treatment are then divided by the expected impact of treatment on lifetime health as measured in quality-adjusted life years (see chapter 10, this volume, for a more detailed discussion).

What Kamlet and colleagues found was that maintenance pharmacotherapy was cost-effective in the strongest sense of the term compared to both pill-placebo and maintenance IPT. Maintenance pharmacotherapy both improved the patients' expected lifetime health (as measured in quality-adjusted life years) and reduced direct medical care costs (relative to maintenance IPT). Combined treatment and (to a lesser extent) maintenance IPT both improved expected lifetime health but did not necessarily reduce direct medical costs (that is, each was more expensive, relative to the benefit provided, than maintenance pharmacotherapy alone). Thus, whereas the clinical efficacy analysis suggested that combined treatment was comparable in efficacy to maintenance medication alone (and that both were superior to IPT alone or pill-placebo), the economic analysis indicated that adding IPT to maintenance medication drove up the cost of treatment with little added benefit.

This was an interesting study that could well serve as a model for the economic analysis of differential treatment effects. Nonetheless, several comments are in order. First, the findings observed were relevant only to the treatments as actually provided. Although pharmacotherapy was continued at full-strength throughout the maintenance interval, session frequency was reduced from once per week to once per month in IPT, in effect a fourfold decrease in treatment "dosage" for the psychotherapy condition. While more frequent sessions would have driven up the cost of treatment, they might also have increased the efficacy of IPT alone.

Second, the only outcome considered when estimating the effects of treatment on expected quality of life was recurrence of depression. Although this was the main outcome examined in the original efficacy study, it is not the only possible outcome of interest. As described above, previous studies typically have found that IPT enhances the quality of social functioning relative to pharmacotherapy (see Weissman & Markowitz, 1994). Although patients already may have received as much benefit as they were going to obtain from IPT with respect to the quality of their relationships (all patients had received several months of IPT in combination with medications during initial treatment), it is also possible that consideration of the effects of treatment on social adjustment would have enhanced the value of maintenance IPT (alone or in combination) relative to maintenance pharmacotherapy.

Finally, although the economic analysis described was both elegant and thorough, it is not clear that it provided any novel information with respect to the specific study in question. Even a casual reading of the original efficacy manuscript suggested that maintenance medication was more effective than maintenance IPT alone and that adding IPT did little to enhance the effects of medication, at least with respect to the prevention of recurrence. Given that IPT was more expensive than maintenance medication and given that combined treatment was obviously more expensive than either single modality, it is not clear that a complex economic analysis was required to indicate that drugs were more cost-effective than psychotherapy (alone or in combination). Although economic analyses are becoming increasingly fashionable, they really must say something that is not already evident from the efficacy data alone if they are to justify their additional expense.

The economic analysis of drugs and psychotherapy in the treatment of bulimia appeared to do just that. In the original efficacy study, Agras and colleagues (1992) found CBT (with or without medications) to be superior to pharmacotherapy alone (desipramine) with respect to both acute response and the maintenance of treatment gains. Nonetheless, in a subsequent cost-effectiveness analysis of these data, the investigators found that brief pharmacotherapy alone (16 weeks) was the most cost-effective intervention shortly after treatment termination, whereas extended pharmacotherapy (24 weeks) was the most cost-effective intervention one year after study initiation (Koran et al., 1995). Why this should be the case is not immediately clear, but it merits further consideration.

In essence, what Koran and colleagues did was to estimate the cost of treatment for each intervention and to relate it to the proportion of patients who were abstinent with respect to both binge and purge behaviors at two subsequent points in time, shortly after treatment termination (32 weeks after entering the program) and after an extended treatment-free interval (52 weeks after entering the program). What they found was that rates of abstinence at 32 weeks were worse for patients receiving brief pharmacotherapy (16 weeks) than for patients receiving combined treatment with extended pharmacotherapy (24 weeks), but that this poorer performance was offset by the lower cost of treatment. Thus, the cost per abstinent patient was lower in brief pharmacotherapy than it was in extended combination treatment (CBT alone was intermediate in both respects). Rates of abstinence for brief pharmacotherapy were sufficiently reduced at the one-year follow-up so that they could not be offset by the lower costs of treatment, but extended pharmacotherapy did sufficiently well to appear to be more cost-effective than other comparably effective treatments (extended combined therapy or CBT alone). Thus, in this study, the conclusions that might be drawn about cost-effectiveness (Koran et al., 1995) did not coincide with those that would be drawn from an examination of the efficacy data alone (Agras et al., 1992).

As the authors pointed out, their study highlights the complexity inherent in using economic analyses to guide policy decisions. If only short-term findings were considered, brief pharmacotherapy might have been preferred, since it cost less per abstinent patient, despite the fact that it was only about half as effective as CBT (either alone or in combination with extended pharmacotherapy). Thus, failure to consider the extended effects of treatment would have greatly altered the decisions that might be made about the relative values of the different treatments. Moreover, the choice of outcome measures strongly influenced the results of the analysis, since only CBT and combined treatment with extended pharmacotherapy were superior to brief psychotherapy in reducing overall rates of binge eating (as opposed to the proportion of patients abstinent) through the one-year follow-up (Agras et al., 1994). (In fact, it was curious that patients treated with extended pharmacotherapy alone were more likely to be abstinent at the one-year follow-up than they were shortly after medication withdrawal.) In general, combined treatment with extended pharmacotherapy produced the most consistent pattern of good results across the various measures of outcome, although it was more expensive to provide than extended pharmacotherapy alone.

Nonetheless, these studies both appear to suggest that drugs are more cost-effective than psychotherapy. This may lead some third-party payers to prefer pharmacotherapy, despite consistent indications that patients typically prefer psychotherapy (Munoz, Hollon, McGrath, Rehm, & VandenBos, 1994; Seligman, 1995). Of course, these estimates depend heavily on the nature of the medication provided, the frequency of the contacts required, and the level of training of the professionals involved. For example, both studies examined the cost-effectiveness of tricyclic antidepressants (TCAs), although most patients are now treated with SSRIs, which have lower side effect profiles and are less likely to be lethal if taken in overdose. Given that the SSRIs are still under patent, they are considerably more expensive to prescribe than the TCAs. If the studies had used SSRIs rather than TCAs, the costs involved in providing the medications alone would have nearly doubled and might well have affected the results of the cost-effectiveness analyses. Similarly, IPT in the study analyzed by Kamlet and colleagues was conducted far less frequently during the maintenance phase than it was during acute treatment; maintaining session frequency might have led to better sustained response. Finally, who provides the psychotherapy in part determines how much it will cost. If paraprofessionals or caregivers with lesser degrees can match the quality of care provided by professionals, as has often been suggested, then the costs of psychotherapy may be reduced (Christensen & Jacobson, 1994). Of course, the same could be true of pharmacotherapy if the burden of providing ongoing medications could be shifted to nonpsychiatric physicians or nonmedical personnel.

However, the most important potential qualification to the notion that drugs are less expensive than psychotherapy has to do with the possibility that the psychosocial interventions produce broad and enduring effects that last beyond the end of treatment. There is little evidence that pharmacotherapy of any kind has a lasting effect once treatment is over. Pharmacotherapy for the more severe disorders like schizophrenia or mania is already thought of as an ongoing process that will last for the rest of the patient's life. Increasingly, the same is being said of unipolar depression, at least with respect to those patients with a propensity for recurrence (who represent the majority of patients with affective disorders). If psychotherapy has broader or more enduring effects, as has long been suggested, then it may prove more cost-effective in the long run than simply providing medications. Clearly, these effects will have to be demonstrated in controlled empirical trials, but the existing literature, although not yet conclusive, does suggest that they might exist for at least some types of psychotherapy (Hollon & Beck, 1994; Weissman & Markowitz, 1994).

Conclusions

With respect to efficacy, it appears that medication is essential to the treatment of the more severe disorders, but that psychosocial interventions (particularly the newer skills training and psychoeducational family interventions) can play a key adjunctive role. With respect to the less severe disorders, recent evidence suggests the psychosocial interventions are often at least as effective as pharmacotherapy and may be broader and more enduring in their effects. However, the empirical support for these latter effects is not yet conclusive, and there is a clear need for additional studies in this regard. Whether combining drugs and psychotherapy provides sufficient incremental benefit to justify the additional cost is likely to depend upon the nature of the disorder. Answering that question will require more definitive knowledge regarding psychotherapy's putative impact on breadth and stability of response.

Treatment effects detected in controlled research often do not generalize well to applied clinical settings, but it remains unclear whether that is due to differences in the populations studied or the nature of the treatments and the competence with which they are implemented. It is probably more difficult for innovations in psychotherapy to penetrate applied settings than is the case for pharmacotherapy, although studies of actual clinical practice suggest that there are problems with respect to each. At the same time, there are persistent concerns that the treatment efficacy literature has systematically underestimated the effectiveness of the more traditional approaches to psychotherapy typically preferred by practitioners in the field. This is another area in which additional information is clearly needed.

Finally, although the few economic analyses currently available have suggested that drugs are more cost-effective than psychotherapy, this literature is still in its infancy and has yet to take into account the indications of greater breadth of response and more enduring change suggested for at least some of the psychosocial interventions. Moreover, given that such analyses require large samples and the inclusion of personnel with training in health care economics, cost-effectiveness studies must provide novel information (beyond what is evident from a simple reading of the efficacy literature) if they are to justify their additional expense. It is likely that this will prove to be the case, but it will probably require a "period of adjustment" as researchers from the different perspective learn to work together within a common protocol.

Acknowledgments This chapter draws heavily on an earlier presentation by Ellen Frank on drugs and psychotherapy at the NIMH conference on the cost-effectiveness of psychotherapy on which this book is based. Although she should not be held accountable for any errors in judgment or fact that I may have made, I was strongly influenced by the clarity and wisdom of her presentation and can only regret that her schedule prevented her from writing this chapter herself.

References

Agras, W. S., Rossiter, E. M., Arnow, B., Schneider, J. A., Telch, C. F., Raeburn, S. D., Bruse, B., Perl, M., & Koran, L. M. (1992). Pharmacological and cognitive-behavioral treatment for bulimia nervosa: A controlled comparison. *American Journal of Psychiatry, 149*, 82–87.

Agras, W. S., Rossiter, E. M., Arnow, B., Telch, C. F., Raeburn, S. D., Bruce, B., & Koran, L. M. (1994). One-year follow-up of psychosocial and pharmacologic treatments for bulimia nervosa. *Journal of Clinical Psychiatry, 55*, 179–183.

American Psychiatric Association. (1993a). Practice guideline for major depressive disorder in adults. *American Journal of Psychiatry, 150*, 792–794.

American Psychiatric Association. (1993b). Practice guideline for major depressive disorder in adults. *American Journal of Psychiatry, 150*, Suppl. 1–26.

Barlow, D. H. (1980). Behavior therapy: The next decade. *Behavior Therapy, 11*, 315–328.

Barlow, D. H. (1981). On the relation of clinical research to clinical practice: Current issues, new directions. *Journal of Consulting and Clinical Psychology, 49*, 147–155.

Barlow, D. H., Hayes, S. C., & Nelson, R. O. (1984). *The scientist-practitioner: Research and accountability in clinical and educational settings*. New York: Pergamon Press.

Chevron, E. S., & Rounsaville, B. J. (1983). Evaluating the clinical skills of psychotherapists: A comparison of techniques. *Archives of General Psychiatry, 40*, 1129–1132.

Christensen, A. C., & Jacobson, N. S. (1994). Who (or what) can do psychotherapy: The status and challenge of nonprofessional therapies. *Psychological Science, 5*, 8–14.

Christensen, H., Hadzi-Pavlovic, D., Andrews, G., & Mattick, R. (1987). Behavior therapy and tricyclic medication in the treatment of obsessive-compulsive disorder: A quantative review. *Journal of Consulting and Clinical Psychology, 55*, 701–711.

Clark, D. M., Salkovskis, P. M., Hackmann, A., Middleton, H., Anastasiades, P., & Gelder, M. (1994). Comparison of cognitive therapy, applied relaxation and imipramine in the treatment of panic disorder. *British Journal of Psychiatry, 164*, 759–769.

Clarkin, J. F., Glick, I. D., Haas, G. L., et al. (1990). A randomized clinical trial of inpatient family intervention: 5. Results for affective disorders. *Journal of Affective Disorders, 18*, 17–28.

Cochran, S. D. (1984). Preventing medical noncompliance in the outpatient treatment of bipolar affective disorder. *Journal of Consulting and Clinical Psychology, 52*, 873–878.

Cohen, L. H., Sargent, M. H., & Sechrest, L. B. (1986). Use of psychotherapy research by professional psychologists. *American Psychologist, 41*, 198–206.

Craighead, L. W., & Agras, W. S. (1991). Mechanisms of action in cognitive-behavioral and pharmacological interventions for obesity and bulimia nervosa. *Journal of Consulting and Clinical Psychology, 59*, 115–125.

Depression Guideline Panel. (1993). *Depression in primary care: Vol. 2. Treatment of major depression* (Clinical Practice Guideline No. 5, AHCPR Publication No. 93-0551). Rockville, MD: Department of Health and Human Services, Public Health Service, Agency for Health Care and Policy Research.

Elkin, I., Shea, M. T., Watkins, J. T., et al. (1989). NIMH Treatment of Depression Collaborative Research Program: 1. General effectiveness of treatments. *Archives of General Psychiatry, 46,* 971–982.

Fairburn, C. G., Jones, R., Peveler, R. C., Hope, R. A., & O'Connor, M. (1993). Psychotherapy and bulimia nervosa: Longer-term effects of interpersonal psychotherapy, behavior therapy and cognitive behavior therapy. *Archives of General Psychiatry, 50,* 419–428.

Frank, E., Kupfer, D. J., Perel, J. M., et al. (1990). Three-year outcomes for maintenance therapies in recurrent depression. *Archives of General Psychiatry, 47,* 1093–1099.

Hollon, S. D., & Beck, A. T. (1978). Psychotherapy and drug therapy: Comparisons and combinations. In S. L. Garfield & A. E. Bergin (Eds.), *Handbook of psychotherapy and behavior change: An empirical analysis* (2nd ed., pp. 437–490). New York: Wiley.

Hollon, S. D., & Beck, A. T. (1994). Cognitive and cognitive-behavioral therapies. In A. E. Bergin & S. L. Garfield (Eds.), *Handbook of psychotherapy and behavior change* (4th ed., pp. 428–466). New York: Wiley.

Hollon, S. D., & Fawcett, J. (1995). Combined medication and psychotherapy. In G. O. Gabbard (Ed.), *Treatments of psychiatric disorders* (2nd ed., pp. 1221–1236). Washington, DC: American Psychiatric Press.

Hollon, S. D., Shelton, R. C., & Loosen, P. T. (1991a). Cognitive therapy and pharmacotherapy for depression. *Journal of Consulting and Clinical Psychology, 59,* 88–99.

Hollon, S. D., Shelton, R. C., & Loosen, P. T. (1991b). Research considerations in evaluating combined treatment. In B. D. Beitman & G. L. Klerman (Eds.), *Integrating pharmacotherapy and psychotherapy* (pp. 353–375). Washington, DC: American Psychiatric Press.

Jacobson, N. S., & Hollon, S. D. (1996a). Cognitive behavior therapy vs. pharmacotherapy: Now that the jury has returned its verdict, its time to review the rest of the evidence. *Journal of Consulting and Clinical Psychology, 64,* 74–80.

Jacobson, N. S., & Hollon, S. D. (1996b). Prospects for future comparisons between drugs and psychotherapy: Lessons from the CBT vs. pharmacotherapy exchange. *Journal of Consulting and Clinical Psychology, 64,* 104–108.

Kamlet, M. S., Paul, N., Greenhouse, J., Kupfer, D., Frank, E., & Wade, M. (1995). Cost utility analysis of maintenance treatment for recurrent depression. *Controlled Clinical Trials, 16,* 17–40.

Keller, M., Lavori, P., Klerman, G., Andreasen, N. C., Endicott, J., Coryell, W., Fawcett, J., Rice, J., & Hirschfeld, R. (1986). Low levels and lack of predictors of somatotherapy and psychotherapy received by depressed patients. *Archives of General Psychiatry, 43,* 458–466.

Kessler, R. C., McGonagle, K. A., Zhao, S., Nelson, C. B., Hughes, M., Eshleman, S., Wittchen, H. U., & Kendler, K. S. (1994). Lifetime and 12-month prevalence of DSM-III-R psychiatric disorders in the United States: Results from the National Comorbidity Survey. *Archives of General Psychiatry, 51,* 8–19.

Koran, L. M., Agras, W. S., Rossiter, E. M., Arnow, B., Schneider, J. A., Telch, C. F., Raeburn, S., Bruce, B., Perl, M., & Kraemer, H. C. (1995). Comparing the cost-effectiveness of psychiatric treatments: Bulimia nervosa. *Psychiatry Research, 58,* 13–21.

Krupnick, J. L., & Pincus, H. A. (1992). The cost-effectiveness of psychotherapy: A plan for research. *American Journal of Psychiatry, 149,* 1295–1305.

Liberman, R. P. (1994). Psychosocial treatments for schizophrenia. *Psychiatry, 57,* 104–114.

Luborsky, L., Singer, B., & Luborsky, L. (1975). Comparative studies of psychtherapies: Is it true that "Everyone has won and all must have prizes"? *Archives of General Psychiatry, 32,* 995–1008.

Marks, I., & O'Sullivan, G. (1988). Drugs and psychological treatments for agoraphobia/panic and obsessive-compulsive disorders: A review. *British Journal of Psychiatry, 153,* 650–658.

Mental health: Does therapy help? (1995, November). *Consumer Reports, 60*(11), 734–739.

Munoz, R. F., Hollon, S. D., McGrath, E., Rehm, L. P., & VandenBos, G. R. (1994). On the AHCPR *Depression in Primary Care* guidelines: Further considerations for practitioners. *American Psychologist, 49,* 42–61.

National Advisory Mental Health Council. (1993). Health care reform for Americans with severe mental illnesses: Report of the National Advisory Mental Health Council. *American Journal of Psychiatry, 150,* 1447–1465.

Persons, J. B. (1991). Psychotherapy outcome studies do not accurately represent current models of psychotherapy: A proposed remedy. *American Psychologist, 46,* 99–106.

Regier, D. A., Hirschfeld, M. A., Goodwin, F. K., Burke, J. D., Lazar, J. B., & Judd, L. (1988). The NIMH Depression Awareness, Recognition and Treatment Program: Structure, aims and scientific basis. *American Journal of Psychiatry, 145,* 1351–1357.

Sackett, D. L., & Torrance, G. W. (1978). The utility of

different health states as perceived by the general public. *Journal of Chronic Disease, 31*, 697–704.

Seligman, M. E. P. (1995). The effectiveness of psychotherapy: The *Consumer Reports* study. *American Psychologist, 50*, 965–974.

Smith, M. L., & Glass, G. V. (1977). Meta-analysis of psychotherapy outcome studies. *American Psychologist, 32*, 752–760.

Stiles, W. B., & Shapiro, D. A. (1989). Abuse of the drug metaphor in psychotherapy process-outcome research. *Clinical Psychology Review, 9*, 521–543.

Sturm, R., & Wells, K. B. (1995). How can care for depression become more cost-effective? *Journal of the American Medical Association*, 273(1), 51–58.

Task Force on Promotion and Dissemination of Psychological Procedures. (1995). Training in and dissemination of empirically-validated psychological treatments: Report and recommendations. *The Clinical Psychologist, 48*, 3–23.

Thase, M. E. (1994). After the fall: Perspectives on cognitive behavioral treatment of depression in the "post-Collaborative" era. *the Behavior Therapist, 17*, 48–51.

Waltz, J., Addis, M. E., Koerner, K., & Jacobson, N. S. (1993). Testing the integrity of a psychotherapy protocol: Assessment of adherence and competence. *Journal of Consulting and Clinical Psychology, 61*, 620–630.

Weissman, M. M., Klerman, G. L., Paykel, E. S., Prusoff, B., & Hanson, B. (1974). Treatment effects on the social adjustment of depressed patients. *Archives of General Psychiatry, 30*, 771–778.

Weissman, M. M., Klerman, G. L., Prusoff, B. A., Sholomskas, D., & Padian, N. (1981). Depressed outpatients one year after treatment with drugs and/or interpersonal psychotherapy (IPT). *Archives of General Psychiatry, 38*, 51–55.

Weissman, M. M., & Markowitz, J. C. (1994). Interpersonal psychotherapy: Current status. *Archives of General Psychiatry, 51*, 599–606.

Weisz, J. R., Weiss, B., & Donenberg, G. R. (1992). The lab versus the clinic: Effects of child and adolescent psychotherapy. *American Psychologist, 47*, 1578–1585.

Wells, K. B., Katon, W., Rogers, B., & Camp, P. (1994). Use of minor traquilizers and antidepressant medications by depressed outpatients: Results from the Medical Outcomes Study. *American Journal of Psychiatry, 151*, 694–700.

Wilson, G. T. (1996). Manual-based treatments: The clinical application of research findings. *Behaviour Research and Therapy, 34*, 295–315.

Yates, B. (1994). Toward the incorporation of costs, cost-effectiveness analysis, and cost-benefits analysis into clinical research. *Journal of Consulting and Clinical Psychology, 62*, 729–736.

3

Linking Efficacy and Effectiveness Research in the Evaluation of Psychotherapies

A. John Rush

Efficacy Research

Typically, efficacy research aims at determining the *comparative clinical effects* (usually defined by symptoms), *tolerability* (e.g., as evidenced by the percentage of patients who complete treatment), and *safety* (e.g., as evidenced by the number of suicides, arrests, etc., during treatment) of a *treatment* (e.g., cognitive therapy, interpersonal therapy) on the particular domain(s) of outcome that is deemed most likely to be remediated by the treatment (e.g., depressive symptoms for antidepressant medications) in *patients selected as most likely to benefit* from the treatment (e.g., patients with uncomplicated, nonchronic, nonpsychotic major depressive disorder), *delivered for a specified time period* (e.g., 10–20 weeks, chosen as that time period during which a therapeutic response is most likely, and during which a nonspecific response is least likely) using *specified procedures* (e.g., according to a manual) delivered by selected practitioners (e.g., therapists assessed on the Cognitive Therapy Rating Scale, or CTS; Vallis, Shaw, & Dobson, 1986; Young & Beck, 1980).

In essence, efficacy trials are designed to have highly interpretable negative outcomes, as well as highly replicable positive outcomes, should such occur (i.e., the highest internal validity) (see chapter 2, this volume). The rationale is that if negative outcomes occur (and are replicated), but few or no positive outcomes occur, the treatment is rejected both from further study and from "export" to clinical practice. If positive results occur, all of the major ingredients to be used to execute the requisite replications are known. If sufficient positive replications occur, "export" to clinical practice is advised, assuming that the safety, tolerability, and efficacy are at least comparable to those of the other available treatments.

Efficacy studies of psychotherapies have generally revealed better results with the therapy of interest than with wait list controls (i.e., doing something is better than doing nothing) (see chapter 20, this volume). The acute phase safety and tolerability of studied therapies is generally high.

Efficacy studies of medications employ a pill-placebo because (1) safety and tolerability can thereby be easily evaluated, and (2) specific efficacy (i.e., that obtained with the chemical agent per se over and above that obtained with pill-placebo) can thereby be evaluated objectively to determine whether the overall benefits outweigh the risks (meaning personal discomfort, injury, or death). Pill-placebos are feasible because the active ingredient—the chemical agent—is known at the outset.

On the other hand, a "placebo" control, meaning the delivery of all treatment elements save for the active ingredient(s), cannot be used in psychotherapy trials because the active ingredient(s) is not known (Parloff, 1986). Furthermore, it is logical to expect that the active ingredient(s) in psychotherapies is likely to be multidimensional. The specific active ingredients in a therapy package are likely to differ across patient groups, disorder subtypes, and therapist types, as well as across the diverse interpersonal contexts that distinguish one patient from another.

The notion that the active ingredient(s) within a standardized therapy differs for particular patients in different contexts or when delivered by different therapists logically follows from the idea that behavior is overdetermined. For example, episodes of inappropriate sadness may be reduced if the patients can reframe their views of the precipitants of sadness, or if they modify their environmental interaction patterns to reduce their exposure to such precipitants. Furthermore, the notion of a diversity of active ingredients is consistent with the views that there are common factors across therapies that contribute to positive outcomes (Garfield, 1992), as well as useful differences among schools in practice (Beitman, 1992). Such a view argues for a matching of therapy and problem (Norcross, 1995).

Our lack of knowledge regarding the specific active ingredient(s) in psychotherapy, however, does not prevent an overall evaluation of safety, tolerability, and comparative efficacy in randomized controlled trials (RCTs) of specific psychotherapies. This situation is analogous to evaluating the combination of two medications used together or to the evaluation of multistep medication algorithms, sometimes called *disease management protocols*. In both cases, the beneficial effect(s) cannot be definitively attributed to one element or step in the package, since there is potentially more than one active ingredient in any package. Conversely, the overall utility of the package can be compared with alternative treatments or with subunits of the total package. Indeed, the latter approach has been used in so-called dismantling studies of psychotherapy packages in attempts to identify which steps are the active ingredients.

Effectiveness Research

Overall, effectiveness research aims at defining how treatments are actually delivered or how treatments might be efficiently delivered, or at evaluating the comparative effects of treatments on representative populations of patients, practitioners, or systems of care. When effectiveness research evaluates different treatments, the patients, practitioners, practices, and/or systems of care are all chosen to closely mirror routine practice. That is, external validity is of paramount importance (see chapter 2, this volume).

Clinical mental health services research regards the patient as the unit of analysis. Results directly inform patients and providers and indirectly also inform administrators, policymakers, and payers. Commonly, clinical mental health services research extends evaluations of the effects of treatment to a wider domain of outcome variables (e.g., symptoms, function, satisfaction, quality of life, service utilization) as delivered by a wider domain of representative practitioners functioning in representative systems of service delivery treating typical patients.

Mental health systems services research uses the system as the unit of analysis. It informs mainly administrators, policymakers, and payers especially in regard to resource allocation. Results may indirectly inform patients or providers.

Service systems research primarily addresses questions of *how* to deliver the treatment(s) at the system level, often comparing diverse delivery systems. Results comment on *whether* to make accommodations (e.g., to reallocate resources) based on the costs and benefits attributable to the treatment(s) in the system of interest (i.e., results inform the choices that payers and administrators must make in setting priorities for the use of available resources).

In an oversimplified shorthand, efficacy research aims primarily at defining the treatment and whether it is worth pursuing (i.e., Does it have efficacy? Is it safe and tolerable?). It is assumed that practitioners would preferentially implement those treatments whose efficacy, safety, and tolerability have been demonstrated. Effectiveness research aims primarily at evaluating what is actually delivered in practice, how it is delivered, to whom is it delivered, and what are the effects of such treatments on broad domains of outcome.

Are Efficacy and Effectiveness Research Distinct?

Efficacy and effectiveness research are distinct, but to varying degrees, depending upon the treatments or interventions under investigation. The newer the treatment is to practice, the greater the distinction between efficacy and effectiveness research. The more the treatment is a modification of existing procedures, the closer conceptually are efficacy and effectiveness research.

The following two examples, hopefully, serve to illustrate these points. The first example comes from pharmacological development, where safety and tolerability are the initial critical issues. The second example illustrates how psychotherapy can be evaluated with different steps from those used for medication development, because safety and tolerability are known to be great, but efficacy/effectiveness and how to deliver the treatment are critical first issues.

Example 1

Let us assume that an entirely new treatment is developed. *New* means that no practitioner has ever used the treatment or any variation of it. Further, let us assume that the treatment has an unknown but significant potential for harm (e.g., a new medication for a disorder never previously treated with medication). Here the classic phases, defined by the Food and Drug Administration (FDA) for approval and licensing, apply. Safety and dosing are initially established in Phase I and II trials. Comparative efficacy with placebo is evaluated in late Phase II and Phase III trials. Efficacy, tolerability, and safety are compared to those of other already-established medications (if available) and evaluated in Phase III trials. Phase IV (postmarketing research) evaluates how practitioners use the treatment, as well as its tolerability and safety with a wider range of patients, providers, practice settings, and systems of care.

In this case, effectiveness research is rather analogous to Phase IV pharmaceutical development efforts. It cannot proceed until safety and efficacy data are available and a policy decision to use the medication in practice is made. Only then will services researchers want to even consider which patient populations, treated by which practitioners, in what ways (e.g., weekly, biweekly, monthly visits) will benefit and at what costs.

The above case is clear because the safety and tolerability of the treatment are the critical issue. Until safety is established, efficacy and effectiveness are of secondary interest.

Example 2

On the other hand, if the new treatment entails a very low likelihood of direct harm and, further, if it involves modifications of existing treatments (e.g., a new psychotherapy), then *how* to implement the treatment and what is its efficacy/effectiveness, rather than safety, are the first issues. In this case, efficacy may be evaluated more rapidly by directly modifying "real-world" practices (i.e., adopting the new therapy) and evaluating its effects (reduced symptoms, reduced disability) compared to those of alternative treatments (e.g., treatment as usual). That is, effectiveness and efficacy can be established simultaneously by RCT methodologies.

Since both efficacy and effectiveness are major early considerations in developing a psychotherapy, the question of *how* to implement the treatment (i.e., how to modify existing practice procedures) is critical. In a nutshell, efficacy/effectiveness is of little matter if the treatment is not feasible. That is, if psychotherapies, even those with substantial efficacy, cannot be implemented in actual practice by reasonably representative practitioners receiving modest training, no practical utility follows.

Psychotherapy Packages and Disease Management Protocols: Birds of a Feather?

Disease management protocols (sometimes referred to as *treatment algorithms*) are analogous to psychotherapy packages. Each "package" involves multiple steps, usually conducted in a semispecified sequence that is recommended by the protocol but defined, in part, by the patient's response to prior steps in the package. Populations suitable for treatment with such packages are broadly defined, yet there is a recognition of the need to tailor the steps in each package to individual patients, a question based on the general principles of pharmacology, psychology, or psychopathology. That is, each step is believed to be effective for some but not all patients. For medications, there is evidence of safety and efficacy for each step in the medication algorithms based on RCTs of each medication. For psychotherapy, there is an empirical or theoretical basis for each step in the package.

For investigators of treatment algorithms, as well as psychotherapeutic treatment packages, the key issue is the benefits and costs of the overall package compared to those of alternative approaches (e.g., treatment as usual or other packages). Whether a particular step is effective is not of interest. In fact, since "carryover" or "priming" effects are inherent in multistep treatment programs, attempts to isolate active ingredients for particular patients treated with multiple steps are logically likely to be fruitless.

In summary, treatment algorithms and psychotherapeutic packages are similar, since each consists of a number of steps from which the practitioner selects, the selection being based on patient status and response to prior steps, so as to individually tailor the overall approach according to the general principles and assumptions underpinning the treatment and the psychopathology to be treated.

Implementation is the Key Issue

Of critical importance in the evaluation of either treatment algorithms or psychotherapy packages are implementation issues in various care systems and practice settings (e.g., Which practitioners? What degree of training? With what system support?). In essence, both psychotherapy and disease management protocols must be directly evaluated for efficacy/effectiveness *early* in broadly defined patient groups because these interventions are designed at the outset to address broadly defined patient and provider groups, as well as broader domains of outcome (i.e., *efficacy* and *effectiveness* become nearly synonymous).

For psychotherapies, the "how to do it" in routine clinical practice is a critical question that must be answered clearly if research is to have results that change practice (i.e., if findings are to be of sufficient importance so that systems and practitioners will or should change their usual behaviors). Similarly, the tactics of how to implement treatment algorithms (multistep clinical decision trees) that typically aim at broadly defined patient samples and broader domains of outcome are critical (Rush & Prien, 1995). When to change steps, how often to see patients, and how to gauge outcomes at each step are implementation issues.

Debates about treatment algorithms center on three key issues: (1) how to define the steps in the algorithm (e.g., which medication is to be used first, which second, etc.); (2) how to describe the algorithm (i.e., the level of specificity to be provided to the practitioners who are to implement the package); and (3) how to implement the algorithm (e.g., How long should the patient tolerating but not responding to Step 1 continue before Step 2 is taken?).

For example, should a particular drug be specified at each step, or should a class of drugs be specified, or should only the principles and parameters that surround each choice at each step be given, so that practitioners make all the specific choices? It is logical to expect greater patient retention and greater provider participation if the general principles and a range of choices are included in the algorithm, as opposed to providing a highly specific recipe of steps that may be less applicable to particular patients and less affected by ongoing observations during the course of treatment. Conversely, if the "algorithm" provides no specifics beyond principles found in textbooks of psychopharmacology, for example, it risks both difficulties in replication and an unacceptably wide range of provider behaviors, so that the algorithm has been neither concocted nor evaluated.

These issues are entirely analogous to debates about how to define, frame, specify, and implement psychotherapies. While the general principles for selecting among and implementing a complex set of steps in the psychotherapy package rest on the theoretical underpinning of the treatment, whether to provide a recipe of steps to be followed in all cases, or rather to provide general principles of treatment, with illustrations of how and when to use certain techniques during treatment—so that the selection and tailoring of techniques are left to clinicians' judgment—remains an issue.

As with treatment algorithms, neither efficacy nor effectiveness studies of the psychotherapy package aim primarily at defining which step was the "active ingredient," though dismantling studies attempt to address this issue. Rather, the overall benefit of the treatment package or protocol taken as a whole for the population is the critical issue. Thus, the efficacy and effectiveness of psychotherapy are defined by comparisons with either no treatment (e.g., wait list), treatment as usual, or other defined treatment packages, whether psychotherapy or medication.

Authors of psychotherapy manuals usually assume that less complex forms of therapy (i.e., fewer steps and more limited goals for less complex patients or conditions) require less highly trained providers, who in turn need more highly specified manuals, much like the technical manuals for troubleshooting automobile maintenance problems. On the other hand, more steps and a more complex and abstract reasoning from general principles may be needed to redress more complex problems in more complicated patients. The assumption here is that more highly trained therapists or providers will be needed to execute these procedures, and that the general principles of treatment and listing of optional treatment tactics and techniques, rather than a highly specific, inflexible recipe of steps, are called for. That is, the level of provider interacts with patient complexity and the complexity/flexibility of the psychotherapy or algorithm.

In sum, for both psychotherapies and medication algorithms, who is to implement the treatment and how are the critical issues. In addition, which patient groups are benefited? When? To what degree? And in what domains (i.e., symptom, psychosocial function, service utilization)? These are important early questions for both psychotherapy treatments and medication algorithms.

Can Efficacy be Established When Effectiveness is Evaluated for Psychotherapy?

Historically, classical efficacy researchers studying psychotherapy have been prominently concerned with how to sufficiently define the new psychotherapy in order to evaluate its efficacy in comparison to other treatments. Thus, manual development, therapist training, and ongoing evaluations to ensure adherence have been routine components of efficacy testing for psychotherapy. Once efficacy is established, the issues of what *types of providers* (e.g., degree, training, background, and experience) with what *personal characteristics* (e.g., empathetic versus task-oriented) and what *level of training* in the new treatment are needed for acceptable implementation in routine practice become important. These issues are rarely empirically tested, yet they are critical to the transfer of treatments with established efficacy into clinical practice. In short, how to transfer the new treatment is rarely studied, even though there is evidence from efficacy trials that better adherence to the particulars of a treatment appears to be associated with better outcomes than poorer adherence (Frank, Kupfer, Wagner, McEachran, & Cornes, 1991; Luborsky & Barber, 1993; Luborsky, McLellan, Woody, O'Brien, & Auerbach, 1985).

It is logical to reconsider aspects of this classical track entailed in psychotherapy development, efficacy testing, and ultimate implementation in practice. The evaluation of services may provide key leads for psychotherapy research (i.e., studies of what works in actual practice can lead to treatment innovations, as well as theoretical revisions).

Second, if the psychotherapy is specified in sufficiently general terms to be applicable to a widely representative patient population, and the presumed requisites (e.g., system requirements, therapist training requirements) are also specified, then initial efficacy testing can occur immediately in patients who are more representative of actual practice with a wider domain of outcomes than are currently routine in classical efficacy trials. Informative comparison groups can (and should) be included in such trials, and randomization and blinded outcome evaluations remain essential.

An example of such a trial is that by Mynors-Wallace, Gath, Lloyd-Thomas, and Tomlinson (1995). They trained (six training cases) general practitioners in the British health system to deliver time-limited, problem-solving psychotherapy. They then compared this approach to amitriptyline and to pill-placebo in the acute phase treatment of patients with major depression presenting to routine general practice. The results revealed both active treatments to be equal and better than pill-placebo.

In essence, this trial leapfrogged over several steps classically involved in establishing efficacy, yet it was not a classical effectiveness trial (e.g., certain concurrent illnesses led to exclusion; a minimal level of symptom severity was required; symptoms [but not cost], service utilization, or function was the main outcome; a selected practice setting was used; treatment delivery was ensured by home visits). As this was a hybrid study, the results spoke not only to efficacy but also to feasibility and generalizability to a largely representative general-practice patient population.

Is it possible to streamline the time-consuming process of developing, testing, exporting, and evaluating new forms of psychotherapy in routine practice? The short answer is it must be. The analogy to medication algorithms is pertinent here. One can take a form of therapy and design a manual with a certain range of providers in mind. For example, more "recipe-like" manuals may be better suited for less complex patient groups and less highly trained providers, while manuals that outline the principle and illustrate its application by clinical vignettes may be more suitable for more highly trained therapists who are dealing with more complex patients. That is, the description of how to conduct the treatment must inherently take into account for whom the treatment is provided and for whom the treatment is being used. Efficacy trials can then be conducted directly in ongoing systems of care but *only* if the system administrators allow for randomization to the "new" treatments versus routine care, and only if providers can be engaged and trained (and be paid while being trained) to provide both the standard and the new treatments. Alternatively, two versions of the therapy, one for more highly trained providers (e.g., PhDs) and one for less highly trained providers (e.g., licensed practical counselors, or LPCs), could be developed and compared in RCTs to determine efficacy and potentially suitability, for diverse patient groups.

How to Facilitate the "Export" of Efficacy-Tested Psychotherapies

While in the last two decades efficacy research has focused on the development and testing of manualized versions of time-limited psychotherapies, many training programs have not focused exclusively on empirically tested psychotherapies as part of their training (Chambless, 1993). Given the as yet incomplete scientifically based evaluations of a diverse number of psychotherapies, such decisions may not be irrational. That is, what has not yet been evaluated may indeed be effective.

In actual practice there is a plethora of psychotherapeutic approaches, most of which have not been evaluated for either efficacy or effectiveness. The "real world" has not readily adopted those forms of psychotherapy with established efficacy. Thus, patients usually receive whatever treatment the provider is skilled in administering rather than treatments with demonstrated efficacy. There is a problem in adopting research findings into practice.

Whether this situation, however, results in less than optimal outcomes has not been clearly defined by RCTs. Furthermore, whether manualized therapies can be taken into routine clinical practice and whether they will produce results as good as or better or worse than those obtained in RCTs used to define efficacy initially is unknown. However, such attempts (e.g., Persons, Burns, & Perloff, 1988) suggest that what "glitters" in RCTs may not be "gold" in clinical practice (see chapter 2, this volume).

Thus, a critical research question, especially for psychotherapies, is how to "export" (meaning adapt to both the usual patients and the usual practitioners) to routine practice those psychotherapies for which efficacy has been either well established or at least suggested by RCTs.

In the interim, we have begun to function in ever more organized systems of care. Providers and available services are selected, monitored, capped, or otherwise rationed. Each clinical step is reviewed and then authorized or not authorized. Some even talk of one to two sessions of psychotherapy as sufficient. These policy decisions are being made in spite of efficacy trial data that suggest the futility of such efforts. For example, the NIMH Treatment of Depression Collaborative Research Program (Elkin et al., 1989) revealed that less than one half of the final full response to either IPT or CT was obtained after 4 weeks of treatment. Furthermore, even in responders to the full acute phase trial, relapse and recurrence were common in the subsequent 18-month follow-up (Shea et al., 1992). Thus, policy decisions to restrict the number of psychotherapy sessions fly in the face of available scientific data.

It is also logical to assume that these systems of care would want to preferentially underwrite those forms of psychotherapy for which efficacy has been demonstrated and would further allocate sufficient resources to properly execute these types of treatment (i.e., the proper number of sessions, the proper training of providers) (see chapter 29, this volume). In addition, innovations to "save money"—for example, the use of licensed practical counselors with only bachelor-level training—to provide a form of psychotherapy that has only been tested with MSWs or PhDs as providers logically requires scientific documentation to demonstrate that efficacy (or in this case, effectiveness) is equivalent to that found in RCTs conducted with more highly trained and closely monitored therapists.

In my view, those responsible for authorizing care also inherit the responsibility for conducting scientifically objective evaluations of their decisions whether or not to authorize particular treatments, to pay particular types of providers, and to continue (or discontinue) authorizing additional sessions. Such systems, however, have yet to produce peer-reviewed published results that evaluate these policy decisions. On the other hand, there is every reason to believe that some of these policy decisions will affect cost, the quality of services, and, consequently, outcome (i.e., health and well-being). If these treatments, as delivered, are found to be efficacious, a dose response curve is likely. The regulation of dosage by defining number of allowable sessions will clearly affect efficacy.

Much as on product liability issues, those who take it upon themselves to change the product (e.g., in order to make it less expensive) have the burden of demonstrating the quality of the "new" product. It is my view that such institutions should face the legal, economic, and ethical consequences of failing to provide such documentation.

Research, whether supported by the government, foundations, and the public, or by private-for-profit health care systems, must be aimed at determining how to optimally export and implement psychotherapies so that both efficacy and effectiveness can be evaluated. This effort includes defining which providers, with what kinds of training, with what level of training in the particular mode of therapy, are beneficial, and to what degree, to which duration and to which patients. There is an immediate need to evaluate various methods by which to implement psychotherapies, as well as to evaluate the efficacy/effectiveness of these treatments. Efficacy and effectiveness constitute closely intertwined issues in the psychotherapies (as well as in disease management protocols and medication algorithms). Systems of care that must define preferred treatments and the methods to implement these treatments have an opportunity (if not an obligation) to conduct efficacy/effectiveness research in psychotherapy. If such resources were available, psychotherapy development and evaluation could be made both consistently more efficient and far more clinically relevant.

Acknowledgments This report was supported in part by the Sarah M. and Charles E. Seay Center for Brain and Applied Research in Psychiatric Illness and by a grant from the National Institute of Mental Health (MH-41115; MH-53799). I appreciate the secretarial support of Mr. David Savage and Fast Word, Inc., of Dallas and the administrative support of Kenneth Z. Altshuler, MD, Stanton Sharp Distinguished Chair and Chairman, Department of Psychiatry, University of Texas Southwestern Medical Center at Dallas.

References

Beitman, B. D. (1992). Integration through fundamental similarities and useful differences among the schools. In J. C. Norcross & M. R. Goldfried (Eds.), *Handbook of psychotherapy integration* (pp. 202–230). New York: Basic Books.

Chambless, D. (1993). *Task force on promotion and dissemination of psychological procedures*. Report adopted by Division 12 of the American Psychological Association, Washington, DC.

Elkin, I., Shea, T., Watkins, J. T., Imber, S. D., Sotsky, S. M., Collins, J. F., Glass, D. R., Pilkonis, P. A., Leber, W. R., Docherty, J. P., Fiester, S. J., & Parloff, M. B. (1989). National Institute of Mental Health Collaborative Research Program. General effectiveness of treatments. *Archives of General Psychiatry, 46*, 971–982.

Frank, E., Kupfer, D. J., Wagner, E. F., McEachran, A. B., & Cornes, C. (1991). Efficacy of interpersonal psychotherapy as a maintenance treatment of recurrent depression: Contributing factors. *Archives of General Psychiatry, 48*, 1053–1059.

Garfield, S. L. (1992). Eclectic psychotherapy: A common factors approach. In J. C. Norcross & M. R. Goldfried (Eds.), *Handbook of psychotherapy integration* (pp. 169–201). New York: Basic Books.

Luborsky, L., & Barber, J. P. (1993). Benefits of adherence to psychotherapy manuals, and where to get them. In N. E. Miller, L. Luborsky, J. P. Barber, & J. P. Docherty (Eds.), *Psychodynamic treatment research: A handbook for clinical practice* (pp. 211–226). New York: Basic Books.

Luborsky, L., McLellan, A. T., Woody, G. E., O'Brien, C. P., & Auerbach, A. (1985). Therapist success and its determinants. *Archives of General Psychiatry, 42*, 602–611.

Mynors-Wallace, L. M., Gath, D. H., Lloyd-Thomas, A. R., & Tomlinson, D. (1995). Randomized controlled trial comparing problem solving treatment with amitriptyline and placebo for major depression in primary care. *British Medical Journal, 310*, 441–445.

Norcross, J. C. (1995). Dispelling the dodo bird verdict and the exclusivity myth in psychotherapy. *Psychotherapy, 32*, 500–504.

Parloff, M. B. (1986). Placebo controls in psychotherapy research: A *sine qua non* or a placebo for research problems? *Journal of Consulting and Clinical Psychology, 54*, 79–87.

Persons, J. B., Burns, D. D., & Perloff, J. M. (1988). Predictors of dropout and outcome in cognitive therapy for depression in a private practice setting. *Cognitive Therapy and Research, 12*, 557–575.

Rush, A. J., & Prien, R. (1995). From scientific knowledge to the clinical practice of psychopharmacology: Can the gap be bridged? *Psychopharmacology Bulletin, 31*, 7–20.

Shea, T., Elkin, I., Imber, S. D., Sotsky, S. M., Watkins, J. T., Collins, J. F., Pilkonis, P. A., Beckham, E., Glass, D. R., Dolan, R. T., & Parloff, M. B. (1992). Course of depressive symptoms over follow-up: Findings from the National Institute of Mental Health Treatment of Depression Collaborative Research Program. *Archives of General Psychiatry, 49*, 782–787.

Vallis, T. M., Shaw, B. F., & Dobson, K. S. (1986). The Cognitive Therapy Scale: Psychometric properties. *Journal of Consulting and Clinical Psychology, 54*, 381–385.

Young, J., & Beck, A. T. (1980). *Cognitive therapy scale: Rating manual.* Unpublished manuscript. Philadelphia: Center for Cognitive Therapy.

4

Philosophical and Ethical Considerations in the Evaluation of the Effectiveness and Cost-Effectiveness of Psychotherapy

Jodi Halpern

This volume seeks "to move the field away from an exclusive emphasis on what is available in the corpus of psychotherapy research literature on short-term, symptomatic outcomes [toward] considering the impact of psychosocial interventions, as practiced in the community, on costs, quality of life, and functional capacities over the long term" (Introduction, this volume). This mission statement condenses two steps that researchers are taking to move beyond traditional psychotherapy research; the first step is from efficacy to effectiveness research, and the second step is from effectiveness to cost-effectiveness research. These shifts need to be distinguished because each carries different ethical opportunities and challenges.

The first shift constitutes a move from a traditional clinical research perspective to a health services research approach. This change in methodology has implications for which patients can be studied. Psychotherapy efficacy research involves randomized, controlled clinical trials, utilizing standard manualized treatments targeted to relatively narrow patient populations. Such an approach has made an essential contribution to the treatment of mental illness but needs to be expanded because sicker patients, patients with comorbid illnesses, and those who are socially disadvantaged tend to be poorly represented in such studies. In addition, clinical trial outcomes tend to be focused largely on symptomatic change, narrowing the stated goals of psychotherapy as practiced in the community, raising questions pertaining to the ends of psychotherapy. Which outcomes, ranging from symptom relief to social functioning to self-realization, are most important, and which should federal research support or emphasize?

The second shift, from a services effectiveness perspective to a cost-effectiveness perspective, entails moving from the question "Which treatments are effective?" to asking, "How much effective treatment can be obtained per dollar expended?" The benefit of researching cost and effectiveness together is that such studies provide a common currency for assessing individual and societal benefits from psychotherapy and broaden the scope of outcomes considered in policy decisions.

However, in adopting the methods of economic analysis to study mental health care, researchers may also adopt an economic conception of values, choices, or utilities as the basis for decisions about the worth of psychotherapy. Problems with relying on measures of choice to determine a fair basis for health care allocation are discussed below. An additional problem is that since the methods of cost-effectiveness research are highly variable, depending on how the question is posed, different results can be produced depending upon the normative assumptions guiding the research. For these reasons, it is critical to scrutinize the choice of problem studied, the measure of outcome utilized, and the manner in which research findings are likely to be used (for example, by an HMO rationing services). These issues will also be addressed.

Ethical Issues Regarding Randomized Clinical Trials of Psychotherapy

The fact that psychotherapy is highly valued by patients (Mental Health, 1995) contrasts starkly with the disproportionate erosion of psychotherapy benefits compared to other aspects of psychiatric care. In an era in which the American public is ambivalent about supporting basic health care for everyone, the status of psychotherapy as a necessary or appropriate component of health care services is increasingly in question. This lack of support for psychotherapy represents, in part, a reflection of the more general failure to adequately recognize and treat mental illness (chapter 1, this volume).

Against this backdrop, researchers have sought to demonstrate the medical value of psychotherapy by showing that standardized, targeted psychotherapies are as efficacious as medications for the treatment of key psychiatric disorders (for example, depression, panic disorder, obsessive-compulsive disorder). Information delineating appropriate and inappropriate treatment-"disease" pairs constitutes an indisputable benefit of standardization and randomized controlled clinical trials. However, in order to validate psychotherapies by the gold standard of medical research—the randomized controlled clinical trial (RCT)—researchers have by necessity focused on a narrow subset of patients and on very few of the types of psychotherapy widely practiced in the community.

The narrow focus that the RCT methodology involves needs to be expanded because several issues need to be addressed. These issues, framed in terms of their ethical import, include who receives psychotherapy (distributive justice), what are the shared goals of psychotherapy (patient values vs. managed-care organization values vs. provider values vs. broader societal values), and who should provide psychotherapy (physician-patient relationship). First, narrow sample selection criteria in clinical trials may lead to exclusion of patients with the most complex conditions, who require more intensive treatments. These patients, however, are the very population already at risk of being undertreated under the auspices of managed mental health care systems. The ethical argument for spending federal dollars differentially to study patients with more complex conditions who may not respond adequately to brief standardized treatment in managed care is based on notions of distributive justice. If patients who are sicker and already societally disadvantaged are not given adequate treatment, they lack a fair chance of functioning at a baseline level in society.

Second, whereas efficacy research has successfully delineated short-term, symptomatic outcomes of psychotherapy, health services research can expand the focus to capture the range of functional outcomes that makes psychotherapy valuable to individual patients and society. Evidence suggests that, in addition to alleviating symptoms, psychotherapy may be especially effective at producing functional improvement that medications alone do not produce (Wells, 1995). The discrepancy between high consumer satisfaction with psychotherapy and public skepticism about the utility of psychosocial interventions may reflect insignificant societal awareness of the impact of psychotherapy on such functioning, including improved social and work functioning. However, in an era of cost containment, it is possible that even if such treatment benefits were recognized, they would not be seen as fitting within the boundaries of medicine's responsibilities. This raises philosophical concerns pertaining to which aims of psychotherapy are viewed by society as appropriate, or even necessary, aspects of medical care, and which are not. The urgency of addressing the question of which outcomes of psychotherapy treatment are most valued by patients is that absent such inquiry, the narrow outcomes assessed in efficacy studies fit too neatly with some managed-care organizations' emphasis on narrowing indications for psychotherapy.

Efficacy research not only involves a narrow range of outcomes but necessarily (because of RCT methods) also focuses on short-term treatment. With the exception of Linehan's randomized controlled trial of cognitive psychotherapy for borderline personality disorder, there has been no research on how much treatment patients with more severe personality disorders and other chronic psychiatric illnesses amenable to psychotherapy require (see chapters 14 and 27, this volume). Because longer term treatments have not been, and are not being, studied, it is increasingly unlikely they will be covered by managed-care organizations in the future.

Third, the issue of who should provide psychotherapy needs to be considered. From the ethical perspective of respect for patients, the question is not about which professional group should have hegemony but about what are the qualities and educational experiences of the therapist that make for a successful therapist-patient alliance. And beyond this issue, the question of whether (and to what degree, and for which patients) continuity of care in the therapist-patient relationship contributes to good outcomes needs to be studied. Many current policies of managed-care companies do not allow for more than four to six visits with the same therapist, and it is unknown how this will affect patient trust and/or treatment outcomes.

There is a need to study therapist effectiveness from a health services perspective because the manner in which randomized efficacy trials are designed and analyzed tends to radically reduce differences in variance of therapist effects (Chris-Christoph et al., 1991). For example, research shows that significant differences exist among therapists in therapeutic success (McLellan et al. 1988; Luborsky et al., 1985, 1986), and that the therapist-patient alliance (Horvath, Gaston, & Luborsky, 1993) constitutes one of the most critical predictors of beneficial outcome across all treatments. Yet, in efficacy studies, where the goal is to maximize fidelity to manualized treatment protocols, there is apt to be decreased variability of patient-therapist alliance measures. Therefore, the relative influence of this important predictor of therapeutic effectiveness in everyday clinical practice remains unknown. In summary, while efficacy studies of psychotherapy have constituted an important approach to delineating which types of patients respond best to which treatments, the methodology required for such studies entails leaving certain questions unanswered. The ethical reason for expanding to a health services research perspective is that questions about who receives psychotherapy, and for what ends, have remained unaddressed by such studies. Effectiveness research, however, can address concerns regarding the fair allocation of treatment and can expand the range of outcomes studied to include measures of functioning and quality of life. Issues relating to the duration and frequency of psychotherapy, and to the qualities of the therapist-patient relationship, which are key to the effectiveness of psychotherapy, could also be encompassed by a health services research approach.

Shift from Efficacy to Effectiveness Research

The shift from efficacy to effectiveness research involves a reflective turn from studying the mechanism of action in "psychotherapy" and studying differential efficacy of two or more targeted treatments, to studying how psychotherapy services are provided and the effectiveness of actual services received. This perspective encompasses questions regarding naturalistic outcomes, as well as access to treatment. Effectiveness research can therefore shed light on whether what patients value about psychotherapy is adequately captured by outcome measures, whether those most in need of psychotherapy are able to access treatment, and if not, why not. Health services research expands the potential for addressing such issues because it makes use of a wider array of methodological and disciplinary approaches (including epidemiology and the social sciences) than does efficacy research.

For example, effectiveness studies can evaluate the effect of undertreatment. Epidemiological methods allow comparisions between those who receive psychotherapy and those in need who do not receive such services in the community. Health services research also makes use of the methods of the social sciences to identify underlying societal factors such as economics, which not only influence the effectiveness of psychosocial interventions but often also determine access to treatment. For instance, domestic violence, absence of child care, culturally specific health beliefs, and convictions about self-efficacy may all differentially influence utilization of psychotherapeutic services.

Consider the issue of whether the benefits patients value from psychotherapy are adequately included in outcome measures. In the absence of societal discussion, researchers (like policymakers) implicitly decide what they think the goals of psychotherapy are when they design outcome measures. However, as Docherty and Rush note (see chapters 1 and 3, this volume), there has been little clarity or agreement about the appropriate goals of psychotherapy in this country. Psychotherapy meets a wide range of medical and nonmedical goals, ranging from the treatment of depression to self-realization.

In the absence of explicit goals, health policy decisions regarding treatment appropriateness are already widely inconsistent. For example, two recent practice guideline panels of the Agency for Health Care Policy and Research (AHCPR) addressed the question of when, in addition to medication, psychotherapy is indicated. One panel addressed psychotherapy for the treatment of cancer pain (Jacox, Carr, & Payne, 1994); the other addressed psychotherapy for the treatment of depression in primary care (Rush et al., 1993). Interpreting the goals of medicine according to a biopsychosocial model, the cancer pain panel included the patient's personal development and spiritual goals, as important reasons for treatment. In contrast, the depression panel interpreted the goals of treatment according to a strictly biomedical model, emphasizing the need to treat depression as a medical illness in the context of a primary-care setting. As a result of different underlying assumptions about which goals of psychotherapy were most important, the panels arrived at disparate decisions. The cancer pain panel determined that adjuvant psychotherapy is appropriate for as long as a patient has a psychosocial, social, or spiritual need, which can only be ascertained by carefully eliciting a detailed account of the patient's subjective illness experience. In contrast, the depression panel concluded that adjuvant psychotherapy is appropriate only when a clinician using a symptom checklist could show objective change by 6 weeks (Halpern, 1995). Thus, the actual goals of psychotherapy, as well as the subsequent treatment indications, were defined far more narrowly for depression than for cancer pain.

Given that patients benefit from psychotherapy for depression in ways that include biopsychosocial dimensions it may be unfair to treat cancer patients and depression patients differently regarding these treatment goals. The point is not that value judgments regarding the goals of medicine should, or even could, be avoided altogether. Rather, it is to draw attention to the fact that no purely scientific observation can delineate when psychotherapy is beneficial in the absence of an agreed upon standard for psychotherapy's aims and purposes, grounded in a coherent conception of the purposes of health care. Significantly, more explicit attention is needed to assess the underlying values that influence decisions made about the effectiveness of psychotherapy. Only then will patient needs rather than provider or plan assumptions determine psychotherapy indications.

The possibility of studying factors that impede the provision of quality care leads directly to the second ethical opportunity that effectiveness research offers, which is the examination of the distribution of psychotherapy services in this country. This issue is important, given evidence that there exists an inadequate allocation of psychotherapy for most members of society according to their needs (both as compared to other aspects of health care, and as measured absolutely). In addition, evidence also suggests that those who are socially disadvantaged are less likely to receive psychotherapeutic services. This disadvantage is intensified by the fact that the mentally ill in the United States are undertreated—more than two thirds of patients with depression, three fourths of those with anxiety disorders, and four fifths of childen with diagnosed mental disorders do not get treated (see chapter 1, this volume).

The fact that so many suffer unnecessarily motivates a utilitarian argument to relieve suffering and improve well-being in this area of great need (mental illnesses across the board). A utilitarian approach would construe fair allocation as that distribution of services that does the greatest good for the greatest number. One limit of such an approach is that it does not address societal injustices that lead to the inequitable distribution of resources. Rather, a utilitarian goal for health services research would seek to improve care now rather than redress previous wrongs.

A second ethical approach to studying determinants of access to effective psychotherapy, however, would begin with the fact that such services are particularly underused by people with less education and lower socioeconomic status. In addition to economic factors, there may be other societal barriers to access, such as diverse beliefs about treatment efficacy, therapist-patient ethnic differences, and language barriers. If such variables create barriers to obtaining care for those with treatable mental illness, then their impact results in substantial maldistribution of resources. In situations where those resources are conceived of as part of society's obligation to help those in need, such maldistribution is considered unfair. To date, however, these issues of distributive justice have received little attention from psychotherapy researchers.

Researchers can address problems of distributive justice at one level not only by examining structural barriers to accessing care, but also by evaluating the societal prejudices that influence decisions about which types of patients benefit from psychotherapy: What tacit, value-based factors constitute barriers to availability, successful access, or completion of a course of psychotherapy? What is the impact of variables such as education, socioeconomic status, culture, gender, and age? Are there medical diagnoses, such as substance dependence or being HIV-positive, that make it less likely that a person will be offered potentially beneficial psychotherapy? Moreover, what value judgments ultimately influence the selection of biological or other approaches to psychological suffering, including nontreatment? Are there particular institutional values that implicitly shape selection of certain modes of psychiatric treatment? For instance, how does the stringency of cost containment in managed-care organizations, and/or rewarding providers for limiting psychiatric referrals, impact the distribution of psychotherapy services?

Beyond this, effectiveness researchers can contribute to fairer social policies by openly evaluating the societal ethics reflected in their own, and in federal, research agendas. For example, an important societal ethical question that has not been openly confronted as yet is how much federal funding, given limited resources, should be earmarked for improving the efficacy of psychotherapies for those who seek them, and how much should be allocated to studying access issues in order to distribute such services more fairly.

The ethical norm influencing practicing psychotherapists has been the Hippocratic ideal of maximizing the care of the individual patient, with the hope that this will turn out to be best for society as well. However, this ideal has been challenged as insufficient to address the issues of efficient resource use and fairness currently in the forefront of health policy in this country (Boyle & Callahan, 1995). We need to consider what kind of ethical concepts would be adequate for adjudicating between the Hippocratic ideals and utilitarian and justice-based conceptions of allocating psychotherapy services.

Since psychotherapy services are distributed unfairly from the perspective of need (see chapter 7, this volume), it is clear that any attempt to meet justice-based ideals would require massive shifts in access to, and delivery of, care; many patients who are in intensive long-term treatments might no longer be seen as most in need of treatment, yet Hippocratic ideals call for treating such patients. This clash between Hippocratic and justice-based approaches to allocating services has yet to be addressed because it is the third, utilitarian paradigm that is currently in strong ascendance in health policy. In part, this paradigm appears to bypass the conflict between individual and societal interests by seeking to guide allocation by the priniciple of getting the most benefit for services expended. This ideal is the philosophical driving force for the shift from the effectiveness to cost-effectiveness research paradigm.

The Shift from Health Services (Effectiveness) Research to Cost-Effectiveness Research

The current political agenda of "accepting limits" in spending for social goods like health care, and of striving to use limited health care dollars more efficiently, has been adopted by ethicists, researchers, and health care payers as the primary agenda for health policy in the 1990s (Boyle & Callahan, 1995). There is therefore a need for cost-effectiveness research to inform policy decisions in the allocation of health care. Such research has the potential to bring a standard common denominator to evaluating the societal, individual, plan, and provider benefits accrued in the provision of psychotherapy. By providing a common currency according to which the value of any treatment may be judged, cost-effectiveness methodology expands the range of policy-relevant research that can be done. For example, researchers can differentially compare the economic, social, and emotional impact of mental illness with that of physical illness or highlight social cost offsets of treatment, ranging from fewer sick days and enhanced productivity to decreased jail time and social welfare payments.

Superficially, cost-effectiveness research appears to reflect an unproblematic utilitarian spirit, given that an aim of such research is to identify the maximally efficient way to provide services in order to yield the optimal "overall" benefit. However, three ethical concerns arise when efficiency of production is taken as a norm for determining access to, and delivery of, psychotherapy services.

First, the goal of maximization of a good is blind to the distribution of that good, so that, for example, there is no independent attention to level of patient need as a basis for service distribution. Second, the notion of "maximizing" benefits tends to be misleading because it implies there is a fixed, homogeneously defined universe of "benefit" that can be tapped into, in proportion to dollars spent. But this is far from the case—cost-effectiveness studies are quite heterogeneous in the benefits and costs they recognize, so that their conclusions are often inconsistent. Third, despite increasing tendencies to adopt economic conceptions of value and economic methods of analysis in cost-effectiveness studies, such measures may not always be optimal approaches for meeting mental health needs.

Consider the first problem, that maximizing efficiency in producing health and mental health outcomes does not necessarily provide care to patients according to their needs. Whether efficient resource use will be proportionate to need depends upon whether those with the greatest need can be helped efficiently. Economic theory applied simplistically ignores this problem: For those with many goods, such as food or entertainment, for example, if one already has little, an increase is worth a lot; if one has a lot, then an increase is worth a little—so efficient distribution turns out to be fair, in the sense of meeting needs proportionally. But from what is known regarding mental health needs and psychotherapy utilization, there is little reason to presume symmetrical balance between need and efficient use of services (see chapters 5 and 7, this volume). If helping sicker patients requires more intensive, expensive services to produce less dramatic outcomes, how do such patient needs fit into policies guided by cost-effectiveness?

There are various approaches to this ethical issue that researchers can take in cost-effectiveness studies. One approach is to segregate patients into groups by severity, then to determine how to treat individuals more efficiently within each subgroup. This approach appears to be more ethically informed, because it gives sicker patients a fair chance of getting the treatment they need without requiring them to compete with easier-to-treat patients.

Another approach researchers are taking is to develop more broad and subtle outcome measures that reflect the complex needs (including social deficits) of sicker patients. For example, Lehman's Quality of Life interview for schizophrenic patients includes outcomes like homelessness, jail time, and victimization, thus allowing for estimates of the societal costs of nontreatment of these chronic mentally ill patients (see chapter 17, this volume). Broadening the scope of relevant outcomes and costs, including societal costs, in cost-effectiveness analysis also allows psychiatric patients to be treated more fairly in comparison with other medical patients. For example, in the Medical Outcomes Study (MOS; see chapter 6, this volume), researchers showed that patients with depression had more lost work days and days in bed than did patients with cardiac disease or arthritis.

These expanded research methodologies address the risk that cost-effectiveness studies, because of their emphasis on efficiency, will disadvantage sicker, more difficult-to-treat patients. However, a second ethical concern about such studies is that there exists neither consensus nor impartial criteria for determining which benefits and costs should be studied. Although there are limits to objectivity in all research, cost-effectiveness studies are particularly dependent on what costs and benefits the designers of the study have reason to care about. For example, the cost-effectiveness of treating schizophrenic or depressed patients intensively will vary, depending upon which stakeholder vision defines the relevant outcomes (see chapter 17, this volume).

A managed-care organization may not be interested in more general quality-of-life or societal functioning measures for schizophrenic patients, since they are not responsible for social costs incurred (such as jail time) through the undertreatment of such patients. Yet the same organization may seek such indicators for employed, depressed patients because work time lost by depressed patients is likely to have significantly more negative repercussions for such plans (which are paid for by employers). If outcome selection in cost-effectiveness research is not based on more impartial criteria than the needs of the organizations that fund the research, then such studies will emerge as ethically problematic, in that they will import narrow organizational interests into the arena of public policy decisions.

A more subtle ethical problem with cost-effectiveness research is that not only the outcomes studied but also the core methodology of such research varies with the perspective of the researchers. For example, according to Sturm and Wells (1995), most cost-effectiveness analysts focus on which interventions will reduce the use of an expensive but ineffective treatment, thus saving the most money, whereas a more clinically oriented approach is "to first focus on treatments with demonstrated efficacy that are simple and inexpensive." For example, from a clinical perspective, they recommend an approach to making treatment of depression more cost-effective that begins with increasing effective use of antidepressants. In contrast, from a payer's perspective, a cost-effectiveness methodology might begin with the elimination of minor tranquilizers prescribed excessively for depression. The former will yield much better patient outcomes than the latter, yet both may appear cost-effective.

Because there are no impartial criteria guiding the conduct of cost-effectiveness studies thus far, both the *New England Journal of Medicine* (editorial, September 1994) and the *Annals of Internal Medicine* (editorial, July 1995) have emphasized that such studies pose ethical risks. They say that there is a need to regulate the conduct of such studies because of their "values sensitivity." Accordingly, both journals recommend that all private sector funds for such research be channeled through a nonprofit scientific advisory board/organization.

However, in my view, it is unclear how a panel of scientific advisers could adjudicate such issues as which outcomes to measure and whether to emphasize improving clinical care first or reducing costs first, and so on, without paying explicit attention to the ethical question of what, as a society, we think are the goals of health care. That is, in order to develop an impartial basis for determining which outcomes and costs of psychotherapy are to be included in cost-effectiveness studies, a conceptual schema ranking the goals of psychotherapy in light of individual and societal values is needed. Impartiality in such research cannot mean that it is value-free, since trading off clinical goals for cost savings is a fundamentally morally laden endeavor. Rather, impartiality could be approached by making such value judgments a topic for explicit societal debate and consensus.

There are two kinds of societal ethical questions that cost-effectiveness research requires us to address. The first is the same question that all health services decisions depend upon, which is how we rank, in order of importance, the various goals of health care (in this case, the goals of psychotherapy), such as alleviating suffering, improving work and/or social functioning, and preventing recurrence. The second is what conception of distributive justice we have in mind in conducting such research. Are we most concerned with economizing because of a commitment to reduce perceived overuse of psychotherapy? Are we most concerned with using psychotherapy more appropriately to address both undertreatment and overtreatment issues? Are we concerned with issues of fairness that might require less cost-efficient resource use in order to treat sicker patients or to improve access to care for patients of lower socioeconomic status?

Some cost-effectiveness researchers have presumed that these kinds of ethical issues are not central to their endeavors because they can handle values questions by measuring patient (or consumer or plan) utilities or preferences for different treatment outcomes. It may appear that measuring preferences could address the first question of ranking the goals of treatment. However, although it is important to study what patients actually prefer (or would prefer under ideal conditions of full information, absent external influences), such studies are not sufficient for resolving the question of which goals of medicine we as a society think are of most importance for our individual members. And measuring individual preferences cannot address the second question of distributive justice.

In Holland, the Dunning Commission (1994) recognized the need to explicitly address the competing values at stake in health care in order to guide the development of health services and research. According to their societal values, they said that in the case of the treatment of individuals, the first goal of health care is to restore people to adequate participation in social life, rather than to save more lives or extend years of life. Perhaps in this country, a different ranking of goals of health care would occur, for example, placing preventing death and restoring people to work functioning above all else. In any case, such societal consensus could inform specific research regarding the effectiveness and cost-effectiveness of treatment. For example, research that does not include outcomes measuring social functioning would not be seen as adequately grounded in Holland.

In summary, we have come full circle to see that cost-effectiveness researchers cannot avoid addressing the gap in values at the heart of effectiveness research simply by ranking treatments in terms of their cost-effectiveness. As Sturm and Wells show, there is no one way to make such recommendations, and which way one chooses will reflect implicit values, for example, valuing improving the clinical care of each patient first, or reducing waste first. While such research can never be impartial in the sense of value-free, it can be more fairly representative of our societal ideals if it is explicitly guided by some consensus regarding which benefits of psychotherapy are most important and how to distribute such benefits fairly. With such explicit ethical standards, it would become possible for investigators to frame cost-effectiveness research as optimizing the treatment benefits obtainable per (societal) dollar spent.

Conclusions

The ethics of health services begins with considering two fundamental questions: What are the ends or goals of health care, and how is health care to be allocated fairly? Both of these questions are particularly salient, yet they are difficult to address when the treatment under investigation is psychotherapy. Regarding the goals of medicine, it is as yet unestablished whether in this country (as compared with Holland) there is broad endorsement for a biopsychosocial conception of health versus a more narrow biomedical conception. Regarding the more specific area of cost-effectiveness and psychotherapy services, we have not, as a society, addressed the thorny problem of evaluating the relative worth of competing goals of treatment. Given the emphasis in American medical ethics on the importance of respecting autonomy and diverse value systems, it may be particularly difficult for our society to face such difficult comparisons as that between expanding psychotherapy services for the treatment of depression in primary care, which will both alleviate suffering and decrease lost workdays, and expanding psychotherapy services for the treatment of spiritual suffering at the end of life, which may not be as directly productive, in economic terms, but may have great existential benefits. Cost-effectiveness researchers need to educate the public regarding not only the benefits, but also the limitations of economic analysis for ranking the relative worth of treatments whose ends meet fundamentally different ethical ideals. In particular, producing improved functioning efficiently is not the only end of health care, which has always also been about alleviating human suffering.

Similarly, in researching cost-effectiveness, the goal should not be to narrowly delineate the least costly approach to a problem. Rather, such research should begin by defining the range of treatment benefits and evaluating, in clinical and ethical terms, the relative worth of such benefits. This would be followed by defining relevant outcome measures, and then by focusing on the most economically efficient way to produce these outcomes. This recommendation is not meant to represent a call to return to the "purity" of the efficacy studies of old, in that such studies, while extremely valuable, involved the limitations mentioned at the outset. Effectiveness research makes it possible to move from more clinically based symptomatic outcomes to more patient-centered and society-centered outcomes, including work and social functioning and economic costs and benefits. In addition, health services research makes it possible to study issues that impact access to care and the fair allocation of psychotherapy services, including cultural differences, severity of illness, and comorbidity. The effects of undertreatment and both short-term and long-term outcomes of psychotherapy can be studied with health services methodology. The need for the field to shift from its exclusive emphasis on efficacy is clear; however, this shift should be made with the caveat that in services research on psychotherapy, economic conceptions should not be the sole arbiters of value; rather, they should be integrated with clinical, ethical, and social science perspectives in evaluating the worth of various psychotherapies.

Finally, in evaluating psychotherapy services research in "naturalistic settings" including managed-care organizations, it is crucial not to assume falsely that such research is impartial in its orientation. Rather, an advisory panel, such as that suggested by the *New England Journal of Medicine* and the *Annals of Internal Medicine*, is needed to reflectively consider the agenda and goals of the researchers and whether they are adequately responsive to our societal conception of what and whom health care is for. Such an approach would be strengthened if there were an explicit public policy delineating the values at stake in psychotherapy services delivery, perhaps as the product of a societally representative consensus panel (meeting perhaps over a more extended period than practice guideline panels do). Defining such a policy would be difficult and would require diverse expertise and patient representation in order to adjudicate between heterogeneous conceptions of the goals of medicine; the product of such a panel would surely lack full objectivity and would require public scrutiny and revision. However, we need to overcome our very American sense that talking about heterogeneous values with the aim of rationally persuading each other of the greater importance of some goals of psychotherapy over others is itself immoral. Only by developing an explicit approach to the value trade-offs inherent in the delivery of psychotherapy services can we begin to guide our services research and health policies by ethical, and not just market, principles.

References

Boyle, P. J., & Callahan, D. (1995). Managed care in mental health: The ethical issues. *Health Affairs, 14*(3), 7–33.

Dunning et al. (1992). *Choices in Health Care: A Report by the Government Committee.* The Netherlands: Dunning Commission.

Crits-Christoph, P., et al. (1991). Meta-analysis of therapist effects in psychotherapy outcome studies. In N. E. Miller, L. Luborsky, J. Barber, & J. Docherty (Eds.), *Psychodynamic treatment research: A handbook for clinical practice.* New York: Basic Books.

Halpern, J. (1995). Can the development of practice guidelines safeguard patient values. *Journal of Law, Medicine and Ethics, 23,* 75–81.

Hillman, A. L., et al. (1995, March). Economic analysis of health care technology: A report on principles. *Annals of Internal Medicine, 123,* 61–70.

Horvath, A., et al. (1993). The therapeutic alliance and its measures. In N. E. Miller, L. Luborsky, J. Barber, & J. Docherty (Eds.), *Psychodynamic treatment research: A handbook for clinical practice.* New York: Basic Books.

Jacox, A., Carr, D., Payne, R., co-chairs. (1994, March). Management of Cancer Pain, *Clinical Practice Guideline Number 9.* Rockville, MD: U.S. Department of Health and Human Services, Public

Health Service, Agency of Health Care Policy and Research, No. 94-0592.

Kassirer, J., & Angell, M. (1994). The journal's policy on cost-effectiveness analyses. *New England Journal of Medicine, 331*(10), 669–670.

Luborsky, L., et al. (1985, 1986). Therapist success and its determinants. In N. E. Miller, L. Luborsky, J. Barber, & J. Docherty (Eds.), *Psychodynamic treatment research: A handbook for clinical practice*. New York: Basic Books.

McLellan, A. T., et al. (1988). Is the counselor an "active ingredient" in methadone treatment. In N. E. Miller, L. Luborsky, J. Barber, & J. Docherty (Eds.), *Psychodynamic treatment research: A handbook for clinical practice.* New York: Basic Books.

Mental health: Does therapy help? (1995, November). *Consumer Reports, 60*(11), 734–739.

Sturm, R., & Wells, K. B. (1995). How can care for depression become more cost-effective? *Journal of the American Medical Association,* 273(1), 51–58.

Wells, K. B. (1995). Care for depression in a changing environment. *Health Affairs, 14*(3), 78–89.

II

PSYCHOTHERAPY SERVICE UTILIZATION PATTERNS

The United States

5

Outpatient Psychotherapy in the United States

The National Medical Expenditure Survey

Mark Olfson & Harold Alan Pincus

Surprisingly little is known about broad patterns in the provision, utilization, and financing of outpatient psychotherapy in the United States. There are major deficits in our understanding of who provides, who uses, and who pays for psychotherapy. In particular, we lack basic information concerning the characteristics of individuals who receive outpatient psychotherapy, the reasons they use psychotherapy, and the intensity or duration of this use. Without such data, policymakers have little sense of current expenditure profiles, and psychotherapy is left vulnerable to the stereotyped criticism that it is usually consumed in a casual or discretionary manner.

One reason that so little is known about the utilization of psychotherapy is that most large surveys of mental health service utilization lack the detail necessary to distinguish psychotherapy from other ambulatory mental health services. For example, neither the NIMH Epidemiologic Catchment Area (ECA) study nor the National Comorbidity Survey (NCS) specifically assessed psychotherapy provision. The 1987 National Medical Expenditure Survey, which is described in this chapter, provides a rare glimpse into psychotherapy provision in the United States.

In this chapter, an analysis is provided of outpatient psychotherapy utilization in the United States based on results from the National Medical Expenditure Survey (NMES; Olfson & Pincus, 1994b, 1994c). These data were collected in 1987, before the large-scale implementation of managed care in outpatient mental health services. The NMES findings thus provide a baseline against which to measure changes in psychotherapy provision that coincide with the spread of managed care.

The 1987 National Medical Expenditure Survey

The 1987 National Medical Expenditure Survey, which was organized by the Agency for Health Care Policy and Research (AHCPR), drew on a national probability sample of the U.S. noninstitutionalized civilian population. A complex four-stage sampling design was employed. Information was collected from a designated informant about all related persons who lived at the selected address or dwelling unit. A total of 15,590 dwelling units were targeted for sampling, and the overall response rate was 85.4%. Results are based on 38,446 individuals (Edwards & Berlin, 1989).

Households selected for the panel survey were interviewed four times to collect information concerning a 12-month reference period. Respondents were asked to record medical events including medication prescriptions as they occurred in a calendar/diary that was reviewed as part of each of the four interviews.

AHCPR devised a system of weights to correct for the complex design to yield approximately unbiased national estimates from survey results. The means and percentages presented in this chapter are based on this weighting system.

We focus on psychotherapy visits provided in nonhospital settings such as physicians' and other health care professionals' offices, medical clinics, mental health clinics, and family health centers. The estimated 4.2 million psychotherapy visits provided in hospital outpatient clinics were not queried in detail and so are not analyzed in this chapter.

Survey respondents were considered users of psychotherapy if they reported making a visit to a nonhospital setting for the main *reason* of receiving psychotherapy during 1987. Psychotherapy was listed as one of several different possible main reasons (e.g., general checkup, immunizations, well child exam, vision exam) for making an outpatient visit. It is not known what specific criteria individual respondents used to determine whether they considered a particular visit as constituting "psychotherapy."

The survey also asked respondents (i.e., patients) the primary *condition* for each ambulatory health care visit. This information was coded according to the *International Classification of Diseases* (Ninth Revision). It is important to note that information was not available on the clinical diagnoses that patients actually received from health care professionals during the health care visits.

Expenditures for psychotherapy were calculated by summing total expenses associated with each individual psychotherapy visit. No effort was made to adjust for increases in medical services that occurred between 1987 and 1996.

Detailed information was collected on the specialty of the medical provider of each adult and child visit to a nonhospital setting. However, for 11.0% of the psychotherapy visits, the provider specialty could not be ascertained.

Findings from the National Medical Expenditure Survey

Who Provides Psychotherapy?

In 1987, Americans made approximately 79.5 million outpatient psychotherapy visits to nonhospital settings. The overwhelming majority of these visits were to a mental health specialist such as a psychiatrist, psychologist, social worker, mental health counselor, counselor, therapist, or occupational therapist. When the provider was known, fully 9 out of 10 (90.7%) of the psychotherapy visits were to a mental health specialist.

General medical professionals played only a modest role in the provision of psychotherapy. Only 9.3% of the psychotherapy visits to known providers were provided by general medical professionals. Most of these visits were to nonpsychiatrist physicians (5.3%), such as a family practitioner or a general practitioner, rather than to a nonphysician general medical professional (4.0%), such as a nurse or a physician assistant. In this context, it is important to remember that the NMES may have failed to capture many of the psychological interventions provided in general medical settings.

Survey respondents described each of their health care visits in terms of a single main reason for the visit. In a variety of general medical settings, less formal psychological interventions may be provided during visits which have as their primary focus the provision of another medical service. It is unlikely that respondents would identify these visits as primarily "psychotherapy." If a broader term such as *counseling* had been used to quantify psychological interventions, it is possible that many more such visits would have been identified as provided by a general medical professional. Primary-care physicians, for example, report extensive involvement in counseling their patients who have psychiatric problems (Orleans, George, Houpt, & Brodie, 1985; Robbins et al., 1995).

Psychologists and psychiatrists together provided more than three quarters (88%) of the psychotherapy visits to mental health specialists. Much of the predicted cost savings from managed care rests on the presumed decreased costs associated with substituting less expensive for more expensive health care professionals (Mechanic, Schlesinger, & McAlpine, 1995). As cost containment mechanisms are increasingly applied to outpatient mental health care, it is likely that there will be a reduction in the proportion of psychotherapy provided by doctoral-level providers (psychiatrists and psychologists) and an increase in the role played by bachelor's- and master's-level therapists. The effects of such "substitution of labor" on the quality of care is an important area for future research.

How Many Visits?

The mean number of psychotherapy visits (10.9) made by the average psychotherapy user is in the range previously reported by provider surveys (Garfield, 1986) but hides the highly skewed distribution of visits across users. Approximately one third of users (34%) made only 1 or 2 visits, and nearly three quarters of users

(71%) made fewer than 10 visits. Only a relatively small proportion of users (16%) made more than 20 visits.

An important issue for future research is to examine the health outcomes of the large number of psychotherapy patients who receive very short-term care. It is not known whether these patients are predominantly premature dropouts as the psychotherapy literature would suggest (Garfield, 1986; Phillips, 1985) or whether they include substantial numbers of individuals who received useful brief crisis intervention.

Who Pays for Outpatient Psychotherapy?

In 1987, self-pay (45%), private insurance (26%), and Medicaid (17%) together accounted for more than three quarters of the estimated $4.2 billion spent for outpatient psychotherapy in nonhospital settings. Medicaid payments accounted for a larger proportion of the payments for longer term (more than 20 visits) than shorter term users (20 visits or less) psychotherapy (19% vs. 11%). The reverse was true of private insurance (longer term use, 22%, vs. shorter term use, 33%). In other words, Medicaid (19%) and private insurance (22%) accounted for an approximately equal proportion of psychotherapy expenditures made by patients who received 20 or more psychotherapy visits.

As managed care rapidly spreads through outpatient mental health care, public and private third-party payment for longer term psychotherapy will become increasingly threatened. Under such conditions, the proportion of long-term psychotherapy financed directly by the users themselves is likely to rise, and the total volume of longer term psychotherapy is likely to fall (Frank & McGuire, 1986).

Why Do People Use Psychotherapy?

When a specific reason for using psychotherapy was reported by NMES respondents, it was almost always reported to be for the treatment of a mental condition (86%). Among the mental conditions, depression was the most common reason for using psychotherapy (27%), followed by anxiety disorders (15%), and adjustment disorders (13%). Only a relatively small proportion of the psychotherapy visits for mental conditions was for the treatment of drug or alcohol problems (5%). It is possible that many of the respondents had multiple reasons for using psychotherapy (e.g., depression, marital conflict, alcoholism), and that the social stigma associated with treatment of substance use disorders decreased the frequency with which treatment for these conditions was reported.

Who Uses Psychotherapy?

When psychotherapy visits are aggregated by individual respondent, 3.1% (national estimate: 7.3 million) of the noninstitutionalized population were estimated to have made a psychotherapy visit to a nonhospital setting. The likelihood of using psychotherapy was higher for females (3.6%) than males (2.5%), higher for those with at least 16 years of education (5.4% vs. 1.7%), and higher for whites (3.4%) than blacks (1.4%) or other nonwhites (1.9%).

Use of outpatient psychotherapy was also higher for separated or divorced persons (6.8%) than for married (2.7%), widowed (1.7%), or never-married persons (3.9%). However, the rates of psychotherapy use varied little with income level (high, 3.6%; middle, 2.5%; low, 3.1%; near poor, 2.3%; poor, 3.5%) and employment status (employed, 3.5%, vs. unemployed, 3.2%). Younger persons (<18 years of age, 2.3%) and those over 65 years of age (1.0%) had comparatively low rates of psychotherapy utilization.

The rate of psychotherapy use among adults increased with higher levels of self-reported nervousness and depression and poorer general health (Table 5.1). Adults who rated their general health as poor were more than twice as likely to use outpatient psychotherapy than those who rated their health as excellent (Table 5.1).

What Proportion of Psychotherapy Users Also Purchase Psychotropics?

Approximately one third (31.1%) of psychotherapy users reported that they purchased a prescription antianxiety/hypnotic (16.6%), antidepressant (15.9%), antipsychotic (9.4%), lithium (3.2%), or psychostimulant (2.0%) during the survey year. This is in the range previously reported for psychotropic drug prescription to patients of psychiatrists (Shappert, 1994) and other mental health care providers (Knesper, Pagnucco, & Wheeler, 1985).

What About Other Types of Outpatient Mental Health Care?

NMES data make clear that psychotherapy is only one type of outpatient mental health care (Figure 5.1). According to the NMES, the most common indicator

Table 5.1 Rates of Psychotherapy Use in the 1987 NMES Sample Stratified by Selected Health and Mental Health Measures[a]

Measures	Number of Respondents	Number of Psychotherapy Users	Rate of Psychotherapy Use per 100 Respondents[b]
Total Sample	22,460	642	3.28
General Health			
Excellent	9,632	243	2.76
Good	14,340	357	2.85
Fair	4,929	171	3.97
Poor	1,137	53	5.59
Health keeps subject from job, housework, or school	2,810	141	5.98
Health limits the kind of work subject can perform	4,424	187	4.98
Health limits performance of moderate physical activity	3,755	132	4.19
Depressed mood, past month			
None of the time	6,300	67	1.22
Little of the time	7,980	199	2.99
Some of the time	4,599	162	4.09
Good bit of the time	1,238	91	8.16
Most of the time	711	69	10.35
All of the time	250	23	11.36
Nervousness, past month			
None of the time	6,377	72	1.35
Little of the time	6,914	176	2.99
Some of the time	4,732	142	3.40
Good bit of the time	1,587	92	6.66
Most of the time	1,107	90	8.94
All of the time	375	38	11.21

[a]Results are for respondents who were at least 18 years of age, except general health (*) which includes all ages.
[b]Based on weighted sample.

of outpatient mental health service use is the purchase of a psychotropic medication. An estimated 15 million persons (6.2% of the population) purchased a psychotropic medication in 1987. The overwhelming majority of these individuals (85%) did not report receiving outpatient psychotherapy. More specifically, only a minority of the individuals who received anxiolytics (11%), antidepressants (24%), stimulants (30%), or antipsychotics (34%) reported making a psychotherapy visit.

Approximately 2.2% of the population (5.2 million persons) made a total of 54.8 million outpatient visits to mental health specialists in 1987. Most (86%) but not all of these patients received psychotherapy. At the same time, 3.4% of the population (8.0 million persons) made visits for the primary purpose of treating a mental health condition. Approximately one third (2.8 million) of these individuals did not report receiving psychotherapy.

These findings underscore the importance of distinguishing among the various major classes of outpatient mental health care. While there is some overlap among users of psychotherapy, psychotropic medications, mental health specialists, and visits for mental health conditions, there are important differences as well. Compared with people who purchase psychotropic medications, for example, users of psychotherapy are substantially younger (mean age = 33.5 years vs. 53.3 years), are more often employed (65% vs. 38%), less often report that their general health is fair or poor (23.8% vs. 50.3%), and less often report that health keeps them from their job, housework, or school (18.7% vs. 35.2%). Policymakers should be aware that

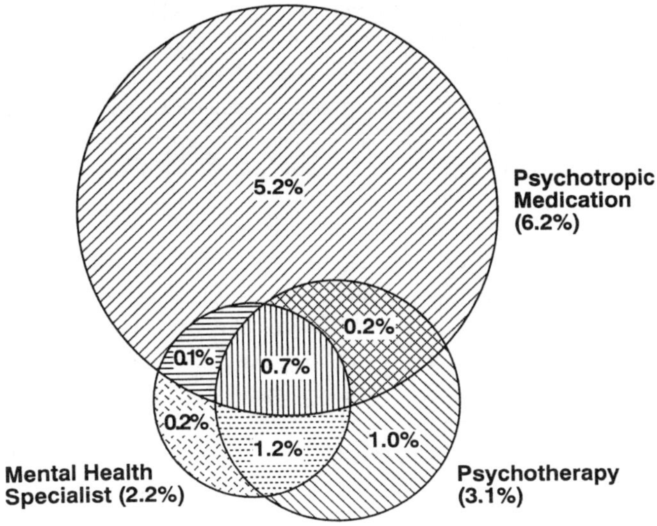

Figure 5.1 Overlapping relationships between the percentage of the population who receive psychotherapy, purchase a psychotropic medication, and visit a mental health specialist. (Data from the 1987 National Medical Expenditure Survey.)

different definitions of outpatient mental health service utilization identify different populations (Olfson & Pincus, 1994a).

Perspective

The NMES provides an overview of the size, scope, financing, and costs of outpatient psychotherapy in 1987. The results indicate that utilization of psychotherapy was common (79.5 million visits a year), expensive ($4.2 billion), and unevenly distributed across the population. Certain groups, such as whites, females, the highly educated, and separated or divorced persons, used psychotherapy at comparatively high rates. As might be expected, users of outpatient psychotherapy commonly reported anxiety, depressed mood, and impaired general health.

The costs of psychotherapy were highly skewed toward longer term users. In 1987, the 16% of psychotherapy users who made more than 20 visits accounted for nearly two thirds (63%) of total outpatient psychotherapy expenditures. A substantial proportion of this care (19%) was financed by the Medicaid program. As organized cost containment mechanisms spread to Medicaid and other publicly financed health care, it can be expected that the provision of longer term psychotherapy will be monitored very closely. Managed-care providers (for public or private purchasers) that assume financial risk are particularly averse to the high costs associated with long-term psychotherapy. How patients who have historically received longer term psychotherapy will fare in the new managed-care environment remains an important and unresolved issue.

A recent review of cost containment efforts for mental health services suggests that cost savings can often be achieved without apparent adverse effects on patient outcomes (Wells, 1995). At the same time, however, certain patient groups are especially vulnerable to potential detrimental consequences of cost containment policies. Specifically, individuals with low income and poor mental health—an important subgroup of long-term psychotherapy users—may be particularly susceptible (Wells, 1995). With respect to psychotropic drug use, Medicaid claims data indicate that prescription payment caps are associated with immediate reductions in use of antipsychotic drugs and sharp increases in emergency mental health services use and partial hospitalization (Soumerai, McLaughlin, Ross-Degan, & Casteris, 1994). There is a need to conduct similar research on the consequences of cost containment initiatives in the psychotherapy area.

Another vulnerable group is women who require treatment of psychiatric conditions during pregnancy and the postpartum period (when use of psychotropic medications is contraindicated) (Wolk & Weissman, 1995). Limits on psychotherapy coverage may have particularly serious consequences for such women. In 1987, over half of all psychotherapy visits were made by women during the childbearing years.

Substantial gaps remain in our understanding of the provision of psychotherapy in routine outpatient practice. With the NMES, it is possible to get a rough indication of who uses and who does not use psychotherapy. The current findings suggest that nonwhites, the young, the elderly, and the less-than-college-educated use psychotherapy less often than expected based on the prevalence of mental disorders within these sociodemographic groups (Robins & Regier, 1991). Considerable attention has been devoted to examining factors that either facilitate or impede use of mental health services in the general population (Gallo, Marino, Ford, & Anthony 1995; Leaf et al., 1988; Regier et al., 1993). Large-scale utilization surveys such as the NMES provide opportunities to contribute to this literature. If future surveys include a broader range of mental health indicators, it will be possible to examine access to outpatient psychotherapy in greater depth.

While a building literature supports the efficacy of manual-based psychotherapies for specific mental disorders (Elkin et al., 1989; Foa, Kozak, Steketee, & McCarthy, 1992), almost nothing is known about the content and effectiveness of psychotherapy as it is practiced in the community. There is a critical need to examine the practice of psychotherapy in the community in a manner that resembles the research on psychotropic medication prescribing in routine practice (Keller, Klerman, Lavori, Coryell, & Endicott, 1982; Olfson & Klerman, 1992).

One approach to researching current clinical practice is to engage clinicians in the research itself. One such promising initiative is the American Psychiatric Association's (APA) Practice Research Network (PRN). The APA PRN is a group of practicing psychiatrists who collaborate to collect data and conduct research in a wide range of clinical settings.

Pilot data from the APA PRN indicate that psychiatrists commonly provide psychotherapy. According to a recent APA PRN survey, the average psychiatrist treats approximately one third of his or her outpatients with major depression (mild severity) with psychotherapy alone (American Psychiatric Association, 1996). A considerably larger proportion of psychiatric patients with major depression receive psychotherapy in combination with an antidepressant. In addition, many patients under the medical care of psychiatrists receive ongoing psychotherapy from other providers such as social workers and psychologists. Through the APA PRN, practicing psychiatrists and mental health services researchers have a rare opportunity to study a variety of psychotherapeutic interventions used in daily practice and to examine the associated clinical outcomes.

An important methodological challenge is the development of measures that rapidly and reliably characterize the nature and intensity of psychotherapeutic processes without unduly burdening the delivery of routine care. Such measures need to be applicable to a range of different psychotherapeutic approaches yet should be focused on specific actions or behaviors, rather than attitudes or opinions. One such measure is the Therapeutic Procedures Inventory (TPI; McNeilly & Howard, 1991), which queries therapists about a variety of specific actions. The TPI measures psychotherapy sessions along three subscales or dimensions: directive/behavioral, psychodynamic/past-focused, and affective.

In the current health care climate, managed-care companies and psychiatric carve out organizations have a strong incentive to monitor the cost-effectiveness of the mental health services they finance. Unfortunately, these evaluations are seldom published, are often colored by the culture that produces them, and are not readily available to inform public policymaking.

Data from publicly financed medical utilization surveys remain an important, if often overlooked, source of information concerning mental health care in America. Brief psychometrically valid mental health indicators have the potential to greatly enhance the relevance of these surveys for mental health planners. Repeated cross-sectional surveys provide opportunities to observe secular change. Without such data, we are left speculating and trading anecdotes on the broad effects that managed care and other powerful forces exert on the mental health care landscape.

References

American Psychiatric Association, Office of Research, Practice Research Network. (1996). *Summary report: Study of the treatment of adult depression.* Washington, DC: Author.

Edwards, W. S., & Berlin, M. (1989). *National Medical Expenditure Survey: Questionnaires and data collection methods for the household survey and survey of American Indians and Alaska Natives.* DHHS, Pub. No. (PHS) 89-3450. Washington, DC: U.S. Government Printing Office.

Elkin, I., Shea, T., Watkins, J. T., et al. (1989). National Institute of Mental Health treatment of depression collaborative research program: General effectiveness of treatments. *Archives of General Psychiatry*, 46, 971–982.

Foa, E. B., Kozak, M. J., Steketee, G. S., & McCarthy, P. R. (1992). Treatment of depressive and obsessive-compulsive symptoms in OCD by imipramine and behavior therapy. *British Journal of Psychiatry*, 31, 279–292.

Frank, R. G., & McGuire, T. G. (1986). A review of studies of demand and utilization of specialty mental health services. *Health Services Research*, 21, 321–340.

Gallo, J. J., Marino, S., Ford, D., & Anthony, J. C. (1995). Filters on the pathway to mental health care: 2. Sociodemographic factors. *Psychological Medicine*, 25, 1149–1160.

Garfield, S. L. (1986). Research on client variables in psychotherapy. In S. L. Garfield & A. E. Bergin (Eds.), *Handbook of Psychotherapy and Behavior Change* (3rd ed.). New York: Wiley.

Keller, M. A., Klerman, G. L., Lavori, P. W., Coryell, W., & Endicott, J. (1982). Treatment received by depressed patients. *Journal of the American Medical Association*, 248, 1848–1855.

Knesper, D. J., Pagnucco, D. J., & Wheeler, J. R. C. (1985). Similarities and differences across mental health services providers and practice settings in the United States. *American Psychologist*, 40, 1352–1369.

Leaf, P. J., Bruce, M. L., Tischler, G. L., Freeman, D. H., Weissman, M. M., & Myers, J. K. (1988). Factors affecting the utilization of specialty and general medical mental health services. *Medical Care*, 26, 9–26.

McNeilly, C. L., & Howard, K. I. (1991). The Therapeutic Procedures Inventory: Psychometric properties and relationship to phase of treatment. *Journal of Psychotherapy Integration*, 1, 223–324.

Mechanic, D., Schlesinger, M., & McAlpine, D. D. (1995). Management of mental health and substance abuse services: State of the art and early results. *Milbank Quarterly*, 73, 19–55.

Olfson, M., & Klerman, G. L. (1992). The treatment of depression: Prescribing practices of primary care physicians and psychiatrists. *Journal of Family Practice*, 35, 627–635.

Olfson, M., & Pincus, H. A. (1994a). Measuring outpatient mental health care in the United States. *Health Affairs*, 13, 172–180.

Olfson, M., & Pincus, H. A. (1994b). Outpatient psychotherapy in the United States: 1. Volume, costs, and user characteristics. *American Journal of Psychiatry*, 151, 1281–1288.

Olfson, M., & Pincus, H. A. (1994c). Outpatient psychotherapy in the United States: 2. Patterns of utilization. *American Journal of Psychiatry*, 151, 1289–1294.

Orleans, C. T., George, L. K., Houpt, J. L., & Brodie, H. K. H. (1985). How primary care physicians treat psychiatric disorders: A national survey of family practitioners. *American Journal of Psychiatry*, 142, 52–57.

Phillips, E. L. (1985). *Psychotherapy revised: New frontiers in research and practice*. Hillsdale, NJ: Earlbaum.

Robins, L. N., & Regier, D. A. (Eds.). (1991). *Psychiatric disorders in America*. New York: Free Press.

Shappert, S. M. (1994). *Office visits to psychiatrists: United States, 1989–90*. Hyattsville, MD: Division of Health Care Statistics, National Center for Health Statistics.

Soumerai, S. B., McLaughlin, T. J., Ross-Degan, D., & Casteris, C. S. (1994). Effects of a limit on Medicaid drug-reimbursement benefits on the use of psychotropic agents and acute mental health services by patients with schizophrenia. *New England Journal of Medicine*, 331, 650–655.

Wells, K. B. (1995). Cost containment and mental health outcomes: Experiences from US studies. *British Journal of Psychiatry*, 166(S), 43–51.

6

A Naturalistic Study of Psychotherapy

The Medical Outcomes Study Approach

Lisa S. Meredith, Roland Sturm, & Kenneth B. Wells

An increasing emphasis on containing the high costs of delivering health care in the United States through gatekeeper policies and prepaid financing could affect the ability of depressed patients to receive care from mental health specialists and affect the overall quality of care delivered. The availability of psychotherapy in benefit plans and insurance coverage for patients with depression and other emotional and family problems is particularly vulnerable to the impact of policy shifts. To better guide policy decisions in achieving cost-effective care for depression, it is necessary to assess changes in practice patterns and predict their consequences. Such an assessment requires a framework to identify the cost-effectiveness of counseling for depression across specialty sectors, across payment systems, determining how it compares to alternative therapies. Counseling may be a cost-effective form of therapy for some patient groups, but this requires determining which components of counseling in typical practice are associated with improved quality and outcomes and how to furnish the appropriate incentives for providers to deliver quality counseling therapies.

While numerous studies provide evidence for the efficacy of psychotherapy based on clinical trials (Depression Guideline Panel, 1993), few naturalistic studies offer data of sufficient depth for understanding how psychotherapy is actually used to treat depressed patients in typical settings. Nevertheless, a number of effective therapies studied in these trials have the potential for success in naturalistic settings if implemented properly (Brody et al., 1994). Techniques of cognitive, behavioral, and interpersonal therapy hold promise for these settings because they require less intensive training and may be effective in their brief forms. The Medical Outcomes Study (MOS) is one of the first studies undertaken encompassing such a broad view in describing the psychosocial treatment of patients with depressive disorder, across both general medical and mental health specialty treatment settings. The MOS also provides data about how alternative financing strategies affect psychosocial treatment for depression.

Prior to the development of the MOS, no established framework or set of operational definitions was available for use in assessing psychotherapy service utilization patterns in large health care policy studies. Most information about psychotherapy for depression (Depression Guideline Panel, 1993) was based on studies documenting efficacious care. Thus, it was not generalizable across diverse populations or treatment sectors in that it was based on highly controlled clinical trials, using a select subpopulation of patients from mental health specialists (Beck, Rush, Shaw, & Emery, 1979; Klerman & Weissman, 1993). Only a few studies have examined briefer forms of counseling in patients of general medical providers (Brodaty & Andrews, 1983; Mynors-Wallace, Gath, Lloyd-Thomas, & Tomlinson, 1995; Pfeiffer, 1986). While work on efficacy of psychotherapy for depression has been significant, a broader approach to conceptualizing effectiveness of cross-sector care is needed.

In this chapter, we describe the MOS approach, which emerges from a health services research perspective, to conceptualize and evaluate the use of psychotherapy for depression in typical practice settings. We characterize psychotherapy as typically provided, including all forms of usual counseling, discussing what has been learned about psychotherapy utilization, and providing evidence for its cost-effective use. Continued research to characterize the content of counseling as typically provided can help guide policy decisions, assist in the implementation of feasible and effective care in managed-care settings, and shed light on how to best finance such care.

Conceptualization and Measurement of Psychotherapy in the MOS

Because the MOS is a large health policy study, our approach required the translation of counseling concepts from clinical research into a health services research framework. This framework was intended to be applicable across a variety of typical practice settings, so a very broad definition of counseling, combined with a more detailed characterization of specific counseling domains, was used. Figure 6.1 illustrates the MOS approach to conceptualizing counseling as the extent to which patients use mental health services and the clinician style of counseling. Operationalization of these concepts is described later in the chapter. The framework facilitates comparisons among specialists who provide a range of counseling techniques in treating depressed patients. Under this rubric, psychosocial interventions could range from briefer forms of informal counseling—consisting mostly of education and advice typical of general medical clinicians—to the formal varieties of psychotherapy based on standardized protocols more typical of mental health specialists and clinical investigators. Under this broad definition, counseling encompasses a variety of different purposes, ranging from detection, evaluation, and assessment to psychoanalysis and medication management for depression.

First, it was determined whether patients identified as having depression received at least brief psychosocial counseling and, if so, whether the mode was individual or group format. Data were based on clinicians' responses to a single item asking whether they counseled each patient about depression for at least 3 minutes during the screening visit. This operational definition of psychotherapy, which differs from that used in manual-based studies, where clinicians always counsel for more than 3 minutes, reflects psychotherapy in typical practice settings. To more fully understand use of counseling, frequency of using health care services for mental health reasons was assessed, and provider continuity as an indicator of extent and quality of patient's relationship with the study clinician was also measured. This set of measures is referred to as the *patient use of counseling for depression.*

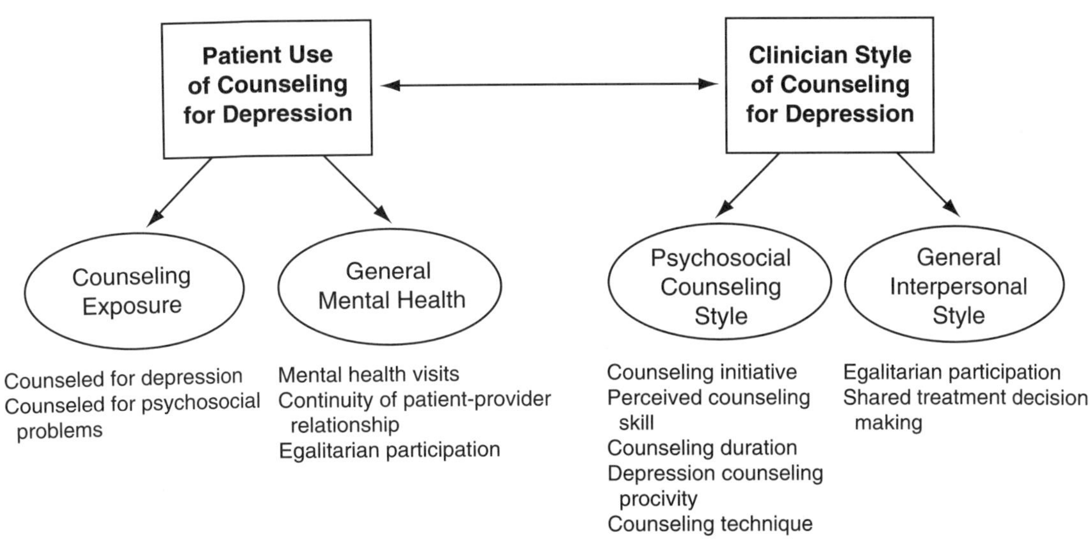

Figure 6.1 Components of "usual" counseling for depression.

We were also interested in the clinician's usual style of counseling depressed patients. Clinician style is defined as a multidimensional set of constructs tapping various domains of counseling and interpersonal style of care. The domains of clinician style were based, when possible, on established theoretical or empirical approaches. The components of usual counseling style were adapted from the framework for assessing clinicians' style in counseling about health promotion activities from Wells, Ware, and Lewis (1984a, 1984b); in particular, variables utilized included the initiative taken in counseling or the tendency of clinicians to raise issues with patients, intensity of counseling in terms of duration, and comprehensiveness of counseling in terms of range of techniques used. The concept of perceived skill in counseling was also derived from this framework, adapted from Social Cognitive Theory (Bandura, 1977, 1986), and from the Health Belief Model (attitudes that facilitate a health promotion behavior) and applied subsequently to physician counseling behavior (Rosenstock, 1974; Wells et al., 1984b).

The interpersonal style measures have a different origin. The concepts of egalitarian participation style (extent to which clinicians convey dominance, directiveness, or superiority over patients) and sharing treatment-related decisions in the patient-clinician relationship derive largely from the constructs initially identified as generic components of interaction during psychotherapy sessions. Kaplan and her associates (Greenfield, Kaplan, Ware, Yaho, & Frank, 1988; Kaplan, Greenfield, Gandek, Rogers, & Ware, 1996; Kaplan, Greenfield, & Ware, 1989) later applied these concepts as key targets of patient activation interventions to improve the process and outcomes of care for diabetes.

Measuring and Evaluating Psychotherapy

Assessing psychotherapy in the context of usual care was a particular challenge, because the relationship of specific psychotherapies to "counseling" in the context of usual care is not known. Our strategy was to determine from providers whether patients had received counseling for depression or for any emotional or personal problem in the screening visit. To obtain information pertaining to the content of such counseling, detailed reports of clinicians' usual counseling style for treating depression were collected to serve as a proxy for what might have actually occurred during the counseling session. Given the large set of objectives addressed by the MOS (Tarlov et al., 1989), budget constraints precluded the collection of detailed accounts of each counseling session. Because counseling in naturalistic settings involves interpersonal style of care in general, several aspects of clinician relationships with patients were also included. The whole set of clinician usual practice and attitudes toward care was described as *clinician style of care for depression*.

Method

Study Design

A brief overview of the design of the MOS is provided here. For additional details regarding the conceptual framework, study design, and data collection methods, see Tarlov et al. (1989) and Rogers et al. (1992).

The MOS is an observational study designed to compare the processes and outcomes in clinicians' practice styles and patient outcomes in different health care systems (health maintenance organizations, or HMOs; large multispecialty groups, or LMSGs; and solo practices, or SOLO) in three geographic sites (Los Angeles, Boston, and Chicago). Within each system of care, a representative sample of 523 clinicians was selected from the specialties of family medicine, general internal medicine, cardiology, endocrinology, psychiatry, and clinical psychology. Patient participants were a representative cross section of 22,399 adults visiting study providers during an average 9-day period in the summer of 1986. During this time, patients and clinicians completed screening questionnaires following the office visit. Both clinician and patient information from these instruments was used to identify those with hypertension, diabetes, heart disease, or depression.

Depressed patients ($N = 3{,}456$) were identified using a two-stage screening procedure based on criteria met at the time of the visit. First, patients completed a brief eight-item screening instrument for depressive symptoms (Burnam, Wells, Leake, & Landsverk, 1988) that identifies those with a high probability of having current major depression or dysthymia. Second, eligible participants who exceeded the cut point on the first-stage screen were identified according to *DSM-III* criteria for having current depressive disorder (Robins, Helzer, Croughan, & Ratcliff, 1981). A subset of patients who exceeded the initial screener cutoff were asked to participate in the longitudinal portion of the study (N = 974), with 743 meeting full Diagnostic Interview Schedule (DIS) criteria for current major depression or dysthymia.

Sources of Data and Study Measures

Measures of counseling data were derived from both patient and clinician reports. Data on *patient use of counseling for depression* came from both patient and clinician and were evaluated with the individual patient as the unit of analysis. Data on exposure to counseling were obtained from clinician reports of counseling (as a proxy for psychotherapy) during specific patient encounters, and from clinician reports of usual counseling style. In the screening visits, clinicians were asked whether they had provided 3 minutes or more of face-to-face counseling for depression, anxiety, coping with a medical problem, or personal, emotional, or family problems. Counseling for emotional problems other than depression were included to measure broader psychosocial counseling activity. A 3-minute threshold for counseling was used because counseling lasting less than 3 minutes was considered inappropriate interpersonal care for a patient with acute depression. We also asked patients about the modality used for therapy received. At 6 months following the baseline patient assessment, patients reported whether the counseling they received for personal or emotional problems was in the individual, group, or family modality. Information was also collected on use of counseling services from patient reports of outpatient visits specifically for mental health reasons, distinct from visits for general medical reasons. These measures are described in Wells, Sturm, Sherbourne, and Meredith (1996) and reported in Sturm et al. (1995).

In addition to counseling exposure, continuity of care for psychosocial problems was examined (see Sturm, Meredith, & Wells, 1996). It is possible that patients may have received counseling from providers other than the MOS clinician visited at the screening visit, so patients were asked at baseline whether they had visited a mental health specialist in the prior 6 months and, if so, what kind of counseling they had received. The continuity measure tracked whether or not the patient was still seeing the initial MOS clinician over time. Discontinuities in the patient-clinician relationship may indicate poor-quality care for depressed patients, and this, in turn, could be associated with adverse outcomes. At the patient screening, patients were also asked about the the extent to which they felt that the doctor or other health care professional just seen would allow them to participate in treatment decisions (Kaplan, Greenfield, Gandek, Rogers, & Ware, 1996).

Data on *clinician counseling style for depression* were taken from clinician reports of care 3 months *prior* to the patient screening visit and were evaluated with the individual clinician as the unit of analysis. Based on clinician's reports of their practice patterns with patients, the following variables were examined: *counseling initiative*, which refers to whether the clinician or the patient routinely initiates discussions about various psychosocial problems and, if so, how routinely counseling occurs; *perceived skill*, which reflects the self-efficacy or beliefs about the ability of the clinician to counsel effectively; *intensity*, or duration of counseling, refers to the amount of time the clinician typically spends counseling during any given encounter; and *proclivity to counsel depressed patients*, refers to the likelihood of counseling across depressed patients differing in presence of and type of medical comorbidity (Meredith, Wells, & Camp, 1994). Various counseling *techniques* are reflected by the type and number of five specific counseling activities typically used (i.e., education and advice, interpretation or confrontation, counseling of family members, behavioral treatment, or psychodynamic therapy). Two clinician-report measures addressed interpersonal style in general. These include *egalitarian participation*, or level of authority or influence assumed by the clinician, which derives from studies of authoritarian personality style, and *sharing of treatment decisions*, or the clinicians' tendency to share control over and responsibility for treatment decisions with patients.

Results

Tables 6.1 and 6.2 summarize the MOS findings for specialty and payment differences across the various domains of counseling. Because many of these results are reported elsewhere, we focus on highlighting some of the key findings here.

Differences by Specialty and Payment in Patient Use of Counseling

Figure 6.2 shows large average differences by specialty, and payment within specialty, in percentage of depressed patients counseled for depression or other personal problems. Patients of general medical clinicians received significantly less counseling of either type than

Table 6.1 Summary of Specialty Effects on Usual Counseling for Depression[a,b]

Counseling Measure	Patients Seen in Mental Health Specialty or Mental Health Specialists (vs. General Medical Clinicians):
Patient use of counseling	
Counseled for depression	are *more* likely to be exposed to counseling
Counseled for psychosocial problems	are *more* likely to be exposed to counseling
Mental health visits	have *more* mental health visits
Continuity of patient-clinician relationship	have *more* continuity in relationship
Egalitarian participation style	have *similar* levels of egalitarian style in the patient-clinician relationship
Clinician counseling style	
Counseling initiative usually taken	take *similar* levels of counseling initiative
Perceived counseling skill	have *higher* amounts of skill
Counseling duration	are *more* likely to spend more than 10 minutes counseling patients
Depression counseling proclivity	have *higher* rates of counseling
Advice-oriented counseling technique	do *less* advice-oriented counseling
Psychodynamic-oriented counseling technique	do *more* psychodynamic counseling
Egalitarian participation style	have *similar* levels of egalitarian style in the patient-clinician relationship
Shared treatment decision making	have *higher* tendencies to share decision making with the patient

[a]Differences are significant at $p < .05$.

[b]Multi-item measures were scored by averaging responses across items and rescaled to range from 0 to 100. A high score on these scales reflects a *stronger counseling orientation* and, for the patient scale, stronger perceptions of egalitarianism. All multi-item scales exceeded the standard cutoff of .60 for adequate internal consistency (Cronbach, 1951). For additional information about scoring these measures and their psychometric properties, see Meredith, Wells, Kaplan, and Mazel (1996) and Wells et al. (1996).

Table 6.2 Summary of Payment Effects on Usual Counseling for Depression[a,b]

Counseling Measure	Patients in Prepaid Plans or Clinicians Who Treat Mostly Patients in Prepaid Plans (vs. Fee-for-Service):
Patient use of counseling	
Counseled for depression	are *more* likely to be exposed to counseling
Counseled for psychosocial problems	are *more* likely to be exposed to counseling
Mental health visits	have *more* mental health visits
Continuity of patient-clinician relationship	have *less* continuity of relationship
Egalitarian participation style	have *lower* levels of egalitarian participation
Clinician counseling style	
Counseling initiative usually taken	take *similar* levels of counseling initiative
Perceived counseling skill	have *similar* amounts of counseling skill
Counseling duration	are *less* likely to spend more than 10 minutes in counseling
Depression counseling proclivity	have *lower* proclivity to provide depression counseling
Advice-oriented counseling technique	do *more* advice-oriented counseling
Psychodynamic-oriented counseling technique	do *less* psychodynamic-oriented counseling
Egalitarian participation style	have *similar* levels
Shared treatment decision making	have *similar* tendencies

[a]Differences are significant at $p < .05$.

[b]Multi-item measures were scored by averaging responses across items and rescaled to range from 0 to 100. A high score on these scales reflects a *stronger counseling orientation* and, for the patient scale, stronger perceptions of egalitarianism. All multi-item scales exceeded the standard cutoff of .60 for adequate internal consistency (Cronbach, 1951). For additional information about scoring these measures and their psychometric properties, see Meredith, Wells, Kaplan, and Mazel (1996) and Wells et al. (1996).

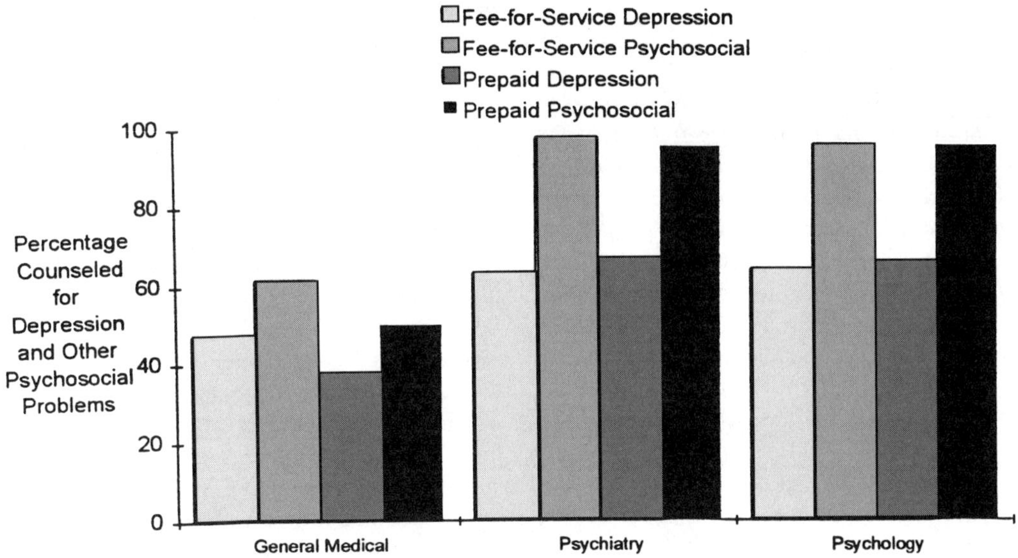

Figure 6.2 Adjusted percentage of patients counseled for depression (baseline sample: current depressive disorder).

patients of either psychiatrists or psychologists ($p < .05$). These patterns held across three different samples of depressed patients, that is, a screener sample of over 3,000 patients with either depression symptoms or current disorder, a longitudinal panel of about 1,000 depressed patients (either symptoms or disorder), and a subset of about 700 patients with current depressive disorder at baseline. Significant payment differences were found in the percentage of patients receiving psychosocial counseling: Within the general medical sector, prepayment was associated with counseling rates up to 11 percentage points lower than fee-for-service, but within the mental health specialty sector, prepayment was only 5 percentage points lower than fee-for-service. Most patients who visited a mental health specialist in the past 6 months received individual therapy rather than group therapy.

Differences by Specialty and Payment in Clinician Counseling Style

Average differences in clinician-style-of-care scores differed substantially by specialty. Specialty is a relevant policy variable because managed-care trends such as increased gatekeeping may shift more depression care out of the specialty sector and into primary care. These results are adjusted for clinician demographic factors and practice characteristics such as percentage of patients who are prepaid. On most measures of psychosocial counseling or interpersonal style, mental health specialists were more inclined to report high levels of counseling or participation in the patient-doctor relationship. Psychiatrists relied more on psychodynamic approaches to counseling and psychologists on behavioral therapies, but both specialty groups provided more intensive sessions and more formal psychotherapeutic techniques than did general medical clinicians.

Type of patient payment for health care services is another relevant policy variable for which we would expect differences in style of care. We found relatively few differences in clinician style of care for clinicians treating a high versus low proportion of patients under prepaid arrangements. However, clinicians who treated a greater proportion of patients in prepaid plans reported a significantly lower proclivity to provide face-to-face counseling for personal or emotional problems, were slightly less likely to spend over 10 minutes of an office visit dealing with psychosocial problems, and were 9 percent more likely to provide either education and advice than were clinicians in practices treating primarily fee-for-service patients. Our sample size for group therapy recipients was too small to determine whether payment affects use of group compared to individual therapy.

Association of Clinician Counseling Style with Counseling Delivered

Table 6.3 summarizes these findings by showing the magnitude of the relationships between selected measures of clinician counseling style and the percentage of patients who received different therapies for depression during the index encounter. Specifically, the percentage of patients for high and low values on these 0–100 scales (25th and 75th percentile scores) that were measured before the encounter was calculated. The actual differences between low and high values on these continuous scales range from 20%–40%, depending on the measure. Patients of clinicians who perceived their psychosocial counseling skills to be higher were significantly more likely to be exposed to counseling (this reflects a 41% difference in perceived skill, which is equivalent to a 10% difference in counseling). Patients of clinicians who report a low proclivity to provide face-to-face counseling compared to those who report a higher preference to counsel (a 28% difference) were less likely to receive counseling for depression (10%) or other psychosocial counseling problems (15%). Patients of clinicians scoring high on egalitarian participation compared to those scoring low (a 21% difference) were also significantly more likely to receive depression counseling (25%). There was no effect on the tendency for clinicians to share treatment-related decisions with their patients.

Discussion

Lessons Learned About Studying Psychotherapy in the MOS

Simple and direct measures of psychotherapy were found to be useful across a range of depressed patients in addressing policy-related questions about the health care process. Measures of counseling exposure and usual clinician style of mental health care were found to reveal significant differences by specialty and, to a lesser extent, by payment type. These measures provided data complementing more traditional quality-of-care indicators, and informing policy decisions about how counseling is typically provided.

While nearly all depressed patients of mental health specialists received counseling for at least 3 minutes, only half of depressed patients in the general medical sector received brief counseling (even among the subset of patients with current depressive disorder). In terms of payment, counseling exposure rates were lower under prepaid than under fee-for-service care, and this was especially true in general medical practices. In the MOS, nearly all patients who had visited a mental health specialist in the past 6 months had received individual forms of therapy rather than group therapy. However, this may be changing as the nation moves toward greater use of managed care to contain costs, since group forms of therapy are likely to be less costly.

In terms of the type of counseling provided, psychiatrists relied more on psychodynamic approaches and psychologists more on behavioral therapies, but both specialty groups provided more intensive sessions and used more formal psychotherapeutic techniques (e.g., interpretation) than did general medical clinicians. Clinicians treating more prepaid patients in their practice reported a lower preference for face-to-face counseling and spent less time when counseling than clinicians treating more fee-for-service patients.

The clinician-based measures of usual counseling and interpersonal style of care provide complementary information that helps inform the meaning of differences in counseling exposure; that is, they help to

Table 6.3 Summary of the Effects of Clinician Counseling Style on Therapies for Depression

	% Increase in Patients Receiving Clinical Treatment			
Clinician Usual Counseling Style (% difference from 25th to 75th Percentile Value on 0–100 Scale)	Detection of Depression	Depression Counseling	Psychosocial Counseling	Effective Use of Antidepressant Medication
Perceived counseling skill (41%)	10	0	10	0
Counseling duration 10 minutes or more vs. under 10 minutes	0	0	0	39
Depression counseling proclivity (28%)	12	10	15	0
Egalitarian participation style (25%)	12	25	0	0

open the "black box" of psychotherapy. Because these measures rely on only a single clinician questionnaire, they are easier to administer and are related to aspects of clinician treatment practice with depressed patients, especially with counseling and assessment practices. One measure, proclivity to counsel depression, predicted actual counseling behavior with patients and patient outcomes. Thus, it may be useful as a screen to identify clinics and physician groups that may be useful targets for more intensive quality review efforts. We caution, however, that these measures, with moderate reliability, tend to be most appropriate for group rather than individual comparisons, and further study is needed of their discriminant validity. Because associations with outcomes are more uncertain and need to be evaluated further, we do not view these measures as substitutes for the direct, patient-based assessment of quality of clinical treatments. Rather, they provide the descriptive context, and some (depression counseling proclivity) may be useful for screening purposes at a clinician or group level. These findings suggest that these measures may be a useful means of understanding clinician variability in style of care for depression, for example, as an efficient means of obtaining information that can be used to design quality improvement or continuing medical education interventions.

Is "Counseling" for Depression Cost-Effective?

The most convincing argument in favor of a procedure is that it increases the value of care; that is, for any amount of money spent, it provides higher health benefits than alternative procedures. Unfortunately, cost-effectiveness analyses of counseling and psychotherapy remain largely absent. Sturm and Wells (1995) studied the cost-effectiveness of higher quality care for depression and concluded that quality improvement is cost-effective because the incremental costs of additional health gains (measured in terms of the number of functional limitations removed) are substantially smaller than the average costs incurred by managed-care organizations to achieve similar gains. Therefore, improving the quality of care for depression is a high-value strategy.

In their cost-effectiveness analysis, Sturm and Wells (1995) found that the simple measure of at least brief exposure to counseling (for at least 3 minutes), which was described earlier in this chapter, was associated with improved outcomes for the sickest depressed patients (Rogers, Wells, Meredith, Sturm, & Burnam, 1993). Specifically, among seriously depressed patients, this counseling measure, as well as antidepressant medication use, was significantly associated with improved functioning.

Counseling for depression at the screening visit was associated with an additional 11.4 mental health visits in the next year, in comparison to no counseling. This may explain why this simple measure predicts functioning outcomes, with counseling in this context serving as a marker for an entire episode of follow-up care, even for patients seen by primary-care clinicians. Similarly, use of appropriate antidepressant medication was associated, on average, with 4.5 additional mental health visits in a year. These visit costs need to be taken into account in a cost-effectiveness comparison.

The cost-effectiveness ratio gives the additional expenditures necessary to achieve additional health improvements. The lower the cost-effectiveness ratio, the more health improvements can be bought for each additional dollar. Because counseling is associated with more than twice as many additional visits as antidepressant medication therapy, the outcome effect of counseling needs to be about twice as that for counseling to have a better (lower) cost-effectiveness ratio than antidepressant medication, or visit costs for counseling need to be lower than visits associated with medication use (for example, through group therapy). Nevertheless, even if this is not the case, the cost-effectiveness ratio for counseling (including the additional visit costs) is only a fraction of what practices currently pay per unit of health improvement, so increased counseling is a high value strategy.

Intensity of visits and continuity of the patient-provider relationship were found to differ by payment, especially among patients of psychiatrists (Sturm et al., 1996). These concepts may be operationalized as provider choice (psychiatrist vs. non-M.D. mental health specialist vs. general medical provider) and duration of the provider relationship over time. They are often considered aspects of utilization rather than counseling style, but studies preferring a comprehensive overview of counseling differences by payment and specialty should integrate dimensions of quality and style of counseling with utilization measures because they reflect additional dimensions of the mental health care process. Future studies might also explore further components of counseling modality with direct cost implications—such as group versus individual psychotherapy.

Informing the Policy Process About Psychotherapy for Depression

Psychotherapy findings from the MOS have several implications for mental health policy. They suggest that policies geared toward shifting patients into prepaid care or limiting access to mental health specialty care could affect the access to and utilization of psychosocial counseling for depression. That is, more patients will receive their mental health care in primary-care settings. Without health care systems-level policies that equip providers to effectively manage depression in practice (e.g., whether extending durations of visits, scheduling follow-up visits, obtaining support, or being able to refer patients to specialty care), counseling is likely to become less than optimally useful. Significantly more research is needed to determine what works in typical practice. Reliable and valid measures of psychotherapy as typically practiced, using data collected in the context of observational study, can help guide mental health policy by providing information about use of quality treatments, and in developing measures of episodes of appropriate care. Currently, episodes of care are defined solely on the basis of visits with no link to management and treatment data (e.g., data on quality of care). Unfortunately, information on long-term treatment decisions was not available in the MOS, nor were sample sizes sufficient for detecting effects of such decisions on outcomes. Future work using repeated measurements should determine whether continuing counseling improves outcomes for patients with depression.

The MOS framework, including more concrete, patient-specific measures of quality of clinical treatments and measures of usual counseling style, represents a starting point for development of further measures of psychotherapy of depression in usual practice. Methodological improvements in this area are likely to provide a richer framework for cost-effectiveness analyses beyond determining the cost of a generic mental health visit. Specifically, studies are needed to determine which particular domains of the counseling visit provide the most value over time for health care dollars spent on depression.

Conclusion

The MOS health services approach to measuring psychotherapy or counseling has provided valuable lessons for guiding future studies of mental health care. Although the MOS measures are defined more broadly than in clinical studies, they are easy to administer and give practitioners, researchers, and policymakers a clearer view of psychotherapy as it is usually provided within a typical practice context. An enhanced view of usual care counseling will aid efforts to improve the quality of care for depression because it is typical care that is the target of quality improvement.

Experience in the MOS underscores the importance of findings from large health services research studies and suggests next steps for the field. First, there is a need for development of measures applicable to usual treatment settings, particularly given the increasing move toward managed-care practice. A number of barriers exist in these settings that may be unique and not reflected in the highly controlled clinical studies that have guided the field to date. Not only is it necessary to understand counseling overall, but it is also even more important to understand what is meant by *counseling* in managed primary-care settings, which, for many individuals, is the only outlet for care of depression.

Another consideration of this research on psychotherapy for depressed patients has to do with research access in the "real" world. Today, it is exponentially more difficult to obtain access to naturalistic settings to carry out research. Some of these obstacles to conducting research that can be applied to naturalistic health care (e.g., establishing trust with top-level managed-care representatives, dealing with the complexity and transitory nature of health care organizations, and funding the delivery of treatment through health care plans) could be ameliorated by changes in the way that the federal government supports such research. For example, more attention could be paid to supporting intervention costs. This will become increasingly important in future studies of the care typically provided, especially for patients with chronic illness like depression and depression combined with other illnesses. To facilitate progress in this field, it will be necessary to provide more of an infrastructure for research demonstration projects.

To carry out such an agenda, it will be essential to recruit talented professionals into the field. Special training programs in "psychotherapy services research" will be needed to address issues not typically covered by traditional mental health services research agendas. For example, how do investigators collaborate with private organizations whose chief concern is economic survival? The future of the field requires developing a policy-relevant subspecialty of psychotherapy services research, to include collaborations among psychotherapy researchers, economists, policy analysts, and others in the health services research field. While this constitutes a daunting task, if it is successful the future of psychosocial treatment will benefit substantially from these "naturalistic experiments." The likelihood of conducting such research will be determined largely by the ability of researchers to attract managed-care providers and foster ongoing relationships with these and other forms of health care organizations.

While the MOS health services approach to understanding counseling as it is typically provided has yielded useful information, the methods could benefit substantially from more detailed analyses of its components. In particular, little is known about what actually happens during encounters with primary-care physicians and depressed patients. Is what clinicians report as counseling consistent with the types of verbal interaction associated with manual-based psychotherapy of demonstrated efficacy? In future studies, it will be particularly important to move toward classifying the actual content of counseling, in terms of the "fit" with formal psychotherapies of established efficacy. Is this the type of care that can become part of routine treatment protocols? Because counseling therapies, when appropriately implemented, may be cost-effective, continued research in the integration of these therapies in typical general medical settings will help ensure that patients will receive quality care. The development of "psychotherapy services research" is likely to require extensive qualitative, as well as quantitative, research, methods development, and research training.

References

Bandura, A. (1986). *Social foundations of thought and action*. Englewood Cliffs, NJ: Prentice-Hall.

Bandura, A. (1977). *Social learning theory*. Englewood Cliffs, NJ: Prentice-Hall.

Beck, A. T., Rush, J. A., Shaw, B. F., & Emery, G. (1979). *Cognitive therapy of depression*. New York: Guilford Press.

Brodaty, H., & Andrews, G. (1983). Brief psychotherapy in family practice: A controlled prospective intervention trial. *British Journal of Psychiatry, 143*, 11–19.

Brody, D. S., Thompson, T. L., Larson, D. B., Ford, D. E., Katon, W. J., & Magruder, K. M. (1994). Strategies for counseling depressed patients by primary care physicians. *Journal of General Internal Medicine, 9*, 569–575.

Burnam, M. A., Wells, K. B., Leake, B, & Landsverk, J. (1988). Development of a brief screening instrument for detecting depressive disorders. *Medical Care, 26*, 775–789.

Cronbach, L. J. (1951). Coefficient alpha and the internal structure of tests. *Psychometrika, 16*, 297–334.

Depression Guideline Panel. (1993). *Depression in primary care: Detection, diagnosis, and treatment: Quick reference guide for clinicians*. Number 5. U.S. Department of Health and Human Services, Public Health Service, Agency for Health Care Policy and Research, AHCPR Publication No. 93-0552. Rockville, MD: AHCPR.

Greenfield, S., Kaplan, S. H., Ware, J. E., Yano, E. M., & Frank, H. J. L. (1988). Patients' participation in medical care. *Journal of General Internal Medicine, 3*, 448–457.

Kaplan, S. H., Greenfield, S., Gandek, B., Rogers, W., & Ware, J. E., Jr. (1996). Characteristics of physicians with participatory decision-making styles: Results from the Medical Outcomes Study. *Annals of Internal Medicine, 124*, 497–504.

Kaplan, S. H., Greenfield, S., & Ware, J. E., Jr. (1989). Assessing the effects of physician-patient interactions on the outcome of chronic disease. *Medical Care, 27*, S110–S127.

Klerman, G. L., & Weissman, M. M. (1993). *New applications of interpersonal psychotherapy*. Washington, DC: American Psychiatric Press.

Meredith, L. S., Wells, K. B., & Camp, P. (1994). Clinician specialty and treatment style for depressed outpatients with and without medical comorbidity. *Archives of Family Medicine, 3*, 1065–1072.

Meredith, L. S., Wells, K. B., Kaplan, S. H., & Mazel, R. M. (1996). Counseling typically provided for depression: Role of clinician specialty and payment system. *Archives of General Psychiatry, 53*, 905–912.

Mynors-Wallace, L. M., Gath, D. H., Lloyd-Thomas, A. R., & Tomlinson, D. (1995). Randomised controlled trial comparing problem solving treatment with amitriptyline and placebo for major depression in primary care. *British Medical Journal, 310*, 441–445.

Peiffer, S. I. (1986). Brief office counseling and the primary care physician. *Southern Medical Journal, 79*, 721–722.

Robins, L. N., Helzer, J. E., Croughan, J., & Ratcliff, K. S. (1981). The National Institutes of Mental Health Diagnostic Interview Survey: Its history, characteristics, and validity. *Archives of General Psychiatry, 38*, 381–389.

Rogers, W., McGlynn, E., Berry, S. H., Nelson, E. C., Perrin, E., Zubkoff, M., Greenfield, S., Wells, K. B., Stewart, A. L., Arnold, S. B., & Ware, J. E., Jr. (1992). Creation of data bases on the health of individuals. In A. L. Stewart & J. E. Ware, Jr. (Eds.), *Measuring functioning and well-Being: The Medical Outcomes Study approach* (pp. 24–41). Durham, NC: Duke University Press.

Rogers, W. H., Wells, K. B., Meredith, L. S., Sturm, R., & Burnam, M. A. (1993). Outcomes for adult depressed outpatients under prepaid and fee-for-service financing. *Archives of General Psychiatry, 50,* 517–525.

Rosenstock, I. M. (1974). Historical origins of the health belief model. *Health Education Monographs, 2,* 328–335.

Sturm, R., Jackson, C. A., Meredith, L. M., Yip, W., Manning, W. G., Rogers, W. H, & Wells, K. B. (1995). Mental health care utilization in prepaid and fee-for-service plans among depressed patients in the Medical Outcomes Study. *Health Services Research, 30,* 319–340.

Sturm, R., Meredith, L. S., & Wells, K. B. (1996). Provider choice and continuity for the treatment of depression. *Medical Care, 34,* 723–734.

Sturm, R., & Wells, K. B. (1995). How can care for depression become more cost-effective? *Journal of the American Medical Association, 273,* 51–58.

Tarlov, A., Ware, J. E., Jr., Greenfield, S., Nelson, E. C., Perrin, E., & Zubkoff, M. (1989). The Medical Outcomes Study: An application of methods for monitoring the results of medical care. *Journal of the American Medical Association, 262,* 925–930

Wells, K. B., Sturm, R., Sherbourne, C. D., & Meredith, L. M. (1996). *Caring for depression.* Cambridge: Harvard University Press.

Wells, K. B., Ware, J. E., Jr., & Lewis, C. E. (1984a). Physicians' attitudes in counseling patients about smoking. *Medical Care, 22,* 360–365.

Wells, K. B, Ware, J. E., Jr., & Lewis, C. E. (1984b). Physicians' practices in counseling patients about health habits. *Medical Care, 22,* 240–246.

7

Entering Psychotherapy

Probabilities, Routes and Finances

Robert J. Lueger, Stephen M. Saunders,
Kenneth I. Howard, John T. Vessey,
& Pierre R. Nunez

The *efficacies* of specific psychotherapies have been established in numerous controlled studies. Meta-analyses of these controlled studies indicate that a complete trial of psychotherapy commonly yields an effect size of .88 (Lipsey & Wilson, 1993). In more meaningful terms, an effect size of .88 indicates that a person treated with psychotherapy has a .77 probability of being better off than an untreated person (Howard, Krause, & Vessey, 1994). Controlled trials represent the more ideal conditions of service delivery. The manner in which patients seek mental health services, enter psychotherapy, and persist in therapy are encompassed in the *effectiveness* of psychotherapy. This chapter examines who seeks mental health services and addresses the probability of entering psychotherapy given demographic and clinical characteristics. We also explore the routes to treatment and discuss the role of finances in seeking and persisting in psychotherapy. An understanding of these effectiveness parameters is important to assessing the cost-effectiveness of psychotherapy as a form of mental health services.

Evidence of a Service Gap

There are two consistent findings in mental health services research. First, there is a substantial proportion of the population that are now suffering, have suffered within the past year, or will suffer at some time in their life from a diagnosable mental disorder. For example, the National Institute of Mental Health (NIMH) Epidemiologic Catchment Area (ECA) study estimated that 28% of the adult population of the United States will experience a mental illness in any given year (Regier et al., 1993), a rate similar to the estimate generated by the National Comorbidity Survey (NCS; Kessler et al., 1994). Second, most individuals with mental problems do not receive any professional help. The ECA program found that only about one fourth of diagnosable persons received any such service and that less than half of them saw a mental health professional (Regier et al., 1993). With regard to utilization, the NCS figures are considerably lower (Kessler et al., 1994). The "service gap" (Stefl & Prosperi, 1985) between mental health need and utilization of mental health services demands a careful examination of what is known about persons who do obtain such services.

Probability of Making a Mental Health Visit

Several large epidemiological surveys were conducted in the 1980s to assess the prevalence of mental health disorders. Respondents in those surveys were asked whether or not they discussed their problems with a mental health professional or a primary-care physician. Whereas a "mental health professional" was defined as a psychiatrist, psychologist, or social worker, none of these surveys distinguished between a mental health visit and *psychotherapy*. Moreover, no single survey contained enough respondents who made a mental health visit to conduct subsample analyses.

In an effort to address these two issues, Vessey and Howard (1993) combined the results of three surveys based on national probability samples: the Epidemiologic Catchment Area surveys (ECA; Regier et al., 1984); the National Medical Care Utilization and Expenditure Survey (NMCUES; Taube, Kessler, & Feuerberg, 1984); and the National Survey of Access to Health Care (NSAHC; Freeman, 1989). Collectively, these three surveys included over 40,000 respondents. Two of these three surveys—NMCUES and ECA—inquired about the number of visits made. From the three surveys, 1,429 individuals made at least one mental health visit.

The demographic breakdown of people who made at least one mental health visit, whether or not a diagnosis was given, indicated that about two thirds were female, about 50% had at least some college education, about half were currently married, 90% were white, and 75% were between 21 and 50. The probabilities of making at least one visit to a mental health professional by various categories of gender, education, marital status, race, income, and age are presented in Table 7.1. Women, college graduates, those separated or divorced, whites, those with incomes over $35,000, and in their 30s were most likely to make a visit to a mental health specialist.

Probability of Entering Psychotherapy

Does a mental health visit constitute psychotherapy? Although psychotherapy begins with a mental health visit, we have used a more traditional concept of psychotherapy based on the generic model involving contract, goals, processes, and outcomes (Orlinsky & Howard, 1987). Thus, more than one visit probably is necessary to constitute psychotherapy. But how many visits are necessary to yield an episode of psychotherapy? The dose-response model of psychotherapy indicates that approximately eight sessions of psychotherapy are needed to produce a 50% improvement rate when one considers all possible outcomes (Howard, Kopta, Krause, & Orlinsky, 1986). Because the goals of the mental health visits are not specified in the epidemiological surveys, we adopted a definition of psychotherapy as consisting of a minimum of eight sessions. Of those who made a mental health visit, college graduates, whites, those with higher incomes, and those in their 20s were more likely to have this utilization pattern.

The relationships between education, the prevalence of a diagnosable psychiatric condition, and making a mental health visit are particularly noteworthy. Figure 7.1 shows the lifetime probabilities of having a *DSM-III* disorder and of making at least one mental health visit for each of five levels of education. There is a perfect rank order negative correlation between the likelihood of having a diagnosable psychiatric disorder and the likelihood of making a mental health visit. The least educated were the most likely to have a diagnosable condition and the least likely to make a mental health visit. The most educated were least likely to have a diagnosable condition and the most likely to make a mental health visit. In short, those most in need of mental health services were the least likely to have received services.

Routes to Treatment

The discrepancy between need and utilization of services emphasizes the importance of understanding mental health help-seeking behavior, which is conceptualized as progressing from needing to seeking services (cf. Cleary, 1989). Various models of health-related behavior exist, such as the health belief model (Rosenstock, 1974), which asserts that health behaviors are the result of risk-benefit analysis, symptomatology, and enabling factors. In such a paradigm, mental health service utilization has been found to be related to gender, age, education, race, urbanization, attitude toward services, treatment fearfulness, and insurance coverage (Farina, 1982; Horgan, 1985; Keeler, Wells, Manning, Rumpel, & Hanley, 1986; Leaf, Bruce, & Tischler, 1986; Stefl & Prosperi, 1985; Taube et al., 1984; Wells, Manning, Duan, Newhouse, & Ware, 1986).

Research has also examined the process of seeking professional or formal help for emotional distress. Most agree that the process can be usefully viewed as comprising stages, beginning with problem recognition and ending with contact with the mental health system. Kadushin (1969), for example, concluded that the process of going to a psychiatrist involves realizing there is an emotional problem, consulting one's social support network, choosing the type of professional to consult, and selecting a specific practitioner. In comparison, Mechanic (1976a, 1976b) identified three stages of the help-seeking process. According to this conceptualization, the mental illness exists and is recognized,

Table 7.1 Probabilities of Making a Mental Health Visit and the Subsequent Probabilities of Entering Psychotherapy

	At Least One Visit	Entering Psychotherapy
Gender		
Male	.026	.37
Female	.039	.38
Education		
Grammar school or less	.019	.23
Some high school	.025	.28
High school graduate	.030	.35
Some college	.041	.39
College graduate	.057	.51
Marital status		
Married	.025	.34
Widowed	.015	.27
Separated, divorced	.061	.45
Never married	.048	.43
Race		
White	.036	.41
Nonwhite	.021	.28
Income (1975 dollars)		
Under $10,000	.038	.32
$10,000–14,999	.033	.38
$15,000–19,999	.034	.44
$20,000–24,999	.034	.40
$25,000–34,999	.032	.46
$35,000 and over	.045	.52
Age		
18–20	.034	.58
21–30	.037	.39
31–40	.063	.43
41–50	.042	.44
51–60	.028	.24
61 and over	.012	.22

prompting illness behavior that, for some, will include seeking professional help.

Still other researchers have focused on the barriers to treatment. Meile and Whitt (Meile & Whitt, 1981; Whitt & Meile, 1985) have argued that attributing problematic behavior to mental illness is neither automatic nor easy but is usually a last resort, with the result that most mentally ill persons do not seek appropriate help. Similarly, Veroff and colleagues (Veroff, Douvan, & Kulka, 1981; Veroff, Kulka, & Douvan, 1981) found that some survey respondents who did not seek psychiatric help realized, in retrospect, that they had failed to recognize that there was a problem.

Saunders (1993) reviewed research into the process of seeking mental health services and proposed a model of the process. The model focuses or centers the process on the help-seeking individual and the decisions that must be made. The first step is recognizing that a problem exists, whether or not it is attributed to an emotional disorder (Kadushin, 1969; Meile & Whitt, 1981). There is research that suggests that making such an attribution increases the likelihood of obtaining help, but apparently, it is not necessary (Davies, Sieber, & Hunt, 1994; Yokopenic, Clark, & Aneshensel, 1983). The transtheoretical model of change, proposed by Prochaska, Di Clemente, and Norcross (1992), in similar fashion holds that prior to trying actively to change, persons languish in the "precontemplation" stage, in which they do not realize that there was a problem.

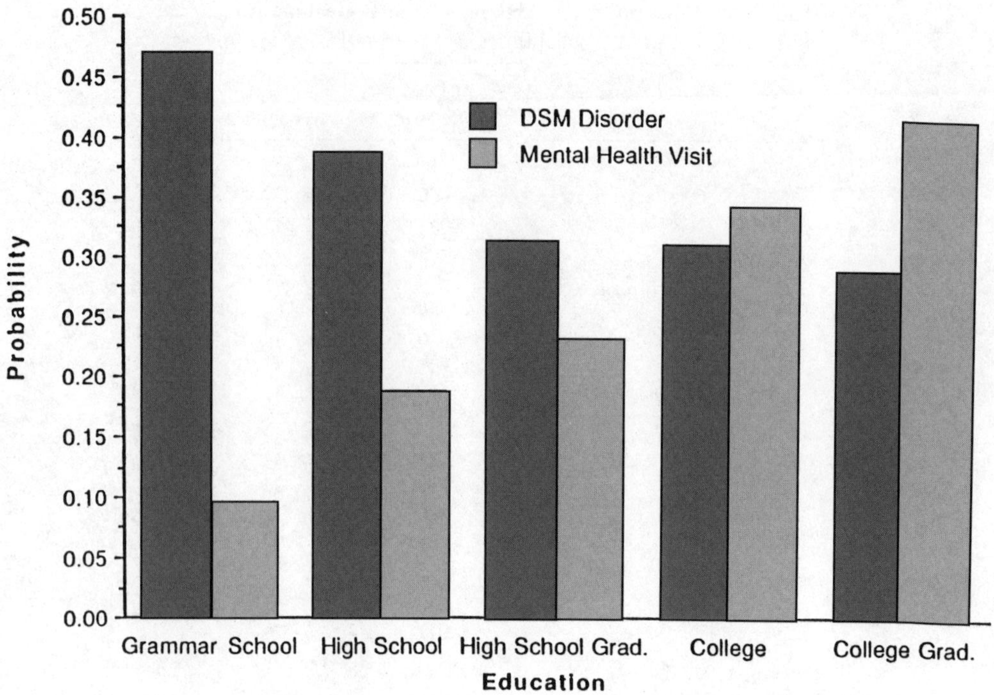

Figure 7.1 Probabilities of having a psychiatric disorder and making a mental health visit by level of education.

The second step is deciding that seeking professional mental health help would be an appropriate way to try to solve the problem, and this is clearly related to, but distinct from, recognizing the problem. Most persons will attempt some coping strategy when faced with a problem, such as talking with friends, waiting for the problem to go away, and seeking help from medical practitioners (e.g., clergy) or even nonprofessionals (Horgan, 1985; Larson et al., 1988; Veroff et al., 1981). In other words, one must conclude that seeking professional mental health help is a distinct coping strategy. Direct support for this conclusion comes from Kessler, Brown, and Broman (1981). They reanalyzed data from four large-scale surveys and found that about 23% of persons who made both of these decisions (i.e., recognized the emotional problem and believed that psychological help was necessary) contacted a mental health professional. In contrast, less than 3% of those who did not perceive a need for professional intervention and only 0.4% of those reporting that they did not have an emotional problem made such contact.

The third step in the process is deciding to seek therapy. Seeking formal help does not happen automatically after the person has decided that doing so might be appropriate (Cohen, Barbano, & Locke, 1976). Perceived stigma about using mental health services (Farina, 1982) and a self-reliant attitude (Warren, 1983) make deciding to seek formal help, regardless of one's opinion about its appropriateness, less likely. Yates (1992) found that experimental subjects' rating of the appropriateness of professional help seeking was related to the severity of a prior, traumatic event. Thus, although generally considered to be appropriate, there do appear to be unspoken "decision rules" regarding whether one should actually seek professional help.

The final step in the process of seeking formal help is actually contacting a professional helper (cf. Kadushin, 1969). Phillips and Fagan (1981) reported that almost half of the initial appointments scheduled at a counseling center failed to appear (see also Sue, McKinney, & Allen, 1976). Garfield (1994) reviewed the research on "refusal of therapy" and concluded, generally speaking, that there is no adequate explanation for why some persons decide to seek therapy and then fail to come to either the intake interview or the first session. Actually contacting a mental health professional appears to be a distinct step that, obviously, marks the end of the help-seeking process.

In a study conducted at Northwestern University's Institute of Psychiatry (Howard, Davison, O'Mahoney, & Orlinsky, 1988), a community mental health center in downtown Chicago, Saunders (1993) explored the difficulty and time needed for therapy applicants to complete the process of seeking mental health services, operationalized as these four steps. Psychotherapy applicants ($n = 275$) completed the Process of Seeking Therapy Questionnaire (PSTQ), developed to assess therapy applicants' experience of seeking therapy according to this model. Most respondents were female (73.5%) and had had previous psychotherapy (60%), with a mean age of 32.0 ($SD = 8.4$), and almost 90% had at least some college. The first question asked respondents how long the problem for which they were seeking psychotherapy had existed. the PSTQ repeated three questions at each of the four steps: how difficult the step was; how long it took; and who, if anyone, helped them achieve it (or, at the final step, whether anyone referred them to the institute).

Almost three fourths of the respondents indicated that the problem had lasted at least one year. Results indicated that the first step in the process, realizing that there is a problem, was the most difficult and took the longest, and that subsequent steps got progressively easier and were achieved more quickly. Over half indicated that realizing there was a problem was at least "somewhat hard," and just less than half needed about a year or more to do so. In contrast, almost 64% rated that last step, making an appointment, as at least somewhat easy, and 60% had done so within a week of deciding to seek therapy. Nonetheless, it is worth noting that about 5% of the respondents had an "extremely hard" time making an appointment and the 9.5% took about a year or more to do so, even though they had decided to seek therapy. It seems that none of the steps in the process are altogether quick or easy. In some of the correlates of the process, the results indicated that distress was curvilinearly related to difficulty; that is, the least and most distressed reported having the most difficulty. Education level was related to time needed to recognize the problem; the better educated respondents took significantly longer to achieve this step.

It is increasingly recognized that the process of seeking professional help involves consulting with non-mental-health professionals and with one's social network of family, friends, and acquaintances. The ECA program explicitly recognized that this is a distinct sector of the mental health service delivery system, that is, the "voluntary support network (VSN) of self-help groups, family, and friends," and that many persons who utilize mental health services do so within this sector only (Regier et al., 1993).

There is not a clear-cut or simple relationship between informal and formal help. Research suggests that social support ameliorates stress and thus the need for formal help (Birkel & Reppucci, 1983; Linn & McGranahan, 1980). Likewise there is evidence that inadequate or deteriorating informal resources are related to seeking formal help (e.g., Goodman, Sewell, & Jampol, 1984; Phillips & Murrel, 1994). Many persons prefer informal resources, such as friends, family, and clergy (e.g., Husaini, Moore, & Cain, 1994), and such preferences may be related to ethnicity, age, and other sociodemographic factors (e.g., Narikiyo & Kameoka, 1992; Yoder, Shute, & Tryban, 1990).

The social network can facilitate the process of seeking professional help by helping identify mental problems (Gourash, 1978), by acting as an important source of information about available services (Friedson, 1960), or both. In contrast, the social network can hinder recognition of the need for help and may convey negative attitudes about mental health services. For example, Horwitz (1977, 1978) found that women were more likely than men to seek informal support and to self-label problems, and that family members were more reluctant than friends and coworkers to attribute a problem to mental illness or to refer to a mental health professional. Ginsberg and Brown (1982) examined why a sample of depressed females did not receive formal help, and they found that the initial consultants (e.g., friends) attributed the depression to life stress and advised against professional intervention.

Saunders (1995) also assessed the influence of the social network on the steps in the process of seeking treatment. Between 55% and 65% of the respondents talked with another person about the first three steps, and fully 72% sought a referral from someone at the fourth step. Who the individuals consulted at each step varied considerably. In the first three steps, when they were deciding whether there is a problem and whether to seek professional help for it, the most frequent sources of consultation were family members and friends (82–93% of respondents consulted with someone at these steps). At the fourth step, almost two thirds of those seeking a referral consulted a professional, usually a medical doctor but occasionally a mental health professional. These results suggest that one's social network of family and friends is important in helping one recognize a problem and what to do about it, whereas professional consultations are most important as sources of referral to particular clinics or practitioners.

Terminating Psychotherapy

A cursory review of the literature suggests that mental health professionals generally don't know why persons stop coming to therapy. Some patients are clearly improved and discuss termination with the therapist; the dyad then comes to a mutual decision that treatment has succeeded and should end. In many cases, however, the patient feels better and unilaterally decides to terminate treatment. Unfortunately, many patients stop coming to therapy for other reasons as well, such as ongoing or recent barriers, or because they feel that therapy is not helping. Occasionally, a therapist and patient will discuss treatment nonresponse and mutually agree that the most logical course of action is to terminate and refer to others. It is our suspicion that this happens fairly infrequently, however.

It is clear that a model for treatment termination is needed, just as a model for the process of seeking treatment has been useful. It may be, for example, that at some point in therapy patients reassess both the problem and the treatment. Perhaps at the next step, they decide that therapy is no longer necessary or is actually not helping alleviate the problem at all. The decision to stop therapy and the actual termination of therapy may be distinct (similar to Steps 3 and 4 in the process of seeking treatment). Issues as to whether the decision is unilateral or by mutual agreement need to be addressed in any such model, as does the issue of whether a dose of therapy was obtained.

Financing and Utilization of Mental Health Services

Nunez (1991) extended the work of Saunders on routes to psychotherapy by examining the influence of form of financing. He examined outpatients seeking psychotherapy at a medical-school-based psychotherapy clinic. The presenting patients, although serviced by the same therapist pool, had different forms of financial coverage. Nunez compared user members of a health maintenance organization (HMO) with users having fee-for-service (FFS) insurance coverage and those choosing to pay for psychotherapy out of pocket (self-pay, or SP). HMO users did differ from FFS and SP patients on important demographic variables. They were better educated, more fully employed, and more likely to be women. Despite these characteristics, HMO users of psychotherapy did not have an easier time deciding to seek psychotherapy. HMO members did make greater use of primary-care physicians in deciding to seek psychotherapy and in making contact with the clinic for an appointment. Self-payment patients were more likely to be unemployed or to be employed part time and were less likely to be college graduates than HMO members.

The three groups did not differ in the duration of their problems before seeking help. All three groups averaged a problem duration of about 2 years. HMO users did report themselves to be functioning better and to be experiencing less psychological distress at the time help was sought. Whereas FFS and SP users described their functioning as "so-so," HMO users were slightly but significantly better, describing themselves as between "fairly well" and "so-so." Form of financing did not influence the self-reported length of time or difficulty recognizing the presence of a problem (Step 1) or labeling the problem as psychological (Step 2). Likewise, form of financing was unrelated to Steps 3 and 4, deciding to seek help and contacting the clinic for an appointment. HMO members did expect shorter durations of treatment than self-payment patients (about 2–6 months *vs.* 6–12 months), and HMO members expected less practical difficulty ("a little difficult") than self-payment patients ("pretty difficult"). HMO patients did place less importance on entering psychotherapy and were less confident that psychotherapy would be successful than FFS and SP patients.

HMO and FFS patients did not differ in the percentage of no-shows at the first scheduled appointment (less than 10% for each form of payment), while the no-show rate of the self-payment group was about 30%. Thus having mental health benefits is more likely to result in keeping a scheduled mental health visit.

Is form of financing related to the likelihood of entering psychotherapy given a mental health visit has been made? Table 7.2 presents the therapy episode durations for psychotherapy patients having each of the three forms of payment. Slightly less than one half of all self-pay patients attended more than 10 sessions, whereas about five of every eight patients with mental health benefits attended more than 10 sessions. In summary, the availability of financing through mental health benefits was related to moving from making a mental health visit to entering psychotherapy.

Table 7.2 Treatment Duration of Patients Making at Least One Mental Health Visit by Mode of Finance

	Mode of Finance (%)		
Sessions	HMO ($n = 90$)	FFS ($n = 97$)	SP ($n = 66$)
1–10	36.7	35.1	53.0
11–20	17.7	15.4	13.6
Over 20	45.6	49.5	3.4

Several interesting observations on psychotherapy duration and financing were made by Nunez (1991). Despite exhausting mental health benefits, a significantly high proportion of patients in each payment form group continued in psychotherapy. HMO patients did not receive payment beyond 40 sessions, and FFS beyond 20 sessions. Yet about 17% of HMO patients continued in psychotherapy beyond 40 sessions, and 50% of FFS patients continued beyond 20 sessions. By contrast, 15% of self-pay patients attend more than 40 sessions, and 33% attended more than 20 sessions.

Summary and Future Directions

A service gap exists between needing and receiving mental health services. Those most in need, the least educated, are least likely to receive services. The process of help seeking has been conceptualized as recognizing a problem, deciding to seek some kind of professional help, deciding to seek psychotherapy, and actually making contact with a mental health professional. Of these processes, the first, problem recognition, is the most difficult and takes the longest, generally from 1 to 2 years. Although this process is facilitated by a social support network, there is little evidence that the form or payment source of mental health benefits influences the difficulty or duration of psychotherapy help-seeking behavior. Payment source does influence whether psychotherapy will occur after an initial visit to a mental health professional. Once psychotherapy is under way, session limitations in payment plans often are exceeded as patients elect to continue in psychotherapy.

Collectively considered, the research reviewed above has implications for health policy. Educational programs directed at recognizing the existence of problems are likely to have the greatest impact on the service gap. The Depression Awareness, Recognition and Treatment program initiated by NIMH with primary-care physicians and other gatekeeper groups in the 1980s is one example of such an effort. Elementary-school-based self-awareness programs taught by school counselors are another example. These educational programs aimed at problem recognition would best be focused on the less well educated. Beyond deciding to get help, seeking psychotherapy, and making an appointment, the presence and type of funding for mental health services influences how much psychotherapy will be delivered to meet patient needs, but not necessarily whether treatment will continue after the limits of payment are exhausted.

References

Birkel, R. C., & Reppucci, N. D. (1983). Social networks, information-seeking, and the utilization of services. *American Journal of Community Psychology, 11*, 185–205.

Cleary, P. D. (1989). The need and demand for mental health services. In C. A. Taube, D. Mechanic, & A. A. Hohmann (Eds.), *The future of mental health services research* (DHHS Publication No. ADM 89-1600, pp. 161–184). Rockville, MD: National Institute of Mental Health.

Cohen, J. B., Barbano, H., & Locke, B. Z. (1976). How biased is the tip of the iceberg? Characteristics of persons who seek help as a subset of persons who indicate they feel they are in need of help. *American Journal of Epidemiology, 104*, 323–324.

Davies, R. M., Sieber, K. O., & Hunt, S. L. (1994). Age-cohort differences in treating symptoms of mental illness: A process approach. *Psychology and Aging, 9*, 446–453.

Farina, A. (1982). The stigma of mental disorder. In A. G. Miller (Ed.), *In the eye of the beholder* (pp. 305–363.). New York: Praeger.

Freeman, H. E. (1989). *The National Survey of Access to Healthcare, 1986*. Princeton, NJ: Robert Wood Johnson Foundation.

Friedson, A. M. (1960). Client control of medical practice. *American Journal of Sociology, 65*, 374–382.

Friedson, E. (1960). Client control of medical practice. *American Journal of Sociology, 65*, 374–382.

Garfield, S. L. (1994). Research on client variables in psychotherapy. In A. E. Bergin & S. L. Garfield (Eds.), *Handbook of psychotherapy and behavior change* (4th ed., pp. 190–228). New York: Wiley.

Ginsberg, S. M., & Brown, G. W. (1982). No time for depression: A study of help-seeking among mothers of preschool children. In D. Mechanic

(Ed.), *Symptoms, illness behavior, and help-seeking* (pp. 87–114). New York: Prodist.

Goodman, S. H., Sewell, D. R., & Jampol, R. C. (1984). On going to the counselor: Contributions of life stress and social supports to the decision to seek psychological counseling. *Journal of Counseling Psychology, 31*, 306–313.

Gourash, N. (1978). Help-seeking: A review of the literature. *American Journal of Community Psychology, 6*, 413–423.

Horgan, C. M. (1985). Speciality and general ambulatory mental health services. *Archives of General Psychiatry, 42*, 565–572.

Horwitz, A. (1977). The pathways into psychiatric treatment: Some differences between men and women. *Journal of Health and Social Behavior, 18*, 169–178.

Horwitz, A. (1978). Family, kin and friend networks in psychiatric help-seeking. *Social Science and Medicine, 12*, 297–304.

Howard, K. I., Davison, C. V., O'Mahoney, M., & Orlinsky, D. E. (1988). *Long-term psychotherapy: Patients, processes and outcome*. NIMH Grant Proposal. (Available from K. I. Howard, Northwestern University, Evanston, IL 60208.)

Howard, K. I., Kopta, S. M., Krause, M. S., & Orlinsky, D. E. (1986). The dose-response relationship in psychotherapy. *American Psychologist, 41*, 159–164.

Howard, K. I., Krause, M. S., & Vessey, J. T. (1994). Analysis of clinical trial data: The problem of outcome overlap. *Psychotherapy Research, 31*, 302–307.

Husaini, B. A., Moore, S. T., & Cain, V. A. (1994). Psychiatric symptoms and help-seeking behavior among the elderly: An analysis of racial and gender differences. *Journal of Gerontological Social Work, 21*, 177–196.

Kadushin, C. (1969). *Why people go to psychiatrists*. New York: Atherton.

Keeler, E. B., Wells, K. B., Manning, W. G., Rumpel, J. D., & Hanley, J. M. (1986). *The demand for episodes of mental health services*. (National Institute of Mental Health Publication R-3432). Santa Monica, CA: Rand Corporation.

Kessler, R. C., Brown, R. L., & Broman, C. L. (1981). Sex differences in psychiatric help-seeking: Evidence from four large-scale surveys. *Journal of Health and Social Behavior, 22*, 49–64.

Kessler, R. C., McGonagle, K. A., Zhao, S., Nelson, C. B., Hughes, M., Eshleman, S., Wittchen, H., & Kendler, K. S. (1994). Lifetime and 12-month prevalence of DSM-III-R psychiatric disorders in the United States: Results from the National Comorbidity Survey. *Archives of General Psychiatry, 51*, 8–19.

Larson, D. B., Hohmann, A. A., Kessler, L. G., Meador, K. G., Boyd, J. H., & McSherry, E. (1988). The couch and the cloth: The need for linkage. *Hospital and Community Psychiatry, 39*, 1064–1069.

Leaf, P. J., Bruce, M. L., & Tischler, G. L. (1986). The differential effect of attitudes on the use of mental health services. *Social Psychiatry, 21*, 187–192.

Linn, J. G., & McGranahan, D. A. (1980). Personal disruption, social integration, subjective well-being, and predisposition toward the use of counseling services. *American Journal of Community Psychology, 8*, 87–100.

Lipsey, M. W., & Wilson, D. B. (1993). The efficacy of psychological, educational, and behavioral treatment. *American Psychologist, 48*, 1181–1209.

Mechanic, D. (1976a). Illness, illness behavior, and help-seeking: Implications for increasing the responsiveness of health services. In D. Mechanic (Ed.), *The growth of bureaucratic medicine* (pp. 161–176). New York: Wiley Interscience.

Mechanic, D. (1976b). Stress, illness and illness behavior. *Journal of Human Stress, 2*, 2–6.

Meile, R. L., & Whitt, H. P. (1981). Cultural consensus and definition of mental illness. *Social Science and Medicine Part A: Medical Sociology, 15*, 231–242.

Narikiyo, T. A., & Kameoka, V. A. (1992). Attributions of mental illness and judgments about help seeking among Japanese-American and white American students. *Journal of Counseling Psychology, 39*, 363–369.

Nunez, P. R. (1991). *HMO membership and the process of seeking therapy*. Unpublished doctoral dissertation. Northwestern University, Evanston, IL.

Orlinsky, D. E., & Howard, K. I. (1987). A generic model of psychotherapy. *Journal of Integrative and Eclectic Psychotherapy, 6*, 6–27.

Phillips, E. L., & Fagan, P. J. (1981, August). *Attrition: Focus on the intake and first therapy interviews.* Paper presented at the annual convention of the American Psychological Association, Washington, DC.

Phillips, M. A., & Murrell, S. A. (1994). Impact of psychological and physical health, stressful events, and social support on subsequent mental health help seeking among older adults. *Journal of Consulting and Clinical Psychology, 62*, 270–275.

Prochaska, J. O., Di Clemente, C. C., & Norcross, J. C. (1992). In search of how people change: Applications to addictive behaviors. *American Psychologist, 47*, 1102–1114.

Regier, D. A., Myers, J. K., Kramer, M., Robins,

L. N., Blazer, D. G., Hough, R. L., Eaton, W. W., & Locke, B. Z. (1984). The NIMH Epidemiological Catchment Area Program. *Archives of General Psychiatry, 41*, 934–941.

Regier, D. A., Narrow, W. E., Rae, D. S., Manderscheid, R. W., Locke, B. Z., & Goodwin, F. K. (1993). The de Facto US mental and addictive disorders service system. *Archives of General Psychiatry, 50*, 85–94.

Rosenstock, I. M. (1974). Historical origins of the Health Belief Model. *Health Education Monographs*, 2, 328–335.

Saunders, S. M. (1993). Applicant's experience of the process of seeking psychotherapy. *Psychotherapy*, 30, 554–564.

Saunders, S. M. (1995). *Social support in the process of seeking psychotherapy.* Manuscript submitted for publication.

Stefl, M. E., & Prosperi, D. C. (1985). Barriers to mental health service utilization. *Community Mental Health Journal, 21*, 167–178.

Sue, S., McKinney, H. L., & Allen, D. B. (1976). Predictors of the duration of therapy for clients in the community mental health system. *Community Mental Health Journal, 12*, 365–375.

Taube, C. A., Kessler, L. G., & Feuerberg, M. (1984). Utilization and expenditures for ambulatory mental health care during 1980. *National Medical Care Utilization and Expenditure Survey*, Data Report 5. U. S. Department of Health and Human Services.

Veroff, J., Douvan, E., & Kulka, R. A. (1981). *The Inner-American: A self-portrait from 1957 to 1976.* New York: Basic Books.

Vessey, J. T., & Howard, K. I. (1993). Who seeks psychotherapy? *Psychotherapy Research, 30*, 546–553.

Warren, L. W. (1983). Male intolerance of depression: A review with implications for psychotherapy. *Clinical Psychology Review*, 3, 147–156.

Wells, K. B., Manning, W. G., Duan, N., Newhouse, J. P., & Ware, J. E. (1986). Socio-demographic factors and the use of outpatient mental health services. *Medical Care, 24*, 75–85.

Whitt, H. P., & Meile, R. L. (1985). Alignment, magnification and snowballing processes in the definition of symptoms of mental illness. *Social Forces, 63*, 682–697.

Yates, S. (1992). Lay attributions about distress after a natural disaster. *Personality & Social Psychology Bulletin, 18*, 217–222.

Yoder, C. Y., Shute, G. E., & Tryban, G. M. (1990). Community recognition of objective and subjective characteristics of depression. *American Journal of Community Psychology, 18*, 547–566.

Yoder, C. Y., Shute, G. E., & Tryban, G. M. (1990). Community recognition of objective and subjective characteristics of depression. *American Journal of Community Psychology, 18*, 547–566.

Yokopenic, P. A., Clark, V. A., & Aneshensel, C. S. (1983). Depression, problem recognition and professional consultation. *Journal of Nervous and Mental Disorders, 171*, 15–23.

III

ASSESSING COSTS AND BENEFITS OF PSYCHOTHERAPY

The Economic Evaluation of Psychotherapy Services

8

Integrating Cost-Effectiveness Analyses Within Clinical Trials of Treatment for Major Depression in Primary-Care Practice

Judith R. Lave & Herbert C. Schulberg

The continuous rise in expenditures for mental health services and the attendant efforts to contain them have led to increased interest in assessing the clinical effectiveness and cost-effectiveness of various psychiatric treatments (Elixhauser, Luce, Taylor, & Reblando, 1993; Knapp & Kavanagh, 1992; Office of Technology Assessment, 1980). In the near future, information on clinical effectiveness and cost-effectiveness will play a larger role in guiding both coverage decisions (i.e., the services and providers to be covered under public and private health insurance plans) and clinical practice as the principles and constraints of managed care permeate the health delivery system.

Systematic dialogue on the relationships between monetary and other costs, treatment techniques and treatment delivery systems, and psychological and economic outcomes will grow increasingly critical in the years to come. Mental health researchers and practitioners need to understand economic concepts if they are to feed their expertise into the public policy debate and provide scientifically and economically sound information for state- and national-level decision makers. However, at the present time, most mental health research fails to analyze costs (Yates, 1994). With the aim of promoting that dialogue, and of helping mental health researchers to participate in it, this chapter first defines the terms *efficacy*, *effectiveness*, and *cost-effectiveness*. It then describes the types of information needed to conduct a cost-effectiveness study and presents three generic approaches for obtaining data needed to conduct research, with particular attention paid to assembling information from randomized clinical trials. Issues arising from adding a cost-effectiveness component to a clinical trial will be illustrated with a case example wherein the clinical effectiveness of standardized treatments of major depression were assessed when transferred from psychiatric to primary medical care settings.

Defining Efficacy, Effectiveness, and Cost-Effectiveness

In discussing the outcomes of treatment, it is useful to distinguish between a treatment's efficacy and its effectiveness. The term *treatment* here is broadly construed to include a range of interventions (drug and psychotherapy), settings (inpatient and outpatient), and providers (specialty mental health clinicians as well as generalist physicians). The term *efficacy* generally describes the benefits generated by a treatment when provided under ideal conditions. Measures of a treatment's efficacy are most often obtained from a clinical trial where patients are selected according to specified inclusionary and exclusionary criteria and then randomized to treatment and control groups to eliminate the confounding of patient selection factors and clinical outcomes. *Effectiveness* describes the benefits of efficacious treatments that are realized under clinical conditions in treatment settings that reflect the usual circumstances of delivering medical care.

Efficacy and effectiveness studies can also be related to the terms *internal* and *external validity*. Clinical trials are designed to have considerable internal validity; that is, they are designed so that one can be certain that the effect of the treatment under investigation can be measured. However, since clinical trials are often conducted under idealized situations, they may not have much external validity; that is, the findings observed under the experimental conditions may not be replicated when the treatment spreads into practice. Effectiveness studies have external validity. However, one needs to control for selection bias for them to have internal validity.

In recent years, the concept of treatment effectiveness has been expanded to include not only the clinical benefits obtained under conditions of normal practice, but also a much broader range of outcomes than those traditionally examined as end points in clinical trials. Thus, quality of life (Gill & Feinstein, 1994), general health (Hays, Wells, Sherbourne, Rogers, & Spritzer, 1995), and social/vocational functioning (Mintz, Mintz, Arruda, & Hwang, 1992; Von Korff, Ormel, Katon, & Lin, 1992) are now typically included as outcome measures along with the standard indices of symptomatic remission. These differing uses of the term *effectiveness* are often blurred. Sometimes *effectiveness* is used to describe clinical outcomes observed in usual practice, sometimes it encompasses a broader array of outcome variables, and sometimes its dual meanings are applied simultaneously.

Cost-effectiveness, cost-utility, and cost-benefit analyses are analytic methods that enumerate the costs and consequences associated with alternative programs (see chapters 10 and 16, this volume). These analytic methods arise from economic policy analysis and were designed to help policymakers make decisions about whether to proceed with specific projects, particularly large-scale public investment ones such as the building of dams and the siting of airports.

As applied to the health field, these methods differ in how they value the consequences of treatments. In a cost-effectiveness analysis, the basic health effects are examined and measured. Estimates are made of the cost per life year gained, the cost per life saved, the cost per quality life year gained, and so on across the treatments being compared. In a cost-utility analysis, health consequences are transformed to a utility scale (Kamlet, 1992), and findings are presented in terms of cost per quality life year gained. Some analysts define cost-effectiveness very narrowly; their analyses focus solely on programs that are designed to accomplish the same goals. Most analysts, however, view cost-effectiveness as a more generic approach that subsumes cost-utility analysis (Kamlet, 1992). In a cost-benefit analysis, all benefits and costs are measured in common units, which traditionally are dollars.

In an ideal world, all outcomes would be aggregated into a single measure (i.e., cost per quality life year gained). Thus, one could compare the cost-effectiveness of all treatment types (medical, mental health, etc.) across all categories of patients and service delivery settings, with the findings used to allocate resources among all these programs (Spiegelhalter et al., 1992). In the real world, however, researchers frequently cannot create such a unitary measure, and so the comparisons are limited to a more narrow set of comparisons. Furthermore, there are highly contentious issues, such as how to add benefits across different types of individuals (Spieghelhalter et al., 1992).

Several analysts have specified the basic steps needed to conduct a cost-effectiveness, cost-utility, or cost-benefit study (Kamlet, 1992; Lave & Lave, 1978; Office of Technology Assessment, 1982). These steps include: (a) stating the objectives of the health care technologies being assessed; (b) identifying the alternative treatment technologies being evaluated (a treatment may be assessed against the status quo, or two treatments may be compared); (c) identifying all positive and negative consequences that may result from the intervention and, to the extent possible, measuring them; (d) identifying, measuring, and analyzing all expected program costs; (e) establishing the analytic perspective (although most effectiveness analyses take a social perspective, the implications could differ depending on the payer) (Weisbrod, 1983; Weisbrod, Test, & Stein, 1980); and (f) recognizing uncertainties and conducting sensitivity analyses of the basic assumptions. Other requisite steps for cost-effectiveness studies include the consideration of ethical issues, assessment of the distributional implications of alternative treatments (the explicit consideration of "who benefits from" and "who pays for" a given intervention, with particular reference to the family income of the relevant groups) and the discounting of future benefits and costs where relevant. (Discounting is the process by which costs and benefits occurring in the future are valued in present dollars, or present quality life years, by dividing these future costs and benefits by a rate of interest.)

In general, the following three aspects of a cost-effectiveness analysis need to be stressed:

1. Cost-effectiveness studies must address *both* the resources used in providing the treatments being compared (the costs) *and* clinical and other outcomes (the effectiveness).
2. Cost-effectiveness is a relative construct. Among two competing programs, one is the more cost-effective if its costs per unit of similar "output" are lower than those of the other. However, a program that increases both costs and benefits relative to the status quo could be deemed cost-effective if the additional benefits associated with the higher costs were judged as "worth it."
3. Cost-effectiveness and cost saving are distinct, rather than synonymous, concepts. Thus, a treatment producing outcomes identical to the status quo but at lowered costs would indeed be both cost saving and cost-effective. However, an intervention that both increased costs and improved outcomes relative to the status quo would not save costs but would be cost-effective if its marginal-cost-to-marginal-benefit ratio were similar to that of other ongoing programs. In this case, the marginal costs are the additional costs incurred as a result of the program, and the marginal benefits are the additional ones associated with the treatment. (This point relates to the preceding one.)

Data Sources for Cost-Effectiveness Studies

There is a range of approaches to conducting cost-effectiveness studies (Kossirer & Angell, 1994). At one extreme are the studies that rely entirely on secondary data assembled from various sources such as expert opinion and the pertinent findings of other investigators. At the other extreme are self-contained cost-effectiveness studies that gather primary data on the costs and consequences of the treatments under consideration. The full range of methodologies includes database studies, case control studies, pre-post studies, prospective cohort studies, and randomized clinical trials. Thus, researchers can select from among several approaches for obtaining information on the clinical effectiveness and cost-effectiveness of different treatments. We now consider advantages and disadvantages of the following three methodologies: database studies, prospective cohort studies, and randomized clinical trials.

Database Studies

The cost-effectiveness of alternative treatments for a given illness may be analyzed through claims files contained in large administrative databases such as those of Medicare and commercial insurance firms. The researcher must use the diagnoses entered in the claims data to identify comparable patient groups that have received different treatments and then use information embedded in subsequent claims to identify outcomes. This approach has been applied more frequently in studies of somatic than in studies of psychiatric disorders. For example, McClellan, McNeil, and Newhouse (1994) used data from the Medicare administrative files to assess the clinical effectiveness of invasive cardiac procedures following an acute myocardial infarction (i.e., whether they led to increased life expectancy).

Mental health services researchers have applied claims data information in studying whether utilization of mental health services leads to decreased caregiving costs (i.e., to determine whether mental health services may be cost-saving, also known as "cost offset," approaches; see chapter 11, this volume). For example, Schlesinger, Mumford, Glass, Patrick, and Sharfstein (1983) used insurance claims data from the Blue Cross/Blue Shield Plan for Federal Employees to identify cohorts that did and did not receive mental health treatment during a particular time period, as well as their patterns of health services utilization in subsequent years. These researchers found that use of physical health services decreased after mental health treatment. However, it is impossible to ascribe the differential utilization patterns to the receipt of mental health services since the two groups may have differed in significant ways.

There are several advantages of claims-based research. These administrative claims data usually contain huge numbers of observations. There is no respondent burden, and the cost per study case is very low. However, research making such use of claims data is both in its infancy and very controversial since it encounters difficulty controlling for possible bias in the patient selection process. It is very difficult to use these data in assembling comparable cohorts, that is, patients with similar levels of illness who would be expected to act like each other. Thus, patients who visit primary-care physicians for help with depression may differ in some fundamental demographic or clinical characteristic from those who visit psychiatrists, even after controlling for level of present depressive severity (Schulberg et al., 1991). Furthermore, it is difficult to use claims data to measure meaningful mental health outcomes. Survival or mortality, which is a major outcome for some medical treatments and which is easily determined through claims data, is of less importance to researchers dealing with chronic psychiatric conditions. Finally, many of the mental health services provided people with insurance coverage may not be captured in the insurance claims data base, for example, when physicians obscure a psychiatric diagnosis (Rost, Smith, Matthews, & Guise, 1994). Researchers seeking to measure all utilization and costs of services associated with psychiatric treatment through an extant database, therefore, may be limited in their ability to derive valid conclusions. On balance, claims data have limited value in the study of the clinical effectiveness and cost-effectiveness of mental health services.

Cohort Studies

Prospective cohort studies select individuals manifesting particular characteristics and observe them over specified periods of time. The investigator can build a data collection strategy into well-designed prospective research (e.g., the RAND Medical Outcomes Study; Tarlov et al., 1989) to ensure that standardized outcome measurements are obtained, standardized coding systems are used, and the relevant cost data are collected. When study patients receive different treatments, the costs and outcomes associated with each intervention can be measured and analyzed.

Prospective cohort studies have several methodological and practical strengths. First, as noted above, the research can readily be designed to collect information on both costs and outcomes. Second, since service utilization and outcomes are being observed under conditions of routine practice, cohort studies provide information which is more generalizable than that obtained under the more artificial conditions of a clinical trial. Third, cohort studies typically can be conducted at lower costs than clinical trials. Fourth, all individuals are assessed by the researchers at the beginning of the study period. For much research, this means that accurate diagnostic information (independent of clinician diagnosis) is available. Despite these advantages, the validity of conclusions to be drawn from cohort studies is constrained by potential selection biases. While the relative effectiveness of two treatments is determined by statistical methods that define groups of comparable patients and measure their differential outcomes, the statistical methods may fail to account for unassessed critical intergroup variations. For example, patients who seek treatment from specialty care providers rather than primary-care providers, or who prefer medication rather than psychotherapy for treatment of a depressive episode, may differ in ways that are not captured by the study design and its analytic strategy. A recent study that examined the cost-effectiveness of mental health services provided by psychiatrists relative to those provided by primary-care physicians (Sturm & Wells, 1995) is an excellent illustration of using modern statistical techniques to control for selection bias.

Clinical Trials

A third major data source in studying cost-effectiveness is the randomized clinical trial. The basic advantage of the clinical trial is that it avoids or limits various threats to the validity of its findings, for example, subject selection bias and the confounding of treatment and outcome variables (Grof, 1994). (However, there may be some bias with respect to which patients choose to enter a trial; Heckman & Smith, 1995). One can conceptually distinguish clinical trials that seek to determine the efficacy of treatment and those explicitly assessing a treatment's clinical and cost-effectiveness. Despite their methodological sophistication, randomized clinical trials of cost-effectiveness are rarely undertaken given their high cost and design complexities (Adams, McCall, Gray, Orza, & Chalmers, 1992; Strain, Hammer, & Fulop, 1994).

Researchers can augment a clinical trial in various ways to obtain the information needed for a cost-effectiveness analyses. The outcomes examined should be expanded to include measures of quality of life, general functioning, labor force participation, ability to perform usual activities, and so forth. Furthermore, at a minimum, the researcher should collect information on the use and cost of studied treatments, as well as other relevant services that are used concurrently or subsequently. Since many have hypothesized that the use of mental health services leads to decreased utilization of physical health services (i.e., that there is a cost offset effect), information should be gathered on the use and cost of physical health services prior and subsequent to the psychiatric intervention.

Adding cost-effectiveness components to clinical trials has several advantages. First and foremost, observed outcomes are most likely to be related to the treatment. Second, quality of the outcome information should be high. Third, the additional costs of the cost-effectiveness component are relatively small compared to the cost of the trial itself, since much of the information needed to assess cost-effectiveness is also needed to evaluate clinical and other outcomes.

It should be emphasized that this research augmentation strategy has several disadvantages as well. First, a cost-effectiveness component increases the data-gathering complexity of the clinical trial and could possibly lead to problems in conducting it. (For example, if the additional information needed for the cost-effectiveness components contributes to significant respondent burden, then the quality of the data for the trial per se could suffer.) Second, since most randomized clinical trials are of the efficacy rather than the effectiveness type, patients are carefully selected and the interventions rigorously standardized. The treatment size effects, therefore, may be greater than those to be observed after the intervention has been diffused into the community and delivered within routine care. Third, the sample size needed to observe significant clinical differences is likely to be markedly smaller than the numbers needed to test for cost, or even quality-of-life, differences. Therefore, a clinical trial may lack the statistical power needed to test hypotheses of specific interest to a health economist. Fourth, the addition of a cost-effectiveness component to a clinical trial brings together disciplines that are not used to working with each other (i.e., the clinical scientist and the social scientist). Each needs to understand the other's culture, concepts, methodologies, and analytic strategies. Fifth, study sections reviewing grant applications that propose to investigate clinical as well as cost outcomes may lack the expertise needed to judge the merit of research in both of these scientific domains.

Types of Cost-Effectiveness Data to Be Collected in a Clinical Trial

What types of information should be collected if a clinical trial is expanded to analyze cost-effectiveness? Economists have identified various costs and consequences associated with illness. These include (a) direct costs, which include the expenditure of specific resources used in treating the disorder, for example, physician services, hospital services, and pharmacy (included as well are the "time" costs involved in getting to and receiving the treatments); (b) indirect costs or consequences, which include the loss of productivity associated with morbidity and mortality; (c) psychosocial consequences, that is, the deterioration in the quality of life associated with illness; and (d) family burden consequences. The data collection strategy, therefore, needs to address all of these costs but must be judicious in doing so, given the expenses entailed in a comprehensive data-gathering program. (It should be noted that these are the same kind of data that would need to be added to a prospective cohort study.)

The specific types of data to be collected and the particular methods for collecting them will vary according to the focal problem under study (Hargreaves, Shumway, Hu, & Cuffel, 1998). For example, individuals with schizophrenia and major depression exhibit differing symptoms and functional limitations. Thus, data collection strategies for determining the cost-effectiveness of alternative treatments for these two illnesses also should be quite different. For instance, Weisbrod and colleagues (1980, 1983) examined a wide range of costs and benefits in their evaluation of the benefits and costs of an innovative community-based program developed by the Mendota Mental Health Institute as an alternative to hospitalization. Their approach reflects a conceptual model that acknowledges that caring for the mentally ill in communities engenders numerous expenses beyond those of the psychiatric treatment per se. Therefore, the two groups' differential use of law enforcement services and social services was included in the analysis. However, in a study of the cost-effectiveness of treatments for depression in primary care, Lave and colleagues (1998) did not collect such data, since illegal activities are rare among depressed primary-care patients. Given the low probability of such events and the major expense of acquiring data about them, such costs were not considered critical for inclusion in the depression primary-care cost-effectiveness study.

Adding an economic component to a clinical trial is rare. Adams, McCall, Gray, Orza, and Chalmers (1992) reviewed 50,000 such published trials and found that only 121 (0.2%) included an economic analysis. Moreover, they deemed the quality of even this limited body of research to be inadequate. Among the most common deficiencies identified were the investigators' failure to include some aggregated index measuring benefits, or effectiveness, and the misidentification of appropriate costs and benefits.

Adding a Cost-Effectiveness Component to a Clinical Trial: A Case Study

Designing a Randomized Clinical Trial of Treatments for Major Depression in Primary-Care Practice

By the late 1980s, the efficacy of various pharmacological and psychotherapeutic treatments for major depression had been demonstrated in numerous randomized clinical trials conducted with ambulatory and hospitalized psychiatric patients. Internists and family physicians were being urged to use these state-of-the-art interventions with their own patients since major depression has a point prevalence of 6–8% in primary-care practice (Katon & Schulberg, 1992), it produces disability resembling that of various chronic physical illnesses (Wells et al., 1989), and it generates a large economic burden for the United States (Greenberg, Stiglin, Finkelstein, & Berndt, 1993). However, the propriety of transferring these clinical technologies from the specialist to the generalist health care sector remained questionable. Earlier studies reviewed by Schulberg, Block, and Coulehan (1989) highlighted uncertainties pertaining to the etiology, nature, severity, and course of major depression manifested in patients presenting in ambulatory medical settings. This research also highlighted the absence of clinical studies regarding treatment effectiveness with this population.

Given these unresolved questions about how best to treat major depression in the generalist, as opposed to the specialist, mental health care sector, Schulberg and colleagues conducted a randomized clinical trial testing whether standardized treatments for this disorder produce better outcomes for depressed primary-care patients than does a primary-care physician's "usual care."

In brief, protocol patients were recruited for the study if they met clinical criteria for a current major depression of sufficient severity to warrant treatment in the primary-care setting, but not so severe that it required management in the mental health specialist sector, for example, if the patient was suicidal or had had a past psychotic episode. The assessment process involved the following three phases: (a) screening all patients presenting in health center waiting rooms with the Center for Epidemiologic Studies-Depression (CES-D) Scale to identify those scoring ≥22; (b) administering the Diagnostic Interview Schedule-Depression section to patients scoring ≥22 to identify those meeting *DSM-III-R* criteria for a current major depression; and (c) evaluating patients assigned this diagnosis in a psychiatric interview to ascertain that they met the protocol's inclusionary requirements and were not to be excluded for medical or psychiatric reasons. Of the 7,652 primary-care patients screened with the CES-D at four health centers, 283 were subsequently judged clinically eligible for the protocol (Schulberg et al., 1995). Almost all eligible patients ($N = 276$) then provided informed consent for a randomized treatment assignment.

The study investigated whether pharmacotherapy (nortriptyline) and interpersonal psychotherapy (IPT) delivered within treatment manual standards achieve significantly better clinical outcomes than outcomes resulting from a physician's "usual care" of major depression. Thus, primary-care physicians were rigorously trained in pharmacotherapy procedures and mental health specialists in procedures specific to IPT. All patient-doctor sessions in these two arms of the clinical trial were audiotaped and monitored by the investigators to ensure the integrity and quality of the standardized treatments. Frequent follow-up assessments conducted by blinded evaluators included administration of the Hamilton Rating Scale-Depression (HRS-D) and the Beck Depression Inventory (BDI) to detect symptomatic changes in severity of the mood disorder, as well as the Global Assessment Scale and the Medical Outcomes Study Short Form-36 to capture changes in broader functional domains.

In summary, this study included design features pertinent to the validity of both efficacy and effectiveness analyses (Schulberg et al., 1993). Procedures enhancing the former analyses (i.e., their *internal* validity) included standardized psychiatric screening and assessment procedures, standardized pharmacotherapy and psychotherapy interventions, and the administration of structured outcome measures by blind evaluators. Protocol elements maximizing effectiveness considerations (i.e., the study's *external* validity) included the case-finding strategy of screening all health center patients rather than only those patients referred by their physicians or those who spontaneously volunteered; conducting all diagnostic and treatment procedures in the health centers so that study subjects retained their identity as medical rather than psychiatric patients; and using primary-care physicians as the clinicians for two of the study's three treatments (pharmacotherapy and usual care). Given this unusual combination of design features, the study may be conceived of as an efficacy-effectiveness hybrid. Its scientific rigor exceeded that of prior primary-care treatment trials, but the generalizability of its findings did not achieve that possible in more naturalistic cohort studies.

Designing the Cost-Effectiveness Component

The randomized trial initially was stimulated by the investigators' desire to answer pressing problems in the clinical management of depressed primary-care patients. It sought to determine whether standardized, depression-specific treatments produced better clinical outcomes than the nonstandardized, heterogeneous variety of interventions utilized by physicians in their "usual care" of major depression. However, since costs varied among the three treatments provided depressed patients, it seemed critical to ask whether one approach would be more cost-effective than the others. Later reports, such as those about treatment outcome and cost variations by health care setting (Frank & Kamlet, 1990), differences in the physician's diagnostic accuracy in relation to the patient's type of health care coverage (Rogers, Wells, Meredith, Sturm, & Burman, 1993), the failure of a family practitioner's psychotherapy/counseling to significantly reduce medical costs (Richman, 1990), and psychotherapy's overall failure to document its cost-effectiveness (Krupnick & Pincus, 1992), have only reinforced the value of studying the cost as well the clinical effectiveness of treatments delivered in this project.

In adding a cost-effectiveness component to the clinical trial, the data collection strategy was expanded in two directions. First, the clinical outcome measures already being assessed were expanded to include the number of restricted-activity days reported by patients before and after they were randomized to one of the study's three treatment conditions. (Broadhead, Blazer, George, & Tse, 1990, had found this rate to differ significantly among the Epidemiologic Catchment Area program sample in relation to degree of depressive symptomatology.) Second, a strategy was developed to gather information on the patients' use of health care services. Information on the use of protocol-related services was obtained from the clinical trial's study team. Information on the use of other services inside the participating health centers was obtained from administrative records; information on the use of services outside the health centers was obtained through patient questionnaires. (The decision was made not to examine claims data filed by study subjects with health insurance companies or with the state Medicaid program since this process would generate a very mixed yield. Some patients were uninsured, data were lacking for others, and the remainder had a wide variety of third-party coverage.) The health service utilization data included use of mental health services (outside the protocol), use of physical health services, hospitalizations, emergency room use, and participation in peer-support services.

As noted earlier, adding cost-effectiveness research to a randomized clinical trial is relatively efficient, since many of the needed tasks are budgeted within the clinical investigation. In this case, adding the cost-effective component to the clinical trial increased the project's total cost by 20%. However, a key reason for the rather high costs of the cost-effectiveness component is that it extended the follow-up period by a year. Thus, the randomized clinical trial supported follow-up assessments through the 8-month period of acute and maintenance treatments, while the cost-effectiveness research supported follow-up assessments at 12 and 18 months postrandomization. The cost-effectiveness follow-up period was extended for two interrelated reasons: (a) Studies of the effect of treatment for major depressive disorder (MDD) frequently assess patients at 18 months to determine whether there is a relapse or early recurrence of the disease (Coryell, Endicott, & Keller, 1990; Frank, Kupfer, & Perel, 1989; McLean & Hakistan, 1990), and (b) researchers of the offset effect argue that patients should be followed for more than 12 months after psychiatric treatment is initiated to determine its true impact (Hankin, Kessler, Goldberg, Steinwachs, & Starfield, 1983). Table 8.1 summarizes the types and sources of data pertinent to the cost-effectiveness analyses and distinguishes data available through the clinical trial from those collected for the health economics research.

Table 8.1 Information Source for Cost-Effectiveness Study

	Clinical Trial	Cost-Effectiveness Component
Utilization		
IPT sessions	X	
Drug management sessions	X	
Blood draws	X	
Physical health services		X
Specialty mental health services		X
Health status		
Hamilton Depression	X	
Medical Outcomes SF-36	X	
Drug side effects	X	
Global Activity Score	X	
Beck Depression Inventory	X	
Restricted activity days		X

Implementing the Cost-Effectiveness Component

Which of the generic problems associated with adding an economic component to a clinical trial that we discussed above did we encounter? What has been our experience in implementing such research, and what issues will require consideration when we move to the data analysis phase of our work?

We encountered relatively few problems with respect to incorporating the cost-effectiveness data collection elements into the project's larger assessment package. Perhaps the greatest constraint imposed on our health economics data collection was the barring by health center study sites of questions to patients about their wages and income. However, since only 43% of study subjects were working full or part time at the point of randomization, it is unlikely that we would have been able to detect an effect of treatment on productivity.

Another data collection problem was that a growing number of protocol patients dropped out of treatment and were lost to follow-up with the passage of time. Furthermore, even patients who participated in the full treatment protocol did not comply with all scheduled follow-up assessments. In addition, a number of usual care patients were lost to follow-up. Such problems are familiar to clinical researchers, who have developed statistical strategies such as the random effects model (Gibbons et al., 1993) to estimate missing data points. However, these problems are daunting to health economists, who are more familiar with intact secondary data sets.

Turning to anticipated data-analytic concerns, the clinical trial's total sample of 276 patients permitted the assessment of numerous questions but not others. Thus, the costs associated with actually rendering the protocol treatments, as well as the costs associated with all other mental health treatments (regardless of who provided them), can be examined for both protocol and usual care patients. Second, it is possible to examine whether utilization of ambulatory health services, a common event, was more affected by a depression-specific treatment or usual care. However, hospitalization events, which are more uncommon, probably cannot be analyzed given the study's sample size. Other rare clinical events, such as suicide attempts associated with each of the study's three treatments and their costs to the health care system, will be impossible to analyze with a total sample of only 276 patients.

Since the data collection strategy was determined by the clinical trial, and since respondent burden was already high, a quality-of-well-life instrument (i.e., Kaplan & Anderson, 1988) was not administered, nor was utility measurement undertaken directly. Thus, creative, outcome measures that incorporate both clinical and functional variables were constructed (Lave, Frank, Schulberg, & Kamlet, 1998). Specifically, data from the depressive rating scales were used to create a measure called depression-free days. These were then transformed to quality-adjusted days using utility weights for depression reported in the literature.

Conclusion

Researchers and providers of mental health services continue to be queried about the cost-effectiveness of alternative treatments. Thus, it is necessary to expand our research models and techniques if we are to answer questions. We consider clinical trials one important source of needed data and urge researchers to expand the focus of such trials by including information about nonpsychiatric outcomes, as well as data on the cost of service delivery. The expense of expanded data collection can be controlled if it is restricted to conceptually pertinent, rather than all possible, indices of outcome and utilization. By adhering to this principle, cost-effectiveness concerns can be efficiently integrated into a clinical trial.

This integration, however, is but one step on the road to constructing improved data bases for decision making. Lingering problems include the fact that clinical trials often enroll a relatively small number of subjects, so that it is difficult to generalize from a single study. This problem should be seen as a challenge with at least two possible solutions. First, where clinically and fiscally possible, increase the sample size. Second, encourage researchers to collect a standard set of outcome measures so that findings from different trials can be assembled for meta-analyses. Despite these problems, clinical researchers and health economists should consider the strengths of randomized trials, and alternatively, prospective cohort studies to obtain information about both costs and treatment effectiveness. Such collaboration by investigators who typically have pursued independent agendas carries the potential for synergistic contributions far exceeding the value of each specialty's autonomous endeavors.

References

Adams, M., McCall, N., Gray, D., Orza, M., & Chalmers, T. (1992). Economic analysis in randomized control trials. *Medical Care, 30,* 231–243.

Broadhead, E., Blazer, D., George, L., & Tse, C. (1990). Depression, disability days, and days lost from work in a prospective epidemiologic survey. *Journal of the American Medical Association, 264,* 2524–2528.

Coryell, W., Endicott, J., & Keller, M. (1990). Outcome of patients with a chronic affective disorder. *American Journal of Psychiatry, 147,* 1627–1633.

Elixhauser, A., Luce, B., Taylor, W., & Reblando, J. (1993). Health care CBA/CEA: An update on the growth and composition of the literature. *Medical Care, 31,* JS1–JS17.

Frank, E., Kupfer, D., & Perel, J. (1989). Early recurrence in unipolar depression. *Archives of General Psychiatry, 46,* 397–400.

Frank, R., & Kamlet, M. (1990). Economic aspects of patterns of mental health care: Cost variation by setting. *General Hospital Psychiatry, 12,* 11–18.

Gibbons, R., Hedeker, D., Elkin, I., Waternaux, C., Kraemer, H., Greenhouse, J., Shea, T., Imber, S., Sotsky, S., & Watkins, J. (1993). Some conceptual and statistical issues in analysis of longitudinal psychiatric data. *Archives of General Psychiatry, 50,* 739–750.

Gill, T., & Feinstein, A. (1994). A critical appraisal of the quality of quality-of-life measurements. *Journal of the American Medical Association, 276,* 619–626.

Greenberg, P., Stiglin, L., Finkelstein, S., & Berndt, E. (1993). The economic burden of depression in 1990. *Journal of Clinical Psychiatry, 54,* 405–418.

Grof, P. (1994). Designing long-term clinical trials in affective disorders. *Journal of Affective Disorders, 30,* 243–255.

Hankin, J. R., Kessler, L. G., Goldberg, I. D., Steinwachs, D. M., & Starfield, B. H. (1983). A longitudinal study of offset in the use of nonpsychiatric services following specialized mental health care. *Medical Care, 21,* 1099–1110.

Hargreaves, W., Shumway, M., Hu, T. W., & Cuffel, B. (1998). Cost-outcome methods for mental health. San Diego: Academic Press.

Hays, R., Wells, K., Sherbourne, C., Rogers, W., & Spritzer, K. (1995). Functioning and well-being outcomes of patients with depression compared with chronic general medical illnesses. *Archives of General Psychiatry, 52,* 11–19.

Heckman, J. J., & Smith, J. A. (1995). Assessing the case for social experiments. *The Journal of Economic Perspectives, 9,* 85–110.

Kamlet, M. (1992). The comparative benefits modeling project. A framework for cost-utility analysis of government health care programs. Washington, DC: Department of Health and Human Services. Public Health Service.

Kaplan, R. M., & Anderson, J. P. (1988). A general health policy model: Update and applications. *Journal of Health Services Research, 23*(2), 203–235.

Katon, W., & Schulberg, H. (1992). Epidemiology of depression in primary care. *General Hospital Psychiatry, 14,* 237–242.

Knapp, M., & Kavanagh, S. (1992). Health economics relevant to developments in community psychiatry. *Current Opinion in Psychiatry, 5,* 314–319.

Kossirer, J., & Angel, M. (1994). The journal's policy on cost-effectiveness analyses. *New England Journal of Medicine, 331,* 669–670.

Krupnick, J., & Pincus, H. (1992). The cost-effectiveness of psychotherapy. *American Journal of Psychiatry, 149,* 1295–1305.

Lave, J., & Lave, L. (1978). Cost-benefit concepts in health: Examination of some prevention efforts. *Preventive Medicine, 7,* 414–423.

Lave, J. R., Frank, R. G., Schulberg, H. C., & Kamlet, M. S. (in press). Cost-effectiveness of treatments for major depression in primary care practice. *Archives of General Psychiatry.*

McClellan, M., McNeil, B., & Newhouse, J. (1994). Does more intensive treatment of acute myocardial infarction in the elderly reduce mortality? *Journal of the American Medical Association, 272,* 859–866.

McLean, P., & Hakistan, A. (1990). Relative endurance of unipolar depression treatment effects: Longitudinal follow-up. *Journal of Consulting and Clinical Psychology, 58,* 482–488.

Mintz, J., Mintz, L., Arruda, M., & Hwang, S. (1992). Treatments of depression and the functional capacity to work. *Archives of General Psychiatry, 49,* 761–768.

Office of Technology Assessment, U.S. Congress. (1980). *The implications of cost-effectiveness analysis of medical technology.* Washington, DC: U.S. Government Printing Office.

Office of Technology Assessment, U.S. Congress. (1982). *Strategies for medical technology assessment.* Washington, DC: U.S. Government Printing Office.

Richman, A. (1990). Does psychiatric care by family practitioners reduce the cost of general medical care? *General Hospital Psychiatry, 12,* 19–22.

Rogers, W., Wells, K., Meredith, L., Sturm, R., & Burnam, A. (1993). Outcomes for adults outpatients with depression under prepaid or fee-for-service financing. *Archives of General Psychiatry, 50*, 517–525.

Rost, K., Smith, G., Matthews, D., & Guise, B. (1994). The deliberate misdiagnosis of major depression in primary care. *Archives of Family Medicine, 3*, 333–337.

Schlesinger, H., Mumford, E., Glass, G., Patrick, C., & Sharfstein, S. (1983). Mental health treatment and medical care utilization in a fee-for-service system: Outpatient mental health treatment following the onset of a chronic disease. *American Journal of Public Health, 73*, 422–429.

Schulberg, H., Block, M., & Coulehan, J. (1989). Treating depression in primary care practice: An application of decision analysis. *General Hospital Psychiatry, 11*, 208–215.

Schulberg, H. C., Block, M. R., Madonia, M. J., Scott, C. P., Rodriguez, E., Imber, S. D., Perel, J., Lave, J. R., Houck, P. R., & Coulehan, J. L. (1995). Treating major depression in primary care practice. *Archives of General Psychiatry, 53*, 913–919.

Schulberg, H., Coulehan, J., Block, M., Lave, J., Rodriguez, E., Scott, C., Madonia, M., Imber, S., & Perel, J. (1993). Clinical trials of primary care treatments for major depression: Issues in design, recruitment, and treatment. *International Journal of Psychiatry in Medicine, 23*, 29–42.

Schulberg, H., Coulehan, J., Block, M., Scott, C., Imber, S., & Perel, J. (1991). Strategies for evaluating treatments for major depression in primary care patients. *General Hospital Psychiatry, 13*, 9–18.

Sheldon, T. (1994). Please bypass the port. *British Medical Journal, 309*, 142–143.

Simon, G., Wagner, E., & VanKorff, M. (1995). Cost-effectiveness comparisons using "real world" randomized trials: The case of new antidepressant drugs. *Journal of Clinical Epidemiology, 48*, 363–373.

Spiegelhalter, D., Gore, S., Fitzpatrick, R., Fletcher, A., Jones, D., & Cox, D. (1992). Quality of life measures in health care: 3. Resource allocation. *British Medical Journal, 305*, 1205–1209.

Strain, J., Hammer, J., & Fulop, G. (1994). APM Task Force on Psychosocial Interventions in the General Hospital Inpatient Setting: A review of cost-offset studies. *Psychosomatics, 35*, 253–262.

Sturm, R., & Wells, K. (1995). How can care for depression become more cost effective? *Journal of the American Medical Association, 273*, 51–58.

Tarlov, A., Ware, J., Greenfield, S., Nelson, E., Perrin, E., & Zubkoff, M. (1989). The Medical Outcomes Study: An application of methods for monitoring the results of medical care. *Journal of the American Medical Association, 262*, 925–930.

Von Korff, M., Ormel, J., Katon, W., & Lin, E. (1992). Disability and depression among high utilizers of health care. *Archives of General Psychiatry, 49*, 91–100.

Weisbrod, B. (1983). A guide to benefit-cost analysis, as seen through a controlled experiment in treating the mentally ill. *Journal of Health Policy Politics and Law, 4*, 808–843.

Weisbrod, B., Test, M., & Stein, L. (1980). Alternative to mental hospital treatment: 2. Economic benefit-cost analysis. *Archives of General Psychiatry, 37*, 400–405.

Wells, K., Stewart, A., Hays, R., Burnam, A., Rogers, W., Daniels, M., Berry, S., Greenfield, S., & Ware, J. (1989). The functioning and well-being of depressed patients. *Journal of the American Medical Association, 252*, 914–919.

Yates, B. (1994). Toward the incorporation of costs, cost-effectiveness analysis, and cost-benefit analysis into clinical research. *Journal of Consulting and Clinical Psychology, 62*, 729–736.

9

Measuring Psychotherapy Cost and Effectiveness

William A. Hargreaves, Martha Shumway, & Teh-Wei Hu

As more people have insurance coverage for psychotherapy, employers who pay for insurance and companies that market insurance have introduced controls on expenditures. Copayments, utilization management, capitation, medical necessity criteria, and treatment guidelines are common elements of the attempt to limit "runaway" costs. Third-party payers increasingly influence treatment choices that were once solely between client and therapist. The effects of these management techniques on psychotherapy access and outcome are largely unknown and have been a source of controversy among mental health professionals (Borenstein, 1990; Sharfstein, 1990). In particular, the very limited evidence about the relative cost-effectiveness of treatment choices in mental health care, including the psychotherapies and their alternatives, leaves clinicians with inadequate tools for shaping the management of mental health care and maintaining its quality.

Good-quality evidence about cost in relation to outcome for particular types of psychotherapy for particular conditions is essentially nonexistent (Krupnick & Pincus, 1992). The authors are aware of only two published psychotherapy cost-outcome experiments (Kamlet et al., 1995; Koran et al., 1995). In the absence of such evidence, stigmatizing attitudes about psychotherapy and its insurance coverage are widespread among policymakers (chapter 13, this volume). This is not to say that knowing the cost-effectiveness of a particular psychotherapy answers whether it should be covered by insurance plans, or what that coverage will cost. Cost-effectiveness research informs somewhat different policy questions, usually questions about the choice of alternate treatments for a particular condition.

Recent studies of cost-effectiveness of mental health treatments have focused on treatment for depression (Hatziandreu et al., 1994; Jonsson & Bebbington, 1994; Kamlet et al., 1995) and schizophrenia (Essock, Hargreaves, Covell, Goethe, 1996a; Essock, Hargreaves, Dohm et al., 1996b; Goldberg, 1991, 1994; Knapp et al., 1994; Meltzer et al., 1993). There is a longer history of cost-effectiveness studies of assertive community treatment (Bond, 1984; Bond et al., 1988; Burns & Santos, 1995; Olfson, 1990; Weisbrod, 1983; Weisbrod, Test, & Stein, 1980). Standard textbooks are available (Drummond, Stoddart, & Torrance, 1987; Warner & Luce, 1982). Several authors have recently provided overviews of cost-effectiveness methods in mental health care (Hargreaves, Shumway, Hu, & Cuffel, 1998; Knapp, 1995; Netten & Beecham, 1993; Revicki & Luce, 1995; Zarkin, Grabowski, Mauskopf, Bannerman, & Weisler, 1995).

At present, a large percentage of cost and outcomes research in mental health is being mounted by pharmaceutical firms. It is not relevant to the marketing concerns of these firms to compare medication treatments to psychosocial interventions such as psychotherapy. Governments of several industrialized nations have recently begun defining standards for cost-effectiveness evidence that pharmaceutical firms must produce regarding new compounds, further spurring commercial cost-effectiveness research efforts. These forces threaten to produce a rather unbalanced literature on the cost-effectiveness of mental health interventions.

Psychotherapy does not have a large proprietary research and marketing support base. The incentive for introducing a new psychotherapy "product" is dwarfed by the potential profit from developing another popular antidepressant. Therefore cost-effectiveness research on psychotherapy will probably depend on the interest of university psychotherapy researchers and their funding agencies. If this means that the field does not pursue serious cost-effectiveness research on psychotherapy, the public policy priority accorded psychotherapy may continue to rank near cosmetic surgery and adult recreational programs.

Approaches to Cost-Outcome Research

Terms like *cost-effectiveness analysis* and *cost-benefit analysis* are used broadly and variably, generally indicating joint attention to costs and to noncost outcomes. These terms can refer to a wide range of research designs. The gold standard is a randomized trial specifically designed to estimate relative costs and outcomes of alternative treatments under conditions of usual health care practice. In health services research, this is called a *medical effectiveness study* and is contrasted to an *efficacy* study designed to estimate the relatively short-term effects of a drug or surgical treatment on symptoms of a specific disease state. The parallel *efficacy* study in psychotherapy research might focus on cognitive and interpersonal effects on symptoms or coping strategies, comparing different types of closely monitored psychotherapy delivered by expert therapists to clients who suffer from a specific psychiatric disorder and do not have complicating comorbid conditions—in other words, what in clinical research is considered a well-designed randomized controlled trial. In contrast, psychotherapy cost-effectiveness research aims for generalizability to the clinician skills and client selection typical in ordinary clinical practice. Hoagwood, Hibbs, Brent, and Jensen (1995) have expanded on the efficacy-effectiveness distinction as it applies to research on child and adolescent psychotherapy, in an introduction to several papers that discuss issues in demonstrating generalizability of efficacious psychotherapies to usual care settings (Clarke, 1995; Henggeler, Schoenwald, & Pickrel, 1995; Kendall & Southam-Gerow, 1995; Weisz, Donenberg, Han, & Weiss, 1995).

Psychotherapy quality and client suitability are certainly relevant in cost-effectiveness research. Controls on the quality of psychotherapy in an effectiveness experiment might not be typical of current practice but would consist of quality control techniques that could be applied in usual care. Study findings would then be generalizable only to situations in which comparable quality controls were employed. If certain client characteristics were thought necessary for the effectiveness of the intervention under study, then one might measure "suitability" variables for use in the analysis but nevertheless ensure that the subject sample was representative of the range of clients seen in usual care. Findings regarding suitability may provide relevant information to consumers seeking psychotherapy and clinicians recommending psychotherapy. Further relevance to settings other than private-pay psychotherapy may be limited, unless the suitability measures can be monitored validly by a supervisor or funder, not just by a therapist or client.

Other designs than the full medical effectiveness experiment are also used in cost-outcome research. While inferences from alternative designs may be difficult, such studies may nevertheless contribute useful information. A common practice is to add cost assessment to efficacy studies. Costs may be assessed prospectively during the study or may be restricted to data that can be gathered retrospectively. A variety of quasi-experimental designs are used. Some cost studies use large administrative databases, typically with little or no information on outcome. Finally, modeling studies may be based entirely on literature review and expert opinion about treatment choice and outcome. Modeling studies, for all their limitations, may be the only evidence available during the years it takes to complete randomized medical effectiveness studies, or the only way to estimate lifetime effects of alternative treatments. Any of these research designs may be implied by the broad term *cost-effectiveness analysis*.

Regardless of design, there are specific differences between cost-efficiency, cost-benefit, cost-effectiveness, and cost-utility studies, related to the way that noncost outcomes are treated. In cost-efficiency research, one assumes that noncost outcomes are equivalent, while in cost-benefit research, one converts all outcomes to monetary equivalents. Neither model is likely to be relevant to psychotherapy cost-outcome research. In cost-effectiveness research, noncost outcomes are measured in their natural units, so this method will seem the most familiar to psychotherapy researchers. Cost utility research is an extension of, or alternative to, cost-effectiveness research in which a judgment procedure is used to scale outcome configurations into their overall subjective preferability, or utility, for the client or others who have a stake in study outcomes. Healey and Knapp (chapter 12, this volume) provide greater detail on these cost-outcome models.

Conceptual Framework of Cost Evaluation

A standard definition of cost is essential to meaningful cost analysis of mental health services. Investigators need a definition that allows accurate measurement, can be reported clearly, and can be replicated reliably. The scope of costs considered must be comprehensive enough to account for likely cost shifting among types of services and payers. The definition developed in health economics to meet these needs is called the *societal cost of illness* (Rice, 1966).

In some respects, the concept of societal cost echoes features of a widely used economic indicator of the value of goods and services produced in a country, the gross national product (Alchian & Allen, 1967) or the more recently adopted gross domestic product. The gross national product provides an index of the general economic health of a nation as a whole in a given year, a shared community value not specific to any one individual. It counts consumption expenditures, investments in production, net exports, and government purchases. It does not count unearned income such as capital appreciation, pensions, or welfare payments. It uses market prices to establish value.

Similarly, the societal cost of emotional disturbance is equivalent to the value of resources consumed or lost by the ill person and by treatment providers, government entities, or other segments of society as a result of the disorder. The terms *value* and *resources* are key and are carefully defined. *Resources* include time inputs by psychotherapists and other health care providers, medication, supplies, and space. Resources are counted in their natural units. *Value* is the worth of one unit of a specific resource. The task of cost evaluation is to identify the resources used or lost, enumerate the quantities of these resources, and assign appropriate monetary values to each resource. Then, the unit value of each resource is multiplied by the number of units used or lost, and the total cost is calculated as the sum of all resource costs.

The first task is to define the types of resources that should be counted, while considering the available data sources. For each type, the countable unit of that resource must be identified, a unit to which one will be able to assign a meaningful monetary value. For example, one needs to consider whether the unit of individual psychotherapy should be a visit or a time unit such as a quarter hour, if data sources will support either definition. One might start with a list of units used in another study of psychiatric services and tailor the selection to the target population of interest in the planned study. Some units may occur rarely and can be omitted or combined with others. Other units may be so prominent that subdividing them will help reveal the way resources are used. Unit definitions should match the units in data sources or match combinations of data source units. If a data source unit is to be subdivided, methods for dividing both the count and the value of the units will need to be developed.

It is usually more difficult to assign appropriate monetary values than to count the units of resources used and lost. Market price is the most desirable valuation. If there is a competitive market for a resource, the market value reflects the best compromise between producers' and consumers' valuations of the resource. If there is no market for a resource, we have to impute its value using other information.

It is usually useful to distinguish direct costs, the value of resources consumed, from indirect costs, the value of resources lost (Hu & Jerrell, 1991; Rice, 1966). A common way resources are lost is when someone who would ordinarily be working (thereby producing resources) is not able to work because of his or her disorder. Psychotherapy may improve work productivity, reducing the loss of economic resources. Lost work time by family members because they have to care for a disabled family member is another example of an indirect cost of a disorder.

Deciding whether a particular cost results from an emotional disorder can be difficult. For example, physical health care may or may not have resulted from an emotional disorder. Fortunately, in experimental studies, one does not need to attribute specific costs to a disorder and can instead simply observe whether a treatment under study leads to greater consumption of a resource than does the control or comparison condition. The investigator will decide to include a cost if the cost is likely to be relevant to the disorder, the cost will be at least a few percentage points of the costs incurred by the average member of the target population, and the cost could differ as a result of the treatment group to which the subject is assigned.

Avoiding too narrow a definition of cost may be

important for understanding policy implications of research findings. One usually would not want to count only a single payer's costs. For example, an investigator would not count only an insurer's expenditures on psychotherapy if the treatment innovation under study could shift cost from the insurer to the client or to some other payer. Resources beyond mental health care are usually included. Physical health care costs are almost always important, since emotional disorder is often seen to lead to increased physical health care expense. If a very disabled client population is being studied, the investigator may decide to include social service, vocational rehabilitation, and criminal justice costs, and even the economic loss of productivity due to premature death. One would also usually measure the sources and amounts of income each client receives.

Lost wages are often included as an indirect cost of illness. If psychotherapy enables clients to return to productive work or to lose less sick time from work, that is certainly a desirable outcome. Wages are the market's value placed on the production of resources through work and are included in the gross national product. Therefore, economists often include improvement in work performance as a monetary outcome in cost-effectiveness analyses, valuing increased work time at the specific wage rate for the type of work performed. Evaluating the value of work at the person's typical wage (called the *human capital approach*) reflects the value of the work to the economy (Max, Rice, & MacKenzie, 1990; Rice, 1967; Robinson, 1986). Other ways of valuing work are sometimes appropriate, especially unpaid work such as time spent by a family member in caring for a mentally ill relative. In this case, one might value this work at the typical hourly wage for a home health care worker.

Sometimes, including the monetary value of work on the cost side of the analysis raises some troubling problems. While valuing work at its market rate reflects its economic value, it may not reflect its broader social value. For example, is it three times as valuable for psychotherapy to enable an economist (or psychotherapist, or attorney) to work compared to enabling a sales clerk to work, because the economist earns three times as much? These considerations might reasonably lead an investigator to treat time worked as a noncost outcome, an aspect of effectiveness, rather than converting time worked to its economic value. If time worked is treated as an aspect of effectiveness, this is equivalent to treating the *social* value of an hour of work as equal for all persons.

Another confusing issue is the treatment of transfer payments, such as welfare payments to a disabled person or a parent's support of a disabled adult child. These are called *transfer payments* because, from a societal perspective, the payment reflects not the production or consumption of a resource, but only the transfer of a resource. That is why transfer payments are not included in the gross national product. Whether they represent a cost depends on whether one is taking the perspective of the society as a whole or of a particular payer. From a parent's perspective, support of an adult child is a cost. From a taxpayer's perspective, welfare payments are a cost. From the recipient's perspective, welfare payments are income. Note, however, that it is appropriate to consider the cost of administering welfare payments a societal cost.

This brings us to the primary modification needed in the standard societal cost perspective, namely, the addition of payers' perspectives. Policy application almost always depends on both cost and who pays. Therefore, it is good practice to record who is paying for each resource unit and to analyze costs from different payer perspectives. Often, it is important to distinguish whether the payer is the client or client's family, an employer or employer-paid insurance company, health service payers supported by tax funds, or nonhealth tax-supported payers. Among tax-supported payers, it is often of interest whether the tax-collecting authority is national, state, or local. These issues are especially important when the treatment innovation is likely to shift costs from one payer to another.

There is not a simple formula for designing cost assessment for cost-effectiveness studies of mental health services. Thoughtful consideration in collaboration with a skilled health economist can lead to methods that fit the type of service comparison, address the important policy issues, and allow replication by other investigators. Eight design principles summarize the issues we have raised about cost measurement:

- The initial selection of resource units defines the overall scope of the cost analysis one wishes to undertake. It is best to define resource units that match data sources.
- Separating the counting of units from the task of assigning values to each type of unit enables one to recalculate costs with different definitions of value, to determine whether different valuation methods alter the cost comparison.
- Market price is the preferred criterion for valuing each type of resource unit. Other methods must be used for resources that are not in a market.

- It is best not to decide in the field during data collection which instances of resource consumption are the result of emotional disorder, since such judgments can be unreliable. Instead, one decides on the types of cost to be included and records them for every subject.
- In selecting costs to include, the costs selected may go well beyond the cost of psychotherapy itself and may include other mental health services, physical health care, loss of productive time from work, school, or homemaking, and sometimes social service, vocational rehabilitation, and criminal justice costs.
- We urge investigators not to restrict costs to those incurred by only one type of payer when there could be cost shifts to other payers, and to analyze costs from different payer perspectives.

Measuring Costs: Counting Resources Consumed

We discuss six categories of cost: mental health care, physical health care, other services, family and informal care, lost productivity, and research costs.

Mental Health Care

Mental health care for most psychotherapy clients includes more than just the cost of psychotherapy itself. Clients may consume days of inpatient care, skilled-nursing care, residential treatment, emergency visits, ambulance trips, medication visits, nonpsychotherapy outpatient visits, case management hours, day services, partial hospitalization days, medication, and laboratory procedures. Data on publicly sponsored programs are generally available in existing databases maintained at the local or regional level. Such databases are desirable sources because data are collected routinely and all providers are subject to common data collection and reporting requirements. In some cases, however, existing databases may not provide the data required for a specific cost analysis. For example, if private practice activities or other private mental health programs are not included or necessary data on different components of a treatment are not available, it may be necessary to collect additional utilization data from agency records or to monitor directly the provision of treatment.

Physical Health Care

In cost analyses of psychotherapy, it is often informative to examine data on physical health care because emotional disorders and their treatment may affect medical care utilization. Some individuals seek assistance for their mental health problems from primary-care providers because appropriate mental health services are unavailable or unappealing. In other cases, mental health treatment may link clients to necessary medical services that they would not have obtained on their own. Medical treatment includes inpatient, outpatient, and emergency visits; laboratory procedures; and nursing care. The wide variety of providers, insurance plans, and payment options makes it more difficult to obtain complete data on medical care utilization than to obtain data on mental health care utilization. Data on public insurance payments can be obtained from public claims databases such as Medicaid and Medicare, and data on private payments can be obtained from private claims databases. Individual hospital or provider billing records may also be useful in some situations. Given the vast array of medical illnesses and procedures, all of these data sources tend to be difficult to access and complex and costly to analyze. Often, one seeks information about medical care use from the client, obtains signed release forms, and then verifies specific utilization through provider or insurance sources. While physical health care may sometimes be utilized because of a mental disorder, one need not (and cannot) make this determination when gathering data, so data are obtained on essentially all medical care utilization.

Other Services

Persons receiving psychotherapy occasionally utilize social or vocational services or incur criminal justice costs. Data on the costs of these resources should be collected if they are deemed relevant to the client group under investigation. Criminal justice resources include police contacts, arrests, court appearances, attorney services, jail, probation, and conservator services. Collecting data on these activities is much more difficult than collecting data on mental health or medical care. Most criminal justice agencies do not routinely generate billing or cost reimbursement data. Data are scattered at different locations, and tracing relevant records is complex and time-consuming. These records are often difficult to access and interpret, and special confidentiality rules may apply.

Data on social services, such as mental health conservatorship or guardianship, supported housing, and rehabilitation services are often collected from client interviews and/or clinician or public guardian records.

Information on sources and amounts of income can be obtained from client interview.

Family and Informal Care

When clients are seriously disabled by their emotional disturbance, they may require assistance with food, lodging, transportation, clothing, and shopping above and beyond services that treatment programs provide. Family and friends often provide this informal care. Interviews with clients or caregivers are usually the only way to collect data on this kind of resource use. Parents may also provide direct financial support. While many parents provide financial assistance to their adult children, parents typically contribute much more to offspring with a serious mental illness (Clark & Drake, 1994).

Lost Productivity

Lost productivity, which may result from emotional disturbance and is often affected by mental health care (Mintz, Mintz, Arruda, & Hwang, 1992), is an important variable to measure well in cost-effectiveness studies of psychotherapy. Information on work performance must often be gathered from client interview and not from the employer. It is important that the client not be expected to recall details for longer than a few weeks. Given the importance of this variable in studies of employed persons, it may be useful to ask study subjects to keep a diary of time lost from work, including all time formally counted as medical leave, vacation, and all other reasons. They might also be asked to note periods when any events, feelings, interpersonal conflicts, or actions by others reduce their ability to function up to their best level of productivity. They might be asked to rate the percentage of the best level of productivity they attained each workday. It may be desirable to examine the psychometric properties of work-functioning measures and adopt a common instrument in psychotherapy cost-effectiveness research (see, for example, Endicott & Nee, 1997).

Research Costs

Research costs, such as study recruitment or assessment interviews and special laboratory tests, should not be included in treatment costs. While research contacts with patients or their families may have incidental psychotherapeutic benefits, the usual practice is not to count them when the primary purpose of these contacts is research data collection.

It should now be clear that collecting utilization data can be difficult, time-consuming, and expensive. In a "medical effectiveness study" that is specifically designed to assess relative cost-effectiveness, the research cost of measuring utilization of resources is about as great as what psychotherapy investigators are accustomed to spending on assessing outcome. Useful cost-effectiveness data can sometimes be obtained by adding relatively simple cost measures to the typical randomized controlled (efficacy) trial, but this usually involves several design compromises, since the experiment may not examine psychotherapy practice under usual service conditions and with a subject population that is known to be representative of the target population that will be considered for the particular type of psychotherapy under study (Drummond & Davies, 1991; Simon, Wagner, & VonKorff, 1995).

Measuring Costs: Assigning Value to Resource Units

A crucial aspect of any cost evaluation is assigning appropriate monetary values to resource units. If values are readily available, such as unit costs of mental health services, which may be available in agency databases, then the investigator (or collaborating health economist) should review agency cost-accounting and cost-allocation procedures to determine whether the values accurately represent the true cost. If no resource values are available, then the investigator needs to impute costs. Several common issues in valuation and cost assignment arise during this process.

Charges vs. Costs

Most private sector providers and some public sector providers send bills to patients, government agencies, or insurance companies reflecting their charges for specific services. Although they are often easier to obtain than costs, charges are usually not accurate proxies for the true cost of the resources used to provide services. Charges commonly include a share of the cost of uncompensated care for other patients or reflect cost shifting between different departments in a hospital or clinic. Charges may also reflect profits to private sector providers. One provider's charge for the same service may vary from patient to patient if the provider has negotiated special rates with a government program or a private insurance plan.

In some circumstances it is possible to determine costs from charges. Many institutions prepare a Medicare cost report for the Health Care Financing Administration for reimbursement purposes, and the charge-to-cost ratios contained in these reports can be used to adjust charges to yield cost estimates. For example, if the charge for an inpatient day in a private hospital is $900 and the hospital's charge-to-cost ratio for inpatient care is 1.44, the actual cost would be $625 per day. Likewise, costs of physician time and medication can be calculated from similar standard reports, such as the Medicare physician fee schedule or actual payment data from patient claims files. If cost data are not available, payments may provide a superior alternative to charges, since payment is likely to reflect negotiation of an amount closer to actual cost than the original charge.

These important concerns about the distinctions between costs and charges may not be applicable to all of the public sector services that provide mental health care. Many public health agencies operate services directly or contract for services at cost. Thus, in some cases, costs may equal charges. However, even with such publicly provided services, there may be cost sharing and cost shifting among different departments or treatment programs, and the cost-accounting procedures used to compute costs and charges should be examined before equivalence is assumed.

Capital Costs

Capital costs are the value of land and buildings used to provide treatment. It is essential to consider capital costs because they may constitute a major cost component that will determine the balance of some cost comparisons (Cannon, McGuire, & Dickey, 1985; McGuire, 1991; Weisbrod, 1983). Capital costs are estimated by means of the basic economic principle of "opportunity cost," which is the cost of the best alternative use of a resource.

If a program rents space, capital costs do not need to be independently calculated because rent is a negotiated market estimate of the opportunity cost that is already included in the unit costs for treatment. However, when a treatment program owns the building in which it operates or is located in a publicly owned building, the cost of the space and hence the cost of the treatment are at least partially subsidized. The opportunity costs of such buildings may vary a great deal, depending on factors such as the age and location of the building. Four types of methods have been used to determine the capital cost of such a building. One could use the historical value of a building, an estimate of the replacement cost, the current assessed value, or the fair market rental price for similar space. The use of historical cost may underestimate the current value of property, while the replacement cost or assessed value may overestimate the value. For simplicity, the literature indicates that a sensible approach would be to use the regional rental price listings, such as the list compiled by the U.S. Office of Economic Development, in combination with estimates provided by community realtors (McGuire, 1991; Rosenheck, Frisman, & Neale, 1994).

Allocation of Joint Costs

Joint costs are incurred when one program or facility provides two or more distinct services—for example, day treatment and outpatient psychotherapy—and the two services share resources such as space or staff. Two general methods are used to allocate joint costs between the services that share them. One is based on the amount of inputs used (i.e., the amount of time space is used or the time spent by a clinician) and the other is based on the amount of outputs produced (i.e., the number of patients treated).

When the first, input-based approach is used, if 5% of emergency room clinician time was devoted to serving mentally disordered patients then the total cost of emergency room clinician time for these patients would be equal to 5% of the cost of all clinician time, and the unit cost would be that amount divided among the number of service units provided to mentally disordered patients. When the second, output-based approach is used, if 8% of the clients seen in the emergency room were mentally disordered then the cost of services for these clients would be 8% of the total emergency room cost, and the unit cost would be that total divided by the number of service units provided. Similarly, the joint costs associated with a case management program could be calculated by the input-based approach by computing the percentage of case managers' time devoted to a specific group of clients. With the output-based approach, the percentage of case-managed clients in that specific group would be calculated.

Some economists (Alchian & Allen, 1967; Enthoven, 1965) have argued that joint costs are not a major concern, since marginal costs—the additional cost of treating one additional client—are more important than average costs. If the marginal cost is constant, regardless of the number of units provided, then the average cost and the marginal cost are equivalent. If the use of a facility by one treatment program does not reduce the ability of another program to use the same facility, then the two treatment programs do not have any joint costs. The more detailed the information on units of inputs and outputs, the easier it is to identify and allocate joint costs.

Criminal Justice Costs

Persons with emotional disorders may have contact with the criminal justice system, and it is possible that these contacts may be related directly or indirectly to emotional disturbance. For severely ill clients, the extent and appropriateness of cost shifting between the mental health and criminal justice systems are of concern. The major challenge in estimating criminal justice costs is the complexity of the process, which can include one or more of the following types of contacts: citation, arrest, hearing, court trial, sentencing, jail, probation, or conservatorship. All of these processes may involve multiple agencies, each with its own information needs and data management systems. In one California county, a colleague of the authors obtained criminal justice data through the sheriff's office, which functioned as a central source of interagency data. Some localities prepare cost reports and cost analyses that include calculations of unit costs for different types of criminal justice contacts. Others have computerized cost-accounting systems that facilitate data acquisition.

If local cost data are not available, national estimates may be used. For example, the U.S. National Institute of Justice has estimated offender-processing costs by type of offense in five locations across the country (Jacoby, McEwen, & Guynes, 1987; Wayson & Funke, 1989). Such estimates, adjusted for inflation and regional cost differences, can be used as estimates of local criminal justice costs.

There is evidence that criminal justice costs are often underestimated because many of the initial stages of the process, such as citation and arrest, are underreported (Clark et al., 1994). Criminal justice records may be difficult for outsiders to interpret, and expert advice is necessary if these data are to be meaningfully incorporated into a cost analysis. While only a small percentage of emotionally disturbed clients are involved in the criminal justice system, several studies suggest that those few individuals who are involved incur substantial costs (e.g., Wickizer, Wagner, Atherly, & Beck, 1993). Thus, the average cost per client in a treatment program could be relatively low, but the distribution of these costs is likely to be highly skewed.

Family and Informal Care Costs

There are two approaches to valuing the assistance with daily living activities that family members and other informal caregivers provide to persons with a mental disorder (McGuire, 1991). One approach treats informal caregiver time as an indirect cost reflecting resources lost as a result of the illness. With this approach, if a caregiver forgoes competitive employment to care for an ill friend or relative, this time is valued at the opportunity cost of the informal caregiver's time. This opportunity cost is typically the wage the caregiver earns from his or her competitive employment. Such estimates correctly reflect the economic costs incurred by the individuals being studied, but there may be great variability in these estimates due to occupational, gender, and age differences in wage rates unrelated to the amount or quality of care. The second approach treats informal care as a direct cost related to treatment and values time spent providing informal care at the market value of the type of assistance provided rather than at the wage rate of the person providing the care. Wage rates for home health workers or housekeepers often provide the best estimate of the market value of these resources. This method may permit more objective comparison of treatments, because informal care provided by an appropriate paid provider could be incorporated into the cost of a treatment program.

Time Costs

There are two categories of time costs. One is the amount of time clients (and perhaps family members) spend in treatment, traveling to treatment, or waiting for treatment. These time costs would usually be considered direct costs of the illness. The second time cost is the value of productive activity that clients lose because of their emotional disturbance, which is the most prominent indirect cost of illness. In evaluating the cost of psychotherapy, the value of the time a client spends in therapy would usually be considered a direct cost of psychotherapy, and this time should be valued at the opportunity cost of that time. Thus, if the client must leave competitive employment to participate in treatment, then the opportunity cost is the client's wage rate at that job. However, if the client is not in the job market, the opportunity cost of time spent in treatment would be zero.

Lost work productivity due to emotional disturbance is an indirect time cost. The appropriateness of treating lost work productivity as an economic cost depends on the level of disability of the target population. In a study of persons who are mostly employed or have a recent employment history, one can make reasonable estimates of wage rates. In a study of chronically disabled persons, this is more of a problem, since disability that begins before individuals are fully established in the labor market makes it difficult to assign a meaningful value to their time. Given this high level of inaccuracy and variability, it may be advisable not to use typical wage rates for estimation in studies of clients who are severely disabled. Instead, investigators might use data on earnings from competitive employment and other measures of productive activity as noncost outcomes, or one facet of psychotherapy effectiveness.

Maintenance Costs

The issue of whether maintenance costs, such as food, lodging, clothing, and transportation, should be included in the costs of treatment is debatable. When clients are in jail, in an inpatient facility, or other supervised housing or treatment facility, maintenance costs are usually incorporated in the unit cost of treatment and are included in cost analyses.

There are two different approaches to estimating the value of treatment related maintenance costs. One approach is to treat all maintenance costs as treatment costs (Rice, Kelman, & Miller, 1992), and the other is to treat only a portion of the total as treatment costs (Dickey, Cannon, McGuire, & Gudeman, 1986). The justification for including all maintenance expenses is that these expenditures are an integral part of the treatment, and the amount often reflects the relative share of burden incurred by different parties (e.g., government, families). The rationale for using only a proportion of maintenance costs is that some level of food, clothing, and room expense is necessary for every individual whether healthy or ill, and only the extra costs of providing these necessities in a special setting are a true societal cost of treatment.

Maintenance costs incurred while living with family members or alone in a house or apartment are not usually considered treatment costs because these maintenance expenditures are part of daily living expenses, even for persons who are not ill. However, there are two types of situations in which maintenance costs may be considered direct costs. Costs of employing a paid caretaker to assist a client with basic daily living activities should be included. Similarly, if family members or others make extensive contributions to a client's basic living expenses, these contributions are clearly a cost of emotional disturbance and are ideally included as a family cost. However, information on the frequency and value of these contributions must be obtained through lengthy and complex interviews with family members or caretakers, so the investigator needs to consider their feasibility and value in relation to the study questions.

Transfer Payments

While transfer payments are not considered costs from a societal perspective, they may nevertheless be an important focus in a study of psychotherapy services if a large part of the target population is disabled. The cost of administering transfer payments, which can be calculated as a percentage of the payment (Frisman & Rosenheck, 1994), may appropriately be included as a societal cost. Transfer payments are a cost from the taxpayer's perspective and can be a large portion of cost for those payers. For example, Wolff, Helminiak, and Diamond (1995) found that maintenance payments and subsidies were 33.5% of total costs for a group of disabled persons with mental illness who were receiving assertive community treatment ($7,713 out of $23,061 per year in, 1988 dollars).

Discounting and Adjusting for Inflation

When evaluating treatment effects that extend over more than one year, it is standard practice in medical economic studies to adjust both costs and outcomes in later years to reflect their present value. This adjustment is called *discounting*. The rationale for discounting is that something valuable that one has today is worth less if it is not received until later (Detsky & Naglie, 1990; Luce & Elixhauser, 1990). For example, if one could earn a 6% return (above inflation) on a forgone investment, the present value of a $100 cost one year from now would be $100/1.06, or $94.34. Similarly, an outcome (e.g., relief from pain) is more valuable if received immediately rather than delayed into the future. The higher the discount rate, the lower the present value of a cost or outcome that is delayed several years into the future. In practice, health economists use discount rates from 3% to 6% and vary discount rates from 0% to 10% in a sensitivity analysis (Revicki & Luce, 1995).

Inflation is also taken into account by expressing all costs in terms of a particular base year. Cost estimates from other years are usually adjusted to the base year by use of the medical care part of the consumer price index.

Viewing Effectiveness Data

The multitude of relevant effectiveness measures and their usual low intercorrelation leads to some special problems in cost-effectiveness studies of psychotherapy. If one study group shows lower total costs and better effectiveness on most measures, policy inferences are easy to draw. But if an innovative psychotherapy is both more expensive and more effective than usual care, the analysis must give the policymaker a sense of the meaning of the increment in effectiveness purchased by each increment in investment in the more expensive service. If, as is often the case, there are many effectiveness measures, only some showing an advantage for the more expensive service, how is one to make a judgment that the improved outcomes are worth the added cost?

A common analytic strategy in previous years was to calculate cost-effectiveness separately for each outcome and allow each reader to decide which treatment is most cost-effective overall (Warner & Luce, 1982, p. 106). The influence of implicit but unexpressed individual preferences can lead to subjective and variable conclusions (Read, Quinn, & Hoefer, 1987). This limitation is particularly problematic if there are important cost trade-offs. For example, antidepressant medications may reduce symptoms or prevent relapse at the expense of unwanted or even disabling side effects. It is also possible that different stakeholders have different opinions about the acceptability of trade-offs.

A commonly proposed solution is to conduct cost-utility analyses which incorporate stakeholders' preferences in the analysis, (chapter 10, this volume). Depending on how preferences are assessed, each outcome may be multiplied by its preference weight, and all outcomes may be combined into a single composite score, or the client may be asked to make preference ratings about his or her present condition compared to alternatives. Health economists have argued that either method makes direct comparison of the effectiveness of different treatments possible (Froberg & Kane, 1989; Revicki, 1993; Revicki & Murray, 1994; Torrance & Feeny, 1989; Torrance, Boyle, & Horwood, 1982). Preference ratings may be used to calculate the effectiveness advantage of one treatment over another as an increase in what are called *quality adjusted life years,* or QALYs. The latter approach is widely used in medical effectiveness studies. However, an extensive body of research on the preference judgment process in general indicates that many respondents construct their preference attitudes during the time they are doing the rating procedure, and results are greatly influenced by the wording of questions (Slovic, 1995). Further methodological work on preference rating techniques will probably be needed before the mental health research community reaches consensus on the role of utility measures in mental health effectiveness research. Two examples of the estimation of utilities for outcome comparisons in depression are provided by the Kamlet et al. (1995) utility analysis of outcomes from a treatment experiment and the Revicki et al. (1995) modeling analysis of novel antidepressant medications.

When client preference information is not available, a structured, hierarchical approach to the analysis of effectiveness measures may be most meaningful. One might group outcome measures into major content areas, such as instrumental functioning, disorder symptoms, adverse effects problems, and life satisfaction. Ideally, preliminary analyses will have shown that the measures within each content area can be meaningfully combined into one or a few internally consistent dimensions. One might then choose one domain a priori as the most meaningful outcome. In long-term cost-effectiveness studies, one commonly gives primary emphasis to instrumental functioning and less emphasis to disorder symptoms, reversing the emphasis most common in treatment efficacy trials. One then follows the logic that the primary domain will carry the greatest weight in the interpretation of cost-effectiveness, while subsidiary analyses of the other content areas serve primarily as a check that they do not contradict the findings with regard to the primary domain.

Choosing one primary effectiveness domain does not avoid the problem that different stakeholder groups may value different domains differently. The reader should be alert for new findings about stakeholder preferences that may suggest relevant ways to examine the different domains of effectiveness. At this writing, several investigators have unpublished work in progress.

Analyzing Cost-Effectiveness

When a specific measure of cost and a specific measure of effectiveness have been chosen, one is ready to analyze cost-effectiveness. A typical analysis of cost-effectiveness uses two parallel regression models to estimate a cost model and an effectiveness model. For the cost model, cost is regressed onto a treatment assignment "dummy" variable and relevant covariates (e.g., age, gender, site, baseline cost, and baseline level of the effectiveness measure). For the effectiveness model, effectiveness is regressed on the same treatment assignment dummy variable and covariates. Let us assume that the treatment dummy variable is coded 1 for an innovative psychotherapy and 0 for usual care. In that case the raw-scale regression coefficient for treatment assignment in the cost model represents the average additional dollar cost incurred in the innovative psychotherapy compared to usual care, adjusting for the covariates. If this coefficient is significantly different from zero, we conclude that the treatments differ in cost. If it is not significantly different from zero, we cannot necessarily conclude that costs are equivalent. A specific statistical logic is needed to conclude equivalence, a logic that requires very high statistical power (Rogers, Howard, & Vessey, 1993; Stegner, Bostrom, & Greenfield, 1996). Similar logic is applied to the effectiveness model, except that the coefficient of treatment assignment is expressed in units of effectiveness. One might obtain these two parallel regression analyses from a single canonical regression analysis, providing an overall significance test on the two dependent variables (effectiveness and cost) to protect the analysis-wise significance level. Whether overall treatment effects are significant or not, confidence intervals will be estimated for cost, effectiveness, and effectiveness/cost differences between treatments.

The interpretation of the results may be clear at this point, if the analysis reveals either that the innovative treatment is not more expensive than usual care and is more effective, or that the innovative treatment is not less effective than usual care and is less costly. If we conclude that the innovative treatment is both more costly and more effective, or less costly and less effective, we then must attempt to interpret the relative cost-effectiveness of the two treatments. The ratio of adjusted mean difference in effectiveness to adjusted mean difference in cost is an effectiveness-cost ratio, an estimate of the increment in effectiveness obtained for each dollar of greater cost (or equivalently, the inverse, an estimate of the cost of gaining one unit of better effectiveness). Since this logic depends in some cases on evidence for equivalence, the simple report of a substantively important "negative" finding without discussing equivalence logic can be very misleading, especially to a reader disposed to believe in equivalent effects in the absence of evidence to the contrary.

Straightforward interpretation of an effectiveness-cost ratio requires that there be no interaction effects involving treatment assignment. Interaction effects mean that the relative cost-effectiveness of the innovative treatment depends on the level of one or more covariates (site, client subgroup, etc.). Interactions are examined by adding a set of product terms (treatment assignment by covariate) to the cost and effectiveness regression equations to test whether significant increased variance is accounted for. It is often wise to determine in preliminary analyses whether such interactions can be assumed to be small. If such an assumption is not supported, one would report this and estimate separate effectiveness-cost ratios for subgroups in order to describe these interactions with treatment assignment.

It will often be valuable to explore an alternative analysis approach recently suggested by Siegel, Laska, and Meisner (1996). An effectiveness-cost ratio is first computed for each subject and then regressed on the treatment assignment dummy variable and other covariates as above. This examines a conceptually different end point. Average effectiveness is not compared to average cost, and it is possible to examine independent variables that identify types of clients who are more cost-effectively served by the innovative treatment. While the main effect of nontreatment variables on individual cost-effectiveness reveals differential prognosis, the interactive effect of such variables with treatment assignment identifies subgroups for whom the innovative treatment is more or less cost-effective. Since the traditional cost-effectiveness analysis and the Siegel et al. variation may reveal complementary information, it may be useful to employ both. If one has adequate statistical power, it may also be informative to estimate cost functions and production functions (chapter 12, this volume).

Using Cost-Effectiveness Results

What kinds of policy questions are informed by information on the relative cost-effectiveness of two treatments? Until recently, cost-effectiveness results were thought to inform primarily the individual clinician's decision about what to recommend to clients. Dissemination of cost-effectiveness findings was seen as progressing through review articles to incorporation in textbooks and other summary recommendations to clinicians.

The widespread implementation of the variety of insurance benefit management techniques known collectively as *managed care* has changed this perception. So has the national effort to develop consensus on treatment guidelines. The managed-care environment has emerged as a strong influence on clinical decisions through mechanisms such as prior and concurrent authorization for services. Detailed public and private guidelines have been developed for this authorization process, specifying what characteristics of the patient's condition and situation should usually be present to authorize a procedure and, if these conditions are not present, what further factors should be considered in reaching an authorization decision. Few aspects of these guidelines are based on specific efficacy or cost-effectiveness research. "Medical necessity" criteria and treatment guidelines are becoming major influences on access to mental health services and therefore are a matter of public policy concern. One can anticipate that much future cost-effectiveness research will be focused on the appropriateness of specific treatment guidelines.

In the pharmaceutical industry, there is a broad perception that drug-purchasing decisions regarding newly marketed compounds are increasingly influenced by formulary decisions. Formulary committees are expected to be very aware of and responsive to empirical cost-effectiveness information about newly marketed drugs. The industry is responding by initiating cost-effectiveness research as part of the premarketing or early postmarketing development of new compounds.

These same forces are also coming to bear on the funding of psychotherapy. Authorization decisions about approving brief psychotherapy and approving additional visits beyond a brief course are already a part of managed-care procedures. This suggests that controlled cost-effectiveness studies of alternate authorization guidelines can have important effects on the availability of psychotherapy services and should be pursued vigorously as a part of the national and international investment in psychotherapy research.

References

Alchian, A. A., & Allen, W. R. (1967). *University economics.* Belmont, CA: Wadsworth.

Bond, G. R. (1984). An economic analysis of psychosocial rehabilitation. *Hospital and Community Psychiatry, 35,* 356–362.

Bond, G. R., et al. (1988). Assertive case management in three CMHCs: A controlled study. *Hospital and Community Psychiatry, 39,* 411–418.

Borenstein, D. B. (1990). Managed care: A means of rationing psychiatric care? *Hospital and Community Psychiatry, 41,* 1095–1098.

Burns, B. J., & Santos, A. B. (1995). Assertive community treatment: An update of randomized trials. *Psychiatric Services, 46,* 669–675.

Cannon, N. L., McGuire, T. G., & Dickey, B. (1985). Capital costs in economic program evaluation: The case of mental health services. In J. Catterall (Ed.), *Economic evaluation of public programs: New directions for program evaluation* (Vol. 26, pp. 69–82). San Francisco: Jossey-Bass.

Clark, R. E., & Drake, R. E. (1994). Expenditures of time and money by families of people with severe mental illness and substance use disorders. *Community Mental Health Journal, 30,* 145–163.

Clark, R. E., Teague, G. B., Ricketts, S. K., Bush, P. W., Keller, A. M., Zubkoff, M., & Drake, R. E. (1994). Measuring resource use in economic evaluations: Determining the social costs of mental illness. *Journal of Mental Health Administration, 21,* 32–41.

Clarke, G. N. (1995). Improving the transition from basic efficacy research to effectiveness studies: Methodological issues and procedures. *Journal of Consulting and Clinical Psychology, 63,* 718–725.

Detsky, A., & Naglie, G. (1990). A clinician's guide to cost-effectiveness analysis. *Annals of Internal Medicine, 113,* 147–154.

Dickey, B., Cannon, N. L., McGuire, T. G., & Gudeman, J. E. (1986). The quarterway house: A two-year cost study of an experimental residential program. *Hospital and Community Psychiatry, 37,* 1136–1143.

Drummond, M. F., & Davies, L. M. (1991). Economic analysis alongside clinical trials: Revisiting the methodological issues. *International Journal of Technology Assessment in Health Care, 7,* 561–573.

Drummond, M. F., Stoddart, G., & Torrance, G. W. (1987). *Methods for the evaluation of health care programmes.* Oxford: Oxford University Press.

Endicott, J., & Nee, J. (1997). Endicott Work Productivity Scale (EWPS): A new measure to assess treatment effects. *Psychopharmacology Bulletin, 33,* 13–16.

Enthoven, A. (1965). Appendix: The simple mathematics of maximization. In E. Hitch, & R. McKean (Eds.), *The economics of defense in the nuclear age*. New York: Atheneum.

Essock, S. M., Hargreaves, W. A., Covell, N. H., Goethe, J. (1996a). Clozapine's effectiveness for patients in state hospitals: Results from a randomized trial. *Psychopharmacology Bulletin, 32*, 683–697.

Essock, S. M., Hargreaves, W. A., Dohn, F-A., Goethe, J., Carver, L., & Hipshman, L. (1996b). Clozapine eligibility among state hospital patients. *Schizophrenia Bulletin, 22*, 15–25.

Frisman, L., & Rosenheck, R. (1994). *The treatment of transfer payments in cost-effectiveness and cost-benefit analysis*. Unpublished.

Froberg, D. G., & Kane, R. L. (1989). Methodology for measuring health-state preferences: 3. Progress and a research agenda. *Journal of Clinical Epidemiology, 42*, 675–685.

Goldberg, D. (1991). Cost-effectiveness studies in the treatment of schizophrenia. *Schizophrenia Bulletin, 17*, 453–459.

Goldberg, D. (1994). Cost-effectiveness in the treatment of patients with schizophrenia. *Acta Psychiatrica Scandinavica*, 382(Suppl.), 89–92.

Hargreaves, W. A., Shumway, M., Hu, T. W., & Cuffel, B. (1988). *Cost-Outcome Methods for Mental Health*. San Diego: Academic Press.

Hatziandreu, E. J., Brown, R. E., Revicki, D. A., Turner, R., Martindale, J., Levine, S., & Siegel, J. E. (1994). Cost utility of maintenance treatment of recurrent depression with sertraline versus episodic treatment with dothiepin. *Pharmacoeconomics, 5*, 249–264.

Henggeler, S. W., Schoenwald, S. K., & Pickrel, S. G. (1995). Multisystemic therapy: Bridging the gap between university- and community-based treatment. *Journal of Consulting and Clinical Psychology, 63*, 709–717.

Hoagwood, K., Hibbs, E., Brent, D., & Jensen, P. (1995). Introduction to special section: Efficacy and effectiveness in studies of child and adolescent psychotherapy. *Journal of Consulting and Clinical Psychology, 63*, 683–687.

Hu, T-W., & Jerrell, J. (1991). Cost-effectiveness of alternative approaches in treating severely mentally ill in California. *Schizophrenia Bulletin, 17*, 461–468.

Jacoby, J., McEwen, T., & Guynes, R. (1987). *National baseline information on offender processing costs: Source data*. Washington, DC: Jefferson Institute for Justice Studies.

Jonsson, B., & Bebbington, P. E. (1994). What price depression? The cost of depression and the cost-effectiveness of pharmacologic treatment. *British Journal of Psychiatry, 164*, 665–673.

Kamlet, M. S., Paul, N., Greenhouse, J., Kupfer, D. J., Frank, E., & Wade, M. (1995). Cost utility analysis of maintenance treatment for recurrent depression. *Controlled Clinical Trials, 16*, 17–40.

Kendall, P. C., & Southam-Gerow, M. A. (1995). Issues in the transportability of treatment: The case of anxiety disorders in youths. *Journal of Consulting and Clinical Psychology, 63*, 702–708.

Knapp, M. R. J. (Ed.). (1995). *The economic evaluation of mental health care*. Aldershot, England: Arena, Ashgate.

Knapp, M., Beecham, J., Koutsogeorgopoulou, V., Hallam, A., Fenyo, A., Marks, I. M., Connolly, J., Audini, B., & Muijen, M. (1994). Service use and costs of home-based versus hospital-based care for people with serious mental illness. *British Journal of Psychiatry, 165*, 195–203.

Koran, L. M., Agras, W. S., Rossiter, E. M., Arnow, B., Schneider, J. A., Telch, C. F., Raeburn, S., Bruce, B., Perl, M., & Kraemer, H. C. (1995). Comparing the cost-effectiveness of psychiatric treatments: Bulimia nervosa. *Psychiatry Research, 58*, 13–21.

Krupnick, J. L., & Pincus, H. A. (1992). The cost-effectiveness of psychotherapy: A plan for research. *American Journal of Psychiatry, 149*, 1295–1305.

Luce, B. R., & Elixhauser, A. (1990). *Standards for socioeconomic evaluation of health care products and services*. New York: Springer-Verlag.

Max, W., Rice, D. P., & MacKenzie, E. J. (1990). The lifetime cost of injury. *Inquiry, 27*, 332–343.

McGuire, T. G. (1991). Measuring the economic costs of schizophrenia. *Schizophrenia Bulletin, 17*, 375–388.

Meltzer, H. Y., Cola, P., Way, L., Thompson, P. A., Bastani, B., Davies, M. A., & Snitz, B. (1993). Cost-effectiveness of clozapine in neuroleptic-resistant schizophrenia. *American Journal of Psychiatry, 150*, 1630–1638.

Mintz, J., Mintz, L. I., Arruda, M. J., & Hwang, S. S. (1992). Treatments of depression and the functional capacity to work. *Archives of General Psychiatry, 49*, 761–768.

Netten, A., & Beecham, J. (Eds.). (1992). *Costing community care: Theory and practice*. Aldershot, England: Arena, Ashgate.

Olfson, M. (1990). Assertive community treatment: An evaluation of the experimental evidence. *Hospital and Community Psychiatry, 41*, 634–641.

Read, J. L., Quinn, R. J., & Hoefer, M. A. (1987). Measuring overall health: An evaluation of three important approaches. *Journal of Chronic Disease, 40*(Suppl. 1), 7S–21S.

Revicki, D. A. (1993). Health care technology assessment and health-related quality of life. In D. Banta, & B. R. Luce (Eds.), *Health care technology and its assessment: An international prospective.* New York: Oxford University Press.

Revicki, D. A., Brown, R. E., Palmer, W., Bakish, D., Rosser, W. W., Anton, S. F., & Feeny, D. (1995). Modelling the cost-effectiveness of antidepressant treatment in primary care. *Pharmacoeconomics, 8,* 524–540.

Revicki, D. A., & Luce, B. R. (1995). Methods of pharmacoeconomic evaluation of new medical treatments in psychiatry. *Psychopharmacology Bulletin, 31,* 45–53.

Revicki, D. A., & Murray, M. (1994). Assessing health-related quality of life outcomes of drug treatments for psychiatric disorders. *CNS Drugs, 1,* 465–476.

Rice, D. P. (1966). Estimating the cost of illness. *Health Economics Series,* No. 6 (DHEW Pub. No. (PHS)947-6). Rockville, MD: U.S. Department of Health, Education and Welfare.

Rice, D. P. (1967). Estimating the cost of illness. *American Journal of Public Health and the Nations Health, 57,* 424–440.

Rice, D. P., Kelman, S., & Miller, L. S. (1992). The economic burden of mental illness. *Hospital and Community Psychiatry, 43,* 1227–1232.

Robinson, J. C. (1986). Philosophical origins of the economic valuation of life. *Milbank Quarterly, 64,* 133–155.

Rogers, J. L., Howard, K. I., & Vessey, J. T. (1993). Using significance tests to evaluate equivalence between two experimental groups. *Psychological Bulletin, 113,* 553–565.

Rosenheck, R. A., Frisman, L., & Neale, M. (1994). Estimating the capital component of mental health care costs in the public sector. *Administration and Policy in Mental Health, 21,* 493–509.

Sharfstein, S. S. (1990). Utilization management: Managed or mangled psychiatric care: A review of the literature. *American Journal of Psychiatry, 147,* 965–966.

Siegel, C., Laska, E., & Meisner, M. (1996). Statistical methods of cost-effectiveness analysis. *Controlled Clinical Trials, 17,* 387–406.

Simon, G. E., Wagner, E., & VonKorff, M. (1995). Cost-effectiveness comparisons using "real world" randomized trials: The case of new antidepressant drugs. *Journal of Clinical Epidemiology, 48,* 363–373.

Slovic, P. (1995). The construction of preference. *American Psychologist, 50,* 364–371.

Stegner, B. L., Bostrom, A. G., & Greenfield, T. K. (1996). Equivalence testing for use in psychosocial and services research: An introduction with examples. *Evaluation and Program Planning, 19,* 193–198.

Torrance, G. W., Boyle, M. H., & Horwood, S. P. (1982). Application of multi-attribute utility theory to measure social preferences for health states. *Operations Research, 30,* 1043–1069.

Torrance, G. W., & Feeny, D. (1989). Utilities and quality-adjusted life years. *International Journal of Technology Assessment in Health Care, 5,* 559–575.

Warner, K. E., & Luce, B. R. (1982). *Cost-benefit and cost-effectiveness analysis in health care.* Ann Arbor, MI: Health Administration Press.

Wayson, B. L., & Funke, G. S. (1989). *What price justice? A handbook for the analysis of criminal justice costs.* Washington, DC: U.S. Department of Justice.

Weisbrod, B. A. (1983). A guide to benefit-cost analysis, as seen through a controlled experiment in treating the mentally ill. *Journal of Health Politics, Policy and Law, 7,* 808–845.

Weisbrod, B. A., Test, M. A., & Stein, L. (1980). Alternatives to mental hospital treatment: 2. Economic cost-benefit analysis. *Archives of General Psychiatry, 37,* 400–405.

Weisz, J. R., Donenberg, G. R., Han, S. S., & Weiss, B. (1995). Bridging the gap between laboratory and clinic in child and adolescent psychotherapy. *Journal of Consulting and Clinical Psychology, 63,* 688–701.

Wickizer, T., Wagner, T., Atherly, A., & Beck, M. (1993). *Economic costs of drug and alcohol abuse in Washington state.* Olympia: Division of Alcohol and Substance Abuse, State of Washington.

Wolff, N., Helminiak, T. W., & Diamond, R. J. (1995). Estimated societal costs of assertive community mental health care. *Psychiatric Services, 46,* 898–906.

Zarkin, G. A., Grabowski, H. G., Mauskopf, J., Bannerman, H. A., & Weisler, R. H. (1995). Economic evaluation of drug treatment for psychiatric disorders: The new clinical trial protocol. In F. E. Bloom, & D. J. Kupfer (Eds.), *Psychopharmacology: The fourth generation of progress.* New York: Raven Press.

10

Assessing the Cost-Utility of Psychotherapy

Mark S. Kamlet & Leah Kleinman

This chapter is intended to provide an introduction to cost-utility analysis (CUA) with special reference to evaluating mental health interventions in general and psychotherapy more specifically. While empirical CUA research to date, as applied to psychotherapy, has been relatively sparse, many of the challenges facing CUA as it pertains to psychotherapy are common across mental health care evaluation more generally.

The chapter opens with a discussion of the evolution of CUA in the 1970s, where it emerged as one of the most commonly used methods of cost-effectiveness analysis (CEA) and, arguably, the dominant approach to economic evaluation in the field of health care. The next two sections address challenges facing researchers interested in cost-utility analysis of psychotherapy when using data collected from randomized clinical trials. The section that follows discusses two recent empirical studies that highlight some of the methodological challenges to conducting CUA of psychotherapy.

The Evolution of CUA

The roots of CUA date back over 30 years. Beginning in the mid-1960s, there was growing recognition that, in addition to clinical outcomes, there are important "economic" variables that are relevant to the evaluation of health care interventions.[1] Slowly at first, then rapidly accelerating in the 1970s and 1980s, as cost considerations became more prominent in health care policy nationally, a large applied literature began to emerge that examined economic aspects of health interventions.

While program evaluation in the field of economics traditionally had depended upon cost-benefit analysis (CBA), social science researchers were, from the outset, hesitant to consider CBA the primary economic evaluation tool for health care, largely because of a reluctance to attach a dollar value to a life and a similar reticence to attach monetary equivalents to different morbidity states. In part, the reluctance was based on ethical considerations. Thus, in using either the "willingness to pay" or the "human capital" approaches to assessing health monetarily, the value assigned to a given individual's health could depend, in part, on his wealth or income level. The implication that the health (and life) of more wealthy individuals might be considered "more valuable" than those of a less wealthy individual was both ethically troubling and difficult to justify to politicians and practitioners. Ethical qualms aside, the movement away from CBA in health care evaluation also stemmed from a perceived lack of practical, yet compelling, methodological procedures by which to formulate monetary assignments keyed to specific mortality and morbidity outcomes.

Accordingly, beginning in the mid and late 1960s, instead of CBA, a range of related methods evolved for expediting economic program evaluation in health policy. By self-description, most of these approaches fall under the general rubric of cost-effectiveness analysis

(CEA). Analyses within this classification generally included an assessment of the costs of the health intervention (usually relative to some stated alternative of care), measures of health outcome(s) (again, usually relative to some alternative), and an attempt to determine whether, in light of the health care outcomes and the economic costs, the health intervention under consideration provides an adequate health "bang for the buck."

As the field began to develop, the methods employed across CEAs in each of the key aspects of economic evaluation—in determining costs, determining health outcomes, and assessing results—varied widely. By and large, most studies used basic methods set forth in CBA for measuring costs, at least in terms of so-called direct costs (those that constitute the specific medical health care resources entailed in a health care intervention: drugs, health care professionals' time, use of hospital facilities, etc.). Yet, even in the measurement of costs, there was substantial variation across CEA studies in the procedures and methods of analysis. Some studies, for example, included costs borne by all parties, while others focused solely on costs occurring to one party, or to a subset of parties (e.g., the patient, his or her family, the hospital, the insurance company, the government). Moreover, depending on the analysis, some CEA studies borrowed from the cost-of-illness literature, augmenting the "cost" side of cost-effectiveness analysis with so-called indirect costs. (Such costs consisted primarily of lost wages and the like, due to illness or to a health intervention.)

Even less uniformity was evident across studies in assessing and quantifying health outcomes. The approaches in use ranged across a broad spectrum, sometimes based on clinical measures (e.g., blood-pumping capacity of the heart), and often employing disease- and/or health-intervention-specific measures (e.g., number of heart attacks averted, number of individuals stopping smoking).

The use of clinical and disease-specific outcome measures carried a number of immediate drawbacks for CEA. For instance, it was often unclear how clinical measures actually related to the patient's objective experience of overall health. Additionally, the use of different clinical measures across varied illness domains rendered resulting CEAs incomparable. If blood pressure, for example, is used as a clinical outcome measure in a CEA for hypertension, and a Hamilton Depression Index score is used as a clinical outcome measure for CEA in depression, there is little hope of comparing the cost-effectiveness of a given health intervention for hypertension with that of a given treatment for depression.

A final deficiency of clinical measures for CEA stemmed from the fact that the health state associated with any given illness or health intervention generally spans a range of clinical measures. This is especially the case when comparing interventions aimed at the same illness that may manifest different types and levels of side effects. How does one combine into a single outcome measure the effect of a treatment for schizophrenia that both has a certain level of effectiveness in controlling hallucinations, and carries the probability the patient will subsequently develop tardive dyskinesia as a pronounced side effect of treatment? In short, in terms of measurement of both costs and health outcomes, by the mid-1970s, the term *CEA* had grown to embrace a range of procedures and methods so broad and incomparable that future progress in the area was threatened unless greater uniformity could be established.

Before turning to the emergence of CUA as a particular mode of CEA in health care that attempts to overcome these difficulties, two other key trends—emerging in other fields at about the same time as CEA was becoming prominent in health care—are deserving of mention. First was the recognition in health psychology that in considering health outcomes, the individuals experiencing these outcomes care, in the end, not about clinical measures but about the impact of health outcomes on their "quality of life." While there is debate in the health psychology literature about the best way to define quality of life and to specify its component parts, there is general agreement that it includes such considerations as functionality, pain, internal peace of mind, and some aspects of the ability to interact with friends, family, and in society. Stemming from these concerns, new scales for quantitative measurement of health status emerged, such as the Sickness Impact Profile (SIP), as well as new studies, such as the Medical Outcome Study (MOS; see chapters 6, 16, and 17, this volume).

Another field of research of relevance to this discussion also developed in the 1970s, applied decision analysis (DA), and one of its special components, multiattribute utility theory (MAUT). This form of analysis is rooted in von-Neumann Morgenstern utility theory, which since the 1940s has formed the underpinning of neoclassical economic utility theory. The work of Keeney and Raiffa (1976) represents a particularly important contribution from the 1970s, which served to move applied decision theory forward, enabling it to be used as a practical tool for decision makers facing a wide range of types of decisions (where to locate an airport, what new product to bring to market, how to evaluate and compare the desirability of different health states).

As CEA evolved in the mid 1970s, along with the variety of different approaches and methodological procedures discussed above, there slowly evolved one particular set of methods that drew not only from CEA but from the concurrent work in health psychology and applied decision theory. Best set forth at the time by Weinstein and Stason (1977), the approach was not so much new as a codification of certain procedures that were already evolving in CEA and its related fields. To many researchers the approach seemed to represent a way to overcome the plethora of methods then employed, as well as to surmount the problems encountered with comparability of CEAs across (and within) illness domains (see chapter 11, this volume).

The methodology proposed by Weinstein and Stason relied on cost-benefit analysis, as had most methods in CEA, for its definition and measurement of costs. It also adopted from CBA the "societal" perspective, wherein all costs are considered, regardless of who bears them. For health outcomes, the recommended approach introduced the concept of quality-adjusted life years (QALYs), which united within one metric both morbidity and mortality considerations. This outcome measure could be made consistent with von-Neumann Morgenstern utility theory (Pliskin, Shepard, & Weinstein, 1980), at least under certain assumptions. It also shared much with the emphasis found in the health psychology literature on health outcomes' properly reflecting impacts on quality of life. The approach set forth allowed, in principle, for the comparison of virtually any health interventions, providing a common scale that might apply to interventions dealing with heart attacks, cancer, or mental illness.

The key outcome of a cost-effectiveness study, as defined by Weinstein and Stason, was a ratio, the so-called cost-effectiveness (or cost-utility) ratio. The numerator of this ratio captures the differential costs of the given health intervention under consideration (relative to a stated alternative). It is denoted in monetary terms. The denominator of the ratio measures health impacts in terms of quality-adjusted life years (again comparing the difference between the QALYs associated with the given health outcome and a stated alternative). The ratio is thus measured in dollars per quality-adjusted life year (or $/QALY). If this ratio is less than a certain threshold level, the health intervention under consideration is considered cost-effective. If the ratio is greater than said threshold, the health intervention is not considered cost-effective (see chapter 9, this volume).

In practice, rather than a strict threshold, it is often useful to consider zones for cost-effectiveness ratios. For instance, if a given health intervention (when compared to a given alternative) has a cost-effectiveness ratio that is less than, say, $40,000/QALY, then that health intervention would generally be considered cost-effective (relative to the alternative). Conversely, if the $/QALY ratio is greater than, say, $200,000, then the health intervention would generally not be considered cost-effective. A health intervention with a cost-effectiveness ratio falling between these amounts would be considered more ambiguous vis-à-vis its cost-effectiveness.

Weinstein and Stason (1977) used the term "cost-effectiveness analysis" to refer to their method. While this was certainly descriptive, by the time their paper was published the term *cost-effectiveness analysis* had been sufficiently usurped to include many other potential methods and meanings. Accordingly, the term *cost-utility analysis* has often been subsequently used to differentiate this particular approach to CEA from others.

While many features of CUA thus date back 20 years, and the roots leading to that starting point date back another decade at least, the establishment of the basic outlines of CUA by Weinstein and Stason and others in the mid and late 1970s represented more of a beginning than a full fruition of the development of CUA as a methodology of power and usefulness in health policy. In the two decades since, there has been steady progress in developing the tools by which CUA can be used in different areas of health. This has been paralleled by the steady development of common methodological procedures for use within CUA.

Nevertheless, the degree to which CUA even now exists as a methodology with "paradigmatic" status in terms of commonly accepted tools for measurement and use should not be overstated. In some respects, progress has been slower than one might have imagined, partly because CUA borrowed from several literatures and thus did not come into being with the fully developed normative underpinnings of the type that underlie, say, CBA. This has meant, among other things, that when subtle methodological issues have arisen, it has not always been feasible to "go back to first principles" to determine which methodological procedure is right and which wrong. Moreover, since the field of CUA was defined at the intersection of at least four domains—CBA, DA (and MAUT), health psychology, and clinical health policy—that did not share common approaches, definitions, or terminology, those laboring in applied CEA and CUA analysis over the years have had to learn and accommodate to each others' terms and concepts and how they relate to one another.

The reader is referred to Gold, Siegel, Russell, and Weinstein (1996) for a presentation of the state of the field of CEA and CUA in health care as of the mid-1990s. That volume reports on the recommendations and discussion of the Panel on Cost-Effectiveness in Health and Medicine, a panel convened by the Public Health Service and consisting of economists, ethicists, psychometricians, clinicians, and psychologists. It provides a set of detailed recommendations concerning methodological procedures for CEA and CUA and represents a useful consensus on those procedures, on which CUA's in psychotherapy and related areas can be based. Still, while great progress has been made in the 20 years after Weinstein and Stason in developing CUA as an increasingly practical and powerful tool of evaluation in health care, many pragmatic and methodological challenges remain to be worked out as CUA is applied in new areas. Nowhere is this more true than in its application in the area of mental health policy, which is further examined below.

CUA and RCT Data

Some of the challenges faced in conducting CUA in mental health care are shared with doing CUAs in any other area of health care in which data for evaluating health interventions come from randomized controlled trials (RCTs).While RCTs represent the gold standard for clinical research, the data collected in RCTs often are less useful than they could be for CUA. Some difficulties in using RCT data for cost-utility analysis are inherent (e.g., the limited duration of the trial), but others are not. In these latter cases, data collected under the auspices of RCTs can often be made much more useful for CUA at relatively little additional cost, given appropriate and proper planning.

Five common difficulties that frequently arise in using RCT data for CUA will be highlighted below. Each entails a basic problem in measuring the numerator of a cost-utility ratio. Lest these problems seem daunting, it is worth noting that evaluating the numerator of a cost-utility ratio is often the easier half of carrying out CUA in mental health care. Often, evaluation of the denominator is even more challenging, as discussed in the following section.

Opportunity Costs Versus Charges

In CUA costs reflect the (so-called) opportunity cost—sometimes referred to as *economic cost*—of the health care resources used in the health intervention. The opportunity cost of a resource is the value of what else could have been done with that resource if it had been used for some other purpose. So, for instance, if a psychotherapist devotes an hour to treating a given patient but decides not to charge that patient but to volunteer his time instead, the value of the psychotherapist's time remains the same as if he had charged his usual fee, because the opportunity cost of that time (e.g., using that time to treat another patient) remains the same regardless of the amount the original patient is charged.

In competitive private markets, price often represents a good measure of opportunity cost. Unfortunately, in health care, this often is not the case, since the price of goods in the health sector is not always determined in a competitive market. For example, charges made by hospitals or doctors need not be (and generally are not) accurate reflections of economic (opportunity) costs. Instead, to do a CUA, it may be necessary to keep careful records on the actual resources being consumed in the context of a health intervention, and then, to turn to other methods, using data from outside the RCT, to assign per unit economic costs to each unit of resource. Accordingly, detailed charge data collected in the context of an RCT may be of limited use, in and of themselves, for CUA and may require much untangling before they can be combined with external data sources (outside the RCT) to yield the economic cost data required.

Marginal Versus Average Costs

The proper economic cost to assign to a particular resource in CUA is the "marginal," or incremental, cost of that resource. If one is dealing with, say, syringes, which are used daily in a hospital by the hundreds, there is probably no meaningful difference between the average cost of a syringe and the marginal cost of the last syringe. On the other hand, if a hospital has 100 beds but is only using 65 of them, the average cost of the beds spread across the 65 patients will be different, in general, than the marginal cost associated with adding the 65th patient. The reason is that many of the costs associated with hospital beds are fixed costs, and as a result, adding another patient may lead to only a small increase in the overall economic costs that the hospital incurs.

Resource Use Versus Transfer Payments

One of the subtle but important distinctions in measuring costs in CUA is between resource usage and transfer payments. Transfer payments do not represent resources being "used up" in the provision of health care. Instead, they represent instances where some individual—a taxpayer for instance—transfers money to some recipient, say, someone receiving unemployment insurance.

So, for instance, if an illness leads to an individual's losing her or his job, this loss should be counted in some fashion in a CUA. The exact way this should be counted is actually a matter of substantial controversy: The job loss might be reflected in the denominator's representing one quality-of-life component (e.g., the ability to sustain a "role function" in society), or it might conceivably be counted as a cost if assessed in terms of lost wages. But one thing that is agreed upon in CUA is that the magnitude of the unemployment compensation benefits the person receives as a result of job loss is of no consequence in measuring the impact of the job loss in CUA because unemployment insurance is considered a transfer payment; that is, it is a transfer of funds from taxpayers to the unemployed individual. This is not to say that this transfer payment does not affect the recipient and the paying parties involved. It does. But every dollar that a taxpayer pays into the unemployment insurance pool (and treats as a $1 decrement) is exactly balanced by gain of a dollar by the recipient (who views it as a $1 increment). Since CUAs adopt a societal perspective, the two impacts cancel out and lead to no net "cost" associated with transfer payments in CUA.

Often, data on earnings or job status in CUAs have to be gleaned from insurance and other information collected in the RCT. Often, the insurance and financial data collected in RCTs are driven by concerns with insurance eligibility and the like, and reliable data on job status and changes in job status are not available. Similarly, earned-income data may be sparse, and it may be difficult to determine how much different members of a family unit are earning, how much of family income is earned versus transfer payments from government programs, and so forth.

Out-of-Experiment Extrapolation Versus Within-Experiment Data

In CUA, both the numerator and the denominator of a cost-utility ratio capture all impacts of the health intervention, including those that persist well into the future. While many RCTs may run for a number of years, it is still often the case that there are ramifications of the health intervention on the individual well after the RCT is concluded. For health interventions that affect chronic conditions, this impact can extend for the entire future life span of the individual involved. This is especially true of the mental health arena, where illnesses are often chronic, with episodic recurrences. Very accurate information about costs and health outcomes during the brief period of RCT are of little value for CUA if there is no ability to provide information about the relevant costs and health outcomes experienced under the health intervention (and under the alternative) for a significant period following the RCT.

Total Resource Use Versus Health System Use

In many RCTs, great attention is given to the detailed collection of data on resources born by the health care system per se. However, for CUA purposes, it is imperative that all relevant direct resource use should be measured. One of the categories of resource use often neglected in RCT data collection is that of resources contributed by the patient and his or her family. These would include not only out-of-pocket medical costs incurred by the patient, but his or her time (undergoing the health intervention), the time and costs for transportation associated with the healthcare intervention, and so on. It would also include estimates of the burdens borne by the patient's family in time, financial costs, loss of work, and so forth. Finally, the impact of an illness can also significantly affect the direct costs borne by "systems" other than the health care system (e.g., the criminal justice or social welfare system).

In all of these examples cited above, individuals coming from a clinical research tradition will doubtlessly be struck by the degree to which the concepts CUA insists upon, in measuring costs, are not representative of the types of cost data typically collected in the context of clinical studies. In fact, few RCTs are structured ex ante with a data collection strategy oriented toward the successful application of CUA. Since the financial and other data that appear on insurance forms, for instance, are typically not geared to the needs of CUA, substantial additional work and Herculean assumptions are needed before such data can be even minimally useful. Because many of the cost categories mentioned above are neglected in the course of typical RCT data collection strategies, ex post facto use of RCT data for CUA, often resemble an archaeological dig, with investigators returning to the RCT data to determine if it is possible to re-create, from fragments and incomplete data sets, the types of information CUA requires. A priority for more powerful and informative CUAs in mental health care evaluation is to consider the data needs of CUA, along with the clinical data needs, as a key component of prospective RCT data collection design (see chapter 8, this volume).

Outcomes in CUA: The Denominator

Measuring outcomes (the denominator of cost-utility analysis) is, in many instances, the most difficult challenge faced in conducting CUA in mental health. Outcomes of mental health treatments such as psychotherapy are often subjectively based on personal feelings and difficult to quantify. Moreover, treatments typically also involve outcomes on a number of disparate other dimensions in addition to internal mental state, such as ability to maintain interpersonal relationships, ability to function in one's normal role in society, and capability for self-care. Deriving a quantitative measure of health outcomes in mental health adequately incorporating these factors into a metric possessing the properties required for CUA is a dominant challenge for the field.

As discussed above, cost-utility analysis measures health effects of an intervention in terms of quality-adjusted life years (QALYs), which form the denominator of the cost-utility ratio. Several well-established generic scales exist for this purpose. These include the Quality of Well-Being Scale (Kaplan & Anderson, 1988) and the Health Utilities Scale (Torrance et al., 1982). General health as defined by the Quality of Well-Being Scale consists of three dimensions: physical activity, mobility, and social ability, plus a problem/symptom checklist. The Health Utilities Scale also consists of three dimensions: physical function, role function, and social-emotional function. The two scales were developed originally for physical rather than mental illnesses. Although mental illness may affect dimensions such as mobility or role function, it may not occur in a manner easily captured in these generic scales (see chapter 16, this volume). For example, in mental illness, a person's physical activity (e.g., ability to walk without assistance) is not usually affected; however, ability to travel freely may be impeded because of fear of others, inability to use public transportation, drive a car, and so on. In addition, mental health quality-of-life measures may need to include areas such as housing or the justice system, to name two dimensions usually not included in health-related quality of life. As a result, services researchers have chosen to develop mental-health-specific quality-of-life measures.

The majority of quality-of-life measures have been developed specifically for use with the severely and chronically mentally ill (Lehman, 1988, 1992, this volume; Lehman & Burns, 1990). Others have been designed specifically for use in program evaluation, including the Community Adjustment Form, Satisfaction with Life Domains Scale, Oregon Quality of Life Questionnaire, Lehman Quality of Life Interview, and the Client Quality of Life Interview. Each instrument measures multiple dimensions addressing an individual's ability to reside comfortably and safely in the community, and each incorporates measures of respondents' feelings of well-being. Although developed for different program evaluations, the instruments share many dimensions, including housing, family, social relations, use of leisure time, legal issues, employment, income, and overall satisfaction.

Despite their strengths, these instruments were not developed for CUA and are hard to apply to CUA. While all measure multiple dimensions, only the Satisfaction with Life Domains Scale can be summed into a single numeric score, and this is not on the 0–1 scale necessary for QALY research. Moreover, none of the instruments have been scaled, so there is an implicit assumption that the various dimensions and combinations of outcomes are equivalent in value. One method of resolving these issues draws from multiattribute utility theory, discussed in more detail below.

Two Empirical Studies

This section reviews two empirical studies that are of particular relevance for those interested in CUA of psychotherapy. The first, Kleinman (1995), is concerned with developing utility measures for a range of severe mental illnesses. The second, Kamlet et al. (1995), is a CUA of several maintenance interventions, including psychotherapy, for recurrent unipolar depression.

Utility Measure of Mental Illness Severity

Multiattribute utility theory (MAUT) permits the incorporation of the relative importance of different outcomes within the purview of a single measure (Keeney & Raiffa, 1976; von Winterfeldt & Edwards, 1986) and provides a way to describe subjective trade-offs made by individuals. In mental health, for example, such trade-offs might be demonstrated by improving family and social relationships and enhancing one's ability to keep a job through the acceptance of a certain amount of increase in medication side effects. Amounts traded off to achieve certain outcomes differ among individuals. MAUT provides methods to measure and describe such trade-offs in mathematical form, including specifying the degree of interaction among the attributes.

Multiattribute utility theory was used in a recent study, Kleinman (1995), examining preferences for results of outpatient mental health treatment for the severely mentally ill. Focus groups were held with the stakeholders involved in mental health treatment, in order to identify a comprehensive set of attributes that could be considered potential consequences of treatment. Stakeholders, including patients, providers, and family members, all participated in individual focus groups to identify outcomes they considered important. Group participants were asked about the types of treatment outcomes they valued most.

An important point in this approach to utility assessment is the fact that the groups identified all play different roles in mental health treatment. Not unexpectedly, this led to some disagreement as to the importance of various outcomes. For example, insight into illness was perceived as important by the psychiatrists and psychotherapists; however, patients, family, and rehabilitation therapists did not value insight as an important result of treatment. Behavior/symptoms were considered unimportant by many patients, who felt that "society should accept us the way we are"; providers and family members, however, viewed reductions in symptoms as possibly one of the most important outcomes.

Six attributes were chosen as reflective of mental health treatment outcomes: medication side effects, family relationships, planned and regular daily activity, social relationships, community-living skills, and behavior/symptoms. Many of these attributes resemble those used in other instruments designed to measure quality of life in the mentally ill. The final definitions of the attributes allowed preferences for amounts of each attribute to be measured on an interval scale. Each attribute was divided into incremental levels (mutually exclusive stages) reflecting a progression from best to worst.

A utility assessment was conducted with individuals with severe mental disorders (primarily schizophrenia, major depression, and bipolar disorder) and mental health care professionals (therapists, psychiatrists, nurses, etc.). Patients and providers were chosen because of their involvement in the mental health treatment, as well as their accessibility.

Six scaling techniques are commonly used to elicit health utilities: the standard gamble, time trade-off, category scaling, magnitude estimation, equivalence, and willingness-to-pay models (Froberg & Kane, 1989). All provide interval-level utilities. Because those with severe mental illness often have short attention spans and difficulty with cognitive tasks, category scaling was selected as the optimal mode in this instance. Easily understood, it provides a straightforward value technique and has been demonstrated to be valid and reliable (Kaplan, Bush, & Berry, 1979; Patrick, Bush, & Chen, 1973a, 1973b). Participants were presented with an 11-point ladder with 0 representing the worst, or least important, treatment outcome, and 10 representing the best.

The utility instrument was designed to compare and contrast two mathematical forms of a utility function. A utility function provides a mathematical way to characterize a person's overall quality of life by quantifying his or her status on each of the different attributes. It allows the different values, given to each attribute and level, to be incorporated into a single numerical entity representing overall quality of life.

The additive form is the simplest function and the one used most frequently in health utility assessment. It assumes that there are no interactions among the attributes. That is, it assumes that the impact on the overall outcome measure of a given change in any one of the attributes is not affected by the level of any of the other attributes. The multiplicative form allows for one interaction term taken to different powers to represent interactions among all possible subsets of outcomes. Other forms are possible, but the additive and multiplicative are the most popular and are used in the Quality of Well-Being Scale and the Health Utilities Index, respectively.

In this study, category scaling was used to elicit utilities for attributes and levels of attributes. Both additive and multiplicative forms of utility function were examined, and the additive form was judged appropriate. Patient and provider groups were analyzed separately, and as indicated above, their preferences diverged, both with regard to the importance of different attributes relative to one another and with regard to the utility differences assigned to different levels within several of the attributes.

The study described above highlights several difficulties with conducting CUA in the field of mental health. QALYs are measured by a morbidity measure in which, by definition, 1 denotes full health and 0 denotes death. For use in a CUA, outcome measures—in this case, the severity of the mental disorder—must be able to be converted to this type of scale. In the study being described, however, the lower bound on each attribute was set at that point at which it was judged that hospitalization would be required, not that the individual would be dead. It is not clear that the subjects would have been able to reasonably make utility assessments about worse states without changing the elicitation approach substantially. Thus, utilities elicited on scales such as the one described above must be mapped onto the more usual QALY scale before they can be used directly in a CUA.

The utilities elicited from this study were obtained from individuals with severe mental disorders, including schizophrenia, bipolar disorder, major depression, and psychosis. It is unclear whether these results would hold for those with less disabling, or different, disorders. While disease measures have the advantage of being more responsive and better able to detect small and clinically important changes unique to the disease and have dimensions easier to relate to clinical measures (Guyatt, Feeny, & Patrick, 1993), utilities generated by specific instruments cannot be used to compare outcomes across programs (i.e., community treatment for schizophrenics versus psychotherapy for the general public). Generic instruments have been developed precisely for that task.

Another challenge illustrated by this study is deciding which stakeholders' utilities should be used in an economic analyses. Patients in active treatment and mental health professionals hold dissimilar views about the importance of various treatment outcomes. An argument can be made that those who are most affected by a disease represent the most appropriate source of utilities to be integrated into a CUA, since they subjectively comprehend how functioning is impaired in various areas. However, arguments also can be made in favor of taxpayers (the general public), who bear the cost of health programs. While most members of society may not have experienced actual disability due to mental illness, they may have a legitimate role in deciding which treatments (particularly costly ones, with risky or difficult-to-measure outcomes) should be provided. Health care providers also play a role, since they are responsible for the design and implementation of treatment programs. In cases of extremely debilitating diseases, families are called upon to provide much of the day-to-day care and support. Their values should not be ignored. All these stakeholders have an interest (or stake) in the program(s) being evaluated and are important enough so that it has been argued that their interests should be considered (Edwards & Newman, 1982).

CUA of Maintenance Treatments for Recurrent Depression

A second study in the literature highlights an additional set of challenges to conducting CUA in the area of psychotherapy. Clinical unipolar depression is often a recurrent phenomenon. Those who have experienced two depressive disorders have almost a 90% chance of experiencing a third, and once the disorder has become recurrent, rates of relapse are high. Given the debilitating nature of depression and the high rate of relapse, attention has recently focused on ways to treat patients between depressive episodes. Kamlet et al. (1995) analyze three maintenance treatments for recurrent depression: drug maintenance treatment using imipramine, psychotherapy maintenance treatment using interpersonal therapy (IPT), and a combination of the two.

One immediate challenge in this study was dealing with the fact that while the RCT that was the basis for the analysis was unusually long (3 years), the CUA needed to project a much longer period of time because it needed to consider the lifetime impact of the different maintenance treatments. To do this, a relatively simple Monte Carlo simulation model was constructed, in which a patient is modeled as being depressed, not-depressed, or dead (possibly as a result of depression-induced suicide). Data from the RCT are used to model the probabilities and timings of the transitions among these states that an individual using a given maintenance treatment will experience over his or her lifetime. The details of the Monte Carlo model are not discussed here, but the lesson to be drawn is simply that in this CUA, as is the case generally for CUAs dealing with chronic conditions, there is a need to extrapolate beyond the period of the RCT itself to do the analysis.

A related challenge faced in this study was the fact that the RCT did not provide information on some of the key transition probabilities in the Monte Carlo simulation. For instance, the probability that an individual who is depressed will commit suicide was not estimable from the RCT, given its duration and sample size. In this instance and in others, secondary data were necessary to complete the simulation model that lay at the heart of the CUA.

A third challenge faced in this study was the lack of a utility-based mental health severity measure that could translate directly into a QALY format. This pertained both to assigning a quality-of-life measure to the health condition of being depressed and to assigning a quality-of-life measure to the side effects that could occur from the medication. To address these problems, secondary data were used to suggest quality-of-life values for depression based on other studies, and then sensitivity analysis was extensively employed to determine whether the conclusions of the analysis were highly sensitive to different quality-of-life values. (They were not, as it turned out.)

Last, because our understanding of the etiology and life consequences of depression remains far from perfect, a large number of simplifying assumptions had to be made in the Monte Carlo analysis. For instance, it was assumed that the only quality-of-life impacts of depression occur when an individual is depressed, an assumption that ignores the more lasting impacts on friendships, family relations, and employment relations that can occur.

In dealing with each of these methodological challenges, the analysis attempted to make conservative assumptions that would "bias" any conclusions against finding the maintenance treatment cost-effective. In this instance, the results were highly supportive of the cost-effectiveness of the maintenance treatments compared to a placebo, even with the various conservative assumptions. The study found that for the patients meeting the eligibility standards of the RCT being examined, IPT maintenance treatment of recurrent depression led to an estimated cost-effectiveness ratio that was under \$5,000/QALY, well below the typical threshold for judging a health intervention cost-effective. Because these results were so strong, the limitations in the methodology did not prevent conclusions from being drawn.

Conclusions

Treatment options for mental illness have increased substantially over the past several decades. A myriad of approaches available in the field of psychotherapy have been shown to be efficacious. In response to new treatment interventions, mental health services research has become increasingly sophisticated. It is moving from the simple measurement of treatment compliance and symptom reduction outcome rates to more routinely assessing functional skills, employment productivity, family and social interactions, coping skills, and quality of life. Policymakers are increasingly interested in the comparison of costs and outcomes across programs, in an effort to identify the most effective use of public and private resources.

CUA is rapidly becoming the predominant approach to economic evaluation in health care. The challenge to the field of the evaluation of mental health interventions in general and to psychotherapy specifically will be able to identify the costs and health benefits that should be included in the CUA ratio. This entails the identification of all costs, including those placed on the family and the employer, those incurred by contact with the judicial or social welfare system, and so on. It also requires that quality of life be measured either through the use of existing tools or via the development of new, more appropriate ones, geared to the conduct and to outcomes specific to psychotherapeutic treatment.

The "gold standard" of clinical research is the RCT. But as we have seen, the data currently collected in RCTs are often insufficient for easy use in CUA. Often, with better advanced planning, the usefulness of RCT data for CUA and other evaluation analyses could be enhanced substantially at modest cost. If this type of analysis is valued, it is important that there be an integration of economics and health service researchers in future evaluation research in the area of psychotherapy.

While CUAs have been successfully conducted in mental health research, the application of CUA to mental health and to psychotherapy is clearly in its infancy. In applying cost-utility analysis to psychosocial treatment, psychotherapy researchers face a number of absorbing challenges, some of which are shared with the evolution of CUA in health care more generally, and some of which apply more specifically to psychotherapy issues per se.

Yet, without minimizing these challenges, it is important to stress the significant potential benefits that further work in this area is likely to have. Changing social needs, cost pressures, and the development of new methods of treatment and prevention all highlight the value of identifying mental health programs that are effective and efficient. Given these pressures, it is increasingly important to be able to identify mental health interventions that are cost-effective, relative to alternative mental health interventions, and to be able to assess the cost-effectiveness of resources allocated to mental health care compared to other health domains. Cost-utility analysis is the dominant methodology designed to provide information that is useful in exactly those types of assessments, and the field has much to gain from further application in the mental health area. Accordingly, it is essential that CUAs quickly become integrated as a routine aspect of treatment and intervention research.

Note

1. Health care interventions here encompass everything from new drugs and technological procedures, to prevention efforts, health promotion activities, and organizational or institutional features of health delivery systems.

References

Edwards, W., & Newman, R. J. (1982). *Multi-attribute evaluation*. Sage.

Froberg, D. G., & Kane, R. L. (1989). Methodology for measuring health-state preferences: 1. measurement strategies. *Journal of Clinical Epidemiology, 42*, 345–354.

Gold, M. R., Siegel, J. E., Russell, L. B., & Weinstein, M. C. (Eds.). (1996). *Cost-effectiveness in health and medicine*. New York: Oxford University Press.

Guyatt, G. H., Feeny, D. H., & Patrick, D. L. (1993). Measuring health-related quality of life. *Annals of Internal Medicine, 118*, 622–629.

Kamlet, M. S., Paul, N., Greenhouse, J. G., Kupfer, D., Frank, E., & Wade, M. (1995). Cost utility analysis of maintenance treatment for recurrent depression. *Controlled Clinical Trials, 16*(1), 17–40.

Kaplan, R. M., & Anderson, J. P. (1988). A general health policy model: Update and applications. *Health Services Research, 23*, 203–235.

Kaplan, R. M., Bush, J. W., & Berry, C. C. (1979). Health status index: Category ratings versus magnitude estimation for measuring levels of well-being. *Medical Care, 17*, 501–523.

Keeney, R. L., & Raiffa, H. (1976). *Decisions with multiple objectives: Preferences and value tradeoffs*. New York: Wiley.

Kleinman, L. (1995). Preferences for outpatient mental health treatment. Unpublished dissertation, Johns Hopkins University School of Hygiene & Public Health, Baltimore, MD.

Lehman, A. F. (1988). A quality of life interview for the chronically mentally ill. *Evaluation and Program Planning, 11*, 51–62.

Lehman, A. F. (1992). *Measures of humanistic outcomes (quality of life) among persons with severe and persistent mental disorders*. Impacting Mental Health Research Policy: NIMH/CSP Research Demonstration Grantee Workshop, Bethesda, MD.

Lehman, A. F., & Burns, B. J. (1990). Severe mental illness in the community. In B. Spilker (Ed.), *Quality of life assessment in clinical trials*. New York: Raven.

Patrick, D. L., Bush, J. W., & Chen, M. M. (1973a). Methods for measuring levels of well-being for a health status index. *Health Services Research, 8*, 228–245.

Patrick, D. L., Bush, J. W., & Chen, M. M. (1973b). Toward an operational definition of health. *Journal of Health and Social Behavior, 14*, 6–23.

Pliskin, J. S., Shepard, D. S., & Weinstein, M. C. (1980). Utility functions for life years and health status. *Operations Research, 28*(1), 206–224.

Torrance, G. W., Boyle, M. H., & Horwood, S. P. (1982). Application of multi-attribute utility theory to measure social preferences for health states. *Operations Research, 30*, 1043–1069.

von Winterfeldt, D., & Edwards, W. (1986). *Decision analysis and behavioral research*. Cambridge: Cambridge University Press.

Weinstein, M. C., & Stason, W. B. (1977). Foundations of cost-effectiveness analysis for health and medical practices. *New England Journal of Medicine, 296*(13), 716–721.

11

Measuring Medical Offsets of Psychotherapy

T. Michael Kashner & A. John Rush

In the era of managed care, consumers, providers, administrators, and policymakers have become concerned not only over the direct costs of performing a treatment, such as psychotherapy, but also how much providing such services may change the bottom-line, systemwide cost of care (Guadagnoli & McNeil, 1994; Salive, Mayfield, & Weissman, 1990; Shortell & McNerney, 1990). The impact of psychotherapy on systemwide costs is calculated by subtracting from the direct costs of psychotherapy the costs of other mental health services and of general medical care that would have otherwise been consumed had the patient not received therapy. How to calculate these averted care costs, or cost offsets, is the subject of this chapter.

Our focus on total systemwide costs is emphasized in a brief history of health care cost containment in the United States and in a conceptual framework for cost-effectiveness analyses found in the medical literature. Next, we lay the foundation to explain why cost offsets may exist. However, existence of cost offsets may depend on subjects' being serviced by successful managed-care environments. Such environments may be needed to serve as catalysts to help patients benefiting from psychotherapy to adjust their posttherapy care-seeking behaviors to meet declining care needs. We conclude that results from cost offset studies should be evaluated in the context of the patients' managed-care environment and with respect to changes in patients' health outcomes.

The empirical literature leads to inconclusive findings. To improve on these studies, we describe a method based on economic theory to calculate offsets. This strategy emphasizes the need to examine changes in health outcomes when evaluating cost offsets. Measures of access to care and health outcome are briefly reviewed. The consumer-based approach estimates offsets as a response to changes in access to, rather than in actual use of, psychotherapy. The emphasis on access reflects more realistic decisions that face policymakers, who, in most cases, can control access but not patient use of care. This is further discussed along with other advantages and disadvantages of the economic approach. A mathematical exposition designed for economists is provided in the Appendix.

History of Cost Containment

Concerns over health care costs are not new. During the late 1920s, Ray Lyman Wilbur, a past president of the American Medical Association, and his Committee on the Costs of Medical Care (1932) described medical costs as "inequably distributed." At that time, medical costs amounted to only 4% of the gross domestic product (GDP). By 1960, health care accounted for 5.4% of GDP, and the medical literature began to speak of a U.S. health care "crisis" (Battistella & Southby, 1968). By 1995, the figure had increased to 14.2% with 17.9% projected by 2005 (Burner & Waldo, 1995).

Neither the crisis nor government attempts to solve it are new. Following the Flexner Report (1910) on the quality of medical education, 57% of the nation's medical schools had closed by the early 1940s (Feldstein, 1979) leaving the supply of medical personnel inadequate to meet growing demands for care. To prevent pending medical inflation, government attempted to *expand the supply* of facilities and health professionals. The Hill-Burton Act (1946) financed hospital construction, and the Nurse Training (1964) and Health Professions Education Assistance Acts that began in 1963 expanded enrolments in professional schools. Increasing the supply of health services was expected to moderate fees and help redistribute professionals to underserved specialities and geographic areas.

Facing continued cost increases and maldistributed resources, government also attempted to *plan for health care services*. Building on efforts to coordinate construction of new facilities under the Hill-Burton Act, Regional Medical Programs (1965) linked research centers with diagnostic and treatment stations. Developing rational plans for service expansion was the goal of Comprehensive Health Planning (1966) under the Partnership for Health Act (1967), which linked government, consumers, and health care providers. These planning functions were later consolidated into regional Health System Agencies (1974), which were armed with enforcement powers that included civil sanctions, licensure suspensions, and partial withholding of reimbursement for beneficiaries of federal entitlement programs. The federal Food and Drug Administration's regulation of drugs and new medical devices was extended to reviewing not only safety and efficacy, but also cost-effectiveness of proposed products.

Government has also attempted to *conduct utilization review* to ensure that federally financed patients would only receive medically appropriate care. Originally undertaken by local hospitals under Medicare (1965), the function was later transferred to 195 nonprofit physician groups, called Professional Standards Review Organizations (1972). These organizations were later streamlined to 53 Peer Review Organizations (1982), which, after 1982, could include insurance companies or Medicare fiscal intermediaries. A precursor to managed care, reviews were based on algorithms, provider profiles, criteria screens, and medical chart assessments of cases suspected of having problems.

Government has also attempted to contain costs by *shifting the cost burden onto patients* in federally financed programs through deductibles, coinsurance, and maximum benefit levels. The issue is important in mental health since care-seeking behaviors are generally more sensitive to increases in out-of-pocket prices for mental health than for medical care services (Keeler, Manning, & Wells, 1988).

Another remedy that government tried was to directly *control fees* through wage and price controls. Examples include the Economic Stabilization Program of 1971–1974, prospective payments for inpatient stays based on diagnostic groupings called Diagnosis Related Groups, or DRGs began in 1983, and the Medical Fee Schedule for outpatient clinical procedures based on the Resource Based Relative Value Scale, began in 1989. The DRGs and RBRVS Medical Fee Schedules are legally applicable to Medicare patients, though other third-party payers have adopted the system (Carter, Jacobson, Kominski, & Perry, 1994; McCormack & Burge, 1994). The RBRVS Medical Fee Schedule was designed to redistribute fees to primary care specialties by assessing clinical practice costs, rather than utilizing historical charges based on usual, reasonable, and customary fees.

Finally, to *promote market solutions*, government has encouraged the development of health-maintenance and preferred-provider organizations by providing support for planning and start-up capital (1973) and by granting Medicare waivers for pilot and demonstration programs. With Sherman antitrust protection, third-party payers are now employing managed-care enterprises to regulate expenditures of health care benefits. Under competitive pressures, insurance carriers are expected to pass these cost savings to consumers by reducing premiums and extending benefits.

What we may learn from the history of cost containment is that for these market strategies to work, health plans, their providers, and the patients they serve must have adequate information about not only how well different treatments work, but also how much they cost "on the bottom line."

Offsets and Cost-Effectiveness Analysis

In introducing their analyses to the medical literature, Weinstein and Stason (1977) calculated cost-effectiveness ratios by dividing treatment effects by *"net health care costs."* These net costs are calculated by subtracting the costs of medical and other services that are *averted* as a consequence of the new technology under study, from its *direct* operating costs. In the Weinstein-Stason framework, these averted, or offset, costs are defined as the change in expenditures for health care (excluding a given treatment) per additional dollar spent on a given treatment. Cost-effectiveness ratios are calculated as the change in health outcome per additional dollar spent on *all* health care as patients access a new treatment. Consistent with the Weinstein-Stason framework, estimates of cost offsets are necessary to calculate how much a new technology or treatment will impact total health care costs "on the bottom line."

Basis for Cost Offsets

Some analysts contend that investments in mental health care may reduce medical costs. There are several reasons. Based on a conceptual framework introduced by Donabedian (1976), patients obtaining psychotherapy may need fewer general medical care services (GM) as they

- (*treatment productivity effect*) become more responsive to health care treatment;
- (*compliance effect*) become more willing and able to comply with medical advice;
- (*health effect*) achieve better mental health leading physiologically to better physical health;
- (*substitution effect*) use psychotherapists to replace GM providers who otherwise are treating needs for psychotherapy.

However, medical costs may go up as patients in psychotherapy:

1. (*discovery effect*) discover other medical illnesses in need of care;
2. (*complementary effect*) learn to better value their physical health and thus seek more general medical care;
3. (*longevity effect*) live longer with chronic conditions requiring care;
4. (*income effect*) work more productively and generate earnings to pay for more care;
5. (*system effect*) interact with a health care system that does little to discourage inappropriate use of care.

These issues are empirical ones.

Concern over cost offsets is not new to the medical care literature. In his review, Donabedian (1976) noted higher hospital costs when patients previously insured for hospital care began to receive coverage for outpatient services. Donabedian explained these findings as evidence either of previously unmet patient needs or a health care system that may not efficiently allocate resources on the basis of clinically defined needs.

For psychotherapy, the existence of medical offsets will depend on the performance of the health care system, its providers, and the patients who access its services. After psychotherapy, patients may begin to place a greater value on health and seek care for previously unattended conditions. Thus, medical offsets should be examined in the context of any changes in health outcomes. After psychotherapy, patients may be in overall better mental and physical health but may continue to seek care based on pretherapy schedules. Under these circumstances, cost offsets may only be realized in settings that successfully reinforce and reward optimal use of general medical and mental health services. When evaluating estimates of cost offsets, one needs to consider how the treatments impact patient health outcomes and how the clinical settings monitor and optimize access and use of care.

General Medical Offsets of Mental Health Care

Studies attempting to reveal general medical care (GM) cost offsets to mental health treatments have typically been based on comparing (a) psychiatric symptoms with use of GM, (b) use of GM with mental health care, (c) use of GM services before-after mental health treatment, (d) use of mental health treatment with effectiveness of GM care, or (e) insurance coverage for mental health care with total health care costs. Some investigators have shown that patients with psychiatric symptoms, such as depressive symptoms, tend to incur more medical care costs (Johnson, Weissman, & Klerman, 1992; Kessler et al., 1987; Levenson, Hamer, & Rossiter, 1990; Manning & Wells, 1992; Mechanic, Cleary, & Greenley, 1982; Simon, Von-Korff, & Barlow, 1995).

Naturalistic studies reveal that the use of specialty mental health care has been associated with as much as a 5% decrease in general medical outpatient visits (Patterson & Bise, 1978), an 85% decrease in general medical hospital days (Duehrssen, 1962), a decrease in peak use of primary-care services (Hankin, Kessler, Goldberg, Steinwachs, & Starfield, 1983), and lower cost of general medical and surgical care. On the other hand, medical costs were not seen to decline after patients initiated mental health treatment in a staff model health maintenance organization (Simon et al., 1995). Other investigators have attempted to reveal cost offsets by measuring the change in expenditures for general medical and surgical care per dollar spent on mental health care services. Cost reductions in general medical and surgical care attributed to mental health care were estimated at 133% (Jameson, Shuman, & Young, 1978) or as ranging between 4% and 67% (Jones & Vischi, 1979) of the cost of the mental health care. In a before-after design, Salvador-Carulla, Segui, Fernandez-Cano, and Canet (1995) found a 94% offset following diagnosis and treatment for previously undiagnosed panic disorder. In an often cited study, Mumford found that mental health treatment was followed by a 20% decrease in the use of general medical services (Mumford et al., 1984; Rupp, 1995). A study of Kaiser Permanente enrollees found that patients who averaged 1 to 20 psychotherapy visits per year tended to have fewer combined psychiatric and general medical visits in the year following therapy than the number of general medical visits in the year prior to therapy. However, the offset became negative for patients who began to depend on more and more psychotherapy visits (averaging 48 visits) (Cummings, 1977). An increase in general medical care consumption following the use of specialty psychiatric care, however, has been observed among Mexican-Americans (McHugh, Kahn, & Heiman, 1977).

The existence of cost offsets may also be found in studies that show a positive association between psychiatric symptoms and the effectiveness of GM. For instance, the absence of depressive symptomatology is associated with reduced mortality rates and greater likelihood of recovered functioning among the elderly with hip fractures (Magaziner, Simonsick, Kashner, & Hebel, 1990; Mossey, Mutran, Knott, & Craik, 1989) and myocardial infarctions (Frazier-Smith, Lesperance, & Talajic, 1993).

Methodological design and measurement flaws, however, seriously limit these findings. For example, the before-after cost comparisons may overstate cost offsets, as some patients may seek a specialty mental health care provider only after exhausting general medical alternatives. Recalculating Patterson and Bise's (1978) estimate, Jones and Vischi (1979) found a 1% gain, rather than a 5% drop, in use of GM following a mental health specialty encounter when calculations on prior use of GM excluded visits made during the month immediately preceding the mental health encounter. Simple correlations do not reflect causality and may either overstate or understate the true cost offset. For instance, an inverse correlation between patient use of mental health care and GM services may constitute a statistical artifact in a patient population that correctly selects specialty providers to treat mental and general medical disorders that rarely cooccur by chance. On the other hand, a positive correlation between patient use of mental and GM services may result if patients who seek treatment for mental disorders are more likely to have GM problems needing care. Finally, these studies fail to provide for a sufficient follow-up period (Follette & Cummings, 1967), to apply rigorous criteria to judging the adequacy of the patients' psychiatric diagnosis (Spitzer, Williams, & Gibbons, 1986), to consider the age of onset of the mental disorder (Hankin, 1983), to adequately control for the type or quantity of mental health services used, or to include patient use of care from comprehensive sources of care (Cummings, 1977; Follette & Cummings, 1967; Goldberg, Krantz, & Locke, 1970; Hankin et al., 1983; Kogan, Thompson, Brown, & Newman, 1975).

Finally, some economists doubt the existence of cost offsets in light of evidence (from Keeler et al., 1988) that patients with better coverage for mental health care tend to incur greater health care costs. This is not surprising to those familiar with how costs behaved when inpatient coverage was expanded to include outpatient care during the 1960s and '70s (Donabedian, 1976, described in the previous section). Based on the Weinstein-Stason framework, cost offsets should be evaluated for specific treatments serving patients who satisfy defined diagnostic criteria. Findings should be evaluated in the context of the health care environment where study patients received care and with reference to observed changes in patients' health status.

Econometric Approach

Economic Theory of Demand for Health Care

A theory that explains patient demand for care is needed in cost-effectiveness and cost offset studies whenever the investigator wants to examine treatment performance in actual clinical care environments or when the investigator cannot control patient use of psychotherapy treatment. The emphasis on demand for care to measure costs originates from the idea that costs equal unit costs times quantity of use (chapter 9, this volume). The economic theory of demand for health care is based on the following assumptions:

First, by focusing on consumers and their demands, rather than on patients and their needs, econometric approaches depart from health belief and psychosocial behavioral models to explain use of health care (Andersen, 1973; Becker, 1974; Rosenstock, 1974). Consumers are assumed to know their own preferences for different goods and services, including health. This does not mean that consumers have perfect information by which to execute those preferences. Rather, consumers may rely on professional consults, community leaders, or health professionals who share the consumers' views on health to help them make decisions.

Second, consumers weigh the value of health against the value of alternative uses of scarce resources. While desiring to be healthy, patients will compromise their health in order to accomplish other valued objectives (e.g., to smoke, eat fatty foods, engage in risky sex, refuse psychopharmacological treatment with undesired side effects). Once guided as to the risks and consequences of treatment, consumers and not doctors are assumed to "know best." That is, to the economist, consumer demand for care may be different from clinically assessed needs, as patients may rationally refuse care against medical advice to divert scarce resources to further other interests. To the clinician under the medical model, patients who refuse medically prescribed treatment are said to be "irrational," "in denial," or "noncompliant." Describing the fundamental view of the economic approach, the economist Kenneth Boulding said, "Only the slave has needs, the free man has demands."

Third, economic consumers are assumed to assign a subjective measure of quality of life, called *utility*, to the mix of goods and services they consume. As a ratio scale, utility is subjectively assigned by the patient to be (a) consistent over time for the same consumer; (b) increasing with increasing consumption of one good, but at a declining rate; and (c) incrementally increasing for one good with increasing consumption of other goods, but at a declining rate. The third condition means that satisfaction with one good (food) will depend on consumption of other goods (clean utensils, comfortable environment).

Patients are assumed to behave *as if* they purchased a feasible bundle of market goods so as to maximize their subjective quality of life. A mix of goods is "feasible" if patients can afford the purchase. In the simple model, a mix of goods is feasible if the total purchases times the respective market prices do not exceed the patients' earnings.

Gary Becker (1965) extended this simple economic model by replacing market goods with "commodities" as both the objects of patient satisfaction and the arguments determining utility. This approach attempted to explain how consumers spent their time at home as well as their money in the marketplace. A Becker *commodity* is the final end point of consumer wants, such as housing, food, and recreation. Commodities are produced from activities accomplished at home and from goods or services purchased in the market. For instance, consumers purchase market goods (groceries, cooking stove, electricity) and perform household chores (cooking food, setting the table, cleaning, eating at a table), to produce a commodity (meal) to satisfy a want (hunger).

To produce commodities, consumers are assumed to divide their 24-hour day between employment and household activities. Consumers enter employment, earn income at a defined wage rate, and purchase market goods. Consumers also spend their time at home to use these market goods in household activities to produce commodities. The production of commodities from market goods and household activities is called *household production*. Household activities are tantamount to activities of daily living (Katz, Downs, Cash, & Grotz, 1970).

With limited time and financial resources, patients are assumed to acquire and consume commodities as if to maximize their subjectively determined quality of life, or utility. In a simple economic model, how much consumers can buy is limited by their income and the prices of goods and services in the marketplace. In Becker's model, commodities are produced from goods purchased in the market and from household activities performed at home. Thus, there are two prices. The *money price* equals the average cost of market goods the consumer uses to produce and consume one unit of commodity. The *time price* is the amount of time the consumer uses to perform the household activities required to produce and consume one unit of the commodity. As a single "price" for a commodity, a *full wealth price* equals the money price plus a dollar value for the time price. The dollar value for the consumer's time is estimated by the consumer's wage rate (Rice & Miller, 1993; Rupp, 1995). Thus, patients can consume a feasible mix of commodities, provided that the full wealth price times the quantity of each commodity enjoyed does not exceed the patients' "full wealth." Wealth includes interest-producing assets and the patients' value of the 24 hours per day available to them for market and household activities (including sleep). Again, the patients' value of time equals the patients' wage rate.

Grossman (1972) further expanded Becker's framework by including "health" as a commodity, an object of consumer satisfaction. Thus, demand for care is "derived" from patients' interests in acquiring health. Patients are assumed to want health because health status: (a) is associated with "feeling well" and "avoiding pain" as a direct object of patient satisfaction, (b) enables patients to better enjoy their use of other commodities, and (c) allows consumers to earn higher wages in the labor market, be more productive in household activities, and have more disability-free time that may be allocated to household activities and income-producing employment. More productive consumers produce more commodities, creating for themselves a higher quality of life.

Economically, consumers are assumed to "stockpile" health, adding to it by investing in health care or engaging in healthy behaviors, or subtracting from it through disease, injury, age-related susceptibilities to illness, and health-depreciating market goods (alcohol, drugs, cigarettes). The impact of these factors on patient health will be determined, in part, by an initial health condition, genetics, and environmental and household-related factors. For psychotherapy, "health care" can be divided into psychotherapy care, other mental health care, and GM services.

Patients are assumed to plan their household activities and their purchases of market goods to produce and consume commodities over time. Patients are assumed to select the plan that maximizes the present value of the utility generated by the plan during the patients' lifetime. This issue is important when focusing on estimating long-term costs. The present value of a utility derived from consuming commodities in the future is obtained by discounting the future utility to a present value. Most economists contend that patients prefer present over future consumption (Kashner, 1990). That is, the further in time consequences occur, the less influence the consequences will have on current behavior. The idea has been called *time preferences* (Olson & Bailey, 1981) or *impatience* (Fisher, 1930) in economics, *impulse control* in psychoanalysis (Rapaport, 1950), and *deferred gratification* in sociology (Schneider & Lysgaard, 1953). The present value of lifetime utility is calculated by summing the discounted value of the utility assigned to future consumption. Future utility is discounted to a present value at a rate that reflects how important consumers consider future consequences. When time preferences are large, consumers greatly value the present over the future, generously discount future consequences when making present decisions, live primarily for the moment, and are considered myopic by some economists. On the other hand, future consequences will have significant impacts on present behavior whenever the discount rate is small.

Unlike in simple one-period models, present consumption can be expanded (reduced) by borrowing against (saving for) future income at a rate equal to the market interest rate. Thus, the present value of the cost of consumption equals quantity times the respective full-wealth price, discounted to the present value at a market interest rate, and summed over the patient's lifetime and over all commodities the patient consumes. Just as total purchases cannot exceed the patient's income in the simple model, the present value of the cost of lifetime consumption cannot exceed the present value of the patient's lifetime full wealth. This is called the *full-wealth constraint.*

Grossman (1972) amended Becker's full wealth constraint to include the consumer's health status. Health augments full wealth by increasing the patient's life expectancy, increasing the proportion of time that the consumer lives free of disability, increasing the productivity at household time by effectively lowering time prices for commodities, and increasing labor market productivity by effectively increasing wage rates. Higher time prices reflect patients in poor health who require more time to accomplish similar household activities.

In summary, economic consumers plan their employment so as to purchase market goods and plan their household activities so as to produce and consume commodities over a lifetime to maximize their lifetime quality of life, but so that the total household time and money purchases do not exceed the patients' total wealth.

Estimating Cost Offset and Cost-Effectiveness Ratios

This economic theory is then used to derive statistical models to calculate Weinstein-Stason cost offsets and cost-effectiveness ratios from empirical data. To derive workable statistical equations, the above model is treated as a problem known among mathematicians as dynamic optimization and optimal control (Kamien & Schwartz, 1991). The solution reduces to a set of simultaneous econometric equations that describes how use of health care, psychotherapy treatment, and health status change over time for a panel of study patients, as a function of patient access to psychotherapy. The complete model contains as independent variables measures of patient access to care and other covariates, including an index variable representing time (month, year), an evaluation of patients' initial health status, a prognosis of how quickly the patients' future health is likely to deteriorate with time (usually related to patient age and presence of risk factors), patients' ability to earn income in the labor market including patient education level and current wages, the market interest rate, and time preferences measuring how patients value the future relative to the present (Kashner, 1990).

"Access to psychotherapy" is a contrived measure intended for use in estimating cost offsets and cost-effectiveness ratios. The data design includes screening patients who satisfy criteria for specific psychiatric disorders. It is preferred that patients be randomized into treatment and control groups. Patients assigned to the treatment group will have improved access to specific psychotherapy treatments. Those assigned to the control group will have traditional, or, if practical, no, access to psychotherapy.

The traditional approach to measuring health care offsets to psychotherapy compares patient use of health care with patient use of psychotherapy. Though mathematically equivalent, the new approach computes offsets by determining the change in the cost of health care (excluding psychotherapy), in response to changes in access to psychotherapy, divided by the change in the cost of psychotherapy, in response to changes in access to psychotherapy. Similarly, the cost-effectiveness ratio may be computed by determining the change in health status, in response to changes in access to psychotherapy, divided by a total change in health care costs, in response to changes in access to psychotherapy. These changes in response to access to psychotherapy care are computed from the estimated statistical models.

Measuring Access, Utilization, and Outcome

Access to Care

Measures of access are of interest primarily as instrumental variables necessary to calculate cost offsets. To improve statistical power and reduce biases associated with model misspecification, if feasible, it is preferable to randomly assign patients to different levels of access. Penchansky and Thomas (1981) have classified measures of access into:

1. *Availability*: Does the provider exist?
2. *Accessibility*: How do patients physically get to the provider, and what geographic barriers do they face?
3. *Affordability*: Can patients afford needed services?
4. *Accommodation*: Do providers offer adequate facilities and working hours to accommodate patients' schedules?
5. *Acceptability*: Do patients feel safe and welcome in the facility?

Investigators may control access by offering selected patients extended insurance coverage to reduce out-of-pocket expenditures, making available a health clinic or care provider, assigning priority in appointment scheduling to reduce waiting time, and providing for the patients' transportation.

Utilization and Cost of Care

Use of care may be classified by *type* (general medical, surgical, psychotherapeutic, addiction treatment), *setting* (inpatient, outpatient, day treatment, residential care), specific *procedure*, *provider* (MD, RN, PhD), and *unit of analyis*. Unit of measuring patient use of care may be represented as dichotomous variables indicating whether the patient receives care, and numeric variables counting the number of services the patient receives during a given time. Services may be counted in terms of inpatient days, visits, procedures done, encounters, and so on. The cost of care is calculated by multiplying a unit price times the quantity of care consumed for each service and is summed over all services (see chapter 9, this volume).

Outcomes of Care

Health outcomes may be measured in different ways depending on study objectives. Methods may be based on:

1. *Diagnosis*, including the presence or absence of specific diagnoses.
2. *Conditions*, including the number of *conditions* reported as "chronic," treated with medication, diagnosed by a qualified clinician, or causing problems for the patient. Methods based on *symptoms* include the presence or absence of specific symptoms, symptom counts, or symptom counts weighted by degree of severity. Examples include the Brief Psychiatric Rating Scale (Overall & Gorham, 1962) and the Inventory for Depressive Symptomatology (Rush, Giles, Schles-

ser, Fulton, Weissenburger, & Burns, 1986; Rush, Gullion, Basco, Jarrett, & Trivedi, 1996).

3. *Functioning*, including counts of disability days, days of restricted activities for health reasons compared to the patients' usual activities; days of restricted activities for health reasons compared to the patients' normal activities for persons of the same age, gender, and other circumstances; bed disability days for health reasons; capacity to perform physical activities of daily living (eating, dressing, grooming, walking, transferring, bathing, and toileting) and instrumental activities (taking medication, using telephone, getting to places out of walking distance of residence, shopping, preparing meals, doing household chores and handling money) (Katz et al., 1970); and social capacity to engage in and interact with people at work and in the community, and with family and friends (Weissman & Bothwell, 1976).
4. *Global health measures*, including physical, mental, or social health, bodily pain, and general health perceptions. Examples include the SF-36 Medical Outcome Study Short Form (McHorney, Ware, Lu, & Sherbourne, 1994; Ware & Sherbourne, 1992).
5. *Quality-adjusted health status*, including methods that assign values, or worth, to different levels of health status. These values are assigned based on patient behavior in the market (Kashner, 1990), court documents granting cash awards to plaintiffs seeking restitution for measurable injuries (Rosser & Watts, 1972), or patient responses to hypothetical situations in order to psychometrically measure patient willingness to pay for, or to avoid, specific health outcomes (Hogness & Van Antwerp, 1991; Maynard, 1990) (see chapters 10, 16, and 17, this volume). This method is growing in popularity, though we advise some caution when applying and interpreting results from these measures. Findings are likely to be sensitive to, among other things, sample selection and data collection methods.
6. *Utilization of care*, to the extent that patient use of services reflects patient health outcome (Wennberg, Roos, Sola, Schori, & Jaffe, 1987). For example, acute psychiatric admissions may indicate poor health, while keeping follow-up appointments may indicate good health. Since care is responsive to other factors such as access to care (Horgan, 1986; Taube, Kessler, & Burns, 1986), inferring patient health from use of care is not advised.

Advantages and Disadvantages of the Econometric Approach

The econometric approach as described here manifests both disadvantages and advantages.

On the negative side, the model does not provide a basis for explaining how and why consumers value health. The model is based on the assumption that consumer preferences for health and other commodities remain consistent over time and operate in markets that have "cleared." Markets clear when suppliers are willing to supply, and consumers are willing to purchase, all services at agreed-upon and negotiated prices. This may not be true in health care when changes in technology are quick but responses by providers and patients are slow.

However, the model may be usefully extended to account for markets that fail to clear quickly and for patients and providers who may "learn as they go" about the cost and effectiveness of treatment. The model may also be extended to explain how patients use health care when their preferences are influenced by providers and when they are faced with uncertain health outcomes and life expectancies.

The econometric approach does contribute important theoretical and empirical advantages. Theoretically, the model

1. provides a unified framework that encompasses key elements commonly used in cost-effectiveness studies.
2. makes important distinctions. For example:

   "Substitution in demand," reflecting patient wants, is distinguished from "substitution in production," reflecting the efficacy of clinical procedures (Knesper, 1989).

   Discounting a present value for future health is distinguished from discounting to calculate a present value of future costs (chapter 9, this volume).

   Time costs are distinguished from money costs.

   Need for care, based on clinical recommendations, is distinguished from demand for health, based on consumer preferences (Donabedian, 1973).

3. focuses on access as a more realistic view of how managed care and health insurance plans are likely to impact health care. Administrators of a health plan can only modify its benefits and guidelines, making services more or less accessi-

ble to consumers. On the other hand, they cannot force its subscribers to use beneficial services in either a clinically appropriate or a timely manner. By focusing on access, investigators may better explain to plan administrators the consequences of proposed changes in policies on patient use of care, costs, and health outcomes.
4. derives statistical models from mathematical statements of theory that allow one to trace assumptions regarding patient preferences for health and treatment efficacy.
5. permits analyses of consumer behavior in actual clinical settings, consistent with the outcomes research initiatives (Guadagnoli & McNeil, 1994).
6. accounts for patients who may rationally refuse medically recommended care.
7. accounts for the impact of psychotherapy on costs, cost offsets, and health outcomes simultaneously.

The econometric approach has statistical advantages.

First, investigators who evaluate psychotherapy programs may not be able to control the care the study patients use. Thus, experimental "meltdowns" are possible if control patients obtain treatments from nonstudy sources at the same time that experimental patients refuse treatment and threaten to drop out of the study. In other cases, investigators may want to evaluate the performance of psychotherapy under treatment-as-usual clinical care conditions. Under these circumstances, biased estimates of cost offsets and cost-effectiveness ratios are likely if the investigator simply correlates cost and health outcome with "use of psychotherapy." Multiple regression will not correct these biases if "use of psychotherapy care" as an independent variable is correlated with the regression errors, or if the model is misspecified (Kmenta, 1973; Theil, 1971). Typically, these problems are managed by the use of what is called an *instrumental variable technique.* Here, the variable of interest, "use of psychotherapy," is replaced by a conceptually meaningful, but less statistically offending, variable. Based on traditional economic theory, "access to psychotherapy" is an appropriate instrumental variable.

As a second statistical advantage, the proposed methodology does not require psychometric estimates of patient satisfaction or quality of life. Finally, the fact that patients are to be followed as a panel over time allows for a statistical model with greater power, avoids the simultaneity and dual causality problems found in analyses involving simple correlations of cross-sectional data, and permits calculation of how effect sizes change over time (Kashner, Rost, Smith, & Lewis, 1992).

Since we rely on the validity of the underlying theory to correctly measure cost offsets, it is natural to ask if the economic theory discussed above is empirically valid. There is empirical support for many of the hypotheses that can be inferred from the above model. For instance, mental health care costs are associated with mental status in general (Mechanic et al., 1982) and depressive symptoms in particular (Klerman & Weissman, 1992). Use of care is also responsive to changes in access to care (Frank, 1985; Frank & McGuire, 1986; Horgan, 1986; McGuire, 1981; Taube et al., 1986; Wells, Manning, Duan, Newhouse, & Ware, 1986); need factors (Arce, Tadlock, Vergare, & Shapiro, 1983; Fischer, Shapiro, Breakey, Anthony, & Kramer, 1986); personality traits (Cloninger, 1987); family characteristics (Liepman & Nirenberg, 1989); concern over health (Patek & Hermos, 1981); and gender (Wallen, Roddy, & Meyers, 1986). For a review, see NIMH (1989) and Frank and McGuire (1986).

Conclusion

PPOs, HMOs, and managed-care plans are market strategies intended to contain health care costs. Their birth in the health care industry did not happen over night but in fact evolved from a long history of federal initiatives intended to address the problem of rising costs. What one may learn from this history is that for these market strategies to work, good information must be available to describe how well different therapies and treatments work, how much they cost, to whom, and under what circumstances. The econometric method described here may be used to measure cost offsets and cost-effectiveness ratios consistent with the conceptual framework introduced in the medical literature by Weinstein and Stason (1977). The economic method advanced by Weinstein and Stason focuses on the relationship among *access* to psychotherapy, cost of care, and health outcomes (rather than focusing on the *utilization* of psychotherapy, per se). The focus on access better reflects the choices facing health planners and policymakers, who control patient use of care only indirectly through changing benefit packages and managed-care guidelines. As an instrumental variable, measures of access are better suited to studies common in outcomes research in which investigators have little control over patient use of the treatment under study.

A review of the current literature leads to uncertain conclusions regarding the existence of cost offsets for psychotherapy. To investigate these costs, we recommend patients who satisfy standardized diagnostic criteria be randomized *not* to different treatment protocols, but rather to different health plans that vary with respect to patient access to psychotherapy services. Finally, it is important to measure health outcomes. If patients who receive psychotherapy tend to use more general medical care, it is important to know if the additional costs incurred had a payoff in terms of better overall patient health. On the other hand if cost offsets exist, it is important to know if these offsets occurred at the expense of patient health.

References

Andersen, R., & Newman, J. F. (1973). Societal and individual determinants of medical care utilization in the United States. *Health and Society Milbank Memorial Fund Quarterly, 51,* 95–124.

Arce, A. A., Tadlock, M., Vergare, J. J., & Shapiro, S. H. (1983). A psychiatric profile of street people admitted to an emergency shelter. *Hospital Community Psychiatry, 34,* 812–817.

Battistella, R., & Southby, R. McK. (1968). Crisis in American medicine. *Lancet, 1,* 581–586.

Becker, G. S. (1965). A theory of the allocation of time. *Economic Journal, 75,* 493–517.

Becker, M. H. (Ed.). (1974). *The health belief model and personal health behavior.* Thorofare, NJ: Slack.

Burner, S. T., & Waldo, D. R. (1995). National Health Expenditure Projections, 1994–2005. *Health Care Financing Review, 16,* 221–242.

Carter, G. M., Jacobson, P. D., Kominski, G. F., & Perry, M. J. (1994). Use of diagnosis-related groups by non-medicare payers. *Health Care Financing Administration, 16,* 127–158.

Cloninger, C. R. (1987). Neurogenetic adaptive mechanisms in alcoholism. *Science, 236,* 410–416.

Committee on the Costs of Medical Care. (1970). *Medical care for the American people.* Washington, DC: U.S. Department of Health, Education, and Welfare. (Original work published 1932)

Cummings, N. A. (1977). Prolonged (ideal) versus short-term (realistic) psychotherapy. *Professional Psychology, 8,* 491–501.

Donabedian, A. (1973). *Aspects of medical care administration.* Cambridge, MA: Harvard University Press.

Donabedian, A. (1976). *Benefits in medical care programs.* Cambridge, MA: Harvard University Press.

Duehrssen, A. (1962). Katamnestische ergebnisse bei 1004 patienten nach analytischer psychotherapie. *Zeitschrift für Psychosomatische Medizin und Psychoanalyse, 8.*

Feldstein, P. J. (1979). *Health care economics.* New York: Wiley.

Fisher, I. (1930). *The theory of interest.* New York: Macmillan.

Fischer, P. J., Shapiro, S., Breakey, W. R., Anthony, J. C., & Kramer, M. (1986). Mental health and social characteristics of the homeless: A survey of mission users. *American Journal of Public Health, 76,* 519–524.

Flexner, A. (1960). *Medical education in the United States and Canada.* Washington, DC: Science and Health Publications. (Original work published 1910)

Follette, W. T., & Cummings, W. T. (1967). Psychiatric services and medical utilization in a prepaid health plan setting. *Medical Care, 5,* 25–35.

Frank, R .G. (1985). Pricing and location of physician services in mental health. *Economic Inquiry, 23,* 115–133.

Frank, R. G., & McGuire, T. G. (1986). A review of studies of the impact of insurance on the demand and utilization of specialty mental health services. *Health Services Research, 21,* 241–265.

Frazier-Smith, N., Lesperance, F., & Talajic, M. (1993). Depression following myocardial infarction. Impact on six-months survival. *Journal of the American Medical Assocation, 270,* 1819–1825.

Goldberg, I. D., Krantz, G., & Locke, B. Z. (1970). Effect of a short-term outpatient psychiatric therapy benefit on the utilization of medical services in a prepaid group practice medical program. *Medical Care, 8,* 419–428.

Grossman, M. (1972). On the concept of health capital and the demand for health. *Journal of Political Economy, 80,* 223–255.

Guadagnoli, E., & McNeil, B. J. (1994). Outcomes research: Hope for the future or the latest rage? *Inquiry, 31,* 14–24.

Hankin, J. R., Kessler, L. G., Goldberg, I. D., Steinwachs, D. M., & Starfield, B. H. (1983). A longitudinal study of offset in the use of nonpsychiatric services following specialized mental health care. *Medical Care, 21,* 1099–1110.

Horgan, C. M. (1986). The demand for ambulatory mental heatlh services form specialty providers. *Health Services Research, 21,* 291–320.

Jameson, J., Shuman, L. J., & Young, W. W. (1978). The effects of outpatient psychiatric utilization on the costs of providing third party coverage. *Medical Care, 16,* 383–399.

Johnson, J., Weissman, M., & Klerman, G. (1992). Service utilization and social morbidity associated with depressive symptoms in the community. *Journal of the American Medical Association, 267,* 1478–1483.

Jones, K. R., & Vischi, T. R. (1979). Impact of alcohol, drug abuse and mental health treatment on medical care utilization. *Medical Care, 12*(Suppl.).

Kamien, M. I., & Schwart, N. L. (1991). *Dynamic optimization.* New York: North-Holland.

Kashner, T. M. (1990). Present-future gratification tradeoffs: Does economics validate psychometric studies. *Journal of Economic Psychology, 11,* 247–268.

Kashner, T. M., Rost, K., Smith, G. R., & Lewis, S. (1992). An analysis of panel data: The impact of a psychiatric consultation letter on the expenditures and outcomes of care for patients with somatization disorder. *Medical Care, 30,* 811–821.

Katz, S., Downs, T. D., Cash, H. R., & Grotz, R. C. (1970). Progress in the development of the index of ADL. *Gerontologist, 10*(Part I), 20–30.

Keeler, E. B., Manning, W. G., & Wells, K. B. (1988). The demand for episodes of mental health services. *Journal of Health Economics, 7,* 369–392.

Kessler, L. G., Burns, B. J., Shapiro, S., Tischler, G. I., George, L. K., Hough, R. L., Bodison, D., & Miller, R. H. (1987). Psychiatric diagnoses of medical service users: Evidence from the Epidemiologic Catchment Area program. *American Journal of Public Health, 77,* 18–24.

Klerman, G. L., & Weissman, M. M. (1992). The course, morbidity and costs of depression. *Archives of General Psychiatry, 49,* 831–834.

Kmenta, J. (1973). *Elements of econometrics.* New York: Macmillan.

Knesper, D. J. (1989). Substitution in production as the basis for research and policy relevant to mental health specialists. In C. A. Taube, D. Mechanic, & A. Hohmann (Eds.), *The future of mental health services research.* DHHS Pub. No. (ADM)89-1600. Washington, DC: U.S. Government Printing Office.

Kogan, W. S., Thompson, D. J., Brown, J. R., & Newman, H. F. (1975). Impact of integration of mental health service and comprehensive medical care. *Medical Care, 13,* 934–942.

Levenson, J., Hamer, R. M., & Rossiter, L. F. (1990). Relation of psychopathology in general medical inpatients to use and cost of services. *American Journal of Psychiatry, 147,* 1498–1503.

Liepman, M. R., & Nirenberg, T. D. (1989). Evaluation of a program designed to help family and significant others to motivate resistant alcoholics into recovery. *American Journal of Drug and Alcohol Abuse, 15,* 209–221.

Magaziner, J., Simonsick, E. M., Kashner, T. M., & Hebel, J. R. (1990). Predictors of functional recovery one year following hospital discharge for hip fracture: a prospective study. *Journal of Gerontology: Medical Sciences, 45,* M101–107.

Manning, W., & Wells, K. B. (1992). The effects of psychological distress and psychological well-being on use of medical services. *Medical Care, 30,* 541–553.

Maynard, A. (1990). The design of future cost-benefit studies. *American Heart Journal, 119,* 761–765.

McCormack, L. A., & Burge, R. T. (1994). Diffusion of Medicare's RBRVS and related physician payment policies. *Health Care Financing Review, 16,* 159–173.

McGuire, T. (1981). *Financing psychotherapy: Costs, effects and public policy.* Cambridge, MA: Ballinger.

McHorney, C. A., Ware, J. E., Jr., Lu, J. F., & Sherbourne, C. D. (1994). The MOS 36-item Short Form Health Survey (SF-36): 3. Tests of data quality, scaling assumptions, and reliability across diverse patient groups. *Medical Care, 32,* 40–66.

McHugh, J. P., Kahn, M. W., & Heiman, E. (1977). Relationships between mental health treatment and medical care utilization among low-income Mexican-American patients: Some preliminary findings. *Medical Care, 15,* 439–444.

Mechanic, D., Cleary, P. D., & Greenley, J. R. (1982). Distress syndromes, illness behavior, access to care and medical utilization in a defined population. *Medical Care, 20,* 361–372.

Mossey, J. M., Mutran, E., Knott, K., & Craik, R. (1989). Determinants of recovery 12 months after hip fracture: The importance of psychosocial factors. *American Journal of Public Health, 79,* 279–286.

Mumford, E., Schlesinger, H. J., Glass, G. V., Patrick, C., & Cuerdon, T. (1984). A new look at evidence about reduced cost of medical utilization following mental health treatment. *American Journal of Psychiatry, 141,* 1145–1158.

National Institute of Mental Health. (1989). *The future of mental health services research.* C. A. Taube, D. Mechanic, & A. Hohmann (Eds.). DHHS Pub. No. (ADM)89-1600. Washington, DC: U.S. Government Printing Office.

Olson, M., & Bailey, M. J. (1981). Positive time preference. *Journal of Political Economy, 89,* 1–25.

Overall, J. E., & Gorham, D. R. (1962). Brief psychiatric rating scale. *Psychological Reports, 10,* 799–812.

Patek, A. J., Jr., & Hermos, J. A. (1981). Recovery from alcoholism in cirrhotic patients. *American Journal of Medicine, 70,* 783–785.

Patterson, D., & Bise, B. (1978). *Report to NIMH,* Contract 282-77-0219 MS. Rockville, MD.

Penchansky, R., & Thomas, J. W. (1981). The concept of access: Definition and relationship to consumer satisfaction. *Medical Care, 19,* 127–140.

Rapaport, D. (1950). On the psycho-analytic theory of thinking. *International Journal of Psychoanalysis, 31,* 161–170.

Rice, D. P., & Miller, L. S. (1993). Economic burden of affective disorders. In Teh-Wei Hu & A. Rupp (Eds.), *Advances in health economics and health services research* (Vol. 14). Greenwich, CT: JAI Press.

Rosenstock, I. M. (1974). Historical origins of the health belief model. *Health Education Monographs, 2,* 409–419.

Rosser, R. M., & Watts, U. C. (1972). The measurement of hospital output. *International Journal of Epidemiology, 1,* 261–268.

Rupp, A. (1995). The economic consequences of not treating depression. *British Journal of Psychiatry, 166*(Suppl. 27), 29–33.

Rush, A. J., Giles, D. E., Schlesser, M. A., Fulton, C. L., Weissenburger, J., & Burns, C. (1986). The inventory for depressive symptomatology (IDS): Preliminary findings. *Psychiatry Research, 18,* 65–87.

Rush, A. J., Gullion, C. M., Basco, M. R., Jarrett, R. B., & Trivedi, M. H. (1996). Inventory of Depressive Symptomatology (IDS): Psychometric properties, *Psychological Medicine, 26,* 477–486.

Salive, M. E., Mayfield, J. A., & Weissman, N. W. (1990). Patient outcomes research teams and the Agency for Health Care Policy Research. *Health Services Research, 25,* 697–708.

Salvador-Carulla, L., Segui, J., Fernandez-Cano, P., & Canet, J. (1995). Costs and offset effect in panic disorder. *British Journal of Psychiatry, 166*(Suppl. 27), 23–28.

Schneider, L., & Lysgaard, S. (1953). The deferred gratification pattern: A preliminary study. *American Sociological Review, 18,* 142–149.

Shortell, S. M., & McNerney, W. J. (1990). Criteria and guidelines for reforming the U.S. health care system. *New England Journal of Medicine, 322*(7), 463–466.

Simon, G. E., VonKorff, M., & Barlow, W. (1995). Health care costs of primary care patients with recognized depression. *Archives of General Psychiatry, 52,* 850–856.

Spitzer, R. L., Williams, J. B. W., & Gibbons, M. (1986). *The Structured Clinical Interview for DSM-III-R (SCID).* New York: New York State Psychiatric Institute, Biomedical Research Department.

Taube, C. A., Kessler, L. G., & Burns, B. J. (1986). Estimating the probability and level of ambulatory mental heatlh services use. *Health Services Research, 21,* 321–340.

Theil, H. (1971). *Principles of econometrics.* New York: Wiley.

Wallen, J., Roddy, P., & Meyers, S. M. (1986). Male-female differences in mental health visits under cost sharing. *Health Services Research, 21,* 341–350.

Ware, J. E., & Sherbourne, C. D. (1992). The MOS 36-item Short Form Health Survey (SF-36): 1. Conceptual framework and item selection. *Medical Care, 30,* 473–483.

Weinstein, M. C., & Stason, W. B. (1977). Foundations of cost-effectiveness analysis for health and medical practices. *New England Journal of Medicine, 296,* 716–721.

Weissman, M. M., & Bothwell, S. (1976). Assessment of social adjustment by patient self-report. *Archives of General Psychiatry, 33,* 1111–1115.

Wells, K. B., Manning, W. G., Duan, N., Newhouse, J. P., & Ware, J. E., Jr. (1986). Use of outpatient mental health services by a general population with health insurance coverage. *Hospital and Community Psychiatry, 37,* 1119–1125.

Wennberg, J. E., Roos, N., Sola, L., Schori, A., & Jaffe, R. (1987). Use of claims data systems to evaluate health care outcomes: Mortality and reoperation following prostatectomy. *Journal of the American Medical Association, 257,* 933–936.

Mathematical Appendix

This appendix is designed to assist economists implement the proposed strategy to estimate cost offsets for psychotherapy. It is based on Grossman's modification of Becker's model:

$$\max \int_0^T e^{-\rho\tau} U(H(\tau), X(\tau))d\tau \qquad (1A)$$

subject to:

$$\Delta H(\tau) = I(m(\tau), c(\tau), H_0) - \delta H(\tau) \qquad (1B)$$

$$0 = \int_0^T e^{-i\tau}(wH - \hat{p}_x X - \hat{p}_m m - \hat{p}_c c)d\tau - A_0 \qquad (1C)$$

$$w = w(H(\tau), w_0) \qquad (1D)$$

"U" reflects patient utility at a time τ as a function of $H(\tau)$ health status and $X(\tau)$ other commodities consumed at time τ. For convenience and without loss of generality, health is measured as the proportion of the patient's time that is "disability-free" and suitable for labor and household activities. T is the patient's life expectancy. The term, exp $\{-\rho t\}$, reflects the present value at time τ for $H(\tau + t)$ and $X(\tau + t)$ consumed in t periods and discounted at a time preference rate of "ρ".

Health is produced according to the production function I and depreciated with age at a rate δ. The increment to patient health, as an investment, is a function of patient use of health care (except psychotherapy), $m(\tau)$, psychotherapy, $c(\tau)$, and initial health, H_0, such that $\partial I/\partial m > 0$ and $\partial I/\partial c > 0$; $\partial I^2/\partial m^2 < 0$ and $\partial I^2/\partial c^2 < 0$; and $\partial I^2/\partial m \partial c > 0$ and $\partial I^2/\partial c \partial m > 0$. In the general model, m and c are vectors representing different procedures, setting (inpatient, outpatient) and specialty (internist, psychiatrist, psychologist).

Resource constraints are described in equations 1C and 1D. A_0 is the initial endowment of interest-producing assets; i is the market interest rate; w is the wage rate and a function of the patients' health status at time τ and an initial wage reflecting the patient education and employment opportunities, w_o. The product $w \cdot H(\tau)$ measures the dollar value of the patients' time that is disability-free and available for labor and household activities at time τ. Note that $w \cdot H(\tau)$ declines with deteriorating health as both wages and the proportion of time free of disability fall. p_x, p_m, and p_c are the fixed money prices, and t_x, t_m, and t_c are the fixed time prices for one unit of other goods—health care and psychotherapy, respectively—so that $\hat{p}_x = p_x + w(H(\tau))t_x$, $\hat{p}_m = p_m = w(H(\tau))t_m$, and $\hat{p}_c = p_c + w(H(\tau))t_c$. The model may be "solved" as a problem of optimal control (Kamien and Schwartz, 1991) leading to three equations:

$$m(\tau) = M(\tau, H_0, \delta, w_0, i, \rho, t_m, p_m, t_c, p_c) \tag{2A}$$

$$c(\tau) = C(\tau, H_0, \delta, w_0, i, \rho, t_m, p_m, t_c, p_c) \tag{2B}$$

$$H(\tau) = H(\tau, H_0, \delta, w_0, i, \rho, t_m, p_m, t_c, p_c). \tag{2C}$$

These equations may be converted using a Taylor series expansion to three simultaneous, cross-sectional and time series regressions that are linear in parameters and include first- and second-ordered variables and interaction terms. Assume that predicted minus actual values for m, c, and H are random variates. The parameter coefficients to the linear models may be estimated from a patient population selected and screened for appropriate diagnoses. To improve statistical power, study patients should have uniform access to health care except for randomly selected patients assigned to receive access to psychotherapy treatment. Let $\tilde{p}_c$ be a measure of access to psychotherapy treatment constructed to incorporate both time and money costs to the patient. The change in patient use of health care, use of psychotherapy, and health status associated with changing access to psychotherapy are estimated to be:

$$\frac{\partial m}{\partial \tilde{p}_c} = \frac{\partial \hat{M}}{\partial \tilde{p}_c}, \frac{\partial c}{\partial \tilde{p}_c} = \frac{\partial \hat{C}}{\partial \tilde{p}_c}, \frac{\partial H}{\partial \tilde{p}_c} = \frac{\partial \hat{H}}{\partial \tilde{p}_c}. \tag{3}$$

where $\hat{M}$, $\hat{C}$, and $\hat{H}$ are estimated models for equations 2A–C, respectively.

The change in the cost of health care (except psychotherapy) per additional dollar spent on psychotherapy may be calculated as:

$$\frac{\Delta\, other\ care\ cost}{\Delta\, psych\ therapy\ cost} = \frac{\dfrac{\Delta\, other\ care\ cost}{\Delta\, access}}{\dfrac{\Delta\, psych\ therapy\ cost}{\Delta\, access}} = \frac{\int_0^T e^{-it} P_m \dfrac{\partial m}{\partial \tilde{p}_c} dt}{\int_0^T e^{-it} P_c \dfrac{\partial c}{\partial \tilde{p}_c} dt}. \tag{4}$$

The Weinstein and Stason (1977) cost-effectiveness ratio (annualized) may be calculated by:

$$\frac{\Delta health}{\Delta psych\ costs + \Delta other\ cost} = \frac{\dfrac{\Delta health}{\Delta access}}{\dfrac{\Delta psych\ cost}{\Delta access} + \dfrac{\Delta other\ cost}{\Delta access}} = \frac{\dfrac{\partial H}{\partial \tilde{p}_c}}{P_m\left(\dfrac{\partial m}{\partial \tilde{p}_c}\right) + P_c\left(\dfrac{\partial c}{\partial \tilde{p}_c}\right)} \tag{5}$$

12

Psychotherapy: Individual Differences in Costs and Outcomes

Martin Knapp & Andrew Healey

The Need for Disaggregated Data

In most health care systems of the world, there has been marked growth over at least the past 10 years in demands for evidence on the costs of alternative policies, placements, and treatments. Whether the dominant system of health care finance is public subsidy or private insurance, few policy initiatives today, whether national or local, wide-ranging or narrowly focused, are launched or reaffirmed without checking the likely resource consequences. Of course, that "checking" might be cursory, partial, or simply misdirected, but there is certainly a widespread recognition that it needs to be done. New therapies (both psychosocial and pharmacological) and—increasingly—new ways of organizing mental health services must demonstrate not only their effectiveness in improving patient health and/or quality of life, but also their cost-effectiveness in making good use of available resources.

What are the sources of these demands for better evidence on costs and outcomes? Policymakers in different tiers of government want evidence to guide their strategic planning of services, expenditures, education, and training. In countries with public health systems, taxpayers and government departments financing health services on behalf of patients want to ensure that they are getting good value for money, while health insurance companies that have to reimburse patients' fees in countries with predominantly private health care systems want to scrutinize both the payment schedules and the health-improving achievements. Decision makers lower down in the organizational hierarchies in health care or other agencies—such as case managers, primary-care physicians making referrals, and counselors in social welfare settings—may want information on the wider resource consequences of different treatment or service modalities, as well as data on outcomes, so that they can make more effective placements and/or give better advice. In many circumstances—for example, with health maintenance organizations, general-practice fund holding (introduced in the UK in 1991), or other forms of managed care—key decision makers obviously also need to know the consequences for their *own* budgets of their decisions or recommendations. In all systems, patients will want to be reassured that their treatments are effective and, if they are bearing any of the costs of therapy, that the treatment is worthwhile.

Many of these needs or demands are for fairly broad orders of magnitude—indications of the likely cost and outcome ramifications of different placements, therapies, or other choices for groups of patients, perhaps even for whole populations. But often, the need is for rather more disaggregated data. There are many circumstances when *individual* costs and outcomes must be identified, measured, and employed in key decisions about treatment delivery or organization. Indeed, the trend toward individualization that characterizes many demands for cost evidence has particular pertinence to a field such as psychotherapy, with its strong reliance on the dynamics of the patient-therapist relationship to generate information in delineating need identification, treatment choice, and eventual effectiveness. Individual users of psychotherapy services display markedly different needs and arrive at the therapist's door in markedly different personal, familial, and other circumstances. The most appropriate therapeutic response will consequently often vary between patients.

Therapists themselves have different approaches and work in varying contexts. With or without treatment differences, patients will experience different outcomes—some improving along one dimension of health status or quality of life but not along another; some showing significant changes in a short space of time and others responding only slowly or not at all; some able and willing to terminate the treatment after a few sessions and others needing to continue in long-term therapy. Interpatient differences of this kind generate different resource requirements and impose different costs.

Exploration of individual variations in therapeutic response has been a common theme of research in the psychotherapy literature, although—compared to evaluations of other treatments for schizophrenia—rarely with large samples or randomized designs. There has been much less research on costs, so it is perhaps not surprising that interpatient cost variations have attracted little attention.

The aims of this chapter are therefore to reaffirm the importance of specifying interpatient cost and outcome differences, highlighting the benefits that can flow from individual-level economic studies of psychotherapy; to illustrate how such studies can be done; and to review how evaluations of individual costs and outcomes can guide psychotherapy planners and providers.

Economic Evaluation: The Why and Wherefore

The needs and wants of society will always outstrip the resources available to meet them. Scarcity is endemic. Choices must therefore be made regarding the allocation of resources to activities that produce goods and services valued by individuals within society. For some goods and services, it is accepted that market forces can be relied upon to allocate resources reasonably well to their most highly valued uses, so that aggregate social welfare (the value that members of society derive from the consumption of goods and services) is maximized. When this occurs, freely operating markets are said to *allocate resources efficiently*.

In reality, however, and for various well-known reasons, market forces generally fail to allocate resources efficiently or appropriately: Resources are not used to maximum social advantage, or the burdens and benefits may be distributed inequitably. This is especially likely in health and social care, where evolved systems of finance and provision have incentive structures that lead to inefficient resource allocation, most obviously manifested in some countries in dramatically rising health and social care expenditures. Just as worrisome is the propensity of financing systems based on private insurance to leave a pool of individuals (typically the chronically ill and low paid) without access to effective treatments. "Safety nets" developed by government alongside private insurance markets and publicly financed health care, while mitigating inequities in access to health care, carry their own inefficiencies. Frank and McGuire (chapter 13, this volume) highlight this problem with regard to the U.S. Health Security Act and the extensions of public insurance to cover psychotherapy.

Consequently, decisions as to the allocation of scarce health care resources will need to be influenced in part by evidence from economic evaluations. It is the purpose of economic appraisal to provide decision makers or system stakeholders with information pertaining to the costs and benefits associated with various options for resource investment. There are different types of economic evaluation aimed at informing resource allocation in different contexts. The remainder of this section will provide a brief outline of each evaluative type. Chapter 9 (this volume) also presents a detailed exposition of issues arising when conducting economic evaluations of psychotherapy.

Cost-Benefit Analysis

Cost-benefit analysis (CBA) is unique among economic evaluations in that it addresses the extent to which a particular course of action, such as investment in an outpatient psychotherapy unit or the expansion of community-based mental health services, represents a socially worthwhile use of resources. All costs and benefits are valued in monetary units and can be directly compared; if benefits exceed costs, the evaluation would recommend undertaking the project, and vice versa. The use of CBA in health care evaluation, for some years regarded as infeasible or reductionist, has recently enjoyed a resurgence, with the development of contingent valuation survey methods and the generation of empirical evidence on people's willingness to pay for health care benefits (Jöhanesson & Jönsson, 1991; Tolley, Kenkel, & Fabian, 1994). Critics of the approach typically point to distributional problems of interpretation (willingness to pay is limited by ability to pay), and to the validity that can be attached to survey responses based on hypothetical scenarios. In its favor, the willingness-to-pay approach is the only means of valuation consistent with welfare economic theory, and it provides an explicit means of assessing the importance of public policy that might otherwise be left to the hidden value judgments of decision makers. It also provides a means by which to value in monetary terms those treatment outcomes that have previously tended to be labeled "intangible." The willingness-to-pay approach to benefit valuation is too new to have had much impact on the body of completed evaluations, which is one reason why CBA has had only limited application in the evaluation not only of psychotherapeutic interventions but of mental health services more generally (Drummond, Stoddart, & Torrance, 1987; Ginsberg, Marks, & Waters, 1984; Kavanagh & Stewart, 1995; Weisbrod, Test, & Stein, 1980).

Cost-Effectiveness Analysis

The second mode of evaluation, cost-effectiveness analysis (CEA), is concerned with ensuring that resources allocated to the health care sector are used to maximum effect. More often than not, CEA is employed to help decision makers choose between alternative interventions available to or aimed at specific patient groups. It can address two main types of questions: (a) If two treatment options are of equal cost, which option provides the greater benefits from a given budget? (b) If two options have been found to be equally beneficial in terms of patient or population impact, which is less costly?

Complications arise when one particular intervention is both more costly *and* more effective than the alternative with which it is compared, because the costs and effects are measured in different units. Under these circumstances, decision makers need to determine whether additional expenditure on the more costly intervention is worth the extra benefits gained. Weighing up costs and effects measured in different units, for two or more treatment alternatives, is famously difficult. By implication, decisions of this nature will involve shifting resources away from one health program to use in another, or even taking resources away from a different field of public or private enterprise.

Traditionally, CEAs combine cost data with unidimensional measures of effectiveness to produce cost-effectiveness ratios. Examples include cost per life year saved or cost per successfully treated case. However, measures such as life years gained offer convenience but little else in the evaluation of most mental health interventions: saving lives is not irrelevant, but it is rarely the primary concern. Therapeutic objectives are more likely to be couched in terms of reduced symptomatology, improved social functioning, and enhanced quality of life. Where CEAs have been conducted in the mental health field, they have used batteries of (often condition-specific) functional and symptom-based outcome measures, of the kind familiar to clinical and behavioral evaluators. As we argue later, these data offer a baseline from which to explore cost and outcome variations.

Cost-Utility Analysis

A newer mode of economic evaluation, cost-utility analysis (CUA), is similar to CEA with the important exception that it measures and then *values* the impact of an intervention on a patient's health-related quality of life as well as the cost of achieving that improvement (see chapter 10, this volume). The value of health improvement from a treatment is measured in conflated units of utility, in contrast to the method in CBA, which uses monetary values of the effects. CUAs avoid the potential ambiguities with multidimensional outcomes found in CEAs and can be applied to choices across a range of treatments or diagnoses. The most common value measure of health outcomes used in CUAs is the quality-adjusted life year (QALY) (Torrance, 1986). QALYs are not only convenient summary measures of outcome but also partly a recognition of the inadequacy of using life expectancy data as a generic measure of effectiveness. People value quality as well as length of life, as reflected in some individuals' willingness to trade off better life expectancy against a shorter life in better health. But despite its attractive features and its growing use across a wide span of health care contexts, CUA has rarely been applied to psychotherapy, mainly because of the limited relevance of current QALY measures (Chisholm, Healey, & Knapp, 1996).

The Production of Welfare Framework and Psychotherapy

A Conceptual Framework

The production-of-welfare approach provides a conceptual framework within which to consider, in a more rounded and complete way, the links between patient costs, needs, and outcomes. It can do so because of its emphasis on the individuality of treatment and the impact of situational factors on the achievement of health or other improvements. The label originally attached to the approach—combining the process of *production* familiar to economists with the *welfare* (quality-of-life) focus of social care interventions—may not travel well, but we retain it here to emphasise links with earlier work. It is only a label.

The production-of-welfare approach has been employed to good effect as a framework in the UK and elsewhere for social care and mental health evaluations (Davies & Knapp, 1981; Davies, Bebbington, & Charnley, 1990; Knapp, 1984, 1995; Netten & Davies, 1991). The approach simply argues that patient and family outcomes, as well as quality-adjusted service units or treatment sessions, are determined (or produced) by the level and modes of combination of the resource inputs into the treatment or therapeutic process (particularly therapist time) and the nonresource characteristics of treatment (such as social milieu). (In some respects, the approach might be recognised by health economists as maintaining Grossman's 1972 distinction between health care as a "derived demand" and health per se as a consumption and investment good in its own right, while developing Donabedian's 1980 model of structure, process, and outcome.)

Principal Stages

The framework suggested by the production-of-welfare approach would comprise three principal stages:

- The definition, identification, and prioritization of need
- The employment and combination of resources such as staff and capital in an attempt to meet need
- The achievement of outcomes.

In areas as complex as psychotherapy, treating a diversity of needs and with many nontherapy factors exerting an influence on patient outcomes and service utilization, any evaluative framework must have sufficient breadth and flexibility to encompass the many and often complex linkages between needs, resources, and outcomes. It will rarely be sufficient to compare inputs and outputs, resources and outcomes, or costs and benefits without a good understanding of therapeutic or treatment processes. Many of the key features of these processes are neither outcomes in their own right nor resources that can be expressed in cost terms. These can be called *nonresource inputs*, being potential influences on psychotherapy outcomes that have no direct or readily identified cost, but that have a bearing on the ability of psychotherapy to improve patient health and welfare. They include the nature of the patient-therapist relationship, the social milieu of a care setting, and patient experiences and attitudes. The production-of-welfare approach, with its flexible framework and its ability to draw insights and arguments from a range of disciplines and perspectives, explicitly includes the nonresource inputs. Too many economic evaluations overlook them.

In contrast, a number of psychotherapy evaluations rightly stress the importance of these factors. Indeed, whole libraries of books and journals have unpacked the psychotherapeutic relationship. However, as will be clear from this book, few tackle the resource dimension well, and we are not aware of a disaggregated "model" of psychotherapy that adequately addresses the resource side. What we propose here can, we hope, provide the beginnings of an approach that allows economic evaluations to be integrated within other perspectives on, and theories of, psychotherapeutic interventions.

The objectives of therapeutic interventions are usually specified in terms of health-status, social-functioning, and quality-of-life improvements. This suggests how to approach the definition, measurement, and valuation of *outcomes*. Patient *needs*, by contrast, define the mental-health or quality-of-life shortfalls of individuals with respect to some objective (such as full health or a normal life, however defined). Although the need for and outcomes produced by psychotherapy are distinct concepts, they are clearly interrelated. The extent to which individual needs are met by psychotherapy could be defined as the outcome from the delivery of that service. Provision of services for those in need represents an intermediate stage, or a *means* to producing patient or family outcomes (mental health or other improvements). At an intermediate stage, we can therefore define service or process outputs—quantities of services and their qualities—that are relevant achievements of a health care system even if they are not usually valued as ends in themselves.

In private health care systems, some needs will be registered through demand—requests for treatment backed up by the ability to pay—while other needs will go untreated. The private health care system prioritizes need on the basis of ability and willingness to pay. The public health care system endeavors to use means other than market forces to identify and prioritize needs. In both cases, the therapist has responsibility for conceptualizing and addressing need. Whether one system is more successful than the other, and by what criteria, raises questions beyond the scope of this chapter. The key points, common to both types of health care system, are that needs are registered and treated, and that changes in need help to define outcomes.

The third element of the production process is input deployment. The *resource inputs* of the production-of-welfare process include therapist time, medication, buildings, and administrative support. Many patients who receive psychotherapy, particularly those with long-term mental illness, will require support from a *range* of agencies (public, for-profit, and nonprofit), and perhaps also from family and other informal care networks. These multiservice care arrangements should shape an economic evaluation, for most such evaluations endeavor to adopt a societal perspective. The outcomes of therapy are likely to be influenced by the wide range of resources, not just by psychotherapy itself, and so costs should generally span that same range.

Location and Development

This description of psychotherapy services in terms of inputs and outputs may appear somewhat reductionist and mechanistic, but the production-of-welfare approach, or something akin to it, is actually broadly applicable and seeks only to reflect the reality of treatment in a manner that assists evaluation. For example, the available evidence on the key features of successful therapy and the interconnections between patient circumstances, therapeutic responses, and health outcomes could be located within this framework. At the same time, the approach makes conceptual connections with economic magnitudes and readily suggests empirical techniques for practical research, as we show later. The approach thus tries to locate cost and outcome evaluations of psychotherapy in their practice and conceptual contexts, thereby (a) helping the researcher identify the full range of evaluative dimensions, even if it proves impossible in a particular study to measure every one; (b) suggesting analyses that can tease out key relationships; and (c) aiding the interpretation of findings.

Our introduction of the production-of-welfare structure here is not, in fact, suggesting a radically new approach to evaluating psychotherapy. Fonagy and Higgitt (1989), for example, note the usefulness of distinguishing inputs, activities, and outputs when evaluating the performance of hospital-based departments. Yates and Newman (1980a) have drawn analogies with production processes in recommending that evaluations move away from the purely descriptive (summative studies) to the predictive (formative studies). The heterogeneous nature of psychotherapy in terms of treatment content, practitioner characteristics, and, of course, patients' characteristics is well documented; for example, Andrews (1991) classified psychotherapeutic treatments according to whether they were verbal, behavioral or counseling in nature and used meta-analysis to reveal differences in effectiveness. Variability in treatment approaches within any categorization of therapy—such as dynamic therapy, cognitive therapy, or counseling—is the norm, not the exception. There is also evidence that the level of therapist involvement with patients, and by implication the levels of resource use and cost, can significantly influence patient outcomes (e.g., Howard, Kopta, Krause, & Orlinsky, 1986; Orlinsky & Howard, 1986). Krupnick and Pincus (1992), quoting evidence, note the existence of a learning-curve effect in psychotherapy practice and document that the substitution of nonspecialist for primary-care physician input leads to inferior patient outcomes.

The efficient and equitable allocation of resources in the provision of psychotherapy services thus needs to be based on considerations of how costs, patient characteristics, therapy type and orientation, and outcomes interact with one another. The production-of-welfare approach seeks to make these linkages explicit. In so doing, it makes clear that to rely solely on *average* cost and outcome findings, without exploring the variable impacts of therapy content and patient-related factors, could miss differences in patterns of service provision and their consequences. When the aim is to achieve outcomes from therapy and other resources, this would be unfortunate. Where the production-of-welfare approach can help is in its identification of core elements and their interconnections, and in its analytical sequelae.

Sources of Variation: Research Methods

A well-conducted CBA, CEA, or CUA will tally the costs and effectiveness for each of the therapies or treatments being evaluated and will compare the results. It will essentially describe what *is*, with broad recommendations for decision makers. And it would offer those descriptions and make those recommendations for *groups* of patients. For example, a CEA based on a randomized controlled trial (RCT) would be able to compare the costs and effects of the experimental and control treatments across the full sample of patients.

Although the RCT is widely regarded as the "gold standard" research design, it cannot address every evaluative issue. Health care interventions that are neither monotechnic nor uniform (either across patients or across therapists) or that are liable to be influenced by a multitude of extraneous factors (such as patient histories, or the availability and quality of adjunct services) might be better evaluated by moving beyond the standard RCT. The randomized trial should have considerable power in testing the impact of a single-variable treatment factor but is less helpful when there is interest in other factors that have been partialed out in the research design. By definition, the contextual circumstances should be identical for the two or more arms of an RCT, which puts a limit on its wider relevance. Randomized designs should obviously not be discarded altogether, but their implementation should be carefully considered, as to the appropriate contexts and circumstances. Especially in the case of community psychiatry, when implemented, RCTs often warrant analytic supplementation.

This is not to argue that the randomized trial is in any new sense "wrong," but rather to suggest that the opportunities offered by the data gathered in RCTs often tend to be fully exploited with reference to wider policy and practice questions. Alternatively, multivariate exploration of data is not *always* warranted, even when sample sizes permit, in that some modes of treatment might not repay closer scrutiny, and blatant data mining is methodologically dangerous. Nevertheless, experience gleaned from research undertaken on a number of studies would suggest that new insights are often forthcoming from further analysis of this kind. This is particularly the case in moving down from aggregate to disaggregate analyses, so that adjustments are necessary in order to compare like with like, which in turn generates a need for multivariate methods to interrogate the data. A case study approach might also be initiated, although this would be less likely to produce the kinds of robust evidence on the often complex interconnections of factors that a well-conducted multivariate analysis can offer.

Certain forms of modeling, including cost and production functions, have the potential to make descriptions at a lower level of aggregation, for example, at the level of the individual patient. Another reason for pursuing such analytic methods is to vary certain parameters and/or variables in the estimated functions for the psychotherapeutic processes in order to understand some of the complexities of the relationships between costs and outcomes and to appreciate the consequences of different resource contexts, patient groups, and treatment arrangements for either costs or outcomes. The central argument of this chapter is that information benefits can flow from the careful exploration of cost and outcome variations, both for the purposes of more accurately describing psychotherapy, and for making informed predictions of the consequences of changes in the resource or treatment environments.

Cost Functions

As their name suggests, cost functions seek to explain differences in costs. They are estimated equations that link variations in the observed costs of treatment to differences in patient needs and other characteristics, input prices, outcomes, occupancy or throughput rates, treatment characteristics and quality, and the location of facilities. Developed originally from economic theories of production relations and processes, and—more specifically in the social care and health fields—from an appropriate conceptual analogy, such as the production of welfare approach, cost functions seek to quantify the effects of a host of hypothesized factors. Provided that the necessary data are available on sufficient numbers of observations (in this case, on a sufficiently large sample of psychotherapy patients—less than 50 would generally be too few; more than 100 would be a lot safer), functional relationships are estimated by appropriate statistical methods (usually ordinary least squares or some close relative).

Early work on "statistical cost estimation" established methodological and empirical baselines for the approach (Dean, 1976; Johnston, 1960). While the use of the cost function approach is now seen to confer many potential advantages (Knapp, 1996), realization of these advantages in practice depends on data volume and quality. The cost function, for example, can provide policymakers with information on the marginal cost implications of providing psychotherapy to patients with different demographic and familial characteristics and varying levels of need and can yield data pertaining to the marginal costs of achieving such outcomes. It can make plain the resource consequences of treating different health problems for different groups in the population.

A recent study by Goodman, Holder, Nishiura, and Hankin (1992) provides an example of the insights to be gained from unpacking individual cost variations. The study was based on a cost function analysis of patients receiving short-term treatment for alcoholism. Using two-stage modeling, the investigators were able to assess the effects of comorbidity on choice of treatment location (outpatient or inpatient/outpatient mix) and the impact of severity of alcoholism and presence of comorbidity on patient costs once treatment location had been chosen.

While finding out what factors are important in influencing the costs of psychotherapy, cost functions can also strengthen the scientific rigor of the experimental design in studies where intervention and control groups have not been adequately matched, perhaps as a result of sample attrition or in instances where randomization is impractical or unethical, thereby leading to the adoption of a quasi-experimental design (e.g., Knapp et al., 1996). In addition, the cost function can help to unravel some of the complexities of the psychotherapeutic process (in an evaluative sense), distinguishing core from peripheral influences on cost and outcome.

Production Functions

An estimated production function examines the reasons for differences in outcome: Which treatment components, therapeutic interventions, and professional inputs (and in which combinations) lead to changes in patient health and quality of life? Production functions have a more basic position in economic theory than cost functions, summarizing the process whereby resource inputs are turned into outputs. More specifically, a production function can be defined as a technical relationship that specifies the maximum level of output that can be achieved with given combinations of inputs. Multiple regression analyses are usually employed to obtain empirical representations of production functions.

There are numerous examples of estimated production functions, but none for psychotherapy. Much of the branch of applied economics concerned with production functions has concentrated on industrial or agricultural processes, for example, looking at how automobiles are produced by combining labor inputs, capital, and power, or how much grain can be produced from different combinations of land, machinery, and farmworkers (Fuss & McFadden, 1978). In health and social care, while physical resource inputs of this kind are important, we have already noted the potentially important influences of so-called nonresource inputs such as the care milieu, staff attitudes, or patients' previous treatment histories. Moreover, the emphasis switches away from physical, tangible units of outputs to *outcomes*—changes in the health status or general well-being of those who enter treatment. Production is now often assumed to take place at the level of the individual patient, being behavioral and biological rather than mechanistic, although production function analyses could be pursued at the level of the individual therapy practice, or at the facility level (but generally with more practical difficulties).

Yates and Newman (1980a) have previously suggested that production functions might deliver evaluative insights for psychotherapy. It is important, however, that these functions be located within a framework of the breadth offered by the production-of-welfare framework, which has direct implications for the quantity and quality of data to be collected. In these circumstances, production functions could quantify the productivity of identified treatments and their component resource and nonresource inputs, that is, their impacts on patient health and quality of life. For example, what improvements in patient health follow from an additional session of therapy, or from a therapist trained in one way rather than another, or from inpatient rather than outpatient treatment, or from some change in the social and interpersonal environments of a residential care setting? What are the interdependent impacts of other service components of treatment packages (including drugs)? Production functions can point to the substitutability or complementarity of inputs in their outcome impacts. With good enough data, they would help to unravel (although not actually to solve) the age-old conundrum about who benefits, in which ways, from what kinds of psychotherapy. From a methodological standpoint, insights of this kind do not come cheap. *In principal,* the production function—like the cost function—has much to contribute, but it needs good data on the full range of outcomes, as well as resource and nonresource inputs for a sample of sufficient size to allow for careful statistical modeling of the underlying relationships.

Disaggregated Analyses

Almost all clinical or social evaluations need to collect information at the individual patient level, even if they conduct their analyses and present their results at an aggregate level. It is usually relatively straightforward to collect supplementary economic data for individual patients. With individualized data on sufficient numbers of patients, and by employing appropriate multivariate statistical techniques, cost and production functions can help integrate economic with clinical data and thereby build on the better known evaluative modes of CBA, CEA, and CUA. Disaggregated analyses can expand the information base for resource allocation decisions and can allow the evaluation to assign cost and effectiveness and/or benefits to different processes used in psychotherapy, in order to identify the mixture of processes that maximizes cost-effectiveness or cost-benefit (Yates & Newman, 1980a).

It is important to stress, however, that these are *supplements* to, not replacements for, other modes of evaluation and have yet to be widely employed. Although data generated by randomized controlled trials are eminently suitable for this purpose, cost and production functions can also be particularly helpful when randomization is not possible between control and intervention groups.

Putting Methods into Practice

Examining disaggregated, patient-specific data by putting into practice the principles of cost and production functions in an area as complex as psychotherapy requires attention to many issues, from study design and data collection to statistical analysis and the informed interpretation of results. There are too many such issues and too many requisite details to develop in the space available here, but fortunately, other chapters in this volume cover many of them. We therefore address only a few of the methodological issues faced while conducting research on the disaggregated cost-effectiveness of psychotherapy: study design, service recording, costings, and outcome measurement.

Study Design

Cost and production function estimation typically calls for large samples, with N greater than 100 usually being best for robust estimation. The more complex the therapeutic context, the more specific the research question or the larger the number of outcomes to be measured, the larger the sample that will be needed to support reliable analysis. In contrast, psychotherapy research has typically employed small samples and intensive, qualitative evaluations. While often insightful studies, such investigations cannot provide the information baseline necessary for cost or production function estimation. Apart from this sample size constraint, almost any study design would be suitable for the kinds of statistical examination of interpatient variation discussed in this chapter. Classical experimental designs are usually deemed to be the most powerful in most contexts, including situations where modeling is to be undertaken (Sheldon, 1996). However, it has been increasingly argued that randomized experimental designs, while providing statistically robust indications of the efficacy of psychotherapy, typically fail to provide meaningful assessments of the real-world effectiveness of treatment (see, for example, Fonagy & Higgitt, 1989; Parry, 1992).

Service Recording

Techniques are needed to record the services used by patients and their associated costs. We treat these as two separate activities. It is necessary at the outset to decide on the breadth of an economic appraisal. The extent of service or cost coverage will depend on the viewpoint that a decision maker wishes to take (Drummond et al., 1987), ranging from consideration of the costs falling exclusively on a particular health service budget (the psychotherapy service, for example), or the impact of a treatment option across all parts of the health care system, or on all public sector agencies, to a fully comprehensive analysis of costs to the wider society.

Generally, service descriptions and costings should aim to be as comprehensive as possible, covering the full range of potential resource impacts (Knapp, 1995; Knapp & Beecham, 1990). Because people with mental health problems living in community settings often have a variety of needs, a range of services are typically involved. These additional services also need to be costed in evaluative inquiries, particularly because of the interpatient variations that they reveal. Comprehensiveness is therefore important, first, where an evaluation examines the appropriateness of alternative settings, such as institutional/residential versus community settings, and second, when the provision of psychotherapy within a health service setting may have secondary impacts on the health care sector and elsewhere (for example, among UK studies, see Menzies, Dolan, & Norton, 1993; Tarrier, Lowson, & Barrowclough, 1991).

On occasions when comprehensiveness is impossible or difficult, or when the resources made available for the research might not permit a full collection of service use data, it might be legitimate to focus on one part of the care system, or to aim to collect information on a subset of services expected to make the largest contributions to total costs. For example, an ongoing economic appraisal of UK government policy of transferring patients with chronic mental health problems from institutional to community settings found that accommodation and living expense accounted for three quarters of the total cost associated with community reprovision. Health service day care, hospital inpatient services, social services day care, and voluntary sector support accounted for most of the remainder. This approach of identifying key cost components is based on post hoc examination of the contributions to total cost of "reduced lists" of services (Knapp & Beecham, 1993). Of course, such reduced lists are country- and context-specific, constituting evidence-based selections of services that require some degree of prior information. But when such information is available, it makes sense to use it to practical advantage when research resources are limited.

Many instruments have been developed to collect service utilization data. They are often labeled the *economic questionnaire*. An instrument developed for mental health economic evaluations in the UK and now employed in more than 60 separate studies in the UK and elsewhere is the Client Service Receipt Inventory (CSRI) (Beecham, 1995; Beecham & Knapp, 1992). The CSRI assesses services used, accommodation arrangements, employment (informal) caregiver support, and other dimensions linked to the measurement of costs. A variant of the CSRI is used in each of our psychotherapy evaluations and is usually integrated into broader assessment sessions with patients or social service workers. Additionally, we endeavor to collect confirmatory or supplementary evidence from hospital records and other computerized information systems.

Costings

The economic cost of a resource input is defined as the value of the benefits forgone from not using that resource in its highest valued alternative use. This is the concept of *opportunity cost*. Given that all resources are finite in their availability, any health care activity will impose an opportunity cost even where apparently provided free of charge (for example, the use of volunteer or family caregivers). Most resources used directly in the provision of a course of psychotherapy (therapist time, buildings, equipment, administrative resources) will have market values: They are bought and sold in markets where the forces of demand and supply interact to set prices, even if imperfectly. In ideal circumstances, these values reflect the opportunity costs of the resource input. In reality, the hourly cost of providing specialist therapy from social workers, psychiatrists, and clinical psychologists might not equal the private or social opportunity cost of an hour's use of their time, but pragmatism dictates that these values are probably the best estimates likely to be reached.

Beecham (1995) details a general methodology for costing the service inputs provided by a range of professionals and in a number of accommodation and other congregate settings. Beyond the costing of the human input into patient care, it is also vital to recognize the full range of operating and capital costs associated with delivery of a service, including those associated with administrative and other overheads. For the UK, there is now an annual publication, *Unit Costs of Community Care*, that provides costings for more than 50 health and social welfare services, together with guidelines as to how these are to be employed for different purposes (Netten & Dennett, 1996). We are currently developing equivalent unit cost lists for mental health services in Italy (Amaddeo et al., 1995), Spain, and Canada, and there are similar moves afoot in other European countries and in the United States (Dickey, Latimer, Beecham, & Powers, 1995). These constitute national or regional unit cost estimates, whereas local figures may be more suitable for some evaluations. Most of our own studies use local figures for those services that are likely to figure significantly in the total costs of treatment and/or that have features that might be particular to that service, team, facility, or therapist and therefore potentially of influence in determining the pattern of outcomes.

Outcome Measurement

In the measurement of treatment effectiveness or outcomes, most evaluations of psychotherapy employ a mixture of clinical and functional outcomes (Krupnick & Pincus, 1992; chapter 18, this volume). Clinical outcomes include the use of psychometric tests and behavioral checklists in assessing therapy, whereas functional outcomes go beyond clinical assessment of improvements in patient health to focus on both monetary and nonmonetary functional benefits. A functional approach to outcome measurement was adopted, for example, in a study comparing inpatient therapy with day treatment therapy for patients suffering from a range of chronic mental health conditions (Washburn, Vannicelli, Longabaugh, & Scheff, 1976). Outcome measures included subjective distress, ability to function in the community, and family burden. The monetary aspects of functional outcome are prevalent in studies reviewed by Yates and Newman (1980b), which include measures of improved productivity at work, "cost offset" effects relating to reductions in the overutilization of medical services, and consideration of the broader implications of therapy outside the health care sector.

The emphasis on measuring financial savings generated by psychotherapy in general medical settings is not surprising, given the emphasis on cost containment within the U.S. health care system, the UK National Health Service, and elsewhere. Furthermore, given that many U.S. health insurers have doubted the effectiveness of psychotherapy and have regarded its use as a costly excess, it remains in the best interest of the psychotherapeutic provider community to demonstrate its worth. Similar pressures are emerging in the UK (see chapter 29, this volume). But cost offset measures can provide only a very partial assessment of the potential benefits to society from psychotherapy, and studies that confine themselves exclusively to cost differences or savings have rightly been criticized for their methodological and practical limitations (see chapter 11, this volume).

Many clinical and functional approaches to outcome measurement are now being recognized as too narrow in approach, and more attention is being given to the development of instruments that accurately reflect the impact that treatment has on quality of life. For example, Hunt and McKenna (1993) suggest that "the aim of quality of life measurement is to quantify the impact of both clinical condition and treatment on wider aspects of the patient's life beyond physician-dominated indicators of the patient's progress" (p. 346). Although outcome measures that concentrate on symptoms and social functioning reflect various aspects of quality of life, it is useful to utilize specifically developed instruments to assess this dimension. If individuals value health care because it can improve their quality of life, then the allocation of resources to, and the economic evaluation of, differing alternatives to treatment should be couched in these terms.

Global measures of quality of life that could prove useful in economic evaluations of psychotherapy include the Oregon Quality of Life Questionnaire (Bigelow, McFarland, & Olson, 1991), the Lehman Quality of Life Interview (Lehman, 1988), and the Lancashire Quality of Life Profile (Oliver, 1991), all of which have been employed in the evaluation of mental health services more generally and have been translated into various languages (see chapter 16, this volume). Some health economists now aim to take the measurement of health-related quality of life further by *valuing* improvements afforded by treatment. As noted earlier, valuation can mean either assessing the utility attached to different health states or determining how much people are willing to pay to avoid decrements or to enjoy improvements in health-related quality of life.

Economists are also interested in the *externality* effects of treatment—those costs and outcomes that fall on people other than the direct users of services. In some mental health contexts, these external effects can be sizable (e.g., Kavanagh & Knapp, 1995). The external benefits of therapy are perhaps easier to identify than any external costs and may include, for example, reductions in resource costs or improvements in the general quality of life of informal caregivers. Similarly, the financing of psychotherapy that mitigates extreme forms of individual behavior or improves compliance with medication regimens could provide public safety benefits.

Conclusions

Differences in costs or outcomes between individuals are rarely entirely random. For example, cost variations usually reflect, in part, a systematic relationship between the marginal cost of providing treatment and a range of influences including, for example, patient outcome, need, severity of condition, and other characteristics of the individual, as well as characteristics of the treatment setting. These cost variations need to be understood, for they reflect upon the targeting and efficiency of provision. Equivalently, interpatient variations in outcome are rarely happenstance and reflect the (partly) predictable consequences of applying different treatment resources and orientations to meet the assessed needs of patients who present themselves to therapists with different histories, personalities, expectations, and constraints.

For these reasons, economic evaluations should pay more attention to disaggregated data, and to the reasons for and implications of interindividual differences. Conventional economic evaluations—cost-effectiveness, cost-benefit, and cost-utility analyses—can compare psychotherapy to other treatments but generally do so only at the aggregate or group level. Cost and production functions can be useful supplements, providing the means to analyze disaggregated cost and outcome data more thoroughly, and thereby to reflect on the consequences of targeting therapy or other treatments on particular patient groups.

As we have argued, interpatient cost and outcome variations are the norm, not the exception. They are especially pertinent to psychotherapy with its patient-centered modus operandi. Clearly, then, the cost-effectiveness of psychotherapeutic interventions will vary across different kinds of disorders, patient groups, therapy types, and even health care systems. These differences should be welcomed, not scorned; they should be explored, not ignored; and they should be exploited in practice settings and in policy environments for the efficiency and other improvements that recognition, analysis, and careful interpretation can bring.

Acknowledgments The authors gratefully acknowledge insightful and challenging comments on an earlier version of this chapter from Bill Hargreaves, Kathy Magruder, Nancy Miller, and Agnes Rupp.

References

Amaddeo, F., Bonnizato, P., Rossi, F., Beecham, J. K., Knapp, M. R. J., & Tansella, M. (1995). La valutazione dei costi delle malattie mentali in Italia: Svilippo di una metodologia e possibili applicazioni. *Epidemiologia e Psichiatria Sociale, 4*(2), 145–162.

Andrews, G. (1991). The evaluation of psychotherapy. *Current Opinion in Psychiatry, 4,* 379–383.

Beecham, J. K. (1995). Collecting and estimating costs. In M. R. J. Knapp (Ed.), *The economic evaluation of mental health care.* Aldershot, England: Arena.

Beecham, J. K., & Knapp, M. R. J. (1992). Costing psychiatric options. In G. Thornicroft, C. Brewin, & J. Wing (Eds.), *Measuring mental health needs.* Oxford: Oxford University Press.

Bigelow, D. A., McFarland, B. H., & Olson, M. M. (1991). Quality of life of community mental health programme clients: Validating a measure. *Community Mental Health Journal, 27,* 125–133.

Chisholm, D., Healey, A. T., & Knapp, M. R. J. (1996). QALYs in mental health care. *Social Psychiatry and Psychiatric Epidemiology, 32,* 68–75.

Davies, B. P., Bebbington, A. C., & Charnley, H. (1990). *Resources, needs and outcomes in community-based care.* Aldershot, England: Avebury.

Davies, B. P., & Knapp, M. R. J. (1981). *Old People's Homes and the Production of Welfare.* London: Routledge & Kegan Paul.

Dean, J. (1976). *Statistical cost estimation.* Bloomington: Indiana University Press.

Dickey, B., Latimer, E., Beecham, J. K., & Powers, K. (1995). *Toolkit for estimating per unit mental health programme costs.* Mimeograph, Health Services Research Unit, Harvard University, Cambridge.

Donabedian, A. (1980). *The definition of quality and approaches to its assessment.* Ann Arbor, MI: Health Administration Press.

Drummond, M. F., Stoddart, G. L., & Torrance, G. W. (1987). *Methods for economic evaluation of health care programmes.* Oxford: Oxford Medical Publications.

Fonagy, P., & Higgitt, A. (1989). Evaluating the performance of departments of psychotherapy. *Psychoanalytic Psychotherapy, 4,* 121–153.

Fuss, M., & McFadden, D. (Eds.). (1978). *Production economics: A dual approach to theory and applications.* Amsterdam: North Holland.

Ginsberg, G., Marks, I. M., & Waters, H. (1984). Cost-benefit analysis of a controlled trial of nurse therapy for neuroses in primary care. *Psychological Medicine, 15,* 683–690.

Goodman, A. C., Holder, H. D., Nishiura, E., & Hankin, J. R. (1992). An analysis of short-term alcoholism treatment cost functions. *Medical Care, 30,* 795–810.

Grossman, M. (1972). *The demand for health: A theoretical and empirical investigation.* New York: National Bureau of Economic Research.

Howard, K., Kopta, S. M., Krause, M. S., & Orlinsky, D. E. (1986). The dose-effect relationship in psychotherapy. *American Psychologist, 41,* 159–164.

Hunt, S., & McKenna, S. (1993). Measuring quality of life in psychiatry. In S. Walker & R. Rosser (Eds.), *Quality of life assessment: Key issues in the 1990s.* Amsterdam: Kluwer Academic.

Jöhannesson, M., & Jönsson, B. (1991). Economic evaluation in health care: Is there a role for cost-benefit analysis? *Health Policy, 17,* 1–23.

Johnston, J. (1960). *Statistical cost analysis.* New York: McGraw-Hill.

Kavanagh, S., & Knapp, M. R. J. (1995). At the crossroads of health policy, health economics and family policy: Whose interest to provide a family oriented service? In M. Gopfert & J. Webster (Eds.), *Disturbed mentally ill parents and their children.* Cambridge: Cambridge University Press.

Kavanagh, S., & Stewart, A. (1995). Economic evaluations of mental health care: Modes and methods. In M. R. J. Knapp (Ed.), *The economic evaluation of mental health care.* Aldershot, England: Arena.

Knapp, M. R. J. (1984). *The economics of social care.* London: Macmillan.

Knapp, M. R. J. (Ed.). (1995). *The economic evaluation of mental health care.* Aldershot, England: Arena.

Knapp, M. R. J. (1998). Making music out of noise: Understanding cost variations. *British Journal of Psychiatry* (supplement, forthcoming).

Knapp, M. R. J., & Beecham, J. K. (1993). Costing mental health services. *Psychological Medicine, 20,* 293–908.

Knapp, M. R. J., & Beecham, J. K. (1990). Reduced-list costings: Examination of an informed short-cut in mental health research. *Health Economics,* 2, 313–322.

Knapp, M. R. J., Marks, I., Wolstenholme, J., Beecham, J. K., Audini, B., Astin, J., & Connelly, J., & Watts, V. (1998). Home-based versus hospital-based care for serious mental illness. *British Journal of Psychiatry, 172,* 506–512.

Krupnick, J. L., & Pincus, H. A. (1992). The cost-effectiveness of psychotherapy: A plan for research. *American Journal of Psychiatry, 149,* 1295–1305.

Lehman, A. F. (1988). A quality of life interview for the chronically mentally ill. *Evaluation and Programme Planning, 11,* 51–62.

Menzies, D., Dolan, B. M., & Norton, K. (1993). Are short term savings worth long term costs? Funding treatment for personality disorders. *Psychiatric Bulletin, 17,* 517–519.

Netten, A., & Davies, B. P. (1991). The social production of welfare and consumption of social services. *Journal of Public Policy, 10,* 331–347.

Netten, A., & Dennett, J. (1996). *Unit costs of community care 1996.* Canterbury: Personal Social Services Research Unit, University of Kent.

Oliver, J. P. J. (1991). The social care directive: Development of a quality of life profile for use in community services for the mentally ill. *Social Work and Social Sciences Review,* 3, 5–45.

Orlinksy, D. E., & Howard, K. J. (1986). Process and outcome in psychotherapy. In S. L. Garfield & A. G. Bergin (Eds.), *Handbook of psychotherapy and behaviour change* (3rd ed.). New York: Wiley.

Parry, G. (1992). Improving psychotherapy services: Applications of research audit and evaluation. *British Journal of Clinical Psychology, 31,* 3–19.

Sheldon, T. (1996). Problems of using modelling in the economic evaluation of health care. *Health Economics,* 5, 1–11.

Tarrier, N., Lowson, K., & Barrowclough, C. (1991). Some aspects of family interventions in schizophrenia: 2. Financial considerations. *British Journal of Psychiatry, 159,* 481–484.

Tolley, G., Kenkel, D., & Fabian, R. (1994). *Valuing health for policy: An economic approach.* Chicago: University of Chicago Press.

Torrance, G. W. (1986). Measurement of health state utilities for economic appraisal: A review. *Journal of Health Economics,* 5, 1–30.

Washburn, S., Vannicelli, M., Longabaugh, R., & Scheff, B. J. (1976). A controlled comparison of psychiatric treatment and in-patient hospitalisation. *Journal of Consulting and Clinical Psychology, 44,* 665–675.

Weisbrod, B. A., Test, M. A., & Stein, L. I. (1980). Alternatives to mental hospital treatment: Economic benefit-cost analysis. *Archives of General Psychiatry,* 37, 400–405.

Yates, B., & Newman, F. L. (1980a). Approaches to cost-effectiveness analysis and cost-benefit analysis of psychotherapy. In G. R. Vandenbos (Ed.), *Psychotherapy: Practice, research, policy.* London: Sage.

Yates, B., & Newman, F..L. (1980b). Findings of cost-effectiveness and cost-benefit analyses of psychotherapy. In G. R. Vandenbos (Ed.), *Psychotherapy: Practice, research, policy.* London: Sage.

13

Pricing Psychotherapy

Lessons from Health Care Reform

Richard G. Frank & Thomas G. McGuire

President Clinton's health care reform initiative in 1992 and 1993 was initially viewed by many, including most of the mental health community, as an opportunity to make right the irrationalities and inequities of the health care system. Mental health advocates had a special set of grievances. Most private insurance placed special limits on hospital care and psychotherapy and was slow in introducing coverage for intermediate levels of care. Larson (1992), summarizing data from the Bureau of Labor Statistics, notes that only 2% of the workforce (in firms with 100+ employees) had parity of coverage for psychotherapy, in comparison with coverage for other outpatient care. The seriously mentally ill were overrepresented in an unevenly and, in many cases, inadequately funded public system for care. The mix of payers—private, Medicaid, and state—contributed to the lack of coordination of care. In this context, for the first time in modern U.S. history, a federal administration articulated a complete vision for the mental health and substance abuse system that would address these shortfalls.

The proposed Health Security Act (HSA) itself, which finally emerged in the fall of 1993, confronted the demands for reform and refinancing with the reality of budget limitations.[1] Frank et al. (1994) estimated that Americans spent roughly $225 per person on mental health and substance abuse treatment in 1990. In the policy development process, it was clear relatively early that reforms that required new funds (after trending forward the 1990 numbers to the relevant years) would simply not be feasible. If coverage were to be extended to the currently uninsured, and if the risk of high-cost illnesses were to be ameliorated, the budget constraint had to be loosened in some other way. This had two immediate effects that were relevant to coverage for psychotherapy under reform. First (and this is a relatively familiar issue), coverage for psychotherapy has traditionally been a target for cost savings. Second, the imposition of a budget constraint on policymaking put pressure on the cost-estimating process. In the presence of "managed care," could benefits be expanded and new populations covered with the "savings" that could be expected by a more efficient management of the benefit?

This chapter uses the experience with estimating costs of the Health Security Act to examine aspects of the cost estimation process that are especially relevant for making payment policy for coverage of psychotherapy. We focus on areas where there was a high degree of uncertainty in making assumptions and on those factors that were central to discussion of the psychotherapy benefit. The paper is organized into four sections. Following the introduction, the second section describes the coverage for mental health care within the Health Security Act proposed by President Clinton. The third section illustrates a number of issues that arise in cost estimation. We focus especially on the costs of insuring the uninsured to underscore the difficulties that arose in making fair estimates of the costs of mental health coverage. The fourth section of the paper briefly draws some lessons from the experiences with national health care reform.

"Discriminatory Coverage" in the Health Security Act

Proposed coverage for psychotherapy in HSA was dependent on time (pre and post full integration in 2001), and on the plan a person or family would select. In a managed-care plan such as a health maintenance organization (HMO) and its variants, coverage for psychotherapy was 30 visits per year with a $25 per visit copayment (not counted toward the overall out-of-pocket limit). In a conventional plan, coverage was also 30 visits but with a 50% coinsurance payment. In both plans, it was possible to trade inpatient days for outpatient visits, a provision that effectively eliminated the coverage limit for most users. The psychotherapy benefit was not much better than what most employed families already had.[2] Screening, medical management, crisis intervention, and case management all would have been covered at parity (20% coinsurance) with other conditions.

One of the reasons coverage for psychotherapy is subject to special restrictions in health insurance is the problem of demand response. A benefit plan for health care has two goals: to encourage cost-effective care and to protect patients from the financial risk of illness. In most discussions of health insurance, these goals are assumed to conflict. The risk protection afforded by insurance comes at the cost of weakening patient incentives to use care efficiently: the "moral hazard" problem in health insurance. Demand response to lower out-of-pocket costs implies that patients use more care when they are insured, and since they would not have purchased this care had they been paying full cost, there is a presumption that the care is "not worth the cost" (Pauly, 1968). The greater the demand response in some area of care, the more is sacrificed in terms of efficient care when insurance is increased. The implication is that care with a high degree of demand response should have less comprehensive insurance coverage.[3]

This argument is the technical counterpart to the popular concern that generous insurance coverage for mental health treatment will lead to unacceptable levels of costs. The response to the price-lowering effects of insurance for mental health is greater than for general medical care taken in the aggregate. Every major study of insurance and demand concludes that demand for ambulatory mental health care is more responsive to insurance coverage than is demand for general medical office care (McGuire, 1989). Results from the Rand Health Insurance Experiment (HIE) are probably most convincing. Keeler, Wells, Manning, Rumpel, and Hanley (1986) found that families with full coverage used about four times as much ambulatory mental health care as families with no coverage, a demand response about twice as great as that found for general medical care. While people with an insurance plan that makes care nearly free use much more care, there was no evidence in the HIE that better coverage improved mental health status (Wells, Manning, & Valdez, 1989).

The arithmetic of demand response and cost saving shows why it is so tempting to cut coverage for psychotherapy. Suppose a plan pays full coverage for psychotherapy, and the total cost of that benefit is $X. What is saved if the coverage is cut to 50%? First, there is the cost shifting. Even if total utilization remains unchanged, the plan saves 50%. But of course, utilization falls with a rise in demand-side cost sharing. A reasonable estimate is that demand falls by half with a move from full to 50% coverage. Thus, the plan pays only half of half of the original utilization, or *25% of the original cost.* Figure 1 makes this point graphically, showing the comparative plan obligations under full and 50% coverage.

Similar reasoning applies, of course, to the coverage of any health service. Differences arise from the degree of demand response. Savings to a plan are greater for psychotherapy because of the high degree of demand response. The theory of optimal insurance is the rationale for a policy to take the savings offered by a service with an unusually high demand response to coverage.

Pricing Psychotherapy in the HSA

Writers on economics and mental health (ourselves included) have pointed to the progress made in the last 20 years in understanding the demand response to health insurance.[4] Although demand response in psychotherapy is greater than the average for other medical conditions, it is not "unlimited" and "uncontrollable" as some have said. It is unfortunately true, however, that there is a great deal of suspicion about psychotherapy in the actuarial community. Employers and governments rely on actuaries for advice about insurance costs. Here is a sample (only slightly biased) of remarks (referring not just to psychotherapy, but to

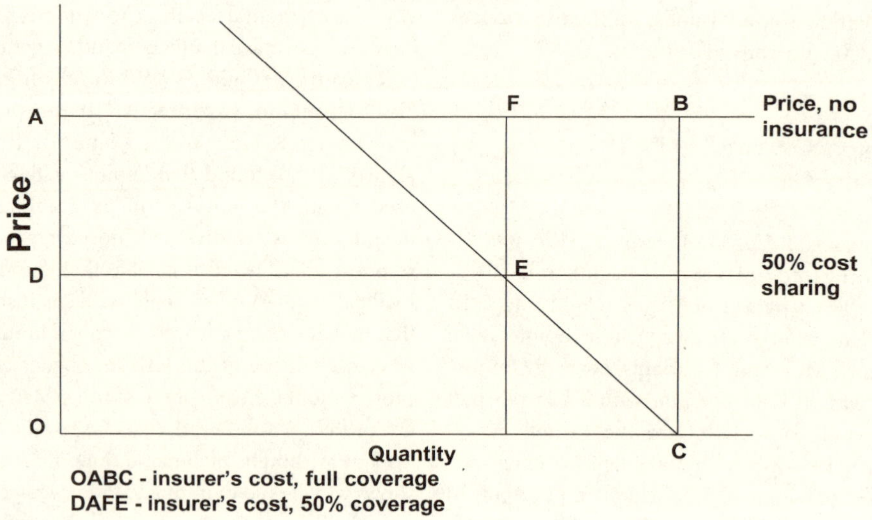

Figure 13.1 Cost shifting and demand response due to benefit change.

all mental health treatment) made at a panel entitled "Managing Mental Health Costs" and published by the Society of Actuaries (1989, 1990):

> None of us can show up at a general hospital and say, "Put me in intensive care." In psychiatry you can walk into any psychiatric or substance abuse treatment facility or general hospital with a psychiatric unit and request admission. And, after careful review of your insurance plan you will have a consensus on that referral.
>
> There are some segments of the population where it is actually a status symbol to say, "I'm going to my therapist."
>
> Providers do not have protocols for treatment.
>
> We are spending a lot more money, taking up a disproportionate share of our resources, and it is not resulting in improved outcome.
>
> There is no standardized treatment. Misdiagnosis is the rule, not the exception. Professional consensus is lacking. Generally speaking, the psychiatrist believes everything can be treated with drugs and is biologically based, the psychologist thinks he can talk you through everything, the clinical social worker thinks the problem is society, and the marriage and family counselors think everything has to do with the relationships within the family.
>
> [Providers] construct a treatment plan which maximizes [the] benefit.

In spite of the information that has accumulated on the cost of mental health benefits and methods for cost estimation, suspicion about psychotherapy leads some actuaries and others in the business of cost forecasting to err on the side of caution, which means, in this case, making sure projections are not too low. Psychotherapy is not the only mental health service subject to this problem, to be sure. The upshot for the proposed legislation was, however, that decision makers were presented with discrepant numbers when it came to the costs of covering mental health care.

The discrepancies between the various cost estimates produced suggested an area of considerable budgetary and political risk that made both the Clinton administration and Congress wary of the Mental Health and Substance Abuse (MH/SA) coverage proposed in the HSA. A contentious debate took place over the MH/SA cost estimates during the larger health reform deliberations. In the end, uncertainty in estimates led the administration and Congress to shy away from including a benefit that would offer broad coverage for MH/SA care.

Estimating the Costs of the Uninsured

One of the components of cost estimation for the HSA involved estimating the costs of coverage for the currently uninsured. A number of groups developed such an estimate. This was an area characterized by an especially high degree of uncertainty. It is therefore instructive to see how one of these estimates was developed, that of the American Association of Actuaries

(AAA). The AAA report spelled out many of the assumptions made in estimating costs of MH/SA coverage for the uninsured. The lack of empirical support provided for many of the assumptions made is quite striking.

The cost per uninsured user of MH/SA care was estimated by taking the aggregate distribution of diagnoses for all state mental hospital and VA psychiatric hospital specialty psychiatric admissions in 1986 and estimating the costs for the same distribution of diagnoses by using data from a large insurer. The diagnostic distribution of cases treated in state mental hospitals and VA psychiatric hospitals was viewed as representative of insured psychiatric inpatients. The resulting expenditure estimates reflect the private insurance payments associated with a set of diagnoses that reflect the illnesses of insured inpatients. The purpose of performing this "matched" estimate was presumably to account for the different pattern of illness (generally more severe) found among uninsured users of public mental health services from the pattern of the insured population. The diagnosis-specific private cost was then increased by a factor of 1.98. The reason given for this adjustment was to adjust for the greater severity of illness (within diagnosis) in the currently uninsured than in the currently insured. The 1.98 factor was put forward without justification or without reference to any data. We know of no data to help with making such a "severity adjustment," but given this is a within diagnosis adjustment, the almost doubling of the cost of treating a case of the uninsured compared to the insured seems very high. The effect of this assumption was to increase and probably overstate the cost of extending care to the uninsured.

In order to estimate the number of users of MH/SA for the uninsured population as coverage was expanded, the AAA relied on prevalence data. It was assumed that the uninsured, once insured, would use MH/SA care at a rate that was 24% higher than that of the currently insured population. The 1.24 adjustment factor was used to account for the higher prevalence of MH/SA illnesses in the uninsured population. To obtain the total cost per insured individual, one combines the two components. That is, one begins with the cost per insured individual, multiplies that number by 1.98 to account for higher costs per user, and then multiplies that product by 1.24 to allow for a higher number of users. The net effect of these assumptions was to project very large increases in the level of utilization by currently uninsured individuals when coverage is extended to them. The AAA report concluded that extending coverage to the uninsured would result in a cost of \$550–\$750 per uninsured person, a cost 245% (1.98 × 1.24) higher than the costs of covering the typical person who is currently insured.

Some of the assumptions in the AAA report (and some of the other reports) could have been made more accurate if the authors had had the resources and time to consult some of the recent research literature, such as the National Comorbidity Survey and the Patient Sample Survey from the Center for Mental Health Services (CMHS). Only the Congressional Budget Office (CBO) analysis made use of these data sets. The prevalence of mental illness is higher among the uninsured population. Data from the National Comorbidity Survey (NCS) shows that approximately 23% of uninsured people have a 30-day psychiatric diagnosis compared to about 17% of the insured population that have such a diagnosis. It is, however, well known that there is a rather weak relation between diagnosis and utilization in mental health. In addition, the uninsured population is different from the insured in other respects. The uninsured tend to be younger, suffer from fewer physical conditions, and are more likely to suffer from substance abuse conditions than are the insured population. These data can help estimate (a) the portion of the uninsured who would use MH/SA services when coverage is extended to them and (b) the cost of care to the insurance plan per user.

Estimates of both components cannot be adequately made from either aggregate health accounts data or simple prevalence data. Answering the first question requires (a) estimating the impact of insurance on utilization, with other factors held constant, and (b) knowing the baseline probability of use for the currently uninsured population. The NCS offers data from a sample of the U.S. population between the ages of 15 and 54 that are relevant to these questions. Analysis of data from the NCS suggests that if coverage were extended to the currently uninsured population, their probability of using MH/SA care would be 0–5% higher than for the currently insured population (Frank, Kessler, & Leaf 1994). This result occurs because the uninsured are generally younger and somewhat healthier, and because the higher prevalence of mental illness in this population is accounted for largely by substance abuse problems, where treatment utilization rates are quite low even among the insured.

One approach to estimating cost per user is to employ the data from demand research. In the cost estimates of the HSA, the assumptions about utilization growth ranged from 45% to about 100% above baseline per user costs. These assumptions about utilization growth ranged from 45% to about 100% above baseline per user costs. These assumptions are consistent with the view that there are high barriers to treatment for individuals who are indigent and mentally ill. There is clearly some truth to the view that all those who could benefit from treatment do not receive care. However, it is also clear that there is a large and active public MH/SA treatment system that provides access to care at no cost to many in this population.

For instance, according to the CMHS, in 1990 there were about as many "public" psychiatric beds (in state mental hospitals and VA psychiatric hospitals) offering free care per 1,000 population as there were "private" psychiatric beds (49.4 vs. 50). In addition, there are about 740 freestanding outpatient psychiatric clinics and 1,249 mental health centers in the United States, where 50% and 61% of the revenues, respectively, come in the form of direct payments from government for treating the idigent mentally ill. These organizations treat about 2 million outpatient MH/SA cases a year. Thus, uninsured people with MH/SA problems have access to a substantial amount of free care. Taking account of the availability of free care is very important in making projections of "new" utilization stemming from insurance coverage. Estimates from demand studies that use differences in use from a no-insurance condition (assuming individuals pay for care themselves) and a full-insurance condition (assuming care is paid for by insurance) to estimate response of the uninsured are likely to overestimate the increase in costs attributable to insurance coverage.

Offsets and Substitution

A second area that is often pointed to in discussion of cost estimates for psychotherapy is the phenomenon of cost offsets. This, too, is an area of considerable uncertainty. Advocates for mental health coverage often point to an "offset effect" to justify including mental health care in an insurance benefit package. An offset effect exists when mental health services lead to a reduction in use of other health care.

Advocates for expanded MH/SA benefits claim that increased coverage for MH/SA services will result in important reductions in medical costs. Some insurance plan designers have advanced the notion that limits on psychotherapy (such as those found in the HSA) can be relaxed in a cost-neutral fashion by allowing individuals to "substitute" coverage for inpatient days in order to expand visits.

The notion that MH/SA problems affect the consumption of medical services is a sensible one. Estimates of the offset effect have ranged dramatically; from 5% to 80% of MH/SA costs have been found to have been offset by reduced medical costs (Fiedler, 1989). Enormous methodological difficulties are associated with obtaining an unbiased estimate of the offset effect. While there is certainly ample reason to believe that the offset effect exists, there remains great uncertainty about its magnitude. An important danger is that given the range of findings reported in the literature, one can find support for assumptions that will generate almost any number between 0 and the maximum premium by any of the groups making cost estimates of the HSA.

If offset effects exist, then any offset from the present set of benefits will have already been built into the current medical-surgical costs. The issue for health reform has to do with a "marginal" offset effect. If we *increase* coverage for psychotherapy above existing norms, will we get *more* offset? The (weak) existing evidence for offset effects has to do with initial treatments, not with marginal treatment. All the estimates of health reform costs disregarded marginal offsets, which was probably the right thing to do.

Another form of substitutability concerns the trading of outpatient for inpatient benefits when limits on psychotherapy visits exist (as they did in the HSA). The study by the AAA offers an example of such an assessment in connection with the HSA. There are a number of controversial policy issues related to the use of such substitution provisions, such as the dilution of coverage for catastrophic costs that such a trade-off may induce. In this paper we limit our discussion to issues concerning the estimation of coverage costs. The AAA, among others, claims that substitution provisions that call for either 3 or 4 visits per inpatient day are cost-neutral, a claim unlikely to be correct. The reasons relate to the basic distributions of MH/SA service utilization. Based on data from the CMHS and MEDSTAT, roughly 0.2% of an insured population stay for more than 30 days of inpatient care, 0.16% stay between 20 and 30 days, and 0.45% use more than 25 psychotherapy visits. Moreover, 84% of those exceeding the 25-visit limit use no inpatient care. Thus, there are many more people likely to trade in their hospital benefit than there are people for whom savings may be realized. In addition, there is no evidence to suggest that improving the outpatient benefit in the context of indemnity insurance will result in reduced inpatient utilization. There is some evidence to suggest that managed care leads to substitution between inpatient and outpatient care, but this is incorporated into the managed-care effect assumptions discussed above. The conclusion we reach from examining the data is that instituting "substitution" between psychotherapy benefits and inpatient care will drive up costs because one is, in effect, lifting a constraint on utilization for a relatively large number of users while realizing offsetting savings from very few individuals.

Discussion

Estimating the costs of mental health and substance abuse coverage has long been a difficult and controversial exercise. Estimating costs of psychotherapy has been among the most contentious aspects of the overall effort. In some ways, this is surprising. From a research standpoint, the data analysis of the demand response for psychotherapy to insurance coverage has been carefully studied, and a broad consensus has been reached regarding the response to cost sharing. The political issues regarding psychotherapy coverage are formidable. Major professional groups have strong commitments to coverage for psychotherapy even if that means limiting coverage for more costly (and therefore financially more risky) forms of care. Uncertainty around the costs of insuring the uninsured, offset effects, and the efficiency of substitution of level of care create opportunities for advocates of various positions to offer assumptions for cost estimation that are favorable to their views. The experience with President Clinton's proposal for national health care reform presents a case study of that situation.

The lessons we believe emerge from the recent experience in pricing benefits are as follows: (a) The predisposition among most groups making estimates of mental health costs is to assume that costs will increase dramatically with expanded coverage; (b) carefully analyzed high-quality data can sometimes be persuasive in influencing the assumptions used for making projections, but not always; (c) counting on offsets and substitution effects to justify expanded-coverage psychotherapy is generally not justified by the data; and (d) substitution of psychotherapy visits for inpatient days as a strategy for relaxing visit limits will increase, not decrease, costs.

Acknowledgments This Research is partially supported by grant K05-MH1263 from the National Institute of Mental Health. The authors are grateful to Kathryn Magruder, Nancy Miller, and Agnes Rupp for suggestions about topics to be addressed in the paper.

Notes

1. See Arons et al. (1994) for a discussion of the Health Security Act, and the reasons that comprehensive reform of mental health and substance abuse financing were not proposed for immediate implementation.
2. Inpatient coverage was for 30 days with 30 additional days possible. A 1-day deductible and 20% coinsurance imposed significant cost sharing on families. Coverage for nonresidential services would have improved dramatically for most working families. Frank, Goldman, and McGuire (1992) discuss the rationale for the cost-sharing features.
3. See an interesting article by Keeler (1995) on the "demand for effective care," offering one interpretation of the relation between the observed demand and effectiveness.
4. See McGuire (1994) for a discussion of the methods of cost estimation in mental health and substance abuse.

References

Arons, B., et al. (1994, Spring). Mental health and substance abuse coverage under "health care reform." *Health Affairs, 13*(1), 192–205.

Fiedler, J. (1989). *The medical offset effect and public health policy*. New York: Praeger.

Frank, R., Kessler, R., & Leaf, P. (1994). *The uninsured and mental health coverage: Duplications for health care reform*. Working paper, Harvard University.

Frank, R. G., Goldman, H. H., & McGuire, T. G. (1992, Fall). A model mental health benefit in private insurance. *Health Affairs, 11*(3), 98–117.

Frank, R., et al. (1994, Spring). Paying for mental health and substance abuse care. *Health Affairs*, 337–342.

Keeler, E. B., Wells, K. B., Manning, W. G., Rumpel, J. D., & Hanley, J. M. (1986). *The demand for episodes of mental health services*. Rand Corporation, R-3432-NIMH.

Larson, M. J. (1992). *Demand for private health insurance provisions, for drug abuse care in medium and large firms, 1989*. Ph.D. dissertation, Brandeis University.

McGuire, T. (1994). Predicting the cost of mental health benefits. *Milbank Quarterly*, 72(1), 3–23.

McGuire, T. G. (1989). Financing and demand for mental health services. In C. Taube, D. Mechanic, & A. Hohmann (Eds.), *The Future of Mental Health Services Research*, DHHS Pub. No.

(ADM) 89-1600, Washington, DC: Government Printing Office.

Pauly, M. (1968, June). The economics of moral hazard: Comment. *American Economic Review*, *58*(3), 531–537.

Society of Actuaries. (1989). Managing mental health cost. *Record*, *15*, 113–123.

Society of Actuaries. (1990). Managing mental health cost. *Record*, *16*, 391–407.

Wells, K., Manning, W., & Valdez, B. (1989, July). The effects of insurance generosity on the psychological distress and well being of a general population. RAND publication R-3682-NIMH/HCFA, Santa Monica, CA.

Part IV

MEASURES FOR STUDYING PSYCHOTHERAPY COSTS AND OUTCOMES

14

The Cost-Effectiveness of Psychotherapy

Dose-Response and Phase Models

Kenneth I. Howard, Robert J. Lueger,
Zoran Martinovich, & Wolfgang Lutz

Psychotherapy works. The evidence supporting this conclusion has accumulated from many sources and research designs. Whether one examines the retrospective survey responses of psychotherapy consumers (e.g., Mental Health: Does Therapy Help? 1995), or the results of many clinical trials (cf. Lipsey & Wilson, 1993), the verdict is that psychotherapy is generally efficacious. Indeed, psychotherapy may be one of the most well-documented interventions in the health care field.

Moreover, psychotherapy works as well as or better than other health care prescriptions and interventions. For example, a review of meta-analyses (Lipsey & Wilson, 1993) conducted on psychotherapy and occupational, educational, and medical treatments showed that psychotherapy produced a rate of positive benefit that surpassed those of many other health interventions. By applying a probabilistic interpretation (Howard, Krause, & Vessey, 1994) of the effect sizes identified by Lipsey and Wilson(1993), we can see in Table 14.1 that patents in psychotherapy had a 75% probability of being better off after treatment than patients who did not receive treatment. This is higher than the probabilities identified with some other common medical interventions.

From Efficacy to Treatment Effectiveness

Efficacy studies, with their careful selection of homogeneous patients and standardized treatment conditions, are critical for addressing the causal sufficiency of a treatment for a prototypical problem. Effectiveness studies establish the generalizability of causal sufficiency under actual practice conditions. Service delivery settings may differ (health maintenance organization, private practice, medical school clinic), providers are the normal employees of those settings, and patients might have comorbid psychiatric and medical diagnoses. In addition, the length of treatment is not a fixed variable. Patients may discontinue psychotherapy after a few sessions or may continue much longer than the 16-session protocol employed in many efficacy studies. It is the effectiveness of therapies over longer periods of time and treatment that is of particular interest, whether the intended treatment is long-term psychotherapy, maintenance or booster treatments, or post-treatment follow-ups. The certainty that the highly controlled conditions of the efficacy study account for alternative interpretations diminishes as more time and events occur from the initiation of any efficacy study. Cost-effectiveness and cost-efficiency analyses require models of patient improvement for effective interpretation of treatment outcome.

The Dose-Response Model

Our work has emphasized both theory and empirically based modeling of patient improvement in psychotherapy. Howard, Kopta, Krause, and Orlinsky (1986) re-

Table 14.1 The Effectiveness of Treatments: Mean Effect Sizes and Probabilities of a Treated Patient Being Better Off Than an Untreated Patient

Effect	Treatment Size	$P(t > nt)$
Psychotherapy (general)	.88	.73
Cognitive behavioral/behavioral	.77	.71
Bypass surgery	.80	.71
Drug treatment for arthritis	.61	.67
Anticoagulants	.30	.58
Aspirin to prevent heart attacks	.07	.52

Based on Lipsey and Wilson (1993).

viewed the relationship between amount of treatment (sessions) and improvement as reported in 15 studies. A probit model fitting the data was identified. The model showed that improvement in psychotherapy followed a log-linear relationship between the log of the number of sessions and and the normalized probability of benefit. The greatest amount of improvement occurred in early sessions. Thereafter, it took more and more sessions of psychotherapy to produce the same amount of benefit. The positively sloped, negatively accelerating curve illustrating this phenomenon is presented in Figure 14.1. From this figure, it can be concluded that it takes approximately 8 sessions of psychotherapy for 50% of patients to achieve improvement, 26 sessions to achieve a 75% improvement rate, and 65 sessions to achieve a near asymptote of 85% improvement rate. The value of the dose-response model is its identification of the pattern of change in response to psychotherapy.

The dose-response model has enabled us to make better sense of other published studies and is highly informative for cost-benefit studies. For example, a reanalysis of the Eysenck data (McNeilly, & Howard, 1991) has qualified Eysenck's (1952) conclusion that spontaneous remission is as effective as psychotherapy. Indeed, it is, if a 2-year end-point analysis is made of the Eysenck data. As Figure 14.2 shows, psychotherapy accomplishes in 16 sessions what spontaneous remission does in 2 years. Half of psychotherapy patients are improved with 8 sessions, whereas the comparable rate of improvement under spontaneous remission conditions takes approximately 1 year. These differences are remarkable, considering Eysenck included any and all other interventions other than psychotherapy under the rubric of "spontaneous remission." The time during which quality of living is improved by psychotherapy over spontaneous improvement can signify real cost-benefit. In health care assessment, the rate of improvement is an important variable for addressing the relevance of a particular intervention.

The dose-response model also is useful for demonstrating the response of different patient conditions to psychotherapy. In Figure 14.3, the response curves of patients with three diagnoses are compared. These are clinician-based diagnoses, not the products of structured interviews. As can be seen, limiting psychotherapy to an arbitrary number of sessions—say, 20—would be more than adequate for most depressive patients and patients suffering from anxiety but would result in little gain for patients with borderline conditions. Yet the patterns of improvement with additional amounts of psychotherapy are in the desired directions.

The Phase Model

The dose-response model showed the pattern of improvement for patients in psychotherapy and was based on global ratings of patient improvement or on measures of symptom change. A large number of outcome constructs and measures has been used in theorizing and measuring treatment results. Casual comparisons of these outcome measures do not always yield rational interpretations. For example, one study will report a large effect size for the treatment of major depression in 6 sessions whereas another study will report modest effect sizes in 16 sessions. Obviously, the outcome of choice matters in the observed effects.

We have proposed a relatively simple model of treatment outcomes, which includes three categories of

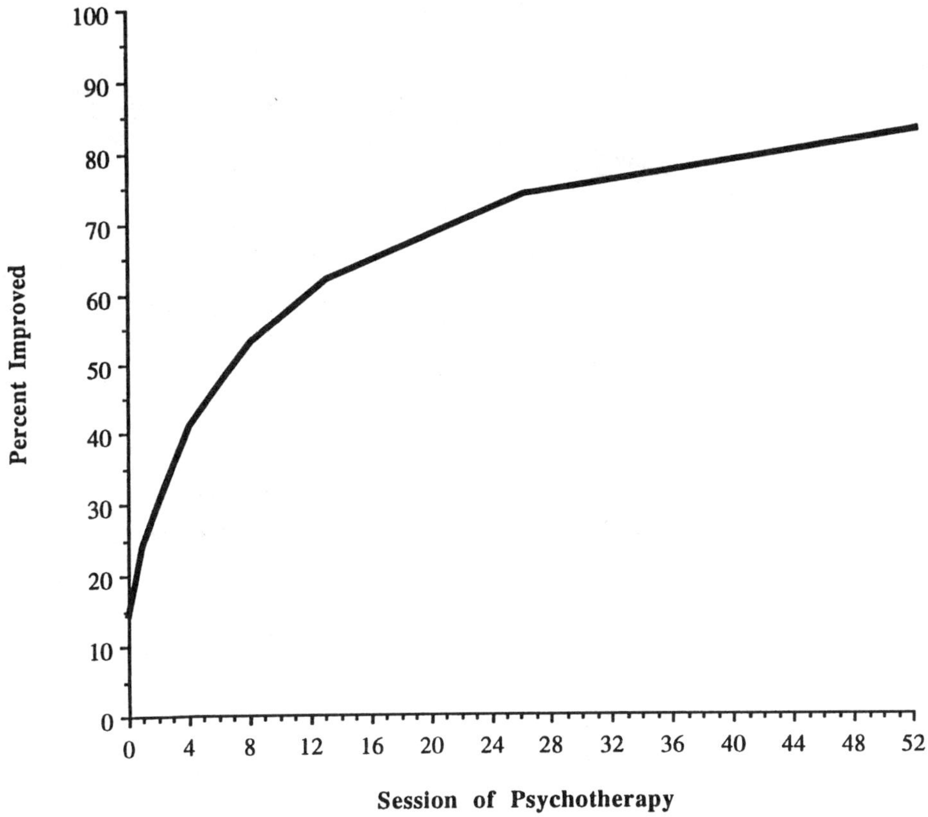

Figure 14.1 The dose-response model of psychotherapy improvement.

outcomes. The first phase, *remoralization*, has been thoroughly described by Jerome Frank (Frank, 1968; Frank & Frank, 1991). The therapist uses a variety of techniques to be supportive. The patient begins to feel better, realizes that she or he is not alone in distress, becomes more hopeful and optimistic, and feels less helpless. For most patients, this response happens relatively quickly, usually in two to four sessions. For many, remoralization is sufficient, and therapy is terminated by satisfied patients. The patients are optimistic and able to use their own coping resources enough to feel in control of their lives and confidently back on their feet.

The second phase, *remediation*, involves the reduction of the patient's symptoms or symptom syndromes. Here, the therapist helps the patient learn to recognize and label symptoms, to gauge their severity and impact, and to learn new or alternative ways of coping. Here also, the theoretical approach of the therapy influences the focus: Interpersonal psychotherapy with depression involves instruction in the symptoms of depression and a session-by-session review of these symptoms prior to exploration of ways the depression is related to role transitions, loss, conflict, or social deficits. Cognitive behavior therapy teaches patients to examine assumptions and attributions about personal contributions to positive or negative outcomes. Short-term psychodynamic psychotherapy focuses on critical conflictual emotional events and provides insight.

We maintain that remediation cannot happen without the patient's remoralization. In fact, we have shown that remoralization is a probabilistically necessary antecedent to remediation of symptoms (Howard, Lueger, Maling, & Martinovich, 1993). Now, some patients, perhaps especially veteran patients, enter psychotherapy with remoralization nearly accomplished. Once the patient is hopeful, the necessary groundwork has been established to work collaboratively with the therapist in whatever technique the therapist introduces to work on the symptoms presented by the patient. Again,

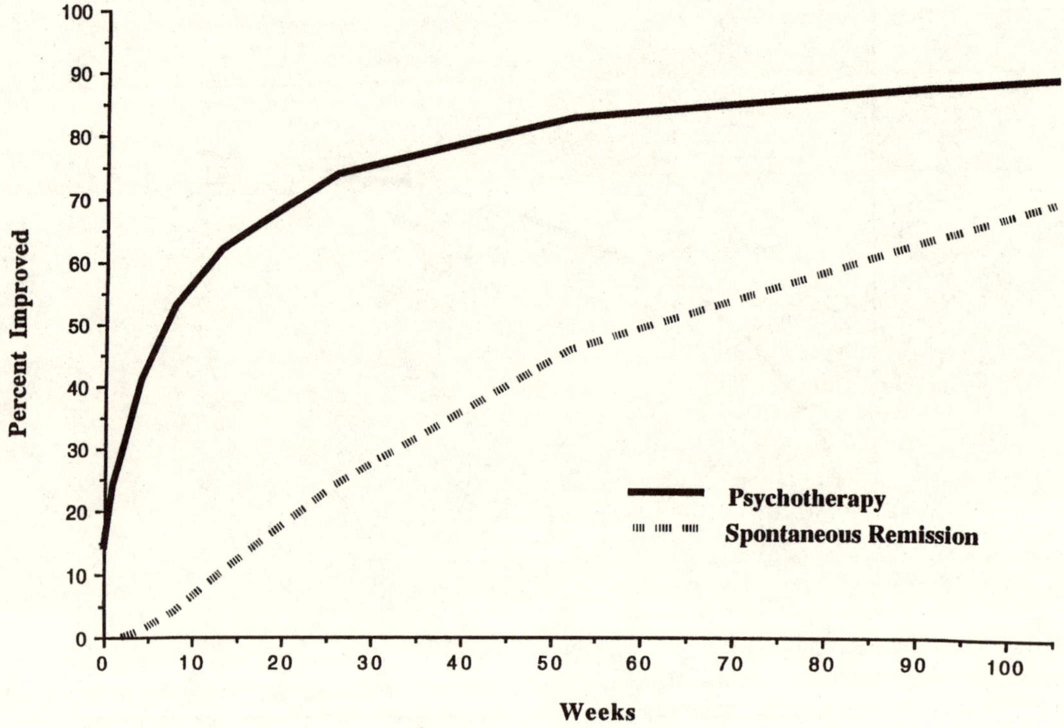

Figure 14.2 Reanalysis of Eysenck's data using the dose-response model.

the reduction of symptoms will lead many patients to terminate treatment. Symptom reduction has received the greatest focus in clinical trials of treatments, especially treatments of diagnostically homogeneous patients. Yet for some patients, symptom reduction is not sufficient, and these patients persist in treatment toward a third category of treatment outcomes.

The third phase, *rehabilitation*, involves repair or improvement of functioning in one or more life roles: work, student, homemaker, parent, and so on. Rehabilitation can mean either a restoration to previous levels of functioning, such as recovering work capacity or establishing a new intimate relationship following a loss, or the learning of new skills or roles. The duration of this phase is perhaps most varied. Patients with a high premorbid level of functioning may return to that previous level of functioning relatively quickly. For others, the acquisition of new skills/roles can take years. For still others, the primary goal of the rehabilitation phase is the maintenance of existing levels of functioning. For example, with chronic patients, the goal of treatment might well be supporting the existing level of functioning and scanning patient behavior for signs of deterioration.

Evidence from other studies supports the necessary sequential pattern between symptoms and rehabilitation. Mintz, Mintz, Arruda, and Hwang (1992) examined the relationship between work functioning and symptom reduction in patients treated for depression in eight clinical trials. They observed that symptom reduction preceded improvement in work functioning. Lueger, Tan, and Howard (1993) conducted a meta-analysis of psychotherapy studies conducted over a 12-year period, categorized the outcome measures according to the phase model, and observed that effect sizes for symptom measures were almost always greater than effect sizes for functioning when treatments were at least eight sessions. Again, our analyses indicate that improvement in symptoms is a probabilistically necessary condition for improvement in functioning (Howard, Brill, Lueger, Maling, Martinovich, 1993).

We believe that this sequence of improvement in psychotherapy—remoralization, remediation, and rehabilitation—is the inverse of the sequence of becoming in need of therapy. That is, most episodes of treatment need begin with at least a partial failure to satisfactorily manage a life change or to meet functional requirements in some domain of life functioning. None

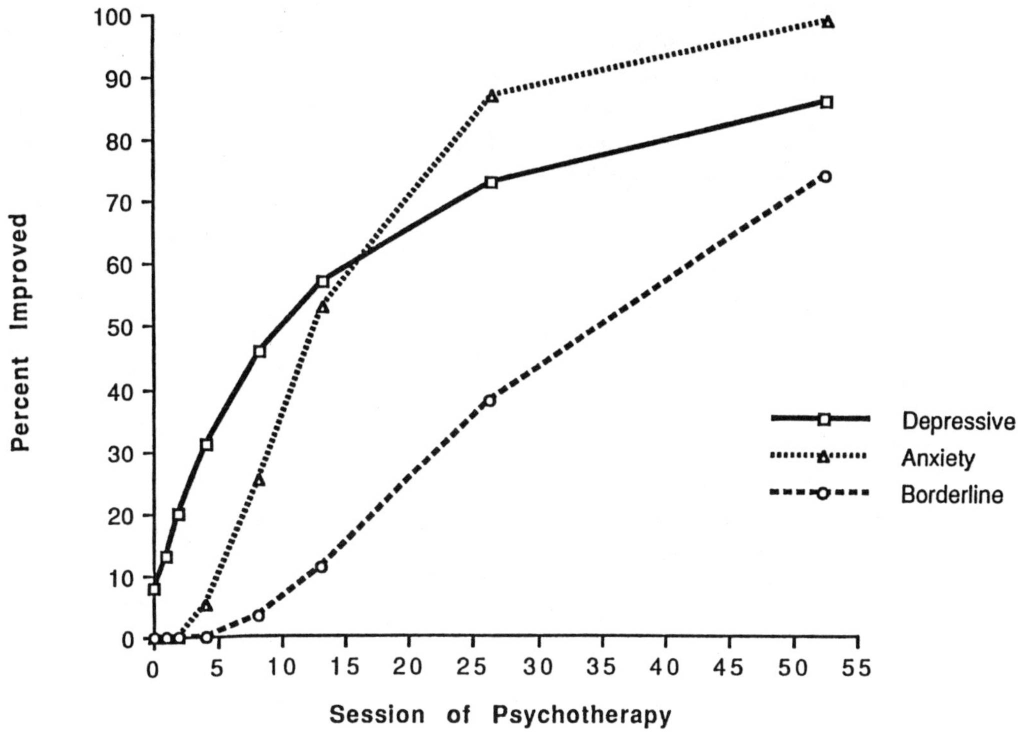

Figure 14.3 Dose-response of patients with three diagnoses.

of us is completely invulnerable to life challenges; when our coping resources fall short and our support systems cannot make up the difference symptoms can develop. The form these symptoms take depends on biological characteristics, cognitive and affective styles, and learned patterns of living. When efforts to curtail, contain, or modify these symptoms are unsuccessful, demoralization sets in. We become hopeless and feel alone and helpless to influence our situation. It is then that some people turn to mental health professionals for help.

Of course, not all psychotherapy patients enter therapy at the point of demoralization. Experienced psychotherapy users may access what has previously been a helpful system before becoming demoralized. Other individuals, recognizing their inadequacy in the face of life challenges, might turn to psychoeducational interventions such as assertion training, career counseling, or relationship enhancement exercises. While not usually categorized as psychotherapies, these psychoeducational interventions serve the function of restoring or enhancing role functioning threatened by situational demands and thus can prevent further deterioration.

Measurement of Phase Model Components

The self-report operational measures (Howard, Brill, Lueger, O'Mahoney, & Grissom, 1993) of the three phase model components are, respectively, Current Well-Being, Current Symptoms, and Current Life Functioning. Current well-being is a four-item measure. It assesses distress, energy and health, emotional and psychological adjustment, and current life satisfaction. The alpha in a sample of 197 patients prior to treatment was .79, and the 1-week test-retest was .82.

The Current Symptoms scale, which measures remoralization, includes 40 items tapping symptoms for eight diagnoses found to account for 92% of patients being serviced at an outpatient psychotherapy clinic. The seven diagnostic areas are Adjustment Disorder, Anxiety Disorder, Bipolar Disorder, Depression, Obsessive-Compulsive Disorder, Phobia, and Substance Abuse. Patients rate the frequency of each symptom in the past month. The alpha for the Current Symptoms total score was .94 on a sample of 160 patients at intake, and the 3-week test-retest reliability on a sample of 53 patients was .85.

The Current Life Functioning scale measures functioning in six domains: self-management, social relationships, work/school/household, intimacy, family, and health/grooming. The 24-item scale has an alpha of .93 ($n = 70$ patients) at intake, and a 3-week test-retest reliability of .76 ($n = 48$ patients). Patients rate the degree to which their emotional and psychological problems are interfering with functioning by using a 5-point scale.

The total scores on each of the three measures—Current Well-Being, Current Symptoms, and Current Life Functioning—can also be combined into a single score, the *Mental Health Index (MHI)*. The MHI reflects the overall status of the patient. Prior to therapy, the MHI had an alpha of .87 ($n = 163$) and a test-retest reliability over a 3-week period of .82 ($n = 213$). In addition to the MHI, we measure the relationship between the therapist and patient as experienced by the patient. The Therapeutic Bond (Orlinsky & Howard, 1987; Saunders, Orlinsky, & Howard, 1989) is measured with a 13-item scale that includes three components: working alliance, empathic resonance, and mutual affirmation. Thus, the Therapeutic Bond scale taps the effort the patient and therapist put into their respective roles, the patient's perception of how well the therapist understands him or her, and the degree of open, caring regard between patient and therapist. The internal consistency of 1,256 session measurements was .88, and the 2-week test-retest reliability (Session 1 to Session 3) was .62.

In addition to patient self-reports, therapists rate the patient's lowest level of current functioning with the Global Assessment Scale (GAS; Endicott, Spitzer, Fleiss, & Cohen, 1976). Similar to Axis V of *DSM-IV*, the GAS is a ladder scale with 10 intervals ranging from 0 to 100. Each interval contains a description of the extent to which symptoms interfere with functioning. Thus, the GAS is an index of severity of the patient's problems as seen by the therapist.

The therapist also rates the patient's functioning on the same six domains included in the Current Life Functioning measure. These scales, the Life Functioning Scales, are ladder scales ranging from 0 to 100, with increments of 5 marking the scale. Five intervals (e.g., 0–20) are labeled from "Severe Impairment, Virtually Unable to Function" to "No Impairment, High Level of Functioning" (80–100). Each interval is anchored with 20- to 50-word behavioral descriptions. A total score summed across the six domains had an alpha of .86 ($n = 1{,}237$) and a 2-week test-retest reliability of .77 ($n = 81$).

The GAS and Life Functioning Scales total scores were correlated .74 ($n = 1{,}459$). These ratings are summed into the *Clinician Assessment Index (CAI)*. The CAI has an alpha of .84 ($n = 1{,}459$) and a 2-week test-retest reliability ($n = 81$) of .77.

Measuring Improvement

The patient self-reports and the therapists' ratings of patients at intake serve as the base for assessing patient improvement. Individual patient intake scores are adjusted for true score to attenuate for regression-to-the-mean effects. *Reliable improvement* is computed in a manner generally following the reliable-change score proposed by Jacobson and Revensdorf (1988) and elaborated in Jacobson and Truax (1991). That is, the standard error of measurement (*SEM*) is computed by use of the reliability index available for each measure. We use a one-tailed confidence bound (90%) because we are interested in whether or not the patient has improved (with deterioration or no change indicating lack of improvement). For most of the phase model measures, any change of approximately one-half standard deviation represents a reliably improved score. *T* scores are employed in such a way that higher scores are indicative of better status and functioning. On the basis of responses provided by patient and nonpatient samples, it can be determined if an observed score should be considered in the normal range (that is, more like a nonpatient than a patient).

Measurement Points

The dose-response model demonstrates that change occurs more rapidly earlier in treatment. So we have included more measurement points among the earlier sessions. We have measured the MHI components at intake; after Sessions 2, 4, 10, 17; and every 10th session thereafter. Not all patients complete self-reports at each measurement point. Moreover, the "surviving" sample of patients still in treatment is characterized by the "psychotherapy decay curve" (Phillips, 1988), a positively accelerating, negatively skewed distribution.

The components of the MHI—subjective well-being, current symptoms, and current life functioning—for 97 successful patients are presented in Figure 14.4. This pattern shows the predicted response curves of the phase model in that subjective well-being increases

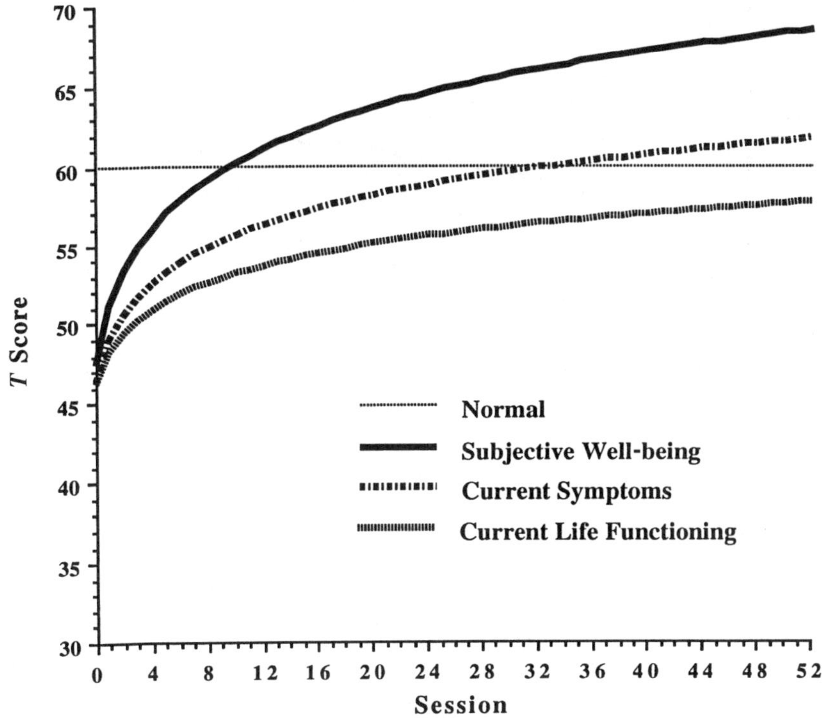

Figure 14.4 Dose-response relationships for the outcome criteria (phase model) for successful psychotherapy patients.

earlier followed by symptom relief, and then by improvement in functioning.

Variations in Improvement Patterns by Diagnosis

As Figure 14.3 indicated, the dose-response patterns of patients who were diagnosed by their therapists with anxiety, depression, and borderline personality disorder diagnoses were different. In the Northwestern Psychotherapy Study, 204 psychotherapy patients were administered the Structured Clinical Interview for Diagnosis of DSM-III-R disorders (SCID; American Psychiatric Association, 1987). Approximately 75% of these patients qualified for at least one Axis I disorder. Of the patients with at least one Axis I disorder, 68% met the criteria for at least one other Axis I disorder. Thus, 50% of the patients who were administered the SCID were comorbid for two or more Axis I disorders. A diagnosis of depression was the primary diagnosis for two of every five patients seeking psychotherapy.

The Mental Health Index scores of patients with depression diagnoses, anxiety diagnoses, and comorbid Axis I diagnoses are presented in Figure 14.5. Clearly, the patterns of change differ for the three groups. The *rate* of improvement is negatively impacted by comorbid diagnosis. It takes more sessions of psychotherapy with comorbidly diagnosed patients who suffer from both anxiety and depression to produce levels of improvement comparable to those of patients with either diagnosis.

Cost-Effectiveness Implications

The value of the dose-response and phase models for understanding the cost-effectiveness of psychotherapy is already evident. In assessing the cost-improvement ratio, the *pattern* of change is important, and the *type or category of outcome* is critical for assessing the value of change. Moreover, patterns of change for patients with high-risk conditions—for example, personality disorders or comorbid Axis I disorders in the *DSM-IV* system—may differ from the patterns of prototypical psychotherapy patient.

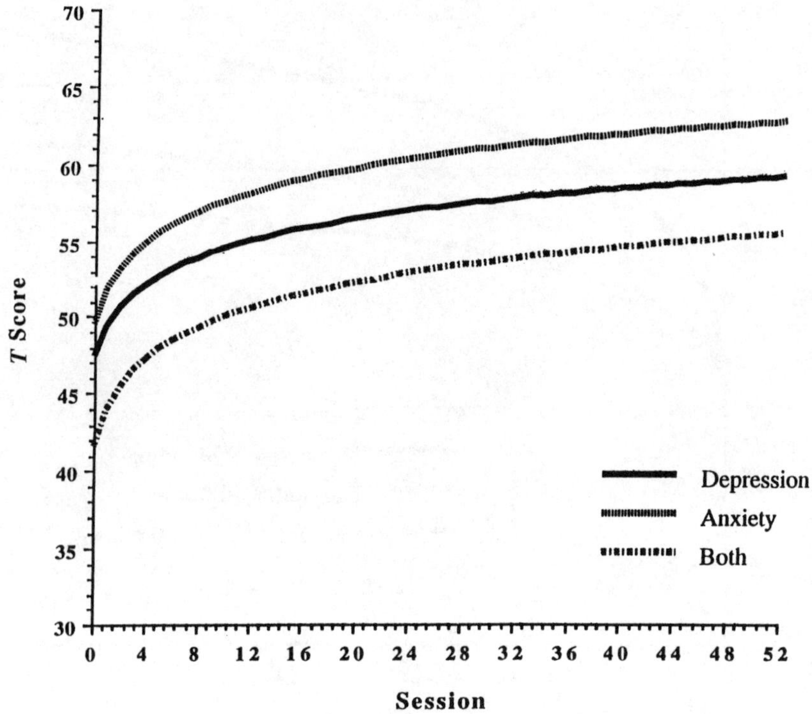

Figure 14.5 Mental Health Index: Estimated mean *t* scores for three diagnostic (SCID) groups.

The values of the various outcome categories identified by the phase model can differ for patients, therapists, significant others, and purchasers of services. Although these groups of interested parties can be overlapping, each is likely to have a particular category of outcome in mind when making cost-effectiveness assessments. Patients usually come to therapy highly distressed and in need of remoralization. Some patients may even come to address repeated failures in one or more areas of life functioning (e.g., failed intimacy relationships, arrested sense of self-development, repeated work frustrations). Therapists often attend to patient symptoms, at least initially, although therapists are unlikely to consider the work of improving functioning ever fully accomplished. Significant others are most likely to be concerned about the patient's distress, but especially about the failures in functioning in work, intimacy, and family. Purchasers, who could well be the patients themselves but often are employers or their proxies, are interested in cost containment, patient satisfaction, and improvement in functional areas such as work. To assess cost-effectiveness, it is important to specify who is the interested stakeholder and which phase of treatment matches the interested party's goals.

The Progress of the Individual Patient

Although groupings of patients by common characteristics such as diagnosis or level of severity are interesting for making broad statements about psychotherapy outcomes, the success of psychotherapy with the individual patient is of paramount interest to consumers, therapists, and purchasers. Likewise, the designation of "success" or "failure" after the therapy has ended is useful for audits of system effectiveness or therapist efficacy. But the most useful information is about the progress of the individual patient assessed in the course of treatment. Is the patient "on track" for a successful outcome? Has the therapy yet achieved success in the outcomes area most important to the patient? To the therapist? To the purchaser? To the significant other?

Although we cannot yet perfectly predict success or failure of the individual case, we can assess a variety of markers that are associated with treatment progress.

The quality of the patient-therapist relationship as assessed by the patient is one important marker. Whether or not the patient has remoralized (achieved improved subjective well-being) in early sessions of treatment is another marker. Congruence between patient and therapist at intake is another marker, especially if the therapist rates the patient significantly worse off than the patient rates herself or himself.

Summary

Assessing the cost-effectiveness of psychotherapy requires attention to the pattern of improvement or rate of change and to the category of outcome. The dose-response and phase models inform the evaluator of the pattern, area of outcome, and sequence of improvements. Those who would evaluate the outcome and assess the costs to produce those outcomes emerge from different constituencies and focus on different areas of outcome. Thus, any assessment of psychotherapy cost-effectiveness must first identify the "client" and the preferred outcome to which costs are relative.

Examination of the improvement patterns of individual patients in subjective well-being, symptoms, and life functioning can reveal useful information for assessing cost-benefit issues related to mental health service delivery. Moreover, monitoring of individual patient progress offers the promise of correcting therapies that are not going well or yielding the expected cost efficiency.

Effectiveness research is concerned with the generalization of results from homogeneous patient and treatment groups to the heterogeneous conditions of unselected clinical practice. In the heterogeneity of the practice context, the focus is on the progress of the individual patient. The development of patient-profiling technology holds considerable promise for evaluating the actual progress of an individual patient against the predicted pattern of change, given characteristics such as treatment history, severity, diagnosis, distress, and functional impairment.

Cost-effectiveness can be addressed with knowledge of rates and amounts of change in individual patients assessed on multiple domains of measurement as seen by different stakeholders.

Acknowledgments This work was partially supported by research grant RO 1 MH42901 and 1 K05 MH00924 from the National Institute of Mental Health.

References

American Psychiatric Association. (1987). *Diagnostic and statistical manual* (3rd ed., rev.). Washington, DC: Author.

Endicott, J., Spitzer, R. L., Fleiss, J. L., & Cohen, J. (1976). The Global Assessment Scale: A procedure for measuring overall severity of psychiatric disturbance. *Archives of General Psychiatry, 33,* 766–771.

Eysenck, H. J. (1952). The effects of psychotherapy: An evaluation. *Journal of Consulting Psychology, 16,* 319–324.

Frank, J. (1968).The role of hope in psychotherapy. *International Journal of Psychiatry, 5,* 383–395.

Frank, J. D., & Frank, J. B. (1991). *Persuasion and healing: A comparative study of psychotherapy.* Baltimore, MD: Johns Hopkins University Press.

Howard, K. I., Brill, P., Lueger, R. J., O'Mahoney, M., & Grissom, G. (1993). *Integra Outpatient Tracking Assessment: Psychometric properties.* Radnor, PA: Integra.

Howard, K. I., Kopta, S. M., Krause, M. S., & Orlinsky, D. E. (1986). The dose-effect relationship in psychotherapy. *American Psychologist, 41,* 159–164.

Howard, K. I., Lueger, R. J., Maling, M. S., & Martinovich, Z. (1993). A phase model of psychotherapy outcome: Causal mediation of change. *Journal of Consulting and Clinical Psychology, 61,* 678–685.

Howard, K. I., Krause, M. S., & Vessey, J. (1994). Analysis of clinical trial data: The problem of outcome overlap. *Psychotherapy Research, 41,* 302–307.

Jacobson, N. S., & Revensdorf, D. (1988). Statistics for assessing the clinical significance of psychotherapy techniques: Issues, problems, and new developments. *Behavioral Assessment, 10,* 133–145.

Jacobson, N. S., & Truax, P. (1991). Clinical significance: A statistical approach to defining meaningful change in psychotherapy research. *Journal of Consulting and Clinical Psychology, 59,* 12–19.

Lipsey, M. W., & Wilson, D. B. (1993). The efficacy of psychological, educational, and behavioral treatment. *American Psychologist, 48,* 1181–1209.

Lueger, R. J., Tan, L., & Howard, K. I. (1993, June). *A meta-analysis of the psychotherapy outcome studies using the phase model.* Paper presented at the annual meeting of the Society for Psychotherapy Research, Pittsburgh, PA.

McNeilly, C., Howard, K. I. (1991). The effects of psychotherapy: A reevaluation based on dosage. *Psychotherapy Research, 1,* 74–78.

Mental health: Does therapy help? (1995). *Consumer Reports, 60,* 734–739.

Mintz, J., Mintz, L. T., Arruda, M. J., & Hwang, S. S. (1992). Treatments of depression and the functional capacity to work. *Archives of General Psychiatry*, 49, 761–768.

Orlinsky, D. E., & Howard, K. I. (1987). A generic model of psychotherapy. *Journal of Integrative and Eclectic Psychotherapy*, 6, 6–27.

Phillips, E. L. (1988). *Patient compliance: New light on health delivery systems in medicine and psychotherapy*. Lewiston, NY: Hans Huber.

Saunders, S. M., Orlinsky, D. E., & Howard, K. I. (1989). The therapeutic bond scales: Psychometric characteristics and relationship to treatment effectiveness. *Psychological Assessment: A Journal of Clinical and Consulting Psychology*, 1, 323–330.

15

Assessing Psychotherapy Outcomes in Clinical Practice for Psychotherapy: Costs and Benefits

James A. Clardy, Ellen P. Fischer, Cindy L. Mosley, Jan A. Hollenberg, & G. Richard Smith, Jr.

Clinicians want good outcomes for the patients whom they treat. This contention is true for all types of health care providers from surgeons to pediatricians to psychotherapists. Until recently, it has been much easier for the surgeon treating a patient with an acute abdomen to tell whether the patient had a good outcome than for the pediatrician treating a child with clinical asthma. Similarly, it has been easier for both of these clinicians to determine whether their patients had good outcomes than it has been for the psychotherapist.

Prior to the last three decades, estimates of how much psychotherapy helped patients achieve good outcomes were largely based on observational studies conducted by proponents of various types of psychotherapy. More recently, large, complex, rigorously designed studies of the efficacy of various types of psychotherapy have been conducted to determine the relative ability of one type of psychotherapy to produce good outcomes compared to another type under clinical trial conditions (Elkin et al., 1989; Luborsky & Singer, 1975).

This rigorous demonstration of efficacy, the effect of treatment under ideal conditions, is in sharp contrast to the demonstration of effectiveness, the effect of treatment under routine clinical conditions, of psychotherapy (Institute of Medicine Core Committee, 1990). Few data are available regarding the effectiveness of psychotherapy as it is currently practiced in routine clinical settings.

In today's rapidly changing, pressured health care environment, payers of health care and managed-care companines are increasingly taking skeptical views of treatments where evidence of effectiveness has not been demonstrated. When this skepticism is combined with the stigma associated with mental health treatment, psychotherapists are likely to find themselves increasingly limited in their ability to be paid to treat patients using even rigorously tested types of psychotherapy. This becomes even more true for the less rigorously defined psychotherapy often provided in routine clinical practice.

In order to be able to provide patients with the psychotherapy that they need, psychotherapists will need to become increasingly sophisticated in understanding how the outcomes of health care are assessed. In fact, they should become active in demonstrating the effectiveness of the treatments they provide.

This chapter provides a brief introduction to the science and technology of patient outcomes assessment as it relates to psychotherapy practice. It uses examples from an ongoing project to assess the outcomes of treatment provided by a large clinical group practice that offers psychotherapy as one of several treatment modalities. Four aspects of outcomes assessment will be discussed: the effect of patient characteristics, the measurement of the types of treatment provided, the importance of selecting which outcomes to assess, and the determination of value for health care expenditures.

Patient Characteristics

The characteristics of patients receiving care are an important, if not the most important, determinant of the outcomes of care. Patient prognostic characteristics, such as socioeconomic status, diagnosis, severity of disorder, and level of social support, have an impact on the patient's outcomes regardless of the type and quality of care provided. For example, consider the impact on the outcomes of an episode of major depression for two patients with different sets of prognostic characteristics. The first patient is a 23-year-old married woman who is a master's degree candidate. She attributes her depression to vocational issues. She has no prior history of depression, is in excellent general health, and has a strong social support system. Compare her to a 55-year-old divorced man seeking treatment for his fifth episode of major depression. Previous episodes have all required hospitalization. His depression is complicated by a personality disorder, excessive alcohol consumption, chronic obstructive pulmonary disease, and limited social support. These very different cases make it clear that even the best therapy would not result in the same outcome. Many other prognostic variables may be equally important, such as attitude toward seeking care and availability of treatment.

When characteristics of groups of patients are being considered, prognostic characteristics are usually referred to as *case-mix characteristics* (Smith, Rost, Fischer, Burnam, & Burns, in press). Case-mix characteristics are what is referred to when one group of patients is said to be "sicker" than another. For instance, tertiary-care centers, such as academic medical centers, generally have patients with more severe case-mix characteristics than do community hospitals.

Case-mix characteristics can influence which patients are offered particular types of treatment. Figures 15.1–15.3 illustrate this with data from the ongoing outcomes assessment project mentioned earlier, including thus far 457 patients.

Outcomes of care are known to vary according to the educational level of the group. Generally, the better educated the group of patients, the better the outcomes. This is true for most medical conditions. From Figure 15.1, it is apparent that the more education a patient had, the more likely he or she was to receive psychotherapy for an episode of major depression. Whether this was a function of the patient's choice, the clini-

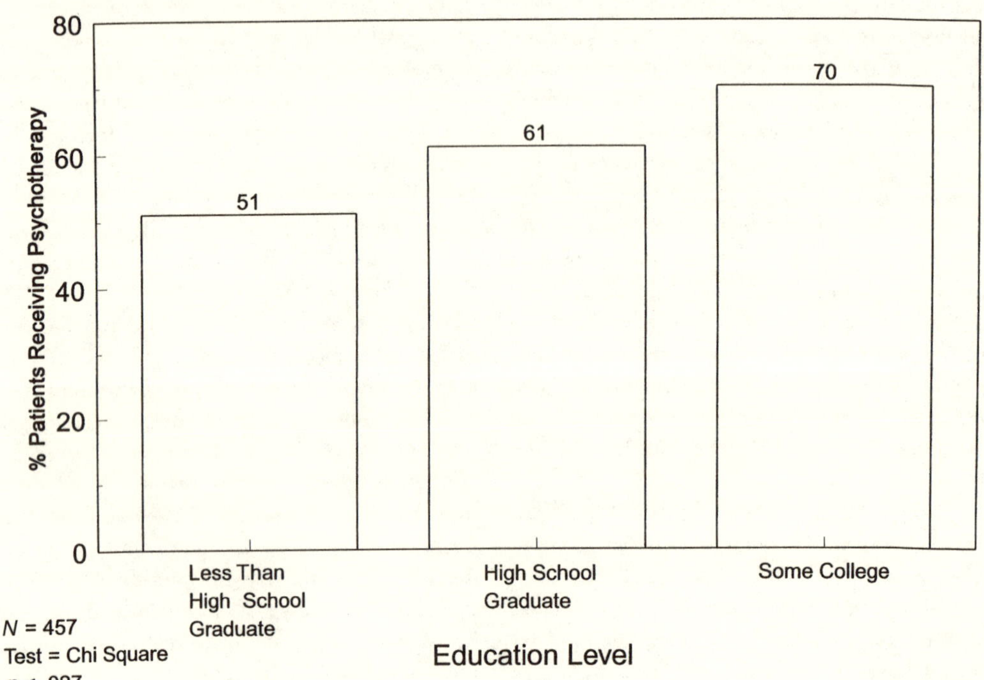

Figure 15.1 The percentage of patients who received psychotherapy according to educational level.

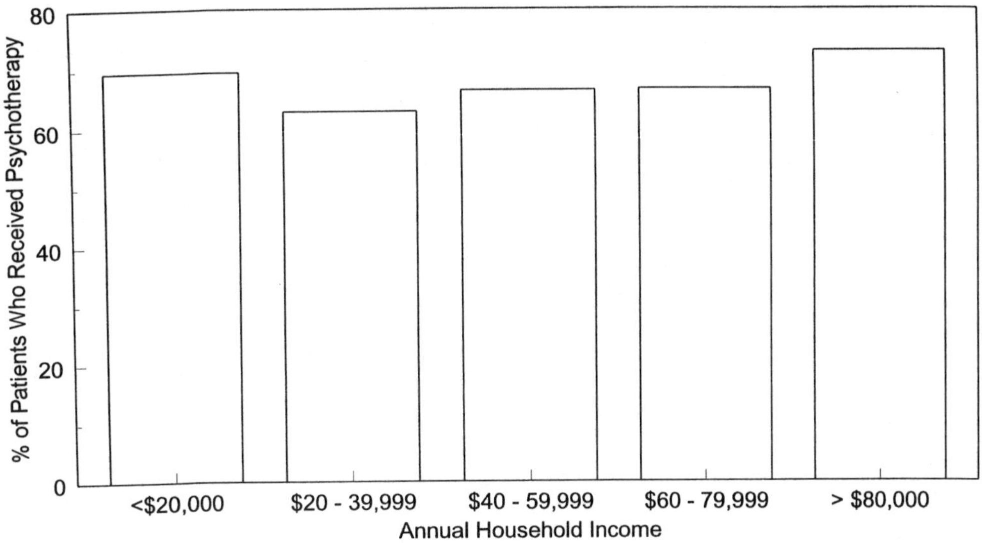

N = 440
Test = Chi Square
p = .780

Figure 15.2 The percentage of patients who received psychotherapy according to annual household income.

cian's recommendation, or both is unknown. However, what is clear is that the educational case mix of those who received psychotherapy was different from the case mix of those who did not. Based on education alone then, the psychotherapy group would be expected to have better outcomes.

Annual household income generally has an impact on outcomes similar to that of education (i.e., the higher the group's income, the better the outcomes). As shown in Figure 15.2, however, the percentage of patients who received psychotherapy did not vary by income. Therefore, outcomes for psychotherapy patients could not be predicted on income alone.

Depression severity is another case-mix or prognostic variable. Severity was measured by means of the score on the Inventory to Diagnose Depression (Zimmerman, Coryell, Wilson, & Corenthal, 1986). In this example, patients who received medication alone for their major depressive episode had more severe depressive symptoms than did those who received psychotherapy alone (see Figure 15.3). Thus, the psychotherapy group started out as less ill than the medications-alone group and would be expected to have better outcomes based on the severity of their depression at the start of treatment.

These three examples illustrate how case-mix or prognostic variables may be used to elucidate differences in outcomes. In comparing outcomes in this group practice for patients receiving psychotherapy versus other treatment modalities, the outcomes would need to be statistically adjusted for group differences in case-mix factors. Outcomes always need to be considered and compared in light of the characteristics of the groups being evaluated.

Treatment Process

The term *process* has dual meanings for the psychotherapist interested in outcomes assessment. Traditionally, *process* within psychotherapy refers to a stage of therapy involving reflection, explanation, and interpretation (Vinogradov & Yalom, 1988). In outcomes assessment, *process* is used to refer to the nature of care (e.g., the types and quantities of services received). It is in the latter context that this chapter uses the term.

Hopefully, the process of care (i.e., treatment) also affects patient outcomes in addition to the characteristics that the patient brings to treatment. Otherwise, the entire treatment endeavor would be wasteful and un-

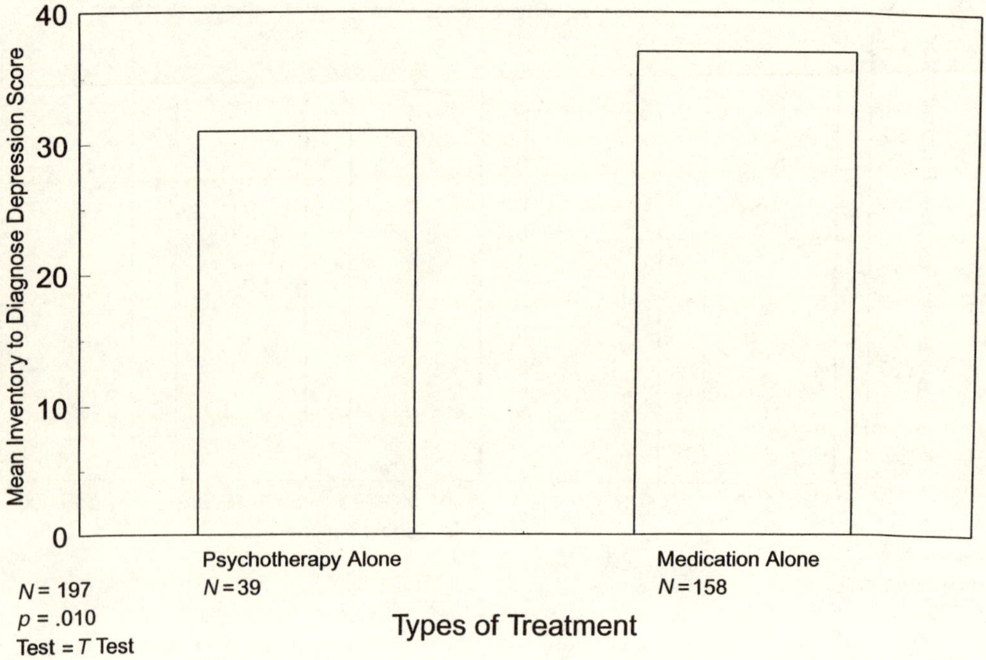

Figure 15.3 The mean Inventory to Diagnose Depression score for those who received psychotherapy alone compared to the score for those who received medication alone. The higher the score, the more severe the depression.

necessary. As part of outcomes assessment, the process of care needs to be assessed to show the relationship between treatment and outcomes.

Assessment of the process of care is usually very basic and straightforward. For instance, in assessing the process of care for major depression, type of treatment, dose and frequency of treatment, and setting of treatment are all that is often collected. Types of treatment in this example include psychotherapy, medication, and/or electroconvulsive therapy, or some combination of the three. Other modalities of treatment (e.g., group psychotherapy) should also be assessed if they are available to patients. Dose and frequency apply to psychotherapy just as the terms do to medication and electroconvulsive therapy. For instance, how long were the psychotherapy sessions, and how frequently did they occur? The setting applies to the location where care was provided, such as the psychotherapist's office, the hospital, the emergency room, or a partial hospital setting.

Often, the simplest analyses of the process of care can be very revealing. In the clinical example being used, information was collected on number of visits for all forms of treatment during the first 4 months following diagnosis of major depression. Patients were divided into two groups: those with less than five visits and those with five or more visits during the 4-month period. This arbitrary division simply shows that it appears unlikely that appropriate care for major depression can be given in less than five visits. This would be especially true if the major treatment modality was psychotherapy. It was found that only 28% of patients received what would be considered a minimally acceptable number (five) of treatment episodes. From Figure 15.4, it is apparent that few patients received psychotherapy alone. A third received medication alone. Slightly more than half received both psychotherapy and medication.

Process-of-care data, such as those presented above, are obviously important to consider when attempting to understand the relationship between treatment and patient outcomes. Additionally, these simple data have a profound potential to be helpful in improving the process of care that an organization provides. For instance, if this group practice determined that patients who received five or more visits had substantially better outcomes than those who received four or fewer visits, then clinicians would have a strong incentive to change their practice by increasing the number of visits.

Types of Patient Outcomes

The systematic assessment of outcomes can take at least two distinct forms: generic or disorder-specific (Smith, in press). "Generic outcomes assessment" measures outcomes in a broad fashion, and frequently, the assessment is the same across diagnoses. Symptoms, functioning, health status, and general mental health status are frequently assessed as part of generic assessment strategies.

"Disorder-specific outcomes assessment" collects information in an in-depth fashion about a particular disorder (Smith et al., in press). Frequently, diagnosis, remission, disease-specific functioning, and disease-specific treatment processes are assessed. Typically, disorder-specific functioning includes brief versions of generic assessment. For disorder-specific assessment of major depression, the measurement of symptoms, function, health status, and general mental health are all appropriate and are usually included.

For the disorder-specific assessment, sufficient information to determine whether the diagnosis is present or absent is collected; data about functioning that may be unique to major depression, such as bed and disability days, are assessed; and specifics regarding treatment, such as type and dosage of antidepressant medication, are measured.

The disorder-specific approach fits well with the use of a tracer condition within a practice setting (Smith et al., in press). A tracer condition is one that is a reasonably frequent health state/trait/disorder, wherein the outcome is affected by an intervention and the state/trait/disorder has a preset standard of care and is generalizable to the mental health care system to the extent of being used as an index of quality of care delivered (Kessner, Kalk, & Singer, 1973).

The assessment of outcomes and process of care will be different from one disorder to the next. For example, in Table 15.1, examples of generic assessment items as well as some aspects of disorder-specific assessments for major depression and panic disorder are

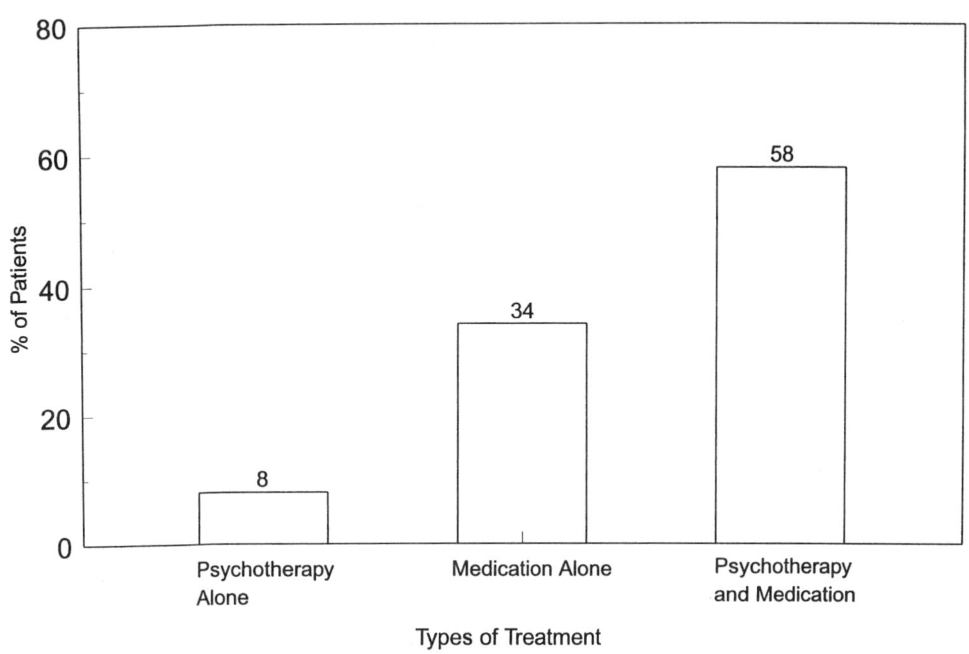

Figure 15.4 The percentages of patients receiving psychotherapy alone, medication alone, or psychotherapy and medication.

Table 15.1 Examples of Generic and Disorder-Specific Assessments for Major Depression and Panic Disorder

	Generic	Depression Specific	Panic Specific
Worthlessness/guilt		X	
Panic attacks			X
Suicidality	X		
Occupational functioning	X		
Social support	X		
Psychomotor retardation		X	
Life satisfaction	X		
Anticipatory anxiety			X

presented. While generic assessments are applicable to many mental disorders, disorder-specific assessments are focused on the particular tracer condition.

Determination of Value for Health Care Expectations

Policymakers and health care payers are beginning to attempt to direct health care toward types of care where increasing value is delivered. An increasingly popular definition of value is the change in health status divided by the cost of care. Change in health status can be defined as the improvement or worsening of health from the time of diagnosis to the end of treatment for a particular episode or time period. The cost of care is simply the total health care expenditure during the same interval. This formula results in a ratio of health status change divided by dollars. While admittedly crude and imperfect, these ratios can be used to compare one treatment approach to another for a particular disorder. For example, one could compare the value ratio for patients treated with psychotherapy alone to those treated with medication alone to those treated with a combination of medication and psychotherapy. With these comparisons, the prospective patient, the clinician, the managed-care company, and/or the health care payer could each weigh which type or types of therapy provide the best value for this patient and this condition.

Several caveats are important when comparing value. First, the ratios should be adjusted for case mix as described above. In the group practice example used above, it appears that patients with a better prognosis received psychotherapy rather than medication. This differential needs to be adjusted for in the calculations prior to comparison. Second, the types of outcomes chosen to be assessed are important. One type of treatment might impact some outcomes differently; therefore, comparisons should be made only in those areas where impact by a treatment is possible or where there is overwhelming agreement about the importance of an outcome (e.g., prevention of suicide). Finally, it is important to remember that the technology of estimating value ratios is a methodology still in its infancy and will therefore require considerably further refinement and development.

Conclusion

It is now just as possible in routine practice to measure the patient outcomes of psychotherapy as it is to evaluate outcomes for patients with, say, an acute abdomen or with chronic asthma. The technology of outcomes assessment is being used with increasing frequency in the health care marketplace. It is imperative that clinicians interested in psychotherapy become familiar with this technology in order to advocate for the benefit of their patients, and for the type of treatment that is best for their patients. It would seem wise for psychotherapists to actively begin determining the outcomes of patients treated in routine clinical practice, in order to better provide the highest quality mental health care.

References

Elkin, I., Shea, T., Watkins, J. T., Imber, S. D., Sotsky, S. M., Collins, J. F., Glass, D. R., Pilkonis, P. A., Leber, W. R., Docherty, J. P., Fiester, S. J., & Parloff, M. B. (1989). National Institute of Mental Health treatment of depression collaborative research program—General effectiveness of treatments. *Archives of General Psychiatry, 46,* 971–982.

Institute of Medicine Core Committee. (1990). Promise and limitations of effectiveness and outcomes research: Summary statement of the IOM Core Committee. In K. A. Heithoff & K. N. Lohr (Eds.), *Effectiveness and outcomes in health care: Proceedings of an invitational conference by the Institute of Medicine* (pp. 8–18). Washington, DC: National Academy Press.

Kessner, D. M., Kalk, C. E., & Singer, J. (1973). Assessing health quality—The case for tracers. *New England Journal of Medicine, 288*(4), 189–194.

Luborsky, L., & Singer, B. (1975). Comparative studies

of psychotherapies—Is it true that "Everyone has won and all must have prizes"? *Archives of General Psychiatry, 32*, 995–1008.

Smith, G. R. (in press). The state of the science of mental health and substance abuse patient outcomes assessment. *New Directions in Mental Health Services*.

Smith, G. R., Jr., Rost, K. M., Fischer, E. P., Burnam, M. A., & Burns, B. J. (in press). Assessing the effectiveness of mental health care in routine clinical practice: Critical components, administration and application of outcomes modules. *Evaluation and the Health Profession*.

Vinogradov, S., & Yalom, I. D. (1988). Group therapy. In J. A. Talbott, R. E. Hales, & S. C. Yudofsky (Eds.), *Textbook of psychiatry* (pp. 951–984). Washington, DC: American Psychiatric Press.

Zimmerman, M., Coryell, W., Wilson, S., & Corenthal, C. (1986). Evaluation of symptoms of major depressive disorder: Self-report vs. clinician ratings. *Journal of Nervous and Mental Disease, 174*(3), 150–153.

16

Health-Related Quality of Life in Mental Health Services Evaluation

Robert M. Kaplan

We are entering a new era in health care. Historically, providers assessed clinical outcomes, such as blood chemistry or disease characteristics. Often, improvements on these clinical parameters went unrecognized by patients. In the new era, patient-reported outcomes are recognized as the goal of medical care (Kaplan, 1990). Measures of health-related quality of life are central to this effort. Evidence presented in this chapter suggests that the general quality-of-life measures may also have validity for studies in mental health. Further, these models may have value for resource allocation decisions that involve mental health along with other aspects of health care.

Quality-of-life measures can provide a common metric that compares different treatments with one another, that compares treatment side effects versus benefits, or that compares the output of different sectors in health care. Competition for health care resources will require mental health providers and psychotherapists to compete with other health care professionals. A general conceptualization of health outcome will allow direct comparisons between the productivity of mental health and other health care providers.

The Economic Crisis

For over 30 years, economists have expressed concern about the increasing proportion of the gross domestic product that is devoted to health care. However, in 1990, the health care cost problem became a major political and social issue. Today, the United States devotes nearly 15% of its gross domestic product to health care, while no other country in the world spends more than 10%. If the United States is to remain competitive in international economic competition, it will be essential to control health care costs. In order to accomplish the best use of available resources, we must evaluate the cost-utility and cost-effectiveness of health care programs. Such analyses require the evaluation of very different types of health care interventions using the same outcome unit. This chapter considers whether mental health outcomes can be evaluated by means of these standard methods.

Accountability in Health Care

Accountability may be the most serious problem with American health care. Psychotherapy interventions have been challenged because their impact upon patient outcomes remains uncertain (Mechanic, Angel, & Davies, 1992). American doctors perform more procedures than their colleagues in any other country in the world. However, we have been unable to document that we live longer or have a lower infant mortality than our trading partners in other developed countries. Like other health services, psychotherapy is also used more commonly in the United States than in other countries. In 1987, Americans made an estimated 79,500,000 visits for outpatient psychotherapy at a cost of $4.2 billion (Olfson & Pincus, 1994a, 1994b). The use of antidepressant medications has also increased in recent years (Olfson & Pincus, 1994c). Psychotherapy is not in a unique position. Indeed, we have remarkably little evidence on the efficacy of many medical interventions. Brook and Lohr (1986) suggest that between 30% and 50% of all health services have little or no effect on patient outcome.

Studies on small-area variation also challenge the value of many medical procedures. Small-area-variation studies simply tabulate the rate at which different procedures are used in different geographic regions. There are significant regional differences in utilization rates for psychotherapy (Kessler et al., 1994: Wittchen, Zhao, Kessler, & Eaton, 1994). These studies tend to show that there is substantial variation in the amount of care delivered, with no consequent difference in health outcomes (Wennberg, 1990). In the southern United States, mental health utilization rates are the lowest, but some epidemiological indicators suggest that population mental health is no better in these areas (Kessler et al., 1994). Utilization rates for surgeries vary substantially. For example, men in the Pacific Northwest are nearly 3 times as likely to receive radical prostatectomy than are men in New England, and men in some areas of Alaska are 20 times more like to get the procedure. However, the rates of death from prostate cancer appear to be about the same in these different regions (Lu-Yao, McLerran, Wasson, & Wennberg, 1993). Increases in the use of cancer screening tests, including prostate-specific antigen, or mammography have not resulted in any reductions in the rates of deaths from these diseases (Fleming, Wasson, Albertsen, Barry, & Wennberg, 1993).

The concept of an opportunity cost is also important to this argument. An opportunity cost is defined as the forgone opportunities attributable to doing one thing rather than another. For example, a decision to regularly offer a particular medical service may necessarily require that we do not offer a different service. With limited resources, a decision to fund liver transplantation from public resources may necessarily mean that we do not provide funding for mental health programs. Or providing coverage for inpatient mental health hospitalization may use so many resources that psychotherapy is deleted as a benefit.

Medical technology has expanded, and we are now blessed with a wide range of desirable services. Since no country in the world can afford to offer all services to all people, allocation decisions must be made. Wealthy countries and poor countries may differ in how they set their priorities, but all face these decisions (Williams, 1988). Previously, these decisions were made arbitrarily.

We propose that formal decision-making models are helpful in prioritizing health care decisions (Kaplan & Anderson, 1990). Central to the general health decision model methodology is the development of a common metric for health outcome. Most health services researchers suggest that mental health outcomes cannot be measured in the same units as other health outcomes (Ware & Sherbourne, 1992). In part, this belief follows from the World Health Organization (1948) definition of health.

WHO Definition

In their charter document, the World Health Organization (1948) defined health as "a state of complete physical, mental and social well-being and not merely the absence of infirmity." Most often, investigators use separate methods for measuring the three components.

The separate category for mental health in the World Health Organization definition prompted many investigators to develop separate measures of mental health functioning. Perhaps the best known effort in this area is the work by Ware and his associates (1984). These investigators adapted Dupuy's (1974) General Well-Being Index and administered it to large numbers of people as part of the RAND Health Insurance Experiment. Ware et al. (1984) argue that the correlation between psychological distress and physical functioning is only .25 and suggested that this confirmed that mental health was a separate dimension. In addition, they offered comparisons between those with no physical limitations but with differences on items about psychological distress. For this high physically functioning group, those with higher scores on mental distress used three times as many mental health services as those low in distress.

The separate measurement of mental health remains a major issue in the conceptualization of general health status (Ware & Sherbourne, 1992; World Bank, 1993). We believe mental health can be conceptualized as an aspect of general health status. Further, separate measurement and specification of mental function may make some analyses difficult or impossible.[1]

A General Health Policy Model

To understand health outcomes, it is necessary to build a comprehensive theoretical model of health status that includes two componenets: mortality (death) and morbidity (health-related quality of life). Diseases and disabilities are important for two reasons: (a) Life expectancy may be shortened, and (b) illness may make life less desirable at times prior to death (health-related quality of life) (Kaplan & Anderson, 1988a, 1988b, 1990).

Over the last two decades, investigators at the University of California, San Diego, have developed the General Health Policy Model (GHPM), which separates aspects of health status and life quality into distinct components. These components include life expectancy (mortality), functioning and symptoms (morbidity), preference for observed functional states (utility), and duration of stay in health states (prognosis).

Mortality. Many public health statistics focus exclusively on mortality through estimations of crude mortality rates, age-adjusted mortality rates, infant mortality rates, and suicide rates. Death is an important outcome that must be included in any comprehensive conceptualization of health.

Morbidity. In addition to death, quality of life is also an important outcome. The GHPM considers functioning in three areas: mobility, physical activity, and social activity. (See Kaplan & Anderson, 1988a, 1990, for descriptions.) Most public health indicators are relatively insensitive to mild to moderate impairment, and disability measures often ignore those in relatively well states. The RAND Health Insurance Study, for example, reported that about 80% of the general population manifest no dysfunction, thereby concluding that 80% of the population is well. However, when symptoms or problems were measured in addition to behavioral dysfunction, only about 12% of the general population was found to report no symptoms on a particular day (Kaplan, Bush, & Berry, 1976). Though some might argue that symptoms are unimportant because they are subjective and unobservable and are highly correlated with the demand for medical services, expenditures on health care, and motivations to alter lifestyles (Kaplan et al., 1976). The quantification of symptoms is therefore very important to any adequate assessment of outcomes.

Utility (Relative Importance). Given that various components of morbidity and mortality can be tabulated, it is important to consider their relative importance. For example, it is possible to develop measures that detect very minor symptoms. Yet because these symptoms are measurable does not necessarily mean they are important. A patient may experience side effects of a medication but be willing to tolerate them because the side effects are less important than the probable benefit of consuming the medication. Similarly, not all outcomes are equally important. A treatment in which 20 of 100 patients die is not equivalent to one in which 20 of 100 patients develop nausea.

An important component of the GHPM is its capacity to scale the various health outcomes according to their relative importance, thereby adding "quality" dimensions to health status. In the preceding example, the relative importance of dying would be weighted more than that of developing nausea. The weighting is accomplished by rating all states on a quality continuum ranging from 0 (for dead) to 1.0 (for optimum functioning). These ratings are typically provided by independent judges who are representative of the general population.[2] With this system, it is possible to express the relative importance of states in relation to the life-death continuum. A point halfway on the scale (0.5) is regarded as halfway between optimum function and death. The quality-of-life weighting system has been described in several different publications (Kaplan et al., 1976, 1978, 1979).

Prognosis. Another dimension of health status is the duration of a condition. A headache that lasts 1 hour is not equivalent to a headache that lasts 1 month. A cough that lasts 3 days is not equivalent to a cough that lasts 3 years. A depressive episode of 1 week's duration is not equivalent to one lasting 6 months. In considering the severity of illness, duration of the problem is central. As basic as this concept is, most contemporary models of health outcome measurement completely disregard duration. This is an important point for mental health researchers, given that most psychiatric disorders are chronic or episodic in nature, whereas most treatment outcome studies focus only on acute results. In the GHPM, the term *prognosis* refers to the probability of transition among health states over the course of time. In addition to consideration of duration of problems, the model considers the point at which the problem begins. A person may have no symptoms or dysfunction currently but may have a high probability of health problems in the future. Patients diagnosed with schizophrenia or bipolar affective disorder may be functioning well now but harbor risk for future exacerbations. The prognosis component of the model takes these transitions into consideration and applies a discount rate for events that occur in the future. Discount rates are used to value resources and health outcomes differently if the onset is delayed as opposed to immediate. Mental disorientation that will begin a year from now may be less of a concern than disorientation that will start immediately. Therefore, greater value may be placed on treating the immediate problem than on preventing the future problem.

Quality of Well-Being Scale (QWB)

The Quality of Well-Being Scale is one of several different approaches for obtaining quality-adjusted life years (Kaplan & Anderson, 1988b). Related approaches include the Health Utility Index (Torrance & Feeny, 1989) and the EuroQol (EuroQol Group, 1990). By means of these methods, patients are classified according to objective levels of functioning. These levels are represented by scales of mobility, physical activity, and social activity (see Table 16.1). In addition to classification into these observable levels of function, individuals are also classified by the symptom or problem that they found to be most undesirable (see Table 16.2). On any particular day, nearly 80% of the general population is optimally functional; however, fewer than half of the population experience no symptoms. Symptoms or problems may be severe, such as serious chest pain, or minor, such as taking medication or a prescribed diet for health reasons.

Human value studies have been conducted to place the observable states of health and functioning on a preference continuum for the desirability of various conditions, with a "quality" rating between 0 for death and 1.0 for completely well. These weights are shown in Tables 1 and 2.

The well-life expectancy is the current life expectancy adjusted for diminished quality of life associated with dysfunctional states, as well as the duration of stay in each state. It is possible to consider mortality, morbidity, and the preference weights for the various observable states of function. The model quantifies the health activity or treatment program in terms of the quality-adjusted life years that it produces or saves.

A mathematical model integrates components of the model to express outcomes in a common measurement unit. With information on current functioning and duration, it is possible to express the health outcomes in terms of equivalents of well years of life, or as some have described them, quality-adjusted life years (QALYs). A *quality-adjusted life year* is defined as the equivalent of a completely well year of life, or a year of life free of any symptoms, problems, or health-related disabilities.

The model for point-in-time quality of well-being is

$$\begin{aligned} QWB = 1 &- (\text{observed morbidity} \times \text{morbidity weight}) \\ &- (\text{observed physical activity} \times \text{physical activity weight}) \\ &- (\text{observed social activity} \times \text{social activity weight}) \\ &- (\text{observed symptom/problem} \times \text{symptom/problem weight}). \end{aligned}$$

The net cost-utility ratio is defined as

$$\frac{\text{net cost}}{\text{net } QWB \times \text{duration in years}} = \frac{[\text{cost of treatment} - \text{cost of alternative}]}{[QWB_2 - QWB_1] \times \text{duration in years}}$$

where QWB_2 and QWB_1 are measures of quality of well-being taken after and before treatment.

Consider, for example, a person who is affected by schizophrenia and in an objective state of functioning (restricted to a hospital) that is rated by community peers as .5 on a 0 to 1.0 scale. If the person remains in that state for 1 year, he or she would have lost the equivalent of one half of 1 year of life. Thus, a person limited in activities who requires confinement to an institution would be hypothetically rated at .50. If confined to that state for an entire year, he or she would lose the equivalent of one-half year of life. However, a person who has acute depression may also be rated as .50. In this case, the symptoms might only last 3 days, and the total loss in well years might be $3/365 \times .50$, which is equal to .004 well years. This may not appear as significant an outcome as manifested by the person with schizophrenia. But suppose that 5,000 people in a community become acutely depressed. The QALYs lost would then be $5{,}000 \times .004$ which is equal to 20 years. Now suppose that a treatment has become available and that acute depression can be eliminated treatment of the 5,000 people in the community. The cost of the treatment is \$100 per person, or \$500,000. The cost-utility of the program would be

$$\frac{\$500{,}000 \text{ (cost)}}{20 \text{ years (utility)}} = \$25{,}000/\text{well year}$$

The GHPM has been used in a wide variety of population studies (Erickson, Kendall, Anderson, & Kaplan, 1989; Anderson et al., 1989). In addition, the methods have been used in clinical trials and studies

Table 16.1 Quality of Well-Being/General Health Policy Model: Elements and Calculating Formulas (Function Scales, with Step Definitions and Calculating Weights)

Step No.	Weight	Step Definition
		Mobility Scale (MOB)
5	–.000	No limitations for health reasons.
4	–.062	Did not drive a car, health-related; did not ride in a car as usual for age (younger than 15 yr), health-related; and/or did not use public transportation, health-related; or had or would have used more help than usual for age to use public transportation, health-related.
2	–.090	In hospital, health-related.
		Physical Activity Scale (PAC)
4	–.000	No limitations for health reasons.
3	–.060	In wheelchair, moved or controlled movement of wheelchair without help from someone else; or had trouble or did not try to lift, stoop, bend over, or use stairs or inclines, health-related; and/or limped, used a cane, crutches, or walker, health-related; and/or had any other physical limitation in walking, or did not try to walk as far as or as fast as others the same age are able, health-related.
1	–.077	In wheelchair, did not move or control the movement of wheelchair without help from someone else; or in bed, chair, or couch for most or all of the day, health-related.
		Social Activity Scale (SAC)
5	–.000	No limitations for health reasons.
4	–.061	Limited in other (e.g., recreational) role activity, health-related.
3	–.061	Limited in major (primary) role activity, health-related.
2	–.061	Performed no major role activity, health-related, but did perform self-care activities.
1	–.106	Performed no major role activity, health-related, and did not perform, or had more help than usual in performance of, one or more self-care activities, health-related.

Calculating Formulas

Formula 1. Point-in-time well-being score for an individual (*W*):

$$W = 1 + (CPXwt) + (MOBwt) + (PACwt) + (SACwt)$$

where "*wt*" is the preference-weighted measure for each factor and *CPX* is symptom/problem complex. For example, the *W* score for a person with the following description profile may be calculated for one day as:

CPX-11	Cough, wheezing, or shortness of breath, with or without fever, chills, or aching all over	–.257
MOB-5	No limitations	–.000
PAC-1	In bed, chair, or couch for most or all of the day, health-related	–.077
SAC-2	Performed no major role activity, health-related, but did perform self-care	–.061

$$W = 1 + (-.257) + (-.000) + (-.077) + (-.061) = .605$$

Formula 2. Well-years (*WY*) as an output measure:

$$WY = [\text{No. of persons} \times (CPXwt + MOBwt + PACwt + SACwt) \times \text{Time}]$$

to evaluate therapeutic interventions in a wide range of medical and surgical conditions. These include chronic obstructive pulmonary disease (Kaplan, Atkins, & Timms, 1984); AIDS (Kaplan et al., 1995); cystic fibrosis (Ornstein & Kaplan, 1991); diabetes mellitus (Kaplan, Hartwell, Wilson, & Wallace, 1987); atrial fibrillation (Ganiats, Palinkas, & Kaplan, 1993); lung transplantation (Squier et al., 1995); arthritis (Bombardier et al., 1986; Kaplan, Kosin, & Anderson, 1988); cancer (Kaplan, 1993c); Alzheimer's disease (Kerner, Patterson, & Kaplan, 1994); sinus disease (Hodgkin, 1994); and a wide variety of other conditions (Kaplan, 1993a). Further, the method has been used for health resource allocation modeling and has served as the basis for an innovative experiment on rationing health care by the state of Oregon (Kaplan, 1993b).

Table 16.2 Quality of Well-Being/General Health Policy Model: Symptom/Problem Complexes (CPX) with Calculating Weights

CPX No.	CPX Description	Weights
1.	Death (not on respondent's card)	–.727
2.	Loss of consciousness such as seizure (fits), fainting, or coma (out cold or knocked out)	–.407
3.	Burn over large areas of face, body, arms, or legs	–.387
4.	Pain, bleeding, itching, or discharge (drainage) from sexual organs—does not include normal menstrual (monthly) bleeding	–.349
5.	Trouble learning, remembering, or thinking clearly	–.340
6.	Any combination of one or more hands, feet, arms, or legs either missing, deformed (crooked), paralyzed (unable to move), or broken—includes wearing artificial limbs or braces	–.333
7.	Pain, stiffness, weakness, numbness, or other discomfort in chest, stomach (including hernia or rupture), side, neck, back, hips, or any joints or hands, feet, arms, or legs	–.299
8.	Pain, burning, bleeding, itching, or other difficulty with rectum, bowel movements, or urination (passing water)	–.292
9.	Sick or upset stomach, vomiting, or loose bowel movement, with or without chills, or aching all over	–.290
10.	General tiredness, weakness, or weight loss	–.259
11.	Cough, wheezing, or shortness of breath, with or without fever, chills, or aching all over	–.257
12.	Spells of feeling upset, being depressed, or crying	–.257
13.	Headache, or dizziness, or ringing in ears, or spells of feeling hot, nervous, or shaky	–.244
14.	Burning or itching rash on large areas of face, body, arms, or legs	–.240
15.	Trouble talking, such as lisp, stuttering, hoarseness, or being unable to speak	–.237
16.	Pain or discomfort in one or both eyes (such as burning or itching) or any trouble seeing after correction	–.230
17.	Overweight for age and height or skin defect of face, body, arms, or legs, such as scars, pimples, warts, bruises, or changes in color	–.188
18.	Pain in ear, tooth, jaw, throat, lips, tongue; several missing or crooked permanent teeth—includes wearing bridges or false teeth; stuffy, runny nose; or any trouble hearing—includes wearing a hearing aid	–.170
19.	Taking medication or staying on a prescribed diet for health reasons	–.144
20.	Wearing eyeglasses or contact lenses	–.101
21.	Breathing smog or unpleasant air	–.101
22.	No symptom or problem (not on respondent's card)	–.000
23.	Standard symptom/problem	–.257
X24.	Trouble sleeping	–.257
X25.	Intoxication	–.257
X26.	Problems with sexual interest or performance	–.257
X27.	Excessive worry or anxiety	–.257

Note. For symptoms 22–27 a standardized weight is used (X) because data are not currently available.

Is the Model Applicable to Mental Health?

Despite widespread interest in the model among practitioners in many different specialties, the concept of a quality-adjusted life year has received very little attention in the mental health field, largely because of the belief that mental health and physical health outcomes are conceptually distinct. As noted earlier, Ware and Sherbourne (1992) have emphasized that since mental health and physical health constitute different constructs, any attempt to measure them by using a uniform measurement strategy is like comparing apples to oranges. While mental and physical health outcomes are distinct and call for measuring the effects of treatment by using different units, it is also important that a common measurement strategy be used to ensure that the productivity of mental health and physical health providers can be directly compared. Since mental health providers compete with all other health care providers for the same resources, a common outcome metric can allow for head-to-head comparisons of treatment effectiveness (Sturm & Wells, 1995).

Several years ago, Kaplan and Anderson (1988a) argued that there are many similarities in mental health and physical health outcomes. The QWB system includes the basic dimensions of observable functioning, symptoms, and duration. Mental health problems, like physical health problems, can be represented by symptoms and by disrupted role functioning. Consider some examples. Suppose that a patient has the primary symptom of a cough. If the cough does not disrupt role function, the QWB score might show a small deviation from 1.0. If the cough is more serious and keeps the person at home, the QWB score will be lower. If the cough is very severe, it might limit the person to a hospital and may have serious disruptive effects upon role functioning. This would necessitate an even lower QWB score. Coughs can be of different duration. A cough associated with an acute respiratory infection may have a serious impact on functioning that may last only a short period of time. This would be indicated by a minor deviation in well years. A chronic cough associated with obstructive lung disease would be associated with significant loss of quality-adjusted life years because duration is a major component of the calculation.

Now consider the case of a person with depression. Depression may be a symptom reported by a patient just as a cough is reported by other patients. Depression without disruption of role function would cause a minor variation of wellness. If the depression caused the person to stay at home, the QWB score would be lower. Severe depression might require the person to be in a hospital or special facility and would result in a lower QWB score. Depressions, like coughs, are of different durations. Depression of long duration would cause the loss of more quality-adjusted life years than would depression of short duration.

Some evidence supports the validity of the QWB in studies of mental health. One recent study evaluated

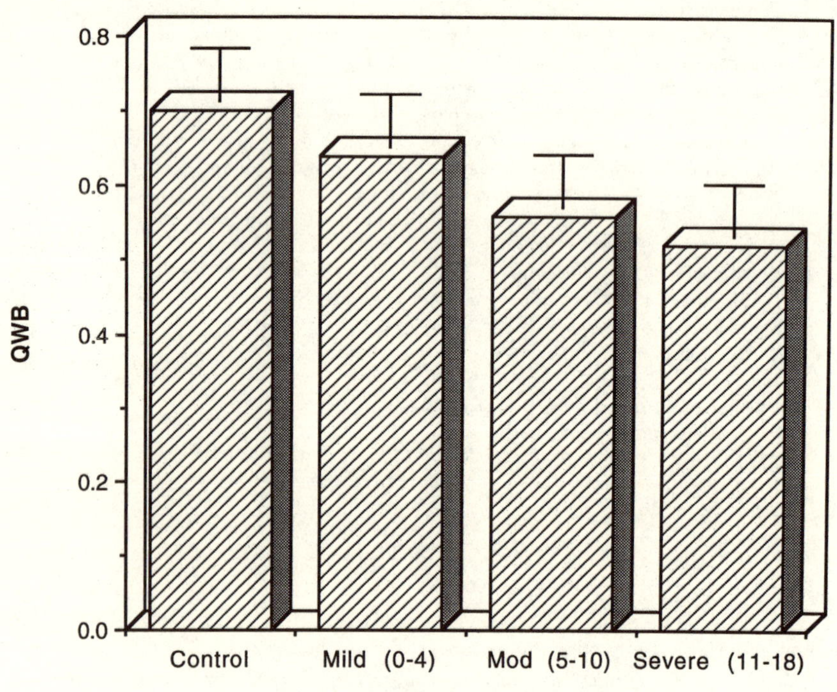

Figure 16.1 Quality of Well-Being Scale (QWB) by Scale for the Assessment of Negative Symptoms (SANS) patient group. Adapted from Patterson et al. (1996).

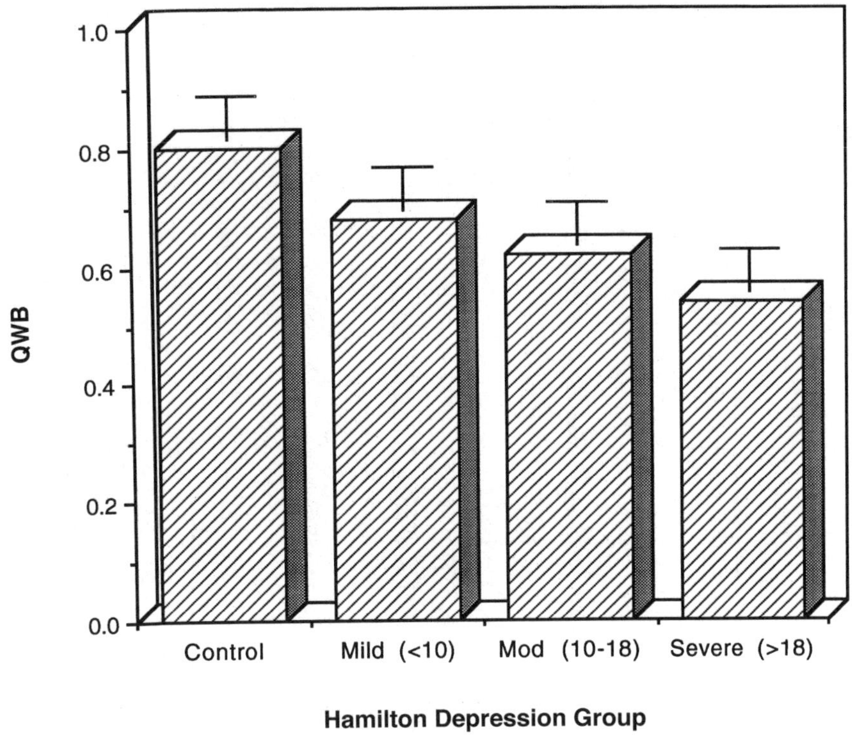

Figure 16.2 Quality of Well-Being Scale (QWB) by Hamilton depression (HAM-D) score in affective disorders clinic. Adapted from Payne et al. (1997).

the validity of the Quality of Well-Being Scale (QWB) as an outcome measure for older psychotic patients. In this study, 72 psychotic patients and 28 matched controls from the San Diego Veterans Affairs Medical Center completed the QWB, the Structured Clinical Interview for the DSM-III-R patient version (SCID-P), scales for the Assessment of Positive and Negative Symptoms (SAPS and SANS), and the Global Severity Index (GSI) from the Brief Symptom Inventory (BSI). The QWB correlated with the SANS –0.52 ($p < .001$), with the SAPS –0.57 ($p < .001$), and with the GSI –0.62 ($p < .001$). Patients and controls were significantly different on the QWB, and there was a linear relationship between QWB and severity of illness (as classified by the SANS; see Figure 16.1) and the SAPS. In addition, component scores of the QWB (i.e., mobility, physical activity, social activity, and worst symptom) were significantly lower among patients than among controls and declined systematically as psychiatric symptoms increased (Patterson et al., 1996).

Pyne and colleagues (1997) compared QWB scores between patients with major depression and controls. Figure 16.2 shows the step-wise decrease in QWB scores for the controls through each of the patient groups according to their Hamilton depression (HAM-D) scores. Similar results were observed for Beck Depression Inventory (BDI) scores. The difference between each of these groups were highly significant ($p < 0.001$). In order to evaluate which of six variables (age, gender, family history, presence of Axis III diagnosis, comorbid Axis I diagnosis, HAM-D) best predicted the QWB score in this patient population, a hierarchical multiple regression analysis was conducted. Although Axis III disorders are significant predictors of QWB, depression (HAM-D and BDI) predicts QWB when Axis III diagnoses are statistically controlled.

In a related study, Rubin and colleagues (1994) administered the QWB and the HAM-D to 285 men with HIV disease and 61 male controls. Men with HIV seropositive infection were divided into those with and without acquired immunodeficniency disease (AIDS) and the presence of depression. Figure 16.3 summarizes QWB scores for controls and for HIV-positive patients with HAM-D scores indicating no depression (0–9), mild depression (10–17), and more serious depression (>17). The analysis shows that QWB scores

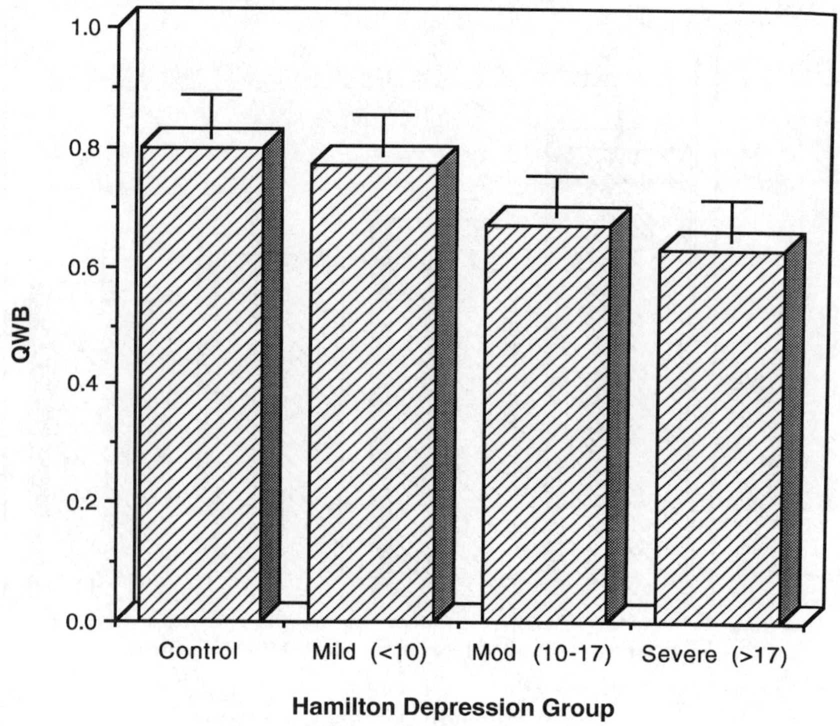

Figure 16.3 Quality of Well-Being Scale (QWB) by Hamilton depression (HAM-D) score in HIV. Adapted from Rubin et al. (1995).

are significantly related to depression. Further, Rubin and colleagues showed that improvement in depressive symptoms over 1 year was associated with improved QWB scores. Those who developed depressive symptoms showed reductions in QWB scores. Overall changes in depression were related to changes in QWB. These findings suggest that depression is difficult to separate from general health status among patients with a serious illness.

Using the general health policy model, it is possible to estimate the benefit of any health care intervention in terms of the quality-adjusted life years the treatment produces. Suppose, for example, that a specific behavioral intervention for anxiety elevates patients from a level of .65 to a level of .75. Suppose further that this treatment benefit lasted for 1 year. Each patient would gain .1 QALY ($.75 - .65 = .10 \times 1$ year = .1 QALY) for each year the benefit was observed. The treatment benefit would be expressed in terms of general QALY units. The productivity of the providers could be compared with that of providers in other aspects of health care, since all providers in health care use resources. (The cost-utility ratio is the ratio of the cost of a treatment divided by the QALYs that the treatment produces.)

Measuring mental health productivity in QALY units would allow the assessment of investments in mental health services to be compared directly to those in other aspects of health care. To date, there have not been systematic trials that have evaluated the effects of psychotherapy in QALY units. This is in contrast to most other areas of medicine, where QALY production reports have become relatively common. In order to compete for resources, psychotherapy researchers may benefit from these analyses.

In summary, the general QWB measure has evidence for validity in a variety of different specific diseases. It has been shown to be responsive to change, and its application has been found to be feasible in a wide variety of different clinical populations. Recent evidence shows that the measure has validity for studies in mental health as well as for studies of nonpsychiatric medical illness. It may be useful for demonstrating the cost-utility of psychotherapy. Examples of applications of these measures in clinical studies and public policy-making are described in the section below.

The World Bank and the World Health Organization have also recognized that traditional health indicators, such as life expectancy and infant mortality, may be relatively unaffected by many of the investments in public health in the developing world. They proposed an index similar to the quality-adjusted life year, known as the *disability-adjusted life year* (DALY) (Murray & Lopez, 1996). In order to calculate DALYs, they considered 109 diseases that represent about 95% of all deaths in the world. Using 1990 mortality data, they estimated the distribution of these diseases by age, sex, and demographic region of the world. Next, they estimated mortality from each of these diseases and created life tables for each condition by each region. The next step involved healthy-life expectancy estimates for these regions by experts who judged the distribution in disability levels by diagnostic category. Finally, expert judgment was used to create qualitative ratings for levels of disability. Using this methodology, they evaluated world health problems. They concluded that too much effort is directed toward infectious diseases, such as the ebola virus. In terms of DALYs lost, mental illness is the leading threat to worldwide health. Noncommunicable problems such as smoking and traffic accidents are second and third. The authors of the study noted that traditional indicators that consider only death tend to ignore some of the most important health problems like psychological and psychiatric illness. However, using a weighted system that places all outcomes in the same measurement units suggests that these problems should be given much higher priority.

Resource Allocation Decisions

One of the advantages of the GHPM is that it allows for comparison between very different types of services, using quality-adjusted life years to provide a common metric. All providers in the health care system have the common objectives of increasing length of life and improving quality of life. The general model allows evaluations of the relative value of investing in each of these specialties in comparison to the resources that they use. Allocating resources based on systematic data has been proposed by several different governments (Neumann & Johannesson, 1994). For example, the Australian government now requires evidence on effectiveness, as do a variety of European governments. Canada has officially proposed the quality-adjusted life year as a basis for making decisions about which drugs will be purchased by the different provinces (Detsky, 1991). This approach has also been considered in the United Kingdom (Williams, 1988).

The GHPM has been used to evaluate outcomes in a variety of settings. Table 16.3 summarizes many of these studies with adjustments to current dollars. As the table suggests, some interventions, such as aerosolized pentamidine for prophylaxis of PCP pneumonia in HIV disease, cost nearly $0.5 million to produce the equivalent of a life year. Traditional medical interventions in prevention, such as cholesterol and blood pressure reduction, may be much less expensive in producing the equivalent of a year of life. However, some nontraditional behavioral interventions, including smoking cessation counseling programs, are even more cost-effective. Interestingly, Table 3 reveals that the most cost-effective program has nothing to do with traditional health care; it involves passing laws that require the use of seat belts in automobiles.

The use of the GHPM, however, requires many heroic assumptions. The data for Table 3 derive from a variety of different studies. In many of these cases, the health benefits were estimated by use of expert judgment. The accuracy of many of these estimates is unknown because they are based on judgments and not empirical studies (Kaplan, 1994). Furthermore, there are important assumptions in the application of the model, including the discount rate and the reliability of the estimate of treatment effectiveness. Despite these limitations, the General Health Policy Model may provide a unique new way of thinking about alternatives in health care.

Formal models of resource allocation have been implemented by at least one state. Oregon has attempted to prioritize the cost-utility of different health services in an innovative experiment with its Medicaid program. One of the landmark features of the Oregon experiment was the attempt to put mental health services and other health services into the same prioritization. In an earlier version of the list, the cutoff for funding was roughly 600. At the top of the list were services such as treatment for rumination disorder of infancy, treatment for delirium resulting from the use of psychoactive substances, and treatment for a single episode of major depression. In the middle of the list were services such as psychotherapy for anxiety disorder and panic disorder and treatment for conversion disorder in childhood. These services would clearly be funded by the program. However, at the bottom of the list were services such as psychotherapy for antisocial personality disorder, psychotherapy for transsexualism, and psychotherapy for pica (Table 16.4).

Table 16.3 Summary of Cost/Well-Year Estimates for Selected Medical, Surgical, and Preventive Interventions[a]

Program	Reference	Cost/well year ($)
Seat belt laws	Kaplan & Anderson (1988a)	0
Antepartum and anti-D injection[b]	Torrance & Zipursky (1984)	1,543
Pneumonococcal vaccine for the elderly	OTA (1979)	1,765
Postpartum and anti-D injection[b]	Torrance & Zipursky (1984)	2,109
Coronary artery bypass surgery for left main coronary	Weinstein & Stason (1982)	4,922
Neonatal intensive care, 1,000–14,999 g	Boyle et al. (1983)	5,473
Smoking cessation counseling	Schulman (1991)	6,463
T4 (thyroid) screening	Epstein et al. (1981)	7,595
PKU screening[c]	Bush et al. (1973)	8,498
Treatment of severe hypertension (diastolic > 105 mm Hg) in males age 40	Weinstein & Stason (1976)	10,896
Oral gold in rheumatoid arthritis	Thompson et al. (1988)	12,059
Dapsone for prophylaxis for PCP pneumonia[d]	Freedberg et al. (1991)	13,400
Treatment of mild hypertension (diastolic 95–104 mm Hg) in males age 40	Weinstein & Stason (1976)	22,197
Oat bran for high cholesterol	Kinosian & Eisenberg (1988)	22,910
Rehabilitation in COPD[e]	Toevs et al. (1984)	28,320
Estrogen therapy for postmenopausal symptoms in women without a prior hysterectomy	Weinstein (1980)	32,057
Neonatal intensive care, 500–999 g	Boyle et al. (1983)	38,531
CABG (surgery) 2-vessel disease[f]	Weinstein & Stason (1982)	39,770
Hospital hemodialysis	Churchill et al. (1984)	40,200
Coronary artery bypass surgery for single-vessel disease with moderately severe occlusion	Weinstein & Stason (1982)	42,195
School tuberculin-testing program	Bush et al. (1973)	43,250
Continuous ambulatory peritoneal dialysis	(Churchill et al., 1984)	54,460
Cholestipol for high cholesterol	Kinosian & Eisenberg (1988)	92,467
Cholestyramine for high cholesterol	Kinosian & Eisenberg (1988)	153,105
Screening mammography	Eddy (1989)	167,850
Total hip replacement	Liang et al. (1986)	293,029
CABG (surgery) 1-vessel heart disease[f]	Weinstein & Stason (1982)	662,835
Aerosolized pentamidine for prophylaxis of PCP pneumonia[d]	Freedberg et al. (1991)	756,000

[a]All estimates adjusted to 1993 U.S. dollars.
[b]Treatment for Rh immunization.
[c]PKU, phenylketonuria.
[d]PCP, pneumocystic carinii pneumonia.
[e]COPD, chronic obstructive pulmonary disease.
[f]CABG, coronary artery bypass graft.

Summary

The American health care system is undergoing significant change. Current directions in health care reform suggest that there will be significant restrictions on the rate of increase in health care spending. Psychotherapy now accounts for about 8% of outpatient medical care costs (Olfson & Pincus, 1994c). In the future, ceilings on health care expenditures are likely. Thus, campaigns to increase funding for some medical services may result in reductions in the availability of funds to support other services.

Mental health service providers must necessarily compete with other health care providers for limited resources. In order to successfully compete, it will be necessary to document that mental health services, including outpatient psychotherapy, provide a benefit to the consumer. General measurement methods that document the effects of interventions upon general health status are now available. The application of

Table 16.4 Examples of Mental Health Items From the Oregon Integrated List

Rank	Item
76	Rumination disorder of infancy
99	Delirium from psychoactive substance use
108	Major depression, single episode
152	Youth abuse of hallucinogen, amphetamine, or alcohol
347	Anxiety disorder
348	Panic disorder
353	Conversion disorder, child
760	Antisocial personality disorder
761	Transsexualism
763	Pica

these methods may help document the benefit and the cost-utility of psychotherapy and of other behavioral interventions.

Notes

1. In some instances where investigators are interested in specific subcomponents of mental health, such as cognitive functioning, more detailed measures might be considered additions to (but not replacements for) the general measures.

2. The model has been criticized for assuming that preference ratings do not generalize from patients to nonpatients. Further, there have been concerns that different social and ethnic groups hold significantly different preferences for health states. This issue was systematically investigated in a series of analyses. The analyses demonstrated that, indeed, the concerns are not well founded. Differences between patients and nonpatients are few, and preferences appear generalizable across different social, ethnic, and gender groups (Kaplan, 1994).

References

Bombardier, C., Ware, J., Russell, I. J., et al. (1986). Auranofin therapy and quality of life for patients with rheumatoid arthritis: Results of a multicenter trial. *American Journal of Medicine, 81*, 565–578.

Boyle, M. H., Torrance, G. W., Sinclair, J. C., & Horwood, S. P. (1983). Economic evaluation of neonatal intensive care of very-low-birth-weight infants. *New England Journal of Medicine*, 308(22), 1330–1337.

Brook, R. H., & Lohr, K. (1986). Will we need to ration effective health care? *Issues in Science and Technology*, 3, 68–77.

Bush, J. W., Chen, M. M., & Patrick, D. L. (1973). Cost-effectiveness using a health status index: Analysis of the New York State PKU screening program. In R. Berg (Ed.), *Health status index* (pp. 172–208). Chicago: Hospital Research and Educational Trust.

Churchill, D. N., Lemon, B. C., & Torrance, G. W. (1984). A cost-effectiveness analysis of continuous abulatory peritoneal dialysis and hospital hemodialysis. *Medical Decision Making*, 4(4), 489–500.

Detsky, A. (1991). *Guidelines for economic analysis of pharmaceutical products*. Toronto: Drug Programme Branch, Ontario Ministry of Health.

Dupuy, H. (1974). Utility of the national center for health statistics general well-being schedule in the assessment of self-representation of subjective well-being and distress. *National Conference on Education in Alcohol and Drug Abuse and Mental Health Programs*. Washington, DC.

Eddy, D. M. (1989). Screening for breast cancer. *Annals of Internal Medicine, 111*, 389–339.

Epstein, K. A., Schneiderman, L. J., Bush, J. W., & Zettner, W. R. (1981). The "abnormal" screening of thyroxine (T4): Analysis of physician response, outcome, cost and health effectiveness. *Journal of Chronic Disease*, 34, 175–190.

Erickson, P., Kendall, E. A., Anderson, J. P., & Kaplan, R. M. (1989). Using composite health status measures to assess the nation's health. *Medical Care*, 27(Suppl. 3), S66–S76.

EuroQol Group. (1990). EuroQol—A new facility for the measurement of health-related quality of life. *Health Policy, 16*, 199–208.

Fleming, C., Wasson, J. H., Albertsen, P. C., Barry, M. J., & Wennberg, J. E. (1993). A decision analysis of alternative treatment strategies for clinically localized prostate cancer: Prostate Patient Outcomes Research Team. *Journal of American Medical Association*, 269(20), 2650–2658.

Freedberg, K. A., Tosteson, A. N., Cohen, C. J., & Cotton, D. J. (1991). Primary prophylaxis for *Pneumocystis carinii* pneumonia in HIV-infected people with CD4 counts below 200/mm^3: A cost-effectiveness analysis. *Journal of Acquired Immune Deficiency Syndromes*, 4(5), 521–531.

Ganiats, T. G., Palinkas, L. A., & Kaplan, R. M. (1992). Comparison of Quality of Well-Being Scale and functional status index in patients with atrial fibrillation. *Medical Care*, 30(10), 958–964.

Hodgkin, P. S. (1994). *Health impact of endoscopic sinus surgery assessed by the Quality of Well-Being (QWB) Scale*. Unpublished, University of California, San Diego.

Kaplan, R. M. (1990). Behavior as the central outcome in health care. *American Psychologist, 45*, 1211–1220.

Kaplan, R. M. (1993a). Application of a general health policy model in the American health care crisis. *Journal of the Royal Society of Medicine, 86*, 277–281.

Kaplan, R. M (1993b). *Hippocratic predicament: Affordability, access, and accountability in health care.* San Diego: Academic Press.

Kaplan, R. M. (1993c). Quality of life assessment for cost/utility studies in cancer. *Cancer Treatment Reviews, 19*(Suppl. A), 85–96.

Kaplan, R. M. (1994). Value judgment in the Oregon Medicaid experiment. *Medical Care, 32*(10), 975–988.

Kaplan, R. M., & Anderson, J. P. (1988a). A general health policy model: Update and applications. *Health Services Research, 23*, 203–234.

Kaplan, R. M., & Anderson, J. P. (1988b). The Quality of Well-Being Scale: Rationale for a single quality of life index. In S. R. Walker & R. Rosser (Eds.), *Quality of Life: Assessment and Application* (pp. 51–77). London: MTP Press.

Kaplan, R. M., & Anderson, J. P. (1990). An integreted approach to quality of life assessment: The general health policy model. In B. Spilker (Ed.), *Quality of life in clinical studies* (pp. 131–149). New York: Raven.

Kaplan, R. M., Anderson, J. P., Patterson, T. L., McCutchan, J. A., Weinrich, J. D., Heaton, R. H., Atkinson, J. H., Thal, L., Chandler, J., & Grant, I. (1995). Validity of the Quality of Well-Being Scale for persons with HIV Infection. *Psychosomatic Medicine, 57*, 138–157.

Kaplan, R. M., Atkins, C. J., & Timms, R. (1984). Validity of a Quality of Well-Being Scale as an outcome measure in chronic obstructive pulmonary disease. *Journal of Chronic Diseases, 37*(2), 85–95.

Kaplan, R. M., Bush, J. W., & Berry, C. C. (1976). Health status: Types of validity and the index of well-being. *Health Services Research, 11*(4), 478–507.

Kaplan, R. M., Bush, J. W., & Berry, C. C. (1978). The reliability, stability, and generalizability of a health status index, *American Statistical Association, Proceedings of the Social Status Section*, pp.704–709. (Volume number not available)

Kaplan, R. M., Bush, J. W., & Berry, C. C. (1979). Health Status Index: Category rating versus magnitude estimation for measuring levels of well-being. *Medical Care, 17*(5), 501–525.

Kaplan, R. M., Hartwell, S. L., Wilson, D. K., & Wallace, J. P. (1987). Effects of diet and exercise interventions on control and quality of life in non-insulin-dependent diabetes mellitus. *Journal of General Internal Medicine, 2*, 220–228.

Kaplan, R. M., Kozin, F., & Anderson, J. P. (1988). Measuring quality of life in arthritis patients (including discussion of a general health-decision model). *Quality of Life and Cardiovascular Care, 4*, 131–139.

Kerner, D., Patterson, T. L., Grant, I., & Kaplan, R. M. (1998). Validity of the Quality of Well-Being Scale in Alzheimer's disease. *Journal of Aging and Health, 10*, 44–61.

Kessler, R. C., McGonagle, K. A., Zhao, S., Nelson, C. B., Hughes, M., Eshleman, S., Wittchen, H. U., & Kendler, K. S. (1994). Lifetime and 12-month prevalence of DSM-III-R psychiatric disorders in the United States: Results from the National Comorbidity Survey. *Archives of General Psychiatry, 51*(1), 8–19.

Kinosian, B. P., & Eisenberg, J. M. (1988). Cutting into cholesterol. Cost-effective alternatives for treating hypercholesterolemia. *Journal of the American Medical Association, 259*(15), 2249–2254.

Liang, M. H., Cullen, K. E., Larson, M. G., et al. (1986). Cost-effectiveness of total joint arthroplasty in osteoarthritis. *Arthritis and Rheumatism, 29*, 937–943.

Lipid Research Clinics Coronary Prevention Trial Results. (1984). Reduction in incidence in coronary heart disease. *Journal of the American Medical Association, 251*, 351—364.

Lu-Yao, G. L., McLerran, D., Wasson J., & Wennberg, J. E. (1993). An assessment of radical prostatectomy: Time trends, geographic variation, and outcomes: The Prostate Patient Outcomes Research Team. *Journal of the American Medical Association, 269*(20), 2633–2636.

Mechanic, D., Angel, R. J., & Davies, L. (1992). Correlates of using mental health services: implications of using alternative definitions. *American Journal of Public Health, 82*, 74–78.

Murray, C. J. L., & Lopez, A. D. (Eds.). (1996). Alternative projections of mortality and disability by cause 1990–2020: Global Burden of Disease Study. *Lancet, 349*(9064), 498–504.

Neumann, P. J., & Johannesson, M. (1994, Summer). From principle to public policy: Using cost-effectiveness analysis. *Health Affairs, 13*, 206–214.

Office of Technology Assessment, U.S. Congress. (1979). *A review of selected federal vaccine and immunization policies: Based on case sudies of pneumococcal vaccine*. Washington, DC: U.S. Government Printing Office.

Olfson, M., & Pincus, H. A. (1994a). Measuring outpatient mental health care in the United States. *Health Affairs, 13*, 172–180.

Olfson, M., & Pincus, H. A. (1994b). Outpatient psychotherapy in the United States: 1. Volume, costs, and user characteristics. *American Journal of Psychiatry, 151*, 1281–1288.

Olfson, M., & Pincus, H. A. (1994c). Outpatient psychotherapy in the United States: 2. Patterns of utilization. *American Journal of Psychiatry, 151*, 1289–1294.

Orenstein, D. M., & Kaplan, R. M. (1991). Measuring the quality of well-being in cystic fibrosis and lung transplantation: The importance of the area under the curve. *Chest, 100*, 1016–1018.

Patterson, T. L., Kaplan, R. M., Grant, I., Semple, S. J., Moscona, S., Koch, W. L., Harris, M. J., & Jeste, D. V. (1994). Quality of well-being in late-life psychosis. *Psychiatry Research, 63*(2/3), 169–181..

Rubin, H. C., Patterson, T. L., Atkinson, J. H., Kaplan, R. M., Koch, W. L., McCutchan, J. A., Chandler, J. L., & Grant, I. (1994). *Tracking effects of depression on life quality in HIV.* Second International Conference on Biopsychosocial Aspects of HIV Infection, Brighton, UK, July 8.

Schulman, K. A., Lynn, L. A., Glick, H. A., & Eisenberg, J. M. (1991). Cost effectiveness of low-dose zidovudine therapy for asymptomatic patients with human immunodeficiency virus (HIV) infection. *Annals of Internal Medicine, 114*(9), 798–802.

Sledge, W. H. (1994). Psychotherapy in the United States: Challenges and opportunities. *American Journal of Psychiatry, 151*, 1267–1270.

Squier, H., Ries, A. L., Kaplan, R. M., Prewitt, L. M., Smith, C. M., Kriett, J. M., & Jamieson, S. W. (1995). Quality of Well-Being predicts survival in lung transplantation candidates. *American Journal of Respiratory and Critical Care Medicine, 152*, 2032–2036.

Sturm, R., & Wells, K. B. (1995). How can care for depression become more cost-effective? *Journal of the American Medical Association*, 273, 51–58.

Thompson, M. S., Read, J. L., Hutchings, H. C., Patterson, M., & Harris, E. D., Jr. (1988). The cost-effectiveness of auranofin: Results of a randomized clinical trial. *Journal of Rheumatology, 15*, 35–42.

Toevs, C. D., Kaplan, R. M., & Atkins, C. J. (1984). The costs and effects of behavioral programs for chronic obstructive pulmonary disease. *Medical Care*, 22, 1088–1100.

Torrance, G. W., & Feeny, D. (1989). Utilities in quality-adjusted life years. *International Journal of Technology Assessment in Health Care, 5*, 559–575.

Torrance, G. W., & Zipursky, A. (1984). Cost-effectiveness of antepartum prevention of RH immunization. *Clinics in Perinatology, 11*(2), 267–281.

Ware, J. E., Jr., Manning, W. G., Duan, N., et al. (1984). Health status and the use of outpatient mental health services. *American Psychologist*, 30, 1090–1100.

Ware, J. E., & Sherbourne, C. D. (1992). The MOS 36-item short-form health survey (SF-36): Conceptual framework and items selction. *Medical Care*, 30, 473–483.

Weinstein, M. C. (1980). Estrogen use in postmenopausal women—Costs, risks, benefits. *New England Journal of Medicine*, 303, 308–316.

Weinstein, M. C., & Stason, W. B. (1976). *Hypertension: A policy perspective*. Cambridge, MA: Harvard University Press.

Weinstein, M. C., & Stason, W. B. (1982). Cost-effectiveness of coronary artery bypass surgery. *Circulation* (Suppl. 3), 56–66.

Williams, A. (1988). The importance of quality of life in policy decisions. In S. Walker & R. Rosser (Eds.), *Quality of life: Assessment and application* (pp. 279–290). London: MTP Press.

Wittchen, H. U., Zhao, S., Kessler, R. C., & Eaton, W. W. (1994). DSM-III-R generalized anxiety disorder in the National Comorbidity Survey. *Archives of General Psychiatry*, 51(5), 355–364.

World Bank. (1993). *World development report.: Investing in health*. New York: Oxford University Press.

World Health Organization. (1948). *Constitution of the World Health Organization*. Geneva: WHO Basic Documents.

17

A Review of Instruments for Measuring Quality-of-Life Outcomes in Mental Health

Anthony F. Lehman

In this age when concerns regarding efficiency and managed care dominate the health care industry, the capacity to demonstrate that the services provided do in fact enhance outcomes in a cost-effective manner has taken on renewed urgency. This is particularly true for treatment interventions for mental disorders, which face additional burdens of stigma, as well as lingering doubts on the part of actuaries and economists (see chapter 13, this volume) regarding whether psychiatry and the related mental health disciplines are adequately based in empirical science.

More than most other aspects of medicine, psychiatry labors under the image of being, at best, a very weakly scientific field and, at worst, just another form of folk art and healing, guided primarily by archetypes and ideologies. Despite its disparaged image as a science, psychiatry has an impressive history of treatment outcomes research. The recent national debate on national health care reform forced a careful inventory of the scientific basis for psychiatric practice, which concluded (Keith & Matthews, 1993) that the scientific evidence for the effectiveness of psychiatric treatments is as impressive as that for many other areas of medical practice. The research findings on the efficacy of many psychiatric treatments have been summarized in special issues of *Psychopharmacology Bulletin* (Vol. 29, No. 4, 1993) and *Schizophrenia Bulletin* (Vol. 21, No. 4, 1995). A recent background report by the Office of Technology Assessment (1995) on considerations for designing health insurance benefits draws much the same conclusion. Because the current wave of health care reform is driven by cost containment, it is imperative that to every extent possible, the critical decisions made in the name of efficiency and responsible resource management be informed by and supportive of the best scientific medical knowledge.

Rationale for Quality of Life as a Health Care Outcome

Quality-of-life (QOL) concerns have gained considerable currency across the field of health care evaluation over the past decade. Several books have been published on the topic (Patrick & Erickson, 1993; Spilker, 1996), entire issues of journals have been devoted to the indexing of QOL measures (see *Medical Care*, 1990, Vol. 28, No. 12; *Journal of Clinical Research and Pharmacoepidemiology*, 1992, Vol. 6, pp. 87–156), and new publications have been created to deal with the volume of research on QOL (e.g., *Quality of Life Research*, *Quality of Life Newsletter*).

Underlying this interest in quality of life is the fundamental question regarding what difference medical treatments *really* make in patients' lives, reflected by the well-known medical aphorism "The surgery was a success, but the patient died." Medical outcome assessments that focus strictly upon the signs and symptoms of disease or disease processes (e.g., tumor size or survival time in cancer, range of motion or "joint counts" in arthritis, expiratory volume in lung disease, seizure frequency in epilepsy, or hallucinations in schizophrenia) have been recognized as essential, but not sufficient, monitors of patient outcome. Hence, driving this movement toward quality-of-life research is a humanitarian concern regarding the overall well-being of patients, and not just the narrow status of their disease processes.

More recently, to this humanitarian focus have been added concerns about costs. For example, pharmaceutical companies now face expectations from the Food and Drug Administration of evidence that new drugs will enhance quality of life, not just reduce symptoms or disease processes, and moreover, that such evidence may be used by hospital formularies in determining the cost-effectiveness of new drugs. Public policymakers and consumer groups also raise the quality-of-life issue in discussions pertaining to which treatments are worth purchasing (Patrick & Erickson, 1993; Spilker, 1996).

Although definitions vary, the quality-of-life concept encompasses three overarching dimensions: (a) what an individual is capable of doing *(functional status)*, (b) *access to resources and opportunities* to use one's abilities to pursue interests, and (c) *a sense of well-being*. The former two dimensions are often referred to as *objective quality of life* and the latter as *subjective quality of life*.

Within these overarching dimensions of quality of life, *life domains* have been identified, for example, health, family, social relations, work, financial status, and living situation. Quality of life is thus a complex notion. Three quality-of-life perspectives can be identified to frame core issues regarding QOL assessment in health care: (1) the *general quality-of-life framework*; (b) the *health-related quality-of-life framework* (HRQL); and (c) the *disease-specific quality-of-life framework*.

The *general QOL framework* underlies the considerable QOL research that has been done with the general population, work that for the most part preceded the more recent development of quality-of-life research in the health care context (Andrews & Withey, 1976; Campbell, Converse, & Rodgers, 1976). The intent of this line of research has been to derive a social perspective about how groups of people are doing and the values that they and their societies place upon various aspects of life experience. Such a perspective may provide insights into what people strive for, why they choose as they do, and how different societies and subgroups within a society fare in their life aspirations relative to others. These insights may guide decisions about how to improve quality of life. Measures based upon this approach typically cover functional status, access to resources and opportunities, and sense of well-being across multiple life domains, some not necessarily directly affected by health care (for example, housing).

The *health-related quality-of-life framework* emphasizes the specific impacts that disease, injury, and their prevention and treatment have on the value of survival (Patrick & Erickson, 1993). The concept of HRQL acknowledges the limited, but often vital, influences that disease and health care have on quality of life and holds health care accountable only for those aspects of quality of life that it may directly affect. The health-related quality-of-life framework focuses on functional status and sense of well-being and within these dimensions covers only those aspects directly related to health (e.g., functional role limitations *due to* emotional or physical illness as opposed to role limitations due to poverty or limited social opportunities). Such HRQL measures offer generic health-related quality-of-life assessments that can be used across most medical conditions.

The *disease-specific quality-of-life framework* presses for an even narrower definition of QOL in health care evaluations, tailored to the potential quality-of-life impacts of a specific disorder and its treatment.

QOL Measures for Persons with Mental Illnesses

Over the past decade, several measures have been developed to assess the quality-of-life experiences of persons with mental illnesses, in particular severe and persistent psychotic illnesses, but more recently, depression and anxiety disorders. These are in addition to the more generic QOL measures that have been developed in general health care and that, to a limited extent, have been applied to persons with mental disorders (Revicki & Murray, 1994).

This section is organized according to the mental illness(es) targeted by the various measures: (a) severe and persistent mental illnesses, (b) schizophrenia, and (c) depression and anxiety disorders. Most take the general QOL framework, but a few disease-specific measures are becoming available. A full review of these measures is beyond the scope of this chapter and is available elsewhere (Lehman & Burns, 1995). The goal here will be to give the reader a flavor of the measures and an entrée into the literature. Each measure is summarized in terms of its name, key reference(s), type of instrument, number of items, length of administration, summary content, psychometric properties, and types of patients studied.

Severe and Persistent Mental Illnesses

1. *Community Adjustment Form* (Hoult & Reynolds, 1984; Stein & Test, 1980). **Type of measure:** Semistructured self-report interview. **Number of items/time to administer:** 140 items/45 minutes. **Constructs assessed:** Leisure activities; Quality of Living Situation; Employment History and Status; Income Sources and Amounts; Free Lodging and/or Meals; Contact With Friends; Family Contact; Legal Problems; Life Satisfaction (21 items); Self-Esteem; Medical Care; and Agency Utilization. **Psychometric assessment:** Not reported. **Types of patients:** Severe mental illness in the community.

2. *Quality-of-Life Checklist* (Malm, May, & Dencker, 1981). **Type of measure:** Checklist completed by a trained interviewer after a semi-structured interview. **Items/time to administer:** 93 items/1 hour. **Constructs assessed:** Leisure Activities, Work, Vocational Rehabilitation, Economic Dependency, Social Relationships, Knowledge and Education, Psychological Dependency, Inner Experience, Housing Standard, Medical Care (Psychiatric and General), Religion. **Psychometric assessment:** Not reported. **Types of patients:** Outpatients with severe mental illness.

3. *Satisfaction-with-Life Domains Scale* (Baker & Intagliata, 1982; Johnson, 1991). **Type of measure:** Self-report scale administered by a trained interviewer. **Items/time to administer:** 15 items/10 minutes. **Constructs assessed:** Satisfaction with housing, neighborhood, food to eat, clothing, health, people lived with, friends, family, relations with other people, work/day programming, spare time, fun, services and facilities in area, economic situation, place lived in now compared to state hospital. These can be summed into a total life satisfaction score. **Psychometric assessment:** + construct validity. **Types of patients:** Severe mental illness in community.

4. *Oregon Quality-of-life Questionnaire* (Bigelow & Young, 1991; Bigelow, Brodsky, Steward, & Olson, 1982a; Bigelow, Gareau, & Young, 1982b; Bigelow, McFarland, & Olson, 1991a; Bigelow, McFarland, Gareau, & Young, 1991b). **Type of measure:** (a) A structured self-report interview, (b) a semistructured interviewer-rated interview; both are administered by a trained (not necessarily clinical) interviewer. **Items/time to administer:** (a) 263 items/45 minutes, (b) 146 items/45 minutes. **Constructs assessed:** Psychological Distress, Psychological Well-Being, Tolerance of Stress, Total Basic Need Satisfaction, Independence, Interpersonal Interactions, Spouse Role, Social Support, Work at Home, Employability, Work on the Job, Meaningful Use of Time, Negative Consequences of Alcohol Use, Negative Consequences of Drug Use. **Psychometric assessment:** + internal consistency, test-retest, interrater reliabilities; + predictive validity. **Types of patients:** Outpatients with severe mental illness.

5. *Lehman Quality of Life Interview* (Franklin, Solovitz, Mason, Clemons, & Miller, 1987; Huxley & Warner, 1992; Lehman, 1983a, 1983b; Lehman, 1988; Lehman, Ward, & Linn, 1982; Lehman, Possidente, & Hawker, 1986; Lehman, Slaughter, & Myers, 1991; Lehman, Kernan, & Postrado, 1995a; Lehman, Rachuba, & Postrado, 1995b; Levitt, Hogan, & Bucosky, 1990; Mechanic, McAlpine, Rosenfield, & Davis, 1994; Rosenfield, 1993; Rosenfield & Neese-Todd, 1993; Simpson, Hyde, & Faragher, 1989; Sullivan, Wells, & Leake, 1992). **Type of measure:** Structured self-report interview administered by trained lay interviewer; two versions available: (a) full, (b) brief. **Items/time to administer:** (a) 143 items/45 minutes; (b) 78 items/15 minutes. **Constructs assessed:** (a) *Objective QOL Indicators:* Residential Stability, Homelessness, Daily Activities, Frequency of Family Contacts, Frequency of Social Contacts, Total Monthly Spending Money, Adequacy of Financial Supports, Current Employment Status, Number of Arrests During the Past Year, Victim of Violent Crime During Past Year, Victim of Nonviolent Crime During the Past Year; General Health Status; (b) *Subjective QOL Indicators:* Satisfaction With: Living Situation, Leisure Activities, Family Relations, Social Relations, Finances, Work and School, Legal and Safety, and Health. **Psychometric assessment:** + internal consistency, test-retest reliability; + construct, predictive, discriminant validity. **Types of patients:** Severe mental illness.

6. *Client Quality of Life Interview* (Goldstrom & Manderscheid, 1986; Mulkern et al., 1986). **Type of measure:** Structured self-report interview administered by a trained lay interviewer. **Items/time to administer:** 46 items rated by the respondent plus 19 interviewer ratings. **Constructs assessed:** Essentials of Life (food, clothing, shelter, health and hygiene, money, and

safety), Job Training and Education, Daily Activities and Recreation, Privacy, Social Supports, Social Time, Self-Reliance, and Peace of Mind. **Psychometric assessment:** None available. **Types of patients:** Outpatients with severe mental illness.

7. *California Well-Being Project Client Interview* (Campbell, Schraiber, Temkin, & ten Tusscher, 1989). **Type of measure:** Self-report questionnaire, three versions: (a) consumer version, (b) family member version, and (c) mental health professional version. **Items/time to administer:** (a) 151 items/time not indicated, (b) 76 items/time not indicated, (c) 77 items/time not indicated. **Constructs assessed:** Adequate Resources, Age, Alternatives to Psychiatric Hospitalization, Aspirations, Benefit Agencies, Board and Care Residents, Boredom, Causes of Psychological and Emotional Problems, Children, Client/Consumer, Conservatorship, Control of Emotional Problems, Creativity, Stereotype of Dangerousness, Discrimination, Electroconvulsive Therapy, Empowerment, Ethnic/Cultural Group, Family Relationships, Freedom, Friends, Gender, General Population, Hallucinations and/or Voices, Happiness, Health, Homelessness, Hospitalization, Income, Informed Consent, Internalized Stigma, Involuntary Treatment/Hospitalization, Labeling, Loneliness/Isolation, Mass Media, Meaningful Work and Achievement/Activity, Medications, Misdiagnosis, Neighborhood Resistance, "Normal" People, Patients' Rights, Personhood, Poverty, Privacy, Pro-Choice, Professional/Client Relationship, Public Policy, Quality of Life, Seclusion and Restraint, Self-Esteem, Self-Help, Sexual Life, Side-Effects, Social Life, Spiritual Life, Stigma, Stress, Tolerance, Stereotype of Unpredictability, Validation, Vocational Rehabilitation, Warmth and Intimacy, Well-Being, and Young Adult Chronic Mentally Ill. **Psychometric assessment:** None provided. **Types of patients:** Persons with severe mental illnesses.

8. *Lancaster Quality-of-Life Profile* (Oliver, 1991–1992; Oliver & Mohamad, 1992). **Type of measure:** Structured self-report patient interview designed for administration by clinical staff in community settings. **Items/time to administer:** 100 items/1 hour. **Constructs assessed:** Work/Education, Leisure/Participation, Religion, Finances, Living Situation, Legal and Safety, Family Relations, Social Relations, and Health. In addition, it includes a measure of General Well-Being and Self-Concept. **Psychometric assessment:** + internal and test-retest reliability; + content, construct, and predictive validity. **Types of patients:** Outpatients with severe mental illness.

9. *Quality-of-Life Self-Assessment Inventory* (Skantze, 1993). **Type of measure:** Self-report inventory completed by patient, followed by a semistructured interview with a clinician to confirm patient's ratings. **Items/time to administer:** 100 items/50 minutes. **Constructs assessed:** Physical Health, Finances, Household and Self-Care, Contacts, Dependence, Work and Leisure, Knowledge and Education, Inner Experiences, Mental Health, Housing, Housing Environment, Community Services, and Religion. **Psychometric assessment:** + test-retest reliability. **Types of patients:** Outpatients with severe mental illness.

10. *Quality-of-Life Index for Mental Health* (Becker, Diamond, & Sainfort, 1993). **Type of measure:** Self-administered questionnaire, with which assistance may be given to more severely impaired patients. Versions exist for (a) patients, (b) families, and (c) clinicians. **Items/time to administer:** 113 items: (a) 20–30 minutes, (b) 10–20 minutes, (c) not specified. **Constructs assessed:** Life Satisfaction, Occupational Activities, Psychological Well-Being, Physical Health, Activities of Daily Living, the Quality of Life Index, Social Relationships, Economics, Symptoms. **Psychometric assessment:** + test-retest, + construct validity. **Types of patients:** Outpatients with severe mental illnesses.

11. *Quality-of-Life Interview Scale* (Holcomb, Morgan, Adams, Ponder, & Farrel, 1993). **Type of measure:** Semistructured interview administered by trained clinical interviewers. **Items/time to administer:** 87 items/time not reported. **Constructs assessed:** Autonomy, Self-Esteem, Social Support, Physical Health, Anger/Hostility, Emotional Autonomy, and Personal Fulfillment. **Psychometric assessment:** + internal consistency reliability; + predictive and discriminant validity. **Types of patients:** Severe mental illness.

Schizophrenia

Although all of the QOL measures reviewed above have been used with patient samples with a predominance of schizophrenia, none was specifically developed as a disease-specific QOL measure. Only one schizophrenia-specific QOL measure exists.

12. *Quality of Life Scale* (Heinrichs, Hanlon, & Carpenter, 1984). **Type of measure:** Semistructured interview rated by trained clinicians. **Items/time to administer:** 21 items/45 minutes. **Constructs assessed:** Commonplace Activities, Occupational Role, Work Functioning, Work Level, Possession of Commonplace

Objects, Interpersonal Relations (household, friends, acquaintances, social activity, social network, social initiative, social withdrawal, sociosexual functioning), Sense of Purpose, Motivation, Curiosity, Anhedonia, Aimless Inactivity, Empathy, Emotional Interaction, and Work Satisfaction. These items reduce to four scales: Intrapsychic Foundations, Interpersonal Relations, Instrumental Role, and Total Score. **Psychometric assessment:** + interrater reliability. **Types of patients:** Schizophrenia.

Affective and Anxiety Disorders

13. *Quality of Life Enjoyment and Satisfaction Questionnaire* (Endicott, Nee, Harrison, & Blumenthal, 1993). **Type of measure:** Self-administered questionnaire. **Items/time to administer:** 93 items/time not reported. **Constructs assessed:** Physical Health, Subjective Feelings, Leisure Time Activities, Social Relationships, General Activities, Work, Household Duties, and School/Course Work. **Psychometric assessment:** + internal consistency and test-retest reliability; + construct, discriminant, and predictive validity. **Types of patients:** Major depression.

14. *SmithKline Beecham Quality-of-Life Scale* (Stoker, Dunbar, & Beaumont, 1992). **Type of measure:** Self-report questionnaire. **Items/time to administer:** 28 items/time not specified. **Constructs assessed:** Psychic well-being, physical well-being, social relationships, activities/interests/hobbies, mood, locus of control, sexual function, work/employment, religion, and finances. **Psychometric assessment:** + internal and test-retest reliability; + construct validity. **Types of patients:** Major depression and anxiety disorders.

15. *Quality of Life in Depression Scale* (Gregoire, de Leval, Mesters, & Czarka, 1994; Hunt & McKenna 1992a, 1992b). **Type of measure:** Self-report questionnaire. **Items/time to administer:** 34 items/time not specified. **Constructs assessed:** Domestic Activities, Interpersonal Relationships, Social Life, Cognition, Personal Hygiene, Leisure Activities and Relaxation. **Psychometric assessment:** + internal consistency and test-retest reliability; + construct validity. **Types of patients:** Depressed outpatients.

Psychopathology and QOL

A critical issue in the utility of QOL measures for assessing outcomes of psychological treatments is the degree to which psychopathology affects QOL. If psychopathology impairs QOL, then it seems reasonable to expect psychological treatments to improve QOL. Although the data are relatively limited, there is in fact good evidence for the premise that psychopathology is associated with impaired QOL experiences.

Two studies comparing persons with mental illnesses with those who are unaffected illustrate the point that mental illnesses are related to impaired QOL. In a study of severely and persistently mentally ill persons living in Los Angeles board-and-care homes, Lehman et al. (1982) found that these patients had significantly lower quality-of-life ratings than the general population. Even after controlling for the effects of poverty, these patients had substantially lower QOL in the areas of family and social relations, financial well-being, and general life satisfaction. More recently, Wells et al. (1988) examined the health-related QOL of depressed outpatients in primary-care settings. They found that the depressed patients had worse physical, social, and role functioning, worse perceived current health, and greater bodily pain than patients with no chronic conditions. Furthermore, among patients with chronic medical conditions, those with depression had greater impairment in health-related QOL than patients without depression. Hence, mental illnesses do appear to detract considerably from QOL.

This association of QOL and psychopathology also extends to specific symptom dimensions of psychopathology although, again, much more work is needed in this area. Lehman (1983a) as shown that symptoms, especially depression, are significantly correlated with patient self-ratings of QOL. For example, he used four different rating scales of symptoms across various studies: two self-report scales (the RAND Mental Health Index—Ware et al., 1979; the Symptom Checklist-90—Derogatis, Lipman, & Covi, 1973) and two clinician rating scales (the Schedule for Affective Disorders and Schizophrenia-Change Version, or SADS-C—Endicott & Spitzer, 1978; the Brief Psychiatric Rating Scale, or BPRS—Overall & Gorham, 1962). By means of these scales, he found that depression scales consistently correlate in the range of −0.4 to −0.5 with general life satisfaction ratings by patients. Anxiety scales showed a similar, but somewhat less strong, correlation with general life satisfaction (−0.25 to −0.3), and psychosis subscales tended not to be significantly correlated (Lehman, unpublished data). These data suggest that affective symptoms are more consistently associated with negative life satisfaction than are psychotic symptoms. The reason may be the variable nature of psychotic experiences, for example, grandiose versus persecutory delusions, but clearly, this area stands in need of further study. Others also have reported a correlation of QOL measures with depression rating scales (Gregoire et al., 1994; Hunt & McKenna, 1992b).

Finally, other dimensions of psychopathology need to be considered in relation to QOL. Unpublished data by Lehman indicate that the presence of an Axis II disorder among psychiatric inpatients is associated with lower life satisfaction (see Table 17.1).

These data build the argument that QOL is affected by psychopathology and that psychosocial interventions designed to alleviate psychopathology should have a positive impact on QOL.

Discussion

It can be argued intuitively that by definition, any treatment that reduces the symptoms and impairments of mental illness enhances QOL. What information might QOL measures add to the evaluation of a behavioral treatment for a mental disorder, above and beyond knowledge gained from assessments of symptoms and functional status?

The rationale for including a QOL assessment in treatment outcome evaluations is that QOL broadly reflects the significance to the patient of improvements in clinical status. As noted earlier, a common complaint of patients and the public about medical care in general is that doctors do not listen to their patients and treat the illness rather than the person. Hopefully, this is less true of mental health specialists in general and psychotherapists in particular, but the caveat remains that unless we ask patients how treatments are affecting their overall well-being, in addition to their target symptoms, we can miss the big picture. QOL assessments attempt to provide this broader view of outcomes from the patient's perspective. This approach is becoming increasingly important with the emphasis on competition among health care plans and the advent of consumer-oriented provider "report cards." Also, consumer and family advocacy is growing nationally and demanding more attention to its perspectives in the evaluation of all aspects of health care.

Table 17.1 Mean Quality-of-Life Scores Among Psychiatric Inpatients According to Presence of a Personality Disorder

Domains	No Personality Disorders ($n = 106$)	Personality Disorders ($n = 187$)
Subjective QOL		
Living situation	5.53	5.05**
Daily activities	4.96	4.42***
Family relations	5.10	4.30***
Social relations	5.31	4.72***
Finances	4.11	3.66*
Safety	5.10	4.33***
Health	5.12	4.72**
Objective QOL		
Daily activities	0.52	0.47*
Family contact	3.95	3.80
Social contact	3.58	3.31*
Financial adequacy	0.77	0.77
Victimization	0.16	0.25
Arrested	0.24	0.31

*$p < .05$
**$p < .01$
***$p < .001$

The major downside to including QOL assessments in the evaluation of treatment is that QOL can be affected by a much broader range of life factors than treatment can fairly be expected to address. For example, poverty, physical illness, and other life adversities can detract from QOL. Although one could argue that psychotherapy can help people deal more effectively with these problems (and hence enhance QOL in the face of them), it seems essential to consider these potential confounding effects in any decision to use a QOL assessment. One will either need to "control" for these factors or need to incorporate them into the theoretical model underlying the impact(s) of a treatment approach.

In developing an assessment of quality of life in a health care context, both the breadth and specificity of the measures must be considered. No single QOL measure will meet all needs. A general QOL approach may raise quality-of-life issues that health care cannot reasonably be expected to address (e.g., decent and affordable housing or access to good jobs) and hence may be insensitive to the effects of health care on quality of life. A disease-specific approach, while sensitive to the quality-of-life issues of concern to patients with a specific diagnosis, lacks generalizability and comparability to other patient groups. General HRQL measures, such as the Duke Health Profile and the MOS SF-36, permit fruitful comparisons across conditions (Wells et al., 1988), but they may lack sufficient specificity to guide improvements in care for persons with specific health problems (see chapter 16, this volume). The information derived from HRQL measures may be too narrow to adequately reflect the needs of persons who are chronically disabled and socially disadvantaged because of medical problems. Great care should be taken in the selection of the most appropriate QOL assessment to address the specific need at hand.

More research is needed if we are to understand the relationship of various aspects of QOL to the various dimensions of mental illnesses. This understanding should aid in focusing QOL assessments to inform practitioners about how treatments affect patients, and about how treatments can be further improved. This information also will inform consumers and payers about what works and is worth purchasing. Existing QOL measures will need to be streamlined and better focused in order to gain widespread utility.

References

Andrews, F. M., & Withey, S. B. (1976). *Social indicators of well-being.* New York: Plenum Press.

Baker, F., & Intagliata, J. (1982). Quality of life in the evaluation of community support systems. *Evaluation and Program Planning, 5,* 69–79.

Becker, M., Diamond, R., & Sainfort, F. (1993). A new patient focused index for measuring quality of life in persons with severe and persistent mental illness. *Quality of Life Research, 2,* 239–251.

Bigelow, D. A., Brodsky, G., Steward, L., & Olson, M. (1982a). The concept and measurement of quality of life as a dependent variable in evaluation of mental health services. In G. Stahler & W. Tash (Eds.), *Innovative approaches to mental health evaluation* (pp. 345–366). New York: Academic Press.

Bigelow, D. A., Gareau, M. J., & Young, D. J. (1982b). A quality of life interview. *Psychosocial Rehabilitation Journal, 14,* 94–98.

Bigelow, D. A., McFarland, B. H., & Olson, M. M. (1991a). Quality of life of community mental health program clients: Validating a measure. *Community Mental Health Journal, 27,* 43–55.

Bigelow, D. A., McFarland, B. H., Gareau, M. J., & Young, D. J. (1991b). Implementation and effectiveness of a bed reduction project. *Community Mental Health Journal, 27,* 125–133.

Bigelow, D. A., & Young, D. J. (1991). Effectiveness of a case management program. *Community Mental Health Journal, 27,* 115–123.

Campbell, A., Converse, & P. E., & Rodgers, W. L. (1976). *The quality of American life.* New York: Russell Sage Foundation.

Campbell, J., Schraiber, R., Temkin, T., & ten Tusscher, T. (1989). *The Well-Being Project: Mental Health Clients Speak for Themselves.* Sacamento, CA: California Department of Mental Health.

Derogatis, D. A., Lipman, R. S., & Covi, L. (1973). SCL-90: An outpatient psychiatric rating scale: Preliminary report. *Psychopharmacology Bulletin, 9,* 13–28.

Endicott, J., Nee, J., Harrison, W., & Blumenthal, R. (1993). Quality of life enjoyment and satisfaction questionnaire: A new measure. *Psychopharmacology Bulletin, 29,* 321–326.

Endicott, J., & Spitzer, R. (1978). A diagnostic interview: The Schedule for Affective Disorders and Schizophrenia. *Archive of General Psychiatry, 35,* 837–844.

Franklin, J. L., Solovitz, B., Mason, M., Clemons, J. R., & Miller, G. E. (1987). An evaluation of case management. *American Journal of Psychiatry, 77,* 674–678.

Gregoire, J., de Leval, N., Mesters, P., & Czarka, M. (1994). Validation of the quality of life in depression scale in a population of adult depressive patients aged 60 and above. *Quality of Life Research, 3,* 13–19.

Heinrichs, D. W., Hanlon, T. E., & Carpenter, W. T. (1984). The quality of life scale: An instrument for rating the schizophrenic deficit syndrome. *Schizophrenia Bulletin, 10,* 388–398.

Holcomb, W. R., Morgan, P., Adams, N. A., Ponder, H., & Farrel, M. (1993). Development of a structured interview scale for measuring quality of life of the severely mentally ill. *Journal of Clinical Psychology, 49,* 830–840.

Hoult, J., & Reynolds, J. (1984). Schizophrenia: A comparative trial of community oriented and hospital oriented psychiatric care. *Acta Psychiatrica Scandinavia, 69,* 359–372.

Hunt, S. M., & McKenna, S. P. (1992a). A new measure of quality of life in depression: Testing the reliability and construct validity of the QLDS. *Health Policy, 22,* 321–330.

Hunt, S. M., & McKenna, S. P. (1992b). The QLDS: A scale for measurement of quality of life in depression. *Health Policy, 22,* 307–319.

Huxley, P., & Warner, R. (1992). Case management, quality of life, and satisfaction with services of long-term psychiatric patients. *Hospital and Community Psychiatry, 43,* 799–802.

Johnson, P. J. (1991). Emphasis on quality of life of people with severe mental illness in community-based care in Sweden. *Psychosocial Rehabilitation Journal, 14,* 23–37.

Keith, S. J., & Matthews, S. (1993). The value of psychiatric treatment: Its efficacy in severe mental disorders. *Psychopharmacology Bulletin, 29,* 427–430.

Lehman, A. F. (1983a). The effects of psychiatric symptoms on quality of life assessments among the chronic mentally ill. *Evaluation and Program Planning, 6,* 143–151.

Lehman, A. F. (1983b). The well-being of chronic mental patients: Assessing their quality of life. *Archives of General Psychiatry, 40,* 369–373.

Lehman, A. F. (1988). A quality-of-life interview for the chronically mentally ill. *Evaluation and Program Planning, 11,* 51–62.

Lehman, A. F., & Burns, B. (1995). Severe mental illness in the community. In B. Spilker (Ed.), *Quality of life and pharmacoeconomics in clinical trials* (2nd ed., pp. 919–924). Philadelphia: Lippincott-Raven.

Lehman, A. F., Kernan, E., & Postrado, L. (1995a). *Quality-of-life toolkit.* Boston, MA: Health Services Research Institute.

Lehman, A. F., Rachuba, L. T., & Postrado, L. T. (1995b). Demographic influences on quality of life among persons with chronic mental illnesses. *Evaluation and Program Planning, 18,* 155–164.

Lehman, A. F., Possidente, S., & Hawker, F. (1986). The quality of life of chronic mental patients in a state hospital and community residences. *Hospital and Community Psychiatry, 37,* 901–907.

Lehman, A. F., Slaughter, J. C., & Myers, C. P. (1991). The quality of life of chronically mentally ill persons in alternative residential settings. *Psychiatric Quarterly, 62,* 35–49.

Lehman, A. F., Ward, N., & Linn, L. (1982). Chronic mental patients: The quality of life issue. *American Journal of Psychiatry, 10,* 1271–1276.

Levitt, A. J., Hogan, T. P., & Bucosky, C. M. (1990). Quality of life in chronically mentally ill patients in day treatment. *Psychological Medicine, 20,* 703–710.

Malm, U., May, P. R. A., & Dencker, S. J. (1981). Evaluation of the quality of life of the schizophrenic outpatient: A checklist. *Schizophrenia Bulletin, 7,* 477–487.

Mechanic, D., McAlpine, D., Rosenfield, S., & Davis, D. (1994). Effects of illness attribution and depression on the quality of life among persons with serious mental illness. *Social Science and Medicine, 39,* 155–164.

Mulkern, V., Agosta, J. M., Ashbaugh, J. W., Bradley, V. J., Spence, R. A., Allein, S., Nurczynski, P., & Houlihan, J. (1986). *Community Support Program Client Follow-up Study.* Report to NIMH.

Office of Technology Assessment. (1995). *The effectiveness of mental health and substance abuse treatment: Considerations for designing health insurance benefits.* Washington, DC: Office of Technology Assessment.

Oliver, J. P. J (1991–1992). The social care directive: Development of a quality of life profile for use in community services for the mentally ill. *Social Work and Social Science Review, 3,* 5–45.

Oliver, J. P. J., & Mohamad, H. (1992). The quality of life of the chronically mentally ill: A comparison of public, private, and voluntary residential provisions. *British Journal of Social Work, 22,* 391–404.

Overall, J. E., & Gorham, D. R. (1962). The brief psychiatric rating scale. *Psychologial Reports, 10,* 799–812.

Patrick, D., & Erickson, P. (1993). *Health status and health policy: Allocating resources to health care.* New York: Oxford University Press.

Revicki, D. A., & Murray, M. (1994). Assessing health-related quality of life outcomes of drug treatments for psychiatric disorders. *CNS Drugs, 1,* 465–476.

Rosenfield, S. (1993). Factors contributing to the subjective quality of life of the chronically mentally ill. *Journal of Health and Social Behavior, 33,* 299–315.

Rosenfield, S., & Neese-Todd, S. (1993). Elements of a psychosocial clubhouse program associated with a satisfying quality of life. *Hospital and Community Psychiatry, 44,* 76–78.

Simpson, C. J., Hyde, C. E., & Faragher, E. B. (1989). The chronically mentally ill in community facilities: A study of quality of life. *British Journal of Psychiatry, 154,* 77–82.

Skantze, K. (1993). *Defining subjective quality of life goals in schizophrenia: The Quality of Life Self-Assessment Inventory, QLS-100: A new approach to successful alliance and service development.* Göteborg, Sweden: Department of Psychiatry, Sahlgrenska Hospital, University of Gothenburg.

Spilker, B. (Ed). (1996). *Quality of life and pharmacoeconomics in clinical trials* (2nd ed.). Philadelphia: Lippincott-Raven.

Stein, L. I., & Test, M. A. (1980). Alternative to mental hospital treatment: 1. Conceptual model, treatment program and clinical evaluation. *Archives of General Psychiatry, 37,* 392–397.

Stoker, M. J., Dunbar, G. C., & Beaumont, G. (1992). The SmithKline Beecham "Quality of Life" Scale: A validation and reliability study in patients with affective disorder. *Quality of Life Research, 1,* 385–395.

Sullivan, G. S., Wells, K. B., & Leake, B. (1992). Clinical factors associated with better quality of life in a seriously mentally ill population. *Hospital and Community Psychiatry, 43,* 794–798.

Wells, K. B., Stewart, A., Hays, R. D., Burnam, A., Rogers, W., Daniels, M., Berry, S., Greenfield, S., & Ware, J. (1988). The functioning and well-being of depressed patients. *Journal of the American Medical Association, 262,* 914–919.

18

The Assessment of Functional Outcomes in Cost-Effectiveness of Psychotherapy Studies

Janice L. Krupnick

In an era of escalating concern about health care expenditures and uncertainty about the value of mental health treatments, research data documenting the broad range of effects produced by psychological interventions are crucial. Without such data, it is inevitable that psychosocial treatments will cease to be reimbursed or will be available only in severely truncated form. In fact, an increasing number of insurance companies have already limited or abolished payment for psychotherapy.

Research studies on treatments for physical illnesses have broadened their assessments to include measures addressing the impact of treatment on patient functioning and well-being in addition to traditionally defined end points, such as survival and dollar costs (Ware, 1992). This perspective, however, has been surprisingly slow to gain acceptance in mental health research, where the conceptual focus in outcome evaluation has typically remained quite narrow (Attkisson et al., 1992; chapters 9 and 19, this volume). Despite the fact that several groups, including clinical investigators, providers, insurance companies, policymakers, and patients, share a stake in obtaining functional outcome data, few studies have explored the nonclinical effects of treatment and the range of domains (e.g., function as a worker, student, marital partner, parent, family caretaker, community member, utilizer of health and/or social services) in which psychotherapeutic intervention might be expected to have an effect. Measurement of symptoms and functioning would permit both researcher and practitioner to observe whether two treatments might be equally effective in symptom remission but might have differential impacts on functioning. Patients, knowing the potential risks and benefits of different therapeutic approaches, would be in a better position to assess their best course of action. Policy analysts, legislators, and managed-care executives, responsible for the allocation of scarce resources, could make more informed decisions regarding mental health care reimbursement. The exploration of a broader range of effects resulting from psychosocial interventions could advance knowledge, enhance clinical practice, and inform public policy (Krupnick & Pincus, 1992).

Accordingly, this chapter aims to (a) review the state of the art in functional outcome measurement in psychotherapy and (b) emphasize routine inclusion of functional and performance measures across all investigations of psychosocial intervention. The pros and cons of existing instruments, reviews of measures adopted by managed-care companies to track outcomes, and recommendations for new measure development will be addressed.

Relevant Services Research Studies

Epidemiological studies in community, primary-care, and outpatient settings (e.g., Broadhead, Blazer, George, & Kit Tse, 1990; Casey, Tyrer, & Platt, 1985;

Wohlfarth, vanden Brink, Ormel, Koeter, & Oldehinkel, 1993) have documented the significant relationship between psychiatric disorder and functional disability. Further, it has been shown that patients who have chronic psychiatric symptoms also experience chronic disability (Ormel et al., 1993; Von Korff, Ormel, Katon, & Lin, 1992). Recent studies (Hays, Wells, Sherbourne, Rogers, & Spritzer, 1995; Ormel et al., 1994) have found that the disability associated with psychiatric disorder exceeds that associated with chronic physical illnesses. Indeed, cost-of-illness studies (e.g., Rice, Kelman, Miller, & Dunnmeyer, 1990; Stoudemire, Frank, Hedemark, Kamlet, & Blazer, 1986) have detailed the billions of dollars spent annually because of psychiatric disability.

The Rand Medical Outcomes Study (MOS), a 2-year observational investigation of 1,790 outpatients (see chapter 6, this volume) that compared the functioning and well-being of patients with depression and those with a variety of chronic medical illnesses, demonstrated that psychiatric illness can be associated with persistent impairment that is at least as debilitating as or more debilitating than many medical conditions. With the exception of patients with congestive heart failure, patients diagnosed with dysthymia reported worse physical functioning than patients in all other groups. Depressed patients had more negative health perceptions and attributed more role limitations to their poor physical health than did patients with general medical conditions. At 2-year follow-up, patients diagnosed at baseline with only subthreshold depression had significantly worse health perceptions, more limitations in physical functioning, greater bodily pain, and more role limitations due to physical health problems than patients with hypertension.

The World Health Organization's collaborative study on psychological problems in general health care showed that in 14 countries around the world, psychiatric disorder was both common and associated with substantial disability, including the inability to care for oneself, perform social roles, and/or work productively (Ormel et al., 1994). Regardless of type of psychiatric disorder, and controlling for demographic characteristics and severity of co-occurring medical illness, disability levels were significantly increased among patients with psychiatric illnesses. This study replicated the MOS finding that the relationship between disorder and disability was stronger for psychiatric illness than for physical illness.

Although these studies, conducted mainly in primary-care settings, highlight the strong association between psychiatric illness and social/physical dysfunction and suggest the potential for psychological treatment's restoring function, psychotherapy studies have tended to give short shrift to assessments of functioning. Thus, Parry (chapter 29, this volume) has concluded that many practitioners are skeptical of the symptomatic change measures commonly used in psychotherapy research because they do not capture the type of changes they aimed for in practice, such as the improvement of functioning and quality of life. As lead consultant for the development and analysis of a survey of almost 4,000 *Consumer Reports* readers aimed at assessing the effectiveness of long-term psychotherapy, Seligman (1995) also emphasized that improvement in general functioning, in addition to symptom relief, is almost always the goal of actual treatment, though this has rarely been the main focus of psychotherapy efficacy studies. Seligman's survey explored self-reported changes in productivity at work, interpersonal relations, well-being, insight, and growth. Citing realism as the main virtue of this approach, Seligman noted that the *Consumer Reports* survey assessed the effectiveness of psychotherapy as actually performed in the field, with the population that actually seeks it. Furthermore, it focused its measurement on areas of interest to both consumers and providers, that is, changes in symptoms as well as the ability to function.

Other authors also have expressed concern about the inadequacy of relying on symptom change as the sole measure of outcome. For example, Norcross (1995) calls it a fallacy to equate outcome with symptom change on self-report measures because patients with comparable changes in symptoms have not necessarily obtained the same benefits. In addition, there are different trajectories for symptomatic and functional recovery. Howard, Kopta, Krause, and Orlinsky (1986) reported that symptomatic improvement precedes, and is probably a necessary precursor to, improvement in functioning. Functional improvement, however, follows a different temporal course than symptomatic change. While 50% of the patients in their study showed symptomatic change after 8 sessions of psychotherapy, that percentage of patients required 28 psychotherapy sessions for work function improvement. Weissman, Sholomskas, and John (1981) and Mintz, Mintz, Arruda, and Hwang (1992) also observed that occupational and social adjustment take considerably longer to achieve than amelioration of symptoms. In addition, Mintz et al. (1992) found that affective impairment associated with depression (e.g., shame about one's work, distress at work, lack of interest in the job) may continue until a total remission of symptoms has been achieved. Functional impairment, such as absenteeism, poor productivity, and interpersonal problems at work, however, were usually ameliorated despite continuing mild to moderate symptoms. Thus, disproportionate emphasis on only symptomatic change may result in misleading conclusions that underestimate the impact of psychosocial intervention. Findings regarding differential trajectories for clinical and functional improvement also have important implications in terms of the timing of measurement and the possible need for longer term treatments to achieve functional gains.

Measures Currently Being Utilized by Managed Care and Behavioral Carve-out Firms

Among the stakeholders with interests in tracking psychotherapy outcomes are managed care companies and behavioral carve-out firms. Dissatisfied with the focus and instrumentation used in existing treatment efficacy studies, several have either adapted existing measures or developed their own instruments to track the outcomes of patients in their health plans (see Table 18.1 for a summary). Their intention in doing this is to redefine outcome measures to answer such specific questions as: Does treatment work in ways that are measurably valuable to the patient in terms of daily functioning level and satisfaction, to the payer in terms of value, to the managed-care organization that is responsible for administering the purchaser's dollars, and to the clinician who is responsible for demonstrating value for the time spent (Migdail, Youngs, & Seltzer, 1995)? Following is a brief description of some of the instruments that are currently being used.

Table 18.1 Measures Being Used by Managed-Care Companies

Instrument	Managed-care company	When introduced
CATOR	New Standards, Inc.	1980
RES*Q	Strategic Advantage, Inc.	1988
HMO Performance Standards	Digital Equipment Corp.	1991
VHP-20	Vista Health Plan	1992
CROSS	Blue Cross/Blue Shield, MA	1992
CQIS	MCC Behavioral Care, Inc.	1993
PROFILE	Foundation Health PsychCare	1993
COMPASS	United Healthcare Services Corp.	1993
Outcome Questionnaire 45.11	Intermountain Health Care	1994

Comprehensive Assessment Treatment Outcomes Research (CATOR) is now being widely used to track the outcomes of chemical dependency treatment programs (Migdail et al., 1995). Using a self-report survey to quantify changes in medical utilization and utilization of other public services, as well as changes in work performance, CATOR follows patients for 2 years and enters all survey information into an aggregate database (the CATOR registry) that can be used to compare the relative effectiveness of different facilities.

The Reliable Electronic Survey Questionnaire (RES*Q) has been developed to assess behavioral health care outcomes and to define optimal patient-treatment–matching algorithms. Using CD-ROM technology to assess both the quality and the cost-effectiveness of care, it aims to create a national database that would allow clients to compare the facilities at which they receive treatment to national norms.

HMO Performance Standards is an instrument developed to assess whether contracting HMOs treating employees under Digital Equipment's health program were maintaining standards established by that firm. Five of the categories of assessment deal with behavioral-health standards with measurement based on the program member's functional status and well-being.

Vista Health Plans developed the VHP-20, an outcome measure for providers to assess their patients' functioning at home and at work. Based on the BASIS 32, an inpatient survey developed at McLean Hospital, it assesses work functioning in terms of ability to perform tasks, concentrate, and get along with coworkers/supervisors. Daily life functioning is defined as getting along with family members, paying bills on time, and having appropriate emotional responses.

The Consumer Reported Satisfaction and Outcome Survey (CROSS) was developed by the Blue Cross/Blue Shield Plan of Massachusetts to assess the effectiveness of the mental health treatments provided to the state's Medicaid population. An adaptation of the SF-36 (MOS 36-item short-form general health survey; Stewart, Hays, & Ware, 1988), the measure of functioning and well-being developed in the context of the Rand Medical Outcomes Study, it includes several open-ended questions aimed at better engaging clients as they describe their level of functioning.

The Clinical Quality Information System (CQIS) assesses patient functioning across nine outcome domains, including work performance, social functioning, legal problems, health status, violent behavior, and medical care utilization. This measure defines treatment effectiveness as the difference in patient functioning before and after intervention.

PROFILE has five items related to functioning and uses a rating scale based on the Global Assessment of Functioning Scale (GAF) (see the next section below). The GAF is a modified version of the Global Assessment Scale (Endicott, Spitzer, Fleiss, & Cohen, 1976). This was first introduced in DSM-III-R and serves as Axis V in DSM-IV. It asks patients to rate their job functioning, marriage/family relationships, interpersonal relationships, current physical health, and, at termination, how well their problem was resolved on a 9-point scale, ranging from "cannot function" to "no problems." This instrument, tested for reliability and validity and compared to the SF-36 (see below), was found to be highly reliable and had a better return rate than the SF-36.

COMPASS, a 24-item measure based on Howard's work on "dose therapy" (Howard, Kopta, Krause, et al., 1986), has patients and therapists rate the patient's progress in work, self-management, intimate relationships, social relationships, family functioning, and health. It has been described as fairly easy to use, relatively free of bias, and apparently meaningful across a wide range of patients (Migdail et al., 1995).

The Outcome Questionnaire 45.11, a 45-item self-report questionnaire, assesses the patient's functioning in terms of family and social relationships and social role performance as a worker, student, or housewife. Although the measure unfortunately combines ratings of symptoms with functioning, it is inexpensive and easy to use and regarded as applicable to a wide variety of patients and disorders.

As can be seen from the brief survey above, it has become common practice for managed-care companies to develop or adapt their own outcome measures. Undoubtedly, this reflects their sense of frustration with existing measures. To their credit, they pay considerable attention, as do health services researchers, to the importance of functioning and disability. It is not clear, however, that all of the managed-care organizations (MCOs) are paying adequate attention to the psychometric properties of the measures they have developed. Since they are more in the business of sales and marketing, it is not apparent that scientific rigor would be a high priority. Furthermore, with each MCO using its own instrument, it becomes increasingly difficult to compare outcomes across health plans, treatment approaches, practitioners, or facilities.

The Status of Functional Outcome Measurement in Psychotherapy Research

Although psychotherapy research studies have not placed adequate emphasis on the measurement of functional status, they have not totally disregarded such assessment. Since the multiaxial system of diagnosis was introduced in *DSM-III* (American Psychiatric Association [APA], 1980), a full diagnostic assessment has included attention to Axis V, the assessment of adaptive functioning.

"Adaptive functioning" in *DSM-III* was measured on a 7-point scale, ranging from "superior" to "grossly impaired." The Global Assessment of Functioning Scale (GAF), a 90-point instrument combining elements of psychological, social, and occupational functioning and based on the widely used Global Assessment Scale (GAS) (Endicott, Spitzer, Fleiss, & Cohen, 1976), was substituted for Axis V in *DSM-III-R*. The perceived advantage of the GAF was that it was based on an instrument that had been used in hundreds of studies and clinical settings.

The GAF has been the target of some criticism, however. Mellsop, Peace, and Fernando (1987) expressed concern about the use of a global rating of functioning because it probably masks significant variability across different domains of functioning. Moreover, because Axis V is not a required element of patient evaluation, it is regarded as only a supplement to official diagnoses (those recorded on the first three axes). Therefore, it is rarely required for insurance company claims and may not be used extensively for either treatment planning or outcome prediction (Goldman, Skodol, & Lave, 1992; Schrader, Gordon & Harcourt, 1986). For these reasons, function measurement has not been accorded the same primacy as symptom assessment. This inequality persists despite data suggesting that symptomatic improvement and functional change, as measured by the GAF, do not go hand in hand in studies of outpatient treatment over time (Gordon, Jardiolin, & Gordon, 1985).

In preparation for *DSM-IV*, a Work Group on Multiaxial Issues was asked to review existing measures of social functioning as potential substitutes for the GAF. In addition to a review of measures typically used in mental health settings, the work group scrutinized

Weissman et al.'s (1981) Assessment of Social Adjustment and Wallace's (1986) Functional Assessment of Social Adjustment.

Goldman et al. (1992) reviewed nearly 30 measures of social functioning and classified them into 7 groups, with each successive group indicating greater utility for Axis V usage. Classification criteria included the following: (a) depth and breadth of the instrument, (b) applicability to the general population, (c) adequate psychometric properties, (d) simplicity, and (e) unidimensionality.

Nine measures (listed in Table 18.2) were regarded as potential substitutes for the GAF. Since none of these instruments appeared to be significantly better than the GAF, and given the requirement that alterations in nosology for *DSM-IV* had to be supported by compelling arguments and extensive documentation (Frances, Pincus, Widiger, Davis, & First, 1990), Goldman et al. recommended retaining the GAF for *DSM-IV*, Axis V. At the same time, however, a modification of the GAF was recommended, in which symptomatic ratings would be separated from ratings of social and occupational functioning. This recommendation was accepted, and a revised measure of disability appears in the *DSM-IV* Appendix B as the Social and Occupational Functioning Assessment Scale (SOFAS).

The SOFAS (APA, 1994, pp. 760–761) is described as differing from the GAF in that it focuses exclusively on the individual's level of social and occupational functioning and is not directly influenced by the overall severity of the individual's psychological symptoms. Additionally, any impairment in social or occupational functional that is due to a general medical condition is considered in making the SOFAS rating.

The general tone of the Work Group's report (Goldman et al., 1992) seemed to reflect the sense of dissatisfaction many psychotherapy researchers feel with regard to available instruments for measuring functioning. There are a number of problems with most of the existing measures, including the GAF, and no satisfactory alternatives, suggesting the importance of developing new measures. The SOFAS addresses two of the most serious problems with the GAF: It separates measurement of functioning and symptoms and takes limitations due to physical health into consideration. Nevertheless, there are very few data on it, it is located in the *DSM-IV* appendix, and, accordingly, it is not clear how much it will be used. The SOFAS has been subjected to psychometric testing in only one study (Patterson & Lee, 1995). A field trial of a modified version of the GAF (GAFSM) supported its construct validity, but no further work is being done on it at this

Table 18.2 Measures Regarded by the *DSM-IV* Work Group on Multiaxial Issues as Potential Substitutes for the GAF

Measure	Authors	Year Published
Structured and Scaled Interview to Assess Maladjustment (SSIAM)	Gurland et al.	1972
Community Adjustment Profile System (CAPS)	Evenson et al.	1974
Standardized Interview to Assess Social Maladjustment (SIASM)	Clare & Cairns	1978
Social Stress and Functioning Inventory for Psychotic Disorders (SSFIPD)	Serban	1978
Social Functioning Schedule (SFS)	Remington & Tyler	1979
Social Adjustment Scale (SAS)	Weissman & Bothwell, Schooler, Hogarty & Weissman	1976 1979
PERI (Social Functioning Scales)	Dohrenwend et al.	1983
Longitudinal Interval Follow-Up Evaluation (LIFE)	Keller et al.	1987
Role Activity Performance Scale (RAPS)	Good-Ellis et al.	1987

time, although that may change when it is time for *DSM-V*.

Measures That Warrant Special Attention

One measure mentioned, but not included, in the *DSM-IV* Work Group's classification system is the SF-36, which includes measurement of the following domains: (a) physical functioning, (b) role limitations due to physical health problems, (c) role limitations due to emotional health problems, (d) social functioning, (e) emotional well-being, (f) pain, (g) energy and/or fatigue, and (h) general health perceptions. The SF-36 has been adapted for use in assessing outcomes in a variety of clinical conditions, including depression (Stewart, Greenfield, Hays et al., 1989), and it is simple to use. As noted earlier, the CROSS was based on this measure, which was also the basis of comparison for the PROFILE, a circumstance suggesting its appeal to insurance and managed-care companies that are tracking outcomes. Blue Cross/Blue Shield of Massachusetts found, however, that this measure was not adequately sensitive to detect differences in lower ranges of functioning, and its pilot data suggested that some dimensions were too long (Migdail et al., 1995). The measure has been primarily used with medically ill patients in primary-care settings. More psychotherapy studies using this instrument are needed to ascertain its validity with psychiatric patients.

One measure included in the *DSM-IV* Work Group's recommendations, the Social Adjustment Scale (SAS; Weissman & Bothwell, 1976), deserves special mention because it is so frequently used in treatment efficacy studies. For example, in Mintz et al.'s (1992) review of 10 studies on treatment efficacy with depressed patients, 7 of the investigations assessed functioning with this instrument. Such frequent usage makes it a likely candidate for inclusion in a core battery of measures (Mintz et al., 1992). Even though the SAS was overwhelmingly the most popular instrument, Mintz et al. discovered that in the 10 studies reviewed, four different versions of the instrument were actually employed. Each had somewhat different item anchors and involved different time frames. Item levels that were defined with relatively mild and benign anchors on one form suggested more severe psychopathology on another. Some forms even omitted critical items, such as those involving major social roles.

Mintz et al. also underscored difficulties with relying solely on self-report data, the type of information obtained with most of the managed-care company measures, with the SF-36, and with the more commonly used version of the SAS. The authors suggest that even such "objective" behaviors as absenteeism can be subject to distortion, through the lens of affective disturbance. It has frequently been noted, particularly with regard to those diagnosed with personality disorders, that patients themselves may not always be the most accurate reporters of their own behavior. Finally, SAS scoring procedures stand in need of review. For example, in at least two of its categories (i.e., functioning as a "homemaker" and as a "friend"), it appears that "more" qualifies as "better," but there is little indication of the validity of this approach. It is possible, for instance, that having a few close friends indicates functioning as good as, if not better than, maintaining multiple superficial ties.

Efforts to Design a Core Outcomes Battery for Use in Psychotherapy Research

While the idea of establishing a core battery of outcome measures to assess psychosocial treatment outcomes was proposed as early as 1975 as a means of increasing standardization of measurement across studies (Waskow & Parloff, 1975), it was almost 20 years before a conference on this issue was convened, under the joint auspices of the American Psychological Association and Vanderbilt University (Strupp, Lambert, & Horowitz, 1997). Staged in 1994, the meeting brought together a small group of researchers with expertise in measurement who agreed on the criteria that should be met by measures of symptomatic distress or functioning: (a) standardized procedures for administering and scoring; (b) norms for patient and nonpatient populations; (c) demonstrated reliability, with reliability appropriate for the corresponding domain; (d) demonstrated validity; (e) briefness, inexpensiveness, and feasibility for use in clinical settings; and (f) relevance to clinical needs. Unfortunately, investigators were unable to reach consensus regarding which actual measures should be included in a core battery. Some of the functioning measures suggested overlapped with the *DSM-IV* Work Group's recommendations (e.g., the Global Assessment of Functioning Scale and the Social Adjustment Scale). Others, such as Howard et al.'s (1993) Life Functioning Scales (the basis for COMPASS), did not. A volume summarizing the conference deliberations has been published (Strupp, Lambert, & Horowitz, 1997), but unfortunately, no further follow-up work on the design of a core battery earmarked for psychotherapy outcome studies is being undertaken.

More recently, the American Psychiatric Association convened a group to publish a Handbook of Psychiatric Measures and Outcomes (Rush, Pincus, & First, in press). Functioning measures that will be evaluated for this volume, based on their psychometrics, include the GAF, the SOFAS, and measures from the MOS (e.g., the SF-36). While it is likely that this group will judge the relative utility of various instruments on functioning, it is not clear whether it will make specific recommendations regarding a core battery.

Recent efforts to standardize psychological treatments include practice guidelines published by the Agency for Health Care Policy and Research (AHCPR, 1993) and by the American Psychiatric Association (APA, 1993). The AHCPR guideline is aimed at the treatment of depression in primary-care settings by primary-care physicians, while the APA guideline addresses the treatment of depression in mental health settings by psychiatrists. The APA also has published guidelines for the psychiatric treatment of substance abuse, bipolar disorder, anxiety, and eating disorders (Zarin, Pincus, & McIntyre, 1993; McIntyre, Charles, Zarin, & Pincus, 1996). Based on available empirical data, the practice guidelines are becoming important foci for research and practice even though they do not address the issue of outcome measurement. Such an emphasis would have constituted a valuable contribution.

Problems with Existing Instruments

Desirable, but missing, qualities in some existing measures of functioning include applicability to a broad population, encompassing not only a broad range of patients with different disorders, as well as various levels of severity within those disorders, but also extending to nonpatient samples of individuals who may be functioning at a very high level. Measures not only should be able to capture the functioning of individuals who require assistance in very basic tasks but should also extend to those who exceed usual standards and expectations.

In addition, most measures do not assess the contribution of physical robustness or impairment to assessments of function, even though functioning in a variety of domains depends on cognitive, emotional, and physical capacities. Given Manton and Soldo's (1992) report that among the elderly, for example, cognitive and physical impairments predict differential needs for service, it may be crucial to understand not only the type of impairment manifested but also the source of that impairment, in order to adequately evaluate and address it.

Breadth of perspective is also absent in many outcome studies, which depend upon a single instrument to assess functioning, thereby capturing only the perspective of the patient or that of the evaluating clinician. There is much to be said for self-reports in that they are inexpensive, and, self-reported disability has been shown to be remarkably valid in predicting medical care usage (Suzman, Harris, Hadley, Kovar, & Weindruch, 1992). As noted earlier, however, self-reports can be subject to distortion based on the rater's emotional state. Evaluating clinicians or therapists may be more objective in some respects, but typically they have less access to the full range of a patient's behaviors. While not always feasible, it is useful to obtain a range of perspectives, including the judgments of therapists, clinical evaluators, and significant others, as well as the patient.

At the NIMH Cost-Effectiveness of Psychotherapy Conference (1994), concerns were raised as to whether the social roles depicted in existing measures were sufficiently broad. Many instruments (e.g., the Social Adjustment Scales) assess functioning as a worker, student, parent, and partner but exclude other important roles. For example, as life expectancy increases, the importance of grandparenting has magnified, yet this role has received scant attention. Many middle-aged children are called upon to care for aging parents, yet the role of adult caretaker of parents is similarly ignored. Existing measures of functioning view the individual as a member of a couple or even a family but do not extend measurement to a view of the person as a neighbor, member of the community, and citizen. Items in the latter domains might tap whether a person voted and/or obeyed the laws of the country, perpetrated violence or civil unrest, volunteered at schools or homeless shelters, and so on. Just as measures of function in medicine assess the individual's robustness in physical terms (e.g., evaluating his or her capacity to walk a quarter mile or to lift 10 pounds), measures in mental health could assess psychosocial robustness (e.g., in demonstrations of generativity to specific individuals, or in caring for the community in general).

Additional concerns focused on the adequacy of current measures to assess certain domains. For example, measurement of work performance tends to be limited (e.g., assessing only absenteeism or length of duration at a particular job). In work functioning, additional variables might include measurement of productivity, earnings, promotions, accidents, and relationships with coworkers and supervisors, in addition to number of "sick days" and job turnover. In another realm, functioning as a student could include information about grades and graduation, as well as class attendance. Levels of personal investment or satisfaction with a given social role may be difficult to obtain but may provide more accurate indicators of functioning.

Finally, establishing the economic value of particular functional outcomes is crucial. As indicated by numerous representatives of managed-care and insurance companies (NIMH Cost-Effectiveness of Psychotherapy Conference, 1994), psychotherapy services are often perceived as expensive, long-lasting, and of questionable value. Without specific figures regarding the costs and economic benefits of psychosocial interventions, such beliefs will only persist and, in times of fiscal austerity, escalate, as increasing caps are placed on health expenditures. Developing methods for calibrating the economic value of social functioning, however, is likely to be difficult.

While individual differences and cultural variations regarding the value of various aspects of functioning must be taken into account, some progress in this area has been achieved, for example, in health care experiments in both Oregon and New York (Oregon Health Services Commission, 1991; Surles & Feiden-Warsh, 1990). In the Oregon model, various health care conditions were paired with appropriate treatments, and the costs of both treating and not treating a condition were assessed. Cost estimates were based on "community values" (i.e., what members of the community said they preferred and were willing to pay for).

The Oregon experience emphasized that mental health outcomes must be considered along with physical health outcomes. While mental illness has often been conceived of as residing solely in the mind, so that the physical suffering, disability, and lowered productivity associated with mental illness has often been minimized, in Oregon the position was taken that there was no principled reason to discriminate between care provided those who suffer from mental illness and care provided those who are physically ill (Boyle & Callahan, 1993). As it turned out, using the same standards for evaluation of treatments for physical and mental health placed mental health services in a favorable light. Moreover, it was found that some mental health services ranked in the highest categories of effectiveness.

Summary and Recommendations

There is still a long way to go in giving functional impairment parity with symptomatic distress in the assessment of psychotherapy outcomes, but there is a groundswell of support among many of the stakeholders regarding psychosocial treatments to move measurement in that direction. As discussed earlier, the issue of "realism" in psychotherapy studies is a current source of some concern among those involved in the health care debate. Providers, consumers, and purchasers want data on the experiences and outcomes of real patients with real problems who undergo treatment as it is actually practiced. Accumulating these data involves the study of clinical populations that experience not only the symptoms but also the functional disability associated with psychosocial disorders, expressed in decreased capacity to carry out a variety of social, occupational, and physical tasks and roles. Measures of function need to take into account the scope of these realities. In addition, it will be essential to track changes in both symptoms and function, not only before intervention and immediately after treatment is concluded, but also over time, given the reality that many emotional disorders are chronic or recurrent. This longitudinal perspective may be of particular importance in the evaluation of function, given the data that suggest the longer time frame needed to evaluate change in disability. Since those who use, provide, and pay for psychotherapy, as well as the families, neighbors, and employers of patients, are often most concerned with the efficacy of a treatment in restoring function, measures are needed that are comprehensive in breadth and duration. It is important to assess not only how much disability can be alleviated, but also how long it will take to achieve various goals and, once achieved, how long such restoration may be expected to be sustained. Assessments of function and changes therein could also be measured across a range of stakeholders, including not only the patients' view, but also those of observers of his or her role performance, such as family members or employers.

While psychotherapy efficacy studies have increasingly moved in the direction of clinical trials, including subjects who are rigorously screened for the presence of *DSM* disorders, the development of functional measures has not kept pace with the evolution of the field. What is needed at this time are new measures that are more diagnosis-focused that could evaluate those areas of dysfunction or disability that are characteristically associated with the disorder under investigation, providing a vehicle for demonstrating the decreased disability that might occur as a consequence of psychotherapeutic intervention.

Another serious problem with many existing measures of function is that they simply do not go far enough in addressing the variety of factors that psychotherapy might influence. It is critical not only to measure functioning broadly and specifically, but also to broaden the domains of functioning that are typically assessed. In order to measure functioning in the most disabled groups (e.g., in patients with schizophrenia), even basic areas of functioning such as self-care must be included. At the NIMH Cost-Effectiveness of Psychotherapy Conference (1994), extensive attention was paid to the domain of work functioning, an arena that carries important economic consequences and that is largely overlooked in psychotherapy outcome studies. In addition, the roles and responsibilities of individuals outside the labor force (e.g., retired persons, homemakers, and volunteers), and the multiple other areas of life outside working hours for those who do hold jobs must be considered. Finding meaningful ways of weighing and calibrating these domains remains a challenge for future instrument development in the psychotherapy field.

Assessment of functioning also must take into consideration the contributions of both emotional and physical difficulties. Boyle and Callahan (1993) observe that it is difficult to disentangle mental and physical symptoms since they often coexist and often give rise to one another. A comprehensive assessment of functioning should take into account the effect that physical disability has on emotional functioning and the impact of psychiatric problems on physical health. Most psychotherapy outcome studies do not focus on physical health outcomes, but given the data that patients with psychological disturbances visit primary-care doctors twice as often as those without such problems (Koss, Koss, & Woodruff, 1993) and findings from the RAND MOS study that suggest considerable physical disability associated with depression, the omission of data on physical functioning and health perceptions seems a serious one.

The use of a core battery presents both advantages and disadvantages but, on balance, seems worth pursuing. On the negative side is the question of whether one or even a limited number of measures could be found to be both valid and reliable across disorders, developmental stages, socioeconomic levels, varying ethnicities and cultures, and treatment settings. Further, given the often conflicting opinions of experts regarding which measures to include in a core battery, it remains unclear whether consensus could be reached on which instruments to include. Nevertheless, a core battery would permit the standardization and generalizability that is crucial in evaluating and comparing the effectiveness of various health care technologies. Only by using the same standardized methods can valid comparisons be made across sites, studies, settings, and disorders.

Finally, it is imperative for psychotherapy and services researchers to collaborate on a regular basis with health economists in order to create models capable of calibrating the value of various functional outcomes in mental health. The creation of interdisciplinary teams, bringing together perspectives from the mental health disciplines and from economics and services research, can be far more productive than each discipline working in isolation. Soliciting input from the consumers of mental health services themselves will constitute a critical ingredient in any research partnership. While some existing measures can be adapted to meet these new paradigmatic needs, it is likely that a new generation of instruments will need to be developed not only to expand the number of roles and domains to be assessed, or to include items and behavioral anchors that are more clinically relevant and valid, but also to ensure that the broad range of economic variables specified elsewhere in this volume are adequately covered.

Great strides have been made over the past decade in recognizing the importance of functional measurement, in acknowledging the potential for mental health treatments to facilitate functional improvement, and in the capacity to assess the costs of mental illness and the economic benefits of treatment. Endeavors such as the RAND Medical Outcomes Study have led the way in giving careful thought to which areas of physical, mental, and social functioning are of significance to broad ranges of individuals.

It is now the time to move forward methodologically, in the interests of good patient care, science, and data-informed policy. In order to provide the kinds of services that are most needed, the availability of valid, reliable data is key. To obtain high-quality data, necessary tools must be forged and methodological advances made. Functional measurement of psychotherapy outcomes represents an area now ripe for further research and development.

References

AHCPR Depression Guideline Panel. (1993). *Clinical Practice Guideline Number 5: Depression in Primary Care, 2: Treatment of Major Depression.* Rockville, MD: U.S. Department of Health and Human Services, Agency for Health Care Policy and Research. AHCPR publication 93-0551.

American Psychiatric Association. (1980). *Diagnostic and statistical manual of mental disorders* (3rd ed.). Washington, DC: Author.

American Psychiatric Association. (1993). Practice guidelines for major depressive disorder in adults. *American Journal of Psychiatry, 150*(Suppl. 4), 1–26.

American Psychiatric Association. (1994). *Diagnostic and statistical manual of mental disorders* (4th ed.). Washington, DC: Author.

Attkisson, C., Cook, J., Karno, M., Lehman, A., McGlashan, T. H., Meltzer, H. Y., O'Connor, M., Richardson, D., Rosenblatt, A., Wells, K., & Williams, J. (1992). Clinical services research. *Schizophrenia Bulletin, 18,* 561–626.

Boyle, P. J., & Callahan, D. (1993). Minds and hearts: Priorities in mental health services. Special Supplement, *Hastings Center Report,* 23,(5).

Broadhead, W. E., Blazer, D. G., George, L. K., & Kit Tse, C. (1990). Depression disability days, and days lost from work in a prospective epidemiologic survey. *Journal of the American Medical Association, 264,* 2524–2528.

Casey, P. R., Tyrer P. J., & Platt S. (1985). The relationship between social functioning and psychiatric symptomatology in primary care. *Social Psychiatry,* 20, 5–9.

Clare, A. W., & Cairns, V. E. (1978). Design development and use of a standardized interview to assess social maladjustment and dysfunction in the community studies. *Psychol. Med.* 8, 589–604.

Dohrenwend, B. S., Dohrenwend, B. P., Link, B., & Levar, I. (1983). Social functioning of psychiatric patients in contrast with community cases in the general population. *Archives of General Psychiatry, 40,* 1174–1182.

Endicott, J., Spitzer, R. L., Fleiss, J. L., & Cohen, J. (1976). The Global Asssesment Scale: A procedure for measuring overall severity of psychiatric disturbance. *Archives of General Psychiatry, 33,* 766–771.

Evenson, R. C., Sletten, I. W., Hedlund, J. L., & Faintich, D. M. (1974). CAPS: An automated evaluation system. *American Journal of Psychiatry, 131,* 531–534.

Frances, A., Pincus H. A., Widiger, T. A., Davis, W. W., & First, M. B. (1990). DSM-IV: Work in progress. *American Journal of Psychiatry, 147,* 1439–1448.

Goldman, H. H., Skodol, A. E., & Lave, T. R. (1992). Revising Axis V for DSM-IV: A review of measures of social functioning. *American Journal of Psychiatry, 149,* 1148–1156.

Good-Ellis, M., Fine, S., Spencer, J., & DiVittis, A. (1987). Developing a role activity performance scale. *American Journal of Occupational Therapy, 41,* 232–241.

Gordon, R. E., Jardiolin, P., & Gordon, K. K. (1985). Predicting length of hospital stay of psychiatric patients. *American Journal of Psychiatry, 142,* 235–237.

Gurland, B. J., Yorkston, N. J., Stone, A. R., Frank, J. D., & Fleiss, J. L. (1972). The structured and scaled interview to assess maladjustment (SSIAM): Description, rationale, and development. *Archives of General Psychiatry, 27,* 259–264.

Hays, R. D., Wells, K. B., Sherbourne, C. D., Rogers, W., & Spritzer, K. (1995). Functioning and well-being outcomes of patients with depression compared with chronic general medical illnesses. *Archives of General Psychiatry, 52,* 11–19.

Howard, K. I., Brill, P. L., Lueger, R. J., O'Mahoney, M. T., & Grissom, G. R. (1993). *Integra Outpatient Tracking Assessment: Psychometric Properties.* Philadelphia: Integra.

Howard, K. I., Kopta, S. M., Krause, M. S., & Orlinsky, D. E. (1986). The dose-effect relationship in psychotherapy. *American Psychologist, 41,* 159–164.

Keller, M., Lavori, P., Friedman, B., Nielsen, E., Endicott, J., McDonald-Scott, P., & Andreason, N. (1987). The Longitudinal Interval Follow-Up Evaluation. *Archives of General Psychiatry, 44,* 540–548.

Krupnick, J. L., & Pincus, H. A. (1992). The cost-effectiveness of psychotherapy: A plan for research. *American Journal of Psychiatry, 149,* 1295–1305.

Manton, K. G., & Soldo, B. J. (1992). Disability and mortality among the oldest old: Implications for current and future health and long-term care service needs. In R. M. Suzman, D. P. Willis, & K. G. Manton (Eds.), *The oldest old* (pp. 199–250). New York: Oxford University Press.

McIntyre, J. S., Charles, S. C., Zarin, D., & Pincus, H. A. (1996). *Practice guidelines*. Washington, DC: American Psychiatric Association.

Mellsop, G., Peace, K., & Fernando, T. (1987). Preadmission adaptive functioning as a measure of prognosis in psychiatric inpatients. *Australia New Zealand Journal of Psychiatry, 21*, 539–544.

Migdail, K. J., Youngs, M. T., & Seltzer, B. B. (Eds.). (1995). *Behavioral outcomes and guidelines sourcebook*. New York: Faulkner & Gray.

Mintz, J., Mintz, L. I., Arruda, M. J., & Hwang, S. S. (1992). Treatments of depression and the functional capacity to work. *Archives of General Psychiatry, 49*, 761–768.

NIMH Cost-Effectiveness of Psychotherapy Conference. (1994). Tyson's Corner, VA.

Norcross, J. C. (1995). Dispelling the dodo bird verdict and the exclusivity myth in psychotherapy. *Psychotherapy, 32*(3), 500–504.

Oregon Health Services Commission. (1991). *Prioritization of health services: Report to the governor and the legislature*. Salem: Author.

Ormel, J., Von Korff, M., Ustun, T. B., Pini, S., Korsten, A., & Oldehinkel, T. (1994). Common mental disorders and disability across cultures. *Journal of the American Medical Association, 272*, 1741–1748.

Ormel, J., VonKorff, M., VandenBrink, W., Katon, W., Brilman, E., & Oldehinkel, T. (1993). Depression, anxiety and disability show syncrony of change. *American Journal of Public Health, 83*, 385–390.

Patterson, D. A., & Lee, M. S. (1995). Field trial of the Global Assessment of Functioning Scale—Modified. *American Journal of Psychiatry, 152*(9), 1386–1388.

Remington, M., & Tyrer, P. (1979). The Social Functioning Schedule—A brief semi-structured interview. *Social Psychiatry, 14*, 151–157.

Rice, D. P., Kelman, S., Miller, L. S., & Dunnmeyer, S. (1990). *The economic costs of Alcohol and drug abuse and mental illness*. San Francisco: University of California, Institute for Health and Aging.

Rush, A. J., Pincus, H. A., & First, M. B. (in press). *Handbook of psychiatric measures and outcomes*. Washington, DC: American Psychiatric Press.

Schooler, N., Hogarty, G., & Weissman, M. M. (1979). Social Adjustment Scale II (SAS-II). In W. A. Hargreaves, C. C. Attkisson, & J. E. Sorenson (Eds.), *Resource materials for community health program evaluators*: Publication ADM 79-328. Washington, DC: U.S. Department of Health, Education and Welfare.

Schrader, G., Gordon, M., & Harcourt, R. (1986). The usefulness of DSM-III Axis IV and Axis V assessments. *American Journal of Psychiatry, 143*, 904–907.

Seligman, M. E. P. (1995). The effectiveness of psychotherapy: The Consumer Reports study. *American Psychologist, 50*(12), 965–974.

Serban, G. (1978). Social Stress and Functioning Inventory for Psychotic Disorders (SSFIPD): Measurement and prediction of schizophrenics' community adjustment. *Community Psychiatry, 19*, 337–347.

Stewart, A. L., Greenfield, S., Hays, R. D., et al. (1989). Functional status and well-being of patients with chronic conditions: Results from the Medical Outcomes Study. *Journal of the American Medical Association, 262*, 907–913.

Stewart, A., Hays, R., & Ware, J. (1988). The MOS short-form General Health Survey. *Medical Care, 26*, 724–735.

Stoudemire, A., Frank, R., Hedemark, N., Kamlet, M., & Blazer, D. (1986). The economic burden of depression. *General Hospital Psychiatry, 8*, 387–394.

Strupp, H., Lambert, M., & Horowitz, L. (1997). *Measuring patient change in mood, anxiety and personality disorders: Toward a core battery*. Washington, DC: American Psychological Association.

Surles, R., & Feiden-Warsh, C. (1990). Mental health coverage in health care reform. Prepared for the Hastings Center Project on Priorities in Mental Health. *Challenges for the 1990s: State Comprehensive Plan for Mental Health Services*, 1990–1995. Albany, NY: Office of Mental Health.

Suzman, R. M., Harris, T., Hadley, E. C., Kovar, M. G., & Weindruch, R. (1992). The robust oldest old: Optimistic perspectives for increasing healthy life expectancy. In R. M. Suzman, D. P. Willis, & K. G. Manton (Eds.), *The oldest old*. New York: Oxford University Press.

Von Korff, M., Ormel, J., Katon, W., & Lin, E. H. B. (1992). Disability and depression among high utilizers of health care: A longitudinal analysis. *Archives of General Psychiatry, 49*, 91–100.

Wallace, C. J. (1986). Functional assessment in rehabilitation. *Schizophrenia Bulletin, 12*, 604–624.

Ware, J. (1992). Measures for a new era of health assessment. In A. L. Stewart & J. E. Ware (Eds.), *Measuring functional status and well-being: The Medical Outcomes Study approach* (pp. 3–11). Durham, NC: Duke University Press.

Waskow, I. E., & Parloff, M. B. (Eds.). (1975). *Psychotherapy change measures*. Rockville, MD: National Institute of Mental Health.

Weissman, M., & Bothwell, S. (1976). Assessment of social adjustment by patient self-report. *Archives of General Psychiatry*, 33, 1111–1115.
Weissman, M. M., Sholomskas, D., & John, K. (1981). The assessment of social adjustment: An update. *Archives of General Psychiatry*, 38, 1250–1258.
Wohlfarth, T. D., vanden Brink, W., Ormel, J., Koeter, M. W. J., & Oldehinkel, A. J. (1993). The relationship between social dysfunctioning and psychopathology. *British Journal of Psychiatry*, *163*, 37–44.
Zarin, D. A., Pincus, H. A., & McIntyre, J. S. (1993). Practice guidelines. *American Journal of Psychiatry*, *150*, 175–177.

19

Assessing Work Function in Mental Health Research

James Mintz, Gary R. Bond,
& Lois Imber Mintz

> The greatest analgesic, soporific, stimulant, tranquilizer, narcotic, and to some extent even antibiotic in short, the closest thing to a genuine panacea known to medical science is work.
>
> Thomas Szasz, *The Second Sin* (1973)

Why Measure Work Functioning?

The capacity to work is generally assumed to accompany good health. In the United States today, the vast majority of healthy adults and most children spend almost half of their waking hours engaged in the work functions associated with their "primary role," be it worker, student, or homemaker. Children and working adults alike understand that missing school or work is socially sanctioned only when one is "really" ill. Hurry, Bebbington, and Tennant (1987) note that "the lay concept of illness is closely related to inability to fulfill social roles" (p. 68). They found that all else being equal symptomatically, individuals with what they termed "social disability" were more likely to be referred for psychiatric services by their general medical practitioners.

It is the linkage between work disability and psychiatric disorder, to some extent real and to some extent a matter of perception and stereotype, that motivates this chapter. For, with the exception of those specialists whose profession directly involves vocational rehabilitation, psychiatric researchers have largely ignored work in their evaluations of how ill people are and how they respond to treatment. Outcome research, particularly in the American mental health research community, has almost exclusively focused on signs and symptoms of disorders as codified in the *Diagnostic and Statistical Manuals (DSM)* of the American Psychiatric Association. In that manual, as in most treatment outcome research, work function appears only tangentially as an associated feature of mental disorder, or the fifth *DSM* axis, where it is amalgamated with a host of social, recreational, and leisure time activities.

Why do we measure the capacity to work? The answers are varied. The psychopathologist may study work function as an indicator of episode severity or residual impairment or may attempt to understand when and how mental disorder manifests itself as impaired functional capacity and when it does not. Treatment researchers may be interested in the process of functional recovery, what Strauss and Carpenter (1972) long ago termed a "quasi-independent" outcome of symptom remission. Vocational rehabilitation specialists directly target the effectiveness with which people can be returned or guided to satisfying, productive activity. Health services researchers may ask questions like how service utilization is affected by "social disability," over and above illness severity. The health economist ponders the cost of illness to society and the cost-benefit ratio of providing treatments, and health policymakers consider the manifold implications of disability. One researcher wants to know if people can work. Another wants to know if they actually do.

Work clearly has personal, familial, and societal value. Each of these varied interests demands a different focus and a different assessment plan. This chapter will focus principally on the measurement of work function in the domains of treatment outcome and vocational rehabilitation, with some attention to cost issues. Several useful summaries of instruments and methods for the assessment of work and, more generally, functional capacity already exist (e.g., Cook et al., 1992; Goldman, Skodol, & Lave, 1992; Vaccaro, Pitts, & Wallace, 1992); accordingly, that will not be repeated here. Rather, this chapter will document how to measure work adjustment in people with mental disorders, given that work is an essential component of the assessment of "mental health," while highlighting some of the difficulties and challenges facing investigators in this domain.

The State of the Field

> Our review of over 4000 research articles found that restoration of work capacity was a sorely neglected topic in the psychiatric treatment literature.
>
> Mintz, Mintz, Arruda, and Hwang (1992)

The fields of psychiatric rehabilitation and psychiatric treatment have existed largely on separate tracks. This division is particularly evident in the research literatures, a schism that Mintz, Mintz, and Phipps (1992) described as both anachronistic and unprofitable. Historically, these research domains have used different methodologies, focused on different kinds of outcomes, and published in different places, to satisfy the needs of distinct audiences. The schism between these domains is exemplified in two important review papers on assessment instruments, one written from the treatment perspective (Weissman, Sholomskas, & John, 1981) and the other from the rehabilitation perspective (Wallace, 1986). Goldman et al. (1992) report that the Workgroup on Multiaxial Issues relied heavily on these two papers as it considered how best to quantify Axis V for the *DSM-IV*. Weissman et al. (1981) reviewed 11 instruments of "social adjustment" (counting 2 versions of her own Social Adjustment Scale only once). Wallace (1986) reviewed 11 measures of "functional living skills" for rehabilitation in their primary table and an additional 8 instruments that received a qualified recommendation "with caveats." Only 3 instruments appeared on the primary lists of both authors. In these reviews, 6 of the 11 measures considered by Weissman and her colleagues, and 14 of the 19 considered by Wallace, were not considered by the other.

In the treatment outcome literature, there has been a general neglect of work and functional outcomes. In treatment outcome research, symptom remission is the principal—indeed, often the only—outcome measure. The favored experimental design is the randomized clinical trial, and great care is typically taken to ensure that samples are carefully diagnosed and highly homogeneous. If work is assessed at all, it is likely to be only as part of a composite social functioning instrument that also includes ratings of social and recreational adjustment, consistent with the broad construct of "adaptive functioning" first introduced as the *DSM-III* Axis V and later revised to assess "psychological, social and occupational functioning" with a single score (Goldman et al., 1992).

Treatment researchers typically believe that valid assessments of work capacity can be obtained from structured clinical interviews and self-report rating scales. When the disorder under consideration is symptomatically episodic, work impairment is often considered a concomitant of symptom episodes that can be expected to remit as symptoms do. In unipolar depression and substance abuse, that may well be the case (Mintz, Mintz, Arruda, & Hwang, 1992; Mintz, Mintz, & Phipps, 1992). For people with schizophrenia, the relationship between work and symptoms is more complicated. Illness episodes may precipitate losing a job, but other factors are also often present (Westermeyer & Harrow, 1987).

In rehabilitation research, on the other hand, work is viewed as essentially an independent outcome dimension, and diagnosis and symptom severity are thought to tell relatively little about capacity to work. Anthony and Jansen (1984) emphasize that

> (a) knowledge of psychiatrically disabled persons' psychiatric symptomatology is *not* a valid indicator of their capacity to work; (b) knowledge of psychiatrically disabled persons' functioning in a nonvocational environment is *not* a valid indicator of their capacity to work; and (c) knowledge of psychiatrically disabled persons' psychiatric symptomatology is *not* a valid indicator of their functional skills. (p. 542; emphasis in original)

In rehabilitation research, samples are typically diagnostically unspecified and quite heterogeneous, although the focus is usually on individuals with serious mental illness (SMI), that is, chronic psychotic disorders. Because symptoms often are not considered to have much to do with work capacity, careful assessment of symptom severity may be lacking. The design is often based on quasi-experimental methodology. One preferred approach to assessment of the *capacity* to work is based on work samples that are obtained in an evaluation workshop setting that simulates the actual workplace. Anthony and Jansen suggest, for example, that the best clinical predictors of future work performance are ratings of a person's work adjustment skills made in a workshop setting or sheltered job site: These results suggest that "The best predictor of future work performance is a structured work evaluation" (p. 540).

Moreover, Bond and Boyer (1988) state that "despite their imperfections, employment measures are objective and verifiable, and they are associated with positive self-regard."

Noting that others have advocated composite indicators as "a reaction to the vocational rehabilitation system's dependence on an oversimplified definition of successful closure," Bond and Boyer conclude that "such indices are one level of abstraction away from the raw data and as such may obfuscate research findings. The advantage of conventional employment measures is that they can be interpreted directly and also analyzed statistically."

In place of composite measures, the authors recommend use of multiple outcome measures:

> Despite possible redundancy, . . . measures should include the percentage of clients in paid employment, the percentage of time employed and total earnings from employment. Studies should also report the percentage of clients in full-time employment and the percentage of clients employed at any time during the follow-up period.

More recently, length of time from program admission to entry into the job market has become a widely used indicator (Bond, Clark, & Drake, 1995; Shafer & Huang, 1995). Furthermore, length of job tenure is being increasingly used in conjunction with survival analysis (Fabian, 1992; Shafer & Huang, 1995). While type and level of occupation is often assessed, in reality, Bond and Boyer (1988) note, "Most graduates of psychiatric rehabilitation programs achieve, at best, entry-level jobs, making this [variable] less relevant." Wages are also sometimes used as a proxy for occupational attainment, and job satisfaction, one of the more qualitative aspects of work adjustment, is often been reported. Although measuring quality of job performance would be a plus, this is methodologically a difficult task. Adequacy of job performance is sometimes assessed indirectly and imperfectly via review of job retention.

One advantage of using situational assessments, or actual employment status, as measures of vocational adjustment is that these can be obtained without dependence on client self-report. People with SMI are sometimes poor historians, raising doubts about reliability of self-report inventories requiring detailed recall or nuanced information. Usually, psychiatric rehabilitation researchers avoid doing assessments of work capacity in artificial settings because the belief in situational specificity is very strong in the rehabilitation tradition, with a substantial research literature to support the view that vocational success in one setting (e.g., the hospital, day treatment, or sheltered work settings) may not generalize to another (e.g., community jobs; Bond, 1994; Test, 1992). An even more extreme position maintained by some adherents of supported employment is a "zero reject model" (Wehman, 1988), which maintains that employability should be discarded as a construct in job placement, with the onus on the employment program to find jobs that suit the abilities of any client, regardless of severity of the disability.

The Lag in Method Development

Although there have been some recent indications of increased interest in work functioning among treatment researchers (see, e.g., Friedman, 1993), there has been very little method development for some time. A very recent review of measures of social functioning that considered the merits of 20 scales as methods for quantifying and assessing the DSM-IV's Axis V (Goldman et al., 1992) is itself heavily reliant on two reviews conducted almost 10 and 15 years ago. As documented in Figure 19.1, the average age of the measures considered by Goldman et al. was about 20 years old. The average year of original publication of the measures was 1974. Only one of the reviewed instruments was introduced after 1980, and most of the psychometric work was accomplished in the early 1970s (the very widely used Social Adjustment Scale was introduced in 1976). The workplace is a continually evolving part of our culture, and it has changed in the past 20 years. The emergence of recent employment strategies, such as supported employment, has led to the necessity for new assessment tools (e.g., Fabian, Waterworth, &

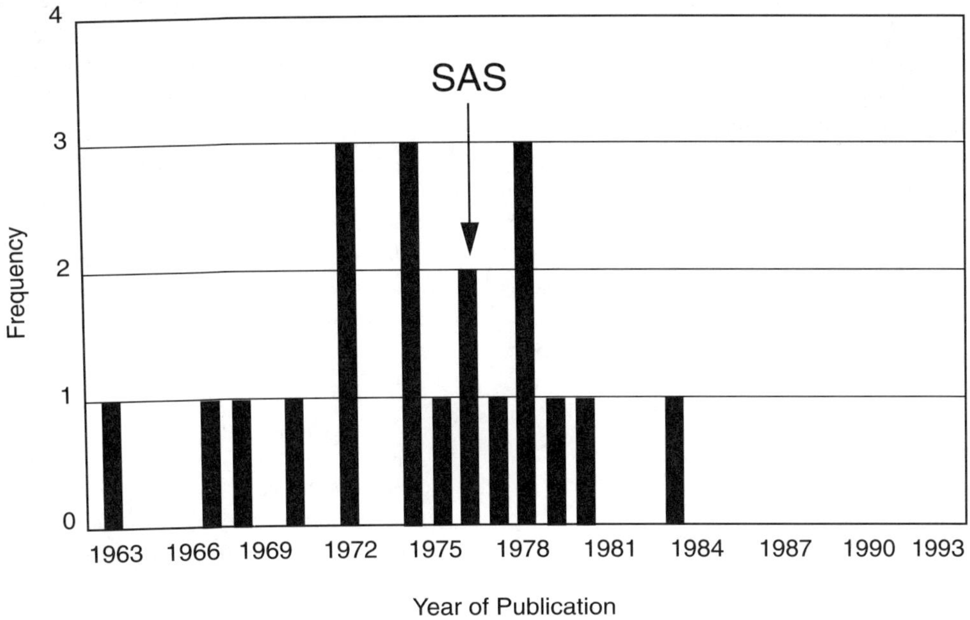

Figure 19.1 Year of publication for 20 measures of social functioning. (Data from Goldman, Skidol, and Lave, 1992.)

Ripke, 1993). Among the groups most caught up in these social evolutions are women, minorities, and people with disabilities. Many of the popular work assessment instruments are manifesting signs of age.

The State of the Art: Some Measures of Work

A recent review of work outcomes reported in treatment outcome studies (Mintz, Mintz, & Phipps, 1992) summarized results in three areas: depression, substance abuse, and schizophrenia. The most commonly used instrument in the area of depression treatment was the Social Adjustment Scale (SAS; Weissman & Bothwell, 1976). The SAS briefly assesses work functioning as a component of a comprehensive overview of social functioning, consistent with the thrust of the *DSM's* Axis V. It exists in both interview-based and self-report formats. Mintz, Mintz, Arruda, and Hwang (1992) developed an operational definition of functional work impairment based on the SAS:

> In most cases, the measure of work impairment was based on items from the SAS [Social Adjustment Scale]. . . . The six SAS Work Role items fall broadly into two categories, which we will call "functional" and "affective." This distinction is based on whether the items measure observable behaviors (absenteeism, performance adequacy, interpersonal conflict) or subjective emotional states (distress, feelings of shame, loss of interest). . . . Subjects were operationally defined as work impaired if they et any one of the following five criteria: (1) absenteeism, i.e., missing half of the scheduled work time or more; (2) performance probelms, i.e., at least moderate impairment or inadequate productivity at least half the scheduled time; (3) interpersonal problems, i.e., many arguments or significant interpersonal conflicts with coworkers or supervisors, moderate friction or significant avoidance of social contact at work; (4) poor overall functioning as indicated by a mean score of 2 or more on these items; and (5) unemployment. (Mintz, Mintz, Arruda, & Hwang, 1992, p. 763)

Norms from community samples of working men and women indicate that most working people report very good work adjustments (Weissman, Prusoff, Thompson, Harding, & Myers, 1978). On the full six-item SAS scale, the average score for over 200 employed community residents of both genders was 1.3 (the scale ranges from 1 to 5), with a standard deviation of .3. A mean SAS Work Role score as low as 2 or more is thus more than two standard deviations above the mean and would clearly place an individual in the lowest 2–8% of average working people in the community. The Addiction Severity Index (ASI; McLellan et al., 1992), a multidimensional instrument that includes assessment of work adjustment, is widely used in substance abuse research. Studies of treatment outcome in schizophrenia have often used simple employment rates, or the Strauss-Carpenter scales (e.g., Strauss & Carpenter, 1972, 1974, 1977).

Goldman et al. (1992, p. 1154) noted that "leaders in general medicine have called for the use of simple measures of functioning in routine clinical practice—to support the need for measures of clinical outcome" and concluded that none of the multi-item instruments they reviewed is "clearly superior" to the use of a single rating item (the Global Assessment of Functioning) as a measure of "adaptive functioning." In fact, most of the popular instruments for assessing work function that are used in both clinical and health services research are quite simple. The SAS, for example, includes only six items in the Work area; Mintz, Mintz, Arruda, and Hwang used only three of them (time missed, productivity, relations with coworkers) to define functional impairment. The four-item Strauss-Carpenter Level of Function scale (reviewed by Weissman et al., 1981; excluded by Wallace, 1986, as too "global") includes only one item measuring work (percentage of time employed). Later adaptations of their prognostic index expand the total to two, providing ratings of both the quantity and quality of work. The Rand 36-item Health Survey (version 1.0), an instrument for epidemiological research used in the Medical Outcomes Study (Stewart et al., 1989) has only three "yes-no" questions:

> During the past 4 weeks, have you had any of the following problems with your work or other regular daily activities as a result of any emotional problems (such as feeling depressed or anxious)?
>
> 1. Cut down on the amount of time you spent on work or other activities?
> 2. Accomplished less than you would like?
> 3. Didn't do work or other activities as carefully as usual?

Although this simple assessment is rather nonspecific, in terms of both the functional and the psychiatric domains involved, it does capture the core issues of diminished time, productivity, and quality of work, and it is certainly easy to incorporate into routine clinical assessment and screening.

In contrast to the brevity that characterizes work assessment in treatment outcome research, rehabilitation specialists have developed very detailed and extensive batteries. These include situational, work sample, and paper-and-pencil assessments that can not only characterize the work capacity and performance of persons with severe mental illness but also describe important features of their work environments. Those instruments have been developed for, and typically are used in, psychiatric rehabilitation settings. Cook et al. (1992) provide an excellent, detailed summary.

A Few Core Constructs That Cut Across Measures

Three items seem to be absolutely fundamental, and appear in even the briefest of measures: Are you working? How much time have you missed in the past month (week, year) due to mental disorder? What is the quality of your work performance? From that common core, scales go on to matters such as the quality of interpersonal relations with coworkers and supervisors, job interest and self-satisfaction, and factors such as those codified in the eleven dimensions of work behavior in the Work Personality Profile (Bolton, 1988):

- acceptance of the work role
- ability to profit from instruction or correction
- work persistence
- work tolerance
- amount of supervision required
- extent trainee seeks assistance from supervisor
- degree of comfort or anxiety with supervisor
- appropriateness of personal relations with supervisor
- teamwork
- ability to socialize with coworkers
- social communication skills

Primary (and Multiple) Roles

Outcome evaluators struggle with the differentiation between work and primary role function. The decision to focus on paid employment, as Bond and Boyer (1988) recommended, leaves a lot of people and activities out of the mix. Examples are the elderly, the retired, children, those temporarily laid off for reasons unrelated to any mental health concern, the very rich, and, most particularly, many women. For many research purposes, it is desirable to have measurement on the entire sample. An alternative to paid employment that meets this requirement is "primary role functioning."

The simple notion that all of these individuals have a primary role to fulfill underlies the structure of the popular Social Adjustment Scale (SAS). The SAS somewhat anachronistically insists that respondents choose only one principal role. Working women are thus forced to "decide" whether they are "housewives" or workers. Many, of course, are both. The same could be said of many students.

Few would question the personal, familial, and social importance of the at-home work role or the profound and often hidden consequences of disability at home. Dual role status may provide additional challenges and stress. The structure of the SAS, however, reflects a notion of gender roles that seems out of date. Many women, perhaps as many as half, given the chance, elect to fill out both the "worker" and "housewife" sections of the Work area (Mintz, 1994). They declare that they have dual roles. It is largely ignored that men typically perform work functions at home as well. Unlike women, however, men very rarely complete the "housewife" items on the SAS, which defines at-home work activities almost exclusively in stereotypically "female" terms. Full consideration of functional living skills must include all significant role activities. On the other hand, Bond and Boyer are probably right to suggest that these various roles are in many respects not comparable. "Housewife" may at times be less a significant work role than a socially sanctioned way of saying one is unemployed.

Is Employment Really a Good Criterion?

Measuring employment obviously makes the most sense when the population under consideration comprises adults prior to the age of retirement who indicate a desire to work. Women (or the occasional man) who identify "housewife" as their main instrumental role do pose a dilemma in the assessment of vocational capacity, not only among persons with SMI, but also in the general population. One strategy, of course, is to take the housewife group out of the denominator and examine it as a separate subgroup (as Mintz, Mintz, Arruda & Hwang did in their analyses of treatment of depression).

The advantages of employment status as an outcome variable are obvious, but there are also major difficulties with this measure. For one thing, employment is affected by a host of factors extraneous to the individual, such as larger economic realities. Use of employment status as an outcome overlooks matters such as job suitability ("underemployment"), the thorny issue of quantifying productivity, interpersonal relations, and affective components such as interest, enjoyment, and job satisfaction. The issue of the desire to work is itself a complex issue. Although studies surveying unemployed public mental health clients suggest that over 70% report a desire to be employed (Rogers, Walsh, Masotta, & Danley, 1991), it is also true that many clients with SMI drop out of vocational programs (Bond, Dietzen, McGrew, & Miller, 1995; Marshak, Bostick, & Turton, 1990), often because of their ambivalence about working. The motivational aspects are clearly a factor clouding our understanding of work capacity.

Certainly, employment status is not work capacity. Work history and "employability" further complicate the interpretation of employment status. People who are otherwise quite capable of working may be unable to find work because of a poor work history. Because of its enormous prognostic significance, assessment of work outcomes is only possible in the context of the work history. As noted above, people may move in and out of work for a variety of reasons. Bond and Boyer (1988) wrote:

> Measures based on employment "at any time" . . . must be interpreted cautiously because of the difficulty clients have in retaining jobs. . . . Full time employment . . . may be too stringent as the sole measure of success. Part-time community employment is an appropriate goal for a large segment of the unemployed mentally ill population. On the other hand, combining paid employment, school attendance, volunteer work, and even, in some instances, attendance in a day program into a single category of productive activity, as do some investigators, dilutes the concept of employment beyond useful limits. Paid employment seems to be a suitable compromise, and should be a major outcome variable.

Particular difficulties attend the assessment of women, who may move in and out of the labor force as part-time workers as a function of factors quite extraneous to their mental health. These difficulties in evaluating the meaning of unemployment among women were dramatized when the following story appeared on page 1 of the *New York Times* (the numerically small percentage change mentioned is a 13% increase, and the "biggest revamping" in history):

> As part of the biggest revamping in the 53-year history of the Government survey that determines the nation's official jobless rate, researchers at the

> Labor Department have discovered a bias in the survey under which many women who were seeking jobs were erroneously described as homemakers, and therefore not counted as being in the work force. . . . The [unemployment] rate for women was 6.8 percent, rather than 6.0 percent. Officials at the Labor Department said they had suspected for some time that the survey . . . was failing to reflect changes in American society. . . . The figures . . . acted as a reminder of the "subjective" element in even the most sophisticated data.
>
> Robert D. Hershey, Jr.
> Special to the *New York Times*
> November 17, 1993, p. 1

Certainly, the benefits accruing from employment include a "cost offset" argument revolving around the fact that clients who are working are much less likely to use expensive mental health services, such as day treatment (Bond, Clark, & Drake, 1995). Several studies examining a cost offset hypothesis suggest that it has some merit (Bond, Dietzen, McGrew, & Miller, 1995; Rogers et al., 1995). Moreover, one mental health center found that converting a day treatment program to supported employment led to a reduction in staff and facilities, with improved employment rates and no observed negative consequences for clients (Drake et al., 1994).

Money and Productivity

Money earned is in many ways an appealing measure. Unlike the elusive construct *productivity*, which may be impossible to define away from the assembly line, earnings are already quantified. Productivity seems to have entirely different meanings across different occupations; not so earnings. A dollar, as they say, is a dollar. It might be argued further that earnings are a direct indication of the social value of an individual's work. Not everyone would agree, however, that low-paying jobs are inherently less valuable than higher pay positions. In fact, the obvious inequities in earnings that exist in society are widely discussed. Extreme examples contrasting the social value of entertainment figures or corporate CEOs with that of fire fighters and teachers bring home the point that there is anything but a one-to-one correspondence between earnings and social value. Studies reporting average hourly wages for individuals with SMI in supported employment programs (e.g., Bond, Dietzen, McGrew, & Miller, 1995; Danley, Rogers, MacDonald-Wilson, & Anthony, 1994) demonstrate the low salary level that most attain.

Earnings from employment are frequently used as the main benefit measure in societal cost-benefit analyses (Weisbrod, 1983). This strategy may involve unwarranted assumptions when investigators extrapolate earnings from a short follow-up period (which is usually the case) to years in the future. As Bond and Boyer (1988) note:

> Methodologies used with other disabilities which project future earnings require unrealistic assumptions when applied to mentally ill clients, who have difficulties with job retention. . . . No completely satisfactory method has yet been proposed which accurately represents long-term benefits.

Gauging the Effects of Financial Disincentives

Some years ago, Rosenhan (1973) discovered that mental health professionals are not very good at detecting faking. He got himself into a mental hospital by faking psychotic symptoms and then had surprising difficulty getting himself out by telling the truth. Most people have little reason to pretend to have mental illness. Some psychometric tests, such as the venerable MMPI, include scales that may suggest malingering. Most clinical scales do not. In the arena of disability, there are powerful monetary disincentives to seeking competitive employment (Walls, Dowler, & Fullmer, 1990; Warner & Polak, 1995). The assumption that people will naturally work to their maximal capacity may be compromised when financial disincentives enter the picture. Accurate assessment of work capacity in such populations will have to develop some approaches to this difficulty. Disincentives to employment may also compromise studies of work outcomes in the community.

Characterizing the Work Setting

One of the very important characteristics of the work setting is whether it is competitive employment or some form of supported work. In fact, there is a continuum of employment settings, from volunteer to sheltered to transitional to mobile work crews to supported to independent employment (Marrone, 1993). People do not work in a vacuum. They work in a physical and interpersonal environment. Even the assessment of work capacity is probably influenced by the setting in which it is observed (Bond & Dietzen, 1993; Schultheis & Bond, 1993). With the passage of the Americans with Disabilities Act, increased attention has been directed to characteristics of the work setting. That legislation requires employers to make "reasonable accommodations" to the needs of disabled employees to enable them to work successfully whenever possible. Work insufficiency on the part of an individual with mental disorder is thus no longer reflexively attributed to the individual as an instance of disability. Instead, it may be viewed as a correctable deficiency in the environment. The notion that features of the work setting may have to be taken into account as part of a valid work assessment is not novel in rehabilitation settings. It is not, however, reflected in any of the standard clinical instruments.

The Timing of Assessments

Cook et al. (1992) emphasize the importance of timing in vocational assessments. If assessments are done too early in the course of rehabilitation, they suggest, staff may "give clients a benefit of a doubt" (p. 10). Too late, and clients may become demoralized with excessive training. More than 10 years ago, Anthony and Jansen (1984) listed as their first research priority the need to determine how long a structured work evaluation needed to be. They were interested in determining the shortest, most cost-effective evaluation. The question of how long to make prevocational assessments is probably a dead issue now, with the advent of rapid-placement supported employment (Bond, Dietzen, McGrew, & Miller, 1995). Another issue, however, is how to evaluate the propensity for decompensation in actual work settings. Individuals may, for example, be quite able to perform simple work tasks in a short-term evaluation setting but unable to sustain effective performance over the long haul.

The Length of the Follow-Up Period

What kind of follow-up protocols make the most sense? Bond and Boyer (1988) assert, "These should be minimum standards: an eighteen-month follow-up period and 80 percent follow-up rate on the initial sample." (p. 254). Timing of assessments is a critical consideration if we are to learn more about the trajectory of work recovery in various populations. For example, work function appears to recover more slowly than symptoms in unipolar depression. Mintz, Mintz, Arruda, and Hwang (1992) reported that symptom remission rates were similar in studies with follow-up periods as short as 4 weeks and as long as 9 months. Work outcomes, however, steadily improved across that time period, even among those whose symptoms had apparently remitted. Very brief study periods may thus be satisfactory for evaluating acute treatment of some rapidly remitting disorders, such as unipolar depression. Even in those conditions, however, adequate assessment of work restoration requires significantly longer follow-up intervals. What does that say about the linkage between symptoms and work function? Why does it happen? Is it diagnostically specific?

Factors Compromising the Validity of Assessments

As in other areas of treatment outcome assessment, multiple sources of information (self-report; employers; "objective" assessments, e.g., workshop tests) are highly desirable. There is, of course, a considerable potential for distortion in self-report. Indeed, one concern is that self-reports may be colored and lack validity. One factor is the current clinical state. The very presence of mental disorder may compromise the validity of self-report measures. On the other hand, direct observational measures may be difficult or impossible to gather. For one thing, confidentiality may be an issue, and there can be significant logistical problems in entering the workplace without unduly disrupting it. The biasing effects of malingering, secondary gain, and financial disincentives (e.g., disability) were discussed earlier. Another factor is the social stigma associated with job loss, being fired, unemployment in general, and mental disorder. Shame, guilt, or embarrassment might well compromise the validity of work assessments.

Coping with Heterogeneity

In all of this, the appeal of having standardized assessment protocols and well-established norms for various populations, normal and otherwise, should be obvious (e.g., Weissman et al.'s 1978 data on a community sample of workers). Structured assessment tools and operational criteria have proven their research utility in the diagnostic realm. The very mention of normative data, however, brings into sharp relief the fact that there are vast differences among various psychiatric populations. As noted above, Mintz, Mintz, Arruda, and Hwang (1992) found that virtually all patients with unipolar depression who responded symptomatically to antidepressant treatment also recovered work functioning, given the passage of enough time (up to 6 or more months). This finding contrasts sharply with most studies of people with serious mental illness, in which employment rates are dismal. In the longitudinal schizophrenia studies reviewed by McGlashan (1988), for example, the nonsheltered employment rate ranged from 6% to 41%, figures that do not take "underemployment" into account (the term refers to working at a lower job level than one's qualifications would ordinarily merit). In studies of clients with SMI receiving community treatment, employment rates are typically 15% or less (Anthony & Blanch, 1987). Moreover, 75% or more of seriously mentally ill clients who do obtain employment through vocational rehabilitation efforts obtain entry-level positions (Kregel, Shafer, Wehman, & West, 1990). The length of employment is not well documented, but it is generally assumed that most jobs obtained by mental health clients in rehabilitation programs are held for an average of about 6 months.

It is therefore understandable that most studies of psychiatric rehabilitation have not focused on the nuances of work capacity but have focused on gross employment rates. We have a "bandwidth fidelity" dilemma. In the metric of the SAS, for example, the adjustment of most normal workers falls well within the top rating point. On the same instrument, samples of clients with severe mental illness such as schizophrenia are likely to cluster in the bottom rating point. At this point, there is no single methodological approach that can effectively be used with both normal workers and the SMI population.

Symptoms and Work: A Complex Reciprocal Relationship

One of the most serious shortcomings of existing instruments for assessing work impairment is that they routinely fail to assess with any specificity why work functioning is impaired. Symptom assessments are done separately from assessments of work functioning, and the "grid" connecting them is never explicitly filled in. Anthony and Jansen (1984) summarized the empirical evidence more than a decade ago, asserting categorically that symptoms were a "poor predictor" of work performance. That "lack of finding," however, begged the question. After all, the concept *psychiatric disability* means an inability to work that is a direct result of *something* about a mental disorder. If it is not its symptoms, what is it?

One possibility is that disability results from associated characteristics of mental disorders that we do not identify as "symptoms." What might these be? In a recent review of research on functional outcome in schizophrenia, Green (1996) concluded that persisting neurocognitive deficits play a role. The only personal characteristics that Anthony and Jansen acknowledged were positively related to work performance (apart from measures of work performance itself) were the "ability to get along with others" and "ego strength." Those associations may well exist, but they are hardly a satisfactory explanation for the pervasive functional devastation associated with disorders like schizophrenia. We can agree with Anthony and Jansen that no particular symptom is "routinely related" to work performance (one possible exception is retardation, which, when present, may cut across diagnostic lines; Liberman, 1990) and still assert that in every individual case of disability due to mental disorder, some pattern of cognitive, affective, motivational, or behavioral deficits associated with that disorder must be accountable for the inability to perform productive work.

More recent work by Anthony himself, and by others, has suggested that the case for the virtual independence of work and symptoms was probably overstated in Anthony's earlier writings (Anthony, Rogers, Cohen, & Davies, 1995; Lysaker & Bell, 1995). Negative symptoms appear to be modest but dependable predictors of work performance. At least in some populations with remitting psychiatric disorders, such as depression, the empirical relationship between work impairment and symptom severity is quite strong and direct (although, for reasons that are still unclear, recovery of work function lags behind symptom recovery considerably; Mintz, Mintz, Arruda, & Hwang, 1992). Even among individuals with chronic and severe disorders, about whom Anthony and Jansen were writing, symptoms and work capacity are related, albeit weakly (the correlations are typically in the vicinity of .30; Liberman, 1990).

Still, more than a decade has passed since Anthony and Jansen's article appeared, and we know surprisingly little about when, how, or why mental disorders become disabling. Part of the issue may be that serious mental illness encompasses a very heterogeneous population. Even when one limits one's focus to schizophrenia, the symptom patterns are more diverse than for other, more circumscribed disabilities. Just as we know that warning signs for relapse are relatively distinctive for each individual (Herz, 1984), so, too, there may be "warning signs" signaling problems in employment. For one person, friction with coworkers may be a critical factor. Stamina may be the Achilles' heel for another, and so on.

Most of the current research tools for assessing work function simply do not provide any insights into these connections. A severely depressed individual may, for example, complain on one research form (say, the Hamilton Rating Scale for Depression) of symptoms, such as lack of energy, irritability, inability to make decisions, and poor concentration. Concurrently, that individual may report loss of interest in work, decreased work productivity, and absenteeism. Across cases, we may find (as Mintz, Mintz, Arruda, & Hwang did find in depression) that these two sets of complaints are positively correlated. Yet we must infer which, if any, of the manifold complaints identified as "depression" actually cause those identified as "work impairment."

Indeed, we can only guess in which direction the causation is going and why the functional impairment appears to persist after the symptoms have lessened in so many cases. Often, any role played by external factors is simply unassessed. It is worth emphasizing that the relationship between symptoms and work functioning is a two-way street. Even among individuals without psychiatric conditions, job loss places people's mental health at risk (Caplan, Vinokur, Price, & van Ryn, 1989). Careful longitudinal studies of exacerbation and recovery that explicitly link features of the disorder to functional consequences would be instructive.

References

Anthony, W. A., & Blanch, A. (1987). Supported employment for persons who are psychiatrically disabled: An historical and conceptual perspective. *Psychosocial Rehabilitation Journal, 11*(2), 5–23.

Anthony, W. A., & Jansen, M. A. (1984, May). Predicting the vocational capacity of the chronically mentally ill: Research and policy implications. *American Psychologist*, 537–544.

Anthony, W. A., & Liberman, R. P. (1992). Principles and practice of psychiatric rehabilitation. In R. P. Liberman (Ed.), *Handbook of psychiatric rehabilitation* (pp. 1–29). New York: Macmillan.

Anthony, W. A., Rogers, E. S., Cohen, M., & Davies, R. R. (1995). Relationship between psychiatric symptomatology, work skills, and future vocational performance. *Psychiatric Services, 46*, 353–358.

Bolton, B. (1988). Vocational assessment of persons with psychiatric disorders. In J. A. Ciardiello & M. D. Bell (Eds.), *Vocational rehabilitation of persons with prolonged psychiatric disorders* (pp. 165–179). Baltimore and London: Johns Hopkins University Press.

Bond, G. R. (1994). Applying psychiatric rehabilitation principles to employment: Recent findings. In R. J. Ancill, S. Holliday, & J. Higenbottam (Eds.), *Schizophrenia: Exploring the spectrum of psychosis* (pp. 49–65). Chichester, England: Wiley.

Bond, G. R., & Boyer, S. L. (1988). Rehabilitation programs and outcomes. In J. A. Ciardiello & M. D. Bell (Eds.), *Vocational rehabilitation of persons with prolonged psychiatric disorders* (pp. 231–263). Baltimore and London: Johns Hopkins University Press.

Bond, G. R., Clark, R. E., & Drake, R. E. (1995). Cost effectiveness of psychiatric rehabilitation. *Psychotherapy and Rehabilitation Research Bulletin, 4*, 26–31.

Bond, G. R., & Dietzen, L. (1993). Predictive validity and vocational assessment: Reframing the question. In R. L. Glueckauf, L. B. Sechrest, G. R. Bond, & E. C. McDonel (Eds.), *Improving assessment in rehabilitation and health* (pp. 61–86). Newbury Park, CA: Sage.

Bond, G. R., Dietzen, L. L., McGrew, J. H., & Miller, L. D. (1995). Accelerating entry into supported employment for persons with severe psychiatric disabilities. *Rehabilitation Psychology, 40*, 91–111.

Caplan, R. D., Vinokur, A. D., Price, R. H., & van Ryn, M. (1989). Job seeking, reemployment and mental health: A randomized field experiment in coping with job loss. *Journal of Applied Psychology, 74*(5), 759–769.

Cook, J. A., Bond, G. R., Hoffschmidt, S. J., Jonas, E. A., Razzano, L., & Weakland, R. (1992). *Assessing vocational performance among persons with severe mental illness.* Chicago: Thresholds.

Danley, K. S., Rogers, E. S., MacDonald-Wilson, K., & Anthony, W. A. (1994). Supported employment for adults with psychiatric disability: Results of an innovative demonstration project. *Rehabilitation Psychology, 39*, 269–276.

Drake, R. E., Becker, D. R., Biesanz, J. C., Torrey, W. C., McHugo, G. J., & Wyzik, P. F. (1994). Rehabilitation day treatment vs. supported employment: 1. Vocational outcomes. *Community Mental Health Journal, 30*, 519–532.

Fabian, E. (1992). Longitudinal outcomes in supported employment: A survival analysis. *Rehabilitation Psychology, 37*, 23–35.

Fabian, E. S., Waterworth, A., & Ripke, B. (1993). Reasonable accommodations for workers with serious mental illness: Type, frequency, and associated outcomes. *Psychosocial Rehabilitation Journal, 17*(2), 163–172.

Friedman, R. (1993, November). Social impairment in dysthymia. *Psychiatric Annals, 23*, 11.

Goldman, H. H., Skodol, A. E., & Lave, T. R. (1992). Revising Axis V for DSM-IV: A review of measures of social functioning. *American Journal of Psychiatry, 149*,(9), 1148–1156.

Green, M. F. (1996). What are the functional consequences of neurocognitive deficits in schizophrenia? *American Journal of Psychiatry, 153*,(3), 321–330.

Herz, M. I. (1984). Recognizing and preventing relapse in patients with schizophrenia. *Hospital and Community Psychiatry, 35*, 344–349.

Hurry, J., Bebbington, P. E., & Tennant, C. (1987). Psychiatric symptoms, social disablement and illness behavior. *Australian and New Zealand Journal of Psychiatry, 21*, 68–73.

Kregel, J., Shafer, M. S., Wehman, P., & West, M. (1990). Policy and program development in supported employment: Current strategies to promote statewide systems change. In P. Wehman, J. Kregel., & M. S. Shafer (Eds.), *Emerging trends in the national supported employment initiative: A preliminary analysis of twenty-seven states* (pp. 15–45). Richmond: Rehabilitation Research and Training Center, Virginia Commonwealth University.

Liberman, R. P. (1990). *Psychiatric symptoms and the functional capacity to work: Final report*, Research Grant (Social Security Administration) 10-P-98193. Los Angeles, UCLA, Department of Psychiatry, and West Los Angeles (Brentwood) VA Medical Center.

Lysaker, P., & Bell, M. (1995). Negative symptoms and vocational impairment in schizophrenia: Repeated measurements of work performance over six months. *Acta Psychiatrica Scandinavica, 91*(3), 205–208.

Marrone, J. (1993). Creating positive outcomes for people with severe mental illness. *Psychosocial Rehabilitation Journal, 17*(2), 43–62.

Marshak, L. E., Bostick, D., & Turton, L. J. (1990). Closure outcomes for clients with psychiatric disabilities served by the vocational rehabilitation system. *Rehabilitation Counseling Bulletin, 33*, 247–250.

McGlashan, T. H. (1988). A selective review of recent North American long-term follow-up studies of schizophrenia. *Schizophrenia Bulletin, 14*, 515–542.

McLellan, A. T., Kushner, H., Metzger, D., Peters, R., Smith, I., Grissom, G., & Argeriou, M. (1992). The fifth edition of the Addiction Severity Index. *Journal of Substance Abuse Treatment, 9*(3), 199–213.

Mintz, J. (1994). Treatments of depression and the capacity to work. Invited address to the Royal College of Psychiatrists, London, England, Winter Meeting.

Mintz, J., Mintz, L. I., & Phipps, C. (1992). Treatments of mental disorders and the functional capacity to work. In R. P. Liberman (Ed.), *Handbook of psychiatric rehabilitation* (pp. 290–316). New York: Macmillan.

Mintz, J., Mintz, L. I., Arruda, M. J., & Hwang, S. (1992). Treatments of depression and the functional capacity to work. *Archives of General Psychiatry, 49*, 761–768.

Rogers, E. S., Sciarappa, K., MacDonald-Wilson, K., & Danley, K. (1995). A benefit-cost analysis of a supported employment model for persons with psychiatric disabilities. *Evaluation and Program Planning, 18*, 105–115.

Rogers, E. S., Walsh, D., Masotta, L., & Danley, K. (1991). Massachusetts survey of client preferences for community support services (final report). Boston: Center for Psychiatric Rehabilitation.

Rosenhan, D. L. (1973). On being sane in insane places. *Science, 179*, 250–258.

Schultheis, A. M., & Bond, G. R. (1993). Situational assessment ratings of work behaviors: Changes across time and between settings. *Psychosocial Rehabilitation Journal, 17*(2), 107–119.

Shafer, M. S., & Huang, H. W. (1995). The utilization of survival analysis to evaluate supported employment services. *Journal of Vocational Rehabilitation, 5*, 103–113.

Stewart, A. L., Greenfield, S., Hays, R. D., Wells, K., Rogers, W. H., Berry, S. D., McGlynn, E. A., & Ware, J. E. (1989). Functional status and well-being of patients with chronic conditions: Results from the medical outcomes study. *Journal of the American Medical Association, 262*, 907–913.

Strauss, J. S., & Carpenter, W. T., Jr. (1972). The prediction of outcome in schizophrenia. *Archives of General Psychiatry, 27*, 739–746.

Strauss, J. S., & Carpenter, W. T., Jr. (1974). The prediction of outcome in schizophrenia, 2. *Archives of General Psychiatry, 31*, 37–42.

Strauss, J. S., & Carpenter, W. T., Jr. (1977). Prediction of outcome in schizophrenia, 3: Five year outcome and its predictors. *Archives of General Psychiatry, 34*, 159–163.

Test, M. A. (1992). Training in community living. In R. P. Liberman (Ed.), *Handbook of psychiatric rehabilitation* (pp. 153–170). New York: Macmillan.

Vaccaro, J. V., Pitts, D. B., & Wallace, C. J. (1992). Functional Assessment. In R. P. Liberman (Ed.), *Handbook of psychiatric rehabilitation* (pp. 78–94). New York: Macmillan.

Wallace, C. J. (1986). Functional assessment in rehabilitation. *Schizophrenia Bulletin, 12*(4), 604–624.

Walls, R. T., Dowler, D. L., & Fullmer, S. L. (1990). Incentives and disincentives to supported employment. In F. R. Rusch (Ed.), *Supported employment: Models, methods, and issues* (pp. 251–269). Sycamore, IL: Sycamore Publishing.

Warner, R., & Polak, P. (1995). The economic advancement of the mentally ill in the community. 2. Economic choices and disincentives. *Community Mental Health Journal, 31.*

Wehman, P. (1988). Supported employment: Toward zero exclusion of persons with severe disabilities. In P. Wehman & M. S. Moon (Eds.), *Vocational rehabilitation and supported employment* (pp. 3–14). Baltimore: Paul Brookes.

Weisbrod, B. A. (1983). A guide to benefit-cost analysis, as seen through a controlled experiment in treating the mentally ill. *Journal of Health Politics, Policy, and Law, 7,* 808–845.

Weissman, M. M., & Bothwell, S. (1976). Assessment of social adjustment by patient self-report. *Archives of General Psychiatry, 33,* 1111–1115.

Weissman, M. M., Prusoff, B. A., Thompson, W. D., Harding, P. S., & Myers, J. K. (1978). Social adjustment by self-report in a community sample and in psychiatric outpatients. *Journal of Nervous and Mental Disorders, 166,* 317–326

Weissman, M. M., Sholomskas, D., & John, K. (1981). The assessment of social adjustment: An update. *Archives of General Psychiatry, 38,* 1250–1258

Westermeyer, J., & Harrow, M. (1987). Factors associated with work impairments in schizophrenic and nonschizophrenic patients. In R. R. Grinker (Ed.), *Clinical research in schizophrenia: A multidimensional approach* (pp. 280–298). Springfield, IL: Charles C Thomas.

Part V

EXAMINING EFFICACY AND COST-EFFECTIVENESS OF PSYCHOTHERAPY

Targeting Interventions for Specific Disorders

Section A

Review of Clinical Trials Data on Treatment of Axis I Disorders

20

Psychotherapy for Major Mood Disorders

From Efficacy to Effectiveness

A. John Rush

The rationale for treating major mood disorders (e.g., major depressive, bipolar, or dysthymic disorders) with psychotherapy is rather clear. These disorders are extremely costly. Greenberg, Stiglin, Finkelstein, and Berndt (1993) indicated that the cost of major mood disorders was over $47 billion per year in the United States. Other systematic economic evaluations of these conditions also reveal high costs (Depression Guideline Panel, 1993a, p. 24). These costs are attributable largely to disability days, which are associated with these often chronic and recurring conditions.

As a treatment, psychotherapy has several potential objectives, including symptom reduction and restoration of normal psychosocial function (e.g., marital, occupational, and parental functioning), as well as preventing return of the current episode (relapse prevention) and preventing a new episode (preventing a recurrence). Depending on the form of psychotherapy, it may also aim, as either a primary or a secondary objective, to increase patient adherence to recommended medication regimens and/or lifestyle change(s), to remediate symptoms of the acute episode, to prevent a relapse, or to prevent a recurrence (Rush, 1986, 1988).

This chapter focuses on evidence for efficacy of psychotherapy for major mood disorders, highlighting the obstacles in translating current findings into routine practice and, conversely, emphasizes issues in evaluating routine practice in light of these efficacy findings.

Efficacy and Effectiveness

Efficacy research aims primarily at deciphering the comparative value of a specified treatment, such as cognitive therapy (CT) or behavior therapy (BT), for selected domains of outcome, such as symptoms or functioning, in comparison to alternative treatments or to predesigned contrast cells that include either none of the elements of active treatment (e.g., wait list control) or some of the elements of the active treatment (e.g., bibliotherapy or pill placebo).

Effectiveness research, on the other hand, attempts to mirror one or more aspects of the "real world" (i.e., to be representative of practice). This mirroring may take the form of including representative patient populations, representative clinical practitioners, and/or representative forms of treatment (e.g., psychotherapy or medication). Basically, the central issue in efficacy research is internal validity, whereas the overriding issue in effectiveness research is external validity (see chapter 2, this volume). Effectiveness research aims at determining how a treatment performs in practice, as compared to some other contrasting group, which may be treatment as usual, or it may entail comparing different practice parameters (e.g., different patient groups, different kinds of practitioners, different systems of service delivery) to determine their effect on outcome.

A number of variables influence the results of efficacy, as contrasted with effectiveness, research in, for example, the utility of psychotherapy for major depressive disorder. These variables include the nature and selection of the practitioners studied, the nature of the patient sample, the homogeneity of the depression evaluated (e.g., level of chronicity or severity), the degree and number of associated comorbidities, the nature and specificity of the treatment delivered, and, finally, the configuration of service system parameters under which treatments are delivered.

A failure to generalize from positive efficacy findings to equivalently positive findings with effectiveness research, as suggested by Hollon, must be elucidated by further studies in order to determine whether, and which of, these various parameters significantly contribute to differences in efficacy and effectiveness.

Establishing Efficacy

Initial suggestions of efficacy are often generated by case reports, regardless of whether the treatment is psychotherapy or pharmacotherapy. While case reports cannot directly test whether a treatment is effective because of lack of a comparison group, such initial efforts are essential in development of the psychotherapeutic package itself, and in providing clues, based on trial and error, to which kinds of patients and/or disorders may find the therapy most useful.

The next step often involves open case series in which consecutive patients are given psychotherapy over time. Case series allow for further adjustment of, and revisions to, the strategies and tactics encompassed by the psychotherapy per se and help tailor the therapy to different kinds of patients and/or disorders. These case series also help develop estimates of attrition and effect sizes and better specify patient populations most suitably treated with the psychotherapy. Case series and case reports often provide the basis for and are included within the treatment manuals used in research (e.g., Beck, Rush, Shaw, & Emery, 1979).

Sometimes, nonrandomized contrasts are conducted to compare the psychotherapy under development with some alternative version of the treatment, or with treatment as usual, a waiting list, or other controls. While nonrandomized comparisons do not provide strong evidence for efficacy, they do allow for further adjustment of the specifics of the psychotherapy and are preparatory for a formal randomized controlled trial (RCT).

To illustrate, Rush et al. (1975) contrasted once-a-week with twice-a-week CT. This contrast was not randomized, however, since those receiving once-a-week CT were treated initially, and then, in the light of high attrition rates, a subsequent cohort was treated with twice-a-week CT. The results suggested that twice-a-week therapy was associated with a lower attrition rate and a more rapid response rate—especially in the first 4 weeks of treatment—which led to recommending that CT be conducted twice a week for the first 4 weeks and then allowing the option of going to once-a-week treatment sessions, depending on patient response. This recommendation was later codified within the treatment manual itself (Beck et al., 1979).

Domains of Outcome

With regard to treatment development and evaluation, broader domains of outcome have historically typified effectiveness, as compared to efficacy research. Early efficacy studies (e.g., Friedman, 1975; Klerman, DiMascio, Weissman, Prusoff, & Paykel, 1974) selected targets that were presumably key intermediate variables to be addressed specifically by the therapy (e.g., social adjustment for interpersonal therapy, or IPT; Klerman, Weissman, Rounsaville, & Chevron, 1984) or marital functioning (for marital therapy). These targets were assessed together with evaluation of depressive symptoms, which were considered the primary measure of successful treatment in acute phase trials of these psychotherapies.

Since that time, psychotherapy efficacy research has relied heavily on symptom measurement, especially for acute phase trials, supplemented with other "process" variable measurements including, for example, change in attitudes and/or automatic thoughts (cognitions) for CT or change in behavioral patterns for BT.

Only very recently has the issue of measuring functional capacity and/or disability become more commonplace in efficacy trials. This development was fostered, in part, by the inclusion of functional impairment as a diagnostic criterion in *DSM-IV* (American Psychiatric Association [APA], 1994) to define the disorder and, in part, by the recognition of researchers, patients, and clinicians that patients who attain a relatively asymptomatic state but who continue to be functionally disabled manifest less satisfactory outcomes than those who attain both symptom remission and psychosocial restoration.

Effectiveness research, on the other hand, typically includes a far wider domain of outcome assessment. Symptoms are often seen as being of secondary importance, or even irrelevant, whereas disability, client satisfaction, quality of life, service utilization, and costs are primary concerns.

This inconsistency in outcome domains of interest—in efficacy, as contrasted with effectiveness, research—rests, in part, on the controversy regarding the relationship among these outcomes. Some believe there is a sequenced relationship between symptom improvement, improved psychosocial functioning, improved quality of life, and consequent reduced service utilization—whether improvement is attained with psychotherapy, medication, or their combination for major mood disorders. The notion is that symptoms of the condition remediate first, and the consequence is improved overall psychosocial functioning (i.e., less disability). Improved psychosocial functioning, in turn, is thought to lead concomitantly, or over time, to improved quality of life; that is, the patient is not only living in a more appropriate (supportive, normative) environment and functioning more ably but also more satisfied with current life circumstances. These improvements in symptoms, disability, and quality of life are often assumed to lead to reduced need for mental health, as well as general medical, services.

The empirical basis for presuming that this sequence is valid, however, is far from established. There is some evidence (Mintz, Mintz, Arruda, & Hwang, 1992) to suggest that at least for outpatients with generally nonchronic, nonpsychotic major depressive disorders, psychosocial restoration, as measured by the Social Adjustment Scale (SAS; Weissman & Bothwell, 1976), follows the reduction of depressive symptoms over several weeks to a month or two. This sequence appears to pertain to treatment with either medication alone or with time-limited, symptom-targeted psychotherapies (i.e., CT or IPT) alone. Conversely, the psychosocial consequences of more chronic forms of depression may well be prolonged, even well after symptom remission. Further studies are needed to better evaluate the validity and generalizability of this alleged causally related sequence.

Evidence for Efficacy of Psychotherapy

While initial studies of psychotherapy alone as a treatment for major depression were disappointing, at least when viewed from the point of view of symptom reduction, in comparison to antidepressant medications (e.g., Friedman, 1975; Klerman et al., 1974), subsequent studies utilizing time-limited psychotherapies specifically designed for depressive conditions (e.g., IPT or CT) revealed promising results. The best studied of these therapies for major depression are BT, CT, and IPT. Results of these time-limited therapies have now been replicated in a variety of formal RCTs. In addition, time-limited psychodynamic psychotherapy has also been evaluated in RCTs.

The majority of available efficacy trials have focused on acute phase treatment and, in particular, on symptom reduction. Patients studied were largely outpatients with nonpsychotic major depression, who generally had minimal concurrent general medical and/or psychiatric comorbidities and who manifested moderate to moderately severe levels of depressive symptomatology.

These studies have been subjected to a variety of meta-analyses (e.g., Depression Guideline Panel, 1993b; Dobson, 1989). Table 20.1 is taken from the Depression Guideline Panel (1993b, p. 76) and presents data from randomized controlled acute phase efficacy trials. The number of studies upon which the overall response rate is calculated appears in brackets. The overall efficacy is shown as a percentage of responders, based on all patients randomized.

The overall response rate (at least a 50% reduction in symptoms), based on a total of 29 cells, which included all of the psychotherapies, was 50% (overall efficacy, bottom of column 1). That is, 50 of 100 patients would show a clinically significant response. When BT was contrasted to wait list controls (five studies), 17.1% of the patients responded to BT but not to wait-list controls. For example, of the 100 patients, 38% might respond to wait list, but 55% might respond to BT. However, it is notable that the standard deviation (34%) is twice the size of the differential effects between BT and wait list controls. This indicates that in some trials, BT was more clearly effective than the wait list control, whereas in other trials, it was minimally different from the wait list control. That is, there is a heterogeneity of response within the patient populations to either the BT or wait list conditions, so that the difference between the two ranged widely across the studies.

This review (Depression Guideline Panel, 1993b) also identified 22 acute phase RCTs conducted with CT alone in adult or geriatric patients (Beck, Hollon, Young, Bedrosian, & Budenz, 1985; Blackburn, Bishop, Glen, Whalley, & Christie, 1981; Covi & Lipman, 1987; de Jong, Treiber, & Henrich, 1986; Elkin et al., 1989; Gallagher & Thompson, 1982; Hogg & Deffenbacher, 1988; Murphy, Simons, Wetzel, & Lustman,

Table 20.1 Meta-Analyses of Psychotherapy Trials in Outpatients with Major Depressive Disorder

Therapy[a,b]	Overall Efficacy	Therapy vs. Wait List	Therapy vs. Placebo	Therapy vs. Other Therapy	Therapy vs. Drug Alone
BT alone[c]	55.3% (9.3)[d] [10][e]	17.1% (34.0) [5]	N/A	9.1% (19.9) [6]	23.9% (11.6) [2]
Brief dynamic psychotherapy alone	34.8% (17.8) [6]	N/A	N/A	−7.6% (14.6) [8]	8.4% (21.3) [2]
CT alone	46.6% (6.9) [12]	30.1% (22.0) [2]	9.4% (8.3) [1]	−4.4% (16.9) [6]	15.3% (26.1) [3]
IPT alone	52.3% (6.1) [1]	N/A	22.6% (8.4) [1]	13.3% (8.6) [1]	12.3% (8.6) [1]
Marital psychotherapy alone	N/A	N/A	N/A	N/A	N/A
Totals	50.0% (5.3) [29]	26.0% (23.5) [7]	15.7% (13.0) [2]	4.7% (8.5) [21]	14.0% (11.2) [8]

Note. From Depression Guideline Panel (1993b, p. 76).
[a]Intent-to-treat sample.
[b]Adult and geriatric patient studies are combined.
[c]Behavioral therapy includes one cell with behavioral therapy plus placebo (Hersen, Bellack, Himmelhoch et al., 1984).
[d]The numbers in parentheses are the standard deviations of the estimated percentage of responders.
[e]The bracketed numbers are the numbers of cells on which estimates are calculated.

1984; Neimeyer & Feixas, 1990; Neimeyer, Heath, & Strauss, 1985; Neimeyer & Weiss, 1990; O'Leary & Beach, 1990; Pecheur & Edwards, 1984; Ross & Scott, 1985; Rush, Beck, Kovacs, & Hollon, 1977; Rush & Watkins, 1981; Scott & Stradling, 1990 [two trials]; Selmi, Klein, Greist, Sorrell, & Erdman, 1990; Steuer et al., 1984; Thompson, Gallagher, & Breckenridge, 1987; Turner & Wehl, 1984). Nearly all were conducted on outpatients.

Certain pivotal studies (e.g., Blackburn et al., 1981) could not be included in the meta-analysis because the number of patients randomized to each cell was not reported in some cases, while in others, outcome was not reported in a categorical form.

In an analysis using the Confidence Profile Method (CPM; Eddy, Hasselblad, & Schacter, 1990; Hasselblad & Eddy, 1992), the overall efficacy of CT alone in adult outpatients was 46.6% for those studies that could be so evaluated. CT was contrasted to wait list control in two studies. Meta-analysis revealed a response rate favoring CT that was greater than the wait list control by 30%. To illustrate the meaning of this number, say, 100 patients were treated with CT, and roughly 50% responded (see column 1, "Overall Efficacy"). Then, only 20% would respond to the wait list control.

Once again, the standard deviation is large, and the estimate rests on only two studies. The number of pill-placebo comparisons was minimal at the time of this review, but results were suggestive of a differential benefit attributable to CT (see below).

The fourth column in Table 1 indicates that the different therapies are basically equivalent, with no statistically significant differences among them.

If we look carefully at the evidence for the efficacy of acute phase psychotherapy when used alone to attain symptom reduction, the findings to date still remain somewhat controversial, although they may be sufficient for making policy decisions as to which forms of treatment are to be reimbursed (see chapter 29, this volume). The controversy is due largely to a lack of consensus in the field with regard to an adequate control or comparison group for psychotherapy treatment. In efficacy trials of medication, the pill-placebo contrast is highly informative because it has within it all of the conditions of treatment (including side effects if an active but nontherapeutic placebo pill is used) as a contrast treatment. Thus, the act of treatment, the act of taking a pill, time with the treating physician, and presumably even expectations surrounding the treatment are comparable between the pill-placebo and active medication treatment cells.

When it comes to psychotherapy, however, the definition of an adequate "placebo" condition is yet to be arrived at. The definition of such a condition would logically require knowledge as to the effective ingredient(s) within the psychotherapy package itself. However, these "active ingredients" are not yet fully known. In fact, the active ingredients within a particular therapy may differ among and between patients, and even within the same patient over time (see chapter 3, this volume).

Comparison groups that have utilized wait list control comparisons have generally found the therapy to be more effective than the wait list (see Table 1). Thus, providing therapy is better than providing no therapy. However, skeptics argue, and properly so, that those in the wait list condition know that they are not in therapy and are receiving, therefore, none of the nonspecific benefits of regularly seeing a helpful person. One might even wonder if the frustration associated with being on the wait list might not sustain depressive symptoms that would otherwise remit spontaneously.

To address some of these issues, a pill-placebo has been used and suggests efficacy in some studies. However, there are only a few pill-placebo comparisons with psychotherapy (Table 1). Second, even if there is a positive between-group difference favoring psychotherapy over pill-placebo, these findings are still subject to the criticism that those in the pill-placebo group spent less time with the therapist than those in psychotherapy. Thus, while pill-placebo can, in part, control for the act of being in treatment, the treatment conditions are not identical.

Another effort to address this problem has been the attempt by some investigators to compare one form of psychotherapy with another. The notion here is that both treatments are equated for frequency, duration, therapist contact time, and credibility. Therefore, between-group differences, if found, are attributable to the content of the treatment. However, as noted in Table 1, such comparisons generally have had equivalent outcomes, at least in terms of acute phase symptom reduction.

Using these results, skeptics have argued that the psychotherapies may, in fact, all be placebo conditions with no specific efficacy among and between them. Note, however, that such a criticism, if leveled against antidepressant medications, would be illogical since all antidepressant medications are equally effective (Depression Guideline Panel, 1993b, pp. 47–53). However, the latter statement (i.e., that antidepressants are effective) is supported by a credible placebo.

Three studies shed further light on this issue. Mynors-Wallace, Gath, Lloyd-Thomas, and Tomlinson (1995) compared pill-placebo with amitriptyline and with six sessions of problem-solving psychotherapy, which, in part, relied on cognitive principles. The outpatients in this trial were those presenting to their general practitioner in the British health care system for treatment of nonpsychotic major depression. Patients received one of three treatments, all of which were delivered (1) by their general practitioner or by the study psychiatrist and (2) either in the primary-care (PC) setting or at the patients' homes.

Results of this acute phase 12-week trial revealed that both amitriptyline (52%) and the therapy (60%) significantly exceeded the response rate to pill-placebo (27%), and the psychotherapy was as effective as amitriptyline.

An as yet unpublished, but publicly presented, acute phase treatment trial found that CT alone was as effective as phenelzine, and both exceeded the efficacy of pill-placebo in outpatients with nonpsychotic major depressive disorder who also had atypical symptom features (Jarrett et al., 1994; Shaffer et al., 1994).

Both of these studies used a pill-placebo and found that medication exceeded pill-placebo, thereby establishing that the populations were medication-responsive. Further, the psychotherapy exceeded pill-placebo in both studies, and in each case, medication and psychotherapy were equally effective. These results add further to the notion of specific efficacy attributable to these time-limited, depression-targeted treatments. One cannot, however, conclude that the same patients were responding either to the psychotherapy or to the medication. That is, the spectrum of action of these two treatments may be different. Thus, from a policy point of view, both medication and at least these two forms of psychotherapy have clinical benefits. These studies, however, are still subject to the critique that there was no match for therapist exposure between those who received the therapy and those who received medication.

Recently, Schulberg and colleagues (1993), in a study of outpatients with nonpsychotic major depression who were recruited from and treated in PC settings, compared nortriptyline, interpersonal therapy, and treatment as usual. Results of that trial (personal communication) revealed the following remission rates, defined here as having achieved a remission (not just a response): nortriptyline (60%), IPT (38%), and treatment as usual (14%).

Both the psychotherapy and the medication performed at overall efficacy rates that were within the range suggested by the prior meta-analysis shown in Table 20.1. Second, both psychotherapy and medication exceeded the efficacy associated with treatment as usual. (It should be noted that treatment as usual was associated with fewer treatment visits by patients to physicians who may or may not have used medication.)

Thus, while the skeptics may continue to clamor for randomized controlled blinded trials of psychotherapy compared with a more adequate inert comparator treatment, there is certainly an abundance of rather convincing evidence that psychotherapy alone is a rational treatment with substantial benefit for many outpatients with these conditions. The main issue remaining for researchers is to determine to what degree this benefit can be uniquely and specifically attributed to the therapy itself, as contrasted with those features that inherently surround the delivery of the therapy (e.g., interactions with a helping agent).

When we turn to the issue of efficacy for psychotherapy combined with medication (see Table 20.1, last column, and Table 20.2), seven acute phase RCTs compared the combination of formal psychotherapy and medication to one or the other treatment alone in depressed adult outpatients (six studies; Beck et al., 1985; Covi & Lipman, 1987; Hersen, Bellack, Himmelhoch, & Thase, 1984; Murphy et al., 1984; Roth, Bielski, Jones, Parker, & Osborn, 1982; Rush & Watkins, 1981) or inpatients (one study; Bowers, 1990). Meta-analyses reveal that the combination treatment had an overall efficacy, for example, for CT combined with medication of 53.7%, based on a total of five comparisons. For BT combined with medication, the overall efficacy was 34.6% based on two comparisons.

When contrasted with either medication alone or psychotherapy alone, the combination was equivalent to either treatment alone, but the combination was not uniquely advantageous. Perhaps because of patient retention in psychotherapy alone (i.e., patients do not attrit early due to medication side effects), psychotherapy may have some advantages over medication or the combination, particularly in those that are less severely ill (see chapter 2, this volume).

However, when interpreting the combined treatment effects, a word of caution is in order. As noted by Hollon and others, these comparisons rest solely on symptom reduction. The combination treatment may well have a wider domain of effects and, in particular, may result in psychosocial restoration not otherwise attained in as timely a fashion as with medication alone. Furthermore, to date, the total number of trials is small.

It should also be noted that the populations entered into these studies were representative of patients who generally enter efficacy trials for major depression. It

Table 20.2 Meta-Analyses of Combined Treatment in Outpatients with Major Depressive Disorder[a]

Combination[a]	Combination Efficacy	Combination vs. Wait List or Placebo	Combination vs. Therapy[b] Alone	Combination vs. Other Therapy Alone[c]	Combination vs. Drug Alone
BT plus medication	34.6% (10.9)[d] [2][e]	N/A	−7.4% (22.3) [2]	−2.2% (11.5) [1]	6.2% (11.4) [1]
Brief dynamic psychotherapy plus medication	N/A	N/A	N/A	N/A	N/A
CT plus medication	53.7% (17.3) [5]	N/A	6.4% (15.3) [6]	35.4% (9.4) [1]	39.4% (32.9) [2]
IPT plus medication	N/A	N/A	N/A	N/A	N/A

Note. From Depression Guideline Panel (1993b, p. 91).
[a]Intent-to-treat sample.
[b]Therapy contrast is that specified in the combination column (e.g., behavioral therapy).
[c]The combination indicated in the first column was compared to a different form of psychotherapy alone.
[d]Standard deviation is in parentheses.
[e]Number of cells in the meta-analysis is in brackets.

is entirely likely and, indeed, many clinicians believe (Depression Guideline Panel, 1993b) that the combination of medication and psychotherapy may be particularly beneficial to those patients with more chronic/complex and/or long-standing depressions that have resulted in more prolonged, profound, and/or generalized psychosocial disabilities. These types of patients have not constituted the majority of subjects who have entered RCT comparisons of the combination and either treatment alone.

Given, however, the few studies of combined treatment, as well as the lack of an entirely acceptable placebo control contrast for the combination and the limited outcome domains evaluated, particular and differential efficacy cannot be attributed to combination treatment at this time. On the other hand, a role for combined treatment is suggested by clinical consensus and some indirect research evidence (Depression Guideline Panel, 1993b) for the more complex or chronically ill depressed patients, or for those who have partial, yet incomplete, response to one of the two treatments. Some have suggested that sequencing these treatments may be clinically useful (e.g., those who have an incomplete response to medication may then benefit preferentially from the addition of psychotherapy or vice versa). Such a sequenced treatment plan would allow one to determine which patients respond sufficiently to monotherapy (thereby abrogating the need for combined treatment) and whether such a sequence is of utility compared to other treatment packages.

The efficacy of psychotherapy for dysthymic disorder has not been formally tested in RCTs. However, there are a number of case reports and case series (reviewed in chapter 23, this volume) that suggest the promise of efficacy for CT and IPT in dysthymic disorder. More recently, an adaptation of CT has been developed (McCullough, 1991) specifically designed for the chronic depressed/dysthymic patient. Again, this form of therapy, while still in development, has not yet been subjected to randomized controlled comparative blinded outcome studies.

Psychotherapy for bipolar disorder has not generally been the subject of formal RCTs. A major problem with bipolar disorder is adherence to recommended medication procedures. Cochran (1984) found that a cognitive/behavioral approach aimed specifically at improving medication adherence did so in patients with bipolar disorder who were being seen in a lithium medication clinic. More recently, Basco and Rush (1996) have developed an extensive cognitive/behavioral package not only to increase adherence but also to assist patients in early detection of illness episodes, in the management of untoward intercurrent life events, and in anticipatory planning for subsequent life difficulties over the longer term in the management of their bipolar disorder. Others have also developed psychosocial treatment packages designed to be used in combination with medication in patients with bipolar disorder (Goldstein & Miklowitz, 1994; Miklowitz, 1989; Miklowitz & Goldstein, 1990). This family-focused treatment approach is currently the subject of RCTs testing the model and associated manuals. In addition, a group at Cornell is currently testing their psychoeducational marital intervention approach to bipolar disorder (Clarkin & Carpenter, 1995). Presumably, some patients may benefit from these treatments, while others may not require it at all, and still others may participate but not benefit.

Generalizing Efficacy Findings to Practice

In addition to difficulties in interpreting the available efficacy data, an even more major stumbling block is the issue of whether efficacy trial findings generalize to "routine practice" with "real-world" patients treated under "routine" treatment conditions. As noted at the beginning of this chapter, several key parameters distinguish efficacy from effectiveness trials. The key parameters that affect the transfer of this knowledge/technology include kinds of patients, presence of general medical and psychiatric comorbid conditions, other disorder factors (e.g., chronicity), diagnostic and treatment procedures utilized in routine care, and service system factors that mitigate or facilitate the implementation of those procedures.

There is some consensus, albeit with only modest data, that the transfer of positive findings from efficacy studies to routine clinical practice is not predictable. Because of fear of the loss of efficacy in this translation (see chapter 2, this volume), questions regarding generalizability have become paramount.

First, consider the nature of patient populations seen in routine clinical practice or evaluated in effectiveness studies (e.g., their social, educational, cultural, ethnic, and other background differences) in contrast to those patients consenting to randomization in efficacy trials.

Determination of which patient population differences actually affect outcome has yet to be fully studied. It is likely, however, that some population differences do matter. For example, even the personal circumstances of patients, as manifested in their marital relationship, can affect treatment and/or relapse rates. Marital dissatisfaction is associated with higher rates of relapse and recurrence following maintenance IPT (Rounsaville, Weissman, Prusoff, & Herceg-Baron, 1979).

Furthermore, efficacy trials often recruit symptomatic volunteers who are sufficiently well not only to provide written and informed consent, but also to be willing to participate in a trial in which one or more of the "treatments" randomly assigned constitutes an inert intervention, such as wait list control or pill-placebo. Clinical experience suggests that the presence of an inert cell may change the nature of the patient population willing to consent to the trial, thereby reducing the participation of those with more chronic and/or disabling forms of depression or patients who have failed to attain symptom remission with prior treatment trials. This recruiting bias could lead to engaging patients in efficacy trials who have major mood disorders that are more likely to respond not only to the particular intervention, but also to the nonspecific features surrounding any intervention (i.e., the presence of active/inert treatment contrasts in RCTs may understate the benefits of the active treatment), while in practice the disorders treated may be more longstanding and complex.

Second, patients seen in routine practice (i.e., effectiveness trials) often have mood disorders with features that may disqualify them from participation in RCTs (e.g., acute suicidal ideation, chronicity, previous failures to respond to several prior treatments, too little or too great symptom severity). Furthermore, the concurrent and comorbid disorders commonly encountered in practice also preclude admission to efficacy trials (see chapter 2, this volume).

Current comorbid conditions are often associated with reduced treatment responsiveness; individuals also may take longer to respond to treatment than those without concurrent illnesses. For example, comorbid personality disorders, which appear to be more commonly found in patients with major mood disorders in routine practice than in those consenting to RCTs, may reduce or slow the response to cognitive, interpersonal, or other time-limited, targeted psychotherapies alone, as well as to medication (Thompson, Gallagher, & Czirr, 1988). Higher levels of neuroticism have been found to be associated with a poor response to both IPT (Frank, Kupfer, Jacob, & Jarrett, 1987; Prusoff, Weissman, Klerman, & Rounsaville, 1980; Shea et al., 1990; Zuckerman, Prusoff, Weissman, & Padian, 1980), CT (Persons, Burns, & Perloff, 1988) and psychodynamic psychotherapy (Gallagher & Thompson, 1982; Steuer et al., 1984). A better response has been found in those without personality pathology (Pilkonis & Frank, 1988).

Third, the treatment procedures used in clinical practice may so insufficiently approximate the procedures used in RCTs that outcomes differ. For example, clinicians are not routinely trained in those forms of psychotherapy that have demonstrated efficacy in RCTs (Chambless, 1993; see chapter 2, this volume). Furthermore, poorer adherence by psychotherapists to the particulars of manualized psychotherapeutic treatments appears to be related to poorer patient outcomes (e.g., see Frank, Perel, Mallinger, Thase, & Kupfer, 1992; Woody, McLellan, Luborsky, & O'Brien, 1990) in the context of efficacy trials.

As is well known, practitioners in daily practice often flexibly titrate the frequency or change the type of therapy as a result of their overall impression of patient response. That is, therapists modify the types of therapeutic tactics and strategies used, depending on response to prior efforts. This adaptable approach is far more difficult to emulate in the manual-driven psychotherapies that are evaluated in efficacy trials. The greater structure and directiveness inherent in manual-driven psychotherapies might either constitute an indirect benefit or be potentially disadvantageous to those treated in the community.

In routine care, practitioners often use pragmatic approaches—adding therapies and/or medications, utilizing treatments in combination, or even presenting a sequence of treatments to patients, none of which are typically mimicked in RCTs. The presentation, or utilization, of multiple options may either undermine the patient's faith in the efficacy of any one treatment (thereby actually reducing responsiveness), or it may potentially enhance the patient's feeling of collaboration with, and trust in, his or her practitioner.

Yet another important difference between efficacy and effectiveness trials is the diagnostic procedures utilized. Those used in efficacy trials (e.g., structured interviews, two clinical diagnostic interviews) may not be mirrored in routine practice, with the result that diagnostically different patient groups are being treated in efficacy, as opposed to effectiveness, studies (Basco et al., 1996). Clinicians, for example, may incorrectly render a diagnosis of major depression when in fact the correct diagnosis is bipolar I disorder. Whether and to what degree such diagnostic discrepancies ultimately affect outcomes in psychotherapeutic treatment has not been systematically evaluated.

Finally, there is most likely a substantial effect of the service system contingencies under which practitioners and patients interact that so modify the delivery of treatment that "routine practice" entails parameters or contingencies that considerably change the efficacy of the treatment being delivered. For example, in managed-care situations, the total number of therapy sessions may be so severely restricted that even the minimal number of sessions required to obtain a clinical response remain undelivered. For example, the delivery system may so curtail the amount of time allocated to therapy sessions that efficacy is reduced for particular patients. Or there may be no resources available to call and follow up patients who miss appointments in practice, yet in efficacy trials, extensive adherence enhancement procedures may be used.

Research to Bridge the Efficacy/Effectiveness Gap

Given the current status of scientific knowledge, it is unclear whether the benefits of psychotherapy alone or in combination with medication (as assessed in the context of RCTs with major mood disorders) actually generalize to routine practice with representative practitioners and patients. Hollon (see chapter 2, this volume) suggests that there is evidence that they do not. Determining which combination of the above causes might explain this presumed phenomenon represents an area of inquiry in need of immediate systematic study.

A stepwise, sequenced research program that better informs practitioners as to when and how to effectively adapt treatment interventions to the world of routine practice is strongly indicated. Research designs controlling for most parameters that might reduce effectiveness are needed in order to enhance understanding of the impact of one particular variable on outcomes derived from actual practice. For example, if the types and diagnoses of patients were matched to those who enter efficacy trials, then population and disease factors would be identical in these two groups. Then, if differences between the efficacy and this "modified effectiveness" trial resulted, they would be attributable either to the procedures used or to the system factors distinguishing the two conditions. For example, if treatment procedures were also kept identical, then differences in patient outcomes could be attributable to system factors. This kind of research represents a hybrid model, which straddles both formal efficacy and classical effectiveness studies, wherein some selected parameters are tightly controlled (as in efficacy trials), while others are designed to mirror key practice parameters (as in effectiveness trials).

An example of such a study is that undertaken by Mynors-Wallace et al. (1995). Patients were gathered from and were fairly representative of PC practice; however, the treatment interventions were defined by research protocols. While the treatments were delivered by general practitioners guided by a brief therapy manual and with modest research oversight, the details of the clinical procedures used were not representative of routine PC practice but were feasible to be delivered in that setting, while the patients and the providers were representative.

Another "hybrid" study, Schulberg et al. (1993), utilized patients gathered from PC settings, but the procedures used to treat them were defined and delivered by clinical researchers for three of the cells, and by PC providers without any influence from the researchers in the fourth cell (treatment as usual).

Such "hybrid" efficacy/effectiveness research studies are likely to generate some of the most interesting and compelling data, providing for determining, with greater specificity and certainty, which of several key parameters most profoundly affect the transfer of findings from efficacy trials into daily clinical practice (Rush & Prien, 1995).

The challenge for those who review grants is to devise methods or mechanisms by which such hybrid research proposals can be fairly reviewed and successfully funded so that they can be properly conducted. Such hybrid studies may lack appeal to reviewers who are fully committed to efficacy research per se, since to date, internal validity has been the cutting variable by which proposals have been judged. Similarly, such a hybrid may not appeal to committed services researchers for whom external validity and generalizability, in particular, constitute an overriding variable for judging research proposals. When logically considered in the context of the current state of knowledge, however, such hybrid studies are urgently needed and, in fact, have already begun to produce useful and interpretable results.

Conclusions

The majority of published evidence to date is consistent with the notion that psychotherapy, either alone or in combination with medication, appears to have efficacy.

While not a panacea for all patients with major mood disorders, these well-researched psychotherapies would appear to have a clear place in routine clinical practice.

The issues confronting researchers are not whether psychotherapy should be provided but the degree to which it is uniquely beneficial and for whom, which outcome domains are preferentially benefited in routine practice, whether maintenance phase psychotherapies result in sustained recovery and limit relapse or recurrence, and whether further posttreatment benefits ensue once treatment is terminated.

For those concerned with benefit design pertaining to whether to pay for psychotherapy, policy decisions cannot await definitive research but must be made now. In contrast to the dramatic cost of untreated major mood disorders, the modest cost of 20 sessions of psychotherapy is, in fact, a trivial expense. While psychotherapy is not uniformly effective for all depressed individuals, neither is any other currently reimbursed medical procedure. Research evidence is sufficiently strong so that from a clinician's point of view, a trial of psychotherapy is called for in the course of treatment of many patients with mood disorders, either alone or in combination with medication (Depression Guideline Panel, 1993b).

When both research and clinical experience recommend particular forms of psychotherapy, and especially when efficacy is equivalent to that of other accepted forms of treatment for major mood disorders, third-party reimbursement is logically called for. Given the high medical utilization rates of those who are clinically depressed but untreated, and given evidence of improved outcomes and reduced utilization when practice guidelines, which include the use of psychotherapy, are implemented (Katon et al., 1995), costs in the longer run may be revenue-neutral or even reduced, should such reimbursement occur.

Finally, given the present state of research data, additional efficacy and effectiveness trials are clearly needed. However, a most compelling case seems to be made for "hybrid" studies that combine the elements from both classical efficacy and effectiveness studies. Such hybrid studies have the potential of defining which of many different parameters (e.g., patients, practitioners, methods of treatment, types of disorders) reduce or enhance outcomes in representative practice arenas.

Acknowledgments This report was supported in part by the Sarah M. and Charles E. Seay Center for Brain and Applied Research in Psychiatric Illness and by grants from the National Institute of Mental Health (MH-41115, MH-53799). I appreciate the secretarial support of Mr. David Savage and Fast Word, Inc., of Dallas and the administrative support of Kenneth Z. Altshuler, MD, Stanton Sharp Distinguished Chair, Professor and Chairman, Department of Psychiatry, University of Texas Southwestern Medical Center at Dallas.

References

American Psychiatric Association. (1994). *Diagnostic and statistical manual of mental disorders* (4th ed.). Washington, DC: Author.

Basco, M. R., Bostic, J. Q., Davies, D., Rush, A. J., Witte, B., Hendrickse, W. A., & Barnett, V. (1996). *Is there a place for diagnostic interviewing in community mental health settings?*

Basco, M. R., & Rush, A. J. (1996). *Cognitive-behavioral therapy for bipolar disorder.* New York: Guilford Press.

Beck, A. T., Hollon, S. D., Young, J. E., Bedrosian, R. C., & Budenz, D. (1985). Treatment of depression with cognitive therapy and amitriptyline. *Archives of General Psychiatry, 42*(2), 142–148.

Beck, A. T., Rush, A. J., Shaw, B. F., & Emery, G. (1979). *Cognitive therapy of depression.* New York: Guilford Press.

Blackburn, I. M., Bishop, S., Glen, A. I., Whalley, L. J., & Christie, J. E. (1981). The efficacy of cognitive therapy in depression: A treatment trial using cognitive therapy and pharmacotherapy, each alone and in combination. *British Journal of Psychiatry, 139,* 181–189.

Bowers, W. A. (1990). Treatment of depressed inpatients. Cognitive therapy plus medication, relaxation plus medication, and medication alone. *British Journal of Psychiatry, 156,* 73–78.

Chambless, D. (1993). *Task force on promotion and dissemination of psychological procedures.* Report adopted by Division 12 of the American Psychological Association, Washington, DC.

Clarkin, J. F., & Carpenter, D. (1995). *Bipolar disorder: A manual for psychoeducational marital intervention.* Unpublished manuscript.

Cochran, S. D. (1984). Preventing medical noncompliance in the outpatient treatment of bipolar affective disorder. *Journal of Consulting and Clinical Psychology, 52,* 873–878.

Covi, L., & Lipman, R. S. (1987). Cognitive behavioral group psychotherapy combined with imipramine in major depression. *Psychopharmacology Bulletin, 23,* 173–176.

de Jong, R., Treiber, R., & Henrich, G. (1986). Effectiveness of two psychological treatments for inpatients with severe and chronic depressions. *Cognitive Therapy and Research, 10*, 645–663.

Depression Guideline Panel. (1993a). *Clinical practice guideline. Number 5. Depression in primary care: Vol. 1. Detection and diagnosis*. Rockville, MD: Department of Health and Human Services, Public Health Service, Agency for Health Care Policy and Research. AHCPR Publication No. 93-0550.

Depression Guideline Panel. (1993b). *Clinical practice guideline. Number 5. Depression in primary care: Vol. 2. Treatment of major depression*. Rockville, MD: Department of Health and Human Services, Public Health Service, Agency for Health Care Policy and Research. AHCPR Publication No. 93-0551.

Dobson, K. S. (1989). A metaanalysis of the efficacy of cognitive therapy for depression. *Journal of Consulting and Clinical Psychology, 57*, 414–419.

Eddy, D. M., Hasselblad, V., & Schacter, R. (1990). A Bayesian method for synthesizing evidence: The confidence profile method. *International Journal of Technological Assessment of Health Care, 6*, 31–35.

Elkin, I., Shea, T. M., Watkins, J. T., Imber, S. D., Sotsky, S. M., Collins, J. F., Glass, D. R., Pilkonis, P. A., Leber, W. R., Docherty, J. P., et al. (1989). National Institute of Mental Health Treatment of Depression Collaborative Research Program: General effectiveness of treatments. *Archives of General Psychiatry, 46*, 971–982.

Frank, E., Kupfer, D. J., Jacob, M., & Jarrett, D. (1987). Personality features and response to acute treatment in recurrent depression. *Journal of Personality Disorders, 1*, 14–26.

Frank, E., Perel, J. M., Mallinger, A. G., Thase, M. E., & Kupfer, D. J. (1992). Relationship of pharmacologic compliance to long-term prophylaxis in recurrent depression. *Psychopharmacology Bulletin, 28*, 231–235.

Friedman, A. S. (1975). Interaction of drug therapy with marital therapy in depressed patients. *Archives of General Psychiatry, 32*, 619–637.

Gallagher, D. E., & Thompson, L. W. (1982). Treatment of major depressive disorder in older adult outpatients with brief psychotherapies. *Psychotherapy: Theory, Research, and Practice, 19*, 482–490.

Goldstein, M. J., & Miklowitz, D. J. (1994). Family intervention for persons with bipolar disorder. In A. B. Hatfield (Ed.), *Family interventions in mental illness* (pp. 23–35). San Francisco: Jossey-Bass.

Greenberg, P. E., Stiglin, L. E., Finkelstein, S. N., & Berndt, E. R. (1993). The economic burden of depression in 1990. *Journal of Clinical Psychiatry, 51*, 405–418.

Hasselblad, V., & Eddy, D. M. (1992). *FAST*PRO Software for Meta-Analysis by the Confidence Profile Method*. New York: Academic Press.

Hersen, M., Bellack, A. S., Himmelhoch, J. M., & Thase, M. E. (1984). Effects of social skills training, amitriptyline, and psychotherapy in unipolar depressed women. *Behavioral Therapy, 15*, 21–40.

Hogg, J. A., & Deffenbacher, J. L. (1988). A comparison of cognitive and interpersonal-process group therapies in the treatment of depression among college students. *Journal of Counseling Psychology, 35*, 304–310.

Jarrett, R. B., Shaffer, M. H., Down, M. M., Cheng, Q. D., Judd, C., & McIntire, D. (1994). A controlled randomized trial of atypical depression: Study design and patient characteristics. *Biological Psychiatry, 35*, 617.

Katon, W., Von Korff, M., Lin, E., Walker, E., Simon, G. E., Bush, T., Robinson, P., & Russo, J. (1995). Collaborative management to achieve treatment guidelines. Impact on depression in primary care. *Journal of the American Medical Association, 273*, 1026–1031.

Klerman, G. L., DiMascio, A., Weissman, M. M., Prusoff, B., & Paykel, E. S. (1974). Treatment of depression by drugs and psychotherapy. *American Journal of Psychiatry, 131*, 186–191.

Klerman, G. L., Weissman, M. M., Rounsaville, B. J., & Chevron, R. S. (1984). *Interpersonal psychotherapy of depression*. New York: Basic Books.

McCullough, J. F. (1991). Psychotherapy for dysthymia: A naturalistic study of ten patients. *Journal of Nervous and Mental Disorders, 179*, 734–740.

Miklowitz, D. J. (1989). *Manual for behavioral family management with bipolar patients*. Unpublished manuscript.

Miklowitz, D. J., & Goldstein, M. J. (1990). Behavioral family treatment for patients with bipolar affective disorder. *Behavior Modification, 14*, 457–489.

Mintz, J., Mintz, L. I., Arruda, M. J., & Hwang, S. S. (1991). Treatments of depression and the functional capacity to work. *Archives of General Psychiatry, 49*, 761–768.

Murphy, G. E., Simons, A. D., Wetzel, R. D., & Lustman, P. J. (1984). Cognitive therapy and nortriptyline, singly and together, in the treatment of depression. *Archives of General Psychiatry, 41*, 33–41.

Mynors-Wallace, L. M., Gath, D. H., Lloyd-Thomas, A. R., & Tomlinson, D. (1995). Randomized controlled trial comparing problem solving treatment with amitriptyline and placebo for major depression in primary care. *British Medical Journal, 310*, 441–445.

Neimeyer, R. A., & Feixas, G. (1990). The role of homework and skill acquisition in the outcome of group cognitive therapy for depression. *Behavioral Therapy, 21,* 281–292.

Neimeyer, R. A., Heath, A., & Strauss, J. (1985). Personal reconstruction during group cognitive therapy for depression. In F. Epting & A. W. Landfield (Eds.), *Anticipating personal construct psychology* (pp. 180–195). Lincoln, NE: University of Nebraska Press.

Neimeyer, R. A., & Weiss, M. E. (1990). Cognitive and symptomatic predictors of outcome of group therapies for depression. *Journal of Cognitive Psychotherapy, An International Quarterly, 4,* 23–32.

O'Leary, K. D., & Beach, S. R. H. (1990). Marital therapy: A viable treatment for depression and marital discord. *American Journal of Psychiatry, 147,* 183–186.

Pecheur, D. R., & Edwards, K. J. (1984). A comparison of secular and religious versions of cognitive therapy with depressed Christian college students. *Journal of Psychological Theology, 12,* 45–54.

Persons, J. B., Burns, D. D., & Perloff, J. M. (1988). Predictors of dropout and outcome in cognitive therapy for depression in a private practice setting. *Cognitive Therapy Research, 12,* 557–575.

Pilkonis, P. A., & Frank, E. (1988). Personality pathology in recurrent depression: Nature, prevalence, and relationship to treatment response. *American Journal of Psychiatry, 145,* 435–441.

Prusoff, B. A., Weissman, M. M., Klerman, G. L., & Rounsaville, B. J. (1980). Research diagnostic criteria subtypes of depression: Their role as predictors of differential response to psychotherapy and drug treatment. *Archives of General Psychiatry, 37,* 796–801.

Ross, M., & Scott, M. (1985). An evaluation of the effectiveness of individual and group cognitive therapy in the treatment of depressed patients in an inner city health centre. *Journal of Royal General Practice, 35,* 239–242.

Roth, D., Bielski, R., Jones, M., Parker, W., & Osborn, G. (1982). A comparison of self-control therapy and combined self-control therapy and antidepressant medication in the treatment of depression. *Behavioral Therapy, 13,* 133–144.

Rounsaville, B. J., Weissman, M. M., Prusoff, B. A., & Herceg-Baron, R. L. (1979). Marital disputes and treatment outcome in depressed women. *Comprehensive Psychiatry, 20,* 483–490.

Rush, A. J. (1986). Pharmacotherapy and psychotherapy. In L. R. Derogatis (Ed.), *Clinical psychopharmacology* (pp. 46–67). Menlo Park, CA: Addison-Wesley.

Rush, A. J. (1988). Cognitive approaches to adherence. In A. J. Frances & R. E. Hales (Eds.), *American Psychiatric Press Review of Psychiatry* (pp. 627–642). Washington, DC: American Psychiatric Press.

Rush, A. J., Beck, A. T., Kovacs, M., & Hollon, S. D. (1977). Comparative efficacy of cognitive therapy and pharmacotherapy in the treatment of depressed outpatients. *Cognitive Therapy Research, 1,* 17–37.

Rush, A. J., Beck, A. T., Kovacs, M., Khatami, M., Fitzgibbons, R., & Wolman, T. (1975). *Comparison of cognitive and pharmacotherapy in depressed outpatients: A preliminary report.* Paper presented at the Society of Psychotherapy Research, Boston.

Rush, A. J., & Prien, R. (1995). From scientific knowledge to the clinical practice of psychopharmaoclogy: Can the gap be bridged? *Psychopharmacology Bulletin, 31,* 7–20.

Rush, A. J., & Watkins, J. T. (1981). Group versus individual cognitive therapy: A pilot study. *Cognitive Therapy Research, 5,* 95–103.

Schulberg, H. C., Coulehan, J. L., Block, M. R., Lave, J., Rodriguez, E., Scott, C. P., Madonia, M. J., Imber, S., & Perel, J. (1993). Clincial trials of primary care treatments for major depression: Issues in design, recruitment and treatment. *International Journal of Psychiatry in Medicine, 23,* 29–42.

Scott, M. J., & Stradling, S. G. (1990). Group cognitive therapy for depression produces clinically significant reliable change in community-based settings. *Behavioral Psychotherapy, 18,* 1–19.

Selmi, P. M., Klein M. H., Greist, J. H., Sorrell, S. P., & Erdman, H. P. (1990). Computer-administered cognitive-behavioral therapy for depression. *American Journal of Psychiatry, 147,* 51–6.

Shaffer, M. H., Cheng, Q. C., McIntire, D., Eaves, G., Kobes, R., Silver, P., & Jarrett, R. B. (1994). A randomized clinical trial of treatment for atypical depression: Preliminary results. *Biological Psychiatry, 35,* 617.

Shea, M. T., Pilkonis, P. A., Beckham, E., Collins, J. F., Elkin, I., Sotsky, S. M., & Docherty, J. P. (1990). Personality disorders and treatment outcome in the NIMH treatment of depression collaborative research program. *American Journal of Psychiatry, 147*(6), 711–718.

Steuer, J. L., Mintz, J., Hammen, C. L., Hill, M. A., Jarvik, L. F., McCarley, T., Motoike, P., & Rosen, R. (1984). Cognitive-behavioral and psychodynamic group psychotherapy in treatment of geriatric depression. *Journal of Consulting Clinical Psychology, 52*(2), 180–189.

Thompson, L. W., Gallagher, D. E., & Breckenridge, J. S. (1987). Comparative effectiveness of psychotherapies for depressed elders. *Journal of Consulting Clinical Psychology, 55*(3), 385–390.

Thompson, L. W., Gallagher, D., & Czirr, R. (1988). Personality disorder and outcome in the treatment of late-life depression. *Journal of Geriatric Psychiatry, 21*(2), 133–146.

Turner, R. W., & Wehl, C. K. (1984). Treatment of unipolar depression in problem drinkers. *Advances in Behavioral Research Therapy, 6,* 115–125.

Weissman, M. M., & Bothwell, S. (1976). The assessment of social adjustment by patient self-report. *Archives of General Psychiatry, 33,* 1111–1115.

Woody, G. E., McLellan, A. T., Luborsky, L., & O'Brien, C. P. (1990). Psychotherapy and counseling for methodone-maintained opiate addicts. *NIDA Research Monograph Series, 140,* 9–23.

Zuckerman, D. M., Prusoff, B. A., Weissman, M. M., & Padian, N. S. (1980). Personality as a predictor of psychotherapy and pharmacotherapy outcome for depressed outpatients. *Journal of Consulting Clinical Psychology, 48,* 730–735.

21

The Costs of Anxiety Disorders

Implications for Psychosocial Interventions

Stefan G. Hofmann & David H. Barlow

The range of services eventually included in any national health care plan will become smaller and more selective (VandenBos, 1993). Most decisions regarding inclusion of specific health and mental health interventions is likely to be made on the basis of two factors: cost and effectiveness. In this chapter, we will review the current literature on the costs of anxiety disorders and discuss the cost-effectiveness of various interventions, with special reference to the suitability of psychosocial interventions to the managed-care environment. Factors impeding dissemination of these interventions will be reviewed.

Description of Anxiety Disorders

The *Diagnostic and Statistical Manual of Mental Disorders* (*DSM-IV*; American Psychiatric Association [APA], 1994) categorizes anxiety disorders into panic disorder without agoraphobia, panic disorder with agoraphobia, agoraphobia without history of panic disorder, specific phobia, social phobia, obsessive-compulsive disorder (OCD), posttraumatic stress disorder, acute stress disorder, and generalized anxiety disorder (GAD). By definition, anxiety disorders cause significant distress or interference with the patient's life, leading to significant personal costs. In addition, anxiety disorders impose significant direct and indirect costs on the nation in medical resources used for care, treatment, rehabilitation, and reduced or lost productivity. Although anxiety disorders are very common mental illnesses (Kessler et al., 1994; Regier et al., 1988), only a few studies have investigated the financial burden of anxiety disorders on society.

Prevalence of Anxiety Disorders

Results from the National Comorbity Survey (Kessler et al., 1994) indicate that 24.9% of the normal population reported at least one anxiety disorder in their lifetime, and 17.2% during the past 12 months. Anxiety disorders are the second most common *DSM-III-R* disorders after substance use disorders, which have a lifetime prevalence rate of 26.6%. The 12-month prevalence rate was highest for simple phobia (8.8%), followed by social phobia (7.9%), generalized anxiety disorder (3.1%), agoraphobia without panic disorder (2.8%), and panic disorder (2.3%).

Similar data were reported from the Epidemiologic Catchment Area (ECA) survey (Regier et al., 1988). Within the category of anxiety disorders, phobic disorders were most common, followed by OCD and panic disorder. The 6-month prevalence rates (for men and women, respectively) were 5.7% and 11.9% for phobias, 1.3% and 1.7% for OCD, and 0.5% and 1.0% for panic disorder (Leon, Portera, & Weissman, 1995). About 0.6% of men and 1.1% of women reported panic attacks in the past 6 months but did not meet *DSM-III* criteria for panic disorder. Furthermore, data suggest (Leon et al., 1995) that 20% of men and 30% of women with the diagnosis of panic disorder have comorbid major depressive disorder (MDD).

Costs of Anxiety Disorders

Health Care and Related Costs

Despite the high prevalence rate, very few studies have reported the direct and indirect costs of panic disorder, GAD, OCD, specific phobias, social phobias, and acute stress disorder. DuPont, DuPont, and Rice (in press) reported that in 1994, the overall cost of mental disorders in the United States was $204.4 billion. Anxiety disorders were among the most costly mental illnesses ($65 billion). Affective disorders (major depressive disorder, dysthymia, and bipolar disorder) accounted for $41.8 billion, for schizophrenia the cost was $44.9 billion, and for other mental disorders, $52.7 billion (DuPont, DuPont, & Rice, in press). Leon et al. (1995) analyzed data from the National Institute of Mental Health ECA Program. These data suggest that individuals with anxiety disorders (panic disorder, OCD, or phobias) manifest elevated rates of financial dependence (disability payments, welfare, and unemployment compensation), unemployment, substance abuse, and substance dependence compared to those in individuals without anxiety disorders. To take one example, 68% of females and 60% of males with panic disorder were unemployed at the time of the evaluation. In addition, 29% of females and 25% of males patients were chronically unemployed for 5 years. Individuals with anxiety disorders more frequently utilize specialized mental health services, are more likely to seek help in emergency rooms and from primary-care practitioners, and have higher rates of alcohol and drug abuse/dependence than those with no anxiety disorder diagnosis.

A recent study by Simon, Ormel, VonKorff, and Barlow (1995) examined the overall health care costs associated with anxiety disorders and depression among primary-care patients. The authors screened 1,962 primary-care patients in a health maintenance organization and selected a subsample for further diagnostic evaluation to assess for *DSM-III-R* diagnoses of anxiety disorders (panic disorder, agoraphobia, or GAD) and depression (major depressive disorder or dysthymic disorder). Total health care costs were calculated for a 6-month period surrounding the time of the assessment. The results showed that the presence of an anxiety or depressive disorder was associated with costs that were almost twice as high as those for individuals without an anxiety disorder or depression ($2,390 vs. $1,397). This difference persisted even after adjustment for differences in medical comorbidity. The cost of treatment accounted for only 10% of the total costs. The higher cost associated with psychiatric disorders was due to greater utilization of all types of inpatient and outpatient medical services, such as outpatient visits, hospitalizations, supplies, and laboratory. Unfortunately, the authors did not provide further detailed information regarding the distribution of total costs, nor did they differentiate the costs of specific disorders. Similar data were reported by DuPont, Rice, Miller, Shiraki, Rowland, and Harwood (1996) who estimated that in 1990, costs associated with anxiety disorders (panic disorder with and without agoraphobia, social phobia, simple phobia, OCD, and GAD) were $46.6 billion, accounting for 31.5% of total expenditures for m ental illnesses. The authors further reported that less than one-quarter of costs associated with anxiety disorders were for direct medical treatment, whereas lost or reduced productivity contributed to three-quarters of the total costs.

Costs of Specific Anxiety Disorders

The few studies that did differentiate specific anxiety disorders suggest that the indirect costs of panic disorder are particularly high (Johnson, Weissman, & Klerman, 1990; Leon et al., 1995; Markowitz, Weissman, Ouellette, Lish, & Klerman, 1989; Sheehan, Ballenger, & Jacobson, 1980; Siegal, Jones, & Wilson, 1990; Weissman, 1991; Weissman, Klerman, Markowitz, & Ouelette, 1989).

Leon et al. (1995) estimate that 56% of female patients with panic disorder and 63% of male patients seek help for emotional, alcohol-related, or drug-related problems; as high as 33% of male patients and 15% of female patients received disability payments in the 6 months prior to the interview. The highest rates of substance dependence were observed in those patients with panic disorder (with or without MDD) compared to the rates in those diagnosed with OCD and phobias. Weissman (1991) reported that compared to patients with other psychological problems, those with panic disorder manifest the most frequent use of the emergency department for emotional problems. Patients with panic disorder utilize medical treatment facilities seven times more frequently and lose work days two times more often than the general population (Siegal et al., 1990). Sheehan et al. (1980) estimated that in

1980 alone, the United States spent $100 million on health care costs and related employment losses for individuals with panic disorder.

Even those with panic attacks not meeting the full diagnostic criteria for panic disorder (subclinical panic) have been found to manifest substantial disability in perceived physical and emotional health, occupational functioning, and capacity for financial independence (Klerman, Weissman, Ouelette, Johnson, & Greenwald, 1991). Compared to the general population, individuals with subclinical panic are at higher risk for other comorbid mental disorders, particularly MDD, alcohol, and other drug abuse; at higher risk for increased use of health care facilities for emotional problems; and at higher risk for increased use of psychoactive drugs. Those with subclinical panic are intermediate in severity between those who meet full criteria for panic disorder, as well as those with other disorders (MDD, dysthymia, bipolar disorder, OCD, schizophrenia or schizophreniform disorder, somatization disorder, alcohol, other drug abuse, or antisocial disorder), and those with no disorder.

Studies comparing MDD and panic disorder indicated that panic disorder is at least as costly as MDD (Johnson et al., 1990; Markowitz et al., 1989). Panic disorder and MDD are both associated with significantly elevated risks of poor marital functioning, impaired social functioning (e.g., contact with friends and relatives, participating in sports or club activities), financial dependence, seeking professional care (both general medical and psychiatric care), using medications (sleeping pills and antidepressants) and alcohol, visiting emergency rooms, and suicide attempts (Markowitz et al., 1989).

The estimated lifetime rate of suicide attempts in people with uncomplicated panic disorder (i.e., without any other Axis I disorder) is 7%, similar to the rate of suicide attempts in those with uncomplicated major depression (7.9%). These rates are significantly higher than for individuals with no psychiatric disorder (1%; Johnson et al., 1990). Rice and Miller (1995) estimate that affective disorders imposed costs of approximately $20.8 billion in 1985 and $30.4 billion in 1990 in the United States. Considering the similarity of indirect costs of MDD and panic disorder, it is estimated that annual expenditures for anxiety disorders are at least as high.

A recent study from France (Souêtre et al., 1994) examined the impact of comorbid diagnoses on the direct and indirect costs of 1,042 patients with GAD. The comorbid diagnoses included medical diagnoses, such as gastroenterological diagnoses (14.6%), gynecological problems (9.8%), and rheumatological problems (8.6%), and psychiatric diagnoses, such as depression (22.7%), addiction (25.0%), and phobias (16.4%). The estimated total costs for a 3-month period per patient was $1,208 among GAD patients with comorbid diagnoses ($N = 604$) and $733 for patients without comorbid diagnoses ($N = 395$). These costs were mainly due to hospitalizations ($423 among patients with comorbid diagnoses and $158 among patients without comorbid diagnoses), lost productivity ($416 and $243, respectively), and outpatient services ($335 and $308, respectively). Other costs were due to emergency room visits, surgeries, internal medicine, psychiatric care, diagnostic and laboratory tests, and medications.

Cost-Effective Treatments for Anxiety Disorders

Offset Effect

The provision of psychological care for the mentally ill can subsequently reduce the inappropriate use of non-mental-health services and other indirect costs and, consequently, can reduce the overall costs of the disorder. This phenomenon is called *offset effect* (see chapter 11, this volume). A recent study from Spain on psychopharmacological treatment of panic disorder (Salvador-Carulla, Segui, Fernandez-Cano, & Canet, 1995) reported an offset effect of 94% following 12 months of psychopharmacological treatment. Specifically, the total direct costs of health care use during the previous year and the year after the diagnosis were $29,158 and $46,256, respectively, whereas the indirect costs of lost productivity were $65,643 and $13,883, respectively. Thus, not treating a disorder is often substantially more expensive than providing the appropriate treatment. This is particularly true if indirect costs are high, and if treatments are efficacious and cost-effective.

Inpatient Versus Outpatient Settings

Outpatient settings are less expensive than inpatient services, yet outpatient treatment is generally as effective as inpatient treatment for most disorders (Lowman, 1991), and most mental health professionals practice in outpatient settings. Souêtre et al. (1994) estimated that over a 3-month period, the average costs per patient with GAD (with medical or psychiatric comorbid diagnoses) is $423 for hospitalization, $335 for outpatient services, and $43 for medications. As recently as 1992, Keisler estimated that inpatient care consumed 70% of mental health dollars under current service delivery systems. With the advent of managed behavioral health care, however, a drastic restructuring of the delivery of mental health services is under way, based on the premise that these services can be delivered as effectively in the form of brief interventions in an outpatient setting, but at a fraction of the cost of treatment in an inpatient unit.

Psychopharmacological Treatments

In the short term, psychopharmacological treatment is a common, relatively effective form of intervention for anxiety disorders. Frequently prescribed drugs for treating anxiety disorders include benzodiazepines, tricyclic antidepressants, monoamine oxidase inhibitors (MAOIs), beta blockers, and, recently, selective serotonin reuptake inhibitors (SSRIs). However, relapse rates can be high once patients stop taking the drug (e.g., Ballenger et al., 1988; Klosko, Barlow, Tassinari, & Cerny, 1990; Telch, 1988; Telch, Tearnan, & Taylor, 1983; Fyer et al., 1987). In the case of panic disorder, for example, between 35% and 50% of patients relapse after they discontinue antidepressant medication (Michelson & Marchione, 1991), with rates approximating 90% for benzodiazepines (e.g., Fyer et al., 1987). Pharmacotherapy may often result in unpleasant side effects, which are associated with discontinuation on the part of the patient, as well as with patient refusal to begin a new trial of treatment.

Psychosocial Treatments

Clinical research has demonstrated that psychosocial treatments, as practiced in outpatient settings, are clearly effective for a number of mental disorders (e.g., Chambless, 1993). Effective psychosocial interventions exist for OCD (Marks & O'Sullivan, 1988; Riggs & Foa, 1993; Steketee, Foa, & Grayson, 1982); GAD (Barlow, Rapee, & Brown, 1992; Borkovec et al., 1987; Brown, O'Leary, & Barlow, 1993; Butler, Fennell, Robson, & Gelder, 1991; Chambless & Gillis, 1993); panic disorder with and without agoraphobia (Barlow, Craske, Cerny, & Klosko, 1989; Clark et al., 1994; Craske & Barlow, 1993; Mattick, Andrews, Hadzi-Pavlovic, & Christensen, 1990; Öst, 1988; Öst & Westling, 1991; Trull, Nietzel, & Main, 1988); specific phobia (Barlow, 1988; Kazdin & Wilcoxin, 1976); posttraumatic stress disorder (Foa, Rothbaum, Riggs, & Murdock, 1991); and social phobia (Heimberg, Dodge, Hope, Kennedy, & Zollo, 1990; Hope & Heimberg, 1993; Mattick & Peters, 1988). Recent studies suggest that many of these interventions are not only more effective than credible psychosocial placebos, alternative psychosocial treatments, or no treatment, but at least as good as existing pharmacological approaches.

For example, previous studies demonstrated that a psychosocial treatment for panic disorder was superior to either the wait list condition, drug-placebo, or alprazolam in terms of percentage of patients who were panic-free immediately following treatment (Brown & Barlow, 1995; Klosko et al., 1990). The psychosocial treatment used, panic control treatment (PCT; Barlow & Craske, 1994; Barlow et al., 1989), concentrates on exposing patients with panic disorder to the cluster of interoceptive sensations that remind them of their panic attacks. The therapist attempts to create "mini" panic attacks in the office, by having patients exercise to elevate their heart rate, or by having them breathe through a thin straw in order to create smothering sensations. Patients also receive cognitive therapy. Attitudes and perceptions concerning fear of the subjectively dangerous, but objectively harmless, sensations are identified, challenged, and modified. In addition to interoceptive exposure and cognitive therapy, patients are also provided with simple techniques to help manage their anxiety and reduce excess arousal.

In intent-to-treat analyses, approximately 80% of patients undergoing this kind of treatment were panic-free following approximately 12 weekly sessions, compared to 40% of patients receiving applied relaxation, and 30–35% of patients from the wait list. Moreover, these effects were maintained at a 2-year follow-up (Craske, Brown, & Barlow, 1991). Study of a very similar treatment approach developed in England by Clark and colleagues (e.g., Clark et al., 1994) revealed that in eliminating panic attacks, brief cognitive behavioral intervention was initially as effective as imipramine by completion of treatment. Moreover, the effectiveness of the psychosocial intervention was retained at 15-month follow-up, wheras the effects of imipramine diminished rapidly following discontinuation.

Combination Treatments

A multicenter comparative treatment outcome study of panic disorder, now nearing completion, was begun in 1990 (principal investigators: M. Katherine Shear at the University of Pittsburgh, Jack M. Gorman at Columbia University, Scott Woods at Yale University, and David H. Barlow at Albany). This randomized controlled clinical trial was designed to determine the comparative efficacy of medication (imipramine or placebo), psychosocial intervention (PCT), and their combination, in the treatment of panic disorder. The hypothesis is that the active treatments in combination (imipramine plus psychosocial treatment) will produce a better effect than either treatment offered in isolation. A total of 480 panic disorder patients with no more than mild agoraphobia are being randomly assigned to one of five treatment conditions: psychosocial treatment (PCT) alone, imipramine alone, pill-placebo alone, a combination of PCT and pill-placebo, and a combination of PCT and imipramine. Each treatment condition consists of a 3-month acute treatment phase and a 6-month maintenance phase. Preliminary results from this study suggest the superior efficacy of combination treatment.

Previous studies have indicated that psychosocial treatments for panic disorder with agoraphobia, such as exposure in vivo, combine well with tricyclic antidepressants (e.g., Mavissakalian, Michelson, & Dealy, 1983; Telch, Agras, Taylor, Roth, & Gallen, 1985), and it is anticipated, though not systematically established, that these results will hold for the SSRIs. For example, results indicate that not only does imipramine enhance the effects of exposure-based psychosocial treatment, but psychosocial treatments in their own right enhance the effects of imipramine. Even when imipramine is discontinued, the effects of psychosocial intervention are maintained at follow-up when the treatment is delivered in a structured manner (Barlow, 1988; Mavissakalian, 1993).

On the other hand, there is some evidence that high-potency benzodiazepines (e.g., alprazolam) may interfere with the effects of exposure treatments over the long term. Whereas initial improvement was approximately equal following cognitive behavioral treatment with or without high-potency benzodiazepines, at follow-up subjects who had received drugs showed substantial relapse (Marks et al., 1993). Additional findings suggest that benzodiazepines may interfere with the effects of PCT (Brown & Barlow, 1995). These findings are consistent with results from animal laboratories indicating that benzodiazepines may interfere with the types of learning that are most powerfully accessed in the context of psychosocial treatment procedures (Barlow, 1988; Wardle, 1990).

Important results on drug-psychosocial comparisons have been reported from a large collaborative study on the treatment of social phobia, carried out under the direction of Richard Heimberg at the University of Albany and Michael Liebowitz at the New York State Psychiatric Institute (e.g., Heimberg, 1993). In this study, cognitive behavioral group treatment was compared with phenelzine, an MAOI. Preliminary results show that psychosocial and psychopharmacological interventions are strong treatments of approximately equal effectiveness. Both are significantly more effective than either a drug-placebo or a credible educational support treatment (a psychosocial placebo). Preliminary follow-up data show continuing comparability. However, again, when medication is discontinued, individuals begin to relapse, whereas psychosocial treatment retains its effectiveness well beyond discontinuation. This result is similar to the findings reported by Clark et al. (1994) that demonstrate a continuation of effect for psychotherapy.

Another relatively unexplored strategy for combining drug and psychosocial treatments was studied by Otto, Pollack, Ball, and Rosenbaum (1993), as well as by Spiegel, Bruce, Gregg, and Nuzzarello (1994). Otto et al. showed that in individuals unable to discontinue, psychosocial treatments can be very effective in helping clients to discontinue high-potency benzodiazepines, such as alprazolam or clonazepam. Spiegel et al. assigned patients treated with alprazolam to either supportive drug maintenance with slow drug taper or a combination of drug maintenance treatment plus cognitive behavioral treatment. Results showed no group differences in the rate of alprazolam discontinuation; 80% of subjects in the alprazolam-only group and 90% of patients in the combined treatment group discontinued alprazolam. However, at 6-month follow-up, 50% of patients in the alprazolam-only condition, but none of those who had received combined treatments, had relapsed and resumed alprazolam treatment. These studies indicate that in cases where immediate relief from panic and anxiety is necessary, a high-potency benzodiazepine may be initiated, but with a firm contract to discontinue its use shortly after beginning a psychosocial treatment. These data again emphasize the importance of considering additional variables, including the clinical course of the disorder once treatment is terminated, treatment compliance, and tolerance to the intervention, when evaluating the cost-effectiveness of any intervention.

Cost-Effectiveness of Psychosocial and Psychopharmacological Treatments

In summary, there is a significant body of evidence pertaining to the effectiveness of psychosocial interventions and, in particular, of cognitive behavioral treatments, across anxiety disorders (e.g., panic disorder with or without agoraphobia, social phobia). To take one example, a meta-analysis of 43 controlled treatment outcome studies of panic disorder with or without agoraphobia showed that psychosocial treatment yielded the largest effect sizes and the smallest attrition rates relative to pharmacotherapy and combined treatment (Gould et al., 1995). The hypothesis that all psychotherapies are of equal effectiveness (the "myth of therapy outcome uniformity"; Kiesler, 1966), with "placebo" factors constituting the mechanism of action, is no longer viable for the majority of anxiety disorders, and it hampers the development of sound treatment and research programs (Beutler, 1995; Norcross, 1995).

It is likely that these psychosocial treatments for anxiety disorders will prove cost-effective, although data are only beginning to appear. For example, Gould et al. (1995) in Boston have estimated monthly costs for a typical course of psychosocial and pharmacological treatment for panic disorder with agoraphobia. They estimated the cost of individual psychosocial sessions of cognitive behavioral therapy (CBT) at $90 per session, group sessions at $40 a session, and a 20- to 30-minute pharmacological management and CBT booster session at $60 per session. The cost of medications—generic versions of alprazolam, imipramine, and branded fluoxetine (Prozac)—in the Boston area were also computed. CBT as administered in Gould et al.'s setting (Massachusetts General Hospital, or MGH) incorporates 12 sessions spread over 3 months, but costs were computed on the basis of 15 sessions, a number that corresponds more closely to that in other programs described in the literature. They also computed the cost of one booster session during the first year of treatment and four during the second year (see Table 21.1).

The cost of drug treatments was based on treatment programs at MGH, where sessions were scheduled twice during the first month and monthly for the first 3 months thereafter and then progress from every other month to every third month by the end of the first year. Treatment then continued for a total of 2 years. Dosages of medication reflected common dosages in drug trials (Pollack et al., 1993). Results are presented in Table 21.1. Lowest costs at the end of 2 years were associated with group cognitive-behavioral therapy ($600) and generic imipramine ($912). Gould et al. conclude that since CBT has approximately the same efficacy as imipramine with a significantly higher rate of retention of patients, the group psychosocial treatment appears to be the most cost-effective treatment.

Despite the impressive results of studies on the effectiveness of psychosocial interventions, when outpatient treatment is considered pharmacological approaches typically receive priority in clinical practice plans, often to the exclusion of psychosocial approaches. As detailed below, the reason why certain psychosocial treatments are still not completely accepted is not effectiveness. Rather, the problem is related to public relations, treatment accessibility, and absence of dissemination and technology.

The Problem of Accessibility and Dissemination of Effective Psychosocial Treatments

Given the consistent findings on the effectiveness of psychosocial treatments across the anxiety disorders, why is it that policymakers have all but ignored these data and, in some instances, downplayed the importance of psychosocial treatments? One major problem seems to be accessibility. Most psychosocial interventions are simply not available to the majority of individuals who would benefit from them. Many individuals suffering from these problems are not even aware that effective psychosocial treatment exists and therefore do not request these interventions.

In the case of phobic disorders, for example, psychotherapists from many theoretical persuasions have concluded that structured, exposure-based exercises appear to be a necessary part of effective treatment, and subsequent evidence has borne out this conclusion (Barlow, 1988). Nevertheless, as indicated in Table 21.2, three recent surveys report that a large percentage of phobic individuals in three major cities are receiving counseling, hospitalization, or medication, but only 15–38% are being treated with effective psychosocial interventions (Breier, Charney, & Heninger, 1986; Goisman et al., 1993; Taylor et al., 1989).

Moreover, national probability samples indicate that only three out of four individuals with panic disorder are receiving any treatment at all, let alone an

Table 21.1 Cost of Different Modalities of Treatment Over a 2-Year Period

Treatment Modality	Months of Treatment 1	2	3	4	5	6	7	8	9	10	12	24
Cognitive-behavior therapy (CBT)												
CBT sessions per month	4	4	2	2	1	1	0	1	0	0		
Cumulative number of sessions	4	8	10	12	13	14	14	15	15	15	15(16)	15(20)
Cumulative CBT sessions cost	360	720	900	1080	1170	1260	1260	1350	1350	1350	1350	1350
Individual with 30 min. booster session every 3 months											1410	1650
Cumulative group tx. session cost	160	320	400	480	520	560	560	600	600	600	600	600
Group with 30 min. booster session every 3 months											660	840
Pharmacotherapy												
Sessions per month	2	1	1	1	0	1	0	1	0	1		
Cumulative number of sessions	2	3	4	5	5	6	6	7	7	8	8	12
Cumulative session cost	120	180	240	300	300	360	360	420	420	480	480	720
Medication costs												
2.5 mg alprazolam	45	90	135	180	225	270	315	360	405	450	540	1080
6 mg alprazolam	108	216	324	432	540	648	756	864	972	1080	1296	2592
150 mg imipramine	8	16	24	32	40	48	56	64	72	80	96	192
20 mg fluoxetine	116	232	348	464	580	696	812	928	1044	1160	1392	2784
Total cumulative pharmacotherapy costs												
2.5 mg alprazolam	165	270	375	**480**	525	630	675	780	825	930	1020	**1800**
6 mg alprazolam	**228**	396	564	732	840	1008	1116	1284	**1392**	1560	1776	3312
150 mg imipramine	128	196	264	332	340	408	416	484	492	560	576	**912**
20 mg fluoxetine	**236**	412	588	764	880	1056	1172	1348	**1464**	1640	1872	3504

Note. Bold numbers signify costs that exceed group CBT and bold and underscored numbers signify those costs that exceed individual CBT.

From "A Meta-Analysis of Treatment Outcome for Panic Disorder," by R. A. Gould, M. W. Otto, and M. H. Pollack, 1995, *Clinical Psychology Review, 15,* p. 841. Copyright 1995 by Elsevier Science Ltd.

Table 21.2 Utilization of Effective Psychosocial Treatments in Cases of Panic and Phobic Disorders

Study	Sample size	Percentage Receiving Effective Psychosocial Treatment
Taylor et al. (1989)	794	15 (Counseling and hospitalization: 50%)
Breier et al. (1986)	60	16
Goisman et al. (1993)	231	38 (Medication: 93%)

Note. Adapted from "Psychological Interventions in the Era of Managed Competition," by D. H. Barlow, 1994, *Clinical Psychology: Science and Practice, 1,* p. 119. Copyright 1994 by the American Psychological Association, D12.

effective one (National Institute of Mental Health, 1991). One possible reason for this state of affairs is that at least some of these psychosocial treatments require skilled administration only available at present from specifically trained mental health professionals.

Disseminating effective psychosocial treatments to the numerous mental health professionals in practice is a challenge we have barely begun to face. As Beutler, Williams, and Wakefield (1993) suggest, it cannot be assumed that new treatments will be disseminated through professional journals. Vehicles for effective dissemination may include, for example, promotion of the development of clinical competence to practice new procedures via continuing education programs that combine structured didactic learning with supervised clinical work. These programs are just beginning. Educating third-party payers and the public at large about the health benefits and effectiveness of psychotherapy should also contribute to dissemination. When psychosocial treatments are better disseminated, more comprehensive analyses of the costs of delivering these treatments in the clinical settings where they are to be offered will be possible.

Conclusions

Anxiety disorders are prevalent and costly. Based on tightly controlled efficacy studies, a number of psychosocial interventions have been shown to be efficacious for treating a range of anxiety disorders. In most cases, these interventions are more effective than credible alternative psychosocial interventions and thereby rule out "nonspecific" or "common" factors as the principal mechanism of action (Barlow, 1994; Nathan & Gorman, 1998; Roth & Fonagy, 1995; Seligman, 1994). While it is likely that these interventions will prove to be cost-effective in terms of both cost offset and a reduction of the direct and indirect costs associated with anxiety disorders, such data are lacking. Furthermore, we still know little about the "clinical utility" of these approaches (American Pyschological Association [APA], 1995) or about their "effectiveness," which refers to the generality of the effects of these interventions across clients, therapists, and settings.

Additionally, the feasibility of these interventions in the clinical settings in which they are offered has yet to be analyzed in any depth, although preliminary results on generalizability and feasibility look promising (Barlow, in press a, in press b). Limitations in generalizing from tightly controlled "efficacy" studies to clinical practice settings have been described in some detail elsewhere (APA, 1995; Barlow, Hayes, & Nelson, 1994; Hayes, Barlow, & Nelson-Gray, in press; see chapter 3, this volume), and studies of cost-effectiveness are most likely associated with services research focusing on the clinical utility of effective interventions. Once again, most of these data have yet to be developed.

One process that should make substantial contributions to data of this type, including data on cost-effectiveness, is the creation of practice research networks such as those recently constituted by the American Psychiatric Association, as well as those under consideration by the American Psychological Association. In these practice research networks, practitioners working in the front lines of mental health service delivery agree to have their practices closely monitored in terms of patients seen, interventions made, and outcomes delivered, so that interventions and their cost can be closely monitored and evaluated (e.g., APA, 1993). These data can then be related to local issues relevant to particular practice settings. Successful adaptations of intervention procedures with proven efficacy, adopted by practitioners in settings in which they practice, could also be noted. Successful innovations could then be evaluated in clinical research centers and communicated widely to other practitioners. In this way, practitioners acting as local scientists can contribute substantially to the production of important data on clinical utility, fulfilling a goal articulated previously (Barlow et al., 1984). It is also likely that these data will be persuasive to those engaged in creating mental health policy, who must decide on appropriate strategies for delivering cost-effective care to those most in need.

References

American Psychiatric Association Guidelines Steering Committee and the Office of Research. (1993). *Development of a psychiatric practice research network: Overview of the purpose and a proposed approach*. Unpublished manuscript.

American Psychiatric Association. (1987). *Diagnostic and statistical manual for mental disorders* (3rd, rev. ed.). Washington, DC: Author.

American Psychiatric Association. (1994). *Diagnostic and statistical manual for mental disorders* (4th ed.). Washington, DC: Author.

American Psychological Association, Task Force on Psychological Intervention Guidelines. (1995, February). *Template for developing guidelines: Interventions for mental disorders and psychosocial aspects of physical disorders*. Washington, DC: American Psychological Association.

Ballenger, J. C., Burrows, G., DuPont, R., Lesser, I., Noyes, R., Pecknold, J., Riskin, A., & Swinson, R. (1988). Alprazolam in panic disorder and agoraphobia: Results from a multi center trial: 1. Efficacy in short term treatment. *Archives of General Psychiatry, 45*, 413–422

Barlow, D. H. (1988). *Anxiety and its disorders: The nature and treatment of anxiety disorder.* New York: Guilford.

Barlow, D. H. (1994). Psychological interventions in the era of managed competition. *Clinical Psychological Science and Practice, 1*, 109–122.

Barlow, D. H. (in press a). The effectiveness of psychotherapy: Science and policy. *Clinical Psychology: Science and Practice.*

Barlow, D. H. (in press b). Health care policy, psychotherapy research, and the future of psychotherapy. *American Psychologist.*

Barlow, D. H., & Craske, M. G. (1994). *Mastery of your anxiety and panic II.* Albany, NY: Graywind.

Barlow, D. H., Craske, M. G., Cerny, J. A., & Klosko, J. S. (1989). Behavioral treatment of panic disorder. *Behavior Therapy, 20*, 261–282.

Barlow, D. H., Hayes, S. C., & Nelson, R. O. (1984). *The scientist-practitioner: Research and accountability in clinical and educational settings.* New York: Pergamon Press.

Barlow, D. H., Rapee, R. M., & Brown, T. A. (1992). Behavioral treatment of generalized anxiety disorder. *Behavior Therapy, 23*, 551–570.

Beutler, L. E. (1995). The germ theory myth and the myth of outcome homogeneity. *Psychotherapy, 32*, 489–494.

Beutler, L. E., Williams, R. E., & Wakefield, P. J. (1993). Obstacles to disseminating applied psychological science. *Applied and Preventive Psychology, 2*, 53–58.

Borkovec, T. D., Mathews, A. M., Chambers, A., Ebrahimi, S., Lytle, R., & Nelson, R. (1987). The effects of relaxation training with cognitive or nondirective therapy and the role of relaxation-induced anxiety in the treatment of generalized anxiety. *Journal of Consulting and Clinical Psychology, 59*, 883–888.

Breier, A., Charney, D. S., & Heninger, G. R. (1986). Agoraphobia with panic attacks: Development, diagnostic stability, and course of illness. *Archives of General Psychiatry, 43*, 1029–1036.

Brown, T. A., & Barlow, D. H. (1995). Long-term outcome of cognitive-behavioral treatment of panic disorder: Clinical predictors and alternative strategies for assessment. *Journal of Clinical and Consulting Psychology, 63*, 754–765.

Brown, T. A., O'Leary, T. A., & Barlow, D. H. (1993). Generalized anxiety disorder. In D. H. Barlow (Ed.), *Clinical handbook of psychological disorders* (pp. 137–188). New York: Guilford.

Butler, G., Fennell, M., Robson, P., & Gelder, M. (1991). Comparison of behavior therapy and cognitive behavior therapy in the treatment of generalized anxiety disorder. *Journal of Consulting and Clinical Psychology, 59*, 167–175.

Chambless, D. L. (1993). *Report of Division 12 Presidential Task Force on Promotion and Dissemination of Psychological Procedures.* American Psychological Association. Unpublished manuscript.

Chambless, D. L., & Gillis, M. M. (1993). Cognitive therapy of anxiety disorders. *Journal of Consulting and Clinical Psychology, 61*, 248–260.

Clark, D. M., Salkovskis, P. M., Hackman, A., Middleton, H., Anastasiades, P., & Gelder, M. (1994). A comparison of cognitive therapy, applied relaxation, and imipramine in the treatment of panic disorder. *British Journal of Psychiatry, 164*, 759–769.

Craske, M. G., & Barlow, D. H. (1993). Panic disorder and agoraphobia. In D. H. Barlow (Ed.), *Clinical handbook of psychological disorders* (pp. 1–47). New York: Guilford.

Craske, M. G., Brown, T. A., & Barlow, D. H. (1991). Behavioral treatment of panic disorder: A two-year follow-up. *Behavior Therapy, 22*, 289–304.

DuPont, R. L., Rice, D. P., Miller, L. S., Shiraki, S. S., Rowland, C. R., & Harwood, H. J. (1996). Economic costs of anxiety disorders. *Anxiety, 2*, 167–172.

DuPont, R. L., DuPont, C. M., & Rice, D. R. (in press). The economic costs of anxiety disorders. In D. J. Stein & E. Hollander (Eds.), *Textbook for Anxiety Disorders.* Washington, DC: American Psychiatric Press, Inc.

Foa, E. B., Rothbaum, B. O., Riggs, D. S., & Murdock, T. B. (1991). Treatment of posttraumatic stress disorder in rape victims: A comparison between cognitive-behavioral procedures and counseling. *Journal of Consulting and Clinical Psychology, 59*, 715–723.

Fyer, A., Liebowitz, M., Gorman, J., Compeas, R., Levin, A., Davies, S., Goetz, D., & Klein, D. (1987). Discontinuation of alprazolam in treatment in panic patients. *American Journal of Psychiatry, 144*, 303–308

Goisman, R. M., Rogers, M. P., Steketee, G. S., Warshaw, M. G., Cuneo, P., & Keller, M. B. (1993). Utilization of behavioral methods in a multi center anxiety disorders study. *Journal of Clinical Psychiatry, 54*, 213–218.

Gould, R. A., Otto, M. W., & Pollack, M. H. (1995). A meta-analysis of treatment outcome for panic disorder. *Clinical Psychology Review, 15*, 810–844.

Hayes, S. C., Barlow, D. H., & Nelson, R. O. (in press). *The scientist-practitioner: Research and accountability in clinical and educational settings* (2nd ed.). New York: Allyn & Bacon.

Heimberg, R. G. (1993, March). *Psychosocial treatment of social phobia.* Paper presented as part of the symposium entitled "Advances in Social Phobia" at the Annual Meeting of the Anxiety Disorders Association of America, Charleston, SC.

Heimberg, R. G., Dodge, C. S., Hope, D. A., Kennedy, C. R., & Zollo, L. J. (1990). Cognitive behavioral group treatment for social phobia: Comparison with a credible placebo control. *Cognitive Therapy and Research, 14*, 1–23.

Hope, D. A., & Heimberg, R. G. (1993). Social phobia and social anxiety. In D. H. Barlow (Ed.), *Clinical handbook of psychological disorders* (pp. 99–136). New York: Guilford.

Johnson, J., Weissman, M. M., & Klerman, G. L. (1990). Panic disorder, comorbidity, and suicide attempts. *Archives of General Psychiatry, 47*, 805–808.

Kazdin, A. E., & Wilcoxin, L. A. (1976). Systematic desensitization and nonspecific treatment effects: A methodological evaluation. *Psychological Bulletin, 83*, 729–758.

Keisler, C. A. (1992). U.S. mental health policy: Doomed to fail. *American Psychologist, 47*, 1077–1082.

Kessler, R. C., McGonagle, K. A., Shanyang, Z., Nelson, C. B., Hughes, M., Eshleman, S., Wittchen, H.-U., & Kendler, K. S. (1994). Lifetime and 12-month prevalence of DSM-III-R psychiatric disorders in the United States. *Archives of General Psychiatry, 51*, 8–19.

Kiesler, D. J. (1966). Some myths of psychotherapy research and the search for a paradigm. *Psychological Bulletin, 65*, 110–136.

Klerman, G. L., Weissman, M. M., Ouellette, R., Johnson, J., & Greenwald, S. (1991). Panic attacks in the community. Social morbidity and health care utilization. *Journal of the American Medical Association, 265*, 742–746.

Klosko, J. S., Barlow, D. H., Tassinari, R., & Cerny, J. A. (1990). A comparison of alprazolam and cognitive-behavior therapy in treatment of panic disorder. *Journal of Clinical and Consulting Psychology, 58*, 77–84.

Leon, A. C., Portera, L., & Weissman, M. L. (1995). The social costs of anxiety disorders. *British Journal of Psychiatry, 116 (Suppl. 27)*, 19–22.

Lowman, R. L. (1991). Mental health claims experience: Analysis and benefit redesign. *Professional Psychology: Research and Practice, 22*, 36–44.

Markowitz, J. S., Weissman, M. M., Ouellette, R., Lish, J. D., & Klerman, G. L. (1989). Quality of life in panic disorder. *Archives of General Psychiatry, 46*, 984–992.

Marks, I. M., & O'Sullivan, G. (1988). Drugs and psychological treatments for agoraphobia/panic and obsessive-compulsive disorders: A review. *British Journal of Psychiatry, 153*, 650–658.

Marks, I. M., Swinson, R. P., Basoglu, M., Kuch, K., Noshirvani, H., O'Sullivan, G., Lelliott, P. T., Kirby, M., McNamee, G., Sengun, S., & Wickwire, K. (1993). Alprazolam and exposure alone and combined in panic disorder with agoraphobia: A controlled study in London and Toronto. *British Journal of Psychiatry, 162*, 776–787.

Mattick, R. P., Andrews, G., Hadzi-Pavlovic, D., & Christensen, H. (1990). Treatment of panic and agoraphobia: An integrative review. *Journal of Nervous and Mental Disease, 178*, 567–576.

Mattick, R. P., & Peters, L. (1988). Treatment of severe social phobia: Effects of guided exposure with and without cognitive restructuring. *Journal of Consulting and Clinical Psychology, 56*, 251–260.

Mavissakalian, M. G. (1993). Combined behavioral and pharmacological treatment of anxiety disorders. In J. M. Oldham, M. B. Riba, & A. Tasman (Eds.), *Review of psychiatry* (Vol. 12) (pp. 565–584). Washington, DC: American Psychiatric Press.

Mavissakalian, M. G., Michelson, L., & Dealy, R. S. (1983). Pharmacological treatment of agoraphobia: Imipramine versus imipramine with programmed practice. *British Journal of Psychiatry, 143*, 348–355.

Michelson, L. K., & Marchione, K. (1991). Behavioral, cognitive, and pharmacological treatments of panic disorder with agoraphobia: Critique and synthesis. *Journal of Consulting and Clinical Psychology, 59*, 100–114.

Nathan, P. E., & Gorman, J. M. (Eds.). (1998). *A guide to treatments that work.*. New York: Oxford University Press.

National Institute of Mental Health. (1991, September). *Treatment of Panic Disorder. NIH Consensus Development Conference Consensus Statement*, 9(2). (Available from the U.S. Department of Health and Human Services. National Institutes of Health. Public Health Service. Office of Medical Applications of Research. Federal Building, Room 618, Bethesda, MD 20892.)

Norcross, J. C. (1995). Dispelling the dodo bird verdict and the exclusivity myth in psychotherapy. *Psychotherapy*, 32, 500–504.

Öst, L.-G. (1988). Applied relaxation vs. progressive relaxation in the treatment of panic disorder. *Behaviour Research and Therapy*, 26, 13–22.

Öst, L.-G., & Westling, B. E. (1991). *Treatment of panic disorder by applied relaxation versus cognitive therapy.* Paper presented at the meeting of the European Association of Behaviour Therapy, Oslo.

Otto, M. W., Pollack, M. H., Ball, S. G., & Rosenbaum, J. F. (1993). Integration of behavioral and pharmacological treatments for panic disorder: Implications for the treatment of substance dependence. In L. S. Onken & J. D. Blaine (Eds.), Integrating behavioral therapies with medications in the treatment of drug dependence (pp. 143–166). NIDA Research Monograph 150. (NIH Publication No. 95-3899). Washington, DC: Government Printing Office.

Pollack, M. H., Otto, M. W., Tesar, G. E., Cohen, L. S., Meltzer-Brody, S., & Rosenbaum, J. F. (1993). Long-term outcome after acute treatment with clonazepam and alprazolam for panic disorder. *Journal of Clinical Psychopharmacology*, 13, 257–263.

Regier, D. A., Boyd, J. H., Burke, J. D., Rae, D. S., Myers, J. K., Kramer, M., Robins, L. N., George, L. K., Karno, M., Locke, & B. Z. (1988). One-month prevalence of mental disorders in the united states. *Archives of General Psychiatry*, 45, 977–986.

Rice, D. P., & Miller, L. S. (1995). The economic burden of affective disorders. *British Journal of Psychiatry*, 116 *(Suppl. 27)*, 34–42.

Riggs, D. S., & Foa, E. B. (1993). Obsessive compulsive disorder. In D. H. Barlow (Ed.), *Clinical handbook of psychological disorders* (pp. 189–239). New York: Guilford.

Roth, A., & Fonagy, P. (1995, February). *National health service report on research on the efficacy and effectiveness of the psychotherapies.* (Available from the National Health Service, Department of Health, Wellington House 135–155 Waterloo Road, London SE1 8UG, Great Britain.)

Salvador-Carulla, L., Segui, J., Fernandez-Cano, P., & Canet, J. (1995). Costs and offset effect in panic disorder. *British Journal of Psychiatry*, 116 *(Suppl. 27)*, 23–28.

Seligman, M. E. P. (1994). *What you can change and what you can't.* New York: Knopf.

Sheehan, D. V., Ballenger, J., & Jacobson, G. (1980). Treatment of enogenous anxiety with phobic, hysterical and hypochondriacal symptoms. *Archives of General Psychiatry*, 37, 51–59.

Siegal, L., Jones, W. C., & Wilson, J. O. (1990). Economic and life consequences experienced by a group of individuals with panic disorder. *Journal of Anxiety Disorders*, 4, 201–211.

Simon, G., Ormel, J., VonKorff, M., & Barlow, W. (1995). Health care costs associated with depressive and anxiety disorders in primary care. *American Journal of Psychiatry*, 152, 352–357.

Souêtre, E., Lozet, H., Cimarosti, I., Martin, P., Chignon, J. M., Adès, J., Tignol, J., & Darcourt, G. (1994). Cost of anxiety disorders: Impact of comorbidity. *Journal of Psychosomatic Research*, 38, 151–160.

Spiegel, D. A., Bruce, T. J., Gregg, S. F., & Nuzzarello, A. (1994). Does cognitive behavior therapy assist slow-taper alprazolam discontinuation in panic disorder? *American Journal of Psychiatry*, 151, 876–881.

Steketee, G., Foa, E. B., & Grayson, J. B. (1982). Recent advances in the behavioral treatment of obsessive-compulsives. *Archives of General Psychiatry*, 39, 1365–1371.

Taylor, C. B., King, R., Margraf, J., et al. (1989). Use of medication and in vivo exposure in volunteers for panic disorder research. *American Journal of Psychiatry*, 146, 1423–1426.

Telch, M. J. (1988). Combined pharmacological and psychological treatments of panic sufferers. In S. Rachman & J. D. Maser (Eds.), *Panic: Psychological perspectives.* Hillsdale, NJ: Erlbaum.

Telch, M. J., Agras, W. S., Taylor, C. B., Roth, W. T. & Gallen, C. C. (1985). Combined pharmacological and behavioral treatment for agoraphobia. *Behaviour Research and Therapy*, 23, 325–335.

Telch, M. J., Tearnan, B. H., & Taylor, C. B. (1983). Antidepressant medication in the treatment of agoraphobia: A critical review. *Behaviour Research and Therapy*, 21, 505–527.

Trull, T. J., Nietzel, M. T., & Main, A. (1988). The use of meta-analysis to assess the clinical significance of behavior therapy for agoraphobia. *Behavior Therapy*, 19, 527–538.

VandenBos, G. R. (1993, March). U.S. mental health policy—Proactive evolution in the midst of health care reform. *American Psychologist*, 48, 283–290.

Wardle, J. (1990). Behaviour therapy and benzodiazepines: Allies or antagonists. *British Journal of Psychiatry*, 156, 163–168.

Weissman, M. N. (1991). Panic disorder: Impact on quality of life. *Journal of Clinical Psychiatry*, 52, 6–9.

Weissman, M. N., Klerman, G. L., Markowitz, J. S., & Ouelette, R. (1989). Suicidal ideation and suicide attempts in panic disorder and panic attacks. *New England Journal of Medicine*, 321, 1209–1214.

22

Psychosocial Treatments for Individuals with Schizophrenia and Related Disorders

Michael J. Goldstein

Approximately 20 million people in the world suffer from schizophrenia. It is a disorder with a relatively low incidence rate (2–4 per 10,000 for persons between 15 and 54 years of age) and a prevalence rate 10 times that amount (World Health Organization, 1990). The disparity between incidence and prevalence is due to the marked chronicity in manifestations of the disorder and its social sequelae, which accounts for the high cost of treating schizophrenia. Despite advances in pharmacological treatment, it is clear that most drugs primarily impact positive symptoms of the disorder, such as delusions, hallucinations, and disordered thought. The reduction in social relationships and functional capacity appear only minimally affected by contemporary medications. This has focused attention on therapies of a psychosocial nature as to their impact on the rehabilitation of persons who have manifested one or more episodes of the active phase of this disorder.

As noted by Parry (chapter 29, this volume) psychologically based treatments fall into three categories: (a) psychological treatments as an integral component of mental health care, (b) eclectic psychological therapy or counseling, and (c) formal psychotherapies. This chapter will consider categories (a) and (c) above. Virtually all writers agree that any psychological treatment for schizophrenia must be part of an integrated mental health care program involving pharmacotherapy, case management, and rehabilitation services. However, it is possible to consider discrete formal psychological therapies within a combined treatment model. This chapter will review extant evidence for the efficacy of individual psychotherapy, for various behavioral therapies, and for family therapy, as applied within the context of an integrated mental health treatment program.

Status of Current Treatments

During the past 5 years, there has been a remarkable acceleration of interest in the development and evaluation of psychosocial treatments for schizophrenia. This renewed interest has been stimulated by a number of factors: the recognition of the limited impact of pharmacological agents in the recovery of social function; the reduction of inpatient length of stay, so that most patients return to the community in states of partial remission; and, finally, the recognition that family members must often function in the role of caregiver for schizophrenic offspring or spouses.

The changing nature of the treatment system in recent years has altered the kinds of questions asked of psychosocial treatment. For example, in the 1950s and 1960s, the primary concern was whether individual psychotherapy, particularly of a psychoanalytic variety, was effective in curing schizophrenia during an extended period of psychiatric hospitalization. This form of psychosocial intervention was evaluated in terms of its effectiveness in resolving the acute psychotic crisis, and in terms of its ability to promote the kind of personal growth that would permit the patient to leave the hospital and to resume relatively normal living. The introduction of effective pharmacological agents in 1954 weakened the rationale for using psychotherapeutic methods for resolving the acute phase of a psychotic episode, and the radical reductions in length of hospital stay eliminated the context in which the second question could be addressed. The classic study by May (1968) further weakened the argument for either function of psychotherapy.

At present, most psychosocial programs begin at time of discharge or thereafter, when patients are living in the community. Clinicians nowadays typically do not hold to a single model for the treatment of schizophrenia, recognizing that an effective program involves prophylactic medication combined with a variety of psychosocial treatment interventions.

Blanket Versus Targeted Administration

Programs can be developed to be uniformly administered to all patients (blanketed usage) or can be targeted only to those patients for whom they are appropriate. In the majority of controlled trials of psychosocial intervention carried out to date, the blanketed format has been most common. The question addressed in these studies is whether the intervention is effective with schizophrenic patients as a class. It has been much more difficult within the clinical trial format to consider the question of individual differences, regarding whether certain types of intervention tend to be more effective than others with particular kinds of patients (or families). A major constraint in staging such studies is that very large sample sizes are required to yield sufficient power to successfully carry out analyses by discrete subgroups. This problem is analogous to the recurrent question in psychopharmacology regarding whether there is an optimal drug for a particular patient.

Early Versus Late Introduction of a Program

Contemporary treatments for schizophrenia can be organized into three temporal phases: the inpatient phase, the postdischarge/stabilization phase, and the maintenance phase. Although not all clinicians utilize operational criteria distinguishing between the stabilization and maintenance phases of aftercare, most investigators (Hogarty et al., 1988; Nuechterlein et al., 1986) define stabilization by 2 to 3 months of consistent (hopefully lower) levels of psychopathology, as indexed by a standard instrument such as the Brief Psychiatric Rating Scale (Overall & Gorham, 1962).

Given this model, the question may be posed whether one particular type of psychosocial intervention is more appropriately introduced and more likely than another to be efficacious in a particular phase of treatment. Premature introduction of a social skills program before the patient is stable, for example, may eventuate in noxious, rather than therapeutic, effects.

The inverse question is also significant, namely, whether a particular psychosocial program has the capacity to accelerate a phase of treatment such as stabilization. In an ongoing multisite study carried out under the auspices of the National Institute of Mental Health (NIMH; Schooler & Keith, 1983), the interaction among three different pharmacological and two different family-oriented psychosocial interventions is being evaluated. The focus of the study is primarily on the postdischarge period. Because it has been found to take some months to stabilize patients clinically, the psychosocial interventions begin shortly after discharge, but randomization to one of the three variants of drug treatment occurs after stabilization. Thus, it is possible to ask whether either form of psychosocial treatment, an intensive or a minimal family-based intervention program, altered the time necessary to achieve clinical stabilization. In fact, Schooler et al. (1989) reported that prior administration of either form of family intervention did not alter time to stabilization, a finding suggesting that this form of psychosocial treatment is not significant for achieving this clinical objective. It remains to be seen whether continuous administration of either form of psychosocial intervention alters the course of disorder during maintenance.

Regarding stabilization, it is impressive (Hogarty et al., 1988; Keith et al., 1989), when systematic criteria are used, how few patients are actually judged clinically stable at discharge, and how long it takes patients to achieve this stability (3–6 months in most cases). It is not clear how often—outside the context of research trials, where the investigators have a strong interest in monitoring symptomatology—patients receive the continuity of care necessary to attain a stable clinical state.

The Deliverability of Psychosocial Intervention

With pharmacological agents, a therapy can be prescribed but not taken or can cause noxious side effects.

Analogous results arise with psychosocial interventions. For example, patients may refuse participation or may be unable or unwilling to remain compliant with an extended program. Patients also may not attain the level of clinical stability required by the demands of a psychosocial program (e.g., they may not be able to pay sustained attention or to inhibit delusional thoughts). Rarely do investigators report how many of a consecutive series of patients enter a clinical trial for a psychosocial intervention. For example, Hahlweg (1989) reported on the deliverability of a form of psychoeducational family therapy, called *behavioral family management* (see Falloon, Boyd, & McGill, 1984), for a consecutive series of schizophrenic patients hospitalized at the Max Planck Institute of Psychiatry, Munich, West Germany. A substantial number of patients had no close relatives available, and others, either patients or relatives, refused the preferred treatment. Ultimately, 21% of the sample entered the trial. Therefore, despite the positive efforts of the psychoeducational family programs, the findings may be applicable only to a limited percentage of patients. It is encouraging to note that Hahlweg (1989) and others have found a strikingly low rate of attrition in these trials (Falloon et al., 1984; Hogarty et al., 1986; Leff, Kuipers, Berkowitz, Eberlein-Fries, & Sturgeon, 1982) once individuals agree to participate. Because only a limited number of patients have available family members to participate in a family-oriented program, it is necessary to pursue alternative strategies of psychosocial intervention focused primarily on the individual patient.

Review of the Efficacy of Diverse Psychosocial Approaches

Individual Psychotherapy

Individual psychotherapy refers to all forms of intervention in which the patient is the primary focus. It refers to approaches that emphasize expression of affect in which the patient is encouraged to explore past and present difficulties in verbal interchange with the therapist.

Research findings on expressive, insight-oriented forms of psychotherapy have largely been negative, whether treatment was initiated during the active phase of disorder or after the schizophrenic patient had achieved some degree of remission. The earliest reports by May (1968) concerning the application of an expressive type of individual psychotherapy during an extended period of inpatient stay were uniformly negative. This form of modified psychoanalytic psychotherapy did not add much to the impact of phenothiazine drug therapy.

More recently, Gunderson et al. (1984) contrasted two forms of individual psychotherapy: a psychodynamically oriented treatment (expressive, insight-oriented) and a supportive form termed *realistic adaptive therapy*, which was designed to assist the patient with day-to-day problems of living. Both therapies were initiated when the patient was hospitalized and continued post-discharge, for a 2-year period. Patients were on variable levels of antipsychotic medication during the trial and were randomly assigned to each treatment condition. Unfortunately, no drug-therapy-only group was present in this study. Even in this study, performed under optimal conditions with expert therapists and multiple outcome measures, there was no evidence that the psychodynamic form of treatment was as effective as the realistic-adaptive form of supportive treatment. In considering outcome variables such as number of days hospitalized or number of days working productively, results strongly favored realistic adaptive therapy. Results for realistic-adaptive therapy were substantially better, in terms of symptomatic and social role functioning, than are typically found for schizophrenic patients on maintenance drug therapy only.

The Gunderson et al. (1984) study involved blanket administration of individual psychotherapy to all schizophrenic patients, but it did not address targeted use of this treatment for selected and appropriate patients. For example, 31% of the patients in that study remained in their assigned therapy condition for 2 years and, in fact, had the best outcomes. This figure is comparable to that reported Alanen et al. (1985), who found that 26% of their sample of schizophrenic patients remained in intensive psychotherapy for the same 2-year period. These patients also had better outcomes than did those who did not remain in therapy; however, in the latter study, those who stayed in treatment also had better prognostic indicators (acute onset, insight into their condition) than did dropouts, a finding that complicates interpretation of the Finnish data.

While it is clear that a subsample (approximately 25%) of schizophrenic patients find a sustained course of individual psychotherapy worthwhile, it has been difficult to prove that such an approach significantly impacts course and outcome.

Two important lessons can be derived from the well-designed Gunderson et al. (1984) study. First, if individual psychotherapy is to be effective with schizophrenic patients, it must operate within a problem-solving model to assist the patient to deal with day-to-day problems of living. Second, it is unrealistic, based on the extremely high dropout rates observed (over 50% by 6 months), to expect the average schizophrenic patient to remain in individual psychotherapy for an extended period of treatment on a regular basis. It is wise to anticipate resistance to continued involvement in psychotherapy, and to adopt strategies for continuing contact with the patient in some form, so that intervention is possible in times of crisis, or when early prodromal signs of an exacerbation are notable.

Behavior Therapy

The origins of behavior therapy for schizophrenic patients derive from work with highly treatment-resistant patients. The work on token economies by Allyon and Azrin (1968), later elaborated in the elegant studies of Gordon Paul (Paul & Lentz, 1977), indicates how ward organization along operant principles can produce substantial normalization of psychotic behavior. The application of these principles has also proved effective in individual behavior therapy where the goal has been to assist the patient to gain some degree of control over psychotic symptoms. Although these forms of behavior therapy have proved valuable, the nature of their interactions with pharmacological therapy has been poorly explored (Schooler & Hogarty, 1987). It remains unclear whether programs of behavior therapy, administered to either individuals or groups, permit reductions in drug dose level at any point in the treatment.

Although control over disabling symptoms is an important goal of behavior therapy for institutionalized schizophrenic patients, it is now recognized to be a very limited one. Resolution of the more disabling symptoms of the active phase of a schizophrenic disorder frequently reveals a person with many negative symptoms, such as evidence of limited ambition and social interest, and deficient social and interpersonal skills. This is particularly the case when patients show some degree of remission of symptoms during hospitalization and then return to community living. For this reason, many behavioral therapists have turned their attention to the development of systematic programs of social skills training oriented to those skills necessary for effective reintegration into the community.

Social Skills Training

A number of different models for social skills training exist for schizophrenic patients. One approach developed by Liberman et al. (1987), for example, has been based on an information-processing model in which there are specific programs for training patients in the "sending" and "receiving" skills essential for effective social interaction. Although numerous case examples concerning the effectiveness of this approach have been published based on single-subject designs, only one controlled trial has been reported by this group, wherein social skills training was contrasted with a program designated as a "holistic health" treatment program in a sample of schizophrenic inpatients. In the latter program, patients were encouraged to participate in a physical exercise routine, utilize healthful dietary habits, practice meditation, and so on. Study results suggest evidence of a modest advantage (Wallace & Liberman, 1985) for the social skills training.

Another study evaluating social skills training in a controlled trial was staged by Hogarty and associates at Pittsburgh. In that study, patients who could be stabilized on injectible phenothiazine medication after discharge from an index episode of schizophrenia were assigned at random to one of three treatment conditions: family intervention only, social skills only, or a combination of the two. Hogarty et al. (1986) reported that social skills training was quite effective in reducing the relapse rate substantially below the rate found in patients who received only maintenance pharmacotherapy. It was as effective as family therapy, and it was most effective when combined with the latter. However, the effects of social skills training alone faded in the subsequent follow-up year.

It is not clear how, and in what ways, the model for social skills training used by Hogarty et al. (1986) differed from that of Liberman et al. (1987; Wallace et al., 1980). However, it appears that the former program, in particular, served as a form of indirect family therapy: A major focus was on methods for alleviating family pressures and conflicts. There are also important differences between the two studies that might account for the marked differences in outcomes. The Liberman et al. study was carried out with patients who resided as inpatients on a special clinical research unit; the Hogarty et al. study was carried out with patients who were in contact with close family members residing in the community, and who had concurrent outpatient pharmacotherapy during involvement in the social skills training.

The third controlled clinical trial of social skills training was carried out by Bellack et al. (1984). In this study, 20 chronic schizophrenic patients were randomly assigned to conventional day-hospital treatment alone, and 44 were assigned to the same program supplemented by comprehensive social skills training. As in other such programs, the social skills training program was conducted in small groups and focused on basic skills necessary to establish a social network and to reduce stress in social encounters. At the end of a 12-week treatment program, there were few differences in clinical state or social skills, but at 6-month follow-up, participants in the social skills training group were improved clinically in their retention of the social skills. However, very disappointing was the finding that 50% of the patients in each group subsequently relapsed and had to be rehospitalized, an outcome indicating that social skills training had had minimal impact on this negative outcome.

The limited impact of these original social skills behavioral programs has led investigators to rethink the appropriate model for such programs. Hogarty, McEvoy, and Munetz (1988) argued cogently that such programs should be guided by a basic model of the psychopathology and psychophysiology of schizophrenia. One approach is the work of Brenner et al. (1989), who designed a cognitive behavioral treatment program for schizophrenia based on a hierarchical model of the nature of deficits in schizophrenic persons. These investigators hypothesized that improvement in deficits at the attentional perceptual level must precede behavioral programs designed to modify more complex social behaviors. In small groups, patients first learn to recognize their cognitive deficits and develop strategies for dealing with them before moving on to work on social information-processing or associated skills. Although only preliminary results of this approach have appeared (Brenner et al., 1989), they appear promising.

Another innovative direction in behavior therapy reflects the psychoeducational approach first articulated in the family intervention programs described below. In this approach, the patient is informed about the nature of his or her disorder is and provided training in self-management. For example, Liberman, DeRisi, and Mueser (1989) developed a series of modules designed to permit clinicians to train patients in self-management. In one study (Eckman et al., 1990), they found that a module on medication management could be taught by clinicians with minimal instruction and could be learned and applied by patients. This module was incorporated with an ongoing clinical trial (Marder et al., 1989) designed to evaluate whether patients in low-dose fluphenazine maintenance treatment exposed to the medication management condition could more readily recognize prodromal signs of exacerbation in themselves and seek appropriate pharmacological intervention than those who had not. Preliminary data in the Marder et al. report indicate that while patients with and without medication management training had a similar number of prodromal signs of exacerbations, those with medication self-management had shorter periods of clinical instability following prodromes.

Over time, distinctions between narrowly defined behavioral therapy programs and total programs of community care for schizophrenic patients have rapidly disappeared. The behavioral model underlying the newer programs is much more sophisticated than the narrow principles of learning that characterized earlier efforts in this area. Also, these now comprise important adjuncts to pharmacotherapy, as well as methods for increasing the impact of drug therapy.

A major unresolved issue has to do with the optimum time for introducing various behavioral programs. It is clear that such programs are not helpful for patients who are highly symptomatic, but the question of when a particular program is appropriate for a remitted patient has not been systematically addressed in research. Hogarty et al. (1988) argued very convincingly for careful research in the sequencing of behavioral therapy programs based on the stages of a patient's disorder, the nature of residual deficits, and the demand characteristics of the patient's phase of rehabilitation (release from hospital or beginning a work training program).

Wallace (1995) has written a comprehensive review of social skills rehabilitation services. He points out that not everyone profits from this type of program, as a certain level of cognitive functioning is necessary to process and retain the skills learned. He also underscores that in a study by Marder et al. (1994) that used the social skills training modules developed by Liberman and colleagues at UCLA (Liberman et al., 1993) to test the interaction of pharmacological and psychosocial treatments, exposure to the model was most effective with patients who had an early onset of disorder that left them with substantial deficits in social and interpersonal functioning. Where social skills were lacking pre-morbidly, social skills training was most useful.

While most recent behavior therapy approaches have focused on increasing the frequency of normal behaviors, there has been a revival of interest in helping patients with treatment-resistant symptoms to deal with them more effectively. Tarrier and colleagues in Great Britain (Tarrier, Beckett, et al., 1993; Tarrier, Sharpe, et al., 1993) have developed and tested, with some success, cognitive behavioral methods for assisting patients to minimize positive symptoms that remain even following sustained pharmacological treatment. Tarrier calls this approach coping-strategy enhancement (CSE), because it builds upon, and reinforces, strategies spontaneously developed by patients to minimize their own residual positive symptoms.

In a similar approach, explicated by Kingdon and Turkington (1994), strategies are used for reducing hallucinations and delusions using some traditional and some unique cognitive behavioral strategies. The essence of both the Tarrier et al. and the Kingdon and Turkington (1994) approaches is that positive symptoms are stress-related responses, which can be modulated, by assisting a patient to utilize more effective coping mechanisms for reducing the impact of stressors.

Behavior therapeutic approaches for schizophrenia have evolved from extensive pilot work and have been tested in controlled trials with modest results. Implementation of and training for delivery of these modules have been notably spearheaded by Liberman and colleagues. The development of videotaped modules, ancillary training materials, and dissemination trials (Eckman et al., 1992) has attempted to determine the most cost-effective approach to training clinicians in these interventions, and to be helpful to schizophrenic patients. The study by Marder et al. (1994) also represents an attempt to determine how well these modules interact with maintenance pharmacological treatment. Despite the modest results from the RCTs to date, treatment development research on social skills training has moved from efficacy to effectiveness work, encompassing a recent focus on cost-effectiveness of treatment delivery.

Family Psychoeducational Programs

In recent years, a strong interest has emerged in family-based intervention programs designed to use resources of the family unit to increase medication compliance, and to reduce the impact of stressors that could serve as triggers of relapse. These family intervention programs have been termed *psychoeducational* by Anderson, Hogarty, and Reiss (1980) because they involved a combination of didactic materials about schizophrenia for patients and relatives, as well as therapeutic strategies designed to improve stress management by all family members through enhanced communication and problem-solving skills.

These psychoeducational family programs received a major impetus from research originating in Great Britain, and subsequently replicated in other countries, on the concept of expressed emotion (EE) (Kavanaugh, 1992). This concept refers to affective attitudes of criticism and/or emotional overinvolvment manifested by the patients' close relatives. It is typically assessed in a semistructured interview conducted during hospitalization of the patient for an episode of schizophrenia. The fact that such assessments correlate with behavioral expression of these attitudes following patient discharge (Hahlweg et al., 1989; Miklowitz, Goldstein, Falloon, & Doane, 1984; Miklowitz et al., 1989) supports them as targets for intervention. Psychoeducational models were accordingly designed to reduce those properties of patient-relative interaction predictive of relapse.

Tactics in Psychoeducational Family Therapy

If the patient is in regular contact with family members, it is advisable to engage these relatives in the patient's care. Most studies suggest that a program which covers a 9- to 12-month period following hospital discharge is acceptable to both patients and their relatives. Table 22.1 presents the essential elements found useful in such a program. Generally, specific components are organized by an orientation to a vulnerability-stress model (Zubin & Spring, 1977), which links theories of etiology and course with a rationale for pharmacological and psychosocial treatment.

Strategic Goals of a Psychoeducational Family Program

All psychoeducational family programs possess similar strategic goals. These involve, first, assisting the patient and his or her relatives to make some sense of the psychotic episode by providing an explanatory model of the disorder; second, assisting all involved in confronting the painful reality that a vulnerability to future episodes exists; third, assisting the patient and family in dealing with continued dependence on medication for symptom control; and fourth, appreciating that stressful life events and how they are dealt with impact

Table 22.1 Common Ingredients in Effective Family Intervention Programs

- Engagement of the family early in the treatment process in a "no fault" atmosphere
- Education about schizophrenia concerning
  - The vulnerability-stress model
  - Etiological theories
  - Variations in prognosis
  - Rationale for various treatments
  - Recommendations for coping with the disorder
- Communication training directed at
  - Improving communication clarity in general
  - Improving ways of providing positive and negative feedback within the family
- Problem-solving training directed at improving
  - Management of day-to-day problems and hassles
  - Management of discrete stressful life events
  - Generalized problem-solving skills
- Crisis intervention
  - In times of extreme stress involving one or more members of the family
  - When incipient signs of recurrence are evident

upon the course of the disorder. Fifth, both patient and relatives need to learn to separate those characteristics of the patient that reflect enduring personality traits from variations in expressions of disorder. Details of how these goals can be approached are described in Goldstein (1995).

Testing the Impact of a Psychoeducational Program on Relapse Prevention

The First Generation of Studies Starting in the late 1970s, a series of six studies (Falloon et al., 1982; Goldstein et al., 1978; Hogarty et al., 1986; Leff et al., 1982; Randolf et al., 1994; Tarrier et al., 1988) was carried out, addressing the issue of whether engagement of the patient's family during the stabilization phase of treatment, when combined with maintenance pharmacotherapy, could reduce risk of recurrence in the short term (9 months to 1 year postdischarge). These programs were designed to address problems observed in both patients and families posthospitalization, modifying intrafamilial processes hypothesized to increase the risk of recurrence. Data from these studies are presented in Figure 22.1. They reveal a notable reduction in relapse rates when family intervention is added to regular medication maintenance.

The Second-Generation Studies: Unique Designs or Treatment Models Recent family intervention studies either have been carried out in unique treatment settings (i.e., another country with a different health delivery system) or have involved notable modifications in the experimental design that narrow the differences between contrasting forms of family intervention. Building on the findings of the first generation of studies demonstrating that family intervention is effective for schizophrenic patients, the second generation of studies used comparison groups that had components of these interventions nested in them, so that the distinction between family-based interventions and non-family-based interventions was less salient.

The Amsterdam Study The study by Linszen (1993) and colleagues was carried out in the adolescent unit at the Amsterdam Medical Center. The 76 patients were young (mean age = 20.5, *SD* = 2.5), and over half were having their first admission for psychosis, so that this was the youngest sample studied to date. In the Netherlands health care system, the period of inpatient stay is substantially longer than is the case in the United States (mean = 13.5 weeks) and is uniformly followed by 3 months of day hospital treatment at the same center with the same therapists. Comprehensive care continued for 9 months, providing a level of continuity of care rarely seen in most U.S. treatment settings.

The design of the study involved the superimposition of a family intervention program along the lines of the Falloon model on what was termed "standard care." Standard care was a very rich form of individual supportive and drug therapy, carried out by a psychiatrist and a psychiatric nurse. It derived from a sophisticated psychoeducational model in which patients were educated about their disorder, taught to recognize stressors, learned coping mechanisms pertaining to recognition of prodromal signs and symptoms, and were taught about the hazards of substance abuse and medication self-management. The study addressed the question of whether the additional involvement of the family added anything to what was already a rich, individually focused treatment system.

Relapse over the 12-month trial was evaluated by combined criteria that relied on Brief Psychiatric Rating Scale (BPRS) ratings periodically collected by a "blind" rater, and on ratings of case notes from the treating clinicians who saw the patient more frequently. According to these conservative criteria, which resembled those used by Hogarty et al. (1986), a low relapse rate of 16% was reported by the end of the 1-year trial. No significant effects on relapse or interaction with family EE status were found as a result of

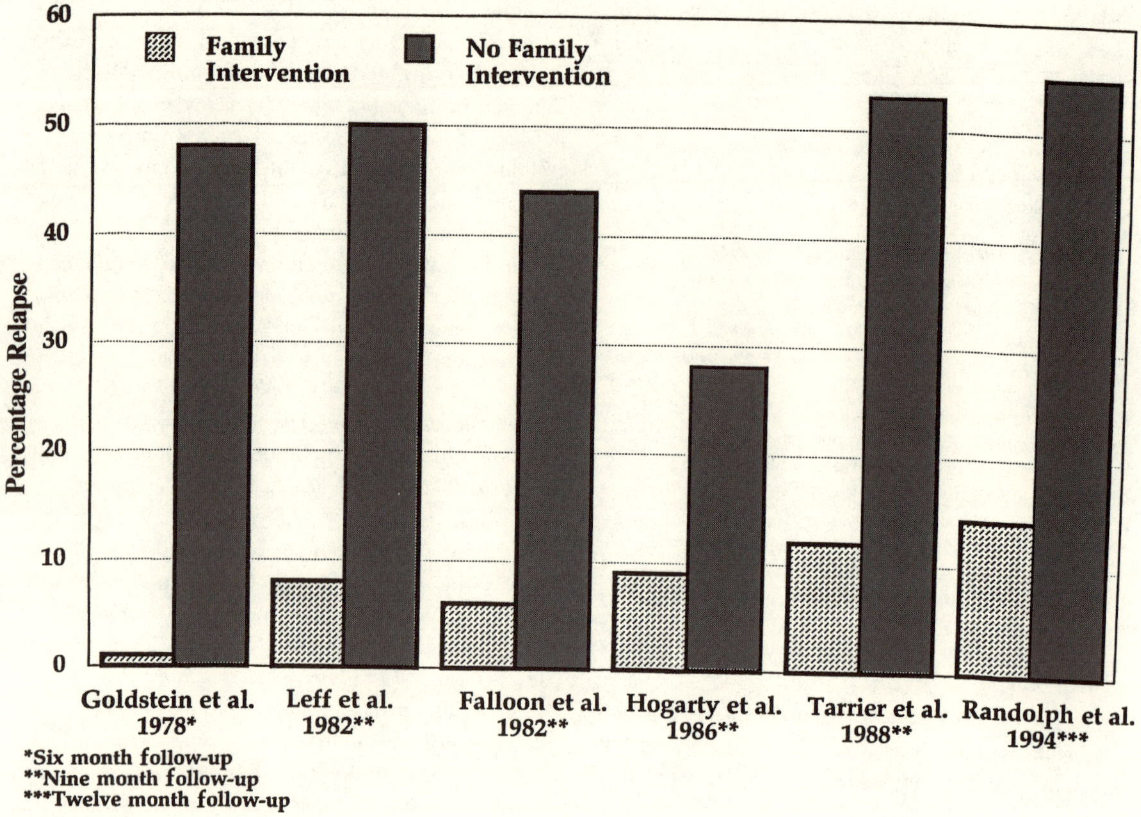

Figure 22.1 Relapse rates from the six first-generation studies, contrasting a family intervention program with the absence of such a program (schizophrenic patients on continuous medication). From Goldstein et al. (1978), Leff et al. (1982), Falloon et al. (1982), Hogarty et al. (1986), Tarrier et al. (1988), and Randolph et al. (1994).

the addition of the family treatment to the standard treatment package.

The NIMH Treatment Strategies Study (TSS) The TSS study (Keith et al., 1989) was recently completed, and the authors' results have been frequently misunderstood. The TSS was a large-scale multisite study initiated by the U.S. National Institute of Mental Health and designed to assess three questions:

1. Are there alternative pharmacological strategies that could reduce risk of recurrence of schizophrenia while preventing unwanted side effects? The study contrasted three medication strategies (termed "standard dose," "low dose," and "intermittent dose"), in which drugs were reintroduced at early signs of a recurrence.
2. Do more intensive, in-home family intervention programs, following the Falloon model (termed "applied family management") in format and schedule, add anything more than intense family involvement (termed "supportive family management"), characterized by a workshop and ongoing monthly group for relatives?
3. Does the addition of more intensive applied family management to supportive family management permit the successful application of a "riskier" pharmacological strategy, such as a lower than standard dose or intermittent medication?

The study involved a 2 × 3 design, with two psychosocial conditions and three medication conditions. All relatives in the applied family management condition also had access to the educational workshop and monthly relatives' groups and attended the latter meetings as often as relatives in the supportive condition, who received nothing but these meetings. Unfortunately, there was not a group in the study in which psychoeducational family treatment was absent.

The answers to Questions 2 and 3 above, the most relevant to this review, were essentially negative: According to various indicators of clinical state or relapse, the data did not support the advantage of adding the applied family management to the supportive family program, nor did the data indicate that the added program improved outcome in low-dose or intermittent medication conditions.

The absence of a non-family-involved or treated condition in the TSS study limits the inferences that can be drawn about effectiveness of family intervention per se. It does raise the question of the nature of the active ingredients in an effective family education program. Is it simply family involvement and education that are the potent ingredients? Or is an essential ingredient a sustained support system for patients and their relatives during the difficult period of transition from hospital to community care?

Psychoeducation in Multiple-Family Groups

An intermediate position between relatives-only groups and programs directed at single-family units is represented by McFarlane and colleagues, who tested the value of multiple-family groups, which included patients, against the same psychoeducational format, delivered to single-family groups. In his original pilot, McFarlane (1990) found that multiplefamily psychoeducational groups were associated with lower relapse rates (12.5% at 12 months; 25% at 24 months) than a similar approach for individual family groups (23.5% at 12 months; 47.1% at 24 months). Both conditions were superior to a multifamily approach not based on a psychoeducational model (42.9% at 12 months; 42.9% at 24 months).

McFarlane (1994) reported data on a multicenter trial contrasting multiple-family and single-family psychoeducational groups carried out in different locations in New York State. The data support the results of the original pilot study, although the differences are not as dramatic. The findings were consistent across sites and, according to McFarlane et al. (1995), extended over a 4-year follow-up period.

Should these data be replicated by others, they suggest a model of treatment combining positive elements of relatives' groups (support, destigmatization, group problem solving) with those of the individual family approach (involvement of the patient in his or her own recovery, emphasis on reciprocal modification of family transactions) in the most cost-effective way.

Conclusion

Several types of family intervention have been described: (a) individual family treatment, which includes the patient as well as key relatives and usually consists of home- or clinic-based education, skill building, problem solving and crisis intervention sessions; (b) relatives' groups, which exclude patients and are oriented around helping relatives to cope with the disorder; and (c) multiple-family groups, which, like relatives' groups, are educational and coping-based but do include patients. Each type of treatment is present-focused, encouraging the patient's gradual reentry into the family milieu and community, as well as the family's reorganization around effectively managing the illness.

How Efficacious Are These Family Programs?

There is now convincing evidence that family interventions are more effective than "routine care," defined as medication management with ancillary crisis intervention in the treatment of schizophrenic patients. There is further evidence from follow-up studies of the first-generation trials (Falloon et al., 1985; Hogarty et al., 1991) that family interventions are more effective over 2-year periods in improving medication compliance, delaying relapse, and improving social functioning, than are individual (supportive or skill-oriented) therapies.

The question of efficacy becomes more complicated when the type and format of family intervention is considered. It is clear that a few sessions of family education, even if involving the patient, are inadequate to bring about long-term changes in the course of schizophrenic disorder (Cozolino, Goldstein, Nuechterlein, West, & Snyder, 1988; Tarrier et al., 1988). Nor is it clear that regular, intensive home-based sessions with individual families are always necessary. Data from several studies (Keith et al., 1989; Leff et al., 1989) suggest that relatives' groups may be as effective as individual family treatments if family members attend them. This is a big "if," in that many relatives cannot be persuaded to attend clinic-based group sessions, often because they are uncomfortable with the stigma of identifying themselves with other families of the mentally ill.

An equally important question is whether family programs add anything, in terms of prophylactic efficacy, to comprehensive systems of care that go beyond mere medication management. The first generation of family studies suggested that family treatments provide clear advantages over medication-only control groups. However, the second generation of studies suggests that results vary considerably depending upon the nature and comprehensiveness of the comparison treatment.

Psychoeducational family intervention has proceeded through pilot development and controlled clinical trials. So far, there has been little effort to develop the most cost-effective means to implement these programs, or to disseminate the most cost-effective methods in regular clinical practice. The TSS study does not address this issue, given that the model disseminated across sites in that study is the original labor-intensive one developed by Falloon, which required extensive training, supervision, and monitoring for adherence. The closest to an implementation phase effort reviewed in this paper is the study by McFarlane, which tested whether a program for groups of families was as effective as one involving one family at a time.

The very promising results from controlled clinical trials indicate that extensive effort in applied effectiveness research is now urgent. Unless more cost-effective methods for delivering psychoeducational family programs can be developed, they will never be incorporated into routine care.

An additional area worthy of attention is the development of programs based on the psychoeducational model for individual patients lacking available relatives. There are elements in the programs originally developed for family units that are adaptable to forms of individual or group therapy for patients. In the Linszen study cited above, the standard care condition contained such a program. Given the good outcomes found for that group, this approach warrants further attention.

Are They Cost-Effective?

The typical psychoeducational family program directed at an individual family has tended to follow the model outlined originally by Falloon et al. (1982). This is a program that begins very soon after discharge and lasts for a minimum of 9 months, sometimes extending longer depending on the needs of the family and the patient. Generally, the program consists of 21 sessions, more intense initially (once per week for 3 months; biweekly for the next 3 months), and at longer monthly intervals in the latter phases of the program. While not essential, most programs have used a cotherapist model, as this has been found useful in dealing with the many crises experienced by the families of psychotic patients, and in providing a support system for therapists. Thus, a 9-month program of 21 sessions involves a minimum of 42 direct contact hours (based on two therapists per session) with a family. When missed or rescheduled appointments and the inevitable crisis calls between sessions are factored in, 50 person hours per 9-month program seems appropriate.

Translating these hourly costs into monetary amounts is difficult because the rates for professional services are dependent on the training experience and professional discipline of the therapists. If we assume that high-level professionals are the psychoeducational family therapists (psychiatrists, psychologists, social workers) and set an average hourly rate of $100 per hour (not an unusual figure in the United States), then a series for one family will cost $5,000 for two therapists, and $2,500 if one therapist runs the family sessions. The latter is certainly a possibility in general practice.

The best estimates regarding the economic benefits come from two major controlled clinical trials conducted in the United States: those of Falloon et al. (1982) and of Hogarty et al. (1986). The former was a 9-month trial and the latter a 12-month trial. Although the models used varied somewhat, both programs showed many common features, as outlined earlier in Table 1. These two trials compared a psychoeducational family program and maintenance drug treatment with the effects of maintenance drug treatment alone in reducing the rate of relapse following discharge from the hospital after an index episode of the disorder. The rates of relapse at 9 months postdischarge in both studies were substantially lower in the groups that received the psychoeducational family programs than in those that received medication alone. While the figures vary between the two studies, the more conservative figures from the Hogarty et al. (1986) study, which found less dramatic group differences, show that the relapse rate was reduced to one third of that seen in the medication-only condition. Note that the medication-only condition is frequently the most common aftercare program in the United States.

If it is assumed that many of these relapses result in the rehospitalization of patients, which, in the United States, involves a minimum cost of $800 per day for an average of 14 days, then the cost of the average relapse is approximately $11,200. This is more than twice the cost of a two-therapist psychoeducational family program, and over four times the cost of a single-therapist program.

Thus, each averted relapse represents a cost savings of approximately $6,200 U.S. The reduction of the relapse rate by one third, which has been found in the controlled clinical trials conducted in both the United States and Great Britain (see Figure 22.1), suggests that routine psychoeducational family programs could be highly cost-effective.

This conclusion does not even address the impact of those programs on symptomatic and social functioning.

References

Alanen, Y. O., Rakkozainen, Y., Riija, R., et al. (1985). Psychotherapeutically oriented treatment of schizophrenia: Results of a five-year follow-up. *Acta Psychiatrica Scandinavica* (Suppl.), *71*, 31–49.

Allyon, T., & Azrin, N. H. (1968). The measurement and reinforcement of behavior of psychotics. *Journal of the Experimental Analysis of Behavior, 8*, 357–383.

Anderson, C. M., Hogarty, G., & Reiss, D. J. (1980). Family treatment of adult schizophrenic patients: A psychoeducational approach. *Schizophrenia Bulletin, 6*, 490–505.

Bellack, A. S., Turner, S. M., Hersen, M., et al. (1984). An examination of the efficacy of social skills training for chronic schizophrenic patients. *Hospital and Community Psychiatry, 35*, 1023–1028.

Brenner, H. D., Boker, W., Hodel, B., et al. (1989). Cognitive treatment of basic pervasive dysfunctions in schizophrenia. In S. C. Schulz & C. A. Tamminga (Eds.), *Schizophrenia: Scientific progress* (pp. 358–371). New York: Oxford University Press.

Cozolino, L. J., Goldstein, M. J., Nuechterlein, K. H., West, K. L., & Snyder, K. S. (1988). The impact of education about schizophrenia on relatives varying in expressed emotion. *Schizophrenia Bulletin, 14*, 675–687.

Eckman, T. A., Liberman, R. P., Phipps, C. C., et al. (1990). Teaching medication management skills to schizophrenic patients. *Journal of Clinical Psychopharmacology, 10*, 33–38.

Eckman, T. A., Wirshing, W. C., Marder, S. R., et al. (1992). Technology for training schizophrenics in illness self-management: A controlled trial. *American Journal of Psychiatry, 149*, 1549–1555.

Falloon, I. R. H., Boyd, J. L., McGill, C. W., et al. (1982). Family management in the prevention of exacerbations of schizophrenia: A controlled study. *New England Journal of Medicine, 306*, 1437–1440.

Falloon, I. R. H., Boyd, J. L., & McGill, C. W. (1984). *Family care of schizophrenia.* New York: Guilford.

Falloon, I. R. H., Boyd, J. L., McGill, C. W., et al. (1985). Family management in the prevention of morbidity of schizophrenia: Clinical outcome of a two-year longitudinal study. *Archives of General Psychiatry, 42*, 887–986.

Goldstein, M. J. (1995). Psychoeducation and relapse prevention. *International Clinical Psychopharmacology, 9*(5), 59–69.

Goldstein, M. J., Rodnick, E. H., Evans, J. R., et al. (1978). Drug and family therapy in the aftercare of acute schizophrenics. *Archives of General Psychiatry, 35*, 1169–1177.

Gunderson, J. G., Frank, A. F., Katz, H. M., et al. (1984). Effects of psychotherapy in schizophrenia: 2. Comparative outcome of two forms of treatment. *Schizophrenia Bulletin, 10*, 564–598.

Hahlweg, K. (1989, November). *Munich project on behavioral family therapy for schizophrenics.* Paper presented at conference on Public and Family Psychiatric Services, Milan, Italy.

Hahlweg, K., Goldstein, M. J., Nuechterlein, K. H., et al. (1989). Expressed emotion and patient-relative interaction in families of recent onset schizophrenics. *Journal of Consulting and Clinical Psychology, 57*, 11–18.

Hogarty, G. E., Anderson, C. M., Reiss, D. J., et al. (1986). Family education, social skills, training, and maintenance chemotherapy in the aftercare of schizophrenia. *Archives of General Psychiatry, 43*, 633–642.

Hogarty, G. E., Anderson, C. M., Reiss, D. J., et al. (1991). Family psychoeducation, social skills training, and maintenance chemotherapy in the aftercare of schizophrenia: 2. Two-year effects of a controlled study on relapse and adjustment. *Archives of General Psychiatry, 4*, 340–347.

Hogarty, G., McEvoy, J. P., Munetz, M., et al. (1988). Dose of fluphenazine, familial expressed emotion and outcome in schizophrenia: Results of a two-year controlled study. *Archives of General Psychiatry, 45*, 797–805.

Kavanaugh, D. J. (1992). Recent developments in expressed emotion and schizophrenia. *British Journal of Psychiatry, 160*, 601–620.

Keith, S. J., Bellack, A., Frances, A., et al. (1989). The influence of diagnosis and family treatment on acute treatment response and short term outcome in schizophrenia. *Psychopharmacology Bulletin, 25*, 336–339.

Keith, S., Schooler, N., Bellack, A., et al. (1989). The influence of family management on patient stabilization. *Schizophrenia Research, 2*, 224.

Kingdon, D. G., & Turkington, D. (1994). *Cognitive-behavioral therapy of schizophrenia.* New York: Guilford Press.

Leff, J., Berkowitz, R., Shavit, N., Strachan, A., Glass, I., & Vaughn, C. (1989). A trial of family therapy versus a relatives group for schizophrenia. *British Journal of Psychiatry, 154*, 58–66.

Leff, J., Kuipers, L., Berkowitz, R., Eberlein-Fries, R., & Sturgeon, D. (1982). A controlled trial of social intervention in the families of schizophrenia patients. *British Journal of Psychiatry, 141*, 121–134.

Liberman, R. P., DeRisi, W. J., & Mueser, K. T. (1989). *Social skills training for psychiatric patients.* Elmsford, NY: Pergamon Press.

Liberman, R. P., Jacobs, H. E., Boone, S. E., et al. (1987). Skills training for the community adaptation of schizophrenics. In J. S. Strauss, W. Boker, & H. D. Brenner (Eds.), *Psychosocial treatment of schizophrenia* (pp. 94–109). Toronto: Huber.

Liberman, R. P., Wallace, C. J., Blackwell, G. A., Eckman, T. A., Vacarro, J. V., & Kuehnel, T. G. (1993). Innovations in skills training for the seriously mentally ill: The UCLA Social and Independent Living Skills modules. *Innovations Research, 3*, 43–60.

Linszen, D. (1993). *Recent onset schizophrenic disorders: Outcome, prognosis and treatment.* Unpublished doctoral dissertation, University of Amsterdam.

Marder, S. R., Van Putten, T., Eckman, T., et al. (1989). Low dose pharmacotherapy and skills training. *Schizophrenia Research, 2*, 211.

Marder, S. R., Wirshing, W. C., Van Putten, T., et al. (1994). Fluphenzine versus placebo supplementation for prodromal signs of relapse in schizophrenia. *Archives of General Psychiatry, 51*, 280–287.

May, P. R. A. (1968). *Treatment of schizophrenia.* New York: Science House.

McFarlane, W. R. (1990). Multiple family groups and the treatment of schizophrenia. In M. I. Herz, S. J. Keith, & J. P. Docherty (Eds.), *Psychosocial treatment of schizophrenia* (pp. 167–190). New York: Elsevier.

McFarlane, W. R. (1994). *Multiple-family groups, psychoeducation and maintenance medication in the treatment of schizophrenia.* Unpublished paper presented at the 11th International Symposium for the Psychotherapy of Schizophrenia.

McFarlane, W. R., Link, B., Dushay, R., Marchal, J., & Crilly, J. (1995). Psychoeducational multiple family groups: Four-year outcome in schizophrenia. *Family Process, 34*(2), 127–144.

Miklowitz, D. J., Goldstein, M. J., Falloon, I. R. H., & Doane, J. A. (1984). Interactional correlates of expressed emotion in the families of schizophrenics. *British Journal of Psychiatry, 144*, 482–487.

Miklowitz, D. J., Goldstein, M. J., Doane, J. A., Nuechterlein, K. H., Strachan, A. M., Snyder, K. S., & Magana, A. M. (1989). Is expressed emotion an index of a transactional process? I. Relative's affective style. *Family Process, 28*, 153–167.

Nuechterlein, K. H., Snyder, K. S., Dawson, M. E., et al. (1986). Expressed emotion, fixed dose fluphenazine decanoate maintenance, and relapse in recent-onset schizophrenia. *Psychopharmacology Bulletin, 22*, 633–639.

Overall, J. E., & Gorham, D. R. (1962). The Brief Psychiatric Rating Scale. *Psychological Reports, 10*, 799–812.

Paul, G. L., & Lentz, R. (1977). *Psychosocial treatment for the chronic mental patient.* Cambridge: Harvard University Press.

Randolph, E. T., Eth, S., Glynn, S. M., et al. (1994). Behavioural family management in schizophrenia: Outcome of a clinic-based intervention. *British Journal of Psychiatry, 164*, 501–506.

Schooler, N. R., & Hogarty, G. E. (1987). Medication and psychosocial strategies in the treatment of schizophrenia. In H. Y. Meltzer (Ed.), *Psychopharmacology: The third generation of progress* (pp. 1111–1120). New York: Raven.

Schooler, N. R., & Keith, S. J. (1983). *Treatment strategies in schizophrenia study protocol.* Rockville, MD: National Institute of Mental Health.

Schooler, M. R., Keith, S. J., Severe, J. B., et al. (1989). Acute treatment response and short term outcome in schizophrenia: First results of the NIMH treatment strategies in the schizophrenia study. *Psychopharmacology Bulletin, 25*, 331–335.

Tarrier, N., Barrowclough, C., Porceddu, K., et al. (1988). The community management of schizophrenia: A controlled trial of a behavioral intervention with families to reduce relapse. *British Journal of Psychiatry, 153*, 532–542.

Tarrier, N., Beckett, R., Harwood, S., Baker, A., Yusupoff, L., & Ugarteburu, I. (1993). A trial of two cognitive-behavioural methods of treating drug-resistant residual psychotic symptoms in schizophrenic patients: 1. Outcome. *British Journal of Psychiatry, 162*, 524–532.

Tarrier, N., Sharpe, R., Beckett, R., Harwood, S., Baker, A., & Yusupoff, L. (1993). A trial of two cognitive-behavioural methods of treating drug-resistant residual psychotic symptoms in schizophrenic patients: 2. Treatment specific changes in coping and problem solving skills. *Social Psychiatry and Psychiatric Epidemiology*, 28, 5–10.

Wallace, C. J. (1995). Social skills rehabilitation services. In *Psychotherapy and Rehabilitation Research Bulletin* (Vol. 4, pp. 17–22). U.S. Department of Health and Human Services, Public Health Service, National Institute of Mental Health.

Wallace, C. J., Nelson, C., Liberman, R. P., et al. (1980). A review and critique of social skills training with chronic schizophrenics. *Schizophrenia Bulletin*, 6, 42.

Wallace, C. J., & Liberman, R. P. (1985). Social skills training for patients with schizophrenia: A controlled clinical trial. *Psychiatrica Res*, 15, 243–248.

World Health Organization. (1990). *Global estimates for health situation assessment and projects*. Geneva, Switzerland: Author.

Zubin, T., & Spring, B. (1977). Vulnerability—A new view of schizophrenia. *Journal of Abnormal Psychology*, 86, 103–126.

Section B

Empirical Evidence Pertaining to Common but Infrequently Studied Disorders

23

Efficacy and Cost-Effectiveness of Psychotherapy for Dysthymic Disorder

John C. Markowitz

Psychiatric outcome research is starting to look beyond symptomatic response to other domains of patient functioning. The economic and social costs of mood disorders are receiving unprecedented interest (e.g., Conti & Burton, 1994; Greenberg et al., 1993), partly because of this expansion of research aims, and partly because of current economic pressures to control the costs of mental health treatment. One by-product of this research has been a new respect for dysthymic disorder, a syndrome often previously dismissed as "subsyndromal" and seen as a poor cousin to major depression (Markowitz, 1995, 1998). In fact, dysthymic disorder may have higher costs and cause greater chronic dysfunction than major depression. This chapter will briefly review—in order of decreasing levels of knowledge—the human and societal costs of dysthymic disorder, the efficacy of psychotherapeutic treatment, and the cost-effectiveness of such treatment. It then offers recommendations for future research.

Before 1980, in the days before *DSM-III*, dysthymic disorder was considered a characterological or neurotic disorder, and psychotherapy was its treatment of choice. In the past 15 years, pharmacotherapy has eclipsed psychotherapy as the first line treatment for chronic depressions. In part, the reason is that research has tested both acute and maintenance applications of pharmacotherapy, whereas there have been few controlled acute trials and no maintenance trials of the psychotherapy of dysthymic disorder. Yet the research evidence for the efficacy of psychotherapy, while limited, is not inauspicious. Psychotherapy particularly deserves consideration for patients who do not respond to, or will not tolerate, antidepressant medication. Psychotherapy may also have important use as adjunctive therapy for some medication responders.

The Costs of Dysthymic Disorder

The costs of this grinding, chronic disorder include emotional suffering, social difficulties, lost productivity, and high medical and mental health utilization.

Dysthymic disorder is common, affecting roughly 3% of American adults, women twice as frequently as men (Kessler et al., 1994; Weissman et al., 1988). The *DSM-IV* (American Psychiatric Association [APA], 1994) defines it as a chronic disorder, with a minimum duration of 2 years (1 year in children). In fact, most adults presenting for treatment have been depressed for decades. Although the severity of their symptoms is less than for major depressive episodes, the burden is still significant and lasts far longer. Moreover, the majority of dysthymic patients seem sooner or later to develop the additional two depressive symptoms needed to qualify for a superimposed major depression (McCullough et al., 1992), thus attaining "double depression" (Keller & Shapiro, 1982). Dysthymic patients frequently have other comorbid conditions on Axes I, II, and III. Common comorbid psychiatric diagnoses include anxiety disorders, substance abuse, and depressively tinged personality disorders: dependent, avoidant, borderline, and self-defeating (Markowitz, Moran, Kocsis, & Frances, 1992). Some of these diagnoses may simply reflect the trespass of chronic depression on other diagnostic criteria sets and may resolve with effective treatment of the underlying dysthymic disorder. In most cases, dysthymic disorder appears to precede comorbid disorders, not to follow them as a kind of secondary demoralization.

Dysthymic patients suffer greatly and seemingly interminably. Many report feeling depressed as long as they can remember—so long, indeed, that depression appears to them part of their personality. They suffer from chronic low self-esteem, low energy, poor sleep, and excessive guilt; because it feels like part of their personalities, they blame themselves for the syndrome as well. Dysthymic disorder is associated with difficulties in both social and occupational functioning (Friedman, 1993). Dysthymic individuals often throw themselves into their work in an attempt to justify what feels like a worthless existence. Despite difficulty concentrating and low energy, their guilt often pushes them to work overtime. Work also provides a relatively comfortable role and social structure. In other social interactions, dysthymic individuals have enormous difficulty. Most dysthymic patients presenting for treatment are not in relationships. Such social dysfunction is indeed a hallmark of the disorder.

Several studies have demonstrated the social and vocational difficulties of dysthymics relative to the population at large (Cassano, Perugi, Maremmani, & Akiskal, 1990; Kocsis et al., 1988; Stewart et al., 1988). The RAND Medical Outcomes Study, which compared 626 outpatients who had major depression, dysthymic disorder, double depression, and subsyndromal depressive symptoms, showed that patients with double depression had the greatest initial symptom severity, but that dysthymic patients with or without superimposed major depression had poor functional status. At the end of a 2-year naturalistic follow-up, dysthymic patients had the worst functional outcomes (Wells, Burnam, Rogers, Hays, & Camp, 1992). Thus, although even subsyndromal depressive symptoms disrupt well-being and work function more than a variety of medical syndromes (Wells et al., 1989), dysthymic disorder is not "subsyndromal" and is associated with still more damage to mental and physical functioning and perceived health. Since it typically has an early onset and long duration, dysthymic disorder may extend throughout a working career.

Although good evidence now exists that both depressive symptoms and social functioning respond to antidepressant pharmacotherapy, dysthymic patients have historically been underdiagnosed and mistreated (Weissman & Klerman, 1977). Like Weissman and Klerman (1977), Wells, Katon, Rogers, and Camp (1994) reported that chronically depressed patients were more likely to receive anxiolytic than antidepressant medication. It may be that the camouflage of comorbid diagnoses distracts clinicians from an underlying dysthymic disorder, that clinicians perceive the dysthymic disorder as secondary to comorbid diagnoses, or that they do not take seriously the relatively recent concept of chronic depression as a mood disorder (Kocsis & Frances, 1987), a construct only included in *DSM-III* in 1980 (APA, 1980). Dysthymic individuals often seek mental health and medical services (Weissman et al., 1988)—another cost of the disorder—but too often are treated either with long-term psychodynamic psychotherapy, which may provide insight without relieving symptoms, or with anxiolytics, which may compound rather than alleviate depression. The appropriate treatments for dysthymic disorder are antidepressant medications and antidepressant psychotherapies, either alone or in combination.

Treatment Efficacy

Because depression tends to recur, its treatment has two goals: acute efficacy and the prophylaxis of recurrence or relapse. The chronic maintenance of euthymia has particular importance for dysthymic disorder: Remission has limited value if it is not sustained.

Pharmacotherapy

Several studies have shown that both depressive symptoms and psychosocial functioning improve in a matter of weeks with acute antidepressant pharmacotherapy of dysthymic disorder (Friedman, Markowitz, Parides, & Kocsis, 1995; Kocsis et al., 1988; Stewart et al., 1988). About half of dysthymic patients are likely to improve with pharmacotherapy. A recent study found that clinical response of chronically depressed patients to a 12-week treatment with sertraline or imipramine had a .59 correlation with subjective improved work performance over the same time period (Finkelstein, Berndt, Greenberg, Parsley, & Keller, 1995). In this study, 86% of subjects ($N = 285$) reported improved work performance by Week 12, and work performance improved on average by 26%. This result supports the intuitive expectation that better work function should accompany clinical remission from chronic depression and in turn suggests the potential cost-effectiveness of such treatment.

Perhaps of still greater importance is recent research demonstrating that maintenance pharmacotherapy over 2.5 years can forestall relapse of dysthymic disorder, whereas dysthymic patients who were randomly assigned to placebo treatment after 6 months of remission were prone to relapse (Kocsis et al., 1996). Analysis of vocational functioning in this study has not yet been completed but is anticipated to show that patients who maintain recovery function more efficiently than those who relapse. A large multisite study now under way will provide more detailed assessment of work function and cost-benefit of chronically depressed patients in maintenance pharmacotherapy.

Psychotherapy

Unfortunately, far less is known about the efficacy of psychotherapy for treatment of dysthymic disorder (Markowitz, 1994), for which the only federally funded study was only recently begun.

Why use psychotherapy at all, if medication has demonstrated efficacy? (See Table 23.1.) One rationale for the use of psychotherapy is that only about 50% of dysthymic patients who receive medication respond. Others cannot tolerate medication side effects, have medical contraindications to taking medication, or simply refuse to take it. Patients who only partially respond to pharmacotherapy may benefit from adjunctive psychotherapy (Markowitz, 1993), which may have particular benefit in remediating the social skills that dysthymic patients typically lack.

Table 23.1 Rationale for Anti-Dysthymic Psychotherapy

1. Lack of medication response
2. Intolerable medication side effects
3. Medical contraindications to pharmacotherapy
4. Patient refusal of pharmacotherapy
5. Patient preference
6. Partial medication response (indication for adjunctive psychotherapy)
7. Demonstrated efficacy of psychotherapies for acute depressive episodes
8. Potential benefits for social skills of dysthymic patients
9. Few psychotherapeutic side effects
10. Nonpsychiatric therapists

The relatively sparse literature on psychotherapeutic treatment outcome for dysthymic disorder has been reviewed elsewhere (Markowitz, 1994). Psychodynamic psychotherapy probably remains the most widely practiced talking treatment in the United States, and dysthymic patients probably account for a significant proportion of the patients in such treatments, yet to date, there have been no outcome studies of its use in chronically depressed patients. One possible technical disadvantage of psychodynamic psychotherapy for chronically depressed patients is the tenet of therapist neutrality, which may lead dysthymic patients to believe that therapists tacitly agree with their self-blame. Another is the therapeutic focus on inner conflict and "personality," which may be epiphenomena of the depressive syndrome. This emphasis may lead patients to believe that they somehow "want to be depressed," rather than that they have a mood disorder which is explicitly defined as not being their fault.

In the past two decades, several time-limited psychotherapies have been developed and tested for patients with mood disorders. The best known and most carefully studied are cognitive behavioral therapy (CBT) and interpersonal psychotherapy (IPT). These treatments focus on the alleviation of a targeted syndrome (e.g., major depression) rather than on character change. Therapy is relatively structured in comparison to an open-ended psychodynamic psychotherapy. Treatment lasts for a predetermined number of weekly sessions, generally between 12 and 20.

Cognitive Behavioral Therapy Cognitive therapy was initially developed as a treatment for outpatients with acute major depression and has demonstrated efficacy in a series of controlled treatment trials (Beck, Rush, Shaw, & Emery, 1979). Cognitive behavioral therapy focuses on the automatic, irrational negative thoughts that depressed patients tend to think, believe, and act upon. Taking a structured approach, the CBT therapist helps patients to recognize and challenge these negative thoughts and thereby to alleviate the depression.

CBT has been applied to the treatment of dysthymic disorder both in its original form, devised for treatment of major depressive episodes (deJong, Treiber, & Henrich, 1986; Fennel & Teasdale, 1982; Gonzalez, Lewinsohn, & Clarke, 1985; Harpin, Liberman, Marks,

Stern, & Bohannon, 1982; Mercier, Stewart, & Quitkin, 1992; Stravynski, Shahar, & Verreault, 1991; Thase et al., 1994), and in a mode specifically adapted for dysthymic disorder (McCullough, 1991). Several of these eight studies have methodological limitations,[1] but their overall reported response rate is 39% for 138 subjects—a response rate approximately 10% lower than that of pharmacotherapy trials, but still considerable (Markowitz, 1994). Some of these studies reported maintenance of gains on follow-up of up to 2 years. A multisite study is comparing acute and long-term efficacy of a modified form of CBT (McCullough, 1992) to that of antidepressant medication.

Interpersonal Psychotherapy Like CBT, IPT was developed as a time-limited, testable treatment for outpatients with major depression. IPT, too, has demonstrated efficacy in the treatment of outpatients with acute and with recurrent major depressive episodes (Klerman, Weissman, Rounsaville, & Chevron, 1984), as well as in the treatment of a variety of subpopulations of patients with depression and nonmood disorders (Klerman & Weissman, 1993). One comparative study for major depression found similar efficacy for IPT and amitriptyline, but subjects who received IPT has gained new social skills at 1-year follow-up, whereas medication yielded no such benefit (Weissman, Klerman, Prusoff, Sholomskas, & Padian, 1981).

The IPT therapist helps depressed patients recognize the connection between their mood and environmental events or the handling of their social role: When upsetting things happen, you tend to feel bad, and when you feel depressed, you handle your social role poorly, and the result is bad events. Patients learn strategies to better handle affectively charged interpersonal problem areas that serve as the focus of the therapy. These potential foci are classified as complicated bereavement, role disputes, role transitions, or interpersonal deficits.

Because IPT addresses the interpersonal difficulties that are a hallmark of dysthymic disorder, a group at Cornell University Medical College has tested its efficacy in an open trial (Markowitz, 1994, 1998; Mason, Markowitz, & Klerman, 1993). In this trial, 17 patients, including 7 (41%) who had failed robust antidepressant medication trials, received IPT from three therapists. None worsened; 11 (65%) reached remission (defined as a Hamilton Depression Rating Scale [Ham-D 1; Hamilton, 1960] score ≤ 8). Mean Ham-D scores fell from 21.5 ± 4.4 at baseline to 7.4 ± 4.7 at the 16-week termination. Several of these subjects have now been followed for more than 2 years in monthly maintenance IPT, and most have remained euthymic. Maintenance sessions appear helpful to patients who, newly remitted after a 16-week acute treatment, benefit from the opportunity to gradually consolidate treatment gains. We are currently conducting an NIMH-funded randomized trial comparing IPT, supportive psychotherapy, and sertraline as treatments for dysthymic disorder. This study also examines the economic outcome of these treatments.

Browne, Steiner and colleagues at McMaster University in Canada have presented preliminary results of their large two-year study of sertraline versus IPT versus sertraline plus IPT for dysthymic primary care patients (Steiner et al., 1997). One year results found sertraline alone ($n = 229$) and sertraline + IPT ($n = 247$) superior to IPT alone ($n = 231$) based on 30% and 40% reductions in depression scores: 71%, 69%, and 61% of subjects reached 30% reduction in scores, respectively, at 1 year. IPT was associated with an economically important reduction in expenditures for health care and social services after one year: hence combined treatment was as effective as but less expensive than sertraline alone.

Combined Treatment Although pharmacotherapy alone may constitute sufficient treatment for some dysthymic patients, some responders to antidepressant medication feel better, but "lost," in their newfound euthymia. They no longer wish to think or act as their dysthymic disorder led them to in the past, but they have yet to establish a new outlook and behavioral "track record." In short, they feel different and want to be different but are not sure how to proceed with this change. Psychotherapy can be a great boon under these circumstances (Markowitz, 1993). Unfortunately, research on combined pharmacotherapy/psychotherapy treatment has been minimal (Markowitz, 1994).

Given such limited research into acute psychotherapy of dysthymic disorder, it comes as no surprise to learn that there have been no maintenance trials to date. Indeed, there have scarcely been any maintenance psychotherapy studies of any kind (Frank et al., 1990; Weissman, 1994). Maintenance therapy might presumably have lower "dosage" or intensity, perhaps monthly or biweekly sessions following a successful acute treatment. Monthly maintenance sessions appeared helpful in our open trial of IPT for dysthymic patients, and monthly IPT has been found to provide helpful prophylaxis in treating patients at high risk for recurrent major depression (Frank et al., 1990).[2]

Cost-Effectiveness of Treatment

The syndrome of depression is extremely expensive. Greenberg et al. (1993) estimated that depression costs $43.7 billion annually in the United States. These authors were unable to differentiate among depressive subtypes in their estimates of some areas of cost: suicide (where dysthymic disorder undoubtedly ranks lower than major depression or bipolar disorder) and direct treatment costs (for which dysthymic disorder presumably accounts for a significant proportion). In the area of work productivity, however, Greenberg et al. did provide a breakdown for the costs of dysthymic disorder. They estimated that there are 2.8 million workers among the more than 4 million Americans who suffer from dysthymic disorder. Greenberg et al. (1993) assume that dysthymic patients do not "experience excess absentee days while suffering" (p. 411), an assumption that some other research would seem to contradict (Broadhead, Blazer, George, & Tse, 1990; Wells et al., 1989, 1992). Ignoring absenteeism, the authors estimate a potential annual work value of $45 billion for dysthymic individuals, of which 20%, or $9 billion, is lost due to the illness. The authors also assume in their calculations that two thirds of dysthymic patients receive treatment, and that treatment reduces the duration of the episode in the current year by a third, from 50 to 33 weeks (Greenberg et al., 1993). Yet whether dysthymic patients actually receive effective treatment for this often mistreated condition is unclear. If dysthymic patients in fact miss work or are subjected to lengthy ineffective treatments, the estimated cost of dysthymic disorder would be still higher. By contrast, effective treatments might well reduce the morbidity of this chronic illness more than Greenberg et al. have estimated, yielding greater savings.

The economics of psychiatric treatment is a topic about which most psychiatrists and other mental health professionals know little. (The author includes himself in this generalization.) Clinicians understand effectiveness of treatment far better than cost-effectiveness. They see the costs of dysthymia as human suffering, in emotional pain, physical symptoms, and suicide, in addition to the "human capital" of job absenteeism and inefficiency when able to work (Rice, Hodgson, & Kopstein, 1985) (see Table 23.2). They recognize that effective treatment of dysthymic disorder can relieve a lifetime of pain. Most clinicians probably assume that the clinical improvement they see in a remitted dysthymic patient must translate into cost savings. These would include gains in work attendance and productivity, lowered health care costs as psychic and somatic concerns subside, and a lowered risk of psychiatric hospitalization—a huge expense—through prophylaxis of the risk of double depression, the acutely worsened state in which dysthymic patients generally present for hospital admission. Prevention of depression also lowers the risk of suicide. Whereas pharmacotherapy requires the ongoing expense of medication, psychotherapy of dysthymic disorder might hope to get by with the cost of relatively infrequent maintenance sessions. Nine billion dollars in lost work productivity—not to mention the other costs of dysthymic disorder—should buy a lot of prevention while still saving money.

Table 23.2 Potential Cost Savings of Anti-Dysthymic Psychotherapy

1. *Human costs*
   a. Reduction in symptoms and suffering
   b. Prevention of suicide
2. *Treatment costs*
   a. Reduction of hospitalization costs
   b. Reduction of outpatient medical and psychotherapy costs for ineffectively treated dysthymic patients (less cost of providing effective acute and maintenance psychotherapy)
   c. Saving of cost of antidepressant medication
3. *Human capital*
   a. Reduced job absenteeism
   b. Higher work productivity
   c. Better social skills

The NIMH Cost Effectiveness of Psychotherapy Conference in January 1994 brought together economists, clinical researchers, and health services researchers. All happily agreed that economic indices should be built into clinical research trials. On the last day of the 3-day meeting, however, it became apparent that economic studies require large numbers of subjects, far surpassing the capacity of most clinical research. Cost-efficacy has thus not been tested in clinical trials with the sophistication that most economists would desire either for psychotherapy generally or the psychotherapy of chronic depression.

Detection of dysthymic disorder is simple and feasible from a brief questionnaire (Burnam et al., 1988). Time-limited, depression-focused psychotherapy such as CBT or IPT, although not yet of clearly proven efficacy, could provide a relatively inexpensive low-tech treatment. If so, psychotherapy could provide enormous savings in all the areas listed in Table 23.2.

Recommendations

It is premature to make treatment recommendations about the psychotherapy of dysthymic disorder, inasmuch as the case for efficacy remains incomplete. It is not too soon, however, to argue for definitively making that case. Now that health services researchers, such as Wells and colleagues, and economic analysts, such as Greenberg and Finkelstein, have demonstrated the huge costs of dysthymic disorder, clinical research must demonstrate the efficacy of psychotherapies to treat it. (Wells himself, 1995, has called for such a demonstration.) This research should explore the potential cost-effectiveness of clinical treatment in lowering other medical costs, increasing work attendance and productivity, enhancing quality of life, and so on (see Table 23.3).

Such research should test the acute and maintenance efficacy of time-limited therapies focused on the alleviation of dysthymic disorder (Markowitz, 1993). IPT and CBT, for which treatment manuals exist (Markowitz & Klerman, 1993; McCullough, 1992), are promising candidates. The time limit of these therapies has obvious—although not formally documented—economic benefits, and they have already shown efficacy in treating other forms of depression. The psychotherapies targeting dysthymic disorder have tended to have an interpersonal focus, which makes sense given the difficulties dysthymic patients have in interpersonal situations.

Particularly interesting would be research examining the serial and combined application of psychotherapy and pharmacotherapy of dysthymic disorder in order to glean some understanding of the differential therapeutics of this disorder. That is, which patients are likely to benefit from psychotherapy rather than medication, vice versa, or a combination of the two approaches? Because of dysthymic disorder's chronicity, follow-up assessments are important to ensure that treatment has more than a transient effect on entrenched symptoms and patterns of functioning.

In trying to answer the question, "How can care for depression become more cost-effective?" Sturm and Wells (1995) found psychotherapy to be an important part of their model. They used the term *counseling* in lieu of *psychotherapy* (see chapter 6, in this volume), noting that "an operational definition of effective psychotherapy in typical practice settings is difficult" (Wells, 1995, p. 52). More work needs to be done to define typical practices, and whether they work. As economic pressures on mental health services increase, and as research and clinical expertise in psychotherapy improve, it increasingly should be possible to define effective and cost-effective psychotherapy for dysthymic patients.

There have been no federally funded studies of psychotherapy outcome research in dysthymic disorder—a terrible oversight, given the prevalence of the disorder and the presumed frequency of the treatment. Nor has there been federally funded research specifically examining service provision of psychotherapy for dysthymic patients. The author fears that the chronic symptoms of dysthymic patients discourage many of their therapists, after which therapy drags on in a long, demoralized dance. An advantage of manualized, targeted antidysthymic treatments is that they give therapists alternatives to demoralization: There's a next step in the therapy if one step fails.

It is essential to test the efficacy of such therapies for dysthymic patients, and to disseminate them once they have been shown to work. Psychotherapy must be tested and accountable, as until recently, it has not been. It should not be abandoned on the eve of demonstrating its utility.

Table 23.3 Recommended Psychotherapy Research on Dysthymic Disorder

1. Time-limited, manualized therapies (e.g., IPT, CBT)
2. Interpersonal focus
3. Serial design
4. Combined treatment trials
5. Continuation and maintenance trials
6. Follow-up assessments
7. Cost assessments of
   a. Work attendance
   b. Work performance
   c. Medical and mental health expenses

Notes

1. Most studies treated small, idiosyncratic samples (e.g., inpatients, patients with varying degrees of antidepressant nonresponse) and used differing outcome measures. None monitored therapist adherence to the psychotherapy protocol. Most reports reflect the work of a single therapist. Most studies did include some degree of follow-up assessment, an appropriate consideration for treatment of a chronic disorder.

2. It should be noted, however, that in the Frank et al. study (1990), low-dose (monthly) maintenance IPT was less protective than high-dose antidepressant medication. Over the 3-year follow-up of the study, no

advantage was found to continuing monthly IPT as an adjunct to continued high-dose medication.

Acknowledgments This chapter was supported in part by grants MH-37103 and MH-49635 from the National Institute of Mental Health, the Nancy Pritzker Foundation and by the Reader's Digest and Community Trust.

References

American Psychiatric Association. (1980). *Diagnostic and statistical manual of mental disorders* (3rd ed.). Washington, DC: Author.

American Psychiatric Association. (1994). *Diagnostic and statistical manual of mental disorders* (4th ed., rev.). Washington, DC: Author.

Beck, A. T., Rush, A. J., Shaw, B. F., & Emery, G. (1979). *Cognitive therapy of depression.* New York: Guilford Press.

Broadhead, E., Blazer, D., George, L., & Tse C. (1990). Depression, disability days lost from work in prospective epidemiologic survey. *Journal of the American Medical Association, 264,* 2524–2528..

Browne, G. (1997, November). Sertraline vs. interpersonal psychotherapy (IPT) alone or in combination for people with dysthymia in primary care. World Psychiatric Association Conference on the Synthesis between Psychopharmacology and Psychotherapy, Jerusalem, Israel.

Burnam, M. A., Wells, K. B., Leake, B., et al. (1988). Development of a brief screening instrument for detecting depressive disorders. *Medical Care, 38,* 775–789.

Cassano, G. B., Perugi, G., Maremmani, I., & Akiskal, H. S. (1990). Social adjustment in dysthymia. In S. W. Burton & H. S. Akiskal (Eds.), *Dysthymic disorder.* London: Gaskell.

Conti, D. J., & Burton, W. N. (1994). The economic impact of depression in a workplace. *Journal of Occupational Medicine, 36,* 983–988.

deJong, R., Treiber, R., & Henrich, G. (1986). Effectiveness of two psychological treatments for inpatients with severe and chronic depressions. *Cognitive Therapy and Research, 10,* 645–663.

Fennell, M. J. V., & Teasdale, J. D. (1982). Cognitive therapy with chronic, drug-refractory depressed outpatients: A note of caution. *Cognitive Therapy and Research, 6,* 455–460.

Finkelstein, S., Berndt, E. R., Greenberg, P., Parsley, R. A., & Keller, M. B. (1995). Improvement in subjective work performance after treatment of chronic depression: Some preliminary results. Poster presentation at the 35th Annual New Clinical Drug Evaluation Unit (NCDEU) Meeting, Orlando, FL.

Frank, E., Kupfer, D. J., Perel, J. M., Cornes, C., Jarrett, D. B., Mallinger, A. G., Thase, M. E., McEachran, A. B., & Grochocinski, V. J. (1990). Three-year outcomes for maintenance therapies in recurrent depression. *Archives of General Psychiatry, 47,* 1093–1099.

Friedman, R. A., Markowitz, J. C., Parides, M., & Kocsis, J. H. (1995). Acute response of social functioning in dysthymic patients with desipramine. *Journal of Affective Disorders, 34,* 85–88.

Friedman, R. A. (1993). Social impairment in dysthymia. *Psychiatric Annals, 23,* 632–637.

Gonzales, L. R., Lewinsohn, P. M., & Clarke, G. N. (1985). Longitudinal follow-up of unipolar depressives: An investigation of predictors of relapse. *Journal of Consulting and Clinical Psychology, 53,* 461–469.

Greenberg, P. E., Stiglin, L. E., Finkelstein, S. N., et al. (1993). The economic burden of depression in 1990. *Journal of Clinical Psychiatry, 54,* 405–418.

Hamilton, M. (1960). A rating scale for depression. *Journal of Neurology and Neurosurgery, 25,* 56–62.

Harpin, R. E., Liberman, R. P., Marks, I., Stern, S., & Bohannon, W. E. (1982). Cognitive-behavior therapy for chronically depressed patients: A controlled pilot study. *Journal of Nervous Mental Disease, 170,* 295–301.

Keller, M. B., & Shapiro, R. W. (1982). "Double depression": superimposition of acute depressive episodes on chronic depressive disorders. *American Journal of Psychiatry, 139,* 438–442.

Kessler, R. C., McGonagle, K. A., Zhao, S. et al. (1994). Lifetime and 12-month prevalence of DSM-III-R psychiatric disorders in the United States: Results from the National Comorbidity study. *Archives of General Psychiatry, 51,* 8–19.

Klerman, G. L., Weissman, M. M., Rounsaville, B. J., & Chevron, E. S. (1984). *Interpersonal psychotherapy of depression.* New York: Basic Books.

Klerman, G. L., & Weissman, M. M. (1993). *New applications of interpersonal therapy.* Washington, DC: American Psychiatric Press.

Kocsis, J. H., & Frances, A. J. (1987). A critical discussion of DSM-III dysthymic disorder. *American Journal of Psychiatry, 144,* 1534–1542.

Kocsis, J. H., Francis, A. J., Voss, C., et al. (1988). Imipramine and social-vocational adjustment in chronic depression. *American Journal of Psychiatry, 145,* 997–999.

Kocsis, J. H., Friedman, R. A., Markowitz, J. V., Leon, A., Miller, N., Gniwesch, L., & Parides, M. (1996). Maintenance therapy for chronic depression: A controlled clinical trial of desipramine. *Archives of General Psychiatry, 53,* 769–774.

Markowitz, J. C. (1993). Psychotherapy of the postdysthymic patient. *Journal of Psychotherapy Practice and Research* 2, 157–163.

Markowitz, J. C. (1994). Psychotherapy of dysthymia. *American Journal of Psychiatry, 151,* 1114–1121.

Markowitz, J. C. (1995). Dysthymia: Respect for the long-suffering. *Psychiatric Services, 46,* 5.

Markowitz, J. C. (1998). *Interpersonal psychotherapy for dysthymic disorder.* Washington, DC: American Psychiatric Press.

Markowitz, J. C., & Klerman, G. L. (1993, November). *Manual for interpersonal therapy of dysthymic disorder* (Edition 2.1). Unpublished manuscript, Cornell University Medical College.

Markowitz, J. C., Moran, M. E., Kocsis, J. H., & Frances, A. J. (1992). Prevalence and comorbidity of dysthymic disorder among psychiatric outpatients. *Journal of Affective Disease, 24,* 63–71.

Mason, B. J., Markowitz, J., & Klerman, G. L. (1993). IPT for dysthymic disorder. In G. L. Klerman & M. M. Weissman (Eds.), *New applications of interpersonal psychotherapy* (pp. 225–264). Washington, DC: American Psychiatric Press.

McCullough, J. P. (1991). Psychotherapy for dysthymia: A naturalistic study of ten patients. *Journal of Nervous Mental Disease, 179,* 734–740.

McCullough, J. P. (1992). *The manual for therapists treating the chronic depressions and using the cognitive-behavioral analysis system of psychotherapy.* Unpublished manuscript, Virginia Commonwealth University.

McCullough, J. P., Klein, D. N., Shea, M. T., et al. (1992). DSM-IV field trial for major depression, dysthymia, and minor depression. *Abstracts of the American Psychological Association Annual Meeting,* Washington, DC.

Mercier, M. A., Stewart, J. W., & Quitkin, F. M. (1992). A pilot sequential study of cognitive therapy and pharmacotherapy of atypical depression. *Journal of Clinical Psychiatry, 53,* 166–170.

Rice, D. P., Hodgson, T. A., & Kopstein, A. N. (1985). The economic cost of illness: A replication and update. *Health Care Financing Review, 7,* 61–80.

Stewart, J. W., Quitkin, F. M., McGrath, P. J. et al. (1988). Social functioning in chronic depression: Effect of 6 weeks of antidepressant treatment. *Psychiatry Research, 25,* 213–222.

Stravynski, A., Shahar, A., & Verreault, R. (1991). A pilot study of the cognitive treatment of dysthymic disorder. *Behavioral Psychotherapy, 4,* 369–372.

Sturm, R., & Wells, K. B. (1995). How can care for depression become more cost-effective? *Journal of the American Medical Association, 273,* 51–58.

Thase, M. E., Reynolds, C. F., Frank, E., Simons, A. D., Garamoni, G. D., McGeary, J., Harden, T., Fasiczka, A. L., & Cahalane, J. F. (1994). Response to cognitive-behavioral therapy in chronic depression. *Journal of Psychotherapy Practice and Research,* 3, 204–214.

Weissman, M. M. (1994). Psychotherapy in the maintenance treatment of depression. *British Journal of Psychiatry, 165*(Suppl. 26), 42–50.

Weissman, M. M., & Klerman, G. L. (1977). The chronic depressive in the community: under recognized and poorly treated. *Comprehensive Psychiatry, 18,* 523–531.

Weissman, M. M., Klerman, G. L., Prusoff, B. A., Sholomskas, D., & Padian, N. (1981). Depressed outpatients: Results one year after treatment with drugs and/or interpersonal psychotherapy. *Archives of General Psychiatry, 38,* 52–55.

Weissman, M. M., Leaf, P. J., Bruce, M. L. et al. (1988). The epidemiology of dysthemia in five communities: rates, risks, comorbidity, and treatment. *American Journal of Psychiatry, 145,* 815–819.

Wells, K. B. Burnam, M. A., Rogers, W., Hays, R., & Camp, P. (1988). The course of depression in adult outpatients: Result from the medical outcomes study. *Archives of General Psychiatry, 145,* 815–819.

Wells, K. B. (1995). Dr. Wells replies (letter). *American Journal of Psychiatry, 152,* 1104–1105.

Wells, K. B., Katon, W., Rogers, B., & Camp, P. (1994) Use of minor tranquilizers and antidepressant medications by depressed outpatients: Results from the medical outcomes study. *American Journal of Psychiatry, 151,* 694–700.

Wells, K. B., Stewart, A., Hays, R. D., Burnam, M. A., Rogers, W., Daniel, M., Berry, S., Greenfield, S., & Ware, J. (1989). The functioning and well-being of depressed patients: Results of the medical outcomes study. *Journal of the American Medical Association,* 262, 914–919.

24

Cost-Effectiveness Issues in the Treatment of Posttraumatic Stress Disorder

Lisa H. Jaycox & Edna B. Foa

Posttraumatic stress disorder (PTSD) is an anxiety disorder with an estimated lifetime prevalence of approximately 9% (Breslau, Davis, Andreski, & Peterson, 1991). This prevalence rate is approximate, because PTSD entered the American diagnostic nomenclature only in 1980 (American Psychiatric Association [APA], 1980), and empirical data are limited. Embedded in the definition of PTSD is its etiology: An individual must have experienced a trauma to become eligible for the diagnosis. PTSD can render an individual extremely dysfunctional because of the anxiety symptoms, and also because of its high comorbidity with depressive symptoms, other anxiety disorders, and substance abuse (Kessler, Sonnega, Bromet, Hughes, & Nelson, 1995). While some effective treatments have been developed to combat this disorder, cost-effectiveness evaluations do not yet exist. This chapter will discuss issues related to costs associated with PTSD and propose directions for investigating cost-effectiveness of psychotherapy for this disorder.

The definition of PTSD and recent changes in the diagnostic criteria for this disorder will be discussed, and implications of the prevalence of trauma and of PTSD for costs to society will be highlighted. Efficacy of treatment and prevention interventions will be reviewed, and critical considerations for next steps in the cost-effectiveness study of psychotherapy will be suggested.

What Is PTSD?

Posttraumatic stress disorder is an anxiety disorder that occurs in reaction to an extreme stressor. The nature of the stressor was defined in *DSM-III-R* as an event that is outside the range of normal human experience and would be markedly distressing to almost anyone (APA, 1987). As will emerge from the forthcoming review of the prevalence of trauma, a normative definition of a trauma is inadequate. Therefore, *in DSM-IV* (APA, 1994), the criteria were amended to include two aspects: the objective characteristics of the aversive event and the subjective experiences of the victim. Specifically, the person must have experienced or witnessed a situation involving actual or threatened bodily injury, death, or physical integrity and must have felt helpless, horrified, or terrified during the experience.

PTSD symptoms fall into three general clusters: reexperiencing, avoidance, and arousal. To be eligible for a diagnosis of PTSD, three criteria must be met. First, the individual must reexperience the trauma in one of the following ways: nightmares, flashbacks, intrusive thoughts, emotional distress, or physiological arousal in response to internal or external cues, which serve as reminders of the trauma. Second, the individual must have at least three of the following avoidance symptoms: avoiding thinking about the trauma, avoiding reminders of the event, emotional numbing, detachment or distance from others, decreased interest in activities, psychogenic amnesia, and a sense of a foreshortened future. Finally, individuals must experience at least two of the following arousal symptoms: sleep disturbance, hypervigilance, exaggerated startle response, irritability or outbursts of anger, and difficulty concentrating. If these symptoms persist for at least 1 month and cause considerable impairment in daily living, a diagnosis of PTSD is appropriate.

Although PTSD cannot be formally diagnosed unless symptoms persist for at least 1 month, most individuals show marked symptoms and impairment immediately after a trauma and may benefit from some psychological intervention. The gap in time between the occurrence of the trauma and eligibility for the PTSD diagnosis is now filled with a new disorder, called Acute Stress Disorder (APA, 1994), which covers dissociative and anxiety symptoms lasting from 2 days to 4 weeks posttrauma.

The costs associated with victimization can be considered on three dimensions: costs to the individual in terms of suffering and distress, costs to his or her immediate environment (family and friends), and costs to society. While this chapter focuses primarily on trauma victims with the full PTSD diagnosis, it should be kept in mind that acute reactions to trauma and subthreshold symptoms would greatly increase calculations of the costs of the spectrum of disorders.

Scope of the Problem

Two prevalence rates are important to consider in PTSD: the number of individuals at risk for developing PTSD by virtue of having experienced a "trauma" as defined in current diagnostic criteria and the prevalence of diagnosable PTSD in traumatized individuals.

The prevalence of trauma and of PTSD is alarming: Researchers estimate that 39% of the general U.S. population has experienced at least one traumatic lifetime event. Lifetime prevalence of PTSD among trauma victims is estimated at 24%, and lifetime prevalence of PTSD in the general population is estimated at 9%, with up to a third (3.4%) of these cases having chronic PTSD (Breslau et al., 1991). In addition, up to 15% of the general population suffer from subthreshold symptoms (Davidson, Hughes, Blazer, & George, 1991). Women appear to be somewhat more likely than men to develop PTSD following trauma, 10.4% for the former and 5% for the latter (Kessler et al., 1995). In a national sample of women, 69% had experienced some type of trauma, and 36% had been victims of crime: sexual assault, aggravated assault, or the homicide of a close friend or relative. The lifetime prevalence of PTSD in this sample was 12.9%, with 6-month prevalence of 4.6% (Resnick, Kilpatrick, Dansky, Saunders, & Best, 1993). Traumas differ in their capacity to cause PTSD; therefore, prevalence rates will be discussed separately for different types of traumatic events.

Combat Exposure

At some point following military service in Vietnam, 31% of male veterans and 26.9% of female veterans reported symptoms of PTSD and over 15% of men and 8.5% of women (over 470,000 individuals) had PTSD at the time of the interview (Kulka et al., 1990). Among male monozygotic twins, 17% of those who served in Southeast Asia met lifetime diagnostic criteria for PTSD related to military service versus 5% of their cotwins who did not serve in Southeast Asia (Goldberg, True, Eisen, & Henderson, 1990). Troops assigned to graves registration duties in Operation Desert Storm showed 48% current and 65% lifetime prevalence of PTSD in deployed troops, compared to no cases of PTSD in nondeployed troops (Sutker, Uddo, Brailey, Vasterling, & Errera, 1994).

Civilians exposed to terrorism and torture are also at risk for PTSD. Examples include a terrorist attack on a Jerusalem bus in which 33% of survivors had PTSD 10 months after the attack (Shalev, 1992) and the torture of Norwegian shipmen in a Libyan port, following which 54% of survivors developed PTSD within two months of the experience (Weisaeth, 1989).

Accidents and Natural Disasters

Millions are affected each year by floods, tornados, earthquakes, hurricanes, and other disasters, and many experience PTSD in the aftermath of such events. One epidemiological study reported an overall prevalence of 4.6% following disasters (Robins et al., 1986); 59% of victims of a tornado and 54% of plane crash survivors met *DSM-III* criteria for acute PTSD (Madakasira & O'Brien, 1987; Sloan, 1988). Notably, such traumas differ in their capacity to produce PTSD: Among flood victims, 4.5% had PTSD after 16 months versus 21% of tornado victims (Steinglass & Gerrity, 1990).

Only a few studies examined the prevalence of PTSD following accidents. Burn injuries severe enough to require hospitalization produced PTSD in 35% of patients 2 months after the injury (Perry,

Difede, Musngi, Frances, & Jacobsberg, 1992). Following a motor vehicle accident, 40% of accident victims met criteria for PTSD initially, although prevalence decreased to 20% 6 months later (Blanchard et al., 1995). In another study, 11.2% of motor vehicle accident victims had a current diagnosis of PTSD (Norris, 1992). These studies highlight the differing ability of different types of trauma to cause chronic PTSD.

In a survey of Alaskan communities differing in degree of exposure to the *Exxon Valdez* oil spill, over 9% had PTSD one year after the disaster (Palinkis, Petterson, Russell, & Downs, 1993). This finding suggests that even those with little or no direct exposure to the trauma can develop PTSD, although the symptom severity is directly related to degree of exposure (March, 1992). *DSM-IV* (APA, 1994) defines victimization as directly experiencing, witnessing, or learning about a traumatic stressor. Thus, symptoms can develop in individuals who are not directly exposed to a trauma, but who view themselves as vulnerable to becoming a victim of such a trauma. Ferry workers, for example, who were *not* on the crew of the capsized *Herald of Free Enterprise* ferry manifested PTSD symptoms, presumably because they identified strongly with coworkers who were in the ferry disaster (Dixon, Rehling, & Shiwach, 1993). This phenomenon has been referred to as the *ripples outward effect.*

Sexual and Nonsexual Assaults

Estimates from a national random sample of women in 1992 showed that 12 million, or 12.9%, had been raped, and 10 million, or 11.1%, had been victims of aggravated assault (National Victim Center and Crime Victim Research and Treatment Center, 1992). In a prospective study, 94% of rape victims met symptom criteria for PTSD 1 month after the assault. Symptoms showed a natural reduction in severity for some women, but 47% continued to meet diagnostic criteria for PTSD 3 months postassault (Rothbaum, Foa, Riggs, Murdock, & Walsh, 1992). Somewhat lower rates were found among female and male victims of non-sexual assault: 42% of women and 32% of men 1 month after the assault, and 21% of women and no men at the 3-month assessment (Riggs, Rothbaum, & Foa, 1995). In a retrospective study, 35% of rape victims and 39% of aggravated-assault victims had a lifetime diagnosis of PTSD, and 13% and 12%, respectively, met current diagnostic criteria (Kilpatrick & Resnick, 1993).

The prevalence of child sexual molestation and domestic violence is astoundingly high. In a national survey, 27% of adult women and 16% of adult men reported abuse or molestation as children (Finkelhor, Hotaling, Lewis, & Smith, 1990). Among children who had been molested, 48% met symptom criteria for PTSD (McLeer, Deblinger, Atkins, Foa, & Ralphe, 1988), and 69% of help-seeking adult women with a history of child sexual abuse had PTSD (Rowan, Foy, Rodriguez, & Ryan, 1994).

Domestic violence tends to be underreported, but prevalence studies indicate that between one fifth and one third of women will be physically assaulted by a partner or ex-partner during their lifetime (Frieze & Browne, 1989). Domestic violence represents a large risk factor for PTSD, with about 45% of such women meeting full criteria for PTSD (Astin, Lawrence, Pincus, & Foy, 1990; Houskamp & Foy, 1991). In studies using standardized self-report or interview measures, estimates of 33% and 58%, respectively, of battered women in shelters and a counseling center were diagnosed with PTSD (Astin, Lawrence, & Foy, 1993; Astin, Ogland-Hand, Foy, & Coleman, 1995).

Vulnerable Professions

Certain professionals are at risk for PTSD by virtue of their increased probability of repeated direct exposure to trauma. In one study, 26% of police officers reported symptoms severe enough to meet symptom criteria of PTSD (Martin, McKean, & Veltkamp, 1986). Symptoms of PTSD have been noted in mental health staff exposed to patient violence: 9% and 12% of clinical staff at two sites met *DSM-III-R* criteria for the disorder (Caldwell, 1992). Fire fighters, emergency medical technicians, emergency room staff, and disaster workers are also thought to be at risk. For instance, 32%, 27%, and 30% of fire fighters of an Australian bushfire were found to have PTSD 4, 11, and 29 months after exposure, respectively (MacFarlane, 1989).

The observation that PTSD-like symptoms are prevalent among individuals exposed to trauma at work led to the development of "critical incident debriefing programs," which aim to prevent or ameliorate symptoms in high-risk individuals (Mitchell & Dyregrov, 1993).

Personal Vulnerability

The studies discussed above suggest that certain traumas are more likely to produce PTSD than other traumas, and that not all trauma victims develop PTSD. Individuals vary with respect to their ability to recover from traumatic experiences. Those with general dysfunction at baseline both appear vulnerable to being exposed to trauma and to developing chronic PTSD. Among psychiatric outpatients, 30% had experienced trauma in the preceding 2 years, and 59% exhibited severe PTSD-related symptoms (Brom & Witztum, 1992). Half to two thirds of homeless individuals had experienced at least one lifetime trauma, and 32% of men and 53% of women had PTSD. Overall, an estimated 18% of homeless men and 34% of homeless women had a lifetime incidence of PTSD. Interestingly, the onset of PTSD preceded homelessness in three quarters of these individuals (North & Smith, 1992). Studies on vulnerable populations suggest a vicious circle of psychological impairment, which leads to increased vulnerability to victimization, exacerbation of PTSD symptoms, and further dysfunction and victimization.

PTSD-Related Problems

PTSD often coexists with physical problems and other psychological difficulties, which complicate treatment and often lead to further impairments in daily living. The most common of these include depression, substance abuse or dependence, poor physical health, and impaired social and occupational functioning.

Depression and Suicide

Traumatic experiences render individuals at risk not only for PTSD, but also for depression and suicide. While some of the symptoms of PTSD and depression overlap (e.g., anhedonia, sleep disturbance), a high prevalence of depression has been found to characterize trauma victims. Rape victims manifest increased depression (Atkeson, Calhoun, Resick, & Ellis, 1982; Frank & Stewart, 1984; Frank, Turner, & Duffy, 1979), and 19.2% of rape victims have attempted suicide, as compared to 2.2% of nonvictims (Kilpatrick et al., 1985). Among individuals with PTSD, 26% to 68% met lifetime criteria for major depression, and 21% to 34% had dysthymic disorders (Keane & Wolfe, 1990; Kilpatrick, Saunders, Veronen, Best, & Von, 1987; Kulka et al., 1990).

Substance Abuse and Dependence

PTSD is often complicated by substance abuse or dependence. This comorbidity can be explained in two ways. First, the use of drugs or alcohol may increase exposure to trauma by placing the addicted individuals in risky environments. Second, victims with PTSD may medicate anxiety symptoms by using drugs or alcohol. Several studies provide support for the second supposition. A strong link has been found between childhood physical or sexual abuse and current alcohol abuse in adult women, even after controlling for factors such as treatment seeking and family background (Miller, Downs, & Testa, 1993). Female drug users in outpatient treatment reported a history of at least one trauma meeting *DSM-III-R* criteria, and 59% met lifetime criteria for PTSD (Fullilove et al., 1993). Among combat veterans treated for PTSD on an inpatient unit, 82% met criteria for alcohol abuse (Murphy et al., 1994).

Very few programs have been developed to treat PTSD and substance abuse disorders with an integrated approach, despite the high comorbidity. One such program has yielded promising results with combat veterans (Abueg, Fairbank, Drescher, Ruzek, & Gusman, 1994). However, more research in this area, with an attention to cost-effectiveness, is clearly warranted.

Medical Problems

Because the diagnosis of PTSD requires exposure to trauma, it is often accompanied by physical injury. Domestic violence injuries alone are estimated to account for more than 1 million emergency room visits per year (Straus, 1986). Physical injuries can exacerbate psychological symptoms. For instance, consider a severe automobile accident in which an individual receives severe back and neck trauma. If the individual experiences symptoms of PTSD following the accident, psychological stress and anxiety can slow the physical healing process or exacerbate pain resulting from the injury. Alternatively, physical pain and limitations in function can serve as reminders of the accident, thereby exacerbating psychological distress. Thus, the combination of physical trauma and PTSD may result in social and occupational dysfunction and lengthened recovery time, thereby augmenting the cost of the accident in terms of lost wages and productivity and increased use of medical and psychiatric services.

In addition to costs associated with actual injury, there is evidence trauma victims experience an increase in health concerns unrelated to injury. Veterans with PTSD have shown increases in incidence of hypertension, bronchial asthma, and peptic ulcers (Davidson et al., 1991) and use more inpatient medical services after discharge (Kulka et al., 1990). Female victims of sexual assault revealed more negative perceptions of health status, more symptoms, more negative health behaviors (e.g., lack of exercise, smoking), more doctor's visits per year, and more reproductive physiology illnesses than nonassaulted women within 2 years of the assault (Waigandt, Wallace, Phelps, & Miller, 1990). Similarly, female victims of criminal assault made twice the number of physician visits, incurring 2.5 times more outpatient costs than nonvictims. Doctor visits increased 15–24% during the year of the crime and 31–56% in the year after the crime, as compared to the 2 years before the crime. Increased violence of crime predicted higher numbers of visits (Koss, Koss, & Woodruff, 1991).

Impaired Social and Occupational Functioning

While impaired functioning is part of the definition of PTSD in the current diagnostic manual, there are specific areas of impairment outside the *DSM* criteria that are especially problematic. For instance, sexual dysfunctions and sexual dissatisfaction are extremely common among victims of sexual assault (Becker & Skinner, 1983; Becker, Skinner, Abel, & Cichon, 1986; Burgess & Holstrom, 1979a, 1979b; Ellis, Calhoun, & Atkeson, 1980). Resick, Calhoun, Atkeson, and Ellis (1981) found that social functioning was impaired in women following a sexual assault; however, function returned to baseline in all areas except work 4 months after the assault. A study of a nationally representative sample of male Vietnam veterans found significant impairment in functioning and quality of life among those with PTSD, even when the effects of comorbid psychiatric and other medical disorders were controlled (Zatzick et al., 1997).

Treatment Efficacy

Several different types of treatment have been suggested for PTSD, including supportive counseling individually or in groups, brief dynamic psychotherapy, hypnotherapy, pharmacotherapy, cognitive behavioral therapy, and, most recently, eye movement desensitization and reprocessing (EMDR). While some of these techniques are used routinely with trauma victims, only a few controlled outcome studies have been conducted. These have focused on efficacy of cognitive behavioral procedures such as systematic desensitization, exposure, and anxiety management techniques (Solomon, Gerrity, & Muff, 1992). An exception is the study (Brom, Kleber, & Defares, 1989) that compared desensitization to hypnotherapy, psychodynamic therapy, and a wait list control group. All treated patients showed a significant decrease in trauma-related symptoms compared to controls.

Outcome studies of cognitive behavioral techniques for PTSD were conducted either on combat veterans or female assault victims. In combat veterans, three controlled studies showed modest efficacy for imaginal exposure compared to no treatment or standard treatment without exposure (Boudewyns & Hyer, 1990; Boudewyns, Hyer, Woods, Harrison, & McCranie, 1990; Cooper & Clum, 1989; Keane, Fairbank, Caddell, & Zimering, 1989). This modest outcome, however, may not reflect accurately the power of this form of treatment, since combat veterans with PTSD seem to be particularly resistant to any form of treatment.

Several studies have examined female assault victims' responses to cognitive behavioral treatment, including exposure to trauma reminders and anxiety management techniques. Anxiety managment (stress inoculation training; Kilpatrick, Veronen, & Resick, 1982), assertiveness training, and supportive counseling were all found to be modestly effective compared to a wait list control, but not different from one another (Resick, Jordan, Girelli, Hutter, & Marhoefer-Dvorak, 1988).

Two studies compared the efficacy of treatments for women with chronic PTSD following rape or nonsexual assault. The first showed that stress inoculation training (SIT) and prolonged exposure were superior to supportive counseling and to a wait list control in reducing PTSD (Foa, Rothbaum, Riggs, & Murdock, 1991). Specifically, 50% of women in the SIT condition and 40% of women in the exposure condition lost the diagnosis of PTSD, whereas only 10% in the supportive counseling condition and none of the women in the wait list control group lost the diagnosis. In the second, the efficacy of SIT, exposure, and a combination of the two was compared to a wait list control condition (Foa et al., 1998). In the treatment groups, 60–70% of women lost the diagnosis of PTSD, with the exposure-alone group showing superiority over the other two groups on a combined measure of PTSD, depression, and general anxiety. In contrast, none of the women in the wait list control group lost the diagnosis of PTSD.

A different cognitive behavioral program called *cognitive processing therapy* (CPT), developed by Resick and Schnicke (1992), was compared to a natural wait list condition, with 50% of treated women manifesting improvement on PTSD measures that was maintained over time. However, the lack of randomization in this study renders the results inconclusive.

A relatively new technique called *eye movement desensitization and reprocessing* (EMDR; Shapiro, 1989) involves exposure along with saccadic eye movements. This technique has generated a lot of interest and some promise as an effective treatment, but its efficacy over and above established exposure therapies remains unclear.

Because only the efficacy of cognitive behavioral therapy had been systematically studied (Solomon et al., 1992), costs of this treatment only are considered below.

Prevention Programs

The concern about development of chronic PTSD in individuals exposed to traumatic events has led to the implementation of critical incident debriefing (e.g., Mitchell & Dyregrov, 1993). Such programs are offered to emergency personnel and victims of natural disaster with increasing frequency, but their efficacy is largely unknown. Rape centers also offer crisis intervention immediately after the assault, and these programs tend to focus on supportive counseling and education about legal and health issues related to assault. Again, while offered in many communities, these programs have not been subjected to controlled efficacy studies.

In a controlled study, Foa, Hearst, and Perry (1995) compared recent assault victims who received a brief (four-session) cognitive behavioral prevention program to women who received assessment only. At 2 months postassault, 10% of the prevention group versus 70% of the control group met criteria for a diagnosis of PTSD.

While the brief prevention program may prove to be cost-effective, given the large number of trauma victims, it may be prohibitive in cost to offer it to every victim. Therefore, studies should focus on predictors of chronic PTSD, so that individuals at risk can be identified and treated.

The Social Context of PTSD

The concern with cost-effectiveness of therapy has special relevance to PTSD because of the strong societal responsibility associated with this disorder. Indeed, PTSD is often caused by an experience that occurs within a societal context and thus has implications for the society at large. For instance, the experiencing or witnessing of sexual or criminal assault, combat exposure, child sexual abuse, work-related accidents, and automobile accidents occurs as part of the fabric of the prevailing societal norms and institutions. Recognition of the responsibility embedded in the circumstances in which PTSD emerges has led to the establishment of social structures aiming to compensate victims of trauma. These include state compensation funds for crime victims, Social Security disability, workmen's compensation, and court awards of monetary compensation for "pain and suffering." Thus, whereas a given society may feel responsible for helping sufferers of mental disorders in general, a moral society feels an obligation to remunerate trauma victims.

Societal responsibility can be envisioned within a variety of frameworks, among them prevention of traumas (e.g., accidents, crime), institution of programs that prevent chronic psychopathology, psychological treatment of victims with chronic symptoms, rehabilitation for trauma-related health problems, and monetary compensation. Programs have been instituted at all of these levels, but the work of evaluating cost-effectiveness is just beginning.

The compensation programs discussed above have at least two obvious cost implications. Not only do they incur direct costs of operation, but they sometimes create indirect costs referred to as *secondary gain*. That is, compensation systems may prevent recovery in some cases because if symptoms disappear, compensation is often discontinues. Before an evaluation of the balance between direct and indirect costs and their benefits, the cost of chronic PTSD to the victim, and to society, will be considered.

Costs Associated with PTSD

The total cost of anxiety disorders in 1990, in terms of both direct and indirect costs, has been estimated to be $46.6 billion dollars, which represents 32% of the mental health costs for that year. These costs had grown at a staggering rate (38%) over those estimated for 1985 (Dupont et al., 1993). The rates for depression were estimated at $43.7 billion per year, which included $23.8 billion in workplace costs, $7.5 billion in mortality costs, and $12.4 billion in direct costs.

The total costs of PTSD are unknown, but the high

comorbidity with depression, substance abuse, and other anxiety disorders suggests that PTSD is equally costly. Moreover, the high prevalence of traumatization (especially among women), the high rates of chronic PTSD among assault victims, and the enormous amount of violence in the United States may render PTSD an ever-growing source of cost if violence is not contained.

Direct Costs

Direct costs are usually defined as the cost of treatment. In the case of PTSD, this often includes an increase in the use of medical as well as psychiatric services. Although there are no good estimates of the costs associated with this disorder, as noted above, such costs include increased doctor visits, emergency room visits, psychiatric hospitalizations, and outpatient psychotherapy.

Because cognitive behavioral treatment has been found efficacious in reducing PTSD symptoms in female assault victims, costs of the treatment will be discussed. The average cost of cognitive behavioral therapy for anxiety disorders has been calculated to range from $1,000 to $6,330, depending on the specific disorder and the complexity of the treatment (Turner, Beidel, Spaulding, & Brown, 1995). These estimates indicate that psychotherapy expenses for core treatment vary considerably but average about $2,800 for the core treatment. It should be noted, however, that many therapists report using "booster sessions" to augment core treatment efficacy.

The standard cognitive behavioral treatment used at the Medical College of Pennsylvania for PTSD in female assault victims averages 9–12 sessions lasting 90 minutes each. At the cost of $100 per hour, total treatment cost ranges between $1,350 and $1,800 for core treatment. This treatment appears to eliminate a diagnosis in about 70% of women who complete the program. While this appears to be a cost-effective means of delivering therapy, there is not yet enough evidence to allow an evaluation of whether changes resulting from therapy translate into reduced physical and mental health costs after therapy ends.

Indirect Costs

Indirect costs include morbidity costs such as missed days at work and decreased work productivity. The symptoms of PTSD include sleep disturbance and loss of concentration, which have implications for productivity. Because these symptoms overlap with the symptoms of depression and other anxiety disorders, it can be argued that the indirect costs of PTSD probably match those of depression. Additional costs of PTSD may include workmen's compensation, litigation, and monetary awards to victims. Since PTSD is especially prevalent in fire fighters, police officers, and medics, the cost of training is another consideration when the presence of PTSD leads to job abandonment.

The Study of Cost-Effectiveness of Psychotherapy for PTSD

While effective short-term low-cost treatments are at least available for female assault victims, many victims still remain somewhat symptomatic, and some do not benefit from treatment. Moreover, little is systematically known about the cost of illness or about the influence of treatment in reducing this cost. Information about the size of indirect costs associated with PTSD remains unavailable, with the exception of data on increased health costs. Thus, does cognitive behavioral therapy result in increased productivity at work? Do patients helped by this treatment report fewer medical problems and utilize fewer medical resources? Do fewer patients rely on workmen's compensation or disability after successful treatment? These questions, so pertinent to cost-effectiveness, need to be further investigated.

Directions for the Future

Education

Individuals with PTSD often have little insight into the reasons for their symptoms before treatment is initiated and tend to report a sense of being out of control, falling apart, or going crazy. Education and training about common reactions to traumatic events helps reduce distress about symptoms, ameliorate stress, and speed up recovery. Given the alarming statistics concerning violence and exposure to other types of trauma, it behooves us to educate the public regarding the psychological and physical consequences of extreme stress—and particularly to target those at high risk of traumatization. While there have been some efforts to increase education about stress reactions and PTSD during training of various professionals, these are not yet part of routine practice.

Delivery of "Effective" Therapies

For those therapies that have been proven in efficacy studies, it is important to remember that this information is derived from studies conducted by experts in speciality clinics. How efficacious this treatment would be in the hands of therapists in community-based clinics is unknown. A therapy that can be delivered effectively by nonexperts who receive minimal training would obviously impact more individuals for less cost than a treatment that can only be delivered by specialists. Supportive therapies and crisis intervention have been traditional modes of psychosocial treatment for trauma victims, but their efficacy and effectiveness have not yet been studied. At the Medical College of Pennsylvania, community counselors are currently being trained to deliver cognitive behavioral therapy to rape victims with PTSD, but it will be several years before the transportability of even this therapy can be determined.

Evaluation of Unproven Therapies

As noted earlier, there is a paucity of efficacy studies on treatment for PTSD, and only a few treatment modalities, mainly cognitive behavioral therapy, have been submitted to rigorous examination. Moreover, most of the treatment studies focused on either war veterans or female assault victims and the generalizability of the results emerging from these studies to victims of other traumas are largely unknown. At present, a variety of treatment modalities, in a variety of settings, are being implemented with trauma victims who manifest trauma-related problems. It behooves us to learn about the efficacy of these widely practiced interventions. Indeed, Seligman (1995) recommended that rigorous evaluations of therapies commonly delivered at clinics should be introduced. Specifically, he proposed that patients be routinely evaluated prior to and after therapy, by the use of sound measures and blind assessors. Introducing an assessment component into already existing treatment centers would be less costly than the traditional efficacy studies and, if applied routinely, would begin to answer questions about what works and for whom. Thus, with limited funding dollars, the addition of routine measurement of services already being offered appears to be the most promising course of action for analyzing the effectiveness of treatment of PTSD.

While these evaluations cannot replace studies of the efficacy of well-delineated manualized interventions, they will at least tell us whether the widely practiced interventions for trauma victims are helpful or whether we are wasting vital community resources.

References

Abueg, F. R., Fairbank, J. A., Drescher, K. D., Ruzek, J. I., & Gusman, F. D. (1994). *A randomized clinical trial examining relapse prevention training in PTSD-Alcoholism.* Paper presented at the 10th Annual Meeting of the International Society for Traumatic Stress Studies, Chicago.

American Psychiatric Association. (1980). *Diagnostic and statistical manual of mental disorders* (3rd ed.). Washington, DC: Author.

American Psychiatric Association. (1987). *Diagnostic and statistical manual of mental disorders* (3rd ed., rev.). Washington, DC: Author.

American Psychiatric Association. (1994). *Diagnostic and statistical manual of mental disorders* (4th ed.). Washington, DC: Author.

Astin, M. C., Lawrence, K. J., & Foy, D. W. (1993). Posttraumatic stress disorder among battered women: Risk and resiliency factors. *Violence and Victims, 8*(1), 17–28.

Astin, M. C., Lawrence, K. J., Pincus, G., & Foy, D. W. (1990). *Moderator variables of posttraumatic stress disorder among battered women.* Paper presented at the annual meeting of the Society for Traumatic Stress Studies, New Orleans, LA.

Astin, M. C., Ogland-Hand, S. M., Foy, D. W., & Coleman, E. M. (1995). Posttraumatic stress disorder and childhood abuse in battered women: Comparisons with maritally distressed women. *Journal of Consulting and Clinical Psychology, 63*(2), 308–312.

Atkeson, B. M., Calhoun, K. S., Resick, P. A., & Ellis, E. M. (1982). Victims of rape: Repeated assessment of depressive symptoms. *Journal of Consulting and Clinical Psychology, 50*(1), 96–102.

Becker, J. V. & Skinner, L. J. (1983). Assessment and treatment of rape-related sexual dysfunctions. *The Clinical Psychologist, 36,* 102–105.

Becker, J. V., Skinner, L. J., Abel, G. G., & Cichon, J. (1986). Level of postassault sexual functioning in rape and incest victims. *Archives of Sexual Behavior, 15,* 37–49.

Blanchard, E. B., Hickling, E. J., Vollmer, A. J., Loos, W. R., Buckley, T. C., & Jaccard, J. (1995). Short-term follow-up of post-traumatic stress symptoms in motor vehicle accident victims. *Behaviour Research and Therapy, 33*(4), 369–377.

Boudewyns, P. A., & Hyer, L. (1990). Physiological response to combat memories and preliminary treatment outcome in Vietnam veteran PTSD patients treated with direct therapeutic exposure. *Behavior Therapy, 21*, 63–87.

Boudewyns, P. A., Hyer, L., Woods, M. G., Harrison, W. R., & McCranie, E. (1990). PTSD among Vietnam veterans: An early look at treatment outcome using direct therapeutic exposure. *Journal of Traumatic Stress, 3*, 359–368.

Breslau, N., Davis, G., Andreski, P., & Peterson, E. (1991). Traumatic events and posttraumatic stress disorder in an urban population of young adults. *Archives of General Psychiatry, 48*, 216–222.

Brom, D., Kleber, R. J., & Defares, P. B. (1989). Brief psychotherapy for posttraumatic stress disorders. *Journal of Consulting and Clinical Psychology*, 57(5), 607–612.

Brom, D., & Witztum, E. (1992). Recent trauma in psychiatric outpatients. *American Journal of Orthopsychiatry*, 62(4), 545–551.

Burgess, A. W., & Holmstrom, L. L. (1979a). Adaptive strategies and recovery from rape. *American Journal of Psychiatry, 136*, 1278–1282.

Burgess, A. W., & Holstrom, L. L. (1979b). Rape: Sexual disruption and recovery. *American Journal of Orthopsychiatry, 49*, 648–657.

Caldwell, M. F. (1992). Incidence of PTSD among staff victims of patient violence. *Hospital and Community Psychiatry*, 43(8), 838–839.

Cooper, N. A., & Clum, G. A. (1989). Imaginal flooding as a supplementary treatment for PTSD in combat veterans: A controlled study. *Behavior Therapy, 20*, 381–391.

Davidson, J., Hughes, D., Blazer, D., & George, L. (1991). Post traumatic stress disorder in the community: An epidemiological study. *Psychological Medicine, 21*, 713–721.

Dixon, P., Rehling, G., & Shiwach, R. (1993). Peripheral victims of the Herald of Free Enterprise disaster. *British Journal of Medical Psychology, 66*, 193–202.

Dupont, R. L., Shirobi, B. S., Rise, D., Miller, L. S., Clayton, R., & Herich, M. (1993). *The economic cost of anxiety disorders.* Paper presented at the Anxiety Disorders Annual Meeting, Charleston, SC.

Ellis, E. M., Calhoun, K. S., & Atkeson, B. M. (1980). Sexual dysfunction in victims of rape. *Women and Health, 5*, 39–47.

Finkelhor, D., Hotaling, G., Lewis, I. A., & Smith, C. (1990). Sexual abuse in a national survey of adult men and women: Prevalence, characteristics, and risk factors. *Child Abuse and Neglect, 14*, 19–28.

Foa, E. B., Dancu, C. V., Hembree, E. A., Jaycox, L. H., Meadows, E. A., & Street, G. P. (1998). A comparison of exposure therapy, stress inoculation training, and their combination for reducing PTSD in female assault victims. Submitted for publication.

Foa, E. B., Hearst, D. E., & Perry, K. J. (1995). The evaluation of a brief cognitive-behavioral program for the prevention of chronic PTSD in recent assault victims. *Journal of Consulting and Clinical Psychology, 63*, 948–955.

Foa, E. B., Rothbaum, B. O., Riggs, D., & Murdock, T. (1991). Treatment of post-traumatic stress disorder in rape victims: A comparison between cognitive-behavioral procedures and counseling. *Journal of Consulting and Clinical Psychology, 59*, 715–723.

Frank, E., & Stewart, B. D. (1984). Depressive symptoms in rape victims: A revisit. *Journal of Affective Disorders, 7*, 77–85.

Frank, E., Turner, S. M., & Duffy, B. (1979). Depressive symptoms in rape victims. *Journal of Affective Disorders, 1*, 269–277.

Frieze, I. H. & Brown, A. (1989). Violence in marriage. In L. Ohlin, & M. Tonry (Eds.), *Family violence.* Chicago: University of Chicago Press.

Fullilove, M. T., Fullilove, R. E., III, Smith, K., Michael, C., Panzer, P. G., & Wallace, R. (1993). Violence, trauma, and post-traumatic stress disorder among women drug users. *Journal of Traumatic Stress*, 6(4), 533–543.

Goldberg, J., True, W. R., Eisen, S. A., & Henderson, W. G. (1990). A twin study of the effects of the Vietnam war on posttraumatic stress disorder. *Journal of the American Medical Association, 263*, 1227–1232.

Houskamp, B. M., & Foy, D. W. (1991). The assessment of posttraumatic stress disorder in battered women. *Journal of Interpersonal Violence, 6*, 365–371.

Keane, T. M., Fairbank, J. A., Caddell, J. M., & Zimering, R. T. (1989). Implosive (flooding) therapy reduces symptoms of PTSD in Vietnam combat veterans. *Behavior Therapy, 20*, 245–260.

Keane, T. M., & Wolfe, J. (1990). Comorbidity in posttraumatic stress disorder: An analysis of clinical and community studies. *Journal of Applied Social Psychology, 20*, 1176–1788.

Kessler, R. C., Sonnega, A., Bromet, E., Hughes, M., & Nelson, C. B. (1995). Posttraumatic stress disorder in the National Comorbidity Survey. *Archives of General Psychiatry, 52*, 1048–1060.

Kilpatrick, D. G., Best, C. L., Veronen, L. J., Amick, A. E., Villeponteaux, L. A., & Ruff, G. A. (1985). Mental health correlates of criminal victimization: A random community survey. *Journal of Consulting and Clinical Psychology, 53*, 866–873.

Kilpatrick, D., & Resnick, H. (1993). Posttraumatic stress disorder associated with exposure to criminal victimization in clinical and community populations. In J. R. T. Davidson & E. B. Foa (Eds.), *Posttraumatic stress disorder in review: DSM-IV and beyond*. Washington, DC: American Psychiatric Press.

Kilpatrick, D. G., Saunders, B. E., Veronen, L. J., Best, C. L., & Von, J. M. (1987). Criminal victimization: Lifetime prevalence, reporting to police, and psychological impact. *Crime and Delinquency, 33*, 479–489.

Kilpatrick, D. G., Veronen, L. J., & Resick, P. A. (1982). Psychological sequelae to rape: Assessment and treatment strategies. In D. M. Dolays & R. L. Meredith (Eds.), *Behavioral medicine: Assessment and treatment strategies*. New York: Plenum Press.

Koss, M. P., Koss, P. G., & Woodruff, W. J. (1991). Deleterious effects of criminal victimization on women's health and medical utilization. *Archives of Internal Medicine, 151*, 342–347.

Kulka, R. A., Schlenger, W. E., Fairbank, J. A., Hough, R. L., Jordan, B. K., Marmar, C. R., & Weiss, D. S. (1990). *Trauma and the Vietnam War generation: Report of findings from the National Vietnam Veterans Readjustment Study*. New York: Brunner/Mazel.

MacFarlane, A. C. (1989). The aetiology of post-traumatic morbidity: Predisposing, precipitating, and perpetuating factors. *British Journal of Psychiatry, 154*, 221–228.

Madakasira, S., & O'Brien, K. F. (1987). Acute post-traumatic stress disorder in victims of a natural disaster. *Journal of Nervous and Mental Disease, 175*, 286–290.

March, J. S. (1992). What constitutes a stressor: The "Criterion A" issue. In J. R. T. Davidson & E. B Foa (Eds.), *Posttraumatic stress disorder: DSM-IV and beyond* (pp. 37–54). Washington, DC: American Psychiatric Press.

Martin, C. A., McKean, H. E., & Veltkamp, L. J. (1986). Post-traumatic stress disorder in police work and working with victims: A pilot study. *Journal of Police Science and Administration, 14*(2), 98–101.

McLeer, S. V., Deblinger, E., Atkins, M. S., Foa, E. B., & Ralphe, D. L. (1988). Post-traumatic stress disorder in sexually abused children. *Journal of the American Academy of Child and Adolescent Psychiatry, 27*(5), 650–654.

Miller, B. A., Downs, W. R., & Testa, M. (1993). Interrelationships between victimization experiences and women's alcohol use. *Journal of Studies of Alcohol, 11*, 109–117.

Mitchell, J. T., & Dyregrov, A. (1993). Traumatic stress in disaster workers and emergency personnel. In J. P. Wilson & B. Raphael (Eds.), *International handbook of traumatic stress syndromes*. New York: Plenum Press.

Murphy, R. T., Bollinger, A., Rosenheck, R., Gusman, F. D., Foy, D., & Abueg, F. R. (1994). *Pilot study of PTSD and alcohol inpatient treatment effectiveness*. Paper presented at the 10th Annual Meeting of the International Society for Traumatic Stress Studies, Chicago.

National Victim Center and Crime Victim Research and Treatment Center. (1992). *Rape in America: A report to the nation* (Research Report #1992-1). Washington, DC: National Victim Center and Crime Victim Research and Treatment Center.

Norris, F. H. (1992). Epidemiology of trauma: Frequency and impact of different potentially traumatic events on different demographic groups. *Journal of Consulting and Clinical Psychology, 60*(3), 409–418.

Palinkis, L. A., Petterson, J. S., Russell, J., & Downs, M. A. (1993). Community patterns of psychiatric disorders after the *Exxon Valdez* oil spill. *American Journal of Psychiatry, 150*(10), 1517–1523.

Perry, S., Difede, J., Musngi, G., Frances, A. J., & Jacobsberg, L. (1992). Predictors of posttraumatic stress disorder after burn injury. *American Journal of Psychiatry, 149*, 931–935.

Resick, P. A., Calhoun, K. S., Atkeson, B. M., & Ellis, E. M. (1981). Social adjustment in victims of sexual assault. *Journal of Consulting and Clinical Psychology, 49*, 705–712.

Resick, P. A., Jordan, C. G., Girelli, S. A., Hutter, C. K., & Marhoefer-Dvorak, S. (1988). A comparative outcome study of behavioral group therapy for sexual assault victims. *Behavior Therapy, 19*, 385–401.

Resick, P. A., & Schnicke, M. K. (1992). Cognitive processing therapy for sexual assault victims. *Journal of Consulting and Clinical Psychology, 60*, 748–756.

Resnick, H. S., Kilpatrick, D. G., Dansky, B. S., Saunders, B. E., & Best, C. L. (1993). Prevalence of civilian trauma and posttraumatic stress disorder in a representative national sample of women. *Journal of Consulting and Clinical Psychology, 62*(6), 984–991.

Riggs, D. S., Rothbaum, B. O., & Foa, E. B. (1995). A prospective examination of symptoms of post-traumatic stress disorder in victims of non-sexual assault. *Journal of Interpersonal Violence, 10*(2), 201–214.

Robins, L., Fischbach, R., Smith, E., Cottler, L., Solomon, S. D., & Goldring, E. (1986). Impact of disaster on previously assessed mental health. In

J. Shore (Ed.), *Disaster stress studies: New methods and findings*. New York: American Psychiatric Press.

Rothbaum, B. O., Foa, E. B., Riggs, D. S., Murdock, T., & Walsh, W. (1992). A prospective examination of post-traumatic stress disorder in rape victims. *Journal of Traumatic Stress*, 5(3), 455–475.

Rowan, A. B., Foy, D. W., Rodriguez, N., & Ryan, S. (1994). Posttraumatic stress disorder in a clinical sample of adults sexually abused as children. *Child Abuse and Neglect*, *18*, 51–61.

Seligman, M. E. P. (1995). The effectiveness of psychotherapy: The Consumer Reports Study. *American Psychologist*, 50(12), 965–974.

Shalev, A. Y. (1992). Posttraumatic stress disorder among injured survivors of a terrorist attack. *Journal of Nervous and Mental Disease*, *180*(8), 505–509.

Shapiro, F. (1989). Efficacy of the eye movement desensitization procedure in the treatment of traumatic memories. *Journal of Traumatic Stress*, *2*, 199–223.

Sloan, P. (1988). Post-traumatic stress in survivors of an airplane crash-landing: A clinical and exploratory research intervention. *Journal of Traumatic Stress*, *1*(2), 211–229.

Solomon, S. D., Gerrity, E. T., & Muff, A. M. (1992). Efficacy of treatments for post-traumatic stress disorder: An empirical review. *Journal of the American Medical Association*, *268*, 633–638.

Steinglass, P., & Gerrity, E. (1990). Natural disasters and post-traumatic stress disorder: Short-term versus long-term recovery in two disaster-affected communities. *Journal of Applied Social Psychology*, 20(21), 1746–1765.

Straus, M. (1986). Domestic violence and homicide antecedents. *Bulletin of the New York Academy of Medicine*, 62(5), 446–465.

Sutker, P. B., Uddo, M., Brailey, K., Vasterling, J. J., & Errera, P. (1994). Psychopathology in war-zone deployed and non-deployed Operation Desert Storm troops assigned graves registration duties. *Journal of Abnormal Psychology*, *103*(2), 383–390.

Turner, S. M., Beidel, D. C., Spaulding, S. A., & Brown, J. M. (1995). The practice of behavior therapy: A national survey of costs and methods. *The Behavior Therapist*, *18*(1), 1–4.

Waigandt, A., Wallace, D. L., Phelps, L., & Miller, D. A. (1990). The impact of sexual assault on physical health status. *Journal of Traumatic Stress*, 3(1), 93–102.

Weisaeth, L. (1989). Torture of a Norwegian ship's crew: The torture, stress reactions, and psychiatric after-effects. *Acta Psychiatrica Scandinavica*, *80*, (Suppl. 355), 63–72.

Zatzick, D. F., Marmar, C. R., Weiss, D. S., et al. (1997). Posttraumatic Stress Disorder and functioning and quality of life outcomes in a nationally representative sample of male Vietnam veterans. *American Journal of Psychiatry*, *154*(12), 1690–1695.

25

Cost-Effectiveness of Psychotherapy for Eating Disorders

James E. Mitchell, Carol B. Peterson, & Stewart Agras

As in many other areas of psychotherapy research, cost-effectiveness in eating-disorder treatment research is only now being considered an important variable to study systematically (Yates, 1994). There are generic reasons for the lack of research in this area. One must consider the field of psychotherapy research in general and the background and training of the researchers who work in the area, most of whom are very skilled and knowledgeable in the areas of psychotherapy and outcome assessment but have little knowledge or expertise in issues related to health economics. Other reasons include the limited funds available for such research, and the fact that knowledge concerning the rigorous methodology needed for such studies is not yet widespread.

However, there are also specific reasons for the paucity of research on the cost-effectiveness of treatments in the area of eating disorder. The first concerns the nature and severity of certain eating disorders. The eating disorder that has been studied for the longest period of time, anorexia nervosa, is a disorder that is difficult to study from a treatment perspective for several reasons: (a) prevalence rates of anorexia nervosa in the general population are quite low even among adolescents and young adult women who are at highest risk (overall about 0.5%); therefore, many potential research sites lack the capacity to collect large enough cohorts of such patients for meaningful treatment studies; (b) many of these patients are adolescents, and issues of informed consent are often problematic; (c) many patients with anorexia nervosa require hospitalization, which introduces a major problem with any sort of randomization and introduces other biases concerning the availability of health insurance benefits, determinants of length of stay, and availability of such services in general (American Psychiatric Association [APA], 1993); (d) these patients are difficult to treat, and both short-term and long-term follow-up studies highlight the problems in working with this patient population, including the substantial morbidity and mortality rates associated with it (Comerci, 1990); (e) most patients require a multiplicity of interventions, including individual counseling, medical management, nutritional therapy, and family therapy (Eckert & Mitchell, 1994), which dictates the need for multiple treatment cells and complex designs and make it difficult to control for all possible therapy confounds (APA, 1993); These difficulties undoubtedly discourage many potential researchers; (f) because of the medical risks involved in this illness, randomization to placebo, waiting list, or minimal intervention control conditions is potentially unethical; and (g) many patients with anorexia nervosa are poorly motivated for treatment, and only seek treatment at the insistence of family members, spouses, or friends; the result is often an unwillingness on their part to participate meaningfully in research trials.

The second major type of eating disorder, bulimia nervosa, is a more obvious choice for studies of cost-effectiveness in psychotherapy research, given that (a) it is a more prevalent condition (1–3% among young women) than anorexia nervosa (Fairburn & Beglin, 1990); (b) patients who have bulimia nervosa generally can be treated on an outpatient basis without hospitalization; (c) patients with bulimia nervosa who present for help tend to be more highly motivated for treatment than anorectic patients; and (d) the number of interventions to which patients need to be exposed can be more easily controlled, so that it is possible to conduct parallel randomized trials. However, despite these advantages, the number of published studies remains modest. Perhaps the main reason is that bulimia nervosa was only described as a distinct diagnostic entity by Gerald Russell in 1979, and controlled treatment trials were not initiated until the early 1980s; therefore, the field has had less than 20 years to develop.

The first level of studies—those that demonstrate the efficacy of specific interventions compared to minimal intervention or waiting-list controls—has now been traversed, and investigators are progressing to second-generation studies that focus on comparing active treatments, dismantling treatment components, and examining predictors of treatment response and mediators of treatment effects (Shapiro, 1995). This area of research has not yet progressed to the point where issues of cost-effectiveness have been addressed empirically in terms of research, with the exception of one study, which will be reviewed (Koran et al,, 1995). Therefore, much of this chapter is more speculative than data-based.

We will attempt to briefly review the psychotherapy literatures that exist on bulimia nervosa (selecting this as an area of focus because of the larger treatment outcome literature than that on anorexia nervosa) and, with this review as a base, will offer some estimates of the costs of treatment to health care systems and patients. The primitive level of sophistication of this methodology will be obvious: Questions concerning quality of life, patient satisfaction, cost of clinical training, and the myriad of other issues that are important in realistically evaluating cost-effectiveness (Yates, 1994) are beyond the scope of this chapter, but for this disorder, few data on such issues exist.

The controlled psychotherapy treatment trials of bulimia nervosa are summarized in Table 25.1. In examining this list, several issues emerge. First, the number of studies is still small but growing. Also, as in much of the recent psychotherapy literature for several other types of psychopathology, there has been a focus on the use of cognitive behavioral therapy (CBT) techniques, perhaps owing to their strong theoretical base, the relative ease of manualizing them, and possibility of applying them in a time-limited format. Indeed, these techniques, when administered in group or individual formats, seem to be effective, although the results in specific studies have been highly variable (Mitchell et al., in press).

Therapies other than CBT have been used experimentally and also appear promising. Of particular note is the study by Fairburn et al. (1991) in which interpersonal therapy, or IPT, was directly compared to cognitive behavioral therapy and to a behavioral therapy that omitted cognitive restructuring. The choice of IPT was particularly interesting since this therapy does focuses not on modifying eating directly, but on changing problematic interpersonal relationships thought to contribute to and maintain bulimic symptoms. Although in the short term, CBT appeared to have advantages over IPT on psychopathological variables (including concerns about weight and shape and dietary restraint, both of which are core features of bulimia nervosa), both CBT and IPT were equally effective in reducing binge eating and vomiting frequency. To the surprise of the investigators and many others who work in this field, at follow-up IPT and CBT were essentially identical in terms of eating behavior and psychopathology (Fairburn et al., 1995). This finding has led to speculation that focusing on interpersonal problems that may perpetuate the symptoms, rather than on the eating-disorder symptoms per se, may lead to long-term improvements in eating patterns and associated psychopathology (Fairburn et al., 1994). While this is a single study that needs to be replicated, it does suggest that more than one type of psychotherapy (e.g., CBT) may be useful in the treatment of bulimia nervosa patients. Of note, both CBT and IPT have also been shown to be effective in the treatment of binge-eating disorder, a disturbance that has certain features in common with bulimia nervosa (Agras et al., 1992; Agras et al., 1994; Wilfley et al., 1993).

Turning to the issue of cost-effectiveness, several alternatives will be considered and compared: Cognitive behavioral techniques appear to hold much promise, and a CBT model that has been used in two large studies and that is currently being used at several centers in additional trials is the individual cognitive behavioral therapy developed by Fairburn et al. (1981, 1986, 1993). An alternative approach, which uses a group format, was developed at the University of Minnesota. This therapy has also been used in two studies that cumulatively have a substantial total sample size (Mitchell et al., 1990, 1993). The costs of providing or

Table 25.1 Controlled Psychotherapy Studies of Bulimia Nervosa

Authors, Year Published	Groups vs. Individuals	Active Treatment Cells	N Start	Complete %	Outcome: % Reduction in Binge Eating Frequency Pre to Post	Outcome: % of Subjects Abstinent at End of Treatment
Lacey, 1983	Ind. + group	Ind. + group	30	100	95	80.0
Connors et al., 1984	Group	Psychoed.[a]	26	77	70	
Yates & Sambrailo, 1984	Group	CBT[b] + BT[c]	24	67		13.0
		CBT				0.0
Kirkley et al., 1985	Group	CBT	14	93	97	
		Nondirective	14	64	64	
Ordman & Kirschenbaum, 1985	Ind.	Full	10	100		20.0
		Brief	10	100		20.0
Lee & Rush, 1986	Group	CBT	15	73	70	29.0
Wolchik et al., 1986	Ind. + group	Psychoeducational	13	85	58	0.0
Wilson et al., 1986	Group	Cog. restruct. + ERP[d]	9	85	82	71.0
		Cog. restruct.	8	67	51	33.0
Fairburn et al., 1986	Ind.	CBT	12	92	87	27.0
		Short-term focal	12	92	82	36.0
Laessle et al., 1987	Group	BT	8	100		38.0
Leitenberg et al., 1988	Group	CBT + ERP (ms)[e]	13	92	67[g]	42.0
		CBT + ERP (ms)[f]	13	85	73[g]	36.0
		CBT	12	100	40	8.0
Freeman et al., 1988	Ind. + group	Ind. CBT	32	66	79	
		Ind. BT	30	83	87	
		Group	30	63	87	
Agras et al., 1989	Group	Self-monitor	19	86	63[g]	24.0
		CBT	22	77	75	56.0
		CBT + ERP	17	94	52	31.0
Mitchell et al., 1989	Group	CBT + placebo	34	85	89	45.0
		CBT + imipramine	52	75	92	56.0
		Imipramine	54	67	49	16.0
Fairburn et al., 1991	Ind.	CBT	25	84	96.7	71.0
		IPT[h]	25	88	98.0	62.0
		BT	25	76	91.3	62.0

Fichter et al., 1991		Fluoxetine + BT	20	100	46.7	
		Placebo + BT	20	100	25.4	
Wilson et al., 1991	Ind.	CBT + ERP	11	82	78	54.6
		CBT	11	73	75	63.6
Laessle et al., 1991	Group	Nutri. mgmt.	27	81	70	50.0
		Stress mgmt.	28	93	70	27.0
Garner, 1993	Ind.	Psychodynamic	30	83	69	40.0
		CBT	30	83	73	11.0
Agras et al., 1992	Ind.	Desipramine—16 wks	12		−12.7[g]	35.0
		Desipramine—24 wks	12		44.1	42.0
		CBT[a] + Desipramine—16 wks	12	83	57.3	65.0
		CBT + Desipramine—24 wks	12		89.2	70.0
		CBT	12		71.3	55.0
Mitchell et al., 1993	Group	CBT				
		High emphasis on abstinence/ high intensity	33	88	76.7	69.7
		High/low	41	88	73.2	73.2
		Low/high	35	86	70.6	70.6
		Low/low	34	82	32.4	32.4
Thackwray et al., 1993	Ind.	Self-monitoring				69.0
		Behavioral	47	82	82	100.0
		CBT			100	92.0
					89	
Goldbloom et al., 1994	Ind.	Fluoxetine	23		52	17.0
		CBT	24		78	43.0
		Fluoxetine + CBT	29		86	27.0

Note. Adapted from Peterson & Mitchell (1995).
[a]Psychoeducational
[b]Cognitive behavioral therapy
[c]Behavioral therapy
[d]Cognitive restructuring + exposure and response prevention
[e]Multiple site
[f]Single site
[g]Reduction in vomiting
[h]Interpersonal psychotherapy

receiving these two programs will be evaluated, while acknowledging that they may not yield comparable outcomes, since they have not been directly compared. However, the percenta reduction in the frequencies of target eating behaviors and rates of abstinence following treatment have been comparable in the published studies using both approaches. The costs of therapists using both master's- and doctoral-level therapists will be addressed.

For purposes of this comparison, a third alternative will be added, which also has its advocates: medication management. The types of medication that have been studied in the largest clinical trials in bulimia nervosa are antidepressant drugs, which were originally used because of the high rate of comorbidity of affective disorders in bulimia nervosa patients (Pope et al., 1983), but which have subsequently been shown to exert a therapeutic effect on bulimic symptoms whether or not patients are depressed at baseline (Crow & Mitchell, 1994). The antidepressant that has been most extensively studied in bulimia nervosa patients is the serotonin reuptake inhibitor fluoxetine hydrochloride (Freeman et al., 1988; Fluoxetine Bulimia Nervosa National Collaborative Study Group [FBNCSG], 1992; Goldstein et al., in press). This drug has been used in two large multicenter studies. Possibly owing to the reduced frequency of visits and attenuated professional time, it is at times assumed that drug therapy is cheaper than psychotherapy. However, in certain situations this may not be the case. Such is the focus of our comparison.

For purposes of our comparison, we will present a rough analysis of the cost of individual psychotherapy using the individual CBT approach of Fairburn et al. (1993) the group CBT approach of Mitchell et al. (1990), and treatment with 60 mg a day of fluoxetine hydrochloride (the dosage that appeared to be optimal in the controlled trials). The two CBT treatments are both manual-based and time-limited. Although the available data suggest that the rates of abstinence achieved with psychotherapy are often superior to those achieved with drug therapy (Mitchell, Hoberman, & Pyle, 1989), for purposes of this analysis, it will be assumed that a course of CBT (group or individual) results in outcomes that are essentially equal to a 1-year course of treatment with fluoxetine hydrochloride. This duration was selected since the data on medication maintenance suggest that there are high relapse rates both with continuation and with discontinuation (Walsh, Hadigan, Devlin, Gladis, & Roose, 1991). For purposes of this analysis the cost of therapist time, MD time, and medication respectively, will be based on billing fees at the University of Minnesota practice group system. Admittedly, such estimates would vary widely at different sites. For the group CBT approach, we offer two different models (A-1 and A-2) that we have studied (Mitchell et al., 1990), one of which requires twice as much therapist time.

As can be seen in Table 25.2, although drug therapy is frequently regarded by many practitioners as relatively inexpensive compared to psychotherapy, this may not always be the case, at least when one is comparing a serotonin reuptake inhibitor—which appears to be the agent of choice in treating bulimia nervosa, given the available evidence—and a time-limited structured psychotherapy approach.

As an alternative, we also will discuss the only systematic study of cost-effectiveness in the treatment of eating disorders, recently completed by Koran et al. (1995) at the Department of Psychiatry and Behavioral Sciences at Stanford University. In the initial report of this study, the investigators demonstrated that 15 sessions of cognitive behavioral therapy combined with desipramine for 16 weeks was superior to CBT alone and to desipramine alone in achieving abstinence from bulimic symptoms at 16 weeks (end of treatment). They also demonstrated that 16 weeks of combined treatment followed by 8 additional weeks of desipramine treatment was superior to 15 sessions of cognitive behavioral treatment followed by 3 monthly sessions, and to 24 weeks of desipramine alone. In this comparison, at the 1-year follow-up, only 18% of those who had received medication for 16 weeks remained abstinent while 78% of those in the combination group who had received medication for 24 weeks were abstinent (Agras et al., 1994). In their cost analysis these investigators used two definitions of effectiveness: (a) the portion of patients who were abstinent from binge eating and purging at 32 weeks (4 to 16 weeks after the end of treatment) and at 1 year from the end of treatment and (b) the portion of patients who engaged in binge eating and purging once a week or less at the same time points. Costs were calculated by multiplying the clinical professional fees by the number of visits in the assigned treatment and adding the cost of medication and serum desipramine levels, with $120 used for the initial assessment, $50 for a brief medication visit, and $95 for a 50-minute individual CBT session. Desipramine at 250 mg a day cost $19.58 per week, and a serum desipramine level was $30. The analysis was based on calculations that produced an average cost per successful patient for each treatment at posttreatment and follow-up.

Table 25.2 Hypothetical Costs of Various Treatments for Bulimia Nervosa

Model	Visits	Duration/ Visits	Therapist	Salary ($)[a]	Cost/Billed ($)[b] per hour	Cost/ Patient ($)	Billed/ Patient ($)
Fairburn et al., 1995	20	50 min	PhD	66,240	46/120	960.00	2,400
Individual CBT	20	50 min	MA	50,400	35/90	700.00	1,800
Mitchell et al., 1993	14	Total time	PhD	66,240	46/44	172.20	990
Group CBT A-2	14	= 22.5 hrs	MA	50,400	35/44	131.25	990
Mitchell et al., 1993	22	Total time	PhD	66,240	46/44	345.00	1,980
Group CBT A-1	22	= 45 hr	MA	50,400	35/44	262.50	1,980
Pharmacotherapy with fluoxetine	13	15–25 min	MD	90,000	31/90	406.25	1,170
		60 mg/day (365 days × $1.70/20-mg pill × 3 pills = $1,861.50)					3,031.50

[a]Includes benefits.

[b]Assumes 6 patients/group; 30 client hours/week; 48 weeks/year. "Cost" is therapist cost to the institution in salary and fringe benefits. Does not include overhead. "Billed" is the amount third-party payers would be billed for this service in our system. Does not include reduced rates for HMO members, etc.

The results indicated that at 32 weeks, medication for 16 weeks was the most cost-effective treatment and the combination for 16 weeks was the least. However, at 1 year, medication for 24 weeks appeared the most cost-effective, and combination therapy for 16 weeks the least. The authors stressed that this analysis made certain assumptions that would not be applicable in all situations, and they stressed the complexity of meaningfully calculating such values. This is perhaps illustrated by our first analysis, which, in examining cost, suggests a possible advantage for psychotherapy over a serotonin reuptake inhibitor when a high dosage is used. This demonstrates that medication costs may have significant impact on cost of care, particularly over long periods of time during maintenance treatment, and on the need to balance cost considerations against issues of efficacy and side effects.

The simplicity of the model for cost as used in this analysis must be underscored. Cost of illness is clearly not equivalent to fees as is well detailed elsewhere in this volume. For example, in chapter 9, by Hargreaves, Shumway, and Hu, the measurements of both cost and effectiveness are complex paradigms, and a meaningful analysis of such issues has really not been conducted yet in eating-disorder psychotherapy research. This point is also illustrated in chapter 16, by Kaplan, which includes a detailed discussion of quality-of-life outcomes and mental health services evaluation. Again, this is an area that has not been meaningfully addressed in eating-disorder research, but one of clear significance given the marked social impairment experienced by many patients with eating disorders.

This review also underscores several other problems in the psychotherapy research of bulimia nervosa that are the subject of a separate report (Mitchell et al., in press) but are summarized here, given their relevance to the issue of cost-effectiveness:

1. Diagnostic criteria for bulimia nervosa have undergone several revisions. The original criteria were included in the *DSM-III* and were revised in both *DSM-III-R* and *DSM-IV*; researchers in the UK have tended at times to use a different set of criteria altogether (Russell, 1979). The revisions have reflected our improved understanding of these disorders and, in particular, have led to a narrowing of the definition of bulimia nervosa in *DSM-III-R* and the subtying of bulimia nervosa in *DSM-IV*. However, these inconsistencies inevitably have made comparisons across treatment studies difficult.
2. Inclusion criteria in treatment studies have varied in other important ways (Mitchell et al., in press). The vast majority of studies excluded adolescents, despite the fact that they make up a significant proportion of these patients. Some studies have excluded patients in older age groups who are seen infrequently, but who nonetheless are of clinical concern. Some studies use overweight subjects while others exclude them. Some exclude those with comorbid conditions, such as affective disorders, while others include them. Most tend to exclude comorbid substance use disorders for obvious reasons, yet there is a frequent co-occurrence of these conditions. There is clearly a need for services research in this area that employs more naturalistic designs, and that includes patient groups usually excluded from treatment studies, most of which are probably particularly difficult to treat and may be particularly prone to relapse if initially

treated successfully. This issue is addressed in chapter 29 of this volume, by Parry, which details how the National Health Service in Great Britain deals with these problems. This has implications for reimbursement as well. A policy that only reimburses therapists for structured manual-based therapies designed for, and proven in, populations of eating-disorder patients with no comorbid conditions would penalize therapists willing to undertake the treatment of more difficult cases and would inhibit the development of innovative therapies for these patients.

3. There are concerns about recruitment. The majority of the studies conducted in the United States have used symptomatic volunteers, while European studies have tended to use patients. It is unclear whether these samples are comparable and whether the results obtained can be equated (Mitchell et al., 1988).
4. Assessments are also of concern. Different instruments have been used by different groups, and psychometric development has been in a state of flux. However, the introduction of the Eating Disorders Examination, a semistructured clinical interview, has provided some much needed stability to the field of assessment (Cooper & Fairburn, 1987; Fairburn & Cooper, 1993).
5. Psychotherapies have not been well standardized. What is considered cognitive behavioral therapy at different sites may vary substantially. More recently, multicentered studies that have controlled for this variation have been initiated and should prove revealing.
6. Concern can also be voiced about the growing reliance on cognitive behavioral therapy as the necessary and sufficient treatment for eating disorders. As noted by Norcross (1995), this reliance may contribute to an "exclusivity myth" that other sorts of therapies are ineffective, and therefore, they may not be tried experimentally. It is only ressonable to assume that one therapy will not be optimal for all patients, given the heterogeneity of these conditions. Also, clinical experience has generated a wealth of observations and information about the treatment of anorexia nervosa, yet there have been few controlled treatment trials. There is also a danger here that psychotherapies applied to anorexia nervosa may not incorporate what has been gained from clinical practice with these patients, and that the research and community treatment sectors may end up pursuing different directions, the former group not adequately informed by the latter group's experiences. That may result in the use of research psychotherapy approaches that may be increasingly divergent from what takes place in practice. The problem of ecological validity has been discussed cogently by Beutler (1995).
7. There has been an unfortunate but strong tendency for many data analyses to focus on treatmnt completers and to exclude or replace dropouts in the analyses, a strategy that may inflate the apparent efficacy of the treatment being examined. Researchers in this area must be very careful to consider and report the results obtained for all available subjects from the point of potential entry, citing the number excluded for vaious reasons, and including dropouts and those who are not compliant in other ways. Only with these sorts of data can the results of research be interpreted in ways that will be useful in the "real-world" setting.

Overall, issues related to the cost-effectiveness of psychotherapy for bulimia nervosa in particular, and for eating disorders in general, are just now becoming the focus of scientific inquiry; however, the field has progressed to the point where questions of cost-effectiveness can and should be addressed in a meaningful way. Unfortunately, there has not been a system for the development and dissemination of psychotherapy research strategies that parallels that in the pharmaceutical industry, and given current budgetary concerns, it is difficult to envisions that adequate resources can be devoted to developing such a system. However, NIH could decide that the partnering of health economics researchers and treatment outcome researchers is a main priority, as the NIMH Conference of Cost-Effectiveness of Psychotherapy held in January 1994 suggested. Given the prevalence of problems of mental illness in this country, the cost to the individuals involved as well as to society in general, and the clear need for meaningful reserch in this area, this would seem to be an important area for focus in funding in the decade ahead.

References

Agras, W. S., Rossiter, E. M., Arnow, B., et al. (1992). Pharmacologic and cognitive-behavioral treatment for bulimia nervosa: A controlled comparison. *American Journal of Psychiatry, 149*, 82–87.

Agras, W. S., Schneider, J. A., Arnow, B., et al. (1989). Cognitive-behavioral and response prevention treatments for bulimia nervosa. *Journal of Consulting and Clinical Psychology, 57*, 215–221.

Agras, W. S., Telch, C. F., Arnow, B., et al. (1994). Weight loss, cognitive-behavioral, and desipramine treatments in binge eating disorder. An ad-

dictive design. *Behavioral Therapy*, 25, 225–238.
American Psychiatric Association. (1993). *Practice guidelines for eating disorders*. Washington, DC: American Psychiatric Association Press.
Beutler, L. E. (1995). The germ theory myth and the myth of outcome homogeneity. *Psychotherapy*, 32, 489–494.
Comerci, G. D. (1990). Medical complications of anorexia nervosa and bulimia nervosa. *Medical Clinic of North America*, *74*, 1293.
Connors, M. E., Johnson, C. L., & Stuckey, M. K. (1984). Treatment of bulimia with brief psychoeducational group therapy. *American Journal of Psychiatry*, *141*, 1512–1516.
Cooper, Z., & Fairburn, C. G. (1987). The Eating Disorders Examination: A semi-structured interview for the assessment of the specific psychopathology of eating disorders. *International Journal of Eating Disorders*, 6, 1–8.
Crow, S. J., & Mitchell, J. E. (1991). Rational therapy of eating Disorders. *Drugs*, 48, 372–379.
Eckert, E. D., & Mitchell, J. E. (1994). Anorexia nervosa and bulimia. In G. Winokur & P. Clayton (Eds.), *Medical Basis of Psychiatry* (2nd ed.). New York: W. B. Saunders.
Fairburn, C. G. (1981). A cognitive behavioural approach to the management of bulimia. *Psychological Medicine*, *11*, 707–711.
Fairburn, C. G., & Beglin, S. J. (1990). Studies of the epidemiology of bulimia nervosa. *American Journal of Psychiatry*, 147, 401–408.
Fairburn, C. G., & Cooper, Z. (1993). Eating Disorders Examination (EDE). In C. G. Fairburn & G. T. Wilson (Eds.), *Binge eating: Nature, assessment and treatment* (pp. 317–360). New York: Guilford Press.
Fairburn, C. G., Jones, R., Reveler, R. C., Hope, R. A., & O'Connor, M. (1993). Longer-term effects of interpersonal psychotherapy, behavior therapy, and cognitive behaivor therapy. *Archives of General Psychiatry*, 50, 419–428.
Fairburn, C. G., Jones, R., Peveler, R. C., et al. (1991). Three psychological treatments for bulimia nervosa. *Archives of General Psychiatry*, 48, 463–469.
Fairburn, C. G., Kirk, J., O'Connor, M., et al. (1986). A comparison of two psychological treatments for bulimia nervosa. *Behaviour, Research and Therapy*, 24, 629–643.
Fairburn, C. G., Marcus, M., & Wilson, G. T. (1993). Cognitive behavioral therapy for binge eating and bulimia nervosa: A comprehensive treatment manual. In C. G. Fairburn & G. T. Wilson (Eds.), *Binge eating: Nature, assessment and treatment* (pp. 361–404). New York: Guilford Press.
Fairburn, C. G., Norman, P. A., Welch, S. L., et al. (1995). A prospective study of outcome in bulimia nervosa and the long term effects of three psychological treatments. *Archives of General Psychiatry* 52, 304–312.
Fichter, M. M., Leibl, K., Brunner, E., et al. (1991). Fluoxetine versus placebo: A double-blind study with bulimic inpatients undergoing intensive psychotherapy. *Pharmacopsychiatry*, 24, 1–7.
Fluoxetine Bulimia Nervosa Collaborative Study Group (FBNCSG). (1992). Fluoxetine in the treatment of bulimia nervosa: A multicenter, placebo-controlled, double-blind trial. *Archives of General Psychiatry*, 49, 139–147.
Freeman, C. P., Barry, F., Dunkeld-Turnbull, J., et al. (1988). A controlled trial of psychotherapy for bulimia nervosa. *British Medicine Journal*, *296*, 521–525.
Freeman, C. P., Morris, J. E., Cheshire, K. E., et al. (1988, April 23). *A double-blind controlled trial of fluoxetine versus placebo for bulimia nervosa.* Presented at the Third International Conference on Eating Disorders, New York.
Garner, D. M., Rockert, W., Davis, R., et al. (1993). A comparison between cognitive-behavioral and supportive-expressive therapy for bulimia nervosa. *American Journal of Psychiatry*, *150*, 37–46.
Goldbloom, D., Olmsted, M., Davis, R., et al. (1994, April–May). *A randomized controlled trial of fluoxetine and individual cognitive behavioral therapy for women with bulimia nervosa: Short-term outcome.* Paper presented at the Sixth International Conference on Eating Disorders.
Goldstein, D. J., Wilson, M. G., Thompson, V. L., et al. (in press). Long-term fluoxetine treatment of bulimia nervosa. *British Journal of Psychiatry.*
Kirkley, B. G., Schneider, J. A., Agras, S., & Bachman, J. A. (1985). Comparison of two groups of treatment for bulimia. *Journal of Consulting and Clinical Psychology*, 53, 43–48.
Koran, L. M., Agras, S. W., Rossiter, E. M., et al. (1995). Comparing the cost-effectiveness of psychiatric treatments: Bulimia nervosa. *Psychiatry Research*, 58, 13–21.
Lacey, J. H. (1983). Bulimia nervosa, binge-eating, and psychogenic vomiting: A controlled treatment study and long-term outcome. *British Medical Journal*, 2, 1609–1613.
Laessle, R. G., Beumont, J. P. V., Butow, P., et al. (1991). A comparison of nutritional management with stress management in the treatment of bulimia nervosa. *British Journal of Psychiatry*, 159, 250–261.
Laessle, R. G., Waadt, S., & Pirke, S. J. (1987). A structured behaviorally oriented group treatment

for bulimia nervosa. *Psychotherapy and Psychosomatics, 48,* 141–145.

Lee, N. L., & Rush, A. J. (1986). Cognitive-behavioral group therapy for bulimia. *International Journal of Eating Disorders, 5,* 599–615.

Leitenberg, H., & Rosen, J. (1989). Cognitive-behavioral therapy with and without exposure plus response prevention in treatment of bulimia nervosa: Comment on Agras, Schneider, Arnow, Raeburn, and Telch. *Journal of Consulting and Clinical Psychology, 57,* 776–777.

Leitenberg, H., Rosen, J., Gross, J., Nudelman, S., Vara, L. S. (1988). Exposure plus response-prevention treatment of bulimia nervosa. *Journal of Consulting and Clinical Psychology, 56,* 535–541.

Mitchell, J. E., Hoberman, H., Peterson, C. B., et al. (1996). Research on the psychotherapy of bulimia nervosa: Half empty or half full? *International Journal of Eating Disorders, 20,* 219–230.

Mitchell, J. E., Hoberman, H., & Pyle, R. L. (1989). An overview of the treatment of bulimia nervosa. *Psychiatric Medicine, 7,* 317–332.

Mitchell, J. E., Pyle, R. L., Eckert, E. D., et al. (1988). Patients versus symptomatic volunteers in bulimia nervosa research. *International Journal of Eating Disorders, 7,* 837–843.

Mitchell, J. E., Pyle, R. L., Eckert, E. D., et al. (1990). A comparison study of antidepressants and structured intensive group psychotherapy in the treatment of bulimia nervosa. *Archives of General Psychiatry, 47,* 149–157.

Mitchell, J. E., Pyle, R. L., Pomeroy, C., et al. (1993). Cognitive behavioral group psychotherapy of bulimia nervosa: Importance of logistical variables. *International Journal of Eating Disorders, 14,* 277–287.

Norcross, J. C. (1995). Dispelling the doddo bird verdict and the exclusivity myth in psychotherapy. *Psychotherapy, 32,* 500–504.

Ordman, A. M., & Kirschenbaum, D. S. (1985). Cognitive behavioral therapy for bulimia: An initial outcome study. *Journal of Consulting and Clinical Psychology, 53,* 305–313.

Peterson, C. P., & Mirchell, J. E. (1995). Cognitive behavior therapy. In G. O. Gabbard (Ed.), *Treatment of psychiatric disorders* (2nd ed.). Washington, DC: APA Press.

Pope, H. G., Jr., Hudson, J. I., Jonas, J. M., et al. (1983). Bulimia treated with imipramine: A placebo-controlled double-blind study. *American Journal of Psychiatry, 140,* 554–558.

Rossiter, E. M., & Wilson, T. (1985). Cognitive restructuring and response prevention in the treatment of bulimia nervosa. *Behaviour, Research and Therapy, 23,* 349–359.

Russell, G. (1979). Bulimia nervosa: an ominous variant of anorexia nervosa. *Psychological Medicine, 9,* 429–488.

Shapiro, D. A. (1995). Finding out how psychotherapies help people change. *Psychotherapy Research, 5,* 1–21.

Thackwray, D. E., Smith, M. C., Bodfish, J. W., 7 Meyers, A. W. (1993). A comparison of behavioral and cognitive and cognitive-behavioral interventions for bulimia nervosa. *Journal of Consulting and Clinical Psychology, 4,* 639–645.

Walsh, B. T., Hadigan, C. M., Devlin, M. J., Gladis, M., & Roose, S. P. (1991). Long-term outcome of antidepressant treatment for bulimia nervosa. *American Journal of Psychiatry, 148,* 1206–1212.

Wilfley, D. E., Agras, W. S., Telch, C. F., Rossiter, E. M., Schneider, J. A., Cole, A. B., Stifford, L., & Raeburn, S. D. (1993). Group cognitive-behavioral therapy and group interpersonal psychotherapy for the non-purging bulimic: A controlled comparison. *Journal of Consulting and Clinical Psychology, 61,* 296–305.

Wilson, G. T., Eldredge, K. L., Smith, D., et al. (1991). Cognitive-behavioral treatment with and without response prevention for bulimia. *Behaviour, Research and Therapy, 29,* 575–583.

Wilson, G. T., Rossiter, E., Kleifield, E. I., & Lindholm, L. (1986). Cognitive behavioral treatment of bulimia nervosa: A controlled evaluation. *Behaviour, Research and Therapy, 24,* 277–288.

Wolchik, S. A., Weiss, L., & Katzman, M. A. (1986). An empirically validated, short-term psychoeducational group treatment program for bulimia. *International Journal of Eating Disorders, 5,* 21–34.

Yates, A. J., Sambrailo, F. (1984). Bulimia nervosa: A descriptive and therapeutic study. *Behaviour, Research and Therapy, 22,* 503–517.

Yates, B. T. (1994). Toward the incorporation of costs, cost-effectiveness analysis, and cost-benefit analysis into clinical research. *Journal of Consulting and Clinical Psycholology, 62,* 729–736.

26

Personality Disorders

Treatments and Costs

Paul A. Pilkonis, Bryan D. Neighbors,
& Elizabeth M. Corbitt

Personality disorders (PDs) are defined as chronic and pervasive maladaptive behavior patterns that begin early in life and cause personal distress, serious dysfunction in major social roles, or both. This chapter reviews literature on the efficacy of psychosocial and pharmacological treatments for personality disorders, discusses the issue of comorbidity (both among Axis II disorders and between Axis I and Axis II disorders), identifies costs associated with personality disorders, and makes recommendations for future work.

In addition to the general definition of PDs, the fourth edition of the *Diagnostic and Statistical Manual of Mental Disorders* (*DSM-IV*; American Psychiatric Association [APA], 1994) describes 10 rigid personality styles sharing the common features of early onset, chronicity, and dysfunction, and it groups these PDs into three clusters: (a) odd or eccentric disorders, including paranoid, schizoid, and schizotypal; (b) externalizing or dramatic disorders, including antisocial, borderline, histrionic, and narcissistic; and (c) internalizing or anxious disorders, including avoidant, dependent, and obsessive-compulsive. Two additional disorders, depressive and passive-aggressive PDs, are listed in an appendix for criteria sets "provided for further study."

The Cluster B disorders (that is, the dramatic, expressive, externalizing diagnoses) are the most socially disruptive and costly PDs, involving behaviors that typically have a negative impact upon and demand a response from the social environment. Patients with severe Cluster B PDs suffer from chronic and debilitating problems that are often treated inadequately by the mental and physical health care systems. Such patients display a pattern of tempestuous and self-defeating interpersonal relationships, emotional instability, poor impulse control, chronic anger, frequent suicidality (manifested in both ideation and behavior), self-mutilation (e.g., episodes of self-inflicted cutting or burning that are not primarily suicidal), eating disorders, and substance abuse. These behaviors can lead to repeated psychiatric and medical hospitalizations, an inability to work or fulfill other social roles (such as parenting), imprisonment, and rates of mortality from suicide several times greater than that of the general population (Frances, Fyer, & Clarkin, 1986; Stone, Hurt, & Stone, 1987).

A monograph (de Girolamo & Reich, 1993) published by the World Health Organization provides a useful summary of data on the epidemiology of PDs. Recent investigations of the prevalence of PDs in the community have produced rather similar findings. In four studies from Germany, the United Kingdom, and the United States, estimates of the prevalence of PDs in the general population ranged from 10% to 13.5%, despite definitional, assessment, and possible cultural differences (Casey & Tyrer, 1986; Maier, Lichtermann, Klingler, Heun, & Hallmayer, 1992; Reich, Nduaguba, & Yates, 1988; Zimmerman & Coryell, 1990). There has been less consistency, however, among prevalence estimates derived from studies of patient populations. Investigations assessing PDs in outpatients have found prevalences ranging from 13% to 81% (Alnaes & Torgersen, 1988; Fabrega, Ulrich, Pilkonis, & Mezzich, 1993; Kass, Skodol, Charles, Spitzer, & Williams, 1985; Pilkonis & Frank, 1988; Shea et al., 1990); those studying inpatients or mixed patient populations have estimated prevalences of PDs from 11% to 67% (Charney, Nelson, & Quinlan, 1981; Jackson et al., 1991; Loranger, 1990; Oldham & Skodol, 1991; Pfohl, Coryell, Zimmerman, & Stangl, 1986; Zimmerman, Pfohl, Coryell, Stangl, & Corenthal, 1988). These ranges are very broad for several reasons, including widely different sample characteristics in terms of demographic features, Axis I morbidity, and Axis II severity; different methodologies for assessing PDs, for example, clinical evaluations, self-report measures, or interview measures; and *DSM-III* versus *DSM-III-R* (and now, *DSM-IV*) definitions.[1]

With the *DSM* nosology, there are serious concerns about the discriminant validity of individual PD diagnoses. The typical finding is that patients meet criteria for multiple diagnoses (Oldham et al., 1992), and the evidence is mixed about whether such diagnoses aggregate within the a priori clusters (A, B, and C) proposed (Bell & Jackson, 1992; Dowson & Berrios, 1991; Kass et al., 1985; Livesley, Jackson, & Schroeder, 1992). These issues have generated a debate about the usefulness of categorical versus dimensional approaches to assessment (Livesley, Schroeder, Jackson, & Jang, 1994; Widiger & Sanderson, 1995), and we consider this topic in more detail below (see "Recommendations").

Treatment Efficacy: Psychosocial Treatments

There are few psychotherapy outcome studies focused exclusively on patients diagnosed with PDs. Among the studies that have been done, methodological difficulties often limit the ability to draw firm conclusions regarding the effectiveness of various therapies with PDs (Aronson, 1989; Shea, 1993). These methodological problems include small sample size, sample heterogeneity, attrition, and differences in diagnostic procedures, therapist skill, and measures for assessing change (Shea, 1993). Despite these limitations, certain studies have made important contributions.

Borderline Personality Disorder

The majority of psychotherapy studies of PDs focus on patients with borderline personality disorder (BPD). Standardized treatment approaches for BPD have been developed from psychodynamic, interpersonal, behavioral, and cognitive frameworks (Shea, 1991). Linehan (1993; chapter 27, this volume) has developed the best known model, a comprehensive treatment approach for BPD called *dialectical behavior therapy* (DBT). This approach combines directive individual therapy with group therapy, and it focuses on enhancing problem-solving, emotional-regulation, interpersonal, and distress-tolerance skills.

Several studies have achieved some success with group psychotherapy in small samples of BPD patients (Blum & Marziali, 1988; Kretsch, Goren, & Wasserman, 1987; Nehls, 1991). Also, despite extensive clinical discussion regarding the link between family pathology and the development of BPD, no empirical study has examined the efficacy of family-oriented therapies in the treatment of this disorder (Aronson, 1989; Clarkin, Marziali, & Munroe-Blum, 1991).

Stone (1987) followed 254 hospitalized borderline patients treated with psychodynamic (expressive) psychotherapy. Patients were judged amenable to dynamic psychotherapy by the absence of eating disorders, concomitant antisocial personality, alcoholism, chronic substance abuse, prominent affective disorder, severe agoraphobia, "tragic" incest history, or a lack of motivation for therapy. The subgroup rated as amenable to such therapy had significantly higher Global Assessment Scale (GAS) scores and a lower suicide rate at follow-up than the group judged not amenable. Overall, 40% of the sample showed "clinical recovery" (GAS > 70) and two-thirds had at least a "good" outcome (GAS > 60).

Antisocial Personality Disorder

Despite widespread public concerns about the prevalence of antisocial behavior, there is a notable absence of information in the research literature regarding the treatment of antisocial personality disorder (ASPD). Although reports of specific treatment efficacy are not available, three studies have identified general predictors of treatment response: the "presence of anxiety" or a diagnosis of depression (Gabbard & Coyne, 1987); the ability to form a working relationship with a therapist (Gerstley et al., 1989); and a lack of psychopathy (Ogloff, Wong, & Greenwood, 1990).

Cluster C Personality Disorders

Behavioral treatment (Alden, 1989) has been shown to produce gains in social behavior and satisfaction for patients diagnosed with avoidant personality disorder (AVPD), especially when combined with an interpersonal process training component (Cappe & Alden, 1986). Also, brief adaptational therapy (BAP) and a similar form of treatment labeled *short-term dynamic psychotherapy* (STDP; Davanloo, 1980) have both proven effective in improving the self-reported functioning of patients diagnosed primarily with Cluster C personality disorders (Pollack, Winston, McCollough, Flegenheimer, & Winston, 1990; Winston et al., 1991, 1994). These two therapies appeared to be equivalent in producing such gains.

Summary

The studies reviewed here are suggestive, but the research literature on the efficacy of psychosocial treatments is more notable for what it does *not* tell us. Most of the personality disorders remain unstudied, and our knowledge regarding those that have been studied is limited by methodological constraints. Shea (1993) has made sound recommendations for future research to remedy many of the methodological problems encountered in this area. For example, sample homogeneity may be increased by focusing on the core pathology of a given disorder, requiring a minimum level of severity and impairment, and excluding patients with certain comorbid Axis I disorders. Attrition may be reduced by making compliance with treatment an early and explicit treatment priority (e.g., Linehan, 1993). In terms of assessment of change, Shea recommends careful evaluation of outcome criteria and extensive training of raters and monitoring of reliability. Also, heavy reliance on self-report may be inappropriate in patients with personality disorders, and the perspective of other informants may be particularly valuable.

Using therapists with considerable experience and skill and encouraging flexibility at the level of "families" of strategies may be particularly important with patients with moderate to severe personality disorders. Norcross (1995) has suggested the potential value of prescriptive patient-treatment matching in terms of relationship styles (rather than treatment packages). Beutler (1995) has also pointed out the importance of individual differences in "receptivity to authority" and therapist directiveness and in patient coping styles (internalizing versus externalizing) as variables needing to be accommodated.

Treatment Efficacy: Pharmacotherapy

Previous studies can be organized into three areas. The first group of investigations includes empirical (but often atheoretical) studies of treatment outcome with different classes of medications. Most of this work has been done with patients with borderline personality disorder (Cowdry & Gardner, 1988; Soloff et al., 1986). Certain studies have examined the implications of comorbid schizotypal personality disorder (Goldberg et al., 1986). Classes of medications investigated have included neuroleptics, tricyclic antidepressants, monoamine oxidase inhibitors (MAOIs), selective serotonin reuptake inhibitors (SSRIs), anticonvulsants, lithium, anxiolytics, and psychostimulants (Gunderson, 1986; Stein, 1992). The most promising leads were initially found with low-dose neuroleptics and MAOIs, but recent findings (Cornelius, Soloff, Perel, & Ulrich, 1993; Soloff et al., 1993) have failed to replicate earlier results with these agents, making conclusions about the medication treatment of severe Axis II patients more, rather than less, equivocal. Future work is likely to focus on the use of SSRIs with these patients (Coccaro, 1993; Cornelius, Soloff, Perel, & Ulrich, 1991; Markovitz, Calabrese, Schulz, & Meltzer, 1991).

The second area of work has been motivated more by theoretical concerns. Several investigators have provided review and conceptual papers, often incorporating supportive data, in attempts to provide models of the psychobiology or genetics of personality disorders that are heuristically useful (Cloninger, Svrakic, & Przybeck, 1993; Coccaro, 1993; Livesley, Jang, Jackson, & Vernon, 1993; Nigg & Goldsmith, 1994; Siever & Davis, 1991). Such psychobiological models are often linked (a) to neurotransmitter systems in the brain and (b) to possible medication strategies using agents that influence these systems. Since SSRIs have the most specific mode of action, much attention is currently focused on their use in attenuating symptoms of impulsivity, disinhibition, aggression, and suicidality, all linked to presumed deficits in serotonin.

The third area of work is represented by attempts

to understand Axis I and II comorbidity as a marker of chronic vulnerability, at least part of which involves some biological or temperamental diathesis. Tyrer's work on the "general neurotic syndrome" (GNS) is prominent here (Tyrer, 1989; Tyrer, Casey, & Gall, 1983; Tyrer, Seivewright, Ferguson, Murphy, & Johnson, 1993). He proposes a broader understanding of the relationships among anxiety, depression, and personality disorder (especially Cluster C disorders, e.g., dependent and obsessive-compulsive personality disorder), arguing that they are part of a single syndrome in many patients. He has also examined the ways in which personality disorders complicate the treatment (both psychosocial and pharmacological) of anxiety and depression.

Comorbidity

Two types of comorbidity are relevant to the discussion of personality disorders. The first is the extensive comorbidity among Axis II disorders themselves, which can be taken as an argument for better conceptual and measurement models. The second is comorbidity between Axis I and II disorders, which complicates the "first-line" treatments for Axis I disorders.

Personality disorders as defined by the DSM-IV (and previously *DSM-III* and *DSM-III-R*) may be diagnosed in the presence of Axis I disorders; also, two or more PDs may be diagnosed in the same patient. Consequently, patients with PDs tend to have complex symptom presentations that often complicate both diagnosis and treatment. As mentioned earlier, investigations have typically found high rates of comorbidity among PDs (Dahl, 1986; Morey, 1988; Oldham et al., 1992; Pfohl et al., 1986; Widiger & Rogers, 1989), with some studies diagnosing patients with an average of as many as four PDs (Skodol, Rosnick, Kellman, Oldham, & Hyler, 1988). To date, the question of the effect of such comorbidity among PDs on the course of illness or treatment has not been adequately addressed in the research literature.

By comparison, the impact of a comorbid PD on the course and treatment of affective disorders has been more thoroughly investigated. Again, comorbidity rates have been found to be high, with studies estimating the prevalence of PDs among depressed patients to range from 30% to 81% (Alnaes & Torgersen, 1988; Charney et al., 1981; Farmer & Nelson-Gray, 1990; Pilkonis & Frank, 1988; Shea, Glass, Pilkonis, Watkins, & Docherty, 1987). In general, the literature indicates that a comorbid PD leads to a worse prognosis for patients with depressive disorders (Frances et al., 1986; Shea, Widiger, & Klein, 1992), with an earlier onset of depression (Charney et al., 1981; Pfohl, Stangl, & Zimmerman, 1984), more suicide attempts and ideation (Black, Bell, Hulbert, & Nasrallah, 1988; Shea et al., 1987), and worse treatment outcome (Charney et al., 1981; Pilkonis & Frank, 1988; Shea et al., 1990; Zimmerman, Coryell, Pfohl, Corenthal, & Stangl, 1986). In particular, borderline PD has been associated with an increased risk of suicide attempts in depressed patients (Friedman, Aronoff, Clarkin, Corn, & Hurt, 1983; McGlashan, 1987; Pfohl et al., 1984), although the judged lethality of such attempts has varied across studies.

Some studies have found that comorbid PDs are equally or even more common with anxiety, somatoform, and substance abuse disorders than with affective disorders (Alnaes & Torgersen, 1988; Koenigsberg, Kaplan, Gilmore, & Cooper, 1985; Nace, Davis, & Gaspari, 1991; Ross, Glaser, & Germanson, 1988). The presence of PDs has also been found to affect adversely the treatment outcome of these other Axis I disorders (Reich & Vasile, 1993; Stein, Hollander, & Skodol, 1993). By contrast, studies concerning the impact of Axis I psychopathology on the treatment of PDs are rare, although the limited findings that do exist indicate that the presence of depression may improve the prognosis of patients with borderline and antisocial PDs (Shea et al., 1992).

"Burden of Illness" Costs

To our knowledge, there are no cost-effectiveness data linked exclusively to PDs although there is an obvious need to collect such information. Clinically, the functional impairment associated with severe PDs suggests major costs that accrue from chronic problems in work, family, and interpersonal functioning; substance abuse; inappropriate utilization of mental and physical health care services; and treatment needs for family members.

The literature on the social costs of PDs consists primarily of anecdotal reports and case studies about the burdens associated with these patients and discussions of the need for more comprehensive approaches to their care (e.g., Cohen, Shapiro, Manson, & Kondi, 1985; Holmes, 1988; Lewis & Sharfstein, 1990; McGlashan, 1993; Nehls & Diamond, 1993). These reports are consistent with the usual clinical wisdom, that is, PD patients create significant interpersonal strains and generate substantial costs within the health care system. Drake, Adler, and Vaillant (1988) found a 22% prevalence of PDs in a community sample that had been followed up from age 14 to age 47. Despite manifesting continuing evidence of impairment and increased rates of morbidity and mortality, few ever received appropriate psychiatric attention or diagnosis. Biological, ego strength, and parenting variables during childhood made significant, independent contributions to the prediction of PD in midlife.

Among the studies that do report on larger samples and include more systematic data collection, the literature can be divided into investigations of the costs and burdens generated within (a) the physical health care system and (b) the mental health care system. In the primary-care system, Casey and Tyrer (1990) found a 28% 1-year prevalence of PDs in two general medical practices in England among 358 patients who had already been identified as having "conspicuous psychiatric morbidity." Patients with PDs had more social dysfunction than those without PDs, and "the robustness of this finding was independent of mental state" (p. 264). In the 3 years following diagnosis, psychologically impaired patients with PDs also displayed greater morbidity and had more frequent contact with psychiatric services (Tyrer & Sievewright, 1988). In a community survey with 249 respondents, Reich, Boerstler, Yates, and Nduaguba (1989) identified 26 persons with *DSM-III* PDs and 167 persons who had no features of personality disorder and served as a comparison group. Individuals with PDs were more likely to have been hospitalized for medical reasons during the prior year (38% vs. 17%). Reich et al. also emphasized the association in women ($r = .50$) between "flamboyant" PD scores and visits to a primary-care physician for mental health reasons. In another investigation focusing specifically on somatization disorder (SD), 61% of 94 patients with this disorder qualified for one or more Axis II diagnoses on the *SCID-II* (Rost, Akins, Brown, & Smith, 1992), and the authors stressed the need for further research to "understand the relationship of personality disorders in SD patients to clinically important variables such as frequency of help seeking, functional impairment, health care expenditures, and readiness for psychiatric referral" (p. 325). Hueston, Mainous, and Schilling (1996) studied 93 patients in primary care. Among these patients, having a personality disorder was "associated with lower functional status, lower satisfaction with health care, and higher risk for depression and alcohol abuse" (p. 54). These investigators also noted a "marked increase" in medical care utilization among patients at high risk for histrionic and dependent PDs specifically. Oldham (1994) has provided a recent summary of "current perspectives" on PDs for a medical audience, and he concluded that "Although it has been less well-studied, there is also evidence that the presence of a PD complicates the assessment and treatment of nonpsychiatric medical illnesses as well" (p. 1773). He included citations of studies of patients seeking plastic surgery, the evaluation of chest pain, a report on 26 "environmentally ill" subjects, somatization disorder, and the management of borderline PD in primary care.

In the mental health care system, borderline personality disorder has been associated with higher levels of service use in emergency room, day care, and inpatient settings (Perry, Lavori, & Hoke, 1987). In this study, patients with BPD were compared to those with antisocial personality disorder and Bipolar II disorder. In a survey of the worst recidivists in 196 state hospitals, patients with diagnoses of schizophrenia, bipolar disorder, and personality disorder were overrepresented (Geller, 1992); the potential severity of the first two diagnoses is often acknowledged, but the major impact of PDs on functional impairment and repeated hospitalization is less frequently discussed.

In ongoing assessment studies of Axis II disorders (Pilkonis et al., 1995; Pilkonis, Heape, Ruddy, & Serrao, 1991), we have collected follow-up data on treatment utilization for a 1-year period. In a sample of 86 patients, those with Cluster B PDs used more treatment sessions than Cluster C patients (23.5 vs. 9.1) and had the highest risk of hospitalization during the follow-up period. Nine patients (10.5%) were hospitalized during follow-up, and all had Cluster B diagnoses.

A comprehensive discussion of the potential social costs of personality disorders should also include some comments about their possible transgenerational effects It is common for both clinicians and social observers to assert that there are consistencies across generations in the occurrence of sexual abuse, physical abuse, family violence, and substance abuse—all frequent markers of PDs. PDs may also exert transgenerational effects in more subtle ways. For example, there is a large body of work examining the influence of maternal depression on early child development that has found depression to be associated with diminished quality of mother-child interaction, decreased likelihood of secure attachment, impaired cognitive development, and less adaptive affect regulation (Gelfand & Teti, 1990). At the same time, a smaller number of studies have emphasized the heterogeneity of maternal and infant behavior in dyads where mothers are depressed (Cox, Puckering, Pound, & Mills, 1987). Very little of this literature has examined the extent to which maternal personality might account for such heterogeneity. In their NIMH longitudinal sample, for example, Radke-Yarrow and Zahn-Waxler (1991) found that as measured on the Personality Disorder Examination, 65% of mothers with affective disorders, but only 19% of control mothers, received a diagnosis of personality disorder. Thus, it is likely that when one compares groups of depressed and nondepressed subjects, one is also comparing groups in which levels of personality disorder differ. In studies that do find differences, it is possible that a chronic condition such as a personality disorder may be more of an influence on maternal interactive capability than an episode of depression.

Recommendations

Need for Dimensional Models

We suggest that future work not be exclusively categorical or restricted to current diagnoses. At present, categorical assessment of PDs tends to neglect severity of pathology and functional impairment, has no adequate resolution for the complexity introduced by the extensive comorbidity among Axis II disorders, and suffers from state-trait confounds (i.e., often patients no longer meet criteria for an Axis II diagnosis after Axis I symptoms have resolved). In the area of personality, dimensional models may be particularly useful, especially if they can be used to define "core" areas of pathology requiring intervention or to generate profiles of patients with the poorest prognoses and a tendency to use the health care system in excessive or inappropriate ways. The important message is that the two approaches—categorical and dimensional—not be polarized but used in complementary fashion. Dimensions are attractive psychometrically; categories are attractive clinically. Neither approach will disappear, so ways to profitably integrate them should be found.

A major problem, however, is the lack of a consensus about the dimensions to be incorporated into comprehensive models of "normal" or "abnormal" personality (Strack & Lorr, 1994). A number of possible candidates are available: the Big Five Factor model (Widiger & Trull, 1992); the factor-analytic studies (and instruments) of Clark (Clark, McEwen, Collard, & Hickok, 1993) and Livesley (Livesley et al., 1992); the Structural Analysis of Social Behavior (SASB) developed by Benjamin (1993); the dimensional model proposed by Siever and Davis (1991); and the psychobiological model of Cloninger and his colleagues (Cloninger et al., 1993).

Need for Common Outcome Measures

It is important to encourage the use of shared assessment tools across treatment outcome studies. There is a broad consensus about the need for assessing symptoms and clinical state, but less attention is paid to assessing functional impairment, social role performance, and quality of life. The state of the art is most limited when assessing complex internal states (e.g., "object relations"; mental representations of self, others, and self in relation to others; measures of self-concept).

Subjective distress, usually operationalized in the form of psychological symptoms, is perhaps the least controversial area requiring assessment. At a minimum, we hope to relieve our patients' symptoms with treatment, and there is evidence suggesting that patients with PDs report more symptomatic distress than patients without these disorders (Shea et al., 1987). Also, there have been some creative attempts to link changes in different symptom complexes to alternative personality constellations (Hull, Clarkin, & Kakuma, 1993).

The greatest immediate progress can probably be made in the second of the areas cited above—measures of impairment and social functioning—and this effort deserves priority (cf. Goldman, Skodol, & Lave, 1992). From a pragmatic perspective, it is useful to identify increases in functional capacities and improvements in role performance as "clinically significant" outcomes that are compelling for patients, therapists, policymakers, economists, and other audiences. Although personality profiles and traits may not change markedly, it is reasonable to expect to see cost-effective benefits in enhanced functioning with efficacious treatments.

More efficient screening tools for PDs that can be used across diverse clinical and community settings are needed in order to investigate the impact of PDs in many different health care contexts and to assess more fully their social costs (see chapters 9, 16, 17, and 19, this volume). Toward this end, we have developed a "Stage I" screening measure (Pilkonis, Kim, Proietti, & Barkham, in press) with items from the Inventory of Interpersonal Problems (Horowitz, Rosenberg, Baer, Ureño, & Villaseñor, 1988) that distinguish among psychiatric patients with no PDs, Cluster B PDs, and Cluster C PDs, a multinomial classification problem that has considerable clinical relevance. The properties of the scale are now being investigated in other patient samples (medical as well as psychiatric) and in community settings.

Need for Better Understanding of Course of Illness and Phases of Treatment

By definition, personality disorders are chronic. Thus, innovative treatment development that incorporates state-of-the-art principles of chronic disease management is needed, with attention to concerns about cost-effectiveness (but not simply attempts at cost containment). There are at least three "families" of treatment alternatives: (a) continuous treatment, at different intensities; (b) acute treatment, followed by maintenance or "booster" strategies; and (c) general practice models (i.e., brief acute treatments at the patient's discretion). "Dosage" guidelines are imperative, and the work of Howard and his colleagues (Howard, Kopta, Krause, & Orlinsky, 1986; Kopta, Howard, Lowry, & Beutler, 1994; chapter 14, this volume) has been seminal in this regard.

Unfortunately, there have been no truly systematic studies of long-term psychotherapy. In addition, little is known about treatments actually being delivered in the community and their effectiveness. Seligman (1995) has generated increased attention to the possibilities of naturalistic research (like the *Consumer Reports* survey) on psychotherapy delivered in typical practice settings. He has characterized the distinctive features of such treatment (e.g., it is not of fixed duration; it is "self-correcting" or at least flexible regarding potential interventions; patients actively choose their treatments and therapists; there are multiple problems and foci; and attention is paid to general functioning beyond symptom relief), and he has made methodological recommendations for surveys of therapy outcome (e.g., they should be prospective; careful diagnostic assessments should be done; untreated comparison groups should be incorporated; behavioral as well as global indicators of outcome should be used; data should be collected from multiple informants).

It may also be useful to develop models of sequential changes in treatment that can be measured reliably; in such models, the ability of patients to go from Stage 1 to 2 to 3 would be an important outcome in itself. Staged models of care would emphasize the goals and tasks of treatment, with guidelines for how they can be accomplished and clear operationalizations of when they have been achieved. For patients with severe PDs, such stages are likely to involve (a) the achievement of physical safety and evidence of day-to-day emotional stability, (b) articulation and "working through" of traumatic historical and concurrent circumstances, and (c) efforts at personal growth and improvements in the quality of life, including the capacity to sustain oneself in the community emotionally and economically (see chapter 28, this volume).

Need for More Sophisticated Longitudinal Studies

Regardless of the treatment modalities used, the use of more data-intensive research designs to evaluate them and the use of more powerful tools to model longitudinal data are needed, rather than the traditional reliance on group averages and pre-post analyses. Longitudinal designs, of course, involve repeated measurements, and repeated measurements introduce certain statistical complexities (e.g., correlated measurement error). In addition, longitudinal designs can be compromised by attrition or missing data at various assessment points, even if subjects are not lost completely. Kraemer and Thiemann (1989) have provided useful suggestions about the analysis of data from such "intensive designs." In a similar vein, Gibbons et al. (1993) and Lavori (1990) surveyed several competing methods for analyzing longitudinal data, including repeated-measures ANOVA, MANOVA, and random regression models. This last approach is especially useful because it can accommodate most kinds of missing data, irregularly spaced measurements, correlated errors of measurement, time-varying and time-invariant covariates, and individual deviations from an aggregate response trend. The general point is that such techniques should become "first-line" approaches to analyzing long-term treatment outcome data. Such models provide more understanding of individual differences among patients and allow inspection of alternative trajectories of change. The rate at which different treatments achieve their effects is a significant concern, especially in the evaluation of modalities of extended care for chronic disorders.

Acknowledgments This work was supported in part by NIMH grants R01 MH44672 (to Paul A. Pilkonis), T32 MH18269 (which provided postdoctoral fellowship support to Bryan D. Neighbors), and T32 MH16804 (which provided postdoctoral fellowship support to Elizabeth M. Corbitt). Bryan D. Neighbors is now in the Department of Psychology, Oklahoma State University, and Elizabeth M. Corbitt is now in the Department of Community Health, School of Medicine, Wright State University. Sally Popper provided the basis for the discussion of possible links between maternal depression and personality disorder.

Note

1. *DSM-III* (APA,1980) marked the first appearance of personality disorders on a separate diagnostic axis, with 11 disorders organized into three clusters. The first cluster of "odd" and eccentric disorders included paranoid, schizoid, and schizotypal PDs. The second cluster of dramatic, emotional, or erratic disorders included histrionic, narcissistic, antisocial, and borderline PDs. The third cluster of anxious or fearful disorders included avoidant, dependent, compulsive, and passive-aggressive PDs. A residual category of atypical, mixed, or other PDs was also allowed. *DSM-III-R* (APA, 1987) maintained the same overall structure but made considerable revisions in the diagnostic criteria for individual disorders and added a new appendix ("Proposed Diagnostic Categories Needing Further Study") that defined two new PDs: sadistic and self-defeating PDs. *DSM-IV* (APA, 1994) made less major changes to the sets of diagnostic criteria, but it eliminated sadistic and self-defeating PDs, moved passive-aggressive PD to the appendix for "Criteria Sets and Axes Provided for Further Study," and added depressive PD to that same appendix.

References

Alden, L. (1989). Short-term structured treatment for avoidant personality disorder. *Journal of Consulting and Clinical Psychology, 57*, 756–764.

Alnaes, R., & Torgersen, S. (1988). DSM-III symptom disorders (Axis I) and personality disorders (Axis II) in an outpatient population. *Acta Psychiatrica Scandinavica, 78*, 348–355.

American Psychiatric Association. (1980). *Diagnostic and statistical manual of mental disorders* (3rd ed.). Washington, DC: Author.

American Psychiatric Association. (1987). *Diagnostic and statistical manual of mental disorders* (3rd ed., rev.). Washington, DC: Author.

American Psychiatric Association. (1994). *Diagnostic and statistical manual of mental disorders* (4th ed.). Washington, DC: Author.

Aronson, T. A. (1989). A critical review of psychotherapeutic treatments of the borderline personality: Historical trends and future directions. *Journal of Nervous and Mental Disease, 177*, 511–528.

Bell, R. C., & Jackson, H. J. (1992). The structure of personality disorders in *DSM-III*. *Acta Psychiatrica Scandinavica, 85*, 279–287.

Benjamin, L. S. (1993). *Interpersonal diagnosis and treatment of personality disorders*. New York: Guilford.

Beutler, L. E. (1995). The germ theory myth and the myth of outcome homogeneity. *Psychotherapy, 32*, 489–494.

Black, D. W., Bell, S., Hulbert, J., & Nasrallah, A. (1988). The importance of Axis II in patients with major depression. *Journal of Affective Disorders, 14*, 115–122.

Blum, H. M., & Marziali, E. (1988). Time-limited group psychotherapy for borderline patients. *Canadian Journal of Psychiatry, 33*, 364–369.

Cappe, R. F., & Alden, L. E. (1986). A comparison of treatment strategies for clients functionally impaired by extreme shyness and social avoidance. *Journal of Consulting and Clinical Psychology, 54*, 796–801.

Casey, P. R., & Tyrer, P. J. (1986). Personality, functioning and symptomatology. *Journal of Psychiatric Research, 20*, 363–374.

Casey, P. R., & Tyrer, P. (1990). Personality disorder and psychiatric illness in general practice. *British Journal of Psychiatry, 156*, 261–265.

Charney, D. S., Nelson, J. C., & Quinlan, D. M. (1981). Personality traits and disorder in depression. *American Journal of Psychiatry, 138*, 1601–1604.

Clark, L. A., McEwen, J. L., Collard, L. M., & Hickok, L. G. (1993). Symptoms and traits of personality disorder: Two new methods for their assessment. *Psychological Assessment, 5*, 81–91.

Clarkin, J. F., Marziali, E., & Munroe-Blum, H. (1991). Group and family treatments for borderline personality disorder. *Hospital and Community Psychiatry, 42*, 1038–1042.

Cloninger, C. R., Svrakic, D. M., & Przybeck, T. R. (1993). A psychobiological model of temperament and character. *Archives of General Psychiatry, 50*, 975–990.

Coccaro, E. F. (1993). Psychopharmacologic studies in patients with personality disorders: Review and perspective. *Journal of Personality Disorders*, 7(Suppl.), 181–192.

Cohen, L. M., Shapiro, E., Manson, J. E., & Kondi, E. S. (1985). The high cost of treating a psychiatric disorder as a medical/surgical illness. *Psychosomatics, 26*, 453–455.

Cornelius, J. R., Soloff, P. H., Perel, J. M., & Ulrich, R. F. (1991). A preliminary trial of fluoxetine in refractory borderline patients. *Journal of Clinical Psychopharmacology, 11*, 116–120.

Cornelius, J. R., Soloff, P. H., Perel, J. M., & Ulrich, R. F. (1993). Continuation pharmacotherapy of borderline personality disorder with haloperidol and phenelzine. *American Journal of Psychiatry, 150*, 1843–1848.

Cowdry, R. W., & Gardner, D. L. (1988). Pharmacotherapy of borderline personality disorder: Alprazolam, carbamazapine, trifluoperazine, and tranylcypromine. *Archives of General Psychiatry, 45*, 111–119.

Cox, A. D., Puckering, C., Pound, A., & Mills, M. (1987). The impact of maternal depression in young children. *Journal of Child Psychology and Psychiatry*, 28, 917–928.

Dahl, A. A. (1986). Some aspects of the DSM-III personality disorders illustrated by a consecutive sample of hospitalized patients. *Acta Psychiatrica Scandinavica*, 73(Suppl.), 61–66.

Davanloo, H. (1980). *Short-term dynamic psychotherapy*. New York: Jason Aronson.

de Girolamo, G., & Reich, J. H. (1993). *Epidemiology of mental disorders and psychosocial problems: Personality disorders*. Geneva: World Health Organization.

Dowson, J. H., & Berrios, G. E. (1991). Factor structure of *DSM-III-R* personality disorders shown by self-report questionnaire: Implications for classifying and assessing personality disorders. *Acta Psychiatrica Scandinavica, 84*, 555–560.

Drake, R. E., Adler, D. A., & Vaillant, G. E. (1988). Antecedents of personality disorders in a community sample of men. *Journal of Personality Disorders*, 2, 60–68.

Fabrega, H., Jr., Ulrich, R., Pilkonis, P. A., & Mezzich, J. E. (1993). Personality disorders diagnosed at intake at a public psychiatric facility. *Hospital and Community Psychiatry, 44*, 159–162.

Farmer, R., & Nelson-Gray, R. O. (1990). Personality disorders and depression: Hypothetical relations, empirical findings, and methodological considerations. *Clinical Psychology Review, 10*, 453–476.

Frances, A., Fyer, M., & Clarkin, J. (1986). Personality and suicide. *Annals of the New York Academy of Sciences*, 487, 281–293.

Friedman, R. C., Aronoff, M. S., Clarkin, J. F., Corn, R., & Hurt, S. W. (1983). History of suicidal behavior in depressed borderline inpatients. *American Journal of Psychiatry, 140*, 1023–1026.

Gabbard, G. O., & Coyne, L. (1987). Predictors of response of antisocial patients to hospital treatment. *Hospital and Community Psychiatry*, 38, 1181–1185.

Gelfand, D. M., & Teti, D. M. (1990). The effects of maternal depression on children. *Clinical Psychology Review, 10*, 329–353.

Geller, J. L. (1992). A report on the "worst" state hospital recidivists in the U.S. *Hospital and Community Psychiatry*, 43, 904–908.

Gerstley, L., McLellan, T., Alterman, A. I., Woody, G. E., Luborsky, L., & Prout, M. (1989). Ability to form an alliance with the therapist: A possible marker of prognosis for patients with antisocial personality disorder. *American Journal of Psychiatry, 146*, 508–512.

Gibbons, R. D., Hedeker, D., Elkin, I., Waternaux, C., Kraemer, H. C., Greenhouse, J. B., Shea, M. T., Imber, S. D., Sotsky, S. M., & Watkins, J. T. (1993). Some conceptual and statistical issues in the analysis of longitudinal psychiatric data: Application to the NIMH Treatment of Depression Collaborative Research Program dataset. *Archives of General Psychiatry, 50*, 739–750.

Goldberg, S. C., Schulz, S. C., Schulz, P. M., Resnick, R. J., Hamer, R. M., & Friedel, R. O. (1986). Borderline and schizotypal personality disorders treated with low-dose thiothixene vs placebo. *Archives of General Psychiatry, 43*, 680–686.

Goldman, H. H., Skodol, A. E., & Lave, T. R. (1992). Revising Axis V for DSM-IV: A review of measures of social functioning. *American Journal of Psychiatry, 149*, 1148–1156.

Gunderson, J. G. (1986). Pharmacotherapy for patients with borderline personality disorder. *Archives of General Psychiatry*, 43, 698–700.

Holmes, J. (1988). Supportive analytical psychotherapy: An account of two cases. *British Journal of Psychiatry*, 152, 824–829.

Horowitz, L. M., Rosenberg, S. E., Baer, B. A., Ureño, G., & Villaseñor, V. S. (1988). Inventory of Interpersonal Problems: Psychometric properties and clinical applications. *Journal of Consulting and Clinical Psychology*, 56, 885–892.

Howard, K. I., Kopta, S. M., Krause, M. S., & Orlinsky, D. E. (1986). The dose-effect relationship in psychotherapy. *American Psychologist, 41*, 159–164.

Hueston, W. J., Mainous, A. G., III, & Schilling, R. (1996). Patients with personality disorders: Functional status, health care utilization, and satisfaction with care. *Journal of Family Practice*, 42, 54–60.

Hull, J. W., Clarkin, J. F., & Kakuma, T. (1993). Treatment response of borderline inpatients: A growth curve analysis. *Journal of Nervous and Mental Disease, 181*, 503–508.

Jackson, H. J., Whiteside, H. L., Bates, G. W., Bell, R., Rudd, R. P., & Edwards, J. (1991). Diagnosing personality disorders in psychiatric inpatients. *Acta Psychiatrica Scandinavica*, 83, 206–213.

Kass, F., Skodol, A. E., Charles, E., Spitzer, R. L., & Williams, J. B. W. (1985). Scaled ratings of *DSM-III* personality disorders. *American Journal of Psychiatry*, 142, 627–630.

Koenigsberg, H. W., Kaplan, R. D., Gilmore, M. M., & Cooper, A. M. (1985). The relationship between syndrome and personality disorder in DSM-III: Experience with 2462 patients. *American Journal of Psychiatry, 142,* 207–212.

Kopta, S. M., Howard, K. I., Lowry, J. L., & Beutler, L. E. (1994). Patterns of symptomatic recovery in psychotherapy. *Journal of Consulting and Clinical Psychology, 62,* 1009–1016.

Kraemer, H. C., & Thiemann, S. (1989). A strategy to use soft data effectively in randomized controlled clinical trials. *Journal of Consulting and Clinical Psychology, 57,* 148–154.

Kretsch, R., Goren, V., & Wasserman, A. (1987). Change patterns of borderline patients in individual and group therapy. *International Journal of Group Psychotherapy, 37,* 95–112.

Lavori, P. (1990). ANOVA, MANOVA, my black hen. *Archives of General Psychiatry, 47,* 775–778.

Lewis, R., & Sharfstein, S. S. (1990). Managed care and the discharge dilemma. *Psychiatry, 53,* 116–121.

Linehan, M. M. (1993). *Cognitive-behavioral treatment of borderline personality disorder.* New York: Guilford Press.

Livesley, W. J., Jackson, D. N., & Schroeder, M. L. (1992). Factorial structure of traits delineating personality disorders in clinical and general population samples. *Journal of Abnormal Psychology, 101,* 432–440.

Livesley, W. J., Jang, K. L., Jackson, D. N., & Vernon, P. A. (1993). Genetic and environmental contributions to dimensions of personality disorder. *American Journal of Psychiatry, 150,* 1826–1831.

Livesley, W. J., Schroeder, M. L., Jackson, D. N., & Jang, K. L. (1994). Categorical distinctions in the study of personality disorder: Implications for classification. *Journal of Abnormal Psychology, 103,* 6–17.

Loranger, A. W. (1990). The impact of DSM-III on diagnostic practice in a university hospital: A comparison of DSM-II and DSM-III in 10,914 patients. *Archives of General Psychiatry, 47,* 672–675.

Maier, W., Lichtermann, D., Klingler, T., Heun, R., & Hallmayer, J. (1992). Prevalences of personality disorder (DSM-III-R) in the community. *Journal of Personality Disorders, 6,* 187–196.

Markovitz, P. J., Calabrese, J. R., Schulz, S. C., & Meltzer, H. Y. (1991). Fluoxetine in the treatment of borderline and schizotypal personality disorders. *American Journal of Psychiatry, 148,* 1064–1067.

McGlashan, T. (1987). Borderline personality disorder and unipolar affective disorder. *Journal of Nervous and Mental Disease, 175,* 467–473.

McGlashan, T. (1993). "Sexual abuse and psychopathology": Commentary. *Psychiatry, 56,* 217–221.

Morey, L. C. (1988). Personality disorders in DSM-III and DSM-III-R: Convergence, coverage, and internal consistency. *American Journal of Psychiatry, 145,* 573–577.

Nace, E. P., Davis, C. W., & Gaspari, J. (1991). Axis II comorbidity in substance abusers. *American Journal of Psychiatry, 148,* 118–120.

Nehls, N. (1991). Borderline personality disorder and group therapy. *Archives of Psychiatric Nursing, 5,* 137–146.

Nehls, N., & Diamond, R. J. (1993). Developing a systems approach to caring for persons with borderline personality disorder. *Community Mental Health Journal, 29,* 161–172.

Nigg, J. T., & Goldsmith, H. H. (1994). Genetics of personality disorders: Perspectives from personality and psychopathology research. *Psychological Bulletin, 115,* 346–380.

Norcross, J. C. (1995). Dispelling the dodo bird verdict and the exclusivity myth in psychotherapy. *Psychotherapy, 32,* 500–504.

Ogloff, J. R. P., Wong, S., & Greenwood, A. (1990). Treating criminal psychopaths in a therapeutic community program. *Behavioral Sciences and the Law, 8,* 181–190.

Oldham, J. M. (1994). Personality disorders: Current perspectives. *Journal of the American Medical Association, 272,* 1770–1776.

Oldham, J. M., & Skodol, A. E. (1991). Personality disorders in the public sector. *Hospital and Community Psychiatry, 42,* 481–487.

Oldham, J. M., Skodol, A. E., Kellman, H. D., Hyler, S. E., Rosnick, L., & Davies, M. (1992). Diagnosis of DSM-III-R personality disorders by two structured interviews: Patterns of comorbidity. *American Journal of Psychiatry, 149,* 213–220.

Perry, J. C., Lavori, P. W., & Hoke, L. (1987). A Markov model for predicting levels of psychiatric service use in borderline and antisocial personality disorders and bipolar type II affective disorder. *Journal of Psychiatric Research, 21,* 215–232.

Pfohl, B., Coryell, W., Zimmerman, M., & Stangl, D. (1986). DSM-III personality disorders: Diagnostic overlap and interconsistency of individual DSM-III criteria. *Comprehensive Psychiatry, 27,* 21–34.

Pfohl, B., Stangl, D., & Zimmerman, M. (1984). The implications of DSM-III personality disorders for patients with major depression. *Journal of Affective Disorders, 7,* 309–318.

Pilkonis, P. A., & Frank, E. (1988). Personality pathology in recurrent depression: Nature, prevalence, and relationship to treatment response. *American Journal of Psychiatry, 145,* 435–441.

Pilkonis, P. A., Heape, C. L., Proietti, J. M., Clark, S. W., McDavid, J. D., & Pitts, T. E. (1995). The reliability and validity of two structured diagnostic interviews for personality disorders. *Archives of General Psychiatry, 52*, 1025–1033.

Pilkonis, P. A., Heape, C. L., Ruddy, J., & Serrao, P. S. (1991). Validity in the diagnosis of personality disorders: The use of the LEAD standard. *Psychological Assessment: Journal of Consulting and Clinical Psychology, 3*, 46–54.

Pilkonis, P. A., Kim, Y., Proietti, J. M., & Barkham, M. (1996). A screening scale for personality disorders developed from the Inventory of Interpersonal Problems. *Journal of Personality Disorders, 10*, 355–369.

Pollack, J., Winston, A., McCullough, L., Flegenheimer, W., & Winston, B. (1990). Efficacy of brief adaptational psychotherapy. *Journal of Personality Disorders, 4*, 244–250.

Radke-Yarrow, M., & Zahn-Waxler, C. (1991). Research on children of affectively ill parents: Some considerations for theory and research on normal development. *Development and Psychopathology, 2*, 349–366.

Reich, J., Boerstler, H., Yates, W., & Nduaguba, M. (1989). Utilization of medical resources in persons with DSM-III personality disorders in a community sample. *International Journal of Psychiatry in Medicine, 19*, 1–9.

Reich, J. H., Nduaguba, M., & Yates, W. (1988). Age and sex distribution of DSM-III personality cluster traits in a community population. *Comprehensive Psychiatry, 29*, 298–303.

Reich, J. H., & Vasile, R. G. (1993). Effect of personality disorders on the treatment outcome of Axis I conditions: An update. *Journal of Nervous and Mental Disease, 181*, 475–484.

Ross, H. E., Glaser, F. B., & Germanson, T. (1988). The prevalence of psychiatric disorders in patients with alcohol and other drug problems. *Archives of General Psychiatry, 45*, 1023–1031.

Rost, K. M., Akins, R. N., Brown, F. W., & Smith, G. R. (1992). The comorbidity of DSM-III-R personality disorders in somatization disorder. *General Hospital Psychiatry, 14*, 322–326.

Seligman, M. E. P. (1995). The effectiveness of psychotherapy: The *Consumer Reports* study. *American Psychologist, 50*, 965–974.

Shea, M. T. (1991). Standardized approaches to individual psychotherapy of patients with borderline personality disorder. *Hospital and Community Psychiatry, 42*, 1034–1038.

Shea, M. T. (1993). Psychosocial treatment of personality disorders. *Journal of Personality Disorders, 7*(Suppl.), 167–180.

Shea, M. T., Glass, D. R., Pilkonis, P. A., Watkins, J., & Docherty, J. P. (1987). Frequency and implications of personality disorders in a sample of depressed outpatients. *Journal of Personality Disorders, 1*, 27–42.

Shea, M. T., Pilkonis, P. A., Beckham, E., Collins, J. F., Elkin, I., Sotsky, S. M., & Docherty, J. P. (1990). Personality disorders and treatment outcome in the NIMH Treatment of Depression Collaborative Research Program. *American Journal of Psychiatry, 147*, 711–718.

Shea, M. T., Widiger, T. A., & Klein, M. H. (1992). Comorbidity of personality disorders and depression: Implications for treatment. *Journal of Consulting and Clinical Psychology, 60*, 857–868.

Siever, L. J., & Davis, K. L. (1991). A psychobiological perspective on the personality disorders. *American Journal of Psychiatry, 148*, 1647–1658.

Skodol, A. E., Rosnick, L., Kellman, D., Oldham, J. M., & Hyler, S. (1988). Validating structured *DSM-III-R* personality disorder assessments with longitudinal data. *American Journal of Psychiatry, 145*, 1297–1299.

Soloff, P. H., Cornelius, J., George, A., Nathan, S., Perel, J. M., & Ulrich, R. F. (1993). Efficacy of phenelzine and haloperidol in borderline personality disorder. *Archives of General Psychiatry, 50*, 377–385.

Soloff, P. H., George, A., Nathan, R. S., Schulz, P. M., Ulrich, R. F., & Perel, J. M. (1986). Progress in pharmacotherapy of borderline disorders: A double-blind study of amitriptyline, haloperidol, and placebo. *Archives of General Psychiatry, 43*, 691–697.

Stein, D. J., Hollander, E., & Skodol, A. E. (1993). Anxiety disorders and personality disorders: A review. *Journal of Personality Disorders, 7*, 87–104.

Stein, G. (1992). Drug treatment of the personality disorders. *British Journal of Psychiatry, 161*, 167–184.

Stone, M. H. (1987). Psychotherapy of borderline patients in light of long-term follow-up. *Bulletin of the Menninger Clinic, 51*, 231–247.

Stone, M. H., Hurt, S. W., & Stone, D. K. (1987). The PI 500: Long-term follow-up of borderline inpatients meeting DSM-III criteria. I. Global outcome. *Journal of Personality Disorders, 1*, 291–298.

Strack, S., & Lorr, M. (Eds.). (1994). *Differentiating normal and abnormal personality*. New York: Springer.

Tyrer, P. (1989). *Classification of neurosis*. New York: Wiley.

Tyrer, P., Casey, P., & Gall, P. (1983). Relationship between neurosis and personality disorder. *British Journal of Psychiatry, 142*, 404–408.

Tyrer, P., & Seivewright, N. (1988). Studies of outcome. In P. Tyrer (Ed.), *Personality disorder: Diagnosis, management and course*. London: Wright.

Tyrer, P., Seivewright, N., Ferguson, B., Murphy, S., & Johnson, A. L. (1993). The Nottingham Study of Neurotic Disorder: Effect of personality status on response to drug treatment, cognitive therapy and self-help over two years. *British Journal of Psychiatry, 162*, 219–226.

Widiger, T. A., & Rogers, J. H. (1989). Prevalence and comorbidity of personality disorders. *Psychiatric Annals, 19*, 132–136.

Widiger, T. A., & Sanderson, C. J. (1995). Toward a dimensional model of personality disorders. In W. J. Livesley (Ed.), *The DSM-IV personality disorders* (pp. 433–458). New York: Guilford Press.

Widiger, T. A., & Trull, T. J. (1992). Personality and psychopathology: An application of the five-factor model. *Journal of Personality, 60*, 363–393.

Winston, A., Laikin, M., Pollack, J., Samstag, L., McCullough, L., & Muran, J. C. (1994). Short-term psychotherapy of personality disorders. *American Journal of Psychiatry, 151*, 190–194.

Winston, A., Pollack, J., McCullough, L., Flegenheimer, W., Kestenbaum, R., & Trujillo, M. (1991). Brief psychotherapy of personality disorders. *Journal of Nervous and Mental Disease, 179*, 188–193.

Zimmerman, M., & Coryell, W. H. (1990). Diagnosing personality disorders in the community. *Archives of General Psychiatry, 47*, 527–531.

Zimmerman, M., Coryell, W., Pfohl, B., Corenthal, C., & Stangl, D. (1986). ECT response in depressed patients with and without a DSM-III personality disorder. *American Journal of Psychiatry, 143*, 1030–1032.

Zimmerman, M., Pfohl, B., Coryell, W., Stangl, D., & Corenthal, C. (1988). Diagnosing personality disorder in depressed patients: A comparison of patient and informant interviews. *Archives of General Psychiatry, 45*, 733–737.

27

Borderline Personality Disorder

Costs, Course, and Treatment Outcomes

Marsha M. Linehan & Heidi L. Heard

Concurrently with the debate on health care reform, clinical researchers in the United States have become increasingly interested and invested in evaluating the cost of providing treatment and other support for the chronically and severely mentally ill. For example, in response to a request from the Senate Appropriations Committee, the National Advisory Mental Health Council (1993) reviewed the costs of treating the severely mentally ill and assessed the efficacy of available treatments. The committee estimated a total annual cost of $74 billion for those with severe disorders. Fortunately, the committee also reported that a wide array of empirically proven efficacious treatments exist to treat those disorders. Unfortunately, borderline personality disorder (BPD) was not among the disorders reviewed, despite its reputation as a chronic, severe disorder.

Although no benefit-cost or cost-effectiveness studies for the treatment of BPD have been conducted, follow-up studies of treatment outcome and natural history suggest that the behaviors associated with BPD render it among the most costly psychiatric disorders, both financially and emotionally. In addition to the obvious mental health costs, the financial costs of BPD are distributed across the entire medical field, social service agencies, and sometimes even the legal system. The emotional costs are paid by family, friends, and therapists, as well as by the patient. Equal to the problems associated with the high costs of the disorder are the problems associated with the absence of treatments with empirically demonstrated efficacy. Results of pharmacotherapy trials with BPD patients have been promising but inconsistent, while only one psychotherapy, dialectical behavior therapy (DBT), has any published outcomes results based on a randomized controlled design. Owing to this double burden of high costs and undemonstrated efficacy, those who treat BPD patients are desperate for the development and evaluation of treatments that address both sides of the equation.

Diagnostic Prevalence and Chronicity

The diagnosis of BPD is prevalent in inpatient and outpatient settings alike. Widiger and Frances (1987) estimated that 11% of outpatients meet criteria for BPD. Estimates of the prevalence of BPD on inpatient units range from 14% to 20% (Kroll, 1981, 1982; Kullgren, 1988; Modestin, Abrecht, Tschaggelar, & Hoffman, 1983; Widiger & Frances, 1987). In addition to this prevalence, follow-up studies consistently indicate that the diagnosis of BPD is chronic, with the number of subjects continuing to meet criteria slowly decreasing over the life span. In a study of diagnostic reliability of personality disorders, Loranger (1987) reported that 65% of subjects diagnosed BPD at index met criteria 6 months later. Short-term follow-up studies of BPD (Barasch, Frances, Hurt, Clarkin, & Cohen, 1985; Stevenson & Meares, 1992) report that 60–70% of BPD subjects continue to meet criteria 2–3 years after their index assessment, while intermediate studies (Pope, Jonas, Hudson, Cohen, & Gunderson, 1983) report that 57–67% of BPD subjects continue to meet criteria 4–7 years after index. A long-term follow-up study by McGlashan (1986) indicates that 44% of subjects continue to meet criteria for BPD 15 years later. The only study that suggests less chronicity of BPD is another 15-year follow-up study (Paris, Brown, & Nowlis, 1987), which found only 25% of subjects continuing to meet criteria.

Follow-Up Studies of Borderline Personality Disorder

A review of short- and long-term follow-up studies of BPD provides a suggestion of the varied and extensive costs incurred by BPD individuals. Below, we review all follow-up studies of BPD published in 1980 or after that we could locate. We have chosen not to review studies published in the 1970s or before because the diagnostic criteria for BPD were poorly defined. Although not reviewed in this chapter, the early follow-up studies that included subjects who would be likely to meet current criteria for BPD (Carpenter & Gunderson, 1977; Grinker & Werble, 1977; Gunderson, Carpenter, & Strauss, 1975; Rifkin, Levitan, Galewski, & Klein, 1972a, 1972b; Werble, 1970) do suggest results similar to those reported by more recent studies. Also excluded from review are a study by Masterson and Costello (1980) because of its focus on adolescents only and a study by Kullgren and Armelius (1990) because it presents results based on Kernberg's construct of borderline personality organization (BPO), a construct that has consistently predicted poorly to a diagnosis of BPD.

The studies reviewed below generally provide naturalistic follow-ups of BPD individuals following an index hospitalization or outpatient treatment program. Table 27.1 provides a summary of these studies. The follow-up periods of the studies vary from short term (follow-up 1–3 years after index, on average) to intermediate (4–7 years) to long term (14–20 years). The different time periods provide complementary data. While the short-term studies may provide information about the disorder at its point of greatest severity, they provide no information about the lifetime course of BPD. In contrast, the long-term studies provide information about the course of the disorder, but without the short-term studies, we generally cannot determine whether the problematic behavior occurred consistently throughout the follow-up period or only near the index period. Some of the studies also provide information about behavior prior to and/or during the index period.

Although the studies provide information on a number of variables related to the cost of BPD, the accuracy and validity of this information remain to be demonstrated owing to several methodological factors. Perhaps the greatest threat to the validity of the data is the method of obtaining follow-up information. In all but a few studies (Linehan, Armstrong, Suarez, Allmon, & Heard, 1991; Linehan, Heard, & Armstrong, 1993; Linehan, Tutek, Heard, & Armstrong, 1994; Perry & Cooper, 1985), researchers did not contact subjects between the index contact and the follow-up contact. This means that the researchers relied on the subjects' memories of events over periods from 1 to 20 years. Memory researchers, however, have demonstrated how unreliable memory can be, even after only 1 year (Loftus, Smith, & Klinger, 1994), with a tendency toward underreporting events. Another problem, as revealed in Table 27.1, is the low rate of subject location at follow-up in a number of studies. In the two that attempted to correct this problem by comparing variables measured at index for those who did and did not return for follow-up, the authors report that follow-up subjects generally did not differ from dropouts (Modestin & Villiger, 1989; Paris et al., 1987).

In addition to the limitations on the ability to interpret the validity of the data, the varying methodologies among the studies make it difficult to compare them. As can be seen in Table 27.1, not only do diagnostic criteria differ among studies but the manner of arriving at diagnosis also differs. Studies also differ in whom they excluded from the subject pool. Some excluded subjects from the BPD sample if they also met criteria for other *DSM* diagnoses that have demonstrated high comorbidity with BPD, such as a major affective disorder (McGlashan, 1986; Plakun, 1991), current substance dependence (Linehan et al., 1991, 1993, 1994; Plakun, 1991), antisocial personality disorder (Plakun, 1991), narcissistic personality disorder (Plakun, 1991), and schizotypal personality disorder (McGlashan, 1986; Mehlum et al., 1991; Modestin & Villiger, 1989). Some studies also excluded males (Kroll, Carey, & Sines, 1985; Linehan et al., 1991, 1993, 1994) or subjects with no history of parasuicidal behavior (Linehan et al., 1991, 1993, 1994). A final problem is that for a given outcome variable, studies differ in the outcome measures used to assess that variable, and follow-up information was collected in a variety of ways: face-to-face interviews, phone calls, and mailed questionnaires. It is impossible to determine which variations in findings between studies are due to differences in subjects' behaviors and which are due to method variance. Given the variations in diagnostic methods, method of follow-up contact, outcome measures, and so on, it is not surprising that some findings vary from study to study. Indeed, given the variability, it is more surprising to see how consistently the studies describe the severity and chronicity of the cost of BPD.

Cost of Borderline Personality Disorder

The greatest health care costs of BPD are due to the lengthy and repeated psychiatric hospitalizations of BPD patients. Table 27.2 presents those studies that reported the lifetime number of admissions to psychiatric hospitals or units prior to index. In the McGlashan (1986) and Skodol, Buckley, and Charles (1983) studies, subjects averaged 6 months and 10.8 weeks, respectively, of preindex psychiatric hospitalization. Of the studies in which index assessment did not occur during a psychiatric hospitalization, two report follow-up data on subsequent psychiatric hospitalizations. Control subjects in Linehan's treatment study (Linehan et al., 1991), were assigned to treatment as usual (TAU) in the community. They thus represent a natural follow-along condition. During the first year of follow-up, 55% had at least one psychiatric hospitalization, and the average subject spent 11% of the year in a psychiatric unit. Stevenson and Meares (1992) report that during their 1-year follow-up, the average subject had 0.73 admissions to and spent 14% of the time in a psychiatric unit. Table 27.3 presents those studies that reported data on psychiatric readmissions and/or length of stay during follow-up. Across these studies, the data suggest that rehospitalization was expected for many patients. It appears that most of the rehospitalizations occurred with 5 years of the index period, although it is difficult to state this with certainty owing to the variability in reported data.

One of the most interesting facts reported by four of the studies in which the index treatment was a psychiatric hospitalization is the length of the index hospitalizations. The historical emphasis on treating BPD patients in psychiatric hospitals and the recent trend toward decreasing inpatient treatment are reflected in these data. The older two studies (McGlashan, 1986; Stone, 1987, 1990; Stone, Stone, & Hurt, 1987) had the longest stays (12.7 months to 2 years), while the more recent studies (Mehlum et al., 1991; Tucker, Bauer, Wagner, Harlam, & Sher, 1987) had shorter stays averaging less than a year. Unfortunately, not all studies using inpatient treatment at index reported the duration of index stays.

Clinical experience would suggest that a primary reason for hospitalizing BPD patients is suicidal behavior. For example, Mehlum, Friis, Vaglum, and Karterud (1994) report that 92% of their sample who had "attempted suicide" were hospitalized at least once following an attempt. One of the hallmark behaviors of BPD is parasuicidal behaviors, which are defined as any overt, acute, self-injurious act engaged in where both act and some harm or injury are intentional, not accidental (Kreitman, 1977). This definition includes acts in which the individual intended to die (i.e., suicide attempts) as well as those with no suicide intent. Of all variables related to cost, parasuicide is the most difficult to compare across studies because of the different definitions used. Parasuicide, self-harm, self-injurious behavior (SIB), suicide attempt, suicide gesture, and self-mutilation can be synonymous, overlapping, or mutually exclusive terms. Unfortunately, the operational definition of the behavior measured, especially whether suicide intent was required as part of the definition, is rarely included, and details of the actual assessment, including assessment of behavioral intent and measurement, are frequently left out.

Table 27.4 presents the lifetime history of parasuicidal behavior prior to index treatment. The table includes several studies that were not designed as follow-up studies but that provide important information on the prevalence of the parasuicidal behavior among borderline individuals. From the studies presented in Table 27.4, it is difficult to estimate the percentage of patients with a history of parasuicidal behavior, primarily because of missing operational definitions and unmeasured reliability of assessments of parasuicidal behavior. Taking at face value the data that are reported and averaging across studies suggest that 67% of subjects who met criteria for BPD had parasuicided at least once prior to index assessment. There are insufficient data to draw any conclusions about the frequency during intermediate or long-term follow-up, since only McGlashan (1986) reports data: 21% of the his subjects parasuicided at least once during follow-up. It is important, however, to remember that the McGlashan sample excluded patients meeting criteria for major depression. At short-term follow-up, Tucker reports that 30% of the subjects parasuicided at least once during the first year of follow-up, and 25% did during the second

Table 27.1 Follow-Up Studies of Borderline Personality Disorder

Study	Follow-up Years		Index Event	Exclusion	N	Traced	Dead	Assessed
	M	Range						
Long term								
1. Community-University Health Care Center, Univ. of Minneapolis Kroll et al., 1985	20.0		Inpatient	??	15	13	4	9 (60%)
2. Austin Riggs Center: Private psychiatric hospital	13.6		1950–1976 Inpatient	<2-mo. stay				
Plakun et al., 1985				None noted	??[a]	??	??	63
Plakun, 1991				MAD, substance dependence, >3 NPD criteria	??	??	??	33
3. Chestnut Lodge: Private psychiatric hospital McGlashan, 1984a, 1984b, 1986, 1987	15.0	(2–32)	1950–1975 <90-day stay	Axis I disorder or schizotypal PD <16 or >55 yrs.	94	81	11	70 (74%)
4. Jewish General Hospital (Montreal) Paris et al., 1987, 1989	15.0		1958–1978 Inpatient (most) and outpatient	None reported	322	165	22	100 (31%)
5. PI-500: New York State Psychiatric Institute: Long-term psychotherapy unit Stone, 1987, 1990; Stone et al., 1987	16.0	(10–23)	1963–1968 Inpatient	<3-mo. stay	224	193	17	176 (79%)
Intermediate term								
6. McLean Hospital: Private psychiatric hospital Pople et al., 1983		(4–7)	Inpatient	<18 years	33	27	2	23 (70%)
7. Psychiatric University Clinic (Berne, Switzerland) Modestin & Villiger, 1989	4.5		1981–1982 Inpatient	Schizotypal PD	26	22	2	18 (69%)
8. General Clinic (Memphis, TN) Akiskal, 1981		(0.5–3)	Outpatient	None reported	100	100	4	96 (96%)
Short term								
9. Bronx (NY) Municipal Hospital Center Skodol et al., 1983	2.0		Recruited from ER, outpatient, ads, probation dept.	Schizophrenia	30	30	0	30 (100%)
10. Payne Whitney Evaluation Service (NY) Barasch et al., 1985	3.0		1979 outpatient	Axis I disorder; <18 yrs. or >45 yrs.	??[b]	??	??	10
11. Cambridge Hospital: Private psychiatric hospital (Boston, MA) Perry, 1985; Perry & Cooper, 1985		(2–3)	Recruited from ER, outpatient, ads, probation dept.	Bipolar II (RDC)	35	??	??	24 (69%)

12. New York Hospital: Private psychiatric hospital (Westchester, NY)	1 & 2		Inpatient	None reported	62	??	??	40 (65%)
Tucker et al., 1987								
13. Area hospitals (Hamilton, Canada)	2.0	(15–3)	Inpatient	None reported	88	83	4	60 (68%)
Links et al., 1990								
14. University of Washington, Psychology Clinic (Seattle, WA)	1 & 2		Outpatient	<2 lifetime parasuicides; current substance dependence; Bipolar I; schizophrenia <18 yrs. >45 yrs., male	DBT: 31[c]	24	1	21 (68%)
Linehan et al., 1991, 1993, 1994					TAU: 32	22	0	22 (69%)
15. Oslo sample	2.8	(2–5)	1982–1985 Day hospital	None reported				
Mehlum et al., 1991					34	34		25 (74%)
Mehlum et al., 1994					41	41		31 (76%)
16. Stevenson & Meares, 1992	1.0		Outpatient	Retardation, language problems, antisocial behavior, missed ≥3 appointments	59[d]	30	0	30 (51%)

Study	Diagnostic Criteria	Follow-up Method
Long term		
1. Community-University Health Care Center, Univ. of Minneapolis	MMPI & DIB	
Kroll et al., 1985		
2. Austin Riggs Center: Private psychiatric hospital	*DSM-III*	Mailed questionnaire
Plakun et al., 1985		
Plakun, 1991		
3. Chestnut Lodge: Private psychiatric hospital	*DSM-III* & Gunderson	In person or phone interview
McGlashan, 1984a, 1984b, 1986, 1987		
4. Jewish General Hospital (Montreal)	DIB	In-person or phone interview
Paris et al., 1987, 1989		
5. PI-500: New York State Psychiatric Institute: Long-term psychotherapy unit	BPO & *DSM-III*	Phone & therapist interview
Stone, 1987, 1990; Stone et al., 1987		
Intermediate term		
6. McLean Hospital: Private psychiatric hospital	*DSM-III*	In-person or phone interview
Pope et al., 1983		
7. Psychiatric University Clinic (Berne, Switzerland)	*DSM-III*	In-person interview
Modestin & Villiger, 1989		
8. General Clinic (Memphis, TN)	*DSM-III*	In-person interview
Akiskal, 1981		

(*continued*)

Table 27.1 (*continued*)

Study	Diagnostic Criteria	Follow-up Method
Short term		
9. Bronx (NY) Municipal Hospital Center Skodol et al., 1983	Gunderson	Clinic records
10. Payne Whitney Evaluation Service (NY) Barasch et al., 1985	*DSM-III*	In-person interview
11. Cambridge Hospital: Private psychiatric hospital (Boston, MA) Perry, 1985; Perry & Cooper, 1985	*DSM-III* & Perry	In-person interview
12. New York Hospital: Private psychiatric hospital (Westchester, NY) Tucker et al., 1987	*DSM-III* Axis II & BPO	Phone interview
13. Area hospitals (Hamilton, Canada) Links et al., 1990	DIB	In-person or phone interview
14. University of Washington, Psychology Clinic (Seattle, WA) Linehan et al., 1991, 1993, 1994	*DSM-III-R* & DIB	In-person or phone interview
15. Oslo sample Mehlum et al., 1991	*DSM-III-R*	In-person interview
16. Stevenson & Meares, 1992	*DSM-III* & DIB	In-person interview

Notes. N = subjects assessed at index; Traced = subjects about whom some data available at follow-up (includes refused and dead); Dead = subjects dead (by suicide or other causes) at follow-up; Assessed = subjects completing assessments at follow-up; ?? = unknown. MMPI = Minnesota Multiphasic Personality Inventory; DIB = Gunderson's Diagnostic Interview for Borderlines; Gunderson = Gunderson's diagnostic criteria predating the DIB; BPO = Kernberg's Borderline Personality Organization; BDP = Perry's Borderline Personality Disorder Scale; DBT = dialectical behavior therapy; TAU = treat as usual in the community.

[a]A total of 878 were followed meeting criteria for BPD, schizophrenia, and other disorders; 626 were traced; 94 were dead; and 237 (27%) were assessed.

[b]The original sample was 76 outpatients meeting criteria for personality disorders; 30 returned for follow-up, of whom 10 were BPD.

[c]Subjects assigned to treatment as usual (TAU) in which subjects may or may not have received treatment.

[d]Number of BPD subjects accepted into studies.

Table 27.2 Mean Number of Lifetime Psychiatric Hospitalizations, at Index

Study	Mean
Skodol et al., 1983	3
McGlashan, 1986	2
Links et al., 1990	49
Linehan et al., 1991	5

year, while Stevenson and Meares (1992) report that subjects averaged 0.83 parasuicides during their 1-year follow-up. Among subjects reporting a history of parasuicide at index, Linehan et al. (1991, 1993) report that 98% of the TAU control subjects parasuicided at least once during the 2-year follow-up, while Mehlum et al. (1994) report a repeat rate of 28.6% during their 3-year follow-up.

Table 27.5 presents those studies reporting the suicide rates in their sample. Summing over studies and recalculating percentages based on sample sizes, we found the estimated suicide rate over the eight studies reporting data is 7.8%. Breaking this down over time periods, we found that for the three studies examining the first 3 years after the index point, the suicide rate was 4.22%. For the six studies estimating suicide rates from 4 to 7 years (three studies) and 13 to 20 years (three studies), suicide rates were 7.53% and 7.65%, respectively. Although suicide rates vary widely across studies, these recalculations suggest that most of the suicides occurred within a few years of the index assessment. Kullgren (1988) and Stone (1990) have noted a higher risk of eventual suicide among borderline subjects with a history of parasuicide. If we reverse the questions, studies of the presence of a diagnosis of BPD among suicides suggest that 12–33% of suicides met BPD criteria (Kullgren et al., 1986; Runeson & Beskow, 1991).

Compared to psychiatric inpatient costs, costs due to outpatient psychotherapy and pharmacotherapy are more difficult to describe owing to their chaotic nature. Table 27.6 presents the history of psychotherapy. The most surprising result of the review is how few studies describe the follow-up history of psychotherapy used. In general, most BPD patients appear to have had a pattern of multiple, discontinuous psychotherapies and pharmacotherapies. In contrast to the pattern for psychiatric hospitalizations, a comparison of short-, intermediate-, and long-term follow-ups suggests that the pattern of psychotherapy use remained consistent throughout the follow-up period. With respect to pharmacotherapy, the studies provide fewer data. During follow-up, subjects in the McGlashan (1986) and Mehlum et al. study (1991) had used psychotropic medication 22.0% and 31.6% of the time, respectively. In the Linehan et al. study (1991), 69% of the TAU control subjects had used at least one psychotropic medication

Table 27.3 Psychiatric Hospitalizations During Follow-Up, Among Studies Using Psychiatric Hospitalization at Index

Study	Number of Admissions	Length of Stay
Long term		
Kroll et al., 1985	11% Ss ≥ 1	
McGlashan, 1986	*M* = 1 to 2	8% of follow-up period
Paris et al., 1987[a]	*M* = 1.32	
	23% Ss ≥ 1	
Stone, 1987, 1990	13% Ss ≥ 1, 6% = 2, 8% ≥ 3	45% Ss ≤ 3 mo., 34% = 3–12 mo.
Stone et al., 1987[b]		17% = 1–3 yr., 4% > 3 yr.
Intermediate term		
Modestin & Villiger, 1989	67% Ss > 1	*M* = 34.8 days
Short term		
Tucker et al., 1987	1st yr.: 17% Ss ≥ 1; 2nd yr.: 7% Ss ≥ 1	
Links et al., 1990		40% Ss > 5% of follow-up
Mehlum et al., 1991[c]	48.3% Ss ≥ 1	10.8% of follow-up

[a]Mean for last 5 years of follow-up only.
[b]Includes only Ss readmitted ≥ 1; BPO diagnosis used.
[c]Index treatment in day hospital.

Table 27.4 Lifetime Parasuicide History, at Index

Study	Percentage	Definition of Parasuicide
Clarkin et al., 1983[a]	75	"Self-damaging act"
Friedman et al., 1983[a,b]	92	"Suicide attempt"
Cowdry et al., 1985[a]	69	"Physically self-damaging acts"
McGlashan, 1987	63	"Self-damaging act"
Tucker et al., 1987	65	"Suicide attempt" and "aelf-destructive act"
Fyer et al., 1988[a]	81	"Serious suicide attempt" and "suicide gesture"
Shearer et al., 1988[a]	88	"Suicide attempt"
Stone, 1990	50	"Suicide attempt" and "suicide gesture"
Plakun, 1991	48	"Self-destructive act"
Mehlum et al., 1994	46	"Suicide attempt—Any deliberate act of self-damage which the person committing the act could not be sure to survive"
Dulit et al., 1994[a]	50	"Self-mutilation (self-injury without suicidal intent)"
Soloff et al., 1994[a]	73	"Suicide attempt"

[a]Not a follow-up study.
[b]Includes only subjects being treated for depression.

during the first follow-up year, with an average of 3.8 medications per patient during the year.

Clinical experience would suggest that in addition to psychiatric costs, many BPD patients accrue substantial nonpsychiatric medical costs, primarily as a result of parasuicidal behavior. The physical effects of parasuicidal behavior range from minor bruises and scratches to burns, cuts, gun wounds, comas due to overdoses, and other bodily injuries requiring medical attention. Stone (1990) writes that among the parasuicides in his sample, some of the parasuicides "were so serious that death would unquestionably have resulted, had not they been rescued by sheer luck or the wizardry of medical technology" (p. 55). Patients frequently seek medical attention for these injuries. Clinical lore suggests that borderline patients may also experience more physical disorders and illness. Unfortunately, most follow-up studies of BPD do not describe nonpsychiatric medical contacts, but there is some evidence that these costs are also significant. Skodol et al. (1983) noted that the BPD subjects in their study used emergency rooms more frequently than subjects with "neurotic disorders," though not as frequently as subjects with schizophrenia. Stevenson and Meares (1992) report that the average patient had 3.5 medical visits per month during the year prior to treatment and 0.5 during the year after treatment. In unpublished data, Linehan found that the average TAU control subject had 6.8 physician visits (3.8 emergency room visits and 3.0 medical hospital days) during the first follow-up year.

Table 27.5 Percentage of Suicide Rate at Follow-up

Study	Percentage
Long term	
McGlashan, 1986	3.0
Paris et al., 1989	8.5
Stone, 1990	8.9
Intermediate term	
Pope et al., 1983	7.4
Modestin & Villiger, 1989	7.7
Short term	
Akiskal, 1981	4.0
Links et al., 1990	6.0
Linehan et al., 1993	3.0

Besides involvement with the medical industry, many BPD individuals are extensively involved with social service agencies in the community. Unfortunately, most follow-up studies of BPD do not describe the social services received by subjects, but several describe employment histories that suggest that a significant number probably receive some combination of unemployment, public assistance, housing subsidies, and so on. We review these studies in Table 27.7. Comparing short-, intermediate-, and long-term follow-ups, subjects' employment status appears to improve by long-term follow-up.

In an ongoing treatment overcome study with women who met criteria for BPD and who had a history of parasuicidal behavior, we have included an assessment of nontreatment costs incurred by subjects. The following data reflect self-reports of the first 20 subjects to complete pretreatment assessment for the year prior

Table 27.6 Follow-Up Outpatient Psychotherapy

Study	Minimum Percentage Ss or Time in Therapy during Follow-up	Percentage Ss in Therapy at Follow-up
Long term		
McGlashan, 1986	$M = 35\%$ of time	46
Paris et al., 1987	$M = 12.6\%$ of time	—
Intermediate term		
Modestin & Villiger, 1989	—	33
Short term		
Tucker et al., 1987	78% Ss in continuously	73
Mehlum et al., 1993	$M = 40.5\%$ of time	—

to entry into the study. The pretreatment assessments indicate that 50% of the subjects reported no employment during the pretreatment year, while another 20% reported at least some months of unemployment during that year. Twenty percent of the subjects also reported receiving "under-the-table" income. No subjects reported receiving unemployment benefits, while 50% reported receiving state and/or federal psychiatric disability for at least 1 month during the pretreatment year, and 30% reported receiving public assistance. These rates are significantly higher than the 0.13–11.96% use rate of Washington State income assistance for the Seattle area in general (Yette et al., 1994). Ten percent of the subjects reported living in a group home for at least 1 month during the pretreatment year, while no subjects reported living in subsided housing or shelters.

As a result of the behaviors that characterize BPD, borderline patients and the communities in which they live incur several other types of expenses that have not been as well documented. For example, a number of BPD individuals become involved with the legal system. The involvement varies from filing for bankruptcy to filing civil suits to imprisonment for criminal offenses. It is difficult to estimate these costs because BPD researchers seldom assess them. Stone (1990), however, found that among the BPD subjects in his study, 11.5% of the males and 2% of the females spent at least one night in jail. Offenses included drug possession, fraud and theft, arson, and manslaughter and murder. He adds that several other patients had "close brushes with the law (their charges were dropped through the influence of their families)" (p. 191). In our current study, 30% of the first 20 subjects described some legal involvement during the pretreatment year.

Table 27.8 presents global functioning as measured across life areas. Although it would be difficult to convert scores of global functioning to monetary values, these scores may suggest how much an individual contributes to or consumes from society. In addition to being suggestive of mental health care costs and employment status, these scores may also be suggestive of the degree to which the patient is a financial burden or asset to family or friends (e.g., family members miss

Table 27.7 Follow-Up Work Functioning

Study	Employment and Financial Status
Long term	
Kroll et al., 1985	44% Ss unemployed & on public assistance at follow-up
McGlashan, 1986	$M =$ employed 68% of follow-up period
Intermediate term	
Modestin & Villiger, 1989	22% Ss receiving disability pension at follow-up
Short term	
Links et al., 1990	23% Ss employed full time throughout follow-up period
Mehlum et al., 1991	56% Ss employed at least part time during follow-up; 38.5% Ss self-supporting at follow-up
Stevenson & Meares, 1992	$M = 1.37$ mo. away from work; 73.3% Ss receiving government financial assistance at follow-up

Table 27.8 Global Functioning Scores

Study	Beginning of Index	End of Index	Follow-up
Long term			
Plakun, 1985	34.9–35.7	—	61.4–67.0
McGlashan, 1986	—	—	64.0
Paris et al., 1987	—	—	63.2
Stone, 1990	—	—	61.0–67.0
Short term			
Barasch et al., 1985	51.4	—	59.2
Perry & Cooper, 1985	—	—	52.1
Tucker et al., 1987	29.7	41.56	50.3 (1st yr.) 56.6 (2nd yr.)
Mehlum et al., 1991	39.4	42.1	49.1
Linehan et al., 1993, 1994			
DBT	37.7	51.4 (1st yr.)	57.4 (2nd yr.)
TAU	33.8	40.4 (1st yr.)	36.1 (2nd yr.)

Note. DBT = dialectical behavior therapy; TAU = treat as usual in the community.

work to care for the patient, patient cannot care for own children). Out of all of the variables, global functioning scores provide the clearest and most consistent indication of improvement over time. Even at long-term follow-up, however, the average patient still reports mild psychiatric symptoms or some impairment in at least one area of life.

In addition to financial costs, the emotional costs of BPD are enormous. BPD individuals describe chronic feelings of anger, emptiness, depression, and anxiety. They experience extreme frustration and anger and occasionally experience brief psychotic episodes. They describe chaotic relationships and "confused identities." Even among those who have not attempted suicide, suicide ideation is common.

Benefits of Treatment

Considering the severity of BPD, the lack of therapies with proven efficacy is disturbing. Pharmacotherapy researchers have conducted a number of controlled studies of pharmacotherapy for BPD (see Brinkley, 1993, for a comprehensive review; Soloff, 1994, for a brief review), with a strong emphasis on examining the effects of neuroleptics and antidepressants. Effects include decreases in anger and other negative emotions, impulsive behavior, psychosis, and other cognitive disturbances and improvements in social and global functioning. However, many of the researchers have not conducted replication studies of their own results, and the results of different studies sometimes conflict with each other. In summarizing the findings of neuroleptic studies, Soloff (1987) concludes that "medication effects are clinically significant but modest in magnitude" (p. 29), a conclusion that may be applied to the other medications as well. Besides modest benefit, however, several of the medications have significant costs in the form of side effects (e.g., Gardner & Cowdry, 1985; Leone, 1982). Finally, the effectiveness of pharmacotherapy, as well as the interpretation of pharmacotherapy studies, is plagued by high rates of attrition (13.7–48.3% in outpatient studies, mean = 38.4%) from treatment (Kelly, 1992).

Although the empirical evidence supporting pharmacotherapy remains equivocal, the empirical evidence supporting psychotherapy for BPD is almost nonexistent. This is particularly distressing in view of the fact that pharmacotherapy researchers suggest pharmacotherapy as an adjunct to psychotherapy (Soloff, 1987). The preponderance of psychotherapy literature for BPD derives from the psychoanalytic/psychodynamic school. Unfortunately, psychoanalytic treatment developers (Adler, 1985, 1989; Buie & Adler, 1982; Kernberg, 1984, 1987; Masterson, 1976, 1981) have thus far supported assertions about the effectiveness of psychoanalysis for BPD only with data from case studies and uncontrolled outcome or longitudinal studies. The results (McGlashan, 1986; Stevenson & Meares, 1992; Stone, 1987, 1990; Stone et al., 1987) suggest that BPD patients do improve over long periods of time, but without a control group, one can not separate treatment effects from factors such as spontaneous remission, maturation, and regression to the mean. Indeed, Stone

(1987) reported that he could find no relationship between treatment received and longitudinal outcome. The one exception to the lack of controlled studies (and an important exception with respect to cost) is Marziali and Munroe-Blum (Clarkin, Marziali, & Munroe-Blum, 1991; Munroe-Blum & Marziali, 1988), who compared psychodynamic group therapy to psychodynamic individual therapy and found no significant differences in outcome between the two modes of treatment. These null findings suggest that psychodynamic individual therapy may not be more cost-effective than psychodynamic group therapy.

To date, only cognitive behavior therapies have shown efficacy for BPD in randomized controlled trials. Dialectical behavior therapy (DBT: Linehan, 1993a, 1993b) was the first psychotherapy for BPD with published outcome results based on a randomized control design. Subjects were randomly assigned to 1 year of standard DBT, in which subjects received concurrent individual psychotherapy and group skills training, or treatment as usual (TAU), in which subjects received referrals to therapists or agencies in the community. At the end of 1 year of outpatient treatment, subjects receiving DBT compared to those receiving TAU had significantly fewer parasuicides, less medically severe parasuicides, higher treatment retention, fewer psychiatric hospital days, less anger, higher social functioning, and higher global functioning (Linehan et al., 1991, 1994). The two conditions did not differ on ratings of depression, hopelessness, or suicide ideation. Results were generally maintained during a 1 year follow-up (Linehan et al., 1993). Preliminary analyses of mental health costs presented in Table 27.9 suggest that compared to TAU, DBT saves $9,000 per patient during the first year of treatment. Thus, DBT appears to have a better benefit-cost value (i.e., monetary value of benefits minus costs) and to be more cost-effective (i.e., ratio of nonmonetary benefits to monetary costs).

A study by Barley et al. (1993) adds further support to Linehan's findings. With a controlled nonrandomized design, Barley and colleagues compared DBT to treatment as usual in an inpatient setting. After adding only the DBT group skills training component to their standard inpatient treatment, they found no differences in the incident rate of parasuicidal behavior. After implementing aspects of individual DBT within their standard milieu and DBT skills training treatment, however, they found a significantly lower incidence of parasuicidal behavior among patients receiving DBT.

Turner (1993) has developed a dynamic cognitive behavioral treatment (DCBT) that is very similar to the treatment developed by Linehan and her colleagues. In a randomized controlled outcome study with BPD outpatients in a community mental health clinic, Turner compared the DCBT to supportive individual psychotherapy. At both the 6-month treatment point and at the 6-month follow-up after treatment, subjects in the DCBT condition had significantly better outcomes. They had less self-harm ideation and behavior; significantly less anger, depression, and anxiety; and significantly better ratings on the Brief Psychiatric Rating Scale.

Future Directions

Our review of follow-up studies and treatment studies suggests that BPD is a severe, chronic, and costly disorder and that we have not yet achieved a "cure." Clearly, the major emphasis of future research must remain on the development and testing of treatments for the disorder. But concurrently with this testing, we should assess both the direct costs of providing the treatment and the effect of the treatment on various areas of potential cost.

In designing a battery to assess costs, two primary methodological issues must be addressed. The first issue is to develop a battery that assesses for the possibility of "cost shifting." Weisbrod (1981, 1983) emphasizes the need for a comprehensive battery that measures cost and benefit consequences for multiple systems because, as he notes, "the dispersion of costs beyond the target group is likely to be especially great in the mental health area." The concern is that the application of the treatment may reduce cost in one area of treatment (e.g., outpatient therapy has lower costs than long-term inpatient therapy) but may shift the costs to another system (e.g., outpatient individuals are more likely to receive transfer payments, spend the night in jail, etc.) and thus overestimate the true cost savings if multiple systems are not assessed. Since BPD patients tend to become involved with multiple systems, they may have a particularly high risk for cost shifting. Additionally, psychological treatments could decrease costs or increase benefits in other systems. For example, treatment can decrease government disability payments by helping the patient gain and maintain stable employment.

The second issue is to develop a battery that assesses costs from various "perspectives." Although the labeling of nonmonetary benefits versus costs generally remains the same across various perspectives, the labeling of

Table 27.9 One-Year Average Health Care Costs in Dollars, by Condition (Linehan Study)

Variable	DBT ($n = 22$)	Control ($n = 22$)	t Value
Individual therapy visits	3,885	2,915	1.71
Group therapy visits	1,514	147	9.68***
Day treatment visits	11	876	1.70
Outpatient therapy total	5,410	3,938	1.58
Psychiatric hospital days	2,611	12,079	2.46††
Emergency room visits	216	543	3.31†††
Medical hospital days	342	1,094	1.30
Physician days	712	621	0.37
Medical total	1,270	2,258	1.53
Grand total	9,291	18,275	2.09†

Note. DBT = dialectical behavior therapy; TAU = treat as usual in the community.

***$p < .001$ at two-tailed.

†$p < .05$.

††$p < .01$, at one-tailed.

†††$p < .01$, at one-tailed.

monetary benefits versus costs depends far more on the perspective considered. For example, a decrease in parasuicide or an increase in global function is generally viewed as a benefit by patient, friends and family, and society. A reduction in disability payments, however, may be viewed as a benefit by the government, as neutral by a managed-care company, and as a cost by the patient. Plotnick (1994) emphasizes the necessity of assessing variables in such a way that they can be analyzed from the view of the treatment "participant," the "nonparticipant," and the "society" as an aggregate whole.

The costs associated with the behaviors and treatment of borderline personality disorder are dramatically high, psychologically as well as financially. Indeed, where comparisons are available, BPD appears to be among the most costly of psychiatric disorders. It can be frustrating, then, to observe that BPD is also among the least studied of psychiatric disorders with respect to the development of empirically demonstrated efficacious treatments. In this era of cost-effectiveness, we must note that none of the long-term follow-up studies of BPD support the hypothesis that the more costly the treatment, the more effective it will be. Ironically, the one treatment empirically demonstrated as effective (Linehan et al., 1991, 1993, 1994) also appears to be less costly than treatment as usual. It can be hoped that the new emphasis on attending to cost in the area of mental health will help to promote the development of efficacious treatments.

Acknowledgments This research was supported by grant MH34486 from the National Institute of Mental Health, Bethesda, Md.

References

Adler, G. (1985). *Borderline psychopathology and its treatment.* New York: Jason Aronson.

Adler, G. (1989). Psychodynamic therapies in borderline personality disorder. In A. Tasman, R. E. Hales, & A. J. Frances (Eds.). *American psychiatric press review of psychiatry.* (Vol. 8, pp. 48–64). Washington, DC: American Psychiatric Press.

Akiskal, H. S. (1981). Subaffective disorders: Dysthymic, cyclothmic and bipolar II disorders in the "borderline" realm. *Psychiatric Clinics of North America, 4,* 25–46.

Barasch, A., Frances, A., Hurt, S., Clarkin, J., & Cohen, S. (1985). Stability and distinctness of borderline personality disorder. *American Journal of Psychiatry, 142,* 1484–1486.

Barley, W. D., Buie, S. E., Peterson, E. W., Hollingsworth, A. S., Griva, M., Hickerson, S. C., Lawson, J. E., & Bailey, B. J. (1993). Development of an inpatient cognitive-behavioral treatment program for borderline personality disorder. *Journal of Personality Disorders, 7,* 232–240.

Brinkley, J. R. (1993). Pharmacotherapy of borderline states. *Psychiatric Clinics of North America, 16,* 853–884.

Buie, D. H., & Adler, G. (1982). The definitive treatment of borderline personality. *International Journal of Psychoanalytic Psychotherapy, 9,* 51–87.

Carpenter, W. T., & Gunderson, J. G. (1977). Five year follow-up comparison of borderline and schizophrenic patients. *Comprehensive Psychiatry, 18*, 567–571.

Clarkin, J. E., Marzialli, E., & Munroe-Blum, H. (1991). Group and family treatments for borderline personality disorder. *Hospital and Community Psychiatry, 42*, 1038–1043.

Clarkin, J. E., Widiger, T. A., Frances, A., Hurt, S. W., & Gilmore, M. (1983). Prototypic typology and the borderline personality disorder. *Journal of Abnormal Psychology*, 92, 263–275.

Cowdry, R. W., Pickar, D., & Davies, R. (1985). Symptoms and EEG findings in the borderline syndrome. *International Journal of Psychiatry in Medicine, 15*, 201–211.

Dulit, R. A., Fyer, M. R., Leon, A. C., Brodsky, B. S., & Frances, A. J. (1994). Clinical correlates of self-mutilation in borderline personality disorder. *American Journal of Psychiatry, 151*, 1305–1311.

Friedman, R., et al. (1983). History of suicidal behavior in depressed borderline inpatients. *American Journal of Psychiatry, 140*, 1023–1026.

Fyer, M. R. (1988). Suicide attempts in patient with borderline personality disorder. *American Journal of Psychiatry, 145*, 737–739.

Gardner, D. L., & Cowdry, R. W. (1985). Suicidal and parasuicidal behaviour in borderline personality disorder. *Psychiatric Clinics of North America, 8*, 389–403.

Grinker, R. R., & Werble, B. (1977). *The borderline patient*. New York: Jason Aronson.

Gunderson, J. G., Carpenter, W. T., & Strauss, S. (1975). Borderline and schizophrenic patients: A comparative study. *American Journal of Psychiatry, 132*, 1257–1264.

Gunderson, J. G., Kolb, J. E., & Austin, V. (1981). The Diagnostic Interview for Borderlines. *American Journal of Psychiatry*, 138, 896–903.

Keller, M. B., Lavori, P. W., Friedman, B., Nielsen, E., Endicott, J., McDonald-Scott, P., & Andreasen, N. C. (1987). The longitudinal interval follow-up evaluation: A comprehensive method for assessing outcome in prospective longitudinal studies. *Archives of General Psychiatry, 44*, 540–548.

Kelly, T., Soloff, P. H., Cornelius, J., George, A., Lis, J. A., & Ulrich, R. (1992). Can we study (treat) borderline patients? Attrition from research and open treatment. *Journal of Personality Disorders, 6*, 417–433.

Kernberg, O. F. (1984). *Severe personality disorders: Psychotherapeutic strategies*. New Haven, CT: Yale University Press.

Kernberg, O. F. (1987). A psychodynamic approach. *Journal of Personality Disorders, 1*, 344–346.

Kreitman, N. (1977). *Parasuicide*. London: Wiley.

Kroll, J. L., Carey, K. S., & Sines, L. K. (1985). Twenty-year follow-up of borderline personality disorder: A pilot study. In C. Stragass (Ed.), *IVth World Congress of Biological Psychiatry*, (Vol. 7). New York: Elsevier.

Kroll, J. L., Carey, K. S., Sines, L. K., & Roth, M. (1982). Are there borderlines in Britain? *Archives of General Psychiatry*, 39, 60–63.

Kroll, J. L., Sines, L., & Martin, K. (1981). Borderline personality disorder: Construct validity of the concept. *Archives of General Psychiatry*, 39, 60–63.

Kullgren, G. (1988). Factors associated with completed suicide in borderline personality disorder. *Journal of Nervous and Mental Disease, 176*, 40–44.

Kullgren, G., & Armelius, B. (1990). The concept of personality organization: A long-term comparative follow-up study with special reference to borderline personality organization. *Journal of Personality Disorders, 4*, 203–212.

Kullgren, G., Renber, E., & Jacobsson, L. (1986). An empirical study of borderline personality disorder and psychiatric suicides. *Journal of Nervous and Mental Disease, 174*, 328–331.

Leone, N. F. (1982). Response of borderline patients to loxapine and chlorpromazine. *Journal of Clinical Psychiatry, 43*, 148–150.

Linehan, M. M. (1993a). *Cognitive behavioral treatment of borderline personality disorder*. New York: Guilford Press.

Linehan, M. M. (1993b). *Skills training manual for treating of borderline personality disorder*. New York: Guilford Press.

Linehan, M. M., Armstrong, H. E., Suarez, A., Allmon, D., & Heard, H. L. (1991). Cognitive-behavioral treatment of chronically parasuicidal borderline patients. *Archives of General Psychiatry, 48*, 1060–1064.

Linehan, M. M., Heard, H. L., & Armstrong, H. E. (1993). Naturalistic follow-up of a behavioral treatment for chronically parasuicidal borderline patients. *Archives of General Psychiatry, 50*, 971–974.

Linehan, M. M., Tutek, D. A., Heard, H. L., & Armstrong, H. E. (1994). Cognitive behavioral treatment for chronically suicidal borderline patients: Interpersonal outcomes. *American Journal of Psychiatry, 151*, 1771–1776.

Links, P. S., Mitton, J. E., & Steiner, M. (1990). Predicting outcome for borderline personality disorder. *Comprehensive Psychiatry, 31*, 490–498.

Loftus, E. F., Smith, K. D., & Klinger, M. R. (1994). *Memory and mismemory for health events*. Unpublished manuscript, University of Washington, Seattle.

Loranger, A. W. (1987). *Personality Disorders Examination (PDE) manual.* Yonkers, NY: DV Communications.

Loranger, A. W., Lenzenweger, M. F., Gartner, A. F., Susman, V. L., Herzig, J., Zammit, G. K., Gartner, J. D., Abrams, R. C., & Young, R. C. (1991). Trait-state artifacts and the diagnosis of personality disorders. *Archives of General Psychiatry, 48,* 720–728.

Loranger, A. W., Susman, V. I., Oldham, J. M., & Russakoff, L. M. (1987). Personality Disorders Examination (PDE): A preliminary report. *Journal of Personality Disorders, 1,* 1–13.

Masterson, J. F. (1976). *Psychotherapy of the borderline adult: A developmental approach.* New York: Brunner/Mazel.

Masterson, J. F. (1981). *The narcissistic and borderline disorders.* New York: Brunner/Mazel.

Masterson, J. F., & Costello, J. (1980). *From borderline adolescent to functioning adult.* New York: Brunner/Mazel.

McGlashan, T. H. (1984). The Chestnut Lodge follow-up study: Follow-up methodology and study sample. *Archives of General Psychiatry, 41,* 573–585.

McGlashan, T. H. (1986). The Chestnut Lodge follow-up study: Long-term outcome of borderline personalities. *Archives of General Psychiatry, 43,* 20–30.

McGlashan, T. H. (1987). Testing DSM-III symptom criteria for schizotypal and borderline personality disorders. *Archives of General Psychiatry, 44,* 143–148.

Mehlum, L., Friis, S., Irion, T., Johns, S., Karterud, S., Vaglum, P., & Vaglum, S. (1991). Personality disorders 2–5 years after treatment: A prospective follow-up study. *Acta Psychiatrica Scandinavica, 84,* 72–77.

Mehlum, L., Friis, S., Vaglum, P., & Karterud, S. (1994). The longitudinal pattern of suicidal behavior in borderline personality disorder: A prospective follow-up study. *Acta Psychiatrica Scandinavica, 90,* 124–130.

Modestin, J., Abrecht, I., Tschaggelar, W., & Hoffman, H. (1983). Diagnosing borderline: A contribution to the question of its conceptual validity. *Archives Psychiatrica Nervenkra, 233,* 359–370.

Modestin, J., & Villiger, C. (1989). Follow-up study on borderline versus nonborderline personality disorders. *Comprehensive Psychiatry, 30,* 236–244.

Munroe-Blum, H., & Marzialli, E. (1988). Time-limited, group psychotherapy for borderline patients. *Canadian Journal of Psychiatry, 33,* 364–369.

National Institute of Mental Health. (1993). *Health care reform for Americans with severe mental illnesses: Report of the National Advisory Mental Health Council* (G. Tucker, Chair). Washington, DC: Government Printing Office.

Paris, J., Brown, R., & Nowlis, D. (1987). Long-term follow-up of borderline patients in a general hospital. *Comprehensive Psychiatry, 28,* 530–535.

Paris, J., Nowlis, D., & Brown, B. (1989). Predictors of suicide in borderline personality disorder. *Canadian Journal of Psychiatry, 34,* 8–9.

Perry, J. C. (1985). Depression in borderline personality disorder: Lifetime prevalence at interview and longitudinal course of symptoms. *American Journal of Psychiatry, 142,* 15–21.

Perry, J. C., & Cooper, S. H. (1985). Psychodynamics, symptoms and outcome in borderline and antisocial personality disorders and bipolar type II affective disorder. In T. H. McGlashan (Ed.), *The borderline: Current empirical research* (pp. 21–41). Washington, DC: American Psychiatric Press.

Plakun, E. M. (1991). Prediction of outcome in borderline personality disorder. *Journal of Personality Disorders, 5,* 93–101.

Plakun, E. M., Burkhardt, P. E., & Muller, J. P. (1985). 14 year follow-up of borderline and schizotypal personality disorders. *Comparative Psychiatry, 26,* 448–455.

Plotnick, R. D. (1994). Applying benefit-cost analysis to substance use prevention programs. *International Journal of the Addictions, 29,* 339–359.

Pope, H. G., Jonas, J. M., Hudson, J. I., Cohen, B. M., & Gunderson, J. G. (1983). The validity of DSM-III borderline personality disorder. *Archives of General Psychiatry, 40,* 23–30.

Rifkin, A., Levitan, S. J., Galewski, J., & Klein, D. F. (1972a). Emotionally unstable character disorder: A follow-up study: 1. Description of patients and outcome. *Biological Psychiatry, 4,* 65–79.

Rifkin, A., Levitan, S. J., Galewski, J., & Klein, D. F. (1972b). Emotionally unstable character disorder: A follow-up study: 2. Prediction of outcome. *Biological Psychiatry, 4,* 81–88.

Runeson, B., & Beskow, J. (1991). Borderline personality disorder in young Swedish suicides. *Journal of Nervous and Mental Disease, 179,* 153–156.

Shearer, S. L., Peters, C. P., Quaytman, M. S., & Wadman, B. E. (1988). Intent and lethality of suicide attempts among female borderline inpatients. *American Journal of Psychiatry, 145,* 1424–1427.

Skodol, A. E., Buckley, P., & Charles, E. (1983). Is there a characteristic pattern to the treatment history of clinic outpatients with borderline personality? *Journal of Nervous and Mental Disease, 171,* 405–410.

Soloff, P. H. (1987). Neuroleptic treatment in the borderline patient: Advantages and techniques. *Journal of Clinical Psychiatry, 48,* 26–30.

Soloff, P. H. (1994). Is there any drug treatment of choice for the borderline patient? *Acta Psychiatrica Scandinavica, 379,* 50–55.

Soloff, P. H., Lis, J. A., Kelly, T., Cornelius, J., & Ulrich, R. (1994). Risk factors for suicidal behavior in borderline personality disorder. *American Journal of Psychiatry, 151,* 1315–1323.

Stevenson, J., & Meares, R. (1992). An outcome study of psychotherapy for patients with borderline personality disorder. *American Journal of Psychiatry, 149,* 358–362.

Stone, M. H. (1987). Psychotherapy of borderline patients in light of long-term follow-up. *Bulletin of the Menninger Clinic, 51,* 231–247.

Stone, M. H. (1990). *The fate of borderline patients: Successful outcome and psychiatric practice.* New York: Guilford Press.

Stone, M. H., Stone, D. K., & Hurt, S. W. (1987). Natural history of borderline patients treated by intensive hospitalization. *Psychiatric Clinics of North America, 10,* 185–206.

Tucker, L., Bauer, S. F., Wagner, S., Harlam, D., & Sher, I. (1987). Long-term hospitalization of borderline patients: A descriptive outcome study. *American Journal of Psychiatry, 144,* 1443–1448.

Turner, R. M. (1993, November). *Dynamic cognitive-behavior therapy for borderline personality disorder.* Paper presented at the meeting of the Association for Advancement of Behavior Therapy, Atlanta.

Weisbrod, B. A. (1981). Benefit-cost analysis of a controlled experiment: Treating the mentally ill. *Journal of Human Resources, 16,* 523–548.

Weisbrod, B. A. (1983). A guide to benefit-cost analysis, as seen through a controlled experiment in treating the mentally ill. *Journal of Health Politics, Policy and Law, 6,* 808–845.

Weissman, M. M., & Bothwell, S. (1976). Assessment of social adjustment by patient self-report. *Archives of General Psychiatry, 33,* 1111–1115.

Werble, B. (1970). Second follow-up study of borderline patients. *Archives of General Psychiatry, 23,* 3–7.

Widiger, T. A., & Frances, A. J. (1987). Epidemiology, diagnosis and comorbidity of borderline personality disorders. In A. Tasman, R. E., Hales, & A. J. Frances (Eds.), *American Psychiatric Press review of psychiatry.* (Vol. 8, pp. 8–24). Washington, DC: American Psychiatry Press.

Yette, R., Hodgson, S., Lund, P. J., Mack, C. E., Mayfield, J., Miller, J. E., & Pavelcheck, D. (1994). *DSHS community data report: Fiscal year 1992.* (DSHS Publication No. 11-78). Olympia, WA: Department of Social and Health Services.

28

Dissociative Identity Disorder

Richard P. Kluft

The treatment of dissociative identity disorder (DID), until recently called multiple personality disorder (MPD), poses significant challenges to the mental health care delivery system. Dissociative identity disorder is a complex chronic dissociative psychopathology characterized by lesions of identity and memory. The *DSM-IV* diagnostic criteria for DID are

A. The presence of two or more distinct identities or personality states (each with its own relatively enduring pattern of perceiving, relating to, and thinking about the environment and self).
B. At least two of these identities or personality states recurrently take control of the person's behavior.
C. Inability to recall important personal information that is too extensive to be explained by ordinary forgetfulness.
D. The disturbance is not due to the direct physiological effects of a substance (e.g., blackouts or chaotic behavior during Alcohol Intoxication) or general medical condition (e.g., complex partial seizures).

(American Psychiatric Association [APA], 1994, p. 487)

The clinical presentation is often confusing and polysymptomatic. It includes dissociative processes and phenomena, amnesia and other disturbances of memory, autohypnotic symptoms, posttraumatic stress disorder symptoms, somatoform symptoms, and affective symptoms (Loewenstein, 1991) in addition to manifestations that may appear psychotic (Kluft, 1987a, 1987b). DID often is associated with considerable comorbidity (Horevitz & Loewenstein, 1994; Kluft, 1991b); it remains uncertain whether apparent co-occurring disorders are more often epiphenomena of the DID or additional psychiatric disorders.

Prevalence

Recent studies screening psychiatric inpatient populations in Canada (Ross, Anderson, Fleisher, & Norton, 1991), the United States (Saxe et al., 1993), the Netherlands (Boon & Draijer, 1993), Turkey (Sar, unpublished data, 1995), and Norway (Knudsen, Haslerud, Boe, Draijer, & Boon, 1995) demonstrate that when investigators use reliable and valid screening measures such as the Dissociative Experiences Scale (Bernstein & Putnam, 1986) to identify patients to be studied further with reliable and valid structured or semistructured interviews (Ross, 1989; Steinberg, 1993), between 3% and 5% or more of psychiatric inpatients (less those with previously diagnosed dissociative disorders) prove to have previously undiagnosed DID.

Ross and his colleagues have explored the prevalence of dissociative disorders (DDs) in other clinical populations. They found 39% of chemical dependency patients had a DD, with14% meeting criteria for DID (Ross et al., 1992); 35% of hospitalized adolescents had a diagnosable DD, with 17% fulfilling criteria for DID (Ross, 1991). Lifetime prevalence of DDs in a random sample of 1,005 citizens of Winnipeg, Canada, was 11.2% (Ross, Joshi, & Curry, 1990). Of women presenting for treatment as survivors of childhood sexual abuse, 88.5% had a diagnosable DD (Ross et al., 1992); 10.5% of an abused subpopulation of 57 patients was found to have DID (Ross, 1991).

Costs

The treatment of DID per se is expensive; in the absence of randomized controlled clinical trials, clinical reports suggest that only long-term individual psychotherapy has proven effective (Kluft, 1995). Additional expenses accrue due to (a) the consumption of inappropriate health services, (b) the consequences of delayed diagnosis, and (c) continued chronicity in the absence of targeted interventions. DID waxes and wanes in its manifest symptomatology but does not improve without treatment that addresses it specifically (Kluft, 1985, 1991b, 1993b). Two keys to cost containment are promotion of rapid diagnosis and appropriate treatment and minimizing expenditures on nonspecific and ineffective treatment.

Early case finding is an extremely important aspect of moving toward the economic treatment of DID, but it is very unusual to identify cases in childhood instead of in adulthood; the average age of diagnosis is early in the fourth decade of life. Putnam, Guroff, Silberman, Barban, and Post (1986) found that their 100 cases had been in the mental health care delivery system for an average of 6.8 years, with symptoms referable to DID prior to being given an accurate diagnosis. This finding has been replicated by other investigators (Boon & Draijer, 1993; Rivera, 1991; Ross et al., 1990). North American series of DID patients have averaged between 6.8 and 7.1 years; a series from the Netherlands averaged 8.2 years. These patients averaged over three previous diagnoses. While some of these other diagnoses were clearly inaccurate in retrospect, others probably were correctly identified concomitant psychopathologies noted prior to recognizing the DID.

In a study of 210 DID patients followed between 3 and 18 years, Kluft (1985, 1993b) found that virtually all patients diagnosed with DID who did not get targeted treatment continued to manifest DID symptoms on follow-up. Those treated by therapists who did not believe in the condition and discouraged discussion of DID-related issues continued to have DID on follow-up. Of patients treated by therapists who treated the patients without specifically addressing the DID, only 2–3% were without DID on follow-up. This suggests that "good general psychotherapy" is not a cost-effective approach to DID.

When the condition is not recognized accurately, the symptomatic DID patient is likely to use medical and psychiatric care extensively in desperate but futile efforts to relieve his or her distress. There is anecdotal evidence that children with DID require less intense treatment and respond to treatment much more rapidly than adults, sometimes in months rather than in years (e.g., Fagan & McMahon, 1984; Kluft, 1984b). In contrast, by adolescence, the condition is difficult to treat, and by adulthood, it is often well entrenched. The persistence of the condition into adulthood has additional economic consequences in terms of the greater likelihood of underachievement, disability, and absenteeism. In the absence of targeted interventions, many DID patients will become chronically ill and incapacitated for considerable periods of time.

Empirical Diagnostic Measures and Structured Interviews

Contemporary diagnostic approaches take a variety of forms, including inquiry about suggestive signs of DID (Kluft, 1987b, 1991a), use of first-rank symptoms (Kluft, 1987a), and direct inquiries that attempt to contact alters (Putnam, 1989). Loewenstein's (1991) specialized mental status examination and the Dissociative Experiences Scale (Bernstein & Putnam, 1986) are useful screens for the likelihood of a dissociative disorder diagnosis in adults.

Structured instruments for the diagnosis of DID include Ross's (1989, 1991) Dissociative Disorders Interview Schedule (DDIS), which is about 90% sensitive with 5% false positives (Colin A. Ross, personal communication, May 1992), and Steinberg's Structured Clinical Interview for the Diagnosis of DSM-IV Dissociative Disorders (SCID-D; 1993), which is over 90% sensitive with few false positives. Psychological testing is moving toward competence in recognizing DID patients, but a large battery of tests and some specialized techniques are necessary (Armstrong, 1991).

The recognition of dissociative disorders in children is less advanced. Several unvalidated screening measures and questionnaires of uncertain reliability have been proposed (listed in Kluft, 1996), in addition to Putnam's reliable and validated Child Dissociative

Checklist (Putnam, Helmers, & Trickett, 1993). No structured interviews for the diagnosis of DID in children or adolescents have been developed.

Targeted Psychosocial Interventions

Herman (1992) has demonstrated a common triphasic structure to the treatment of traumatized patients. A phase of making the patient feel safe, of strengthening the patient and offering support, is followed by a stage of recalling and processing traumatic material. Next, a phase of rehabilitation focuses on helping the patient reintegrate his or her self, repair interpersonal relationships, and reestablish connections with society. Herman summarizes these as the stages of safety, remembrance and mourning, and reconnection.

This triphasic structure underlies the stages of the treatment of DID proposed by modern authors (Braun, 1986; Fine, 1991; Kluft, 1991b, 1993a; Putnam, 1989; Ross, 1989; Turkus, 1991). For example, Kluft (1991b) defines stages of (a) establishing the psychotherapy, (b) preliminary interventions, (c) history gathering and mapping, (d) metabolizing the trauma, (e) moving toward integration/resolution, (f) integration/resolution, (g) learning new coping skills, (h) solidification of gains and working through, and (i) follow-up. Stages (a)–(c) are analogous with Herman's phase of safety, Stage (d) is correlated with remembrance and mourning, and the remainder address reconnection.

Treatment goals encompass alleviating dysfunctional separateness, eliminating episodes of time loss and amnesia (effecting continuity of contemporary memory), relieving interpersonal difficulties, and helping the patient reintegrate himself or herself with respect to the traumas that are believed to have been endured.

A recent survey of therapists treating DID (Putnam & Loewenstein, 1993) found that the primary treatment for DID is long-term intensive psychotherapy with adjunctive hypnotherapy and psychopharmacology. Art therapy and other group modalities are often utilized. The American Psychiatric Association's *Treatments of Psychiatric Disorders*—(1995) states that two 45-minute sessions per week should be regarded as the minimum intensity for effective psychotherapy of DID (Kluft, 1995; Wilbur & Kluft, 1989). The reason such intense treatments are necessary relates both to the nature of the psychopathology and what must be addressed in treatment. DID patients are extremely vulnerable to destabilization (Kluft, 1984a, 1995) yet typically must contend with working through histories of repetitive traumatization. Many DID patients appear unstable and in crisis because their treatments do not offer sufficient intensity and frequency to provide adequate structure and support while attempting such painful work. Treatments have been proposed that focus completely on adaptation while avoiding trauma work, but the long-term effectiveness of such approaches in effecting a definitive cure has yet to be demonstrated. Many DID patients are not candidates for a definitive treatment and must be treated supportively, with palliative goals focused on stabilization and safety. Their therapy cannot move beyond the first phase of trauma treatment.

Therapeutic pluralism characterizes contemporary approaches to the treatment of DID (Kluft, 1988, 1993b). Targeted treatments of DID include strategic integrationalism, tactical integrationalism, adaptationalism, and personality-focused treatments. None have been translated into manual format for research purposes.

Strategic Integrationalism stems from the work of the late Cornelia B. Wilbur (1984, 1986), focusing on rendering dissociative defenses and structures less necessary and less viable by supportive and expressive psychodynamic psychotherapy. Tactical integrationalism emphasizes the application of discrete interventions to accomplish a series of objectives, such as containing flashbacks or isolating an alter prior to dealing with its issues in order to protect the others from being upset. Planful and deliberate, and congenial to the cognitive behavioral paradigm, treatment resembles a series of short-term therapies undertaken within the context of a long-term psychotherapy (as in the writings of Bennett G. Braun, 1986, and Catherine G. Fine, 1988, 1991, 1993).

Adaptationalism prioritizes function and the management of life activities. Integration and dealing with the past are not major priorities but may be addressed. It has been promoted primarily on the basis that more definitive treatments are hard to do, and that cost considerations dictate delivering suboptimal treatment. Neither studies nor anecdotal accounts have demonstrated its effectiveness. Personality-focused treatments owe much to the work of Watkins and Watkins (1993) and the late David Caul (1984). The focus is a problem-solving diplomacy or "family therapy of the self" in which alter personalities are encouraged to collaborate without necessarily moving toward integration.

Outcomes

Two follow-up studies of the treatment of DID patients have been published. Neither utilized stringently operationalized criteria or blind assessments. Working in a state hospital clinic setting, Coons (1986) followed the treatments of 20 DID patients. Most were treated by therapists new to work with DID and were seen an average of once weekly. At an average follow-up of 39 months, two thirds of the patients were described as moderately or greatly improved, and one quarter had achieved integration. Neither measure was operationally defined; determination was by clinicians' judgement.

Kluft (1984c, 1986, 1993b, 1994b) followed 123 DID patients in private practice with an experienced therapist. At last report, 103 had achieved integration and ended treatment; 14 had left treatment prematurely or had had unsuccessful therapies (including 2 suicides); 6 remained in active treatment, and of these, 4 continued to manifest clinical DID and 2 had signs suggestive of dissociative disorder not otherwise specified rather than overt DID. The criteria for successful integration were

> three successive months of 1) continuity of contemporary memory, 2) absence of overt behavioral signs of DID, 3) subjective sense of unity, 4) absence of alters (or the particular alter) on reexploration (preferably involving hypnosis), 5) modification of the transference phenomena consistent with the bringing together of the personalities, and 6) clinical evidence that the unified patient's self-representation includes acknowledgement of attitudes and awarenesses that were previously segregated in separate personalities. (Kluft, 1991b, p. 180)

Patients had to remain integrated an additional 2 years to be regarded as having a stable integration in this series. On follow-up, 94% of the DID patients integrated for 3 months plus 2 years were without overt behavioral DID. Three quarters of them were no longer using pathological dissociative defenses. Residual dissociation generally responded rapidly to additional therapy (Kluft, 1984c, 1986).

While the first 52 to integrate did so in an average of under 2.5 years, the remaining 51 took an average of 7 years. This outcome suggests that (a) DID is heterogeneous with respect to prognosis, and (b) very good results can be achieved for motivated patients in long-term treatment (at an average of two sessions per week) with a therapist who is very experienced in the treatment of DID.

Kluft (1993b, 1994a, 1994b) identified three subgroups of DID patients on the basis of treatment responsiveness: high-trajectory patients with an excellent prognosis; middle-trajectory patients, who were slower to improve and included an unstable group at high risk for suicide; and low-trajectory patients, who may make minimal improvement for long periods of time and may be major consumers of hospital services over periods of months or years. Ross and Dua (1993) also identified three groups of DID patients. The first made rapid gains and resolved their DID within 2–3 years. The second was more complex; patients were enmeshed with their abusive families and required more extensive hospital care. The third did not progress rapidly, but their utilization of inpatient and emergency services declined. Horevitz and Loewenstein (1994) also described three similar subgroups.

Unfortunately, there are no empirical data from controlled clinical treatment trials with DID. Studies in this area are needed. As we enter an era in which the study of the cost-effectiveness of psychotherapy is of paramount importance, minimal data are available pertaining to the economic evaluation of the treatment of DID. Very little research funding has been allocated for its study; the data that are available are incomplete and anecdotal, derived from unfunded clinicians piggybacking their investigative efforts onto clinical work. While such information is far from ideal, it has allowed for preliminary observations.

Cost-Effectiveness Studies

A small number of studies have addressed the issues of cost-effectiveness for the accurate diagnosis and specific treatment of DID. Rivera (1991) outlined the enormous costs incurred by undiagnosed DID patients' consumption of psychiatric, substance abuse, and social welfare services. Ross, Norton, and Wozney (1989) found that DID patients were more likely to use hospital services prior to their accurate diagnosis, a finding indicating the pain and distress of undiagnosed DID patients, and that treatment targeted toward DID reduces the usage of inpatient services.

Ross and Dua (1993) studied 15 inpatients with

DID. They had averaged 8.2 years in treatment prior to accurate diagnosis; an estimation based only on incomplete available records demonstrates that $2,769,997.50 (in 1989 Canadian dollars), or $184,666.50 per patient, had been spent on psychiatric treatment prior to the DID diagnosis. The authors made a series of assumptions about these patients' likely course with specific and nonspecific treatment and calculated that accurate diagnosis and treatment would save $84,900 (1989 Canadian dollars) per patient over the decade subsequent to accurate diagnosis. Further, had the patients been diagnosed in an average of 1 year instead of 8.2 years, a savings of $250,000 (1989 Canadian dollars) per patient, or an aggregate $3.75 million, would have accrued. Had these women been diagnosed prior to age 10, the authors estimate an overall savings on psychiatric, medical, and social services on the order of $10 million (1989 Canadian dollars) might have been realized. Although the assumptions made by the authors can be challenged, and their calculations were based on incomplete records (leading to an underestimation of costs), the take-home message is clear. Early case finding and specific treatment have the potential to save substantial amounts of money.

Fraser and Raine (1992) studied a cohort of 49 Canadian DID patients who averaged 6.9 years of treatment prior to correct diagnosis. Three groups were identified. The first consisted of patients who rapidly forged toward unity. They had averaged $75,000 per patient per year in psychiatric costs for the 3 years prior to diagnosis, and $36,000 for the next 3 years after the diagnosis. However, most of the cost was in the first year: The average for Years 2 and 3 was $10,700.

Their second group had borderline features but no more than 15 alters. They ran a course similar to that of the first group but universally had required one or more stays on a specialized dissociative disorders unit to begin to move forward. Almost all of the patients in the first two groups were out of treatment within 5 years after diagnosis.

A third group had borderline personality disorder features and had more than 15 alters. They had the longest prediagnosis treatment histories, and their costs were four times those of the first group. They did not begin to show a decrease in treatment costs until the sixth year after diagnosis.

Several studies (Fraser & Raine, 1992; Kluft, 1994a, 1994b; Ross & Dua, 1993 see also Horevitz & Loewenstein, 1984) demonstrate the considerable heterogeneity of DID. Treatments for DID appear remarkably effective for the rapidly responding, less severe, or high-trajectory group. Yet results are more problematic for the more seriously affected. Predictors for DID subgroups have not been delineated definitively, although the use of the Dimensions of Therapeutic Movement Instrument (DTMI) has shown some promise in limited open trials (Kluft, 1994a. 1994b).

Research Recommendations Pertaining to Cost-Effectiveness and Cost-Benefits

The most impressive economies may be more easily attained by enhanced case recognition and better training of therapists. It is crucial that systematic data be collected pertaining to the utility and cost-effectiveness of treatment paradigms as applied in the community. Movement toward the more effective diagnosis and treatment of DID in children and an enhanced emphasis on methods of conveying knowledge about the treatment of DID should significantly reduce unnecessary costs in the future.

To address issues of cost-effectiveness and cost-benefit, research must stand aside from the controversies that often surround DID and its treatment. Such concerns must be addressed in other contexts, but with regard to matters of expense, DID patients exist in considerable numbers, their care is costly, and it is important to determine the most effective and efficacious ways to resolve their difficulties.

Recommended research measures must address a number of concerns, some of which were raised in a forward-looking essay by Putnam (1986). It will be crucial to operationalize the definitions of desired treatment outcomes and typical treatment interventions. Although the screening instruments and structured interviews currently available for the assessment of DID in adults are satisfactory, the development of structured instruments for the assessment of children and early adolescents is an urgent priority. The DTMI (Kluft, 1994a, 1994b) is an instrument for use by the therapist; it studies the process rather than the outcome of therapy. It is necessary to develop instruments that are sufficiently operationalized for use by objective observers in the baseline assessment and sequential reevaluation of the impact of treatment on DID patients. This approach will allow the objective assessment of the therapy of DID as it is currently practiced. It will facilitate the completion of crucial multicenter studies, an essential step in moving beyond reliance upon data derived from individuals' reports of their own work (e.g., Kluft, 1984c, 1986) and impressionistic assessments based on secondhand reports (Coons, 1986).

It will be important to manualize one or more approaches to the treatment of DID. The tactical integrationalist model, generally regarded as the easiest major approach to teach, is an excellent candidate for such a project (see Fine, 1991, 1993). The effectiveness and efficacy of manualized and nonmanualized treatments could be compared.

Another important area will be refining understanding of the heterogeneity of DID and its implications for treatment. It should be possible to determine both the response of various subgroups of DID patients to treatment and whether different treatment approaches are more useful for different subgroups. This knowledge may lead to the augmentation of manualized treatments with decision trees to direct treatment of different subgroups and to allow more informed decisions about when it is appropriate for therapy to proceed from one phase to another.

It is essential to promote the teaching of the diagnosis and treatment of dissociative disorders in all training programs, and to mental health professionals who have already completed their training. Because it is already clear that targeted treatment is preferable to nonspecific treatment, and that considerable funds are wasted when the DID diagnosis is not made promptly and/or nonspecific treatment is rendered, such educational efforts should proceed even before the completion of the research studies recommended above.

References

American Psychiatric Association. (1994). *Diagnostic and statistical manual of mental disorders* (4th ed.). Washington, DC: Author.

Armstrong, J. (1991). The psychological organization of multiple personality disordered patients as revealed in psychological testing. *Psychiatric Clinics of North America, 14,* 533–546.

Bernstein, E. M., & Putnam, F. W. (1986). Development, reliability, and validity of a dissociation scale. *Journal of Nervous and Mental Disease, 174,* 727–735.

Boon, S., & Draijer, N. (1993). *Multiple personality disorder in the Netherlands: A study on reliability and validity of the diagnosis.* Amsterdam: Swets & Zeitlinger.

Braun, B. G. (1986). Issues in the treatment of multiple personality disorder. In B. G. Braun (Ed.), *Treatment of multiple personality disorder* (pp. 1–28). Washington, DC: American Psychiatric Press.

Caul, D. (1984). Group and videotape techniques for multiple personality disorder. *Psychiatric Annals, 14,* 43–50.

Coons, P. M. (1986). Treatment progress in 20 patients with multiple personality disorder. *Journal of Nervous and Mental Disease, 174,* 715–721.

Fagan, J., & McMahon, P. P. (1984). Incipient multiple personality in children. *Journal of Nervous and Mental Disease, 172,* 26–36.

Fine, C. G. (1988). Thoughts on the cognitive perceptual substrates of multiple personality disorder. *Dissociation, 1*(4), 5–10.

Fine, C. G. (1991). Treatment stabilization and crisis prevention: Pacing the therapy of the multiple personality disorder patient. *Psychiatric Clinics of North America, 14,* 661–675.

Fine, C. G. (1993). A tactical integrationalist perspective on the treatment of multiple personality disorder. In R. P. Kluft & C. G. Fine (Eds.), *Clinical perspectives on multiple personality disorder* (pp. 135–154). Washington, DC: American Psychiatric Press.

Fraser, G. A., & Raine, D. (1992). Cost analysis of the treatment of MPD. In B. G. Braun (Ed.), *Proceedings of the ninth international conference on multiple personality/dissociative states* (p. 10). Chicago: Rush University.

Herman, J. L. (1992). *Trauma and recovery.* New York: Basic Books.

Horevitz, R. P., & Loewenstein, R. J. (1994). The rational treatment of multiple personality disorder. In S. J. Lynn & J. W. Rhue (Eds.), *Dissociation: Clinical and theoretical perspectives* (pp. 289–316). New York: Guilford.

Kluft, R. P. (1984a). Aspects of the treatment of multiple personality. *Psychiatric Annals, 14,* 51–55.

Kluft, R. P. (1984b). Multiple personality in childhood. *Psychiatric Clinics of North America, 7,* 121–134.

Kluft, R. P. (1984c). Treatment of multiple personality: A study of 33 cases. *Psychiatric Clinics of North America, 7,* 9–29.

Kluft, R. P. (1985). The natural history of multiple personality disorder. In R. P. Kluft (Ed.), *Childhood antecedents of multiple personality disorder* (pp. 197–238). Washington, DC: American Psychiatric Press.

Kluft, R. P. (1986). Personality unification in multiple personality disorder (MPD): A follow-up study. In B. G. Braun (Ed.), *Treatment of multiple personality disorder* (pp. 29–60). Washington, DC: American Psychiatric Press.

Kluft, R. P. (1987a). First-rank symptoms as a diagnostic clue to multiple personality disorder. *American Journal of Psychiatry, 144,* 293–298.

Kluft, R. P. (1987b). An update on multiple personality disorder. *Hospital and Community Psychiatry, 38,* 363–373.

Kluft, R. P. (1988). Today's therapeutic pluralism. *Dissociation, 1*(4), 1–2.

Kluft, R. P. (1991a). Clinical presentations of multiple personality disorder. *Psychiatric Clinics of North America, 14,* 605–629.

Kluft, R. P. (1991b). Multiple personality disorder. In A. Tasman & S. M. Goldfinger (Eds.), *American Psychiatric Press annual review of psychiatry* (Vol. 10, pp. 161–188). Washington, DC: American Psychiatric Press.

Kluft, R. P. (1993a). The initial stages of psychotherapy in the treatment of multiple personality disorder patients. *Dissociation, 6,* 145–161.

Kluft, R. P. (1993b). The treatment of dissociative disorder patients: An overview of discoveries, successes, and failures. *Dissociation, 6,* 87–101.

Kluft, R. P. (1994b). Clinical applications of the Dimensions of Therapeutic Movement Instrument. *Dissociation, 7,* 272–283.

Kluft, R. P. (1994b). Treatment trajectories in multiple personality disorder. *Dissociation, 7,* 63–76.

Kluft, R. P. (1995). Dissociative identity disorder. In G. O. Gabbard (Ed.), *Treatments of psychiatric disorders* (2nd ed., Vols. 1, 2, pp. 1599–1632). Washington, DC: American Psychiatric Press.

Kluft, R. P. (1996). Outpatient treatment of dissociative identity disorder and allied forms of dissociative disorder not otherwise specified in children and adolescents. *Child and Adolescent Psychiatric Clinics of North America, 5,* 471–494.

Knudsen, H., Haslerud, J., Boe, T. Draijer, N., & Boon, S. (1995). Prevalence of dissociative disorders in a Norwegian general psychiatric departments (inpatients and daycare). In O. van der Hart, S. Boon, & N. Draijer (Eds.), *Proceedings of the Fifth Annual Spring Conference of the International Society for the Study of Dissociation* (p. 79). Amsterdam: International Society for the Study of Dissociation.

Loewenstein, R. J. (1991). An office mental status examination for complex chronic dissociative symptoms and multiple personality disorder. *Psychiatric Clinics of North America, 14,* 567–604.

Putnam, F. W. (1986). The treatment of multiple personality disorder: State of the art. In B. G. Braun (Ed.), *Treatment of multiple personality disorder* (pp. 175–198). Washington, DC: American Psychiatric Press.

Putnam, F. W. (1989). *Diagnosis and treatment of multiple personality disorder.* New York: Guilford.

Putnam, F. W., Guroff, J. J., Silberman, E. K., Barban, L., & Post, R. M. (1986). The clinical phenomenology of multiple personality disorder: A review of 100 recent cases. *Journal of Clinical Psychiatry, 47,* 285–293.

Putnam, F. W., Helmers, K., & Trickett, P. K. (1993). Development, reliability, and validity of a child dissociation scale. *Child Abuse & Neglect, 17,* 731–741.

Putnam, F. W., & Loewenstein, R. J. (1993). Treatment of multiple personality disorder: A survey of current practices. *American Journal of Psychiatry, 150,* 1048–1052.

Rivera, M. (1991). *Multiple personality: An outcome of child abuse.* Toronto: Education/Dissociation.

Ross, C. A. (1989). *Multiple personality disorder: Diagnosis, clinical features, and treatment.* New York: Wiley.

Ross, C. A. (1991). The epidemiology of multiple personality disorder and dissociation. *Psychiatric Clinics of North America, 14,* 503–517.

Ross, C. A., Anderson, G., Fleisher, W. P., & Norton, G. R. (1991). The frequency of multiple personality disorder among psychiatric inpatients. *American Journal of Psychiatry, 148,* 1717–1720.

Ross, C. A., & Dua, V. (1993). Psychiatric care costs of multiple personality disorder. *American Journal of Psychotherapy, 47,* 103–112.

Ross, C. A., Joshi, S., & Currie, R. (1990). Dissociative experiences in the general population. *American Journal of Psychiatry, 147,* 1547–1552.

Ross, C. A., Kronson, J., Koensgen, S., Barkman, K., Clark, P., & Rockman, G. (1992). Dissociative comorbidity in 100 chemically dependent patients. *Hospital and Community Psychiatry, 43,* 840–842.

Ross, C. A., Norton, G. R., & Wozney, K. (1989). Multiple personality disorder: An analysis of 236 cases. *Canadian Journal of Psychiatry, 34,* 413–418.

Saxe, G. N., van der Kolk, B. A., Berkowitz, R., Chinman, G., Hall, K., Lieberg, G., & Schwartz, J. (1993). Dissociative disorders in psychiatric inpatients. *American Journal of Psychiatry, 150,* 1037–1042.

Steinberg, M. (1993). *Structured clinical interview for diagnosis of DSM-IV dissociative disorders.* Washington, DC: American Psychiatric Press.

Turkus, J. A. (1991). Psychotherapy and case management for multiple personality disorder: Synthesis for continuity of care. *Psychiatric Clinics of North America, 14,* 649–660.

Watkins, J. G., & Watkins, H. H. (1993). Ego-state therapy in the treatment of dissociative disorders. In R. P. Kluft & C. G. Fine (Eds.), *Clinical perspectives on multiple personality disorder* (pp. 277–299). Washington, DC: American Psychiatric Press.

Wilbur, C. B. (1984). Treatment of multiple personality. *Psychiatric Annals, 14*, 27–31.

Wilbur, C. B. (1986). Psychoanalysis and multiple personality disorder. In B. G. Braun (Ed.), *Treatment of multiple personality disorder* (pp. 133–142). Washington, DC: American Psychiatric Press.

Wilbur, C. B., & Kluft, R. P. (1989). Multiple personality disorder. In American Psychiatric Association (Ed.), *Treatments of mental disorders: A task force report of the American Psychiatric Association* (Vol. 3, pp. 2197–2216). Washington, DC: American Psychiatric Association.

Part VI

PSYCHOTHERAPY SERVICE UTILIZATION PATTERNS

International Perspectives

29

Psychotherapy Services in the English National Health Service

Glenys Parry

The National Health Service (NHS) in Britain provides health services to the public free of charge at the point of delivery, funded through government revenue. Its goal is "to secure, through the resources available, the greatest improvement in the physical and mental health of people in England." The NHS in England is ultimately accountable to Parliament through the Secretary of State for Health, a responsibility that is executed through the Department of Health and its NHS executive. The system in other parts of Britain is very similar but is administered through the relevant government office: the Welsh Office, the Northern Ireland Office, or the Scottish Home and Health Department. In recent years, there have been fundamental changes in the way the NHS is organized, and it is in this context that mental health and psychotherapy services are to be understood.

There are approximately 100 local Health Authorities in England that are apportioned revenue to purchase a range of health services on the basis of having assessed the health needs of their local population. Local needs assessment is important because the populations served by the Health Authorities vary enormously in size and sociodemography, from densely populated inner-city areas to rural areas with few centers of population. The emphasis is on improving the health of local populations by health promotion and by clinically effective treatments and care that yield gains in health. Health care, including mental health care, is provided by family doctors (known as general practitioners) and staff they employ, and by NHS hospitals and community health services. In recent years, the role of local Health Authorities in assessing needs for and purchasing health services has been separated from the function of providing them. Hospital and community services are now delivered through NHS Trusts, provider organizations that have considerable autonomy in organizing, costing, designing, and marketing health care services. General practitioners (GPs) are typically the first point of contact for someone seeking medical or psychological help. They provide primary health care and act as the gateway to specialist services, referring patients to consultant medical staff and other specialist health care professionals. The last government gave some general practitioners a portion of government revenue to *purchase* these services on behalf of their patients, but this system was abolished by the new Labor government in 1998. Instead, larger organizations of GPs with community nurses, Primary Care Trusts, will exert considerable influence on payment for mental health services, including psychotherapy.

Although most decisions about which services are to be provided are made locally, general practitioners, Health Authorities, and NHS Trusts exercise their responsibilities within the context of central health policy, either on an advisory basis or translated into specific guidance on priorities for planning and purchasing. One important central initiative is the "Health of the Nation" policy, launched in 1992 and updated in 1997 to place greater emphasis on the social causes of illness. This gave specific health improvement targets for the country as a whole in key health problems, including mental illness. It was the first time that improvements in the mental health of the nation had been a government health priority, raising the profile of mental health in public policy considerably. This high policy priority continues. For example, standards of mental health provision are to be monitored through a national service framework, the proportion of NHS funding for research in mental health is increasing and clinical effectiveness initiatives are developing in this field.

Review of Psychotherapy Services in England

The high prevalence of mental health problems and the proportion of the NHS resources that is devoted to the treatment and care of people who are mentally ill create a policy imperative that the most clinically effective and cost-effective care will be provided. In 1994, the Department of Health's NHS executive undertook to review policy on psychotherapy services. Psychological therapies complement medical treatments and therefore, make up one of two main classes of treatment for mental health problems. There are many different types of psychotherapy services within the NHS, but they are fragmented and uncoordinated. It was difficult to understand their role in the overall planning for improved mental health services. There were too many unknowns; an unknown amount of revenue was being spent on an unknown range of therapies, of unknown clinical effectiveness, from unspecified practitioners. It was therefore important to understand the actual and potential contribution of psychological therapies across all types of mental illness, as well as the extent to which current provision met basic requirements of safety, appropriateness, and effectiveness.

The project aimed to investigate the current state of NHS psychotherapy services in England: to review existing provision specified in mental health contracts placed by purchasers; to invite and collate evidence on the effectiveness, cost-efficiency, accessibility, appropriateness, and acceptability of current NHS psychotherapy service provision; to report on methods of professionally auditing psychotherapy services and of monitoring quality; to examine research evidence on the effectiveness and cost-effectiveness of the range of psychotherapeutic interventions for different mental health problems; and to investigate methods of epidemiologically based needs assessment in relation to psychotherapy services. The evidence collected will culminate in a series of principles and recommendations about how psychotherapy services are best delivered, consistent with existing policies on mental health.

The policy and research reviews were both published in 1996 (NHS Executive, 1996; Roth & Fonagy, 1996) and have proved influential.

Defining Psychotherapy

The first thing that the policy review revealed was the extent of confusion within the NHS about what is, and what isn't, psychotherapy. A simple working definition in the review documentation failed to clarify this matter because different modes of psychotherapy were actually being practiced within the NHS, and not simply in the sense of psychotherapies from different theoretical schools. An extensive range of therapeutic psychological interventions were found to be delivered in the context of different settings with different client groups. Because of considerable disagreement as to which of these could legitimately be termed *psychotherapy*, three major *types* of psychological therapy being delivered within the NHS were identified:

1. *Psychological treatment as an integral component of mental health care.* A wide range of psychosocial and psychoeducational interventions were found to be offered within mental health services alongside other types of care (e.g., nursing and medical care). In general practice, family doctors and primary-care nurses may provide these services, and in secondary care, psychological interventions may be provided by general psychiatrists, mental health nurses, occupational therapists, and clinical psychologists within community mental health teams. For example, psychiatrists may offer anxiety management advice while also attending to medication side effects during an outpatient appointment. Family interventions in schizophrenia are complemented by pharmacological management and are part of a broader care plan. This type of work is perceived as an integral component of an integrated program of care offered by a particular team or service. It is not, however, offered as a stand-alone therapy.

2. *Eclectic psychological therapy or counseling* is offered in the form of a series of set sessions, ideally following an assessment that generates a therapeutic plan. Although this therapy may be systematic and structured, it does not rely on any single theoretical framework and indeed, in some cases, centers rather

more on practical skills (e.g., listening skills) rather than being systematically linked to theories of psychological dysfunction or personality development. Therefore, it is pragmatic, responding to specific needs and problems of individual patients as they are presented. In primary care in England, counselors often undertake this form of work, without necessarily having a professional mental health qualification.

Eclectic psychological therapy includes both nondirective counseling and psychotherapeutic work using a range of techniques to address different facets of a patient's problem. It is possible to undertake eclectic therapy at an expert level, and it can be theory-based; for example, clinical psychologists frequently work in this way, formulating complex problems from psychological first principles and taking a pantheoretical, problem-focused approach to intervention. Our evidence suggests that of the stand-alone psychotherapeutic work in the NHS, much, if not the majority, falls into this eclectic category.

3. *The formal psychotherapies* are practiced within well-developed bodies of theory, and under the discipline of clear technical guidelines for practice, for example, psychoanalytic or cognitive therapy. Formal psychotherapy is undertaken by, or under the supervision of, a specialist trained in a particular school of formal psychotherapeutic work. In the NHS, such therapists are usually specially trained psychiatrists or clinical psychologists, although there are also a smaller number of career psychotherapists who have trained within this discipline from the outset. Formal psychotherapies are usually provided within a designated psychotherapy or psychology service. Some practitioners have trained and are competent in more than one formal model of psychotherapy.

Formal psychotherapy is sometimes offered in primary care, but more usually, the role of the "formal" psychotherapist in primary care is to offer assessment services, advice, consultancy, and supervision. Formal psychotherapists also have a role in providing such services to those offering therapy as an integral component of a wider mental health programme, or to those offering eclectic psychological therapy or counseling.

Only about half of the Health Authorities in England have any specific contract for psychotherapy services, and where they do, it is often for a formal psychotherapy service, with other psychotherapeutic work remaining unspecified. Where psychotherapy services are covered by formal agreement, there will be an element of basic monitoring, where patient contacts and some basic quality criteria are reported back to the Health Authority. We estimate that the bulk of the psychotherapeutic work undertaken in the NHS is of the first two types and therefore remains largely unmonitored. It is swept into general mental health contracts between Health Authorities or general practitioners, and NHS Trusts.

Clinical psychologists and psychiatrists provide most psychotherapy (across all three types); After medical school or graduate school and registration (licensure) within their professions, they may also undertake further training in the formal psychotherapies and occupy specialist psychotherapy posts in the NHS. A small number of specialists in psychotherapy have no prior training in clinical psychology or psychiatry but are professionally trained as psychotherapists; psychoanalytic child psychotherapists in particular may train in this way. Many other mental health professionals provide psychotherapeutic interventions. Increasingly, mental health nurses are training to provide psychological therapy, particularly cognitive behavioral therapies, as part of their role. A number of other therapy professionals use psychotherapeutic techniques and ideas within their practice to a greater or less extent, including occupational, art, and drama therapists.

In primary care, there has been a steady growth of counseling in the last 20 years or so; this has partly arisen from a need of general practitioners for help with those patients who would not necessarily be seen as a priority for treatment by psychiatric services, but whose psychological difficulties cannot be addressed in the surgery with a standard medical consultation. Sometimes, any form of psychological treatment within primary care is referred to loosely as *counseling*, whichever professional delivers it and whether or not it is, strictly speaking, a counseling intervention.

The role of the private sector varies in different parts of the country. In London, and in most other major cities, there are reputable and well-trained private practitioners, and some psychotherapists practice both within and outside the NHS. General practitioners may know particular private therapists they feel able to refer to on request and, increasingly, can purchase services from directly. There are also not-for-profit therapy services based on the needs of particular groups (women, black and minority ethnic groups, gay people). In other parts of the country, consulting a private psychotherapist can pose difficult choices; this sector is unregulated, and concerns have been raised about the safety and accountability of private practice. In Britain, psychotherapy practice is not restricted to doctors or clinical psychologists, and there is a long tradition of "lay" psychotherapy. However, the competence of those setting themselves up to offer psychotherapy to the public varies widely. Recently, with encouragement from the Department of Health, psychotherapists have begun the process of self-regulation by setting up registers of practitioners who are members of organizations that establish basic training criteria, and that have codes of ethical practice and the means to investigate complaints and to remove practitioners from the register if a complaint is upheld. The United Kingdom Council for Psychotherapy and the British Confederation of Psychotherapists both register practitioners, and a registration body for counselors is being established.

The costs of providing mental health care can be estimated, but it is very much more difficult to estimate the proportion of those costs that can be apportioned to psychotherapeutic work within the three different modes. In 1993–1994, hospital and community health services spending on mental health services was $3.566 million, approximately 12% of total NHS expenditure. The direct costs of psychotropic medication can be estimated at approximately 4% of the mental health expenditure. Social welfare authorities also spent $420 million on mental-health-related social care services, for example, day care. (This amount gives a total spent of approximately $85 per inhabitant in England for secondary mental health services.) There were, at this period, an estimated 2,000 consultant psychiatrists, a similar number of junior psychiatrists, 2,800 clinical psychologists, and 4,700 community mental health nurses. Many of these staff, particularly the nurses, would not be practicing psychotherapy and most would not be full-time or formal psychotherapists.

Questions for Service Commissioners

Those with the responsibility to commission services have some difficult decisions to make. How can *need* be assessed? With such a bewildering range of therapies undertaken by so many different professionals, how closely should health authorities specify which types of therapy they wish to fund? Given the many demands on public finance, how can expenditure on psychotherapies be compared with other priorities? Although there is a heavy demand for psychotherapies, evidenced by the long waiting lists for treatment and complaints about the accessibility of therapy, is there sufficient evidence of their clinical effectiveness? If they are clinically effective, do they represent good value for money? How can quality be monitored? Some of the answers to these questions are emerging from the review.

Levels of Psychotherapy Service Delivery

It is increasingly clear that the levels of disability caused by common mental health problems are considerable, and that good early detection and treatment of depression and anxiety have great potential for health gain and for cost saving. To be cost-effective, psychotherapeutic intervention should be at the least complex, costly, and intrusive level consistent with effective treatment. This means that people presenting for the first time with, say, depression or an anxiety disorder should first be offered low-cost psychological interventions. In addition to drug treatment, simple psychoeducational and bibliotherapeutic approaches might be provided, together with counseling that incorporates basic principles of effective psychotherapy, for example, exposure methods in anxiety.

Many people with more severe or refractory problems can also be helped within the context of the primary-care sector if there is access to a psychological therapy service providing assessment, outreach, and treatment on an outpatient basis. With the advent of fund-holding GPs, these primary-care-focused psychological services became increasingly available, as the GPs exercised their choice to purchase them. This situation has created some concern that funding may be diverted from services for people with the most severe and enduring mental illnesses, although this is not necessarily the case. For example, in some parts of the country, counselors and psychologists work together to offer psychological assessment and brief focal interventions for problems of considerable severity. In this way, they are able to manage the psychotherapeutic care of large numbers of patients who would otherwise be referred to secondary psychiatric services.

Those people with severe and enduring mental illness need a coordinated program of care, where assessment and treatment are multidisciplinary and, often, multiagency. To improve the community care of these patients, the Department of Health has introduced the care program approach (CPA) as a basic requirement for all patients referred to specialist psychiatric services. For the severely mentally ill, CPA includes a multidisciplinary assessment and care plan, with review dates agreed on and a key worker assigned to ensure that all aspects of the plan are delivered. Here the community mental health team will need to ensure that they have members who are well trained in effective psychological therapies that can be a component of care for people with schizophrenia, severe depression, bipolar disorders, severe personality disorders, and the most severe eating disorders.

Fully involving the formal psychotherapies when implementing CPA is proving difficult. At present, although there is evidence that formal psychotherapy services do see patients whose mental health problems are severe, the therapists often operate outside the CPA. With more severe disorders, and the agreement of the general practitioner, the patient is often referred to the psychotherapist from the community team and requires continuing mental health care at the secondary level after psychotherapy. It is rarely appropriate for the psychotherapist to act as the *key worker* in such a care program; it runs counter to the formal psychotherapeutic endeavor to take on a dual role of multidisciplinary or multiagency "case manager." The clinical consensus is that this damages the therapeutic alliance on which, as research evidence indicates, good psychotherapeutic outcomes depend. The psychotherapist should, however, operate *within* the CPA and will be able to inform the key worker if further action by a member of the multidisciplinary team is required. For example, when a patient's mental health deteriorates and a review of his or her medication or hospital admission is indicated, after discussing it with the patient many psychotherapists would request a multidisciplinary review from the community mental health team.

Basing Purchasing Decisions on Research Evidence

The controversial question of whether some forms of therapy should be funded and others not is already exercising many Health Authorities. In general, general practitioners make their funding decisions on a case-by-case basis, making their own best guess of which therapist or service would be helpful for a particular patient. Health Authorities, on the other hand, have a broader-brush approach; less than half have yet attempted to assess needs for psychotherapy services formally. The majority do not specify psychotherapies within their contracts with service providers. A few, however, have taken a look at the research and concluded that there is little enough research evidence for the efficacy of psychoanalytic psychotherapy to make it a priority for investment and have decided that the evidence favors cognitive and behavioral approaches; others have invested in counseling in primary care; and others have specific contracts for specialist psychodynamically oriented services. As we have local decision making on investment, this plurality is not unexpected. However, the NHS review offers a national lead by examining research evidence in more detail than can any one local team, as part of our department's policy on promoting clinically effective and cost-effective care and evidence-based practice.

In Britain, there have been major developments in government policy on the evaluation of health care and coordinated initiatives to improve the clinical effectiveness and cost-effectiveness of services. A formal framework for clinical audit in the NHS (Department of Health, 1989) was followed by a major initiative to promote and fund NHS research and development (Culyer, 1994), including a standing group on health technology assessment (HTA) to assess which are the health technology priorities for research funds (Department of Health, 1992a). For example, two trials of the efficacy of counseling in primary care have recently been funded through the HTA program. The UK Cochrane Centre in Oxford and the York Centre for Reviews and Dissemination systematically review the randomized controlled trials (RCTs) in a given field and disseminate results of research reviews and evaluations. A series of Effective Health Care Bulletins and Health Care Needs Assessments also have a role in promoting awareness of research evidence in clinicians and other decision makers (Stevens and Raftery, 1994). High priority research is commissioned, many larger hospitals and some community trusts have a funded research portfolio. These initiatives have now begun to influence the psychotherapies. For example, there are now NHS projects to promote routine therapy outcome evaluation, clinical databases to support research, and treatment of choice guidelines for the psychological therapies.

The aim now is to apply the same standards to psychotherapeutic practice. There is no doubt that basic and applied research in psychotherapy has had insufficient impact on the organization and delivery of psychotherapy services. The forms of therapy now provided and the ways in which patients are allocated to treatments owe very little to research evidence on effectiveness and far more to the personal allegiences of psychological therapists to specific theoretical schools.

Because research findings on efficacy and clinical

effectiveness of the psychotherapies remain the starting point for evidence-based practice, a review of these studies was commissioned (Roth & Fonagy, 1996). Results of the review demonstrated significant gaps in research findings, particularly a dearth of good studies of psychodynamic modes of treatment. For the main diagnostic groups, therapy methods were identified for which clear evidence of efficacy was available; in addition, promising treatments with preliminary or only limited support were also highlighted. The review found evidence for the efficacy of structured therapies for depression, particularly interpersonal psychotherapy and cognitive behavior therapy, and preliminary evidence for the value of brief structured psychodynamic therapy. On the other hand, there was little evidence to support the benefit of unstructured counseling. The resulting list of effective and promising therapies was broadly similar to the conclusions of the American Psychological Association task force on promotion and dissemination of psychological procedures (Chambless, 1993).

Such results alone, however, will not convince practitioners and trainers to alter their allegiances. There are many reasons why clinicians find psychotherapy research to be of only marginal clinical relevance. Many in Britain argue that it is premature and dangerous to base funding decisions on our current state of knowledge in this field. First, there is a notable absence of research on certain widely practiced modes of treatment, such as psychoanalytic psychotherapy. Second, the weaknesses of psychotherapy research in relation to external validity are severe and lead to incomplete or misleading conclusions by masking naturally occurring interactions among variables in complex service systems. Third, most psychotherapy outcome research is based on comparing two forms of therapy, or therapy and placebo treatment, within specific diagnostic groups. Diagnosis is only one factor on which patients differ, and which is of relevance to choice of therapy; its apparent simplicity can mask the complexity of other variables that have main effects on outcome, such as the capacity to form a therapeutic alliance and the level of social support available to the individual. Fourth, many practitioners are skeptical of the quality of outcome measurement (e.g., symptom change) commonly used in psychotherapy research, believing it not to tap the types of changes commonly aimed for in practice in relation to levels of functioning and quality of life. Finally, many psychotherapists argue that although well-designed group comparisons can yield results that are generally true, the specific applicability of these findings to the individual case remains a matter for clinical judgment. For example, in any group comparison of two treatments, there may be individual patients who benefit more from the treatment that is found to be less effective for the group as a whole.

Achieving evidence-based practice in the psychotherapies is therefore not simple. Some apparently straightforward and justifiable processes—for example, introducing clinical audit systems into psychotherapy services and basing purchasing decisions on research evidence of efficacy—need to be undertaken with care. Otherwise, they can do more harm than good.

Research findings could be misused in the effort to base purchasing decisions solely on the findings of psychotherapy outcome research. There are dangers of health authorities purchasing only a limited range of treatment packages meeting an efficacy criterion for specific diagnostic groups, and withdrawing funds from other therapies. The research review provides backing for the claim that there is no good efficacy evidence, one way or the other, for many clinical practices, for example, many psychoanalytic interventions and the types of "eclectic" practices that characterize much psychotherapeutic treatment in England. Where the appropriate research has not yet been done, the absence of evidence for efficacy is not evidence of ineffectiveness, and valuable approaches that offer appropriate and clinically effective care should not perish for lack of funding. Second, purchasing focused on packages of treatment for predefined diagnostic groups overlooks the very high rate of comorbidity and many other important variables in predicting which psychotherapeutic approach is likely to be most helpful. There is the danger that in a system where public sector funding is the determining influence on psychotherapy service delivery and research, overprescriptive purchasing will stifle innovation and development. One has only to imagine the negative consequences of having implemented such a policy in the 1960s: Many highly valuable later developments such as cognitive and integrationist therapies would have been made more difficult. There is also the problem that those purchasing or commissioning services preempt, through funding decisions, clinical judgments pertaining to, for example, treatment length and modality. Rather than encouraging clinical assessment and formulation to be based on research evidence and fostering a model of evidence-based practice, ironically such a policy could actually delay its development.

A Model for Evidence-Based Psychotherapy Services

The above argument should not be interpreted as special pleading for psychotherapies to be exempt from the requirement to base practice on sound evidence, but it points to the best ways of ensuring this. Figure 29.1 gives a model of evidence-based practice in psychotherapy services. It shows the appropriate relationships between research, standard practice, developments in practice, service evaluation, theoretical developments, clinical audit, and professional training and education. All these activities should work systematically together to improve the quality and effectiveness of psychotherapy services to patients. If this is to be achieved, it requires the collaboration and cooperation of service managers, Health Authority staff, GPs, psychotherapy researchers, and mental health professionals providing psychotherapy services.

The model has a fundamental tenet that standard practice in NHS psychotherapies could be far more clearly specified through clinical guidelines than is currently the case. Psychotherapists are wary of the concept of clinical protocols and guidelines, seeing them as a threat to clinical freedom, but clinical guidelines can be used to benchmark best practice and as to an aid in clinical judgment. They should be informed by service evaluation evidence, formal research findings, and clinical consensus. Research evidence is incorporated into standard clinical practice through these protocols, but it is the prerogative of the clinician to make a judgment in the individual case, on the basis of assessment and case formulation, to do something different. However, the guideline acts as an aide-mémoire to the therapist in formalizing normal expected practice so that deviations from this practice are made thoughtfully and are justified by clinical evidence.

Nor should standard, protocol-based practice be allowed to stifle innovation; rather, it should serve as a springboard to it, since there will always be many situations where there is no research evidence or even clinical consensus to indicate the best approach. Developments in the process of delivering services or experimental clinical techniques first have to be described through case studies or replicated $n = 1$ evaluation of case series.

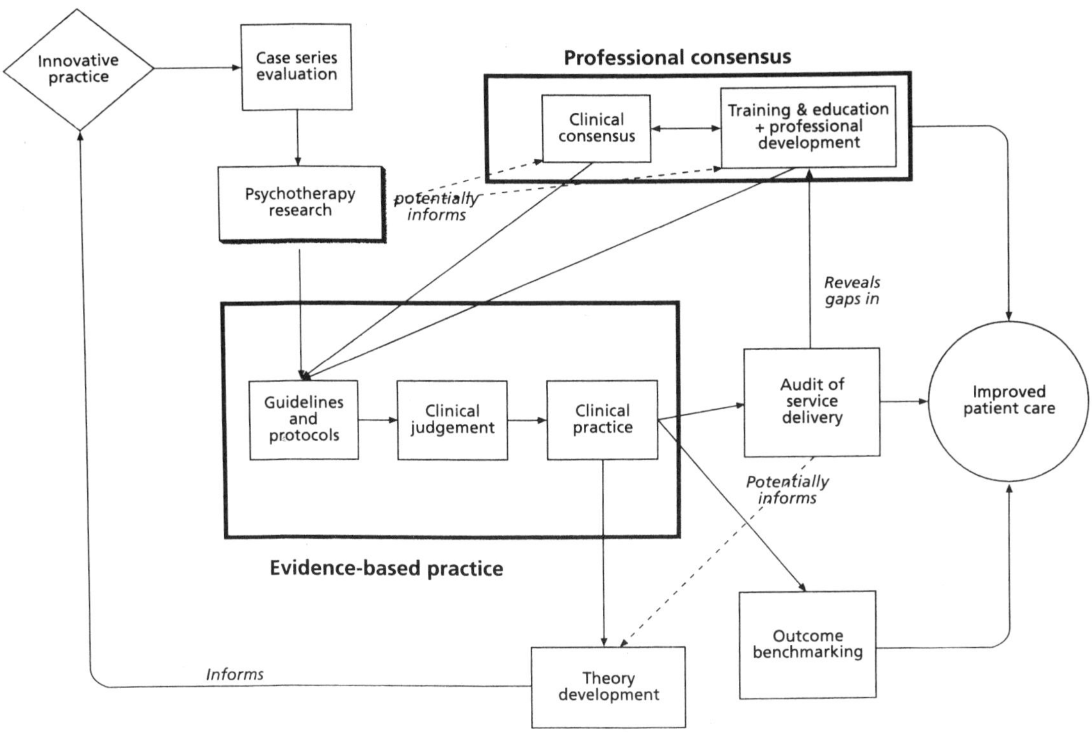

Figure 29.1 A model of evidence-based practice in psychotherapy services.

After a promising new technique or approach has been developed, RCTs can be undertaken to establish whether or not the treatment is efficacious. A well-designed trial is of value to demonstrate efficacy but is not able to establish the clinical effectiveness of the new procedure because of limits on ecological validity (Aveline, Shapiro, Parry, & Freeman, 1995; Seligman, 1995). The effectiveness of the treatment as delivered needs to be tested through field trials and service evaluation methods. (See also chapter 3, this volume, on the need to integrate services and clinical trials research.)

Standard practice that can be described in clinical guidelines also has the great advantage of focusing and clarifying the audit effort, since the guideline states "the right thing to do," whereas the audit asks, "Has the right thing been done?" and "Has it been done right?" By targeting audit on those processes derived from evidence-based protocols, a clear link can be established between research and audit, so that, in turn, gaps in knowledge will be revealed, leading to developments in theory and new hypotheses for formal psychotherapy research.

As clinical and service audit examines the reasons for failures to deliver to a set standard of practice, it can reveal gaps in the skills and competence of psychotherapists that are preventing them from delivering a fully effective service. This highlights quality of professional training, new education and curriculum needs, and questions of professional skills updating. It is likely that it is only by following such a process of service delivery that both pre- and postqualification training in the psychotherapies will become underpinned by links among theory, research, and practice.

In adopting this model, it is now possible to revisit the question of which therapies to purchase, adopting an approach that makes best use of the capacity of the British NHS for coordination among researchers, service evaluators, managers, commissioners, and providers in ensuring clinical effectiveness. Those responsible for purchasing psychological therapies should not fund services or procedures that clear research evidence suggests are ineffective. In addition, a purchasing strategy should drive forward the agenda of evidence-based practice by investing in those services (a) that have clear clinical protocols for standard practice, (b) where the protocols are informed by the findings of research and service evaluation, (c) that specify the patient groups for which the service is appropriate, (d) that monitor outcomes, and (e) that audit key elements of standard practice.

Costs, Effectiveness, and Value for Money

Cost-effectiveness research on psychotherapy in the UK is in its infancy. Given the evidence from economic evaluations in the United States, it is disappointing that when a report was commissioned on the economic evaluation of psychotherapy in the UK (Healey & Knapp, 1995), the authors identified only 10 studies between 1974 and 1994 that incorporated an economic component. These were evaluation studies of clinical services, and all suffered methodological drawbacks, including incomplete or inadequate cost estimation and inadequate follow-up. Healey and Knapp (1995; chapter 12, this volume) conclude that the quantity and quality of such work in the UK will have to increase and improve if economic appraisal is to make any contribution to decision making. They recommend that costs be appropriately and comprehensively measured, and that economic appraisal focus on the marginal cost implications of psychotherapy service provision versus other alternatives for specific groups of patients. In addition to the existing interest in evaluating effects of psychotherapy on costs of NHS service use, emphasis should be placed on evaluating whether psychotherapy offers quality-of-life improvements over and above existing alternatives.

Those UK studies that could be interpreted as true economic appraisals have focused on providing psychotherapy within primary-care settings. Three studies found this to be cost-effective in terms of improvements in clinical outcome and achievement of overall cost savings (Ginsberg & Marks, 1977; Ginsberg, Marks, & Waters, 1984; Robson, France, & Bland, 1984), with a fourth study an exception (Scott & Freeman, 1992). Given that much of the work of both eclectic and formal psychotherapists is undertaken within secondary or tertiary services, further studies are needed.

A systematic approach to cost-effectiveness enhancement for psychotherapy services requires that good estimates be obtained of the numbers of patients receiving psychotherapy through the NHS, of the benefits of the interventions provided, and of the costs of these to patients, families, NHS, criminal justice, and welfare systems. As yet, insufficient data are available to allow cost-utility ratios to be calculated.

Work is being undertaken by the NHS executive in each of these areas, both to measure outcomes in mental health services and to develop better person-based clinical information regarding case mix and care packages delivered. To this end, the NHS executive has commissioned and published advice to researchers on how to include economic analysis alongside controlled clinical trials. It is highly likely that future psychotherapy research and service evaluation in the UK will include economic evaluation (Drummond, 1994). The Mental Health Foundation, a British charity, has recently contributed to this move by funding research on economic evaluation of psychotherapy services.

The costs of psychotherapy services in England are very difficult to estimate, and no study has yet attempted to do so. A survey of Health Authorities and NHS Trusts in England (NHS Executive, 1996) suggests that most psychotherapy is provided by individuals who have other responsibilities as part of their NHS jobs. Accordingly, it is not easy to disaggregate professional time spent on one, rather than another, professional activity.

Despite the difficulties of collecting cost, case mix, therapy type, and outcomes information centrally, pragmatism dictates that much more can be done locally to improve the cost-effectiveness of psychotherapy services. At a local level, Health Authorities are extremely keen to develop strategies that would allow more sophisticated approaches to contracting. It has already been demonstrated, for example, that simple, low-tech cost and outcome reports from routine NHS services are a practical possibility; for example, Marks (1994) at the Institute of Psychiatry, London, demonstrated similar clinical outcomes at 1-month follow-up for patients with obsessive-compulsive disorder (OCD) treated as either outpatients or inpatients. Outpatient costs, however, were less than half those for the inpatients, for clinician time alone. When hotel costs of residence were added, the cost advantage of outpatient treatment was outstanding. This sort of result can inform clinical guidelines for treatment of choice in OCD, particularly if it is possible to investigate what features characterise those patients who *require* an inpatient treatment for a successful outcome.

Some psychotherapeutic treatments have high face validity for cost-effectiveness. For example, because of the very high costs of residential care, family-based interventions for schizophrenia that have been shown to prevent or slow relapse and readmission are now being widely purchased (Mari & Streiner, 1994).

A major determinant of psychotherapy costs is the number of sessions of treatment offered (Watson & Ryle, 1992). There is evidence that patients receiving more psychotherapy benefit more than those receiving less (Orlinsky, Grawe, & Parks, 1994) but that this dose-response relationship is progressively weaker with increasing number of sessions, so that, for example, in outpatients, 52 weekly sessions were reported as the maximum effective dose for uncomplicated depression and anxiety without borderline personality disorder or comorbid conditions (Howard, Krause, & Orlinsky, 1986). Where these were present, however, the dose-response relationship was attenuated, requiring longer treatments. This United States finding has to be replicated in an NHS setting, and attention to the dose-response relationship in different disorders in the context of different psychotherapy services will be of value. While it is important to prevent wasteful overtreatment, there is evidence that longer treatments lead to more extensive gains and are more highly valued by service users (Seligman, 1995). The optimum length of treatment for different conditions has therefore not yet been established, but a purely empirical approach becomes possible when data for a whole service over time are available. In the absence of these data, there is little clinical sense in purchasers' imposing arbitrary funding limits or funding only a preset number of sessions, since the right dosage of psychotherapy varies according to the severity and complexity of the condition. To curtail therapy prematurely when a longer treatment is needed to restore functioning is, of course, as wasteful of resources as overtreatment. In fact, very few English health authorities stipulate lengths of treatment in contracts, although clinical staff feel under pressure to deliver short interventions, often without these decisions being based on effectiveness data.

Another area with potential for improving cost-effective practice is in matching patients to the skill level of the psychotherapist. Systems of triage assessment assign those patients with more complex or difficult conditions to more highly trained (and more costly) specialists, allowing others to be treated by staff with less expertise, working under supervision. Such systems are becoming more common in England, with psychotherapists and counselors working together, agreeing on criteria for assessment and cross-referral between the primary- and secondary-care sectors.

Summary

Three types of psychotherapeutic treatments are available in the NHS through mental health services: those team-based interventions integral to wider mental health care programs, eclectic therapies, and counseling, and the formal psychotherapies provided by the specialty sector. Most therapies are provided by psychologists, psychiatrists, and other staff who are not designated specialists, and who undertake other mental health services work. Formal psychotherapy services staffed by specialists have long waiting lists, and many patients could benefit from such therapies yet do not receive them. Work is under way on improving the clinical effectiveness of NHS psychotherapy services by developing evidence-based practice and promoting cost efficiency through the mechanisms of service agreements, cost and outcome reports, clinical guidelines, clinical audit, improved professional training, triage assessment, and dissemination of research findings on clinically effective psychotherapies.

Acknowledgments Many individuals assisted with the NHSE review of psychotherapy services; in particular, contributions to this chapter are gratefully acknowledged from Dr. Jenny Firth-Cozens, Professor Peter Fonagy, Dr. Keith Hawton, Mrs. Adele Kosviner, Dr. Frank Margison, Dr. Anthony Roth, and Professor David Shapiro.

References

Aveline, M., Shapiro, D. A., Parry, G., & Freeman, C. P. L. (1995). Building research foundations for psychotherapy practice. In M. Aveline & D. A. Shapiro (Eds.), *Research foundations for psychotherapy practice*. Chichester: Wiley.

Chambless, D. L. (Ed.). (1993). *Task force on promotion and dissemination of psychological procedures: A report adopted by the Division 12 Board, October 1993*. Washington: American Psychological Association.

Culyer, A. (1994). *Supporting research and development in the NHS*. London: Her Majesty's Stationery Office.

Department of Health. (1989). *Medical audit: Working paper 6 of working for patients*. London: Her Majesty's Stationery Office.

Department of Health. (1992a). *Assessing the effects of health technologies*. London: Her Majesty's Stationery Office.

Department of Health. (1992b). *The health of the nation: A strategy for health in England*. London: Her Majesty's Stationery Office.

Drummond, M. (1994). *Economic analysis alongside controlled trials*. London: Department of Health.

Ginsberg, G., & Marks, I. M. (1977). Costs and benefits of behavioural psychotherapy: A pilot study of neurotics treated by nurse therapists. *Psychological Medicine, 7,* 685–700.

Ginsberg, G., Marks, I. M., & Waters, H. (1984). Cost-benefit analysis of a controlled trial of nurse therapy for neuroses in primary care. *Psychological Medicine, 15,* 683–690.

Healey, A., & Knapp, M. (1995). *Economic evaluation and psychotherapy: A review of results, methodologies and issues*. A review paper commissioned by the Department of Health.

Howard, K. I., Krause, M. S., & Orlinsky, D. E. (1986). The dose-effect relationship in psychotherapy. *American Psychologist, 41,* 159–164.

Marks, I. M. (1994). *CORM: Clinical outcome and resource measurement: Institute of Psychiatry, London*. London: Institute of Psychiatry.

Mari, D. J. J., & Streiner, D. L. (1994). An overview of family interventions and relapse on schizophrenia: Meta-analysis of research findings. *Psychological Medicine, 24,* 565–578.

NHS Executive. (1996). *A review of strategic policy on NHS psychotherapy services in England*. London: Department of Health.

Orlinsky, D. E., Grawe, K., & Parks, B. K. (1994). Process and outcome in psychotherapy. In A. E. Bergin & S. L. Garfield (Eds.), *Handbook of psychotherapy and behavior change* (pp. 270–376). (4th ed.). New York: Wiley.

Robson, M. H., France, R., & Bland, M. (1984). Clinical psychology in primary care: A controlled clinical and economic evaluation. *British Medical Journal, 288,* 1805–1808.

Roth, A. D., & Fonagy, P. (1996). *The search for effective psychotherapy: Implications and limitations of the research evidence*. New York: Guilford Press.

Scott, A. I. F., & Freeman, C. P. L. (1992). Edinburgh primary care depression study: Treatment outcome, patient satisfaction, and cost after 16 weeks. *British Medical Journal, 304,* 883–887.

Seligman, M. E. P. (1995). The effectiveness of psychotherapy: The Consumer Reports study. *American Psychologist, 50*(12), 965–974.

Stevens, A., & Raftery, J. (1994). *Health care needs assessment: The epidemiologically based needs assessment reviews*. Oxford: Radcliffe.

Watson, J. P., & Ryle, A. (1992). Providing a psychotherapy service to an inner London catchment area. *Journal of Mental Health, 1,* 169–176.

30

Psychotherapy Services and Cost-Effectiveness

A Canadian Perspective

Joel Sadavoy & J. Christopher Perry

Canada has a largely decentralized mental health delivery system that is predominantly the responsibility of each of the 10 provincial governments with some support from the central federal government. Health care is the mandated responsibility of the provinces; however, the federal government has provided "transfer payments" to the provinces that give it some direct control over the development of health care policy. Although some provinces adopted health insurance plans in the late 1950s, the federal government established the formal principle of universal national health care in 1984 through the Canada Health Act. This put pressure on the provinces to abolish all fees beyond those paid fully by provincial health plans for incurred services, with the threat of withdrawal of transfer payments for failure to comply. All other third-party insurers essentially were banned except for services not covered by the government programs. This effectively brought almost all Canadian physicians into an increasingly centralized financial system, with very little practice outside the system. Each province manages its own insurance program; the Ontario system, for example, is called the Ontario Health Insurance Plan, or OHIP. Skyrocketing health costs and declining federal health budgets have weakened central influence on the provinces. Hence, recently, there has been a move to reinstitute some fee-for-service medical activities in some provinces, overtly resisted by the federal government, since universal health care is a deeply cherished right of Canadians.

Because of the structure of health care delivery and payment, it was not possible to locate centralized data on psychotherapy that would adequately permit addressing specific detailed questions about cost-effectiveness for the whole of Canada. Moreover, even at the provincial level, the data with regard to psychotherapy are often imprecise and ineffective for use in evaluating and controlling costs. For instance, the Quebec health insurance agency, Regie de l'Assurance Maladie du Quebec (RAMQ), keeps track of billing by units of time only, without reference to type of psychiatric service offered apart from whether a first consultation visit is billed. Unless otherwise noted, data cited here are derived from primary sources of statistics provided by provincial ministries of health.

Although some national data are included in the chapter, many are derived from the two largest provinces, Ontario and Quebec, which together account for 63% of the Canadian population. Ontario alone accounts for 37% of the Canadian population of 27 million. In examining issues of cost-effectiveness and service delivery in the less populous provinces, one therefore must keep in mind the differences in population distribution (urban versus rural—rural predominating in the smaller provinces, while urban is more the norm in Ontario), as well as efficiencies of scale (i.e., the differences in health care provision in densely populated provinces versus that in some provincial jurisdictions whose total populations may be less than that of a single large city). Figure 30.1

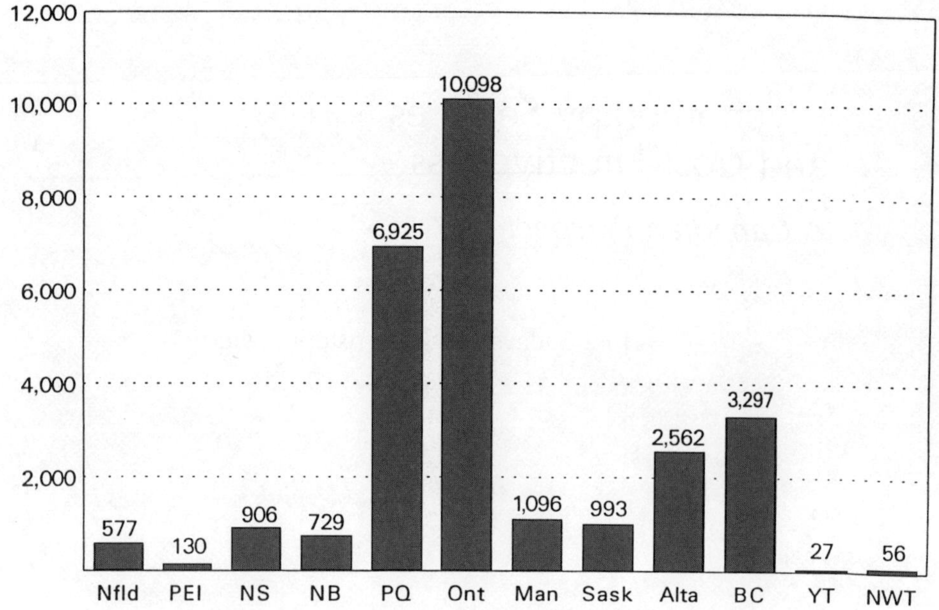

Figure 30.1 Population distribution by province (Canadian Census 1992). Nfld, Newfoundland; PEI, Prince Edward Island; NS, Nova Scotia; NB, New Brunswick; PQ, Quebec; Ont, Ontario; Man, Manitoba; Sask, Saskatchewan; Alta, Alberta; BC, British Columbia; YT, Yukon Territory; NWT, Northwest Territories.

summarizes the population distribution in Canada by province.

Psychotherapy Definitions

While most provincial jurisdictions attempt to define psychotherapy, in general these definitions are very broad and nonspecific. Unlike in Sweden (see chapter 32, this volume), Canadian jurisdictions do not define the required credentials for psychotherapists. The components of the definitions of psychotherapy include the requirement that the therapist deliberately establish a professional relationship, the purpose of which is to treat symptoms and behavior or to promote personality growth. The duration of sessions is specified, usually as 15-minute segments; 25- to 30-minute minimum is often required.

In one jurisdiction, medical psychotherapy is much more specifically defined as follows:

> A series of medical procedures carried out by a physician *trained* to treat mental, emotional and psychosomatic illness through a relationship with the patient in an individual group or family setting, utilizing verbal or non-verbal communication with the patient. Medical psychotherapy always entails continuing medical diagnostic evaluation and responsibility, and may be carried out in conjunction with drug and other physical treatments. Medical psychotherapy recognizes that the psychological and physical components of an illness are intertwined and that, at any point in the disease process, psychological symptoms may arise to substitute for or run concurrently with physical symptoms and vice versa.

Psychotherapy by psychiatrists is not directly rationed in any of the provinces of Canada. In British Columbia, there is a limitation on the duration of the first treatment course, and a rereferral for psychotherapy by a physician is required every 6 months. In that same province, psychotherapeutic intervention by a general practitioner is limited to four sessions a year.

In general, physicians manage their caseloads individually. To date, there is no evident external accountability for taking on new patients. In some jurisdictions, there is increasing political pressure for psychiatrists to address some of the underserved populations (for example, the elderly, children, and those in forensic settings) and to spend more time in their practices treating the seriously mentally ill. This attempt to mold practice patterns has been a particularly important element in the mental health reform process in Ontario. Underlying this is a specific attempt to change a pattern of practice felt to be prevalent in large urban centers, in which psychiatrists are perceived to restrict their practices to traditional forms of dynamic psychotherapy, and to avoid treating the more seriously or acutely psychiatrically ill patient.

Beginning and ending treatment generally remain fully at the discretion of patient and therapist. There are no outcome criteria or effectiveness measures in place in any of the jurisdictions at this time. Waiting lists vary by practitioner but generally are lengthy for long-term individual psychotherapy. Primary-care practitioners, such as family physicians, speak frequently of the difficulty of obtaining psychiatric services, and especially psychotherapy, in a timely fashion.

Psychotherapy that is funded by the Provincial Health Services covers only physicians. One province specifies that the physician (referring to nonpsychiatrists) must have training in psychotherapy, although it does not specify the extent. Otherwise, all physicians may charge the insurance plans for psychotherapy based on the provincial criteria. The only province to limit the practice of psychotherapy for general practitioners is British Columbia. In many circumstances, a "counseling fee" is authorized for nonpsychiatrists, but in many jurisdictions, there is only a small differential between the counseling and psychotherapy provided by nonpsychiatrists and that provided by psychiatrists (Figure 30.2).

As noted, in most jurisdictions, billing by physicians above the sanctioned fee schedule has been banned. The private fee-for-service system is virtually entirely nonmedical, with some minor exceptions, and is conducted by psychologists and social workers. However, if a service is specifically not covered by health insurance—for example, psychoanalysis in some jurisdictions—psychiatrists may provide this service on a private fee-for-service basis.

In Ontario, in 1992–1993, the number of psychotherapy units (one-half hours) provided by nonpsychiatrists MDs was 3 million, of which 2.6 million were individual psychotherapy services units at a total cost of $127 million (Canadian dollars). Psychiatrists provided a total of 3 million individual outpatient services at a total cost of $198 million. Eighty percent of all psychotherapy is carried out by psychiatrists on an individual outpatient basis, the remainder occurring in other settings such as psychiatric hospital units. The average yearly cost per patient (in 1991–1992) was $782, which reflects an average treatment episode duration of 7.8 sessions.

The rate of psychotherapy sessions provided by nonpsychiatrist physicians is rising more rapidly than the rate provided by psychiatrists. In Ontario, in 1993, the total cost of services for psychiatrists and nonpsychiatric physicians was almost equal. As an example of the breakdown of professional disciplines providing psychotherapy, there are more than 1,900 registered psychologists in Ontario, over 400 social workers in private practice, and more than 1,500 psychiatrists. While formal data on fees charged in the private system are unavailable, impressionistically it appears that Ontario psychologists charge 10–50% more than the Ontario Health Insurance Plan Fee Schedule for psychotherapy.

Psychotherapy Costs

Across the country, the patient pays nothing out of pocket to the physician for psychotherapy. Costs are determined on a per patient per service basis. There are few capitated payment plans in Canada although some governments, such as Alberta and Ontario, have begun to enter into alternate payment plans with groups such as hospitals or university departments. In Ontario, these global payment plans are negotiated individually by groups with the government. Under such plans, groups are provided with a global budget from which they pay physicians for all services previously funded by OHIP. In Ontario (until 1996, when there was a change in government), the provincial medical association (Ontario Medical Association) also was actively involved in the negotiations. This tripartite negotiation process was complex. For example, the Ontario Medical Association had to ensure that individual agreements between institutions and government would not draw disproportionately on the OHIP financial pool. Their concern derived from the fact that the OHIP pool is capped. If an institution cut a disproportionately favorable deal with the government, it would have been at the expense of those physicians who were not involved in such alternate plans. The new system places full and exclusive control of fee payment and setting of OHIP reimbursement rates in the hands of the minister of health. The ramifications of this newly legislated system are not yet evident.

Based on the direct fee-for-service process, the Canadian system is constructed so that the number of physician psychotherapists is directly proportional to

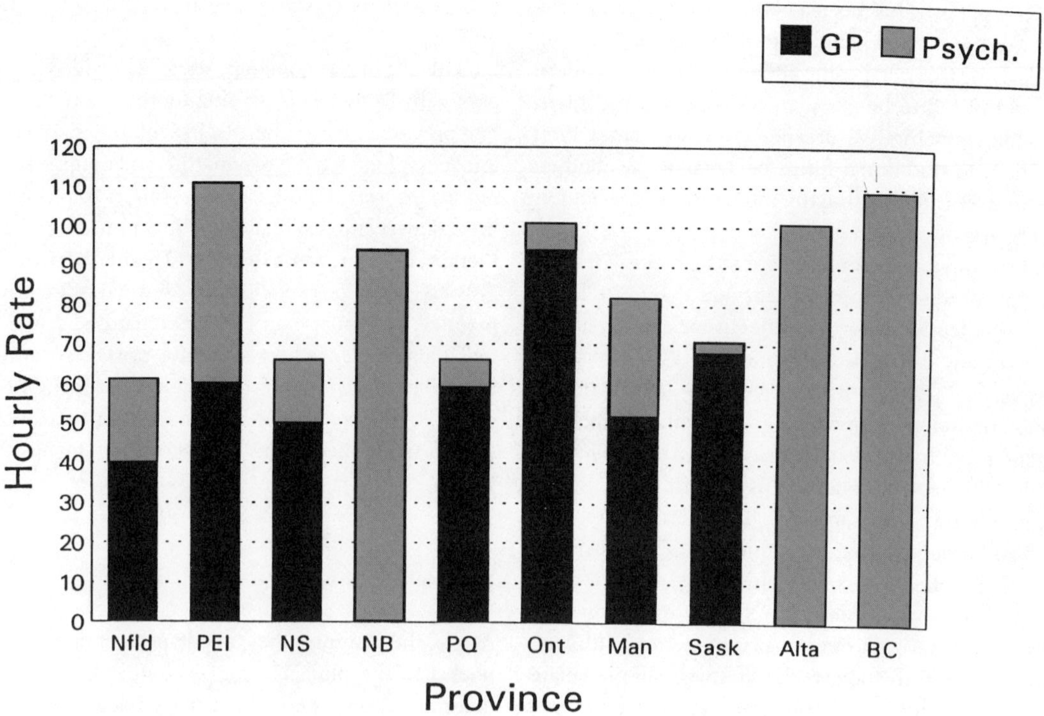

Figure 30.2 Psychotherapy hourly rates by province (GP, general practitioners; Psych., psychologists).

total cost. In a province with a higher ratio of physicians to population, the utilization and cost of psychotherapy are somewhat higher. This is true for all health care costs and has led various jurisdictions, including Ontario, to reduce medical school class sizes and to restrict migration of physicians from one province to another; all in the interest of controlling health care delivery costs. Quebec restricts the number of residency position in psychiatry and regulates the number of new psychiatrists hired in the university hospitals. In addition, the length of the psychiatric residency was increased by the government from 4 to 5 years, an increase that effectively reduces a psychiatrist's lifetime billings.

An example of the mental health expenditure profile may be derived from the Ontario experience. Figure 30.3 shows the approximate percentage breakdown of expenditures for mental health in the province of Ontario. For 37% of the Canadian population, the mental health budget is $1.3 billion (based on the most recent data available). Of all mental health dollars (made up of OHIP, hospital budgets, and community programs), 20% are spent on psychotherapy, an amount that represents approximately 80% of all OHIP payments. While 80% of all individual mental health contacts are labeled *psychotherapy*, it is probable that other forms of therapy, such as pharmacotherapy, also take place under this rubric. A frequent pattern of practice, for example, is for a psychiatrist to see a patient for the required minimum amount of time in order to bill for a legitimate "time period" of psychotherapy, during which pharmacotherapy also will be administered. Consequently, it is impossible to determine how much of the psychotherapy time is actually used for the recognized forms of psychotherapeutic intervention. There is only one province that attempts to define the modes of psychotherapy intervention. Saskatchewan specifies that psychotherapy is a form of treatment for mental illness, behavioral maladaptations, and/or other problems for which a physician establishes a professional relationship with the patient for the purposes of removing, modifying, or retarding existing symptoms or attenuating or reversing disturbed patterns of behavior by one or more approaches or methods from the generally recognized divisions of psychology, that is, analytic, behavioristic, Gestalt, hormic (the term used in the fee schedule), and introspective. Hypnosis is also included in all fee schedules. While more specific defini-

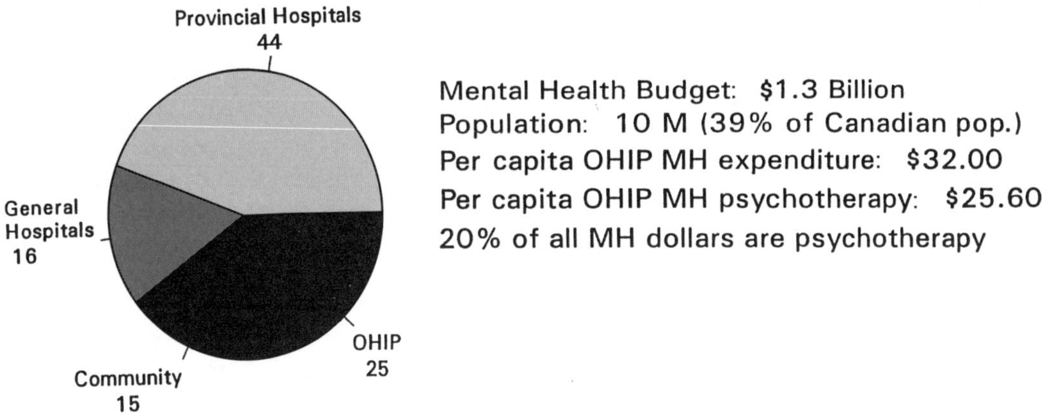

Figure 30.3 Mental health expenditures for the province of Ontario (OHIP, Ontario Health Insurance Plan; MH, mental health).

tions may be desirable, the complexity of implementing a well-defined system is highlighted in Parry's account (chapter 29, this volume) of the English National Health Service's approach to mental health services.

Hourly Fees

The hourly rate for psychiatrists varies substantially across the country by a factor of about 40%. The average annual earnings of a psychiatrist in Ontario is $157,000 (Canadian dollars). However, this includes part-time practitioners and academics. Figure 30.2 shows the psychotherapy hourly rates for all the provinces in Canada and compares the fees for psychiatrists and for general practitioners. New Brunswick, Alberta, and British Columbia have no general practice psychotherapy rate, but all the other provinces do. In many instances, there is a relatively small differential between the rate paid to psychiatrists and the rate paid to general practitioners. Recently, physician reimbursement has been reduced. For example, Ontario has begun to "claw back" 10% of gross physician billings.

The cost of treatment for specific illnesses is unknown for psychotherapeutic practice. An extrapolation from data provided by Doidge et al. (1994) suggests that the mean cost of treatment for a patient in psychoanalysis five times per week is approximately $18,000 per year. In Doidge et al.'s study group, the duration of treatment was 5 years, representing a cost per patient for a course of psychoanalysis of $90,000. Psychoanalysis is fully funded in all but three provinces in Canada. No distinction is made between psychoanalysis and psychotherapy in those jurisdictions where it is funded. In Ontario, there are 174 psychoanalysts who treat an average number of five patients in analysis, with a mean duration of 5 years. The annual cost of psychoanalysis is approximately $15 million, representing a very small percentage of total OHIP expenditures. However, the intensity of the treatment and its high cost per patient led to a recent initiative by the Ontario Ministry of Health to delist psychoanalysis. After significant debate, the initiative was withdrawn, but the cost-effectiveness of analysis remains an active question. Additionally, psychotherapy has come under scrutiny because it takes such a large proportion of the OHIP mental health billings. To date, no specific action has been taken with regard to rationing psychotherapy in Ontario.

In Quebec, where psychoanalysis is not covered, many psychiatrists have both a public psychiatric practice and a private psychoanalytic practice. There is no governmental regulation of psychoanalysis—and no definition of psychoanalysis—nor any training requirement. The allowance of private billing for psychoanalytic practice offers an alternative for patients with personal resources seeking treatment in an environment of scarce psychiatric resources. Psychiatrists bill psychoanalytic hours at around twice the rate of reimbursement for most psychiatric services under Medicare. This de facto two-tiered system essentially is the result of market forces. The government restricts the number of psychiatrists in the province and keeps the Medicare reimbursement rates to one of the lowest in Canada, making regular psychiatric practice both too busy and less remunerative than psychoanalytic practice. Patients complain that finding a psychiatrist who will give them psychotherapy under Medicare is difficult (as opposed to an initial consultation, medication, and clinical management), whereas there is less of a problem finding private psychoanalytic treatment. This has contributed to a robust psychoanalytic environment. There may be some additional effects that warrant study, such as a differential in the level of care offered by the same physician (e.g., more intensive psychotherapy vs. less intensive clinical management of medications), depending on which tier is being accessed rather than on the nature of the psychiatric problem per se. However, while such an occurrence is clearly contrary to the intent of the universal coverage provided by the Canada Health Act, it is an anomaly that has arisen in response to patient need confronting government-controlled rationing of the number of providers. In fact, if private psychoanalytic practice were disallowed, patients would have to seek psychotherapy in the non-medical sector, which is not covered by Medicare anyway. To date, these health care issues have not been adequately studied; rather, they have been treated primarily as economic and political concerns.

Patterns of psychotherapy practice by psychiatrists are not well known in Canada although there are some data. A recent unpublished study by Garfinkel and Voineskos of the psychiatry graduates of Ontario medical schools revealed that 88% of respondents devote over 50% of their time to individual psychotherapy. Similarly, the severity of illness treated by psychotherapy is difficult to determine. While psychiatrists and physicians are required to provide a diagnosis for each service claim, it is common practice, in the interest of confidentiality, to use less specific diagnoses for reporting purposes whenever possible. Doidge et al.'s (1994) study of psychoanalysis reported that the commonest Axis I diagnoses were depression, anxiety, and somatoform disorders. The Garfinkel and Voineskos data revealed similarly that the predominant disorders treated by psychiatrists were mood and anxiety disorders. Patients with schizophrenia, substance abuse, organic disorders, personality disorders, psychosomatic disorders, and childhood disorders seem to be underrepresented in the private practice populations of these therapists.

Conclusion

In the Canadian system, available data on psychotherapy utilization and cost-effectiveness are relatively nonspecific. They do not provide the detail necessary to determine how much psychotherapy is provided for specific diagnostic categories, nor are there any cost-effectiveness data that may be derived. Long-term psychotherapy is a particularly problematic matter. While many of the briefer forms of therapy are systematically studied and many show clear efficacy over short-term follow-up when applied for appropriate indications, the longer term therapies are far more difficult to evaluate in a research mode and hence lack a common body of systematic outcome data. This puts long-term therapies at some risk of attack for lack of sufficient evidence of efficacy. Because of the nonspecific data available pertaining to psychotherapy utilization and the absence of any cost-effectiveness data, caution is advised in drawing conclusions. Debates become polarized between traditional psychotherapists and those who are either biologically focused or advocate brief therapies. The absence of data on the cost-effectiveness of longer term treatments is problematic for policymakers, especially as regards chronic and/or recurrent disorders, which are far less likely to be cured by short-term interventions. This increases the danger that fiscal decisions, rather than data-based decision making, will occur, potentially stripping the profession of certain forms of therapy, particularly long-term psychotherapy, the value of which, for certain populations, may be obscured by the dearth of data. While it is rare that scientific data determine the outcome of political questions, the absence of any data on cost-effectiveness guarantees that fiscal and political expediency will weigh in heavily compared to psychotherapists' and patients' claims of the importance of long-term psychotherapy.

How can we develop such a database on the costs and effectiveness of psychotherapy? One possibility would be to have health funding agencies collect better cost data, including patient diagnosis, level of impairment, specific training of the psychiatrist, type of therapy, length of treatment, and outcome. However, databases of this type may be suspect. For example, "anxiety NOS," a diagnosis commonly used, covers a myriad of disorders, demonstrating how similarly obtained diagnostic or other data may be unreliable. A more productive approach would be the institution of a series of naturalistic cost-effectiveness studies using treatments as they are generally offered in the community. Studying the different psychotherapies by using naturalistic follow-up data would generalize to treatments as they are already being conducted, obviating the generalizability issues that plague manual-based controlled treatment trials, or so-called efficacy studies.

The Kaiser-Permanente study of the treatment of depression is one such an example (Sturm & Wells, 1995; see chapter 6, this volume).

To allow informed decisions about psychotherapy, the database of the provincial ministries of health must be more specific. This begins with the definition of medical psychotherapy, which should differentiate the treatment provided by psychiatrists from that provided by other physicians. The practice of psychotherapy would be strengthened if payment guidelines defined the need for specific psychotherapy training, rather than leaving it to each individual physician and the marketplace to define psychotherapy. These definitions should be based on demonstrable efficacy of treatments. However, the specificity of psychotherapy has not been sufficiently established, and guidelines for therapeutic intervention, therefore, must be left more general at this time.

The relatively brief duration of a course of therapy as reflected in the Ontario data (7.8 sessions per patient) suggests that psychotherapy is being utilized as a billing code for treatment interventions that more properly belong under other headings, such as psychiatric care, pharmacotherapy, and supportive counseling. It is also probable that assessment interviews of one or two sessions are billed under psychotherapy because of the absence of other appropriate billing categories. The addition of assessment codes that are paid at the same level as psychotherapy would help make the data clearer and more reflective of actual practice.

In the search for appropriate methods of cost containment, the profession should work with government to ensure that the widest effective armamentarium of psychotherapies will be maintained, and at the same time to ensure appropriate utilization, for example, through an appropriate peer review mechanism similar to that in British Columbia, but using psychiatrists rather than family doctors as in that jurisdiction. Unlike jurisdictions that take a bureaucratic, as opposed to a therapeutic, approach, however, this review will be most effective if it is based on the therapeutic needs of the patient rather than on arbitrary time and dollar limits. If such peer review strategies are tried, the development of guidelines for when continued treatment is medically necessary and how this should be ascertained would be a prior requirement. Furthermore, such procedures should be studied experimentally to ensure that they will not add an expensive layer of professional/governmental oversight that, in fact, does not cut costs, or that cuts costs only by denying patients needed treatment.

Patterns of psychotherapy use are still poorly understood and studied in Canada. There are indications that the pattern of practice differs in urban and rural settings, with rural practitioners practicing in a necessarily more eclectic and broad-based fashion. Such differences should be documented, and the practices that benefit patients most should be determined. Psychotherapy will undoubtedly need some firm documentation. To the degree that clear cost-effectiveness data are developed, we will have a better chance of informing the health care debates that will arise hand in hand with the political debates over deficit and debt reduction.

References

Canada Year Book. (1994). Ottawa: Communications Division of Statistics Canada.

Doidge, N., Simon, B., Gillies, L., et al. (1994). Characteristics of psychoanalytic patients under a nationalized health plan: DSM-III-R diagnosis, previous treatment and childhood trauma. *American Journal of Psychiatry, 151*(4), 586–590, 1994.

Sturm, R., & Wells, K. B. (1995). How can care for depression become more cost-effective? *Journal of the American Medical Association*, 273(1), 51–58.

31

Psychotherapy Services in the Federal Republic of Germany

Horst Kächele, Rainer Richter,
Helmut Thomä, & Adolf-Ernst Meyer

Historical Development of the Field of Psychotherapy

For historical reasons, the field of psychotherapy in the Federal Republic of Germany (FRG) has largely developed independently from psychiatry and now has achieved the status of a medical specialty (psychotherapeutic medicine) and of a field of applied clinical psychology. The differentiation of psychotherapy from psychiatry began in the second half of the last century with Griesinger's insistence that "mind diseases are brain diseases." This biological focus within German psychiatry was strongly opposed to the developing field of psychotherapy (Alexander & Selesnick, 1969).

Accordingly, the development of psychoanalysis as the leading theoretical and practical movement in psychotherapy after the turn of the century largely took place outside academia. During the Third Reich, psychoanalysis was destroyed. Following closure of the distinguished Berlin Psychoanalytic Institute, which had established the first functioning low-fee outpatient psychotherapy clinic (Fenichel, 1930), the few remaining (non-Jewish) psychoanalysts sought ways to maintain their professional existence. On the one hand, they turned to private practice; on the other, they retained a measure of independence within the German Institute for Psychological Research and Psychotherapy, founded in 1936. During that time, the aim of bringing all schools of depth psychology under one roof was fostered in order to promote a standard form of Aryan psychotherapy. Nevertheless, in his historical review, Cocks (1984) concluded that the gathering of different schools at one institute had long-term consequences that, in his estimation, were positive.[1] The inclusion of different psychodynamic schools in a single institute helped foster the development of consensus pertaining to various issues among advocates of different approaches.

The recognition of psychoanalytic therapy by public health insurance organizations began in Berlin. The Institute for Psychogenic Illnesses (Institut für psychogene Erkrankungen), founded in Berlin in 1946, was the first psychotherapeutic outpatient clinic to be financially sponsored by a semistate organization, the General Communal Health Insurance (Allgemeine Ortskrankenkasse). This represented a first step in the eventual acceptance of psychoanalytic therapy by all public health insurance organizations. Nonmedical psychoanalysts were always active at this clinic and were able later, following the introduction of professional standards for practicing psychologists, to fully participate in the clinical treatment of patients.

Another forceful influence promoting the establishment of psychoanalysis as a key treatment modality in West Germany was the Psychosomatic Hospital at the University of Heidelberg, founded in 1950 with support from the Rockefeller Foundation. Under the direction of A. Mitscherlich, it developed into an institution in which psychoanalytic training, treatment, and research were united under one roof. There, for the first time in the history of German universities, psychoanalysis was able to establish itself in the way Freud (1919) had envisaged.

Many of the first generation of postwar psychoanalysts in Germany began as self-taught practitioners without public support. The slow recovery of the psychoanalytic profession—there were no behavior therapists in those years—was markedly supported by help from German-speaking psychoanalysts living abroad, who put aside personal feelings and offered their assistance.

Key support came from the German Research Foundation (Deutsche Forschungsgemeinschaft), which provided financial support for training and supervisory analyses, as the result of recommendations from a report it had commissioned (Görres, Heiss, Thomä, & von Uexküll, 1964). This report documented the separation of psychotherapy from psychiatry and also made clear that in Germany, psychosomatic medicine had become part and parcel of psychotherapy. Psychotherapy served many patients who were not adequately treated either by psychiatric or by other somatic interventions.

The founding of the Berlin Central Institute for Psychogenic Illnesses in 1946 represented "the first step in the recognition of neurosis as illness by a German public institution. For the first time, one of the institutions in the social insurance system paid the costs of psychoanalysis and other psychotherapeutic treatments" (Dräger, 1971, p. 267). The Central Institute thus made a significant contribution to overcoming the resistance of the social insurance system to psychodynamic treatment. It "provided the German Society for Psychotherapy and Depth Psychology with many of the arguments which, after long and weary years of negotations, finally led to success" (Baumeyer, 1971, p. 231). The acceptance of neuroses as illnesses constituted a precondition for the inclusion of psychotherapy as a benefit in the programs of the major health insurance companies in 1967 and the programs of other public organizations in 1971 (Faber, 1981; Haarstrick, 1976).

Parallel to the recognition of psychodynamic and psychoanalytic therapies as part of the officially funded health insurance service delivery system, German medical faculties revised their curriculum in 1970 to include "psychosomatic medicine and psychotherapy" as an independent field, to be taught mandatorily to all medical students. This necessitated the establishment of departments for psychosomatic medicine and psychotherapy. The first and second generations of chairs of these 33 departments are all psychoanalytically oriented. These institutions have had considerable impact on the further establishment of psychotherapy as an acknowledged form of treatment in medicine.

Later developments in academic clinical psychology, integrating psychotherapy as a field of research and training, evolved largely from behavioral and client-centered orientations. Since many of the professors and lecturers in clinical psychology are not clinically experienced psychotherapists, but qualified as empirical researchers, the standing of psychotherapy within academic psychology is rather poor.

Health Insurance in Germany

In Germany, the health insurance system ensures that necessary outpatient and inpatient medical treatment is available at the time of need for individuals from all strata of society, regardless of financial situation. With few exceptions, the patient pays no more than his or her regular insurance premium (approximately 14% of income). Health insurance companies are legally constrained from demanding any direct contribution toward the costs of either analytic or behavior therapy.[2] As nearly all patients consulting a psychotherapist in the FRG have medical insurance covering the officially admitted forms of psychotherapy,[3] these regulations powerfully shape the nature of the psychotherapy service delivery system.

The system of providing psychotherapy is regulated by a set of agreements between the Kassenärztliche Bundesvereinigung (KBV; the national corporate organization of physicians, which regulates matters of public health and oversees payment of medical care) and the health insurance companies. The German system of third-party payment is explicit about the fact that the patient make no direct payment; instead, he or she requests, by way of the therapist writing a detailed report, that the KBV cover costs for treatment. A body of peer reviewers examines the claim, and if it is approved, the therapist receives the fee via the local branch of the KBV.

It should be emphasized that the patient's right of legal redress is directed not at the state but at the health insurance company, an arrangement dating back to insurance regulations implemented by Bismarck. The German social insurance system is supervised by the state, but it is not a national health service.

Patients know how much is deducted from their salary or wages as their health insurance contribution and can calculate how much they have paid in over the years and how often they have availed themselves of services. They have a free choice of doctors. Just as the public health insurance companies together form a corporate entity, nearly all doctors (and psychotherapists) are members of the KBV.

Fees for psychotherapists' services, as for all doctors' services, are negotiated between these two corporate organizations. Obviously, agreements on rates for medical services entail compromises in which political and economic factors play a considerable part. In many respects, the specific regulations covering the analytic and behavioral psychotherapies, including the guidelines on payment, represent such a compromise.

The Guidelines (Psychotherapie-Richtlinien)

In order to direct the practitioner and to ensure quality of care, clinical guidelines (called *Psychotherapie-Richtlinien*) are continuously monitored by the KBV, which bases its judgments on input from peer reviewers elected from the field.

The clinical indications for psychodynamic therapy and psychoanalytic therapy are

- Psychoreactive psychic disturbances (e.g., anxiety neuroses, phobias, neurotic depression)
- Conversion neuroses
- Autonomic functional disturbances with established psychic etiology
- Psychic disturbances consequent on emotional deficiencies in early childhood; exceptionally, psychic disturbances related to physical injuries in early childhood or to malformations
- Psychic disturbances resulting from severe chronic illness, as long as they offer a basis for the application of psychodynamic or psychoanalytic therapy (e.g., chronic rheumatic conditions, particular forms of psychosis)
- Psychic disturbances due to extreme situations (that evoke grave personality disturbances (e.g., a long prison sentence, severe psychic trauma)

The clinical indications for behavior therapy are

- Psychic disturbances with a delimitated symptomatology (eating disorders, addiction, monosymptomatic phobias)
- Autonomic functional disturbances without established psychic etiology
- Chronic psychiatric disorders without established psychic etiology
- Psychoreactive psychic disturbances (e.g., anxiety neuroses, phobias, neurotic depression) in patients who tend to focus on the actual symptoms instead of reflecting and working through their internal conflicts
- Psychic disturbances resulting from severe chronic illness, as long as they offer a basis for the application of training in and reinforcement of effective coping strategies

The guidelines specify that psychotherapy provided by health insurance is restricted to those illnesses whose course can be influenced for the better. Thus, the patient officially requests insurance coverage, and the psychotherapist is called upon to provide the peer reviewer with evidence suggesting that the intended therapy has the potential to alleviate, improve, or cure the neurotic or psychosomatic disease in question. The psychotherapist is obliged to justify her or his recommended therapy to the insurance company in terms of the triad of necessity, effectiveness, and economy, which govern physicians' diagnostic and therapeutic action in Germany.

Complications inevitably ensue if therapist and patient forget that they are only two sides of a triangle. One cannot behave as if the reviewer were not there; whether therapy is extended or not depends on his or her assessment. In making a decision, the reviewer heeds guidelines pertaining to treatment duration: Analytic psychotherapy should as a rule achieve a satisfactory result in 160 sessions, and in special cases, up to 240 sessions. Further extension to 300 sessions is possible under exceptional circumstances but must be supported by detailed arguments. Even 300 sessions do not constitute an absolute limit, in the event that valid, convincing reasons are presented by the therapist to the peer reviewer. In the unlikely event that therapist and peer reviewer do not agree, a patient may go to court and, in some cases, successfully claim more sessions.[4]

Health insurance companies are obliged to cover costs only when the symptoms constitute an illness, and when the triad of necessity, effectiveness, and economy is also satisfied. Both in diagnosis and in treatment, the German psychotherapist, whether a medical doctor or a psychologist, must keep these criteria in mind. He or she must also remember that neuroses are on a continuum with characterologically determined disturbances, the latter of which, however, are not covered by health insurance. Psychodynamic therapy and psychoanalytic therapy are not covered by public health insurance if they do not have the potential to bring about cure or amelioration of a disease, or to lead to medical rehabilitation. This regulation also disallows interventions intended exclusively for professional growth and development, social adjustment, child-rearing guidance, and other similar measures.

The Two Branches of the Psychotherapy Service Delivery System

The Inpatient System

The German psychotherapy delivery system consists of two branches: outpatient and inpatient. Historically, the development of the inpatient psychotherapy system began with local experimentation by Simmel in Berlin, and by Groddeck in Baden-Baden in the 1920s. Following the war, the joint influence of psychosomatics, as established within university departments of internal medicine (e.g., at Freiburg, Hamburg, and Heidelberg), together with successful efforts to reestablish the tradition of Simmel, led to inpatient psychotherapy's being considered acceptable for insurance coverage long before outpatient psychotherapy became eligible.[5]

As Schepank (1988) makes clear, this trend has been increasing since the 1970s, when those hospitals established for the treatment of chronic somatic diseases (such as tuberculosis) were forced to find a new patient base. Psychosomatic medicine turned out to be a comparatively inexpensive treatment modality and therefore was financially attractive to owners of rehabilitation institutions. Figure 31.1 displays the steeply rising numbers of beds for psychotherapy/psychosomatics in the so-called rehabilitation segment of medical care, as well as the less pronounced growth of psychosomatic beds in community and university hospitals (Lachauer, Neun, & Dahlmann, 1991).

The more than 8,000 beds for short-term inpatient psychotherapy officially provide rehabilitative aftercare for cardiac, pulmonary, orthopedic, dermatologic, and other somatic conditions. Given the large percentage of patients with functional somatic complaints, the system of inpatient rehabilitation over the years has been transformed into a system of inpatient psychodynamic therapy. In recent years, behavioral approaches have also been incorporated, and today, about 25% of inpatient units operate within a behavioral framework. While most of these inpatient facilities operate under the adminstrative-financial auspices of rehabilitation, providing up to 6 weeks of intensive multimodal psychotherapy, some known officially as psychotherapeutic hospitals can provide intensive psychoanalytic inpatient treatment, with duration of stay up to 9 months (e.g., Psychotherapeutic Hospital Stuttgart; Schmitt, Seifert, & Kächele, 1993). Patients hospitalized in the latter facilities tend to be severely and chronically ill psychosomatic and psychoneurotic patients requiring integrated psychosomatic, holistic treatment. A key

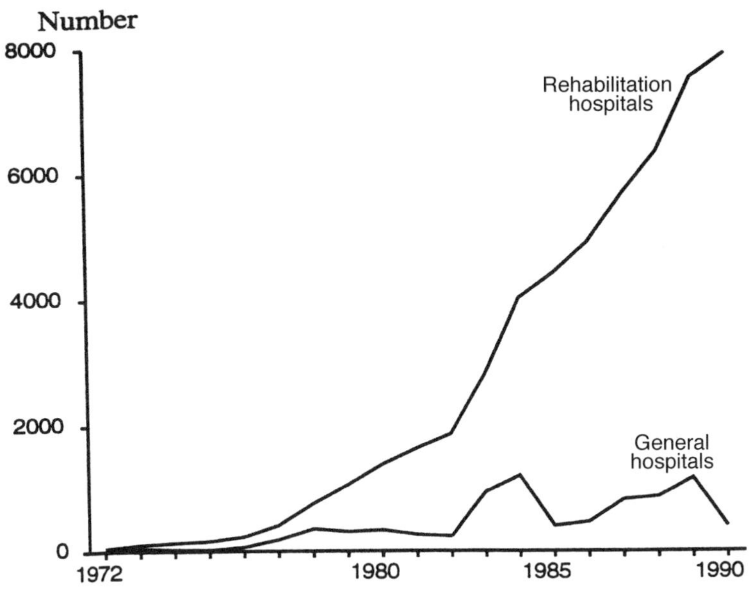

Figure 31.1 Number of beds for inpatient psychotherapy (Lachauer, 1991) in rehabilitation hospitals and general hospitals.

problem of this system, however, is the relative absence of continuity of care postdischarge. Because patients are admitted to intensive therapeutic institutions from all corners of Germany, devising a suitable aftercare system has been difficult.

Though this system of care is unique in providing intensive treatment for a segment of the population that otherwise would not be cared for, scientific questions have been raised regarding whether such a system of inpatient care represents a strategy of treating patients too often and too late. Some have argued that it would be possible to treat all these patients as outpatients if the system of outpatient care were in a position to really draw these patient into treatment. The point of Meyer et al. (1991) decrying the inpatient system as a "misallocation of public means" (p. 41) might be too strong a statement, given that the development of inpatient psychotherapy also represents the growth of wide public acceptance of psychotherapy (Kächele & Kordy, 1996).

Inpatient psychotherapy is more than just psychotherapy in a hospital. Its general goals are based on the assumption that a convenient composition of a variety of therapeutic factors in a suitable structured institutional setting will allow for the optimal treatment of those patients who, when treated in an outpatient setting, are said to have little chances of success.

The sheer number and diversity of psychotherapeutic and psychosomatic hospitals to be found all over Germany[6] as a well established part of the mental health care system may come as a surprise to the Anglo-American reader; nevertheless, it is an established fact that in present-day Germany, nearly 40% of all patients receive their psychotherapy as inpatient psychotherapy (Meyer et al., 1991).

The Outpatient System

The outpatient delivery system in the FRG (1990) comprises a total number of 6,492 trained psychotherapists for adult patients and 740 child and adolescent psychotherapists who are licensed to practice within the German health insurance system.

The present system of funding psychotherapy allows for the regimens shown in Table 31.1, which are detailed in the aforementioned guidelines (Kommentar Richtlinien Psychotherapie; Faber & Haarstrick, 1991).

Funding is easier for short-term psychotherapy than for long-term treatment. Thus, short-term psychotherapy is often indicated for patients in an acute crisis or with a defined and delimited focus, or to test motivation for long-term psychotherapy. There is no differential indication for either brief behavioral or psychodynamic treatment, or for short-term group treatments. As regards long-term treatment, peer review is required at each phase to confirm that further treatment is medically necessary.

The Psychotherapists and the Population

The ratio of psychotherapists to people is 1 : 6,250, or 16 psychotherapists per 100,000 population (1994). Figure 31.2 shows the linear increase in number of psychotherapists from 1982 to 1994. About half the trained psychotherapists are physicians; the other half are clinical psychologists. Neither professional group is qualified to conduct psychotherapy by virtue of an academic degree alone; rather, the members must undergo intensive structured courses of postgraduate education and training (Köhle, Janssen, & Richter, 1996).

Training is provided by private institutions certified by the KBV to provide the necessary qualifications for serving within the medical system. As previously noted, for a long time, psychotherapy training was only provided in psychoanalytic/depth-psychological orientations. Training in behavior therapy was initiated in the 1970s, but only in 1987, after a recommendation from peer reviewers to the KBV and to the insurance companies, was behavior therapy covered by insurance. Since then, the number of institutes providing behavior-oriented training has been increasing rapidly, with a strong preponderance of psychologists seeking that kind of training. In psychoanalytic training institutions, the number of psychologists and physicians is fairly equal.

A report commissioned by the German government estimates that the total number of 7,232 psychotherapists does not cover the actual need for outpatient psychotherapy (Meyer et al., 1991). This estimate is supported by epidemiological data on the prevalence of neurotic, psychosomatic, and personality disorders (Schepank, 1987).

Figure 31.3 highlights data on the 1-week prevalence of mental disorders ascertained from a representative sample drawn at random from a middle-aged municipal population. When screened by an expert group, 25% of the sample received a diagnosis of neurotic, psychosomatic, or personality disorder by the *ICD-9* criteria. Clearly, not all these individuals were motivated to seek out treatment. In a follow-up study, Schepank et al. found that only 35% of diagnosed cases

Table 31.1 Insurance Coverage for Outpatient Psychotherapy Treatment Modalities

		Number of Sessions Allocated
1. Initial interivew and evaluation		5–8
2. Short-term psychodynamic therapy		25
a. Crisis intervention		
b. Focal therapy		
c. Dynamic psychotherapy		
d. Supportive therapy		
3. Short-term behavior therapy		25
4. Psychodynamic therapy	1. Phase	50
	2. Phase	50 + 30
	3. Phase	50 + 30 + 20
5. Psychodynamic group therapy	1. Phase	40
	2. Phase	40 + 20
	3. Phase	40 + 20 + 20
6. Behavior therapy	1. Phase	45
	2. Phase	45 + 15
	3. Phase	45 + 15 + 20
7. Psychoanalytic therapy	1. Phase	160
	2. Phase	160 + 80
	3. Phase	160 + 80 + 60
8. Psychoanalytic group therapy	1. Phase	80
	2. Phase	80 + 40

accepted outpatient individual or group psychotherapy when it was offered (Franz et al., 1990).

Following a review of data from German epidemiological studies, a report commissioned by the German government estimated that 5.3% of the FRG population is in need of outpatient psychotherapeutic care and would accept such treatment if covered by the health care system. This estimate of need cannot be met by the 7,232 insurance-funded psychotherapists.

Using official data from the health care system, the review estimated that only one of seven for whom outpatient psychotherapeutic treatment is indicated is treated in the official health care system. From these studies, it can be deduced that approximately 60 psychotherapists are necessary to cover the needs of 100,000 people, a ratio of 1 psychotherapist for every 1,700 persons. Estimates suggest that the German health system needs six to seven times more psychotherapists than are now available.

Costs and Effectiveness

Although the number of psychotherapists is small relative to the need, it is actually great relative to availability in some other industrial countries. In addition, the budget for outpatient psychotherapy allocated by the health insurance companies is quite small, amounting to only 2.1% of the overall budget for outpatient health care provided by physicians, or amounting to 0.39% of the total budget of the German health insurance companies.

The allocation of the psychotherapy budget to different service components is illustrated in Figure 31.4. Excluding the amount for psychiatric outpatient services, one third of the budget is allocated to basic psychosomatic care (a recently introduced service provided by general practioners with some training in psychological medicine), 43% is allocated to psychodynamic or psychoanalytic treatments, 13% to behavior therapy, 6.4% to psychoanalytic-oriented child and adolescent psychotherapy, and almost 2% to initial evaluative interviews. These data reflect the predominance of the psychodynamic orientation within the German psychotherapeutic health care system; even the provision of basic psychosomatic care is based on psychodynamic principles of training. As noted previously, the reasons for this preponderance reside in the special development of psychoanalysis in the German postwar culture. There is strong societal consensus pertaining

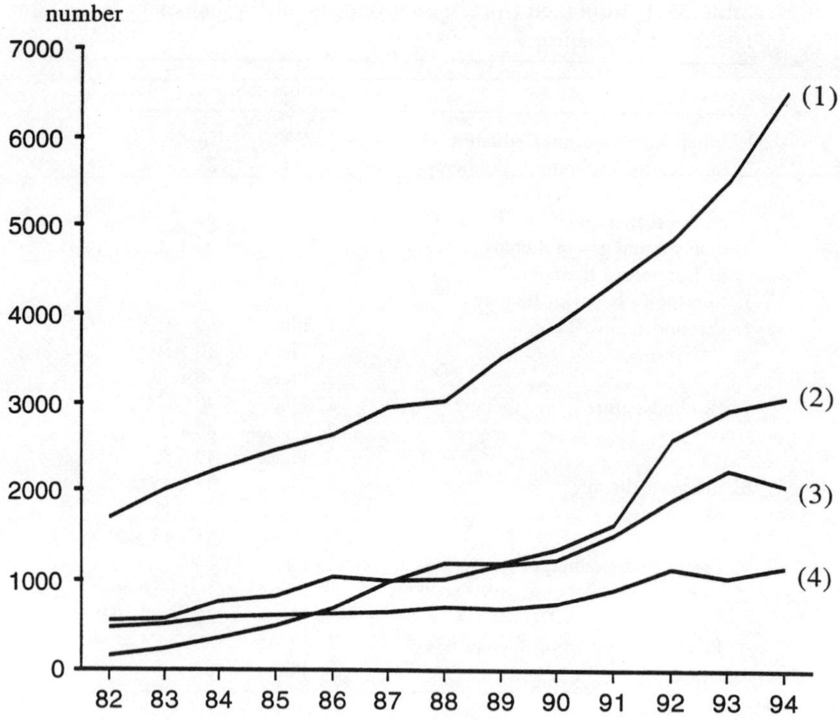

Figure 31.2 Increase in the number of psychotherapists from 1982 to 1994 (recognized by all health insurance companies). (1) Physicians trained for psychotherapy (almost all psychodynamic and/or psychoanalytic therapy): 1994, 6,535; (2) clinical psychologists trained for behavior therapy: 1994, 3,072; (3) clinical psychologists trained for psychoanalytic therapy: 1994, 2,065; (4) child and adolescent psychotherapists (psychoanalytically trained): 1994, 1,057.

to the effectiveness of psychoanalytic psychotherapy. Initial approval for this treatment was based on an empirical study that turned out to be decisive in the process of societal recognition of psychotherapy.

The Berlin Cost-Effectiveness Study

As noted above, the Institute for Psychogenic Illnesses (Institut für psychogene Erkrankungen), founded in Berlin in 1946, was the first psychotherapeutic outpatient clinic to be financially sponsored by a semistate organization. There was early strong interest in evaluating treatment outcomes.

In 1958, a major follow-up study was launched, in which retrospective case histories on 1,427 patients were reviewed. Most patients were treated with individual analytic psychotherapy, one to two times weekly, with an average length of 100 sessions. Five years post-termination, follow-up interviews with the 1,004 successfully terminated cases were conducted by independent experts.[7] The data analysis consisted of systematic scaling of outcome criteria along the dimension of more or less improved. Of the 1,004 successful cases, 845 were interviewed. The outcome data revealed that two thirds of patients remained improved. The more interesting findings of this follow-up study concerned data on successfully treated patients' stay in a general hospital, both before and after treatment. These led to a subsequent study that will be reported in some detail, as it is the basis for key decisions by the insurance companies (Dührssen, 1962).

Dührssen and Jorswieck (1965) drew a random sample of 125 cases from all patients who had received individual psychoanalytic-oriented treatment and had been terminated in 1958. They also drew a random sample of 100 patients from the waiting list. They then checked for the distribution of prognostically favorable and unfavorable cases and balanced the two samples. In addition, they drew another random sample of 100 nonpatients from the general population of the insur-

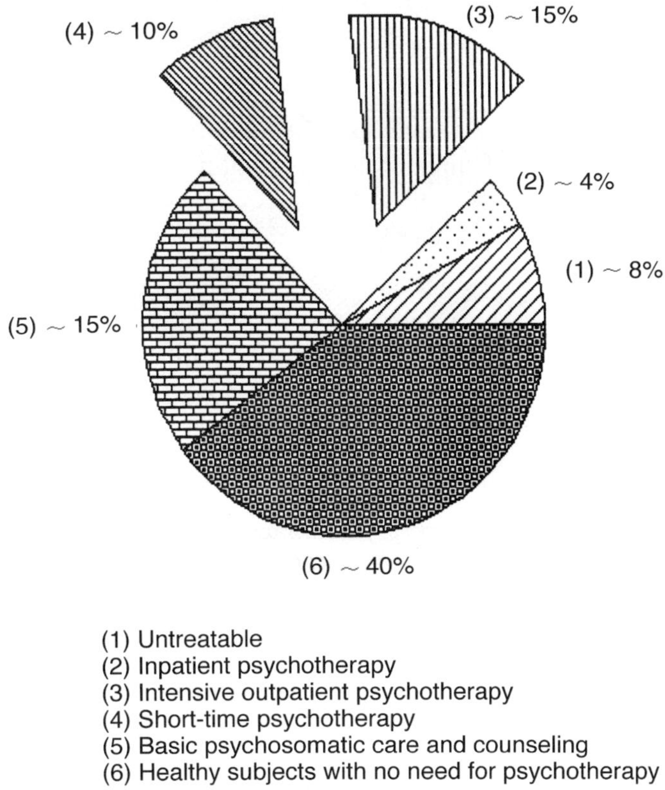

Figure 31.3 Estimated need for psychotherapy in a 25- to 45-year-old randomly selected representative German municipal population (N = 600). From Schepank (1990).

ance files. Using these data, they were able to count exactly the number of days spent in a general hospital—for any reason—in the 5 years preceding and the 5 years following treatment (Table 31.2).

Waiting-list patients required hospitalization for approximately 25 days within the time span of the first and second 5-year evaluation. In the psychotherapy group, however, the number of days of hospitalization decreased from 26 days in the 5-year pretreatment period to only 6 days in the 5-year period following the termination of treatment. The so-called healthy members of the insurance company spent an average of 10 days in the 5-year period before 1958 and 11.7 days in the 5-year period after 1958. This finding was impressive, and it helped support the argument that psychoanalytic therapy should be an integral part of the public health system of care.

Despite this seminal study, true cost-effectiveness or cost-benefit analysis studies of psychotherapy appear rarely in the German literature. The following two studies are mentioned representatively: Deter (1986) studied the effectiveness of psychodynamic group psychotherapy in bronchial asthma. In this controlled study, 57 patients suffering from moderate to heavy bronchial asthma participated in outpatient group therapy for 1 year. The patients were systematically monitored. A randomly selected subsample of 12 patients versus 10 matched controls were further studied. All the differences between the 1-year pre- and 1-year posttreatment period, taken into account in the cost-benefit analysis, were found to be statistically significant.

Three items underscored the benefit of the psychotherapeutic treatment. First, the number of workday absences increased in the control group from 44 to 62 days per year, whereas in the treatment group, absences decreased from 58 days during the pretreatment year to 27 days during the year following therapy. This difference in temporary work disability, expressed as a benefit, was due to both a direct and an indirect decrease in labor costs in the amount of $2,070 per pa-

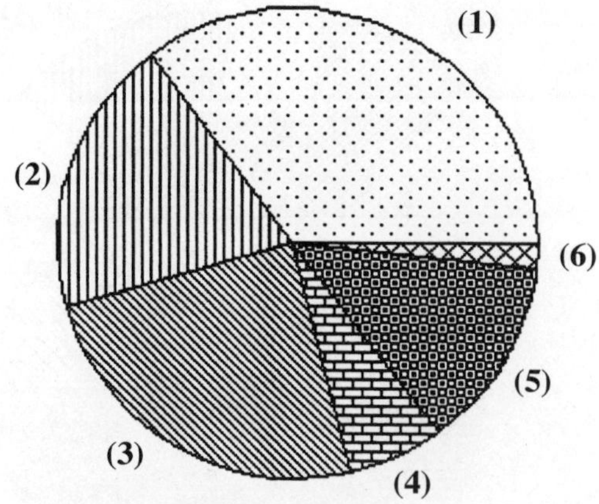

(1)	Basic psychosomatic care	$ 98.0 million
(2)	Psychodynamic psychotherapy	53.0 million
(3)	Psychoanalytic psychotherapy	67.5 million
(4)	Child and adolescent psychotherapy	17.6 million
(5)	Behavior therapy	36.0 million
(6)	Initial interview	5.2 million
		$ 470.8 million

Figure 31.4 Budget of health insurance companies in 1989; $470.6 million = 2.1% of the overall budget for outpatient health care by physicians.

tient. Additionally, while the number of days of hospitalization per year increased in the control group from 11 to 19 days per patient, it decreased from 24 to 3 days in the treatment group. The decrease in costs of hospitalization amounted to $4,410 per patient. Finally, psychotherapy patients were found to visit their general practitioner less often. The authors concluded that a savings of $5,330 per patient was achieved via psychodynamic group therapy.

Zielke (1993) studied 148 patients and calculated the difference between the costs incurred by a chronic psychosomatic disease (treatment costs and labor costs due to temporary work disability) before and after a 60-day inpatient course of behavioral treatment, comparing work disability decreases with treatment costs. He reported a cost-benefit ratio of 1 : 3.5 for working patients (i.e., a direct benefit of $8,871 per patient).

Keller et al. (1995) report a significant reduction

Table 31.2 Number of Days in a General Hospital in the 5 Years Preceding and the 5 Years Following Psychoanalytic Psychotherapy

Group	N	Mean number of hospital days	Standard deviation
1a. Patients before treatment	125	26.1	26.9
1b. Patients after treatment	125	5.9	14.2
2a. Patients waiting before 1958	100	25.6	30.4
2b. Patients waiting after 1958	100	23.9	28.7
3a. Normal subjects before 1958	100	10.0	18.2
3b. Normal subjects after 1958	100	11.7	19.5

Note. From Dührssen and Jorswieck (1965).

in work disability (13.5 versus 41.6 days) and of hospitalization (1 versus 8 days) during a 1-year period subsequent to long-term psychoanalytic therapy in 111 psychoneurotic patients. This effect remained stable over a 5-year period: Sick time was reduced to 8 days per year during the 5 years after termination of therapy, compared to 16 days per year pretreatment.

Economic arguments will become increasingly prominent in the German medical literature in the years to come. Health insurance companies and health administrators will increase pressure on the psychotherapy delivery system to offer treatments that have been proven cost-effective. Accordingly, important new aspects of the evaluation of psychotherapeutic techniques can be expected in the near future.

Notes

1. For further critical comments see Thomä and Kächele (1987, p. xix).
2. To qualify for inclusion in the health insurance system, only those forms of psychotherapy with an etiological theory, specific methods of treatment, and demonstrated effectiveness are acceptable.
3. There are also non-officially recognized forms of psychotherapy (e.g., client-centered and other forms of humanistic psychotherapy) that can be reimbursed based on case-specific decisions by local insurance companies. This "gray market" is quite substantial, accounting for at least 17% of the costs of official psychotherapy (Meyer, Richter, Grawe, Schulenburg, & Schulte, 1991, p. 38).
4. Kächele, Pfäfflin, and Simons (1995) presented a methodology for retrospectively reviewing controversial cases such as one that led a court to rule that the patient should be given 420 sessions of psychoanalytic therapy.
5. A psychosomatic-psychotherapeutic hospital for internal medicine was established in Lübeck in 1946; a hospital for analytic psychotherapy was instituted in Göttingen in 1949, a hospital for psychogenic disorders in Berlin was established in 1948, and a special psychotherapy ward was added to the university hospital for internal medicine in Hamburg in 1950. The Psychosomatic Hospital in Heidelberg was established the same year. Inpatient treatment facilities were also established at universities in Freiburg (1957), Giessen (1962) and Mainz (1965).
6. We are deliberately omitting a description of the former East German psychotherapy system, which has disappeared now and is replaced by the West German system.
7. Why the 152 nonsuccessful cases were not also approached remains a mystery (see Dührssen, 1972, p. 397; for a detailed discussion see Kächele, 1992).

References

Alexander, F. G., & Selesnick, S. T. (1969). *Geschichte der Psychiatrie*. Konstanz: Diana Verlag.

Balint, M., & Balint, E. (1961). *Psychotherapeutic techniques in medicine*. London: Tavistock.

Baumeyer, F. (1971). Zur Geschichte der Psychoanalyse in Deutschland: 60 Jahre Deutsche psychoanalytische Gesellschaft. *Z Psychosom Med Psychoanal, 17*, 203–240.

Boehm, F. (1942). Erhebung und Bearbeitung von Katamnesen. *Zbl Psychother, 14*, 17–24.

Cocks, G. C. (1984). *Psychotherapy in the Third Reich: The Göring Institute*. New York: Oxford University Press.

Deter, H. C. (1986). Cost-benefit analysis of psychosomatic therapy in asthma. *Journal of Psychosomatic Research, 30*, 173–182.

Dräger, K. (1971). Bemerkungen zu den Zeitumständen und zum Schicksal der Psychoanalyse und der Psychotherapie in Deutschland zwischen 1933 und 1949. *Psyche, 25*, 255–268.

Dührssen, A. (1962). Katamnestische Ergebnisse bei 1004 Patienten nach analytischer Psychotherapie. *Z Psychosom Med, 8*, 94–113.

Dührssen, A. (1972). *Analytische Psychotherapie in Theorie, Praxis und Ergebnisse*. Göttingen: Vandenhoek & Ruprecht.

Dührssen, A. M., & Jorswieck, E. (1965). Eine empirisch-statistische Untersuchung zur Leistungsfähigkeit psychoanalytischer Behandlung. *Nervenarzt, 36*, 166–169.

Faber, F. R. (1981). Der Krankheitsbegriff in der Reichsversicherungsordnung. *Psychother Med Psychol, 31*, 179–182.

Faber, F. R., & Haarstrick, R. (1991). Kommentar Psychotherapie-Richtlinien. 2. Auflage. Neckarsulm-München: Jungjohann Verlagsgesellschaft.

Fenichel, O. (1930). Statistischer Bericht über die therapeutische Tätigkeit 1920–1930. In S. Rad, O. Fenichel, & C. Müller-Braunschweig (Eds.), *Zehn Jahre Berliner Psychoanalytisches Institut: Poliklinik und Lehranstalt* (pp. 13–19). Wien: Int Psychoanal Verlag.

Franz, M., Schiessl, N., Manz, R., Fellhauer, R., Schepank, H., & Tress, W. (1990). Zur Problematik der Psychotherapiemotivation und der Psychotherapieakzeptanz. *PPmP Psychother Med Psychol, 40*, 369–374.

Freud, S. (1919). On the teaching of psycho-analysis in universities. *SE, 17*, 169–173.

Görres, A., Heiss, R., Thomä, H., & Uexküll, Th. von.

(1964). *Denkschrift zur Lage der ärztlichen Psychotherapie und der psychosomatischen Medizin.* Wiesbaden: Steiner.

Haarstrick, R. (1976). Kommentierung der Psychotherapie-Vereinbarungen. *Dtsch Ärztebl, 73,* 2084–2087.

Kächele, H. (1992). Psychoanalytische Therapieforschung 1930–1990. *Psyche, 46,* 259–285.

Kächele, H., & Kordy, H. (1996). Outcome research. In Th. von Uexküll (Ed.), *Psychosomatic medicine.* New York: Urban & Schwarzenberg.

Keller, W., Dilg, R., Westhoff, G., Rohner, R., Studt, H. H., & The Empirical Research Group in Analytical Psychology Berlin. (1997). On the efficacy of outpatient Jungian psychoanalyses and psychotherapies. In: Mattoon, M. A. (Ed.), *Proceedings of the 13th International Congress for Analytical Psychology,* Zürich, 1995, Einsiedein, Daimon-Verlag.

Köhle, K., Janssen, P. L., & Richter, R. (1996). Fort- und Weiterbildung unter Berücksichtigung der Entwicklung in der Schweiz und in Österreich. In Th. von Uexküll, R. H. Adler, J. M. Hermann, K. Köhle, O. W. Schoenecke, & W. Wesiack (Eds.), *Psychosomatische medizin* (pp. 93–101). München, Wien, and Baltimore: Urban & Schwarzenberg.

Lachauer, R., Neun, H., & Dahlmann, W. (1991). Psychosomatische Einrichtungen in Deutschland—Eine Bestandsaufnahme. Göttingen: Verlag für medizinische Psychologie.

Meyer, A. E., Richter, R., Grawe, K., Schulenburg, J. M., & Schulte, B. (1991). *Forschungsgutachten zu Fragen eines Psychotherapeutengesetzes.* Universitätskrankenhaus Hamburg-Eppendorf.

Schepank, H. (1987). Psychogene Erkrankungen der Stadtbevölkerung: Eine epidemiologischtiefenpsychologische Feldstudie in Mannheim. Berlin, Heidelberg, and New York: Springer.

Schepank, H. (1988). Die stationäre Psychotherapie in der Bundesrepublik Deutschland: Soziokulturelle Determinanten, Entwicklungsstufen, Ist-Zustand, internationaler Vergleich, Rahmenbedingungen. In H. Schepank & W. Tress (Eds.), *Die stationäre Psychotherapie und ihr Rahmen.* Berlin, Heidelberg, and New York: Springer.

Schmitt, G., Seifert, T., & Kächele, H. (Eds.). (1993). *Stationäre analytische Psychotherapie.* Stuttgart: Schattauer Verlag.

Thomä, H., & Kächele, H. (1987). *Psychoanalytic Practice: Vol. 1. Principles.* Berlin, Heidelberg, New York, London, Paris, and Tokyo: Springer.

Zielke, M. (1993). *Wirksamkeit staionärer Verhaltenstherapie.* Weinheim: Psychologie Verlags Union.

32

Psychotherapy Services in Sweden

Bengt-Åke Armelius

In 1992, large investigation of psychiatry (Psykiatriutredningen) in Sweden was published. The report took a broad view of psychiatry in Sweden, and many of its suggestions and recommendations were accepted by the government during the spring of 1994. This chapter presents some of the facts about psychotherapy that were collected in that investigation.

The problem that is facing the mental health field in Sweden can be summarized in a few facts. There are about 8.5 million inhabitants of Sweden, 2–3% of whom seek psychiatric care during 1 year.

It is estimated that 12–17% of patients in general health care have psychiatric symptoms. The most common psychiatric disturbances are depression and anxiety, which can be seen in 10% of the population. In addition, 2% of the population have psychoses, and about 0.5% suffer from schizophrenia. We estimate 6–7 new cases per 100,000 every year according to a recent study by Alanen et al. (1994).

The total cost of psychiatric care provided by the state in Sweden is estimated to be about $1 billion, or about $125 per inhabitant per year. The average daily cost for inpatient care is around $230. There is a maximum out-of-pocket capital cost for any type of health care in Sweden so that nobody has to pay more than $200 a year owing to a high-cost protection law. The cost per visit for health care is about $20. Very little psychiatric care is provided on a private basis outside the official welfare system.

There are 114 psychiatric sectors that are responsible for all types of care. All kinds of medical services from specialists, whether a knee operation or psychotherapy, should be provided by the state, but in the case of psychotherapy, not all services are yet reimbursed.

There are about 70,000 inhabitants in each sector. The number of specialists in psychiatry is relatively high. We have 10 psychiatrists per 100,000 and 9 psychologists and 9 social workers per 100,000.

In 1960, there were 35,000 inpatient beds; in 1994 there were 14,500. Of those 35,000 beds, 26,000 were in mental hospitals in 1960. In 1994 only 5,000 are left. The mental hospitals have been largely closed down. One third of the beds utilized today are earmarked for acute and short-term treatment. Five percent of inpatients, mostly young schizophrenic and severely disturbed borderline patients, are treated in small treatment homes with active psychotherapeutic intervention over the course of several years. This appears to be a unique form of treatment for severely disturbed patients. A large longitudinal study tracking course and outcome is now investigating about 30 of these treatment homes (Armelius, 1991).

There are 375 mental health centers responsible for outpatient care in the 114 districts, which provide services for approximately 2 million patient visits per year; 85% of the 2 million are return visits, and 10% are estimated to be acute visits. In estimating how much psychotherapy is provided in outpatient psychiat-

Table 32.1 Percentage Visits for "Psychotherapy" and "Supportive Talks" by Professional Groups

Professional Group	Psychotherapy (%)	Supportive Talk (%)
Psychologist	50	32
Psychiatrist	18	67
Social worker	18	67
Nurse	4	46

ric care, a distinction has to be made between "psychotherapy" and "supportive talks," the latter of which may be provided by individuals with only limited training in psychotherapy. In Table 32.1, the percentage of psychotherapy and supportive talks provided by various professional groups is shown.

Table 32.2 shows how these forms of treatment are distributed over different diagnostic groups. On the average, 13% of the 10,773 contacts studied were for psychotherapy, and 42% were for supportive talks.

Psychotherapy is primarily provided to personality-disordered patients, to patients with anxiety and depression, and, to a lesser extent, to patients in crisis. It is infrequently delivered to those with substance abuse or psychosis in outpatient psychiatric care. The current trend in psychiatry in Sweden is to give supportive talks.

We have formal training and authorization of psychotherapists in Sweden, and the term *psychotherapy* is reserved for licenced psychotherapists. In 1979, formal training of psychotherapists started at some universities. We have a two-step model for training. The first step is basic training in psychotherapy, including one and a half years of theory and supervision and 50 hours of personal psychotherapy. This training is included in basic education for psychologists but is only partly available to psychiatrists and social workers. Psychiatrists and social workers do not have personal psychotherapy and have less supervision. They do personal psychotherapy on their own if they want to become psychotherapists. This first step may also be taken by nurses, mental health aides, or any other group that is working with psychiatric patients. Today, the first step is usually provided by psychiatric clinics as part of the job for mental health workers.

The second step is an advanced course for psychotherapists. It is open to psychiatrists, psychologists, social workers, and a few others who may be accepted if they have special qualifications. This step includes 3 years of theory and supervision and 75 hours of personal psychotherapy. Qualifications include completion of Step 1 training and 3 or more years' experience as a psychotherapist under supervision. For those aspiring to be supervisors in psychotherapy, there is an additional 2 years of supervisory education. The system is very well organized, in hierarchical fashion, with a total time in training of almost 10 years beyond completion of a basic education.

In 1985, an authorization was issued to all psychotherapists with the Step 2 level of training. It is protected by law, and today, there are a variety of schools for psychotherapy with Step 2 courses. In the event the school can provide research and theoretical support for its effectiveness, authorization may be given by the health authority. To date, five or six different schools in Sweden have earned such authorization.

In 1994, there were 2,500 psychotherapists, which means 1 psychotherapist for about each 3,200 inhabitants—a fairly dense distribution. In 1991, there were 1,700 psychotherapists, 1,600 of whom answered a questionnaire. About 1,200 of them were classified as psychodynamic, 100 as psychoanalytic, and an equal number as family therapists, while there were fewer than 50 in each of the cognitive and behavioral categories.

Table 32.2 Proportion of Contacts in Open Psychiatric Care That Are Psychotherapeutic and Supportive Talks

Professional Group	Psychotherapy (%)	Supportive Talk (%)
Crisis	12	59
Anxiety	22	44
Depression	14	49
Personality disorder	26	40
Psychosis	4	36
Drug/alcohol abuse	5	43

Table 32.3 Reimbursement Source for Psychotherapy in Private Practice

Reimbursement Source	Percentage
1. Patient himself or herself	47
2. Relative	3
3. Psychiatry contract (Dagmar)	19
4. General health insurance	8
5. The state as employer	8
6. Private company	6
7. Social welfare agency	7
8. Educational services	3

Psychotherapists are employed in different ways. Sixty-two percent of them work in the three biggest cities in Sweden, and an equal percentage are employed by the state in psychiatry, child care, university settings, or some other category. Twelve percent are employed by the community social welfare agencies. Twenty-six percent are in full-time private practice.

Fully 70% of licensed therapists have a small part-time private practice of their own. The average number of patients per therapist is 8 per week. The therapists estimate that they could take another 3,300 patients in therapy if money were available. This would be equivalent to the number of patients estimated to be on waiting lists for psychotherapeutic services.

The reimbursement for psychotherapy in private practice estimated for the 13,287 patients investigated is shown in Table 32.3.

The general health insurance can only be used to reimburse medical doctors, and not, for example, psychologists, a fact that is not well known to the general public. This is one of the recommendations (e.g., that psychologists be eligible for reimbursement) that was not accepted by the government, so that the Dagmar contract, a special temporary fund raised by the government for the support and development of psychiatric care, will have to cover psychotherapy not provided by medical doctors.

In closing, a few general remarks on trends in Swedish psychotherapy are offered: An interesting development is that social welfare agencies are taking responsibility for more and more psychotherapy services, as psychiatry becomes increasingly biological. This is also true for long-term patients, who, by law, are transferred to social welfare, where an integrated system of case management is implemented. This shift represents the main result of the large 1992 national investigation. A second key trend is that psychiatry is reorganizing to develop specialized units for psychotherapy, keyed to specific diagnostic categories (e.g., units for anorectic patients). Finally, and perhaps uniquely, there is a heightened emphasis on early psychotherapeutic treatment of psychotic patients. Scandinavia has a long tradition of implementing psychotherapeutic models for treatment of schizophrenic patients. The study by Alanen et al. (1994) indicates that as much as half of newly diagnosed first-break schizophrenic patients are out of the psychiatric system after 5 years, with no neuroleptic drugs and no residual psychotic symptoms. A great deal of hope has been invested in the hypothesis that a very rapid, early (i.e., within 24 hours of the psychotic break) crisis intervention in the family by multidisciplinary psychotherapeutic teams, together with a variety of intensive psychotherapeutic services, can prevent the onset of chronicity and of other, more insidious forms of schizophrenia.

References

Alanen, Y., Ugelstad, E., Armelius, B-Å., Lehtinen, K., Rosenbaum, B., & Sjöström, R. (1994). *Early treatment for schizophrenic patients: Scandinavian psychotherapeutic approaches.* Oslo: Scandinavian University Press.

Armelius, B-Å. (1991). The borderline patient project in Umeå. In L. Beutler & M. Cargo (Eds.), *Psychotherapy research: An international review of programmatic studies.* Washington, DC: American Psychological Association.

Psykiatrin och dess patienter (Psychiatry and its patients). (1992). Stockholm: Allmänna förlaget. Statens Offentliga Utredningar (SOU), 7 (State official investigations).

Index